Philosophy, Public Policy, and Transnational Law

Series Editor
John Martin Gillroy, International Relations,
Lehigh University, Bethlehem, PA, USA

*Philosophy, Public Policy, and Transnational Law* seeks, uniquely, to publish new and innovative arguments about global law and policy that transcend realist/positivist assumptions and the conventions of current legal/policy discourse. This series means to encourage the application of systematic philosophical and theoretical arguments to practical policy and legal issues that combine domestic, comparative or international law. We will pursue scholarship that integrates the superstructure of the positive law with its philosophical and public policy substructure, and which, in this way, produces a more three dimensional understanding of transnational law and its evolution, meaning, imperatives and future. We seek dissertations, solo and edited volumes, as well as innovative reports that integrate new methods, epistemologies and interdisciplinary perspectives with practical issues on the full range of policy and legal dilemmas challenging transnational relations.

More information about this series at
http://www.palgrave.com/gp/series/14550

Sergio Dellavalle

# Paradigms of Social Order

From Holism to Pluralism and Beyond

Sergio Dellavalle
University of Turin
Turin, Italy

Max Planck Institute for Comparative
Public Law and International Law
Heidelberg, Germany

Philosophy, Public Policy, and Transnational Law
ISBN 978-3-030-66181-6      ISBN 978-3-030-66179-3   (eBook)
https://doi.org/10.1007/978-3-030-66179-3

© The Editor(s) (if applicable) and The Author(s), under exclusive license to Springer Nature Switzerland AG 2021
This work is subject to copyright. All rights are solely and exclusively licensed by the Publisher, whether the whole or part of the material is concerned, specifically the rights of translation, reprinting, reuse of illustrations, recitation, broadcasting, reproduction on microfilms or in any other physical way, and transmission or information storage and retrieval, electronic adaptation, computer software, or by similar or dissimilar methodology now known or hereafter developed.
The use of general descriptive names, registered names, trademarks, service marks, etc. in this publication does not imply, even in the absence of a specific statement, that such names are exempt from the relevant protective laws and regulations and therefore free for general use.
The publisher, the authors and the editors are safe to assume that the advice and information in this book are believed to be true and accurate at the date of publication. Neither the publisher nor the authors or the editors give a warranty, expressed or implied, with respect to the material contained herein or for any errors or omissions that may have been made. The publisher remains neutral with regard to jurisdictional claims in published maps and institutional affiliations.

Cover image: © steve007/Moment/Getty Image

This Palgrave Macmillan imprint is published by the registered company Springer Nature Switzerland AG
The registered company address is: Gewerbestrasse 11, 6330 Cham, Switzerland

# Series Editor's Preface

Of all of the ways in which philosophical argument can approach law and public policy, the concept of the "paradigm" is among the most advantageous. The first reason this is so comes from the fact that human beings approach socio-political ideas and institutions from paradigms of thought, formed from a variety of sources, and from conscious and unconscious predispositions, presuppositions and principles/precepts. The second reason paradigms are important is because change requires them. If the institutions of transnational law and policy are judged to be inadequate, it is only through an understanding and ability to reconstruct or replace their essential paradigms of thought, from which the institutions, laws and practices arise, that change will become truly possible.

While a number of books in this series dance around the edges of this fundamental reliance on paradigms, Sergio Dellavalle takes on this approach directly and consciously. This is the core importance of his argument, and why it fits this Series as an integral effort to both understand the substructure of philosophical concepts that create public international law, and render from these, practical policy arguments to implement change. Dellavalle, with reasoned argument generated from a wealth of both philosophical and legal knowledge, utilizes the idea of paradigms to both trace the history of international legal order and also present essential or core arguments for change in how we conceptualize and work within a transnational legal system.

Specifically, by relating the theoretical development of distinct yet interrelated "paradigms of order", he takes us on a journey through the ever-developing complexity of transnational law, with the end of delineating the core problems that prevent us from handling those dilemmas that transcend the authority of sovereign states. More than this, however, Dellavalle also shows the reader how philosophical concepts and ideas can be utilized as a sound basis for policy and law. This is an important and timely book, especially given the pandemic currently underway, and is applicable to transnational issues from climate change to peace and security, suggesting innovative ways of conceptualizing international law to better fit the policy requirements necessary for a truly twenty-first-century definition of "order".

As the Senior Editor of this Series, I am very please to welcome this innovative, well-thought-out and truly original scholarship to *Philosophy, Public Policy, and Transnational Law*. It not only takes the entire range of issues this Series seeks to explore seriously, but it is testament to how well they can be integrated to make the deepest philosophy relevant to practice and the positive law richer and more conceptually vibrant.

John Martin Gillroy
Lehigh University, Bethlehem, USA

Faculty of Law, CDN, Queen's University
Kingston, Canada

# Foreword

This timely book invites us to rethink the global order. The invitation is extended during the times of the COVID-19 pandemic which engulfed the globe in a matter of weeks if not days. The book reminds us that while often we tend to regard political borders as preordained, perhaps even natural, these are but human constructs, a result of path-dependent decisions and actions. Sergio Dellavalle broadens our horizons and prods us to weigh alternatives that for various reasons—economic, social, cultural or moral—might be regarded as more practical, more moral or more sustainable. A similar prodding results from the new coronavirus which ignores political boundaries, exposes the failure of the current political order to act collectively and demonstrates that no one is safe until everybody is safe and that global solidarity is key to individual survival.

The book turns deep philosophical inquiries into effective, even practical, deliberation over the alternative approaches to order or re-order the world. The book addresses this question from a historical angle, presenting the various paradigms of order in their chronological sequel and addressing the theoretical development within each of them. But all these various approaches are very much en vogue and compete against each other. The earliest paradigm of order is still the most visible politically, as it is based on homogeneous communities, separated by an unruly space subject only to the will of those entities. This vision of order assumes that each of the communities is more valuable than even the sum of the individuals that constitute the community. As Dellavalle convincingly argues, in an increasingly globalized world, the possibility of an alternative, global order of the whole humankind, one which recognizes a well-ordered space for inter-community interaction, becomes more and more appealing from both rational and sociological perspectives. This order also assumes that the (cosmopolitan) community is endowed with a higher value, as a whole, than the individuals of whom it is composed. Yet a third paradigm of order seeks primacy. This is the order founded on the centrality of the individuals and their priority over the whole of the community. In this order, public power is only justified to preserve individuals' rights and interests. This has implications for the common space that is governed by international law which is superior to domestic law. An alternative global ordering envisions non-hierarchical and rather horizontal private ordering of mainly economic private actors.

Which order will gain supremacy in the competition over the anti-COVID treatment and vaccines in short supply? Will the understanding that "as long as there is active SARS-CoV-2 transmission anywhere there will be a risk of transmission everywhere, [and that hence] the equitable allocation of vaccines globally is in all countries' enlightened self-interest,"[1] transform our understanding of which order is more just and efficient? Will the ensuing recognition of "all human beings as having equal moral status and their interests as deserving of equal moral consideration" lead to global commitment to "[e]nsure equity in vaccine access and benefit globally among people living in all countries, particularly those living in low-and middle-income countries"?[2] Most likely, the global debate will continue, but Dellavalle's masterful work will shine a light on the various possible orders and promote deeper and well-informed deliberations. The critique of the lawless global space shared by homogeneous communities has never been more convincing.

Winter 2020

Eyal Benvenisti
University of Cambridge
Cambridge, UK

NOTES

1. WHO Strategic Advisory Group of Experts (SAGE) on Immunization: Values Framework for the Allocation and Prioritization of COVID-19 Vaccination (2020).
2. Among the values articulated by SAGE.

# Acknowledgements

This book being the result of almost twenty years of research, it is easily understandable that many are the friends and colleagues that gave significant contributions to the development of the concepts that build its backbone, as well as of the specific analyses that make up its more detailed contents. In the first place, I want to mention Armin von Bogdandy, the Co-Director of the Max Planck Institute for Comparative Public Law and International Law in Heidelberg, who coordinated—along with me—the research project from which the first idea of a book on the "paradigms of order" arose. Some of the interpretations, which are exposed in detail in the present volume, emerged in their germinal form during our personal dialogues as well as from the activities of the research project in Heidelberg, and found their first expression in co-authored publications. Among the friends and colleagues who—during conferences or presentations, as well as through interactions face-to-face or via mail—commented on some aspects of the theory of the "paradigms of order" or on the analytic approach in its entirety are: Eyal Benvenisti, who invited me to research stays first at the University of Tel Aviv and then at the Lauterpacht Centre for International Law of the University of Cambridge; Mario Dogliani, Raffaele Caterina and Pier Paolo Portinaro from the University of Turin; Mortimer Sellers from the University of Baltimore School of Law; Stefan Kadelbach, Gunther Teubner and Matthias Goldmann from the Goethe-University in Frankfurt; Hannes Hansen-Magnusson and Peter Sutch from the School of Law and Politics of Cardiff University; Joseph H. H. Weiler from NYU; Jochen von Bernstorff from the University of Tübingen; Hanoch Dagan from Tel Aviv University; Anne Peters, the Co-Director of the Max Planck Institute for Comparative Public Law and International Law in Heidelberg; Tomer Shadmy from the Hebrew University of Jerusalem; Alec Walen from Rutgers University; Arif Jamal from the National University of Singapore, Wallace Mlyniec from Georgetown University; Timothy Endicott from the University of Oxford; Ingo Venzke from the University of Amsterdam; Christopher McCrudden from Queen's University Belfast; Massimo La Torre from the University of Catanzaro; Sabrina Zucca from the Helmut-Schmidt-Universität in Hamburg; Peter Hilpold from the University of Innsbruck; Aravind Ganesh from Oxford Brookes University; and Russell Miller from Washington & Lee University. A special thought goes to the memory of Norberto Bobbio, who taught me to love political philosophy and not to shy away from developing unusual views on topics and authors. Furthermore, I am deeply grateful to John Martin Gillroy for always supporting my endeavour and for accepting this book in the series on *Philosophy, Public Policy, and Transnational Law*, and to Rebecca Roberts who, on behalf of Palgrave Macmillan, accompanied the different stages of my work with competence, sensibility and a lot of patience. Finally, I want to thank from the bottom of my heart my wife Eva Birkenstock and my daughters Ariane and Micol for always assisting and encouraging me; with the most heartfelt feelings of love and gratitude, this book is dedicated to them.

# Contents

1 Social Order and Its Paradigms, Or: What Is
  a Paradigm of Order? 1
  1.1 The Concept of Order and the Well-Ordered Society 4
  1.2 Theories and Paradigms 7
  1.3 The Contents of the Paradigms of Order: Continuity
      and Revolutions 13
  1.4 The Structure of the Book 18
  Notes 26

2 Holistic Particularism as the First Paradigm of Order,
  Or: On the Order of Limited and Single Polities
  and the Exclusion of Inter-state Order 29
  2.1 The First Appearance of the Paradigm in Ancient
      Greece 32
      2.1.1 The Justification of Particularism in Thucydides 33
      2.1.2 The Holistic Understanding of Society
            in Ancient Political Philosophy 36
            2.1.2.1 Plato: The Unconditional
                    Identification Between Citizens
                    and Polis 37

|     | 2.1.2.2 | Aristotle: The Enlarged Family as Social Basis of the Political Community | 39 |
|---|---|---|---|
| 2.2 | The Revival of the Paradigm in Early Modern Ages | | 41 |
|     | 2.2.1 | The Independence of Politics from Moral and Religion in Machiavelli's Realism | 42 |
|     | 2.2.2 | Bodin's Concept of Sovereignty | 44 |
|     | 2.2.3 | The Decline of the Familistic Conception of the Polity in Filmer's Patriarcha | 47 |
| 2.3 | Adam Müller, Or: The Forging of the Nation in Political Romanticism | | 49 |
| 2.4 | The Struggle Between Friend and Enemy as the Justification for the Striving for Hegemony in Carl Schmitt | | 56 |
| 2.5 | Three Variants of Holistic Particularism: Realism, Nationalism, Hegemonism | | 60 |
| 2.6 | The Re-foundation of Realism, or the Neo-Realism of the Theory of International Relations | | 63 |
| 2.7 | The Defence of the Nation in the Globalization Era | | 67 |
| 2.8 | Contemporary Hegemonism and Beyond | | 72 |
|     | 2.8.1 | The Theory of the Clash of Civilizations | 72 |
|     | 2.8.2 | Particularism Going Global in the Neo-Conservative Approach | 75 |
| 2.9 | The Dialectics of Holistic Particularism | | 80 |
|     | 2.9.1 | Rational Choice Theory | 81 |
|     | 2.9.2 | Communitarianism | 83 |
| Notes | | | 86 |

3 **Holistic Universalism as the Second Paradigm of Order** 95
   3.1 Universal Logos and World Nomos in the Stoic Philosophy 99
   3.2 The Christian-Catholic Conception of Universalism 104
      3.2.1 The Idea of the City of God in Augustine 106
      3.2.2 The Shaping of Political Universalism 110
         3.2.2.1 Dante's Apology of the Universal Monarchy 110

|  |  | 3.2.2.2 | Francisco Suárez: The Attempt to Reconcile Unity and Diversity in the First Multilevel Conception of Legal Order | 116 |
|---|---|---|---|---|
|  | 3.2.3 | | On Discrimination, Persecution and the Defence of the Status Quo, Or: Can Universalism Be Based on Religion? | 121 |
|  |  | 3.2.3.1 | The Subjugation of the "Others" | 121 |
|  |  | 3.2.3.2 | A Backward-Oriented Conception of Political Order | 128 |
|  | 3.2.4 | | Bartolomé de Las Casas and the Way Beyond Discrimination | 130 |
|  | 3.2.5 | | The Inclusion of the "Other" in the Doctrine of the Second Vatican Council | 133 |
|  | 3.2.6 | | Faith and Logos in the Resumption of Catholic Exceptionalism | 137 |
|  | 3.2.7 | | Towards a "Global Ethic"? | 141 |
|  | 3.2.8 | | The New Frontier of Catholic Theology | 147 |
| 3.3 | The Universalism of Natural Law | | | 149 |
|  | 3.3.1 | | From the Law of God to the Law of Humanity: On the Natural Law Theory from the Middle Ages to the Reformation | 150 |
|  | 3.3.2 | | Human Sociability and the Law of Nations | 161 |
|  |  | 3.3.2.1 | Johannes Althusius: Sociability and Universal Federalism | 162 |
|  |  | 3.3.2.2 | Samuel Pufendorf: The Law of Nations as Pure Natural Law | 165 |
|  |  | 3.3.2.3 | Christian Wolff: The Apotheosis of the Civitas Maxima | 168 |
|  | 3.3.3 | | The New Natural Law | 172 |
|  | 3.3.4 | | The Constitutionalization of International Law | 178 |
| Notes | | | | 183 |

4 **Universalistic Individualism as the Third Paradigm of Order** — 199
 4.1 *The Individualistic Turn in the Western Theory of Knowledge* — 208
 4.2 *Thomas Hobbes's Contractualist Theory of State* — 212

|  |  |  |
|---|---|---|
| 4.3 | Individual Rights and State Power | 217 |
|  | 4.3.1 John Locke's Liberalism | 218 |
|  | 4.3.2 Jean-Jacques Rousseau's Democratic "Social Contract" | 220 |
| 4.4 | The Universalistic Turn of Contractualism and the Cosmopolitan Order in Immanuel Kant | 223 |
| 4.5 | Hans Kelsen and the Priority of International Law | 241 |
| 4.6 | The World Federal Republic as the Only Possibility for Cosmopolitan Order | 254 |
|  | Notes | 258 |

## 5 The Failed Paradigmatic Revolution: Particularistic Individualism, or the Spontaneous Order of Transnational Economic Actors, as a Possible Fourth Paradigm of Order — 269

|  |  |  |
|---|---|---|
| 5.1 | Trade as Instrument of World Order | 275 |
|  | 5.1.1 The Hellenist Doctrine of the Universal Economy | 276 |
|  | 5.1.2 The Lex Mercatoria of the Middle Ages | 278 |
| 5.2 | The Free Trade Theory | 281 |
|  | Notes | 288 |

## 6 The Post-unitary Paradigms of Order I: Systems Theory and the New Lex Mercatoria — 291

|  |  |  |
|---|---|---|
| 6.1 | Niklas Luhmann and the Plurality of Systemic Rationalities | 293 |
| 6.2 | The Law of Globalization and Fragmentation | 302 |
| 6.3 | The Lex Mercatoria of Systems Theory | 306 |
| 6.4 | Supra-Systemic Rationality and the Inescapability of the Public Realm | 311 |
|  | Notes | 320 |

## 7 The Post-unitary Paradigms of Order II: From Modernity to Post-modernity — 327

|  |  |  |
|---|---|---|
| 7.1 | The Philosophical Foundations of Post-modernism | 332 |
|  | 7.1.1 Discovering Contextuality | 334 |
|  | 7.1.2 Beyond Modern Subjectivism | 338 |
| 7.2 | Order as Oppression | 342 |
|  | 7.2.1 Against Empire | 343 |
|  | 7.2.2 The Third World Approach to International Law | 347 |

|  |  |  |
|---|---|---|
| | 7.2.3 Feminist Theory | 350 |
| 7.3 | The Break of Unitary Order as a Chance for Individual Self-realization | 353 |
| | 7.3.1 Legal Pluralism | 353 |
| | 7.3.2 Neo-Liberalism in the Theory of International Relations and in International Law | 355 |
| | 7.3.3 Global Governance | 360 |
| | 7.3.4 Legal Formalism | 363 |
| 7.4 | The Decline of Normativity and Legitimacy | 367 |
| Notes | | 370 |

## 8 The Post-unitary Paradigms of Order III: The Communicative Paradigm 377

|  |  |  |
|---|---|---|
| 8.1 | From Subjectivity to Intersubjectivity—and Back? | 381 |
| | 8.1.1 The Struggle for Recognition and the Hypostasis of Subjectivity in Georg Wilhelm Friedrich Hegel | 382 |
| | 8.1.2 Karl Marx: From the Overcoming of Alienation to the Necessary Dynamics of Historical Evolution | 389 |
| 8.2 | The Intersubjectivity of Political Life | 397 |
| | 8.2.1 The Social and Democratic Dimension of Individual Freedom in John Dewey's Pragmatism | 397 |
| | 8.2.2 Hannah Arendt's Theory of Political Action | 401 |
| 8.3 | The Rationality of Communication | 405 |
| | 8.3.1 The Theory of Language | 405 |
| | 8.3.2 Gnoseology | 410 |
| | 8.3.3 The Communicative Use of Practical Reason | 413 |
| | 8.3.4 Systems and Lifeworld | 417 |
| | 8.3.5 Plurality and the Unity of Rationality | 419 |
| | 8.3.6 Communication in the Political and Legal Dimension | 424 |
| 8.4 | The Conception of Order According to the Communicative Paradigm | 427 |

8.5 *The Perspective of a Cosmopolitan Order of Freedom
and Justice in Difficult Times* 434
*Notes* 438

**Index** 449

CHAPTER 1

# Social Order and Its Paradigms, Or: What Is a Paradigm of Order?

Since the beginning of Western thought, "order" was conceived as the essence of the world. Indeed, the intuition that the world was generated when "order" originated from "chaos" is already expressed as far back in time as in the poetry of Hesiod:

> Verily at the first Chaos came to be, but next wide-bosomed Earth,
> the ever-sure foundations of all the deathless ones
> who hold the peaks of snowy Olympus,
> and dim Tartarus in the depth of the wide-pathed Earth,
> and Eros (Love), fairest among the deathless gods,
> who unnerves the limbs and overcomes the mind
> and wise counsels of all gods and all men within them.
> From Chaos came forth Erebus and black Night;
> but of Night were born Aether and Day,
> whom she conceived and bare from union in love with Erebus.
> And Earth first bare starry Heaven,
> equal to herself, to cover her on every side,
> and to be an ever-sure abiding-place for the blessed gods.
> And she brought forth long Hills, graceful haunts
> of the goddess-Nymphs who dwell amongst the glens of the hills.
> She bare also the fruitless deep with his raging swell, Pontus,
> without sweet union of love.
> But afterwards she lay with Heaven

© The Author(s), under exclusive license to Springer Nature
Switzerland AG 2021
S. Dellavalle, *Paradigms of Social Order*,
Philosophy, Public Policy, and Transnational Law,
https://doi.org/10.1007/978-3-030-66179-3_1

and bare deep-swirling Oceanus, Coeus and Crius
and Hyperion and Iapetus, Theia and Rhea, Themis and Mnemosyne
and gold-crowned Phoebe and lovely Tethys.
After them was born Cronos the wily, youngest
and most terrible of her children, and he hated his lusty sire.[1]

Here, chaos is put at the beginning of time, and *kosmos*—in the sense of "world" as well as of "order"—is not possible before the indistinct condition, in which all elements are melted together, has given place to the manifold appearances of the universe, characterized by clear distinctions and rules. This understanding characterized the whole antiquity, so that the same cosmology—although presented in a less obscure language—can be discovered again in Ovid's *Metamorphoses*, during the flourishing of Roman classics:

Before the seas, and this terrestrial ball,
And Heav'n's high canopy, that covers all,
One was the face of Nature; if a face:
Rather a rude and indigested mass:
A lifeless lump, unfashion'd, and unfram'd,
Of jarring seeds; and justly Chaos nam'd.
[...]
Thus air was void of light, and earth unstable,
And water's dark abyss unnavigable.
No certain form on any was imprest;
All were confus'd, and each disturb'd the rest.
For hot and cold were in one body fixt;
And soft with hard, and light with heavy mixt.
But God, or Nature, while they thus contend,
To these intestine discords put an end:
Then earth from air, and seas from earth were driv'n,
And grosser air sunk from aetherial Heav'n.
Thus disembroil'd, they take their proper place;
The next of kin, contiguously embrace;
And foes are sunder'd, by a larger space.[2]

Following this cosmological approach, nature developed its numerous forms when "order" replaced "chaos". Doubts are justified, from our point of view, on whether nature's evolution really results from the substitution of "chaos" through "order": what happened and happens in the physical world is probably better described as a kind of temporary "differentiation", rather than as an increase of "order", since the rules that nature follows, its laws, are supposed to be stable. The history of life, too, is more exactly explained as a rise of "complexity" than of "order": a unicellular organism is actually no less "ordered" than a human being. Should we say, therefore, that what the ancient authors are telling us is simply meaningless, at least for our understanding of the world? No such radical conclusion should be drawn: we have just to change the focus of our interpretation. What the ancient authors are projecting on the natural world—which emerges from the anthropomorphic presentation of nature in the quoted passages—is their conception of the *social* evolution: it is the advancement to a well-ordered *society*, in which everyone and everything have their places according to rules that did not exist in the previous condition of "chaos", that they had in mind while describing what they thought to be the phenomena of natural history. And it was society that arose from chaos as an ever more complex and inclusive order.

Indeed, no social life is possible without order.[3] Being order the most constituent element of society, it is not surprising that so many theories have been developed to explain what social order is and how it is possible, as well as on the features that social order acquires in its different dimensions. The aim of this inquiry consists—rather unusually in times in which academic research in humanities is principally concentrated on discovering differences—in leading back these many theories of social order to few patterns, or matrices for the use of theoretical and practical reason, which I propose to define as "paradigms of order". The first challenge of the proposed reconstruction lies, thus, in the attempt to reduce the plurality of conceptual constructs regarding social order to just a small number of theoretical patterns. Thereby, an intellectual map is produced in which the most significant distinctions in the approaches concerning order as well as the most relevant breaks in their historical development become evident. To do so, it is necessary to begin by clarifying what is understood, here, by "social order" and what are the advantages of using this concept (1.1). Having specified the methodology of the inquiry as well as the meaning of "theories" and "paradigms" (1.2), the results of both clarifications—of the concept of "order", on the one hand, as well as of the notion of "paradigm" on the other—are brought together, then, so as to give an account of what the "paradigms of order" are assumed to be (1.3). A brief outlook on the structure of the book will conclude the chapter (1.4).

## 1.1 THE CONCEPT OF ORDER AND THE WELL-ORDERED SOCIETY

Generally speaking, an "ordered society" is a human community which is characterized by effective rules that make human interaction predictable. Understood in this sense, the assertion that "a society is ordered" does not imply any assumption concerning the ethical quality of the interactions that unfold within its boundaries. For instance, concentration camps had rules and, in general, these were—unfortunately, we could add—respected; nevertheless, it is difficult to consider them as "ordered societies". Or maybe we can speak in these cases of a "bad" or "wrong order". To define a society as "ordered" in the—also ethically—full sense of the word, we have to further qualify the concept, going from a merely "ordered society" to what can be called a "well-ordered society", or from an "order" as the condition in which rules are followed, without ethical qualification, to a "good" or "just order" with an additional ethical value.

Yet, what is a "well-ordered society"? I propose to define it as the human community in which rules do not only aim at making interactions predictable but also organize social life in a *peaceful* way, allowing for the pursuing of the various interests of all agents involved—however different these interests may be, as long as they do not unduly constrain the justified interests of others—and, in the most ambitious understandings, even facilitating mutual cooperation. Therefore, the first feature of a "well-ordered" society is that its rules guarantee peace to the advantage of all its members. This does not mean that conflicts are avoided or suppressed; to the contrary, conflict is recognized as necessary for the further development of society. From the absence of conflict only stagnation can follow. However, to make social interactions peaceful, conflicts should be conveyed into processes that prevent disruptive consequences for the whole society. Law is the most significant instrument for this purpose, at least if we consider the *reflexive* operationalization of conflicts.

According to this understanding, a "good and just order" is necessarily a condition of peace, where peace is not defined *negatively*, i.e., as the absence of war as the form of unfettered conflict in which at least one involved actor aims at severely damaging the counterpart without— or at least before—searching for a compromise. Nor is peace interpreted only as a *Hegung des Krieges*, i.e., as the "containment of war" praised by Carl Schmitt. Rather, it is understood in its *positive* meaning, as the situation in which the most essential conditions are guaranteed for everyone to see her/his rights or at least her/his social role respected and to realize her/his life projects, albeit within the boundaries of the very uneven chances that different social orders can give. Furthermore, in a "well-ordered society" the illegitimate use of force—in particular, the unleashing of an armed conflict without due legitimation deriving from the authority vested with the power to authorize it, or at least from a putative justification in the case that the authority proves to be incapable to act—is seen as a *pathology* that has to be prevented or healed, not as a political instrument that should only be regulated through the *jus in bello*.

Three specifications should be made to clarify the concept of "order" as it is used in this research. First, I employ the concept of "order" or of "social order", in general, to identify the set of rules on which the functioning of a peaceful society, in the sense explained before, is based in its whole. Concretely, this general set of rules—always following the dominant pattern or "paradigm"—is articulated in more specific sets related to the distinct social subsystems. Therefore, a general theory of social order, concentrated on its general paradigms, has the task of detecting the constants that determine the general conditions for a peaceful interaction within a society. These constants are concretized, then, in the particular rules, for instance, of the political interaction, or of the legal subsystem. In the following, thus, when the focus is on the paradigms that characterize the functioning of the interactions in the society as a whole, I will speak of a "general theory of social order" or, more concisely, "of order"; when, on the contrary, light should be cast on how the general patterns take specific forms, I will use the definition of a "theory of political, legal, or economic order", depending on which subsystem will be at the centre of the analysis.

Secondly, the concept of "order" has the advantage of being applicable to a very large number of social, political, legal and economic institutions, enabling us to find out the invariables that bind them—or the differences that divide them—at a very abstract level, beyond the many particularities that may disperse our insight into the constants of social life. Using a metaphor, we could say that the concept of "order", precisely because of its abstraction, makes it possible to see the forest among the many trees of which it is made. Indeed, just to make a few examples to which the following analysis directly refers, the ancient Greek *polis*, the Roman empire, the *communitas christiana*, the modern state, the international community, as well as functional subsystems, the *lex mercatoria* or the multilevel cosmopolitan constitutionalism, all have specific institutional structures which are—without any doubt—very different from each other. Nevertheless, they all have also a common trait, which is anything but marginal: they all are forms of social order, in the sense that they can be interpreted as institutional shapes in which a specific kind of rules of social interaction is implemented. As variants of social order, they are species of the same genus. By introducing a synthetic concept like "order", we can go beyond the meticulous discovery of distinctiveness—that, although important in principle, should not degenerate into a mere end in itself—pointing out similarities and continuities, or drawing attention on what are the real "breaks" or "revolutions" in the evolution of the forms of human society.

Thirdly, a further advantage in using the concept of "order" refers to the relation between the different disciplines of human science. Although they are, to a certain extent, all connected to one another, and often share a common origin, in the last decades they have been suffering from a serious loss of mutual communication due to the huge increase of knowledge and to a differentiation of methodologies. Surely, the specificity of the language of each human science should be adequately respected and further developed, but the lacking of conceptual bridges between the disciplines runs the risk of impoverishing each of them, inasmuch as it remains entrenched in its bulwark. Instead, dialogue allows the transfer of knowledge deriving from related sciences into the language of one's own discipline, improving this way also its research results. Dialogue, however, needs some conceptual elements in common, which build the bridges of communication and guarantee that the scholars on each side have a chance to understand each other. The notion of "order" is one of such conceptual bridges. Indeed, "order" is a concept that is familiar to philosophers and political scientists, lawyers and sociologists, theologians and economists—and some other categories of experts of human sciences could be added. To be sure, every discipline has its own way to specify what "order" is assumed to be, based on its specific methodology and on the object of its analysis. Nonetheless, provided that the concept of "order" that we adopt is abstract enough to comprise different variants without losing coherence, the fact that each discipline has an *idea* of "order" qualifies this notion—insofar as it is arguably common, in its general features, to all human sciences—as the open gate that allows to introduce new knowledge from outside into the epistemological structures of the specific fields of study.

## 1.2 Theories and Paradigms

The materials of this research are not the phenomena of order as they are displayed within the different social contexts. In other words, the analysis is not concentrated directly on the political order as the rules that govern the political system, or on the rules of the economic interactions, or on the characteristics of the legal system. Rather, its object is made of *theories of order*, i.e., of conceptual constructs that have themselves—in this case directly—the description and evaluation of the concrete phenomena of order at the centre of their interest. Thus, the materials of the book are theories of political, legal and also (but rather marginally) economic order, or, more in general, theories of social order. By trying to extrapolate from this materials similarities and differences, analogies and oppositions, continuity and breaks, the research aims at establishing a second-level theory, i.e., a general theory on the theories of order, or a *metatheory of social order*.

At the basis of the inquiry is the conviction that a metatheory of social order can be realized by leading the many specific theories back to general patterns, here called *paradigms*. From this perspective, if the theories of order are the materials of the inquiry, then the "paradigms of order" are the categories that are used to interpret these materials and to give them a structure. The notion of "paradigm" is often employed—with reference to both the human and the natural sciences, and not just within the academic discourse—but seldom with the necessary clarity. Relying on the studies of Thomas Kuhn as the author who, more than anyone else, influenced the use of the notion in the last decades of academic debates,[4] I define as a "paradigm" the set of concepts and abstract claims to explain those concepts, that serve as the most fundamental requisites for the use of the theoretical and practical reason with reference to a specific field of knowledge and action in a certain period of human history. On these most fundamental concepts, then, are the theories based that describe, explain and predict phenomena, or prescript the right actions, within a certain context and with reference to a specific object. Therefore, we have the paradigms of biology that shape the theories regarding life phenomena in different periods of the evolution of this science. Analogously, we have also the paradigms of physics or of chemistry, and of all other natural sciences. And we have paradigms for the human sciences as well—among them, the paradigms of what I have proposed to call the general theory or metatheory of order.

Nevertheless, some significant differences exist between the paradigms of natural sciences and those of human sciences. The first distinction that attracts our attention is that, while the paradigms of natural sciences seem to have a *serial* character, so that they are seldom co-present in the same period of time, co-presence appears to be the rule for the paradigms of human sciences. In fact, every single period of the history of natural sciences is generally dominated by the patterns of knowledge of just one paradigm. Therefore, when new evidences are discovered which cannot be easily described or explained within the conceptual framework of the dominant paradigm any longer, this is doomed, over a more or less long period of time, to be substituted by a new theoretical pattern. The co-presence of two or more paradigms in the same period of time is seen as the result of an unaccomplished conceptual transition that is destined to be removed as soon as knowledge further increases. Dismissed paradigms, thus, only remain as parts of the history of the discipline, and do not maintain any epistemological value for the current scientific discourse. Sometimes, it may happen that a dismissed paradigm reappears after a long time of oblivion. So did, for instance, atomism that, after being developed for the first time in antiquity by Democritus and Epicurus—with a rather marginal success that never really challenged the dominant metaphysics—and later forgotten for many centuries, was rediscovered in modern physics and influenced decisively the contemporary understanding of the discipline. Yet, modern and contemporary atomism is considerably dissimilar from its ancient predecessor, so that even their being part of the same epistemological pattern has been questioned.[5] Therefore, even if we admit that a paradigm of natural sciences in its more general terms may come back, under certain circumstances, after a long period of time, the features of the new variant are so specific that the assertion of continuity cannot but be partial and cautious. This is not the case, however, for the paradigms of human sciences. In fact, paradigms of social order can look back to histories of very unlike length: since some of them are very old, and others quite new, only the last decades have seen the co-presence of all paradigms developed so far, and for many hundreds of years, in the far antiquity, just one paradigm dominated the understanding of social order. Nevertheless no paradigm, after being introduced for the first time, ever disappeared entirely or lost completely its epistemological and practical appeal. Instead, we see paradigms that went through crises and times of marginality but, when re-proposed with some novelties, were still characterized by largely the same theoretical assumptions as before.

Paradigms of order seem never to die, but just to spend times, even long periods, of recovery, just to reappear in a shape which is thought to be more adequate to meet the challenges of the new era.

But what are the reasons of this eye-catching difference? The most convincing explanation points out that natural sciences have instruments at their disposal which human sciences have not. Due to these instruments, the validity of which is recognized by almost the whole scientific community, the objects of natural sciences can be impartially measured—or, at least, scientists agree on this purpose and share the aim of objectivity, although the concrete possibility to attain objective knowledge is sometimes overestimated—and the results are expressed in mathematic formulas. Because of this common technical and methodological basis, research results can be easily compared and discussed, as well as wrong or obsolete solutions can be dismissed, sometimes after long and fierce debates, but in the end with the support of the large majority of the scientific community. Human sciences do not have such technical supports of undisputed validity, nor can they resort to a definite and unambiguous methodology, generally accepted as the grammar of a serious inquiry. The reason is easy to explain: human sciences are not the result of the observation of phenomena which are regarded as located outside the observers and are thought to be described by them, if not exhaustively, at least with a sufficient degree of impartiality; rather, human sciences are the product of processes of social self-understanding, of narrations developed in order to clarify the sense of our social life.[6] This does not mean that human sciences cannot collect evidences concerning their object or even, in certain disciplines, measure it, but in any case the results of these observations or measurements are far less "objective" than in natural sciences and more open to interpretation. The aim of human sciences, in fact, is not to observe an *external* phenomenon, but to collect data and argumentations on *internal* processes in order to better understand what the fundaments and purposes of our social life are. Since the paradigms of human sciences—much more evidently than those of natural sciences—do not only contain a description of the world but also an assertion on how this world should be interpreted and organized in order to realize a "good" social life, the collection of new data does not condemn necessarily the old paradigm to a definitive end. Rather, it emerges as a kind of challenge, for the supporters of the paradigm, to adapt its fundamental notions, which express a specific idea on the priorities of human life that is supposed to maintain its validity, to the new situation. This explains why paradigms of human sciences, in general, and paradigms of social order in particular, submerge—even for long time—and then re-emerge again while maintaining their fundamental tenets and only changing some of the less essential elements of their construct. Moreover, this accounts for the fact that paradigms of human sciences do not appear—and disappear—serially, but compete in the same time and within the same society for the most convincing arguments on how social life should be understood and organized.

As a consequence, paradigms are located in a context of complex balance between description and prescription, whereas this balance is quite different for the paradigms of natural sciences than for those of human sciences. As regards this issue, two opposite interpretations should be shortly addressed which, precisely because of their one-sidedness, end up being rather unconvincing. The first, which is supported in particular by specialists of the epistemology of natural sciences,[7] claims that the concept of "paradigm" is rather useless from the epistemological point of view since, at least in natural sciences, the development of knowledge has an *incremental* character, being based on the process of ongoing *falsification* of former theories and not on the change of fundamental patterns of knowledge, or—in the vocabulary that I propose here—on "paradigmatic revolutions". This approach seems to underestimate the importance of social discourse—which is included into the theory of the "paradigmatic revolutions", but not into the theory of falsification—for the consolidation of scientific truth. Galilei's trial is probably just the most famous example of the fact that a new understanding of the world— even of the natural world—needs, to be accepted as a "scientific truth", more than only an excellent experimental method and a sound theory: it needs the awareness that the latest discoveries cannot be adequately included into the old-fashioned general categories any longer, so that a strenuous defence of the old trench has become senseless and a new vision of the world has to take over. Yet, the emergence of such an awareness is not primarily an incremental scientific evolution, but essentially a social process, characterized by a non-marginal normative element.

The second assertion that should be shortly addressed takes the opposite standpoint, maintaining that paradigms, in particular in human sciences, should be regarded as largely independent of the examination of empiric data: being just stipulative definitions, they would only need to be self-coherent, i.e., non-self-contradictory, and could refrain from the reference to the outer world.[8] Lacking connections to empiric data, paradigms—if understood this way—could not be falsified by resorting to new evidences. However, if we accepted this interpretation, paradigms would be patterns of a knowledge of the world that is none, being devoid of any content. In the best case, they would be analytic concepts, adorned with the dubious pretension of describing or explaining real phenomena. In the interpretation that I propose here, however, paradigms are not just self-referential and analytic; rather, they are synthetic and related to real contents since they claim to be instruments for a better comprehension of social phenomena. Indeed, though paradigms are directly applied to conceptual constructs—i.e., to theories of order—and not to real facts, these conceptual constructs are themselves descriptions and explanations of real phenomena as well as prescriptions of action in the real world, so that, at least indirectly, also paradigms are linked to real phenomena.

Thus, paradigms—both of human and of natural sciences—combine the descriptive with the prescriptive dimension insofar as they do not just structure, albeit indirectly, real data but contain also a normative assessment concerning the individual and social experience that is related to the production or to the elaboration of those data. In other words, facts of nature or of the social world are the contents of paradigms, but, within the epistemological context of a specific paradigm, they are always related to the social discourse that goes along with the perception of facts and the collection of data. This perception, for its part, influences then the further production of facts. As a consequence, the difference between the paradigms of natural sciences and those of human sciences with regard to the descriptive and the normative components is rather a question of nuances than of antagonism: of the two elements—the descriptive and the normative—the one that prevails in the paradigms of natural sciences is the evidence of objective data, collected by means of generally accepted technical instruments, whereas the social discourse is thought to shape and interpret the data, hereby introducing the normative dimension. To the contrary, the social discourse is the essence of the processes of self-understanding that characterize human sciences and their paradigms; however, these social discourses have always to refer also to empiric evidences to avoid being trapped in self-referential emptiness.

I have already said that the task of a general theory of social order consists in tracing back the manifold variety of the theories on political, legal and economic order to few paradigms. Yet, what is the epistemological gain of such an operation? What do we have, in terms of knowledge, after leading back theories to paradigms, that we did not have already before? The first advantage consists in drawing a map of the theories of order: like in a geographic map, where natural sites and human settlements are located according to their respective position within a coordinate system, theories are situated here according to their relation to the most fundamental and decisive questions, as they are fleshed out in the metatheory of order. Placing the theories on the virtual map of their most essential concepts allows us to understand better how far from—or near to—each other they are. We can see similarities, differences and even oppositions as well as lines of rupture in a more transparent way. By reducing the complexity, the core solutions to the problem of how society can be organized emerge more understandably and the possible thread of a fragile and always threatened historical development of human society becomes visible, both in its potentialities and in its frailty. Furthermore, by leading back theories to their paradigms and by stressing the character, both descriptive and normative, of paradigms, the here proposed conceptual framework challenges the myth of theories that pretend to be just "realist" ascertainments of what the world is, and dismantles the allegations against other theoretical constructs accused of being devoid of the necessary concreteness: actually, every theory of social order is based on an analysis of facts and aims at developing a proposal for "right" action. Still, for some theories this action is limited to the reproduction of a reality that is regarded as the best possible, while some others envisage rather a more or less radical transformation of a social status quo that is considered to be unjust.

A last remark should be made as regards the theories analysed in the inquiry—a remark which is, at the same time, a kind of apology. In fact, the materials on which the research is based are all derived from the history of Western thought. In this sense, the research is located on the backward side of that "Copernican revolution" in consequence of which the theory of international law has expanded its view from an exclusive Western to a more comprehensive perspective.[9] This self-limitation is not due to some kind of bias, but rather to a simple lack of competences. As a result, I can just express my conviction—without having the expertise to support it with adequate evidences—that some of the paradigms described characterize also non-Western traditions. In China and India, for instance, we may find understandings of social, political and legal order that remind us closely of those patterns that I will call, in the following, "particularistic" and "universalistic".[10] For instance, as regards

China, while the philosophies of Confucius and Laozi contain "universalistic" elements, Han Fei and the School of Legalism focus rather on the interests of the single political community, being thus comparable with authors here labelled under the paradigm of "particularism". Analogously, in India the realism of the *Laws of Manu* and the combination of pragmatism and anthropologic pessimism of Kautilya's *Arthashastra*[11] are contrasted by the radical pacifism and universalistic intent of Buddhism.[12] On the other hand, there are paradigms as well, in particular the "individualistic" understanding of social life, which are likely to be exclusive products of the Western philosophical tradition. Lastly, the globalization of knowledge has eradicated the paradigms from the context in which they were first developed, spreading them all over the world and making them a common intellectual legacy of humankind. In any case the analysis, precisely because it is only concentrated on Western traditions, should be seen as an invitation to the scholars endowed with enough proficiency about non-Western conceptions of social order to engage in the discussion, completing and differentiating the conceptual map of the "paradigms".

## 1.3 The Contents of the Paradigms of Order: Continuity and Revolutions

After having clarified what a "well-ordered society" is assumed to be and what the meaning of the concept of "paradigm" is, it is now time to address, more specifically, the question about the content of the "paradigms of order" as the main categories of a metatheory of social order. Putting the previously described concepts together, we can specify that a "paradigm of order" is a set of concepts and abstract claims as definitions of those concepts, which shape the understanding of what are and should be the conditions for a peaceful, mutually advantageous and, in the most favourable situations, even cooperative social interaction in a certain period of human history. Concretely, the set of fundamental concepts that characterizes every paradigm of order necessarily makes a claim on three essential questions concerning how a well-ordered social interaction is and should be organized: its extension and limits, its ontological foundation, and its unitary or pluralist structure, where "pluralist" is assumed to be identical with multilevel or polyarchic.

Let us start with the first question: Is social order inevitably limited in its extension, both as regards the individuals involved and the territorial range, or is it at least potentially unlimited and therefore cosmopolitan? At the beginning of the Western conception of social order, and for many centuries thereafter, no idea of a universal humanity was present, so that the only conceivable order was the one established in the single political communities, whereas between them only containment of disorder was deemed possible. This *particularistic* understanding of order was challenged for the first time—with little practical consequences—by the Stoic philosophy, and was then replaced, as the leading paradigm of order, with the *universalistic* approach of Christendom, when the new religion began to deeply influence political and legal thinking. Albeit with all the significant contradictions that affect its proposal, according to the Christian political and legal philosophy the *communitas christiana* is at the same time a peaceful order, in which war should be seen—and prevented—as the exception and not as the rule, and a potentially universal community. The turn, first introduced by Stoicism and then established by the Christian hegemony on Western culture, marked the *first paradigmatic revolution*, namely the passage from a paradigm characterized by a particularistic vision of order, to a new pattern of order. This was typified by the idea that the whole humanity constitutes just *one* community with shared values and rules. Since then, the dichotomy between "particularism" and "universalism" has divided the theories on international law and relations in two opposite camps,[13] until just a few decades ago first signs of a possible overcoming of the contraposition have emerged as a result of a further paradigmatic revolution—which I will address later—from the unitary to a post-unitary understanding of order.

Although opposed as regards the question of extension and limits of a well-ordered society, the first two paradigms share the same vision with reference to the second assertion that cannot be missing in a paradigm of order, namely the assumption concerning the ontological basis of order. Indeed, order must be based on some social structure that guarantees its stability. In fact, we can find in the first "particularistic" paradigm of order as well as in its first "universalistic" counterpart many different social structures on which social order is founded: the *polis*, the enlarged family, the nation, or the *ethnos*, and the continental hegemony of a *Volk* or of a civilization on the one side; the *communitas christiana* and the community of humanity sharing interests and values on the other. Despite the differences, yet, all these social structures have one essential element in common: they share the same *organic* or *holistic* understanding of society. A social and political community is conceived of in an "organic" way when it is seen as a "body", a *corpus*, the totality of which—its *holon*, according to the old Greek word from which the concept of "holism" is drawn—weights more than the sum of its members. In other words, according to the "holistic" conception the community has, as a "totality", an added value if compared to the individuals who belong to it, with the consequence that the interests of the community deserve more attention than those of its members, and the values embedded in the whole of society are assumed to be superior to the liberty of the individuals living in it. Indeed, the *polis* is believed to have primacy over its citizen, and the same can be said for the enlarged family, the nation or the civilization with regard to their members. Analogously, the *communitas christiana* and the whole of humanity express a value that is higher than the value that characterizes each single individual or even the sum of them. The difference—quite not marginal—is that the *holon* in particularistic perspective is a community of limited range, while in the universalistic perspective the "totality" potentially includes the whole humanity. Attention should be paid, here, to the difference between the *holon*, which means the totality of an entity that can also be of limited range but is characterized by the priority given to the unity and not to the parts, and the *pan*, which refers to an unlimited whole or to the universe. The use of the concept of "holism" follows this distinction, so that we have two forms of it—the "holistic particularism" and the "holistic universalism". They are divided by an opposite understanding of the extension of order, but united by the assumption that order cannot but be based on the idea of the unity and homogeneity of a social community located far above the individuals. As a result, the holistic paradigm can also include communities of non-universal extension, provided that they are typified by the genetic, ontological and axiological superiority of the totality over its components.

While the first two paradigms of order are characterized by the supremacy of the community over the individuals, the *second paradigmatic revolution* turned this hierarchy upside down: with the emerging of the paradigm of *individualism*, in the early Modern Ages, the individuals were not regarded as spinning around the community as the core of social life any longer, but were themselves considered, with their interests, rights and reason, the barycentre of society. Whereas in the former conception the individuals were assumed to have to serve the society, in the individualistic paradigm of order it is the society, with its political and legal institutions, that has to be a helpful tool at the service of the individual priorities. Therefore, while as regards the extension of order the field of the most significant answers is measured by the dichotomy between particularism and universalism, a second dichotomy—this time between holism and individualism—separates the theories on the ontological basis of order in two different camps as well, although the variants within both of them may be in this case even more relevant.

The first paradigm that came to be established after the second paradigmatic revolution combined individualism, after some hesitations, with a cosmopolitan scope of order. Indeed, since the core of a well-ordered society is made of individuals universally defined only on the basis of endowments like rights, reason and rationally justifiable as well as contestable interests, it would be untenable if this kind of well-ordered society were to be subjected to insuperable limitations at the allegedly non-traversable borders of closed and homogeneous communities. If the individuals, who are the fundament of order, are universal in their most essential qualities, then also the order cannot but be universal. However, a second paradigm with individuals at its centre was sketched—in this case without an explicitly universal horizon. It is the paradigm in which the centrality of individuals comes along with a particularistic definition of interests. It has been claimed that, if all individuals are equal, order must be universal. This is true, yet, only if order is understood as *public* and *reflexive*, thus aiming at protecting common interests which are defined as the result of procedures. However, if individuals pursue only *private* interests and common advantage arises exclusively as a quasi-natural—and thus *unreflexive*—consequence of egoistic actions, then order itself will be particularistic, in the sense that it lacks a dimension which goes beyond the egoistic benefit for the single actor. The difference between this kind of *individualistic particularism* and particularism in its holistic form is that order is not identified, here, with the homogenous community, but with the sphere of interests of the private, especially economic, agents. Concretely, this pattern of social order is defined by the rules of interaction between private economic actors independently of public power and priorities. Yet, the third paradigmatic revolution that would have been needed to establish the paradigm of "particularistic individualism" remained unaccomplished, essentially because the theories that could be led back to this new pattern of order never developed its fundamental tenets with sufficient coherence, rather maintaining strong connections, albeit in a quite original way, to the former paradigms.

A *third paradigmatic revolution* occurred much later—actually just a few decades ago—and involved what has been described as the third element that is always present in a paradigm of order, namely the assertion concerning the unitary or non-unitary character of the well-ordered society. Regardless of whether they were particularistic or universalistic on the one hand, holistic or individualistic on the other, the paradigms of order were all characterized, before the third paradigmatic revolution, by a *unitary* idea of order. This means that, in all these previous paradigms, the institutional structure and the system of norms are considered "well-ordered" only if they are organized as a coherent, vertical and hierarchical unity, i.e., as a pyramidal structure in which normative and institutional conflicts can only be settled insofar as the priority of some norms or institutions over the conflicting ones is unequivocally determined. Instead, the third paradigmatic revolution has ushered in an understanding of order in which the well-ordered society is conceived of as a polyarchic, horizontal and interconnected social texture, more in the form of a network than of a pyramid. Within this complex reality, institutional and normative conflicts do not pose a deadly threat to order any longer; instead they are channelled into procedures aiming not to reinforce hierarchy, but to avoid disruptive consequences or even to reach consensus. In some implementations of the post-unitary conception of order a kind of superiority of certain norms or institutions remains; yet, this priority is not grounded in the capability of displaying hard power, but rather in the disposal of superior legitimacy resources.

Since the post-unitary turn in the theories of order dates back to just a few decades ago, the consolidation of its results is still an ongoing process. As a consequence, the research will present three different paradigms as possible outcomes of the third revolution: each of them takes up the new perspective, while outlining distinct aspects and reaching diverging normative conclusions. Whereas for the periods of history located back in time we can reduce the analysis to just those theories and paradigms that stood the test of time, the focus cannot be so clear and reductive for what is happening before our eyes. The scrutiny of contemporary phenomena is—at least in the realms of human sciences—almost necessarily farsighted: somehow Hegel was right when he said that the owl of Minerva only flies at dusk.[14]

## 1.4 The Structure of the Book

The following chapters present the paradigms of order in a chronological sequel as regards both the time of their first development as well as the evolution within each single paradigm. Nevertheless, since changes, crises and advancements are portrayed for each paradigm singularly from its first elaboration to the present time, it will occur that older variants of more recent paradigms will be addressed later than newer variants of the older patterns. To reconstruct the complete timeline of the evolution of the theories of order it will be therefore necessary, for the reader, to cross over between the chapters, filling the time in which a single paradigm may have been affected by a crisis with the variant of another paradigm that has characterized the understanding of social order in that period. Being confronted with the necessity to decide between outlining the synchronic evolution of different conceptions of order, and addressing the theoretical development inside each of them, I decided to prefer the second option—essentially because of the nature of the inquiry, which does not aim at being a historical reconstruction of the ongoing process of formulation and re-formulation of ideas on social order, but tries rather to elaborate a synthetic and systematic analysis of different patterns of social interaction, and of how they adapt themselves to new challenges.

The second chapter focuses on the most ancient of all paradigms of order, namely on the conception according to which order is only possible within limited and rather homogeneous communities, whereas between these social, political and legal communities only containment of dis-order is feasible. Furthermore, order must here be grounded on an ontological basis in which the whole of the community is clearly assumed to have more value than the single individual, or even than the sum of all individuals that constitute the community. Due to the first characteristic this pattern of order is *particularistic*, and due to the second it is *holistic*; therefore, I will call this first paradigm of order *holistic particularism* (2). To elucidate the first formulation of the most essential tenets of the paradigm, we have to go back to Ancient Greece (2.1): while the historian Thucydides laid down the fundamental assumptions of the particularistic vision of order (or disorder) in a way that has remained almost unchanged until today (2.1.1), the philosophers Plato and Aristotle delivered the first justifications of why a society should be conceived of as holistic (2.1.2). The justifications they gave, however, were considerably discordant: Plato saw the ontological fundament of society in a concept of *justice* that, in its organic content, differs significantly from ours, whereas Aristotle proposed to draw the motivation for solidarity and cohesion within the particularistic polity from the assumption that the political community would be nothing else but an *enlarged family*. Although Aristotle's idea of the familistic essence of society lasted as a dominant element of political and social philosophy for almost two thousand years, the paradigm of holistic particularism fell into a deep crisis at the beginning of the Middle Ages, when the emergence of a new pattern of order relegated the old one to a marginal role. The paradigm experienced a revival in the early Modern Ages (2.2) with Machiavelli'a *realism* (2.2.1) and Bodin's theory of *sovereignty* (2.2.2). Yet, this short renaissance only anticipated a new period of obscuration which set in when the familistic theory of society, that had been linked by Bodin and even more by Filmer (2.2.3) to the destiny of the absolutistic power of European dynasties, faded away along with the first revolutionary blows against the crowned heads. A new epistemological, ethical and ontological substrate for the paradigms was needed—and this was found at the beginning of the nineteenth century in the idea of the *nation*, which corroborated the paradigm again and shaped the history of Europe and, as a consequence, of the whole world for at least one and a half centuries (2.3). As the power of the European nation states weakened as the result of an increasingly globalized world and of the appearance on the scene, in the aftermath of World War I, of continental superpowers with global ideological appeal, the paradigm changed once again its shape and, specifically, its ontological fundament, now situating it in an *hegemonic* political entity made cohesive by the opposition to an existentially threatening enemy. Based now on the struggle between friends and enemies, Carl Schmitt's political community is ideologically flexible and territorially large enough to gather sufficient resources for the worldwide fight for survival (2.4).

In the middle of the twentieth century the paradigm of holistic particularism had thus developed three different variants (2.5): *realism*, claiming that any order—or better: any containment of disorder—is the frail result of the quest for power; *nationalism*, asserting that the limited community characterized by a homogeneous identity is the only possible ground for justice and cooperation; and *hegemonism*, seeking a larger and more flexible basis for identity so as to make ordered societies capable of meeting the challenges of a globalized world. Each of these variants of the paradigm has been then taken up and reshaped in the last decades, in an effort to make them fit for the new social, political, economic and ideological situation. As a consequence, the classic realism developed into the structural *neo-realism*, in which the assumption that politics is made of struggles for power is limited to the realm of international relations (2.6). At the same time, supporters of nationalism upheld the centrality of the nation state, even in times of increasing transboundary interconnections, in guaranteeing at least that fragile social order that is deemed achievable (2.7). Lastly, also hegemonism has assumed new features, according to the new needs that emerged in contemporary politics (2.8), taking form either in the theory of the "clash of civilizations" (2.8.1), or in the neoconservative ideology (2.8.2). In a more and more globalized world, however, the idea that the possible horizon of well-ordered social interactions cannot reach beyond the homogeneous community—even if the borders of this community have been increasingly widened through the ongoing development of the variants of the paradigm—is becoming difficult to maintain (2.9). This will be exemplified by focusing on developments occurring within two conceptual strands of the paradigm: first, on how the theory of rational choice and strategic rationality—often used by supporters of holistic particularism to justify the predominance of egoistic attitudes—can be adopted to substantiate a broader horizon of order as well (2.9.1), and, secondly, on how the idea of the specific and unique identity of every political community has overcome—in some communitarian approaches—the most narrow particularistic dimension, so as to embrace the until then unusual perspective of a reconciliation with the cosmopolitan view (2.9.2).

The third chapter focuses on the second paradigm of order, in which it is assumed that the well-ordered society is extended to include, at least potentially, the whole humankind. Like in the older paradigm, however, it is maintained that the community on which the order is based is endowed with a higher value, as a whole, than the individuals of whom it is composed, except that, in this case, this community has a *cosmopolitan* scope (3). The paradigmatic revolution that established *holistic universalism* as the leading paradigm of order was initiated by the *Stoic* philosophers (3.1); yet, the idea of a community of humankind did not become a powerful historical force until Christian thinkers made it to one of the essential tenets of their vision of the world (3.2.1). Since *Christendom* became, in the passage from antiquity to the Middle Ages, the dominant ideology of the Western civilization, it was necessary to articulate the Christian idea of order not just in religious and philosophical but also in *political* terms. Two quite opposite conceptions were thus developed: firstly, the idea of a *universal monarchy*, and secondly, the vision of a *multilevel structure* of legal norms and political institutions that anticipated by many centuries some aspects of the contemporary understanding of international order (3.2.2). Despite the explicitly universal scope of the Christian message of peace and just order, Christendom in general—and, later, Catholicism in particular—never fully lived up to their promises. In particular, two questions remained unanswered: firstly, what had to be done with non-Christian populations? And, secondly, should social and political renewal be simply condemned, or should it be accepted, at least partially, and integrated into the Christian-Catholic understanding of a just order? With arguably the only remarkable exception of Bartolomé de Las Casas and his disciples, whose groundbreaking ideas paved the way for future paradigmatic developments—to some extent even beyond the horizon of holistic universalism—(3.2.4), the prevailing attitude, also among the most outstanding philosophers of the Catholic tradition of the early Modern Ages, lastly justified *discriminations and abuses against non-Christian peoples*, as well as a *short-sighted defence of the political status quo* (3.2.3). This approach characterized the vision of order of the Catholic Church until the Second Vatican Council, during which a first opening took place towards the recognition of the "others" as well as towards modern political ideas such as liberalism, democracy and the priority of human rights (3.2.5). Yet, this renewed approach to modernity was largely repealed in later documents (3.2.6), leaving the task of defending new perspectives to non-institutional personalities within the Catholic community (3.2.7). After decades of restoration, a fresh wind of innovation seems to have recently reached the Vatican Mount again (3.2.8).

In the face of the structural and enduring biases that impoverished the Christian-Catholic vision of a universal order of the whole humankind, an alternative arose which—resorting back to the Stoic assumption of the universal sociability of all human beings—aimed at grounding universalism on *natural reason* alone (3.3). To do so, theologians and philosophers—mostly influenced by the Protestant Reformation—detached natural law from revelation, in an effort to give it, this way, a purely rational basis in the social ontology of human nature. Nevertheless, even if the attempt to separate the idea of order from religious postulations was in principle correct, the purpose of grounding universal order on a lastly unprovable conjecture regarding the "true nature" of human beings proved to be inconsistent, so that even Grotius, probably the most significant exponent of this strand of political thought in early Modern Ages, became entangled in a knot of contradictions (3.3.1). After one and a half centuries in which holistic-universalistic rationalism had consolidated the position of a continental political philosophy which was rather sceptical towards the individualistic approaches coming first from England and then also from France (3.3.2), a long period of decadence began, as individualism and nationalism gained dominance of the scene. The theory of *natural law* was lastly rediscovered in the last decades of the twentieth century, following in particular the breakdown of civilization that occurred during World War II, which seemed to prove that an order without a metapositive foundation cannot stand the challenges of history; nevertheless, the epistemological problems that affected former elaborations of the paradigm can hardly be regarded as definitively resolved (3.3.3). In spite of some unsettled theoretical doubts and deficits, the assumption of a general sociability of humans has moved from moral and legal philosophy into the field of international law, building the conceptual fundament of what has been called the "theory of the constitutionalization of international law" (3.3.4).

The third paradigm of order is presented in the fourth chapter. In contrast to the former patterns, order is here founded on the centrality of the individuals, and public power is only justified to preserve their rights and interests (4). After a short presentation of the epistemological premises of the individualistic turn in Western thought, as they were laid down by Descartes (4.1), the analysis concentrates on the consequences of the paradigmatic revolution for the understanding of political power and legal order, in particular on Hobbes's hugely innovative contractualist theory of state (4.2). In the following, the liberal and democratic outcomes are presented that Locke, on the one hand, and Rousseau on the other drew from the premises laid down by their philosophical predecessor—with the assumptions, respectively, of a minimal public power, or of a political compensation of social inequalities (4.3). It is with Kant, however, that the new paradigm came to develop its full potentialities: in his writings, indeed, *individualism* reaches the universal scope that was already implicit in its theoretical presuppositions (4.4). The paradigm of *universalistic individualism*, brought to its full completion, maintains for the first time the priority of individuals over the whole of the community, combining it with the assumption that the social order created by them— due to the fact that all individuals are identically or at least comparably endowed with rights, reason and interests—cannot but be cosmopolitan. However, if the order should be cosmopolitan, then it is to assume that international law has to enjoy priority over domestic law. This revolutionary turn in the traditional hierarchy of norms was introduced explicitly for the first time by Hans Kelsen (4.5). Kelsen's conception of legal order is surely one of the most courageous achievements in the whole history of the philosophy of law—just as the entire paradigm of universalistic universalism is of paramount importance as the intellectual source of such essential attainments as liberalism, democracy and individual rights. Nevertheless, the paradigm is affected by a substantial deficit: since the unity and truth of knowledge are exclusively grounded, here, on the internal unity and coherence of the *subject*, whereas the social dimension of knowledge is almost completely removed, no other order can be conceived than the one that is itself *unitary, coherent and hierarchical*. The consequence is that a polyarchic structure of institutions and norms is, in principle, not accepted as "true" order, but condemned as disorder and as a threat for social and normative stability. The conviction that a structure of institutions and norms that deserves the appellation of "order" has to be centralized, unitary and hierarchical lies also at the basis of the most recent renewal of the idea of the "federal world republic" (4.6).

The further step, in Chapter 5, consists in outlining what can be called a "failed paradigmatic revolution" (5). Chapter 4 analyses how the individualistic turn in Western thought founded a new conception of public order as well as a new definition of legitimate authority. Nevertheless, individualism as the basis for order can also be understood in another way, namely as the fundament of a merely *private* and spontaneous regulation of the interactions of mainly economic actors. Insofar as the regulation does not aim at establishing a general—maybe even cosmopolitan— public power with the task of guaranteeing shared interests, but only safeguards the private realm of self-realization, this paradigm of order has to be regarded as *particularistic*. Some strands of philosophical, legal and economic thinking made—with intervals of many centuries— at least three attempts to establish a new paradigm of order centred on *particularistic individualism*. None of them, however, was successful in consolidating a truly new vision of social order. The Hellenistic "doctrine of the universal economy" as well as the Lex mercatoria of the Middle Ages, albeit appraising the role of trade for the first time in Western history, did not ultimately conceive of this as being at the service of the private interests of the merchants; instead, the economic activity of the tradesmen was justified as an essential contribution to the establishment—or re-establishment—of an organic world harmony, jeopardized by the unequal distribution of resources. Therefore, rather than setting up a new paradigm, an innovative and unprecedented role was envisaged for trade within the well-known context of the holistic-universalistic understanding of society (5.1). Nor was the third attempt to coin a new pattern of social order—namely the theory of free trade elaborated in England between the second half of the eighteenth century and the beginning of the nineteenth century—successful in construing a coherent conception. In fact, the ultimate task of private entrepreneurship was considered, in this case, the increase of the wealth of the nation, so that the egoistic interests of private actors, far from being the barycentre of order, were positively reappraised just because this was deemed to be the best way to enhance the power of the nation (5.2).

The last three chapters shift the focal point to the post-unitary paradigms of order, or—more precisely—to the theories of social order developed in the last decades that, against the background of a non-hierarchical and rather horizontal epistemological approach, are marking the origin of new paradigms. Chapter 6 concentrates, in particular, on *systems theory* (6). After presenting the most essential features of systems theory as it has been laid down especially by Niklas Luhmann (6.1), the analysis will converge on a significant evolution of the last decades that was made possible precisely by the introduction of the theoretical organon of systems theory (6.2). In fact, since systems theory assumes that society differentiates itself into distinct specialized subsystems, and that each of these subsystems—characterized by a specific functional rationality—is self-referential and independent of the environment made by all other subsystems, it is now possible to conceive of the corpus of norms that regulates the interaction of private economic agents—namely the Lex mercatoria—as a self-regulating order, and therefore as an autonomous paradigm of order. In other words, systems theory provides the theoretical organon that was missing in the former attempts to build a pattern of order only related to the self-organization of transnational economic actors, without any reference to any role possibly or even necessarily played by public power (6.3). The last paragraph of the chapter will be then dedicated to some critical remarks on both the epistemological premises of systems theory in general, as well as on the assumption of an independence of the transnational economic order from national, supranational, international and supra-state public authority (6.4).

Chapter 7 discusses *postmodernism* as the second way to overcome the unitary understanding of order (7). The first paragraph of the chapter focuses on the philosophical renewal that anticipated the rising of postmodern thinking and then went along with its further developments (7.1). The specific feature of this paradigm of order consists in the assumption—made, in such explicit terms and with such a large influence, for the first time in Western thinking—that order, in the sense of rules that the society in its totality has to follow, is in principle something threatening, at least potentially, for the self-realization of the concrete individualities. Whereas order had always been regarded, from the very beginning of Western culture, as the necessary condition for human beings to develop their capacities—or at least to have some chance to do so—postmodernism turns the perspective upside down, looking at the concept of order with unprecedented criticism, if not with a harsh refusal. At this point, two different strands of the postmodern approach develop, both applying the critical look at the world of social, political and legal interactions. The first variant picks up the most radical interpretation of postmodern criticism, maintaining that, insofar as order is oppressive—either in essence or, at least, as expression of patriarchal or colonial rule—the only possibility to make the society more "human" would consist in an uncompromising rejection of the established rules. This approach ultimately aims at substituting traditional ideas of the well-ordered society either with spontaneous forms of self-expression of subjectivity, or with post-patriarchal and non-Western social and normative alternatives (7.2). The second variant is by far less extreme and relies on the more moderate dimension of postmodern critical analysis of the modern society: order in its absoluteness remains threatening, but it does not need to be radically denied and thus subverted; rather, it has just to be de-structured as a whole and split into a plurality of *orders*—in plural. Given the context of plurality, order loses its all-embracing, tyrannical comprehensiveness, and the individuals gain a new and better chance to realize their plans, according to their priorities, within the spaces generated by the break of the former rigid texture (7.3). Concretely, the postmodern conception of the disentanglement of the individuals for their better self-realization in the context of non-hierarchical and network-like structures of institutions and norms takes four different shapes: the theory of *legal pluralism* (7.3.1); the *neo-liberal understanding* of the state as well as of international relations and law (7.3.2); the justification of *global governance* (7.3.3); and the denial of any truth content of the law and, according to the princi*ples of legal formalism*, the plea for the use of legal instruments following individual priorities (7.3.4). Albeit highly innovative, the postmodern overture towards a more pluralistic understanding of order runs the risk of diminishing the former standards for legitimacy and normativity (7.4).

The eighth and final chapter is centred on the third post-unitary pattern of order, i.e., on the *communicative paradigm* (8). Originally, this conception can be traced back to the theory of *intersubjectivity* sketched in Hegel's early writings. Later, it was resumed, although in a quite different form, by the young Marx. In both cases, however, the further development of their philosophical or economic views in the mature writings eventually led to subjectivistic—and thus unitary—outcomes (8.1). After more than a century of subjectivistic domination in Western philosophy, intersubjectivity was rediscovered, first, by Hannah Arendt and by the American pragmatists (8.2). In a second step, then, the authors of the second Frankfurt School, especially Karl-Otto Apel and Jürgen Habermas, further developed the notion of intersubjectivity by integrating the old Hegelo-marxism not only with the theories of political interaction developed by Arendt and the American pragmatism, but also with elements originating from Kant's moral philosophy, Heidegger's social ontology, and the contemporary philosophy of language. After presenting the most essential epistemological assumptions of the communicative paradigm, in particular the concept of communicative rationality and the consensus theory of truth (8.3), I will concentrate on their application to the political realm, both at the domestic and at the international level (8.4). The result is a complex and multilayered vision, in which the clearly expressed preference for democratic legitimacy at any level of governance is reconciled with the necessity of global inclusion, and the recognition of diversity as a value—shared with the other post-unitary understandings— is now linked, much better than in postmodernism or in systems theory, to the high normative standards that characterized the most distinguished achievements of Western modern individualism (8.5).

## Notes

1. Hesiod, *Theogony*, Hugh G. Evelyn-White trans., Harvard University Press, Cambridge (MA) 1914, ll. 116–138.
2. Ovid, *Metamorphoseon libri* (3–8), John Dryden trans., 1717, Liber primus, 5–9, 15–25.

3. Andreas Anter, *Die Macht der Ordnung*, Mohr Siebeck, Tübingen 2004, at 1.
4. Thomas Kuhn, *The Structure of Scientific Revolutions* (1962), University of Chicago Press 1996.
5. Bertrand Russell, *A History of Western Philosophy*, Simon and Schuster, New York 1972, at 66.
6. Jürgen Habermas, *Erkenntnis und Interesse* (1968), Suhrkamp, Frankfurt a. M. 1973, at 221 et seq.
7. Karl Popper, *Conjectures and Refutations: The Growth of Scientific Knowledge*, Basic Books, New York/London 1962.
8. John A. Vasquez, *The Power of Power Politics: A Critique*, Pinter, London 1983, at 4.
9. Antonio Truyol y Serra, *Historia del derecho internacional público*, Tecnos, Madrid 1998, at 13.
10. *Ib.*, at 21.
11. Kautilya, *Arthashastra*, Penguin Books India, New Delhi 1992.
12. Ulrich Schneider, *Einführung in den Buddhismus*, Wissenschaftliche Buchgesellschaft, Darmstadt 1980, at 142.
13. Armin von Bogdandy, Sergio Dellavalle, *Parochialism, Cosmopolitanism, and the Paradigms of International Law*, in: Mortimer N. S. Sellers (ed.), *Parochialism, Cosmopolitanism, and the Foundations of International Law*, Cambridge University Press, Cambridge/New York 2012, 40–117; Armin von Bogdandy, Sergio Dellavalle, *Universalism and Particularism: A Dichotomy to Read Theories on International Order*, in: Stefan Kadelbach, Thomas Kleinlein, David Roth-Isigkeit (eds.), *System, Order, and International Law*, Oxford University Press, Oxford/New York 2017, 482–504.
14. Georg Wilhelm Friedrich Hegel, *Grundlinien der Philosophie des Rechts*, in G. W. F. Hegel, *Werke in zwanzig Bänden*, Eva Moldenhauer and Karl Markus Michel eds., Suhrkamp, Frankfurt am Main 1971 et seq., Vol. 7, at 28 (Engl. translation: G. W. F. Hegel, *Philosophy of Right*, S. W. Dyde trans., Bell, London 1896).

CHAPTER 2

# Holistic Particularism as the First Paradigm of Order, Or: On the Order of Limited and Single Polities and the Exclusion of Inter-state Order

Homer's *Iliad* describes a world dominated by a handful of heroes, while the rest of the population remains in their shadow, doomed to complete indifference or, at best, to the role of passive victims—without too much of a feeling of empathy—of the furious actions of the protagonists. It is the picture of an aristocratic society, in which the stage belongs to few, whereas the many—tied to the rulers by bonds of personal loyalty—are condemned to marginality and insignificance. Yet, between Homer's time and the flourishing of Greek classicism something happened that indelibly changed Western culture: society transformed itself, from its aristocratic origins, into a community of free and equal. Surely, the exercise of political freedom was only reserved to men and, among them, only to those who enjoyed full citizens' rights, while equality was understood, rather than in material terms, as isonomy or as the formal condition in which the whole population is subjected to the same laws.[1] Yet, as a consequence of what has to be nevertheless regarded as a historic passage, a question arose, unknown to the former generations: How can a community hold together if its members do not see themselves as having a personal relationship of tribal dependence from the rulers any longer? Or, in other words, which is the ideological glue that welds together a society made of free and equal?

The first answer to emerge to this fundamental question is testified by the lyricists of the seventh century B.C.E. Kallinos, in particular, exhorts his fellow citizens, in his verses, to fight bravely against the danger of a Cimmerian invasion:

> When will you show some courage, young comrades?
> How long will you lie back and do nothing?
> Lazing in shabby peace on our land bled by war,
> have you no shame before the neighboring townsmen?
> Let each man hurl his spear once more before he dies,
> for glory dazzles on our helmets when we battle
> the enemy for farmland and children and true wife.
> Death will come only when the web of destiny is spun.
> So move out, charge into the barbarous ranks
> with spear held high and shield gripping a brave heart.
> From death there is no escape; all men face the dark,
> even those with blood of gods in their veins.
> Often a man flees from the clash and thud of spears
> and comes home to fall into sudden doom,
> but he is neither loved nor missed by his townsmen.
> Yet when a hero dies the great and small shed tears;
> by a whole people a brave warrior is mourned.
> In life he seems a demigod before the crowd;
> as a marble pillar they look upon his strength,
> for all alone he does the great deeds of an army.[2]

It has been pointed out that these fragments show "an adaptation of Homeric style and language to the demands of the present", in the sense that they focus "on courage as sacrificial patriotism rather than a means chiefly for the acquisition of individual glory".[3] We see already here that the essence of the new community—the principle that holds it together—is the combination of commitment to the whole of the community, compared to which even the lives of the individuals have little meaning, and the fight against the outside enemy. From the very beginning of Western thought, internal cohesion and external opposition are thus the tie that binds the community of the free and equal.

The same understanding of society—maybe with even more explicit words—is expressed in the lyrics of Tyrtaeus, the Spartan national poet:

> It is beautiful when a brave man of the front ranks
> falls and dies, battling for his homeland,
> and ghastly when a man flees planted fields and city
> and wanders begging with his dear mother,
> aging father, little children and true wife.
> He will be scorned in every new village,
> reduced to want and loathsome poverty, and shame
> will brand his family line, his noble figure.
> Derision and disaster will hound him.
> A turncoat gets no respect or pity;
> so let us battle for our country and freely give
> our lives to save our darling children.
> Young men, fight shield to shield and never succumb
> to panic or miserable flight,
> but steel the heart in your chests with magnificence
> and courage. Forget your own life
> when you grapple with the enemy. Never run
> and let an old soldier collapse
> whose legs have lost their power.[4]

The traitor and the coward lose definitively their social bonds and are condemned, along with their families, to miserable isolation and perpetual contempt. Only those who are bound to their society by an unrestrained willingness to sacrifice, which has to be proved in the existential fight against the enemies, are admitted into the new community, founded on the principle of freedom and isonomy. This way, the Homeric tradition was modified "in the direction of a more corporate and collective ethos".[5]

Internal homogeneity of the community and antagonism against other communities are therefore the pillars on which the first understanding of order in Western thought is based. Each single polity has *its* order, but no consistent order is possible *between* polities. Yet, which reasons speak against the possibility of order beyond the borders of the single political communities? And what is the ontological fundament of this *particularistic* order? The rationale of particularism was already conceptualized in classical Greek antiquity, so that the arguments against the feasibility of a supposed supra-state order of peace that were given for the first time almost two and a half thousand years ago have remained largely the same throughout the centuries, even until present time (2.1.1). On the contrary, the ontological element supposed to build the basis for the order of the single communities has changed many times, being adapted from time to time to the requirements of the historical context. The only characteristic that persisted was—and still is—the *holistic* or *organic* nature of the entity that is assumed to be the source of social order. Yet, the general concept of holism or organicism was concretized in many different shapes, from the uncompromising identification of the individual with the polis (2.1.2.1) to the enlarged family (2.1.2.2), and from the nation (2.3) to the existential community struggling with external threats (2.4). As a result, the paradigms developed different variants (2.5), the supporters of which were then confronted with the challenges that the process of globalization poses to the idea that order can only be limited (2.6, 2.7, 2.8). In the last paragraph, I will address how some conceptual tools often used by the exponents of holistic particularism to support their preference, under certain circumstances—and in particular under the pressure of the conditions of an ever more interconnected world—can be almost reversed and put at the service, if not explicitly of a cosmopolitan vision, at least of a less narrow understanding of human interaction (2.9). This way, holistic particularism experiences its own dialectic and opens the gate to broader perspectives.

## 2.1 The First Appearance of the Paradigm in Ancient Greece

The convictions that no order can exist beyond the limited community—or that other orders possibly existing beyond the one that characterizes one's own community are lastly incommensurable with this—and that a community needs a certain degree of homogeneity to be well-ordered were surely not creations of ancient Greece. Rather, we can take for granted that they belonged already to the most essential assumptions of the prehistoric phase of human evolution as well as of all great cultures before the flourishing of Greece. The novelty introduced by the ancient Greek thought was the purpose—or even the necessity—of giving reasons for social order: in a community of free and equal social cohesion was not regarded any longer as self-evident; to the contrary, it had to be justified. Thus, we find in the ancient Greek culture the first well-argued justifications of both components of the earliest conception of order: the *particularistic* idea of a limited order (2.1.1) and the organic, or *holistic*, essence of social bond (2.1.2).

### 2.1.1 The Justification of Particularism in Thucydides

To find the first clearly stated defence of particularism, we have to go back as far as to the second half of the fifth century B.C.E., i.e., to the times of the Peloponnesian War, in which the two most powerful poleis, Athens and Sparta, faced each other in a long and self-devastating struggle for supremacy. In particular, we have to resort to Thucydides as the historian who masterly described the events of the war, while always pointing out the meaning that these could have in the broader perspective of general considerations on the essential tenets of social and political life.

Among the episodes of the war used by Thucydides to raise more general questions, one is of outstanding relevance for an assessment about the possible limits of order. It is the famous description of the siege of Melos by the Athenians and of its final destruction.[6] For a better understanding, it is necessary to briefly locate the facts into their context. The inhabitants of the island of Melos were Lacedaemonian settlers and therefore ethnically related to Sparta. As a result, they had refused to become part of the Attic League, dominated by Athens. However, Athens was not willing to accept that any island stood neutral in the conflict—regardless of the ethnic origin of its settlers—since this could encourage an attitude of resistance against its hegemony at sea, thus jeopardizing the most essential fundament of its strength. During the summer of 416 B.C.E., after fifteen years of almost uninterrupted war against the Spartans, the military commanders of the Athenians decided to break the resistance of Melos and sent a fleet of more than thirty galleys and three thousand soldiers to the Aegean island. After deploying the army in front of the city, the Athenian generals Cleomedes and Tisias ordered the ambassadors to go to the Melian magistrates to present a hideous alternative: either the Melians submitt themselves to Athens and pay tribute, or they would face annihilation. The Melian magistrates countered the Athenian ultimatum with four arguments. The first argument—which refers to the dangers and uncertainties of war that may strike even the most powerful—is merely prudential and lacks, therefore, a consistent normative content. This is not the case for the further claims, which build what has been—and still is—the conceptual nucleus of an idea of political order that goes beyond the selfish interests of the mightiest. To begin with, negotiations should not be initiated after military strength has been displayed to intimidate the counterpart: indeed, talks are thought to seek a just solution, according to the law, and not only to seal an inevitable submission as a result of the disparity of forces. Furthermore, the brutal application of the law of the strongest was a breach of the superior divine law. Finally, the Melians expressed their confidence in the intervention of a neutral third party—in this case, the Spartans—who should restore the principles of impartial justice.

Therefore, Thucydides puts in the mouth of the Melian magistrates the three most relevant elements of a non-particularistic vision of order, namely the conviction that the enforcement of a just legal order should prevail over power and the exercise of brute force; the belief in the existence of a law, dictated by reason or by God, which should keep in check egoistic self-interest by the force of its higher normative value; and the establishment of a neutral institution with the task of guaranteeing peace and justice. On the other hand, he makes the Athenian emissaries reply point by point and harshly express the most fundamental assumptions of the contrary position, i.e., of the particularistic view. Firstly, law has to be considered valid only in interactions between actors of comparable strength; instead, when the position of the actors is unbalanced, we cannot but acknowledge, as a matter of fact, that power necessarily prevails over the law. Secondly, it is the law of the gods themselves, or of nature, that commands that the strong rules over the weak; the contrary postulation is nothing but self-deception. Thirdly, and lastly, no third party can be correctly presumed to be neutral, or to intervene without pursuing self-interest; thus, if it has no individual interest in the question, it will not step in to protect the weak, and, if it has an individual interest indeed, the safeguard of its own interest will be the only criterion that determines the content of its actions. With contempt, the Athenian ambassadors added that no one was used to apply this principle more coherently than precisely those Spartans who had been invoked by the Melians as the defenders of the illusionary principle of a *super partes* legal order. The facts evolved in the most unfavourable and cruel way for the Melians. After they courageously rebuffed the blackmailing offer, the Athenian army laid siege to the city, which surrendered in the following winter. The vengeance coldly put in place by the victorious army was dreadful: breaking the common law of war of ancient Greece, all men of military age were slain, women and children were sold into slavery, and the population of Melos was replaced by Athenian settlers.

In describing the siege of Melos, Thucydides's purpose did not consist only in giving account of the facts and of the brutalization of the Hellenic people as a consequence of the Peloponnesian War but also—and even more—in working out from the story what he regarded as the essential and inescapable rules of the interaction between social and political communities. Even though his attitude is ostensibly free from moral evaluation, the only approach that he considered reasonable and justifiable was to accept what he assumed to be the immutable reality, namely that politics is quest for power, that strength cannot be counterbalanced by norms, and that it is advisable to act prudentially according to these rules. Those who believe in the chimaera of a stable international order are not to be condemned at the moral level; rather, they must be pitied as the Athenians did with their enemies and their hopes: "we bless your innocent minds, but affect not your folly",[7] since "you are the only men ... that think future things more certain than things seen, and behold things doubtful through desire to have them true".[8]

Besides the three features that constitute the core of the particularistic understanding of order—the prevalence of power over law, the rejection of the idea of an inclusive law of reason comprising the whole humankind and the scepticism as regards the role of independent institutions—Thucydides added a fourth element, i.e., a deep pessimism about the nature of human beings. Anthropological pessimism has characterized, in fact, the vision of all supporters of particularism, but is not exclusive to them. Kant, for instance, was profoundly pessimistic as regards the driving forces of human nature; nonetheless, he decidedly endorsed a cosmopolitan vision of order. More specifically, according to the Greek historian human interaction is mainly driven by three sentiments: honour, desire for profit and fear, which, though partially already negative for themselves, generate an even more negative outcome if taken together.[9] In Thucydides's view every political agent, especially if powerful and distinguished by a glorious historical past, develops a sense of honour based on the awareness of its achievements. This strong feeling of pride results, then, in the tendency to dominate over other agents or communities which are perceived as inferior. It is, in fact, a general law that "the weaker [is] ... kept under by the stronger".[10] Thus, desire for profit is added to the sense of honour, insofar as selfish benefit is derived from the resources that the submitted community puts to the service of the interests of the hegemonic polity. Finally, fear emerges, causing the dominant political agent to act with as much determination and violence as it believes that the opposing power or unfaithful ally is endangering its own well-being or even its existence.

Thucydides seems to apply this general rule to all political agents, be they individual or collective, and regardless of whether they operate within the domestic arena or at the international level. In other words, politics appears to be essentially a struggle for power, in which the stronger is destined to dominate and the weaker should be wisely advised to behave cautiously and accept submission in order to avoid annihilation. However, the overall application of what is assumed to be the general rule of politics fails to explain a simple matter of fact, i.e., use of violence and unfettered struggle for power happen quite often in international relations, while they are rather the exception in the domestic domain. Thucydides himself acknowledged that the best that can be accomplished in the relations between individual polities is to limit the harm that they can do to each other; on the contrary, explosions of physical violence within the borders of the polity must be seen as the consequence of an extremely pervasive— and unusual—crisis of the polity, up to the dissolution of its institutions in the convulsions of civil war.[11] Therefore, even if we embrace the particularistic standpoint, admitting that order—in the true sense of the word—is essentially impossible at the international level, we cannot deny that a well-ordered domestic stability exists indeed, which may be always in danger, but is nonetheless far more reliable than the truce that can be realized beyond the borders. Although implicitly assuming the existence of a difference between the domestic and the international domains, Thucydides gave only a couple of clues as regards the rationale behind it. "Kinship" and the "established laws" are mentioned as the factors that guarantee an acceptable level of stability within the healthy polity.[12] Yet, these references are far too marginal to lay down a consistent theory on the fundament of a well-ordered community. To find more sophisticated explications, we have to abandon the field of history and enter the domain of political philosophy.

### 2.1.2 The Holistic Understanding of Society in Ancient Political Philosophy

Thucydides was the first Western thinker who clearly articulated the conceptual fundaments of the particularistic understanding of order. He also implicitly admitted that disorder—given the premises of particularism—is essentially a feature of international relations, while a more stable form of societal interactions characterizes the internal life of the individual polity. However, he did not explain where the borders of a fairly well-ordered society should be located, therefore avoiding the question on how far this can reach. Furthermore, his work does not offer more than marginal hints as regards which ontological basis the well-ordered society would have, although the nature of this ontological fundament also essentially determines the possible extension of order.

To address the problem of the ontological basis for a limited order and, thus, of the social composition and structure of the well-ordered society, we have to turn to the two most outstanding political philosophers of ancient Greece, namely Plato and Aristotle. Both thinkers shared the fundamental conviction that a society, to be well-ordered, must be conceived as a *holon*, i.e., as a "totality" the worth of which has to be regarded as higher than the sum of its individual components. Put in a more visual form, the holistic community is assumed to be a "body", whose limbs are life- and useless without connection to the whole. Yet, whereas the organic understanding of the community builds the general framework of both Plato's and Aristotle's idea of order, the materials respectively used by them to construe the framework differ significantly.

### 2.1.2.1 Plato: The Unconditional Identification Between Citizens and Polis

In two of his most famous dialogues—*Gorgias* and *The Republic*—Plato targeted directly the interpretations of both politics as a quest for power and order as the rule of the mightiest, that had been prominently expressed by Thucydides a couple of decades earlier. In both dialogues, the "realistic" view of politics is advocated by exponents of the Sophist philosophy: Callicles in *Gorgias* and Thrasymachus in *The Republic*. To begin with the *Gorgias* dialogue, Plato makes Callicles explicitly claim that "nature itself shows this, that it is just for the better man to have more than the worse, and the more powerful than the less powerful".[13] Upholding the same view, Thrasymachus coldly states in the *Republic* that "justice ... is the interest of the stronger".[14] As a result, the concept of justice would only be a rhetoric disguise to cover what really matters and is justified by the laws of nature, namely expediency and the ruthless implementation of selfishness.

Plato replies through the words of his master Socrates. More specifically, Callicles's assertion is rejected by pushing it to its final consequences. Indeed, a community based only on the principle of the reckless rule of the most powerful is doomed to self-destruction[15] since no human society can survive without interiorizing a notion of justice that entails shared values.[16] However, it is not only necessary to demonstrate that a society dominated by selfish feelings is destined to succumb to centrifugal forces; it is also indispensable to clarify what is meant by a "true" notion of justice, as well as how a just society can develop and persist. This is the task that Plato takes up in his description of Socrates's answer to Thrasymachus in the *Republic*. After reaffirming that any government finds its raison d'être in pursuing common interests,[17] he turns—to positively define what justice is—to the origins of the social and political community. The rationale of the social bond consists, according to Plato, in the fact that every human being possesses specific abilities, while lacking others.[18] As a consequence, with reference to one's own necessities, every one of us produces too many goods positively related to one's own capacities, whereas she/he may be in want of those commodities, the production of which depends on skills that she/he does not have. Putting themselves together, albeit quite wanting beings if taken singularly, our fellow humans can realize a functioning and "just" *politeia*.

Thus, Plato's notion of justice is characterized by two aspects, which are both rather distant from our contemporary understanding: neither of them, in fact, is intrinsically related to the question of a reasonable justification of the distribution of resources. The first aspect connotes justice as the condition in which everyone implements the activity for which she/he has the most relevant natural predisposition.[19] Thus, a society is "just" if it is conceived of as an organic structure in which every part or member does the work for which she/he has the best aptitude. On the contrary, it is "unjust" if the division of labour is not sufficiently realized and there is a somehow inefficient overlapping of activities as well as a general tendency to interfere with occupations and decisions outside the sphere of one's own competencies. The second feature, instead, turns out to have a strong ethical implication. Indeed, the exchange of commodities and services cannot be based only on the principle of utility: in order to work, it must presuppose an indisputable identification of the citizens with the common good. Otherwise, once again, the political community is doomed to fail. Only if everyone is willing to submit her/his own interests to the common advantage, the community will be able to thrive.

With his theory of justice, Plato developed the first definition and justification of the ontological fundament of the holistic community. In his view, the social bond should include all those who are connected to each other in a process of division of labour and are disposed to identify their individual preferences with the interests of the community, ultimately regarding the latter as prevailing over the former. Given these premises, the inevitable consequence cannot but be that the well-ordered society is limited in composition and extension. In fact, it comprises only those individuals whose direct and predictable interactions unfold within the boundaries of a small territory and who are wholeheartedly committed to the values enshrined into the idea of common good of that specific community and to its well-being. It is almost superfluous to point out that no universalism is thinkable against this background. The horizon of Plato's well-ordered society is the polis, while among the Hellenes only a containment of disorder is possible. Indeed, although Plato distinguished between the conflicts of the Greeks against other peoples—which he called *polemoi* or "wars"—and the conflicts of Greeks among each other—which are defined as *staseis*, i.e., "civil wars" or even "unrest"—[20] nonetheless the content of the common law of the Hellenes is ultimately quite tiny, including only some rules of the law of war.[21]

### 2.1.2.2 Aristotle: The Enlarged Family as Social Basis of the Political Community

Plato's definition of the ontological fundament of the well-ordered society, with its presupposition of ideological and ethical homogeneity and of unrestricted commitment to the values of the community, was perhaps capable of mirroring—in the best case—the situation of the Greek poleis in their golden age. Yet, this time had expired at the latest with the Peloponnesian War, so that Plato's vision was hopelessly backward-oriented already in the time when it was formulated. In general—and even more in a period of great social and political unrest, in which the cohesion of the Greek polis was fading away—the individuals could not see the self-identification with the aims of their *politeia* as the one and only purpose of their life any longer. Social cohesion needed to rest on a new fundament, and the author who gave to this question a groundbreaking answer that deeply influenced political thought for almost two thousand years was Aristotle.

Fully aware of the necessity to develop an innovative political philosophy which could meet the challenges of the new social and political situation, Aristotle introduced three major novelties with respect to his predecessor. First, he gave a new definition of justice, according to which it is essentially related—in a way that is much nearer to our sensibility—to the principles that guide the distribution of resources and advantages following reasonable and justifiable criteria.[22] Therefore, in accordance with Aristotle's definition, a society is "just" not because its members unreservedly accomplish their respective tasks while putting their activities at the service of a shared idea of the common good. Rather, it is "just" insofar as resources and burdens are allocated on the basis of commendable reasons. Unlike Plato's, Aristotle's concept of justice—which is basically *distributive* justice—is thus relational in essence, since it always becomes "effective in relation to somebody else".[23] For that reason, however, justice cannot represent the ultimate goal of moral and political action. Indeed, in Aristotle's interpretation, the ultimate goal of moral and political action must always be an end in itself, i.e., one must do the action exclusively for its own inherent quality, with no relation to other persons or goods.[24] But distributive justice is inevitably realized in the context of relations between individuals and is necessarily related to something which is located outside, namely the goods that have to be distributed. The consequence is that, according to Aristotle's second major innovation, we have to find elsewhere the ultimate goal of our action, more precisely in what the Greek philosopher called *eudiamonìa*, or "happiness".[25] In fact, we can achieve happiness for ourselves and as an end in itself—but what is precisely the content of happiness? Every living being—Aristotle says—is "happy" whenever she/he can fulfil what best corresponds to her/his specific nature. Since the most specific activity that characterizes human beings consists in using their intellectual capacities, the highest goal of practical life should not be in the service for the political community, as in Plato's interpretation, but in what Aristotle defined as the "theoretical" or "contemplative" life.[26]

Despite his redefinition of justice, his conviction that happiness—and not the commitment to the political community—should be the highest goal of practical life, and the assertion that happiness can be best achieved through contemplation, Aristotle maintained—like Plato—that the *politeia* has to be organized as an organic and holistic community. Indeed, not only individuals but also communities should pursue happiness in order to realize their highest purpose.[27] And, to implement a good life in happiness and well-being, a polity has to be an end in itself: thus, as far as possible, it should be autarchic. According to Aristotle, the self-reliance of the *politeia* is best put into practice by the same means that Plato proposed to reach justice, i.e., through division of labour and the unrestrained devotion of each member of the community to the activity which is best suited to her/his skills.[28] Yet, justifying the commitment to the interests of the polity by the individuals becomes quite difficult if their ultimate goal is the essentially self-referential and apolitical pursuit of contemplation. Moreover, why should the members of the political community owe solidarity to each other if their most essential aim consists in living a life characterized by the individual searching for theoretical truth? On which fundament can the loyalty to the social group be based? Aristotle's answer is astonishingly plain and intuitively convincing at the same time: because all members of the political community belong to an enlarged family, so that they have to support the community as every good family member is expected to do as regards her/his relatives.[29] Again, it is self-evident that this bond cannot reach beyond the borders of the single polis, so that Aristotle's familistic holism is even more manifestly particularistic than Plato's civic ethos.

Therefore, in accordance with Aristotle's familistic understanding of the social and political community, the ontological basis for homogeneity and solidarity is natural kinship. Although, within a rather large and complex social bond, we are not able to directly recognize our fellow citizens as our relatives any longer, nevertheless we have to assume that they belong to a kind of enlarged family, to which we owe unrestrained loyalty. In times in which the appeal to political commitment to justify social cohesion was inevitably destined to become a pitiful illusion, the reference to the blood tie—albeit only assumed or even largely invented—seemed to guarantee the most reliable foothold for the idea of a limited and cohesive well-ordered society. Being laid down for the first time by Aristotle in the second half of the fourth century B.C.E., the familistic theory of the political community was a strong anchor of social philosophy for almost two thousand years, before being extinguished at the end of the seventeenth century.

## 2.2 The Revival of the Paradigm in Early Modern Ages

After enjoying a true golden age of unrivalled dominance in classical antiquity, the paradigm of holistic particularism was faced with its first decline, starting with late antiquity and lasting for the whole Middle Ages, when it was sidelined by the new holistic-universalistic understanding of order. It was then rediscovered at the beginning of Modern Ages by two of the most relevant thinkers in the history of political ideas: Niccolò Machiavelli and Jean Bodin. The first created modern political theory, emancipating political concepts from the dominance of theology, while the second decisively shaped the notion of modern sovereignty. Neither of them, however, really renewed the fundamental patterns of the paradigm. In particular, Machiavelli largely limited himself to take up Thucydides's realism, and Bodin made use of Aristotle's familistic theory of the political community. Yet, precisely the way in which Bodin applied Aristotle's conception makes evident that this was changing its original meaning, increasingly becoming a mere support of backward-oriented aristocratic elites. Lastly, Filmer's work showed beyond any doubt that the time of the familistic explication of society was over: as a justification of the holistic community, it had nothing more to offer for the future of political theory.

### 2.2.1 The Independence of Politics from Moral and Religion in Machiavelli's Realism

Since medieval universalism was essentially based on the centrality of the Christian religion, whose message was regarded as being directed to every human being and whose idea of order included—in principle— the whole humankind, it is not surprising that Machiavelli's criticism against universalism began by targeting some fundamental tenets of Christendom. First, Christian religion deduces the principles of the political life of the individual polity from abstract assumptions, which are presumed to be universally valid. In doing so, according to Machiavelli, it ignores the specific political condition of the individual polity. Not by chance, he claimed that the greatness of the ancient poleis and even more of the Roman Republic was grounded on the quite unscrupulous use of religion as an instrument of power (*instrumentum regni*), explicitly excluding the deduction of the state constitution from allegedly higher truths of moral or religious origin.[30] Secondly, while the Christian religion praises "humility, lowliness, and contempt for the things of this world",[31] the ancient one glorified courage and active life. While the former virtues may be good to go to Paradise, the second are surely better suited— Machiavelli argues—when it comes to strengthening the civic life of the mundane polity. Thirdly, Christian religion generally assumes that human beings are essentially good-natured, whereas they are—as the Florentine put it quite bluntly—"ungrateful, fickle, dissembling, hypocritical, cowardly, and greedy".[32]

As a result, if we want to conceive of political theory as the discipline that discovers and describes the way in which political life works, then we have to make it free from moral and religious prejudices. Furthermore, insofar as it should concretely suggest to rulers what to do, it has to make them avert their eyes from the hereafter and concentrate on what politics really is, namely the art of attaining power and making the polity more stable and powerful. This is the most important legacy of Machiavelli, whose work ushered in a new understanding of political theory as a modern discipline, free from any vassalage towards moral or religion. Yet, when Machiavelli moved to specify the elements that constitute the realm of politics, thus the contents of the interactions that uniquely characterize the political field, he failed to elaborate a really forward-oriented vision, abiding largely by the principles which had been enucleated almost two thousand years earlier by Thucydides. Besides the already mentioned, utterly pessimistic view on human nature, Machiavelli identified three driving forces of human action. The first is fear, since every prince or ruler—but we could extend the assumption to political actors in general—"ought to fear two things: the one is domestic and concerns his subjects; the other is foreign and concerns outside powers".[33] Then, fear generates desire for conquest: in fact, Machiavelli specifies, "there are two causes which lead to wars …; one, your desire to be its master, the other the fear lest it should master you".[34] Lastly, successful conquests easily lead to relentless greed because all human beings always have the same "goal … before them, namely, glory and wealth".[35] The combination of fear, desire for conquest and greed for glory and wealth closely reminds us of honour, desire for profit and fear, as the driving forces of politics in Thucydides's interpretation—just in reverse order, to underline Machiavelli's even more pessimistic vision of human disposition. Under these circumstances, no international order can be reasonably considered feasible: in a world of selfishness and struggle for dominance, alliances are always temporary and only justified by the presence of a common threat. In fact, in the political domain, "the causes for union are fear and war".[36]

The analogies between Machiavelli's conception and Thucydides's do not mean, for sure, that he did not introduce anything new, nor do they condemn him to historical marginality. Undoubtedly, his awareness of the necessity to find a new and original fundament for political theory was unprecedented. Furthermore, he underlined much more than his Greek predecessor the differences between the internal condition of the individual polity, which must be grounded on virtue, and the international realm. We should never forget that—besides the *Prince* in which the ruthless art of conquering dominance is described—he dedicated his second most influential work, namely the *Discourses on Livy*, to the most essential tenets of a constitution that is based on virtue and is capable of fostering it. Nonetheless, politics is analysed also in the *Discourses*—like in Thucydides's work—from a strictly "realistic" standpoint: hence, it is essentially interpreted as a quest for power and not as the process of shaping peaceful interactions to develop shared values. Therefore, the question arises again on how virtue can originate and persist, if the social and political interactions are only instrumental, not presupposing or creating a common ethical background. Like Thucydides, Machiavelli let us only guess as regards the possible answer, indicating just two elements—significantly, the same which had been already mentioned by Thucydides. Firstly, he referred to the "same language" and to the "homogeneity of customs" as conditions which decisively favour the construction of a stable political community.[37] Secondly, he praised the quality of legislation, which enables a polity "to live securely", i.e., without internal unrest.[38] Again, however, these references are too thin to really explain—if taken alone— why the interactions within the polity should be more reliable than those outside it. As long as the "realistic" understanding of politics does not prove able to conceptualize—in more than just a couple of clues— the reasons for the gap between internal and external interactions, we cannot but admit that it is still lacking an answer as regards the second question contemplated by every theory of order, namely a convincing and robust assumption about its ontological fundament. Trapped in this shortcoming, "realism" as an all-encompassing way to interpret social and political order (or disorder) both in the external and in the internal domain is doomed to remain incomplete and, ultimately, unconvincing.

### 2.2.2 Bodin's Concept of Sovereignty

Jean Bodin is granted a highly relevant place among the most influential political philosophers of the Western tradition as the very framer of the modern concept of sovereignty. According to Bodin's groundbreaking definition, the public power—or "power vested in a commonwealth (*république*)"—[39] is sovereign insofar as it is "absolute and perpetual".[40] The perpetuity of power means that a political agent can be regarded as a sovereign only if the exercise of its prerogatives has no time limit. In other words, an elected magistrate cannot be seen as a "sovereign": in fact, a true "sovereign" has to be forever "sovereign", and not just for a while. The second essential feature of sovereignty is its absoluteness. This attribute refers to the circumstance that truly sovereign power has to be self-reliant and must not obey any rule coming from outside. Therefore, a sovereign is not bound by laws (*legibus solutus*), and the civil norms promulgated by him, "even when founded on truth and right reason, proceed simply from his own free will".[41] Precisely in this claim lies the contribution that the concept of sovereignty has made to the idea of a public power which should be strictly related to the defence of the interests of the single polity as an individual entity. Before the postulation of sovereignty, public power had to locate its actions within the broader context of a worldwide order so that it had to validate its decisions as consistent with the task of maintaining a stable and well-balanced political structure, in antiquity, or with the aim of implementing the divine law in the theology of the Middle Ages. Sovereign public power, to the contrary, needs a merely self-referential justification, i.e., it is required only to defend its actions by reference to the protection of its own—indeed individual and often openly selfish—interests and priorities.

Bodin did not pass over in silence the boundaries that natural or divine law may impose on the exercise of sovereign power. He conceded that the power of the sovereign may be limited by the Estates as well as by divine and natural law.[42] Nonetheless, both limitations are, in the end, quite modest. Indeed, on the one hand, the Estates have only marginal competences and are strictly submitted to the undisputed hierarchical superiority of the sovereign authority.[43] On the other hand, although Bodin explicitly claimed that the commands of God and nature have to be respected,[44] the sovereign prince, being the secular *imago* of the almighty God, has nonetheless the right to interpret the suprapositive norms freely, i.e., without any secular or ecclesiastic control. Furthermore, no effective remedy against violation is given. Put in the hands of a sovereign power, political decisions will only aim at fostering the advantages of the single polity, so that an order beyond the borders of the single state is made at least unlikely and precarious, if not downright impossible. The particularistic selfishness of the individual *république*, which characterizes Bodin's conception of sovereignty, has thus been condemned—with some good reasons—as being incompatible with the core idea of international law and order,[45] and as a powerful instrument for imperialistic purposes.[46]

To provide the sovereign polity with a solid ontological fundament, Bodin relied—like many other thinkers before him, and some after him—on Aristotle's theory of the familistic origin of the political community. In accordance with this, Bodin stated at the very beginning of his work—echoing Aristotle's assertion—that the *République* "is the well-ordered government of many families and of what is common to them by a sovereign power".[47] According to this conception, the political community is assumed to originate not only genetically but also—which is even more important—conceptually from an association of families. Therefore, since the family "is not only the true source and origin of the commonwealth but also its principal constituent",[48] the organizational structure of the family serves as a model for the political community as a whole. The premise, here, is twofold: firstly, in accordance with the law of nature the power within the family lies—or, I prefer to say, lied in Bodin's times—in the hands of the *pater familias* and cannot—or could not—be contested by any of its members. Secondly, since the political community is nothing but an extended family, that same power which is derived, in the family, from the order established by the law of nature is legitimately placed—if the focus switches from the smallest natural community to that larger family which is the state—in the hands of the no less natural holder of public authority. Nor are the subjects entitled to require any kind of justification for this state of facts, which is supposed to be given by nature. As a result, just as the authority in the family—at least in the male-centred organization of the family that Bodin had in mind—belongs to the patriarch, in the same way the power in the commonwealth has to be bestowed on the head of the state, more precisely on the monarch.

As compared to Aristotle's view, Bodin's understanding of the familistic origin of the polity has a clearly different tone, which corresponds to a no less clearly distinct—to some extent, even opposite—purpose. In fact, in Aristotle's work, the juxtaposition of the institutional structure of the polity to the allegedly natural division of roles and functions in the family served primarily to justify and improve the *horizontal* solidarity among the citizens, in order to make the social bond more stable and the polis stronger, and only secondarily to defend the *vertical* hierarchy that may originate from the organic structure of the social bond. To the contrary, the goal stressed by Bodin consisted, above all, in giving reason for the political system of dynastic absolutism, whereas social cohesion was taken into account only insofar as it could be considered one of its most positive effects. As a result, the further success of the familistic understanding of the political community was indissolubly intertwined with the destiny of absolutistic monarchy: when the latter turned in an unfavourable direction, also the former was ultimately destined to vanish from the horizon of political theory.

### 2.2.3 The Decline of the Familistic Conception of the Polity in Filmer's Patriarcha

In Bodin's political philosophy, the connection between the familistic theory of the political community and the defence of absolutism was still accompanied by a strong—and historically exceedingly successful—proposal on how to make the polity more cohesive inside and stronger outside by basing it on the notion of sovereignty. Less than one century later, the positive dimension of this connection had completely disappeared, so that nothing of the former manifold functions of the familistic theory of the political community was left except a nostalgic, negative, and almost desperate apology of a political condition that could not be justified any longer and, in the meantime, was already on its way to an irreversible decline. No other work testifies this change of perspective better than Robert Filmer's *Patriarcha*, an almost forgotten pamphlet—published in 1680, about thirty years after it had been written—which is recalled, today, mainly for being the target of criticism in the first part of John Locke's incomparably more influential *Two Treatises*.

Whereas in Bodin's conception the defence of dynastic authority still relied on the conviction that this—along with the uncompromising assertion of particularistic sovereignty—had to be regarded as the best solution for the self-affirmation of the polity in the confrontational context of international relations, the references to common interests that can be inferred from Filmer's pamphlet are much thinner and largely inspired by a defensive attitude. Substantially, they can be led back, on the one hand, to the paternalistic conviction that the monarch always and "naturally" keeps in mind the well-being of the subjects, and, on the other, to the rather trivial claim that order should be preferred to anarchy. However, Filmer's idea of order had a significantly more limited ambition than in the political philosophy of his predecessors. In fact, in the decades between the publication of Bodin's *Six Livres de la République* in 1576 and the English Civil War (1642–1651), during which Filmer wrote the *Patriarcha*, a conception which was deeply contrary to the familistic conception of the political community acquired political centrality. It was the idea that political authority should be justified by the people and held responsible in front of it—precisely the conception that was invoked by the supporters of the trial against Charles I.[49] According to this interpretation of social and political order, it is natural reason itself that reveals—if correctly understood—that the internal and external strength of the polity depends on the legitimation that the ruled accord to the rulers. Therefore, the familistic view was deprived of its forward-oriented justification: if the present and future interests of the polity were to be considered the priority, the reference point could not be its familistic structure any longer, but the legitimation of power. Without the possibility of referring to rational justification, which seemed to decisively point in the opposite direction, the legal order envisaged by Filmer could only rely on tradition and on a narrow-minded notion of natural law, then detached from the commands of natural reason. The preservation of the status quo, thus, was the only horizon of Filmer's view, whereas any look beyond it was regarded with a sentiment of fearful contempt.

Given these premises, it is not surprising that Filmer, at the very beginning of his pamphlet, chose Jesuits and Calvinists—namely those schools of thought in which the idea of popular sovereignty had mainly been developed—as the targets of his polemic.[50] Against the theories of those who were seen by him as the most dangerous instigators of social and political unrest, he played off the old-fashioned vision of a natural law which would be embedded in the organic bond of the family, as well as of all broader communities which originate from it. The most outstanding feature of this social bond is that it does not require consent from its members, but only obedience. According to the main assumption of the familistic theory of the political community, the "natural rights" of "the father over one family" and those of "the king, as father over many families", are "without any difference at all but in the latitude or extent of them".[51] As a consequence, as "the father of a family governs by no other law than by his own will, not by the laws and wills of his sons or servants", analogously "the natural institution of regal authority" is "free … from subjection to an arbitrary election of the people".[52] At the same time, as "every father is bound by the law of nature to do his best for the preservation of his family", so is every king too.[53] Quite interestingly, Filmer's conception of the absolute power of kings shows a feature which is rather untypical for the theories that can be referred to the holistic-particularistic paradigm of order. Generally, holistic particularism is regarded as a view that privileges internal homogeneity in order to maximize the assertive position of the polity towards the outside. On the contrary—and this is, once again, a demonstration of the mainly defensive character of Filmer's position—his plea for absolutism is supported by the claim that a regime of absolutistic monarchies would ensure peace between the nations.[54] However, Filmer considered the international order of peace not so much a value in itself, but rather a side effect of—and, occasionally, a supporting condition for—what really mattered to him, i.e., the safeguard of social hierarchy.

Roughly thirty years before *Patriarcha* was published in 1680, a king— namely Charles I of England—had been put to trial, condemned to death and executed, for the first time, by the authority of the parliament, i.e., by the representatives of precisely those subjects who should have owed unrestricted respect to their monarch. The fall of the king delivered a devastating blow to the ideology of the organic unity of the family-like absolutistic monarchy. In the course of these epochal events, the ideology that, following Aristotle, best supported the virtue of organic solidarity among citizens and was laid by Bodin at the basis of the powerful notion of sovereignty was sized down by Filmer to the humble dimension of a weak dam against a wave that could not be stopped any longer. Only eight years after the publication of the *Patriarcha*, the Glorious Revolution buried the last attempt to establish absolutism in England for good— and with it the familistic vision of political power, the destiny of which had been tied to the past. As a result, the paradigm of holistic particularism was left devoid of a convincing idea about the ontological basis for its conception of order. After the long regency of Aristotle's conceptual creation, it was time to start the search for a new leading way of interpreting holism.

## 2.3 Adam Müller, Or: The Forging of the Nation in Political Romanticism

Five major changes affected the political life of Europe and the Western world between the beginning of the seventeenth century and the end of the eighteenth century. The first was the already mentioned crisis of the dynastic understanding of power, with the contemporary rise of a conception according to which authority has to be regarded as legitimate only insofar as it is based on the consent of the people. The rejection of a hierarchy allegedly grounded on natural or divine law had been anticipated—long before the English Civil War—by the Swiss uprising at the beginning of the fourteenth century and, then, by the Dutch Revolt at the end of the sixteenth century, both fought against the House of Habsburg. Yet, these were mainly national uprising against a political authority which was seen as a foreign oppressor. Beginning with the seventeenth century, the character of the fight against the monarchic power changed, especially because it was then backed by a new and alternative political philosophy focused on the necessity of a legitimation "from below". Therefore, the conflicts were either within the nation, as outcomes of an explicit request to overthrow the old-fashioned absolutistic hierarchy—as in England with the Civil War and the Glorious Revolution, as well as in France with the Revolution of 1789—or the fight for national independence was clearly accompanied by an ambitious plan to refound the political community on the basis of a completely new concept, as in the American War of Independence. Anyway, when the crowned heads began to tremble and fall, the paradigm of holistic particularism found itself without one of its essential components: since the familistic conception of the political community had been used for a long time as the ontological basis of the organic social bond, and this conception had been connected to the destiny of dynastic power, the deadly crisis of absolutism inevitably implied the collapse of the familistic theory as well.

The second change brings us to a rather abstract level, since it concerns the epistemological revolution that occurred in the middle of the seventeenth century. Traditionally, the holistic interpretation of society was based on the assumption of an organic osmosis between humans and nature. In other words, the long-established hierarchical structure of society was accepted because it was seen as something natural, whereas no critical control by the individual was deemed possible. Starting with Descartes, the original and immediate unity of human beings and nature was abandoned in favour of a duality between knowing subject—i.e., the individual as the custodian of knowledge, whose critical use of logical categories would guarantee that the content of what we claim to know is true—and the nature outside as the object of the inquiry. Since the idea of an osmosis of subject and object was left behind, the nature was destined to lose its former spirituality, being reduced to an "extended thing" (*res extensa*) to be measured.[55] Even the functions of knowledge were progressively interpreted by Hobbes in an almost completely mechanistic sense, i.e., as reactions to stimuli coming from outside.[56] Yet, even if according to Hobbes no knowledge is possible without materialistic impact from the world outside, at least the reason as the capacity to calculate advantages and losses of possible actions maintains, in his epistemology, a non-deterministic dimension.[57] The ultimate and most radical port of the epistemological journey into the domain of the mechanistic interpretation of the world was reached by the materialists of the French enlightenment. Indeed, in the philosophies of La Mettrie[58] and D'Holbach[59] every human action or knowledge is explained exclusively by resorting to deterministic patterns of action and corresponding reaction. The general meaning of the evolution of the theory of knowledge between the seventeenth and the eighteenth centuries, hence, was that the world outside—or the object of knowledge—was more and more radically interpreted as something exclusively material which can be best described by means of accurate measurements. Furthermore, the systems of nature—and, progressively, also the systems of the social world and of the individual mind—were interpreted in mechanistic terms as characterized by a balance of their components, all of them ultimately characterized by roughly the same inherent value, so that every action is, in fact, nothing but the reaction following a previous action that altered the balance. Given these premises, it was physics—and, in particular, mechanics—which took on the role of the leading science of Western modernity, substituting metaphysics and theology. However, the dominance of physics was hardly suitable for a justification of an organic understanding of the social and political world, as it had been practised by all supporters of holistic particularism until then.

The third change affected the dimension of practical philosophy. In different ways, all conceptions of order until the seventeenth century always assumed that a healthy society must rest, as regards the attitude towards the use of practical reason, on the immediate identification of the individuals with the goals of the community as a whole. It is not that references to situations were lacking, in which the priority of self-interest was the rule; yet, even in the political philosophies of Thucydides and Machiavelli, the prevalence of individual selfishness was seen as the result of the crisis of the polis, or—if the self-interest was the driving force behind the actions of a would-be prince—as the inevitable way to consolidate the cohesion of the community. The barycentre shifted visibly starting with the middle of the seventeenth century. In Hobbes's moral philosophy, for example, searching for individual payoffs was not the expression of the decline of the polity or a necessary means to stabilize it, but rather the only rational choice of the individual. In the same vein, Jeremy Bentham ennobled utility—also a concept with an undeniably non-holistic main content—by putting it at the centre of practical philosophy, thus in the place that had been formerly occupied by the defence of the homeostasis of the *holon*.[60]

The fourth change was about the notion of history. Before the Modern Ages, this was conceived of as an eternal repetition of always the same processes of rise, flourishing and decline. In this sense, it was assumed to be typified by an endless reiteration of cycles, without any sign of linear development. It was the enlightenment that introduced a concept which was largely unknown before: progress. According to the enlightened concept of history—and, in particular, in accordance with the vision of its most outstanding and innovative exponent, namely Nicolas de Condorcet—no limit is set to the improvement of human condition.[61] Given this premise, history could be interpreted as a steady advancement of humanity, heading to freedom from tyranny, prosperity as a result of scientific innovation and universal peace as the overcoming of particularistic selfishness.[62]

The fifth and last change was the outcome of two events that profoundly transformed European society: the industrial revolution and the Napoleonic Wars. On the one hand, the industrial revolution led to a strong urbanization; on the other, the Napoleonic Wars were characterized by the involvement of unusually large masses of young men in long military campaigns, while triggering an unprecedented ideological mobilization. Both events have an important element in common. Indeed, both decisively contributed to putting an end to the prevalence of the passive acceptance of power which was a typical trait of the rural world. Due to the atomization of life in the countryside—which had been even stronger after earlier forms of solidarity in the rural communities had been crushed along with the repression of the many recurrent peasants' revolts—it was almost impossible, for the underprivileged and oppressed, to articulate their claims in a way that could not be easily ignored. Military mobilization and urbanization, to the contrary, granted them a sufficient concentration of forces to make their voices powerful: a society of citizens was arising from the amorphous mass of speechless subjects, vigorously requesting to play a central role in the political life of the larger community.

All these developments undermined severely—each one of them in its own way—what had been for long time the ontological basis of the holistic understanding of the social and political community. To lead the paradigm of holistic particularism out of the second crisis of its history, therefore, its supporters had to create a conceptual framework which could deliver convincing answers to the five following questions. Firstly, a new leading science had to be identified which could withstand the competition with physics and give to the organic vision of the world an innovative and more solid epistemological fundament. Secondly, a conception of the use of practical reason had to be developed, according to which the pursuit of the interests of the community could cope with individual priorities in a more balanced way than in the former realizations of holism. Thirdly, by bringing the attempt to make common interests overlap with individual preferences to the political level, an idea of the political community had to be shaped in which the inclusion of a significantly larger part of the populace was possible. Fourthly, the hereby grounded political community had to support a positive look into the future; in other words, it had to be open for the perspective of progress. Fifthly, and lastly, the respect for traditional hierarchies—an unwaivable point of reference for the most supporters of the holistic-particularistic paradigm—had to result in a clearer commitment of the upper class to the common good, preventing any downfall into that spirit of pure selfishness which had decisively weakened the former absolutistic monarchies. The challenge, consisting in finding a positive answer to all these questions, was met and successfully managed by the German philosopher Adam Müller.

On the whole, Adam Müller must be rather considered as a second-rank political thinker. Nonetheless, he deserves to be granted the unquestionable merit—at least from the standpoint of those who believed, and still believe, in the value of holistic particularism—not only of having rescued this paradigm of order from its decline, but also of having equipped it with a conceptual organon that significantly helped to make it flourish until the present time. As a first step, he counterposed biology to physics as the leading science in the analysis of social phenomena. In fact—Müller claimed—the political community is not a "machine" that can be explained by resorting to physical concepts, and its components are not parts of a "dead clockwork".[63] Rather, the social world is made of organisms which interact with one another in largely the same way as living beings do in the natural realm. By and large, Müller's interpretation of the social and political community as a biological "body" is not essentially different from the traditional organic view of the political life, as it had already been developed in ancient philosophy and was then reintroduced, again and again, throughout the entire history of political ideas. What distinguishes Müller's conception as compared to earlier versions of organicism is that it is assumed to be supported by the findings of the discipline that was establishing itself, between the end of the eighteenth century and the beginning of the nineteenth century, as the most thriving branch of natural sciences.

When it comes to specifying the features of the organisms that struggle for survival in the world of social and political interactions, Müller introduces his most innovative claim, according to which these organisms are the nations. By bringing the concept of nation to the fore in the political debate, he took up one of the ideological banners of the French Revolution, but decisively changed its meaning. In fact, the revolutionary concept of the *nation* was thought to express a sentiment of *civic belonging* to the *community of citizens*. By crossing the Rhine, however, the notion received quite a different connotation. This was precisely Müller's contribution insofar as he merged the French concept with the notion of the *Volk* with its distinctive culture, which had been developed by Johann Gottfried Herder.[64] Following this most outstanding exponent of early German romanticism, human language should not be interpreted as a logical instrument with the function to build abstract concepts for the theoretical and practical use of reason, but as a semantic tool to allow communication.[65] As a result, human language was understood as something deeply tied with concrete and tangible experiences not only because it was seen as non-abstract but also since it was regarded as non-universal. Indeed, according to Herder, human language is always the language of an individual community, of a specific "people" (*Volk*).[66] Thus, since the different languages and cultures are assumed to be intrinsically divisive, the limits of a meaningful communication must coincide with the borders of the community that shares the same cultural preconditions of interaction.[67] By shrouding the revolutionary nation in the guise of the most reactionary romanticism, Müller transformed the concept, which originally was an appeal to civic participation, into a powerful tool to justify uncritical obedience.

More concretely, Müller defined the nation as the community of individuals who have some distinctive traits in common, in particular the same "customs, language, character, art, culture, and national physiognomy".[68] As the fundament of cohesion inside as well as of collision and exclusion outside, the nation plays the same role that was taken on by the unrestrained commitment to the polis in Plato and by the enlarged family from Aristotle to Bodin; yet, it has also some decisive advantages compared to the earlier versions of holism. More specifically, from the point of view of the conception of practical reason, the concept of nation can support a much stronger implementation of individual priorities, while maintaining a no less narrow tie between the individuals and the community. As regards the vision of history, then, Müller asserts explicitly that every individual belonging to a nation "has a past behind him that has to be respected, and a future ahead of him for which he should care".[69] The nation, therefore, is a community of destiny with a positive outlook into the future; in other words, it is not least a project to be realized. Moving on to the political level, the state is conceived of as the political organization of the pre-political nation.[70] Accordingly, its structure is significantly different from the hierarchical absolutism that dominated the last period of the familistic conception of the political community. In fact, although Müller was utterly assertive in defending hierarchy and dynastic power,[71] it is also clear, from the tone and the substance of his analysis, that the hierarchical organization of society had exclusively to be in the service of the organic division of the social functions. Put differently, the exercise of authority had to be unequivocally separated from any personal interest. Moreover, and lastly, the idea of belonging to a nation was conceived in a way that made possible to commit a much larger part of the populace—and with a much stronger intensity—to the common goal of the political community than under the *ancient régime*. Making the nation great was thought as a duty of every single member of the community, to the advantage of each one of them—not for the sake of the rulers' glory.

Since every political community, as a nation, is compared by Müller to a living being competing for dominance and survival against other similar entities in a hostile, quasi-natural world, no stable order of peace and cooperation is thinkable or even desirable at the international level. Müller explicitly states that the "organic state ..., as an individual, enters into an incessant colossal conflict with the other over-dimensioned individuals of its kind, which is a conflict of its own national freedom against the national freedom of the others".[72] Waging war on the competing organic community, thus, is a perspective that should never be ruled out because war, on the one hand, prevents the society from becoming too static and its members from being too self-serving,[73] while making the community, on the other hand, more compact inside.[74] Surely, Müller advocated an exceedingly aggressive understanding of nationalism. Yet, not every version of it is characterized by such an uncompromising attitude. In fact, as nationalism was at its historical apex, European nation states were able to create international humanitarian law, thus ushering in a new dimension of the law of peoples and transforming international law into what has been defined as the "gentle civilizer of nations".[75] Nonetheless, even international humanitarian law—albeit a cornerstone on the way to a humanization of international relations—was little more than a reprise and a deepening of the classical *jus in bello*. As a consequence, as the tensions between nation states progressively increased at the beginning of the twentieth century, it proved incapable of averting the great catastrophe of World War I and even of guaranteeing the safeguard of the most essential principles of humanity during World War II. Insofar as nationalism accepts the idea of the centrality—if not of the exclusivity—of the interests of the nation, taking the well-grounded interests of others into account remains a fair-weather option.

## 2.4 The Struggle Between Friend and Enemy as the Justification for the Striving for Hegemony in Carl Schmitt

Despite the unquestionable and long-lasting historical and political success of the nationalistic project, the ongoing transition—between the second half of the nineteenth century and the beginning of the twentieth century—to an increasingly diverse society filled with social tensions inside and an ever-more-closely interlinked world outside manifested its weaknesses. To meet the conflict-laden internal situation as well as to facilitate a peaceful advance of the external interconnection, legal theory developed an innovative approach—starting with German-speaking countries, but then exercising a significant influence also outside them—which went down in history by the name of "legal positivism". The main assumption of this theory, the most important exponent of which has been Hans Kelsen,[76] was that, to cope with diversity, conflict and a beginning globalization, society had to rely more on law than on politics, and that law itself had to become more formalized. Being detached from the specific social interests represented by political parties or associations, and even from those embodied by nation states, a formalized law would create a neutral framework in which different priorities peacefully conflict with one another, until a compromise is achieved that is acceptable for all parties. It is evident, however, that this conception runs head-on against the most essential assumptions of the holistic-particularistic paradigm, namely that social and political order is limited and, to be effective, has to be grounded not on formalism, but on some kind of substantial homogeneity—or, the other way around, if order must be based on homogeneity, since homogeneity cannot be universal, then order must have clear boundaries. The author who most loudly raised his voice against legal positivism—being, at the same time, the most influential exponent of holistic particularism in the first half of the twentieth century and, probably, until the present day—was Carl Schmitt.

Schmitt viciously attacked legal formalism, slandering it—with racist arguments—as a "Jewish" science, thus alien to the German spirit.[77] Yet, trying to look beyond the sordid attitude of an incorrigible anti-Semite—which is, admittedly, quite difficult—it has to be recognized that the criticism of legal overformalization touches upon a real problem, namely that formalism alone cannot reliably guarantee for social cohesion and solidarity. The readiness to support a fellow citizen or human being must rest on a much more profound involvement of the individuals than the one that can be achieved through mere compliance with the law. However, according to Schmitt, going back to the romantic idea of nation could not be the solution. In fact, an idea mainly concentrated on the protection of the national identity, no matter how small and marginal a nation might be, does not provide the best conceptual precondition for supporting adequately the sometimes fierce worldwide competition for scarce resources. Most nations—and maybe all of them—are actually too weak to compete while relying exclusively on their own assets. It became necessary to find a broader basis for mobilizing human and material resources in order to tackle the demands of the new global game of survival and success. In other words, provided that a really universal perspective was beyond the horizon of the supporters of the holistic-particularistic paradigm, the development of a more comprehensive definition of the political community that could gather more social and economic assets seemed necessary.

Schmitt's answer to the shortcomings of formalism was the proposal to establish a *Reich*, i.e., an institutional organization of the community which should be capable of overcoming the liberal state in two essential dimensions. Firstly, it was not based on the rule of law, but on the deepest existential involvement of all those who essentially and truly belong to the community. In other words, the "true" members of the *Reich* see their belonging as a fundamental condition for their present and future survival as individuals and as a group.[78] In doing so, law is overcome in its pretence to be self-reliant and is led back to politics, which should be seen as the essence of social life.[79] Secondly, the political community was brought to a territorial extent much larger than what the European states, which were national in essence, could ever reach. Yet, which is the fundament of the *Reich* that makes it different from any other realization of the paradigm? Here, Schmitt introduced his most famous contribution to the history of political ideas: starting with the claim that the legal and institutional structure of the community must be interpreted from the standpoint of the "concept of the political"—where the *political* describes the very essence of political interactions, and *politics* is, on the contrary, the practice of those interactions—he identified that concept with the irreducible *contraposition between friend and enemy*.[80] Thus, Schmitt deformalized the legal and institutional structure of the community by making it dependent on the existential fundament of political life, whereas he stylized the essential tenets of the holistic-particularistic paradigm. In fact, bringing the essence of internal cohesion and external struggle for survival to such a flexible formula as the contraposition friend-enemy paved the way for a definition of the particularistic community which could better adapt to specific circumstances, including, if needed, a larger population and a more extended territory, than any former version of the paradigm. The turn to *hegemonism* had begun.

Interestingly, by defining the opposing couple of notions Schmitt focused first and with much more details on what the "enemy" is assumed to be. This approach is insofar important as it shows that his starting point is not the definition of values and interests that bind the members of the community and are shared by them all, but the existential threat that comes from outside. More concretely, Schmitt's "enemy" is—in a quite abstract, but very effective fashion—any individual or group of individuals who or which is felt as a danger for one's own existence.[81] The reasons for this feeling of threat may be very different: the danger can arise from the social, the racial, the cultural, the religious or the economic foe.[82] The only element that must always be present is that no peaceful order can be achieved since the opposition is irreconcilable. Confronted with such a destructive threat, all those who share the same danger will hold together and form the community of "friends". Furthermore, the more fearful the danger is, the more cohesive and homogeneous the community of "friends" should be. The logical—and quite frightening—consequence of this premise is that anyone who could question the racial, linguistic, cultural, religious or social homogeneity of the community—depending on which of these elements constitutes its essential feature—should be treated as an "internal enemy".[83] Thus, she/he should be kept out as a migrant to prevent the problem, or, if the internal minority already exists, it should be forced to assimilation, its identity denied, and in case of resistance, it should be deported.[84]

Since "the political world is a pluriverse, not a universe",[85] and the resulting conflicts cannot be consistently appeased, the possibility to wage war—or, more brutally, to kill the enemy—must be accepted as a legitimate and rightful instrument of international law and relations.[86] In fact, according to Schmitt's view which is actually shared by all exponents of the holistic-particularistic paradigm, the best we can achieve is what he called a "*Hegung des Krieges*" (a "bracketing" or "containment" of war).[87] Moreover, Schmitt states—almost verging on an oxymoron—that we can best realize this containment under the condition that war is recognized as a legitimate and rightful means of politics. This was the case during the golden era of the *Jus Publicum Europaeum*, between the Peace of Utrecht in 1713 and the beginning of World War I in 1914.[88] Leaving aside the question whether wars during those two hundred years really resulted, proportionally, in less casualties then before this period or after it—Napoleonic Wars, in particular, seem to tell a different story—it can be admitted, nonetheless, that the aim of the conflicts of the eighteenth and nineteenth centuries did not consist in annihilating the enemy, but in gaining or consolidating some sort of dominance over the counterpart as well as the advantages that this dominance could bring. Anyway, the golden era of *Jus Publicum Europaeum* ended as the result of three factors which intervened at the beginning of the twentieth century. The first was a change that occurred in warfare: since the military actions were progressively moved from the land to the sea and to the air and, because of that, the victorious army did not need to take any responsibility for what happened in the territory of the enemy any longer, wars became more difficult to "bracket".[89] Secondly, new great powers of continental extent arose, such as the United States and, then, the Soviet Union, which were not only vast in territory, manpower and resources, but also highly ideologized, which made compromises much more difficult to achieve.[90] Thirdly, and most importantly, a tendency to moralize politics emerged again, mainly driven by the Calvinist tradition in the United States, and finally led to the criminalization of war after World War II.[91] The outcome was a renewed brutalization of war since, according to Schmitt, no war is as vicious as the one which is fought in the name of humanity.[92] Odd enough, Schmitt accused the allies of brutality, while simply passing over in silence what his fellow Nazis had done.

Leaving aside the disturbing incongruities of Schmitt's thought, it is nevertheless interesting to focus on his idea of international law and relations. In times of continental superpowers and ideological mobilization within the friend-enemy-divide, we would face an existential alternative: either we accept a worldwide hegemony in the guise of humanity's interests, thus allowing the annihilation of different political identities, or we establish what he defined as the theory of "large-range-order" (*Großraumordnung*).[93] To address the inadequacy of the traditional concept of the nation without falling into a moralizing cosmopolitan order, he advocated his *Großraumordnung* as an idea of global (yet not universal) order based on few great powers, thus allowing those powers to enlarge both the range and meaning of order as well as the resources needed to achieve it. The hegemons should guarantee the governance of their respective spheres of influence, which had to be largely homogeneous in ethnic composition and ideological orientation. Between the spheres of influence, which should not be disturbed by foreign intervention, competition and, if necessary, also armed conflict were accepted as the rule. In Schmitt's conception, the particular community assumes continental proportions due to a more inclusive definition of the reasons of the cohesion: not the language, for instance, but a homogeneous political system; not the national culture, but the race or, as we would say today, the ethnos. In this way, the hegemon is enabled to play the brutal game of survival and annihilation on a global scale, although remaining fully particular in its intents and values. No universal interests or values are recognized by Schmitt to be more than a mere deceit.

Schmitt's political and legal philosophy made the holistic-particularistic paradigm fit for the era of continental conflicts by transforming it into a justification of hegemonism. Though rejecting the perspective of a worldwide rule, hegemonic power was envisaged at the continental level in order to create particularistic entities with enough resources to successfully confront similar "enemies". To achieve this goal, the narrow national identities had to be left aside, while a reckless, but flexible ideological mobilization had to be put in place. A new era of holistic particularism had begun—an era in which particular forms of social identification only matter insofar as they can be functionalized as instruments for global confrontation.

## 2.5 Three Variants of Holistic Particularism: Realism, Nationalism, Hegemonism

Between its first formulations in the fifth century B.C.E. and the middle of the twentieth century, different variant of holistic particularism had been developed. While the most fundamental tenets of particularism remained essentially the same since Thucydides laid them down at the beginning of the history of the paradigm, the answer to the question about the ontological basis of holism relied, in the consecutive phases of the evolution of the paradigm, on quite differing assumptions (or even on no assumption at all). Some of these assumptions—such as Plato's concept of a "just" society, or Aristotle's idea of the familistic nature of the political community—can be regarded as belonging to history for good, but others were still vital after World War II, being destined to further influence the understanding of social and political order until present time. More concretely, three variants of holistic particularistic proved to be able to stand the test of time: realism, nationalism and hegemonism.

*Realism* is the strand of holistic particularism according to which politics in all its manifestations is nothing but a quest for power. In this sense, order is nothing but the always very unstable outcome of a struggle for predominance, which can last for a while, but, in the end, will inexorably fall victim to the next conflict. However, this variant of holistic particularism—at least in the classical versions of Thucydides and Machiavelli— does not address the undeniable difference between internal (limited) order and external dis-order in a theoretically convincing way. As long as this shortcoming persists, the realistic variant of the holistic-particularistic paradigm of order must be regarded as conceptually incomplete and therefore, in the end, flawed.

Following the second variant—i.e., *nationalism*—the ontological basis for the organic well-ordered society is determined by a community of individuals who share specific, distinctly pre-political features, such as culture, language, customs, religion, history and, mostly, also some kind of genetic footprint. None of these characteristics depends on a reflexive choice made by the individuals, or on a political decision taken by them; rather, they simply happen to find themselves being part of the community that is assumed to decisively forge their destiny.

Nationalism relies largely on the construction of a strong collective identity, necessarily including a large number of dimensions of individual identification, which are all essential for the purpose of reinforcing social cohesion. In general, the positive identification of the individuals with the whole prevails, and the distinction from the "others" is seen, as well as their exclusion, as the consequence of the establishment of a distinctive identity. Since this identity is assumed to be very demanding in terms of the individual adoption of the most essential defining features of the community, the unity of the nation is sometimes bought at the cost of its limited size. This is not an absolute rule, evidently, since we have large nations; but, in general, if it is necessary to make a choice, the supporters of the nation will prefer a tiny, but closely united community, to a larger one, but with a weaker positive self-definition. As regards this point, the supporters of the third, and last, variant of the holistic-particularistic paradigm of order—i.e., *hegemonism*—opt for the opposite way. In fact, when confronted with the alternative between the larger size of the community and its stronger and more deep-going cultural identity, they wholeheartedly choose the first option. In order to build a social community which is large enough to meet the challenges of an increasingly globalized competition, they define its identity following a fourfold presupposition. Firstly, the basis for the positive identification of the individual with the community is generally reduced to only one element—for instance, religion, *or* ethnicity, *or* a specific idea of social organization, and so on. Secondly, this element must be flexible and inclusive enough to allow the realization of a large community; indeed, a too strong cultural presupposition can only limit the number of individuals involved and, therefore, the resources that can be mobilized. Thirdly, negative exclusion is at least as important as positive identification; put differently, to know which community I belong to, distinguishing myself from what I am not, often with an utterly confrontational attitude, is no less essential—and may be, in many cases, even more fundamental—than clarifying what I am and insisting on it. Fourthly, the existential involvement—interpreted, once again, in its negative meaning—in the sense of a strong feeling of being threatened in one's very existence by an external entity prevails over the positive cultural bond as the attempt as well as the wish to build a community with those who share the same heritage.

After the end of World War II, the paradigm of holistic-particularistic order suffered another backlash. Indeed, at least two of its variants, namely nationalism and hegemonism, were justifiably held responsible for the moral breakdown that led to two world wars and for the crimes against the most essential tenets of humanity which were perpetrated during both of them and in particular in the course of World War II. The cosmopolitan humanism that prevailed after the victory against the barbarism of the Nazis and of the Japanese occupation advocated values which were precisely the opposite to what is essentially assumed by the supporters of holistic particularism. Furthermore, while the circumstances of the Cold War made at least realism appear capable of providing some useful explication, the fall of the iron curtain sidelined for roughly a decade any variant of holistic particularism by boosting the vision of a cosmopolitan order and by making it apparently feasible in a way which was probably unprecedented in human history. Yet, far from being at the "end of history",[94] the events of the last two decades reinvigorated all three variants of holistic particularism. Before the most ancient paradigm of order came lately to the fore again, supporters of all its declinations elaborated new versions of them which were thought to overcome the former theoretical deficits as well as to cope better with the requirements emerging from globalization. The way in which realism, nationalism and hegemonism were reshaped after World War II and, in particular, during the short period of reigning cosmopolitanism had a decisive influence on how order and, more specifically, its limitations are understood in the present time of resurgent particularism.

## 2.6 The Re-foundation of Realism, or the Neo-Realism of the Theory of International Relations

The most striking shortcoming of "classical" realism had been its incapacity to explain the evident difference between the weak order—or, rather, the almost permanent disorder, interrupted by short phases of unstable order—of the international realm, on the one hand, and the substantial solidity of social and political conditions within the borders of the individual polity on the other. The challenge was taken up by Hans Morgenthau, who not only paved the way for the transition from the "classical" realism of Thucydides and Machiavelli to "neo-realism", but also established a new discipline of political science, namely the theory of international relations.

Like his predecessors, Morgenthau started by assuming that politics is eminently characterized by the struggle for power and influence. At first, this characterization is applied at both the internal and the external domains. In fact, "both domestic and international politics are a struggle for power", since "the tendency to dominate ... is an element of all human associations, from the family through fraternal and professional associations and local political organizations, to the state".[95] Yet, unlike classical realists, he maintained that the tendency to develop struggles for power is "modified ... by the different conditions under which the struggle takes place in the domestic and in the international spheres".[96] Moving on to describe the reasons for the difference, Morgenthau resorted to the concept of nation—to a notion, hence, which was originally alien to realism, while typifying another variant of the holistic-particularistic paradigm of order. Indeed, according to Morgenthau's assumption, the domestic realm is different from the international arena because the first is organized as a national community, thus guaranteeing to the involved actors—more precisely, to the individuals—a level of cohesion that is nearly unconceivable within a larger context.[97] The cohesion is allegedly due to the presence of characteristics that are usually assigned to the national community, i.e., the partaking "of the same language, the same customs, the same historic recollections, the same fundamental social and political philosophy, the same national symbols".[98] Thus, except for some adjustments aiming at deleting the quite widespread "blood and soil" connotation of nationalism, nothing really new is introduced by Morgenthau's use of the concept of nation. What is more interesting, yet, are his considerations on the benefits that can be derived from the existence of the national community. According to Morgenthau, belonging to a national community provides three major advantages that cannot be realized at the international level: suprasectorial loyalties, expectation of justice and the monopoly of organized violence in order to protect social peace.[99] While these benefits can mitigate conflicts within the nation, the cohesiveness of the national community and of its institutions makes sure that the internal tensions as well as the almost natural desire for power are redirected towards the outside.[100]

Therefore, Morgenthau restricted the validity of the fundamental assumption of realism, according to which politics is essentially a quest for power, solely to the realm of international relations. By doing so, he managed to maintain the epistemological quality of this fundamental assumption as a useful instrument for a better knowledge of the world and for a justifiable orientation for action. Following Morgenthau, it is in the international realm—and essentially there—that the struggle for dominance unfolds. But does this mean that this unfolding is destined to happen—due also to Morgenthau's scepticism towards the potentialities of international law—without any significant control, too? Not necessarily. In fact, Morgenthau noted that also the conflicts in the international realm were generally fought without resorting to all instruments of destruction available to the opponents.[101] Hence, there has been some kind of restriction indeed. Furthermore, he pointed out that even in international relations there has always been a tendency to what he called "peace through accommodation", i.e., to the search for a compromise with which both conflicting parties could live.[102] To achieve the accommodation, according to Morgenthau's approach the fulfilment of four conditions is needed. Firstly, and most essentially, it must be accepted, beyond any moralistic prejudices, that conflict is a constituent part of international relations, that it is—unlike what happens in the internal domain—almost inevitable in the relations between nation states, and, therefore, that it cannot be overcome for good. Secondly, the perspective of a perpetual peace or of a world order must be given up in favour of a more "realistic" attitude aiming at limiting harm. Thirdly, every agent must be aware of its own essential interests as well as of what it can bargain away for the sake of a compromise. Fourthly, every agent must also strive to understand the interests of the counterpart, to generally recognize them as legitimate and to distinguish the most fundamental ones from those which can be handled down for exchange.

The outcome of accommodation cannot be the realization of a stable, binding and generally recognized international order, but rather a feasible limitation of disorder. The task of achieving a compromise is assigned, then, to the diplomatic corps. Indeed, in Morgenthau's perspective diplomacy, insofar as it is granted sufficient independence from the political and popular pressure that is expressed in parliamentary assemblies, has some decisive advantages if compared to the institutions which represent popular sovereignty. In particular, the career diplomats from the different countries share largely the same—or, at least, a strongly comparable—social and cultural background, while generally refraining from overburdening their positions with ideological presuppositions, historically rooted hostilities, or national prejudices, so that arrangements are more likely to be found.[103] Interestingly, the period in which diplomacy allegedly displayed its best potentialities is, according to Morgenthau's interpretation, the same that had been identified by Carl Schmitt as the golden era of the *Jus Publicum Europaeum*, namely between 1713 and 1914.[104] And similar, at least partially, are also the reasons given for its decadence, i.e., the re-emergence of ideology as well as of a misleading cosmopolitan emphasis as driving forces of the political action of nation states and, thus, as a substantial element of international relations, which would trigger a new spirit of crusade.[105] Therefore, if it is to guarantee that we achieve what is feasible, namely not a perpetual peace, but a containment of violence in the international arena, then the diplomatic corps should be shielded against the influence of democratic processes.

By limiting the field of application of the realistic core assumptions, Morgenthau made them overcome the main problem that affected the earlier versions of realism. As a result, realism lost its status of a sub-paradigm with the ambition of explaining the whole world of political interactions, but maintained a significant epistemological status within the hereby newly established discipline of international relations. In a certain sense, Morgenthau rescued realism by redirecting its theoretical thrust and by redefining the domain of its "scientific" application. Given this most relevant difference between his approach and the view that characterized the "classical" realism of authors like Thucydides and Machiavelli, there are good reasons to claim that he belongs already to what has been called "neo-realism", or that he downright decisively contributed to found it. Nonetheless, he is often regarded as being part of the old school of realism,[106] more specifically because he still considered the general political tendency to struggle for power—quite like the classical authors—in anthropological terms, i.e., as a consequence of the deepest natural predispositions of human beings.[107] The second step towards the consolidation of a new discipline with a robust and original epistemological organon was made, then, by those authors—led by Kenneth N. Waltz—who deleted all references to anthropological assumptions, creating a more scientifically grounded theory, the so-called structural neo-realism. According to this conception, conflicts within the international arena can be explained by exclusively resorting to the analysis of objective divergences of interests between the involved actors, without any presupposition which could be assumed to anticipate objective observation and defy critical proof as well as falsification.

"Neo-realism", in general, and "structural neo-realism", more specifically, have been extremely influential theories claiming to explain the specific rules of international relations. Laid down in Cold War times, they reflect a reality in which the formulation of a common cosmopolitan idea of order—not to mention its realization—seemed to be a product of day-dreamers, while the only achievement regarded as possible was the limitation of damage. In the face of the present re-emerging of a confrontational multilateralism, realism appears to provide valuable instruments for understanding and practical orientation again. Leaving aside any normative consideration on this point, it has to be underlined, nevertheless, that even in the context of the discipline of international relations, realism has not been the only way to interpret the interactions of relevant actors. Indeed, while the supporters of the theory of "international regimes" have shown that compliance with shared norms—and not only a free-rider-accommodation—may be, under certain circumstances, a more rational choice than selfishness,[108] constructivists have gone even a step further, downright denying self-reliance the status of the only epistemologically consistent basis for the analysis of international relations. On the contrary, the *construction* of cooperative interactions can be no less decisive. Ultimately, the reality as it is, contrary to what realists seem to believe since Thucydides's times, does not amount to a destiny defined by inescapable contrasting interests; rather, it is nothing but a "world of our making".[109]

## 2.7 THE DEFENCE OF THE NATION IN THE GLOBALIZATION ERA

Since the beginning of the nineteenth century, two different concepts of nation are set against each other, at least at first sight. On the one hand, there is the idea of nation elaborated by Adam Müller, according to which the national community is based on *objective* and *substantial* characteristics, so that the personal belonging to one specific community is assumed to be completely independent of individual preferences and choices. On the other hand, we have the notion created during the French Revolution, against which the reaction of Müller's political romanticism arose; this second conception—in fact the older one—sees the nation essentially as the outcome of an act of *subjective will*, so that it can also be interpreted as a "daily plebiscite".[110] Yet, if we look at the question a little more in depth, we must recognize that the two approaches are not as opposing as it may seem at first glance. Indeed, the subjective version of the nation also regards the common history of "sacrifices" as the most essential element on which national solidarity is grounded—and, in the end, shared experiences, in particular those of the past generations which build the irreplaceable glue that holds national communities together, are no less independent of our individual will than the colour of our skin. Nonetheless, it has to be admitted that, whereas in the objectivistic understanding belonging to the nation is simply a matter of fact, which does not need any sort of individual awareness or conscious confirmation, precisely the reiterated acknowledgement of personal solidarity with the national community makes up the nucleus of the subjectivistic variant of the nationalistic ideology.

Regardless of the more or less significant differences between the two strands of nationalism, it is generally assumed that subjectivistic nationalism has been characteristic for Western Europe and North America, whereas the objectivistic variant took root mainly in Central and Eastern Europe.[111] Nonetheless, it is a fact that objectivistic nationalism took the lead, for roughly one and a half centuries, far beyond the frontier along the Rhine, tainting the Western idea of nation with racial prejudices. The reason may be that its more radical attitude made it a better means for the uncritical mobilization of the popular masses that was envisaged by national elites in times of dominant particularism and growing aggressiveness in international relations. Anyway, it is also unquestionable that "blood and soil" nationalism was lastly responsible for the horrors of two World Wars, for the racial hatred that German, Japanese and Italian occupants spread over whole continents, and for the most perversely planned and scientifically implemented genocide in human history. Therefore, it was not surprising that the objectivistic concept of nation factually disappeared from the political agenda for roughly four decades. Around the end of the 1980s, it re-emerged from oblivion, albeit taking then a slightly different guise. Indeed, the fundament of the homogeneous social and political society was identified, for the first time, not in the nation itself, but in what was called the "ethnos" or the "ethnie". In other words, nations can develop and survive only because the population of each one of them shares the same "ethnic origins".[112] More concretely, the *ethnos* is described by Anthony D. Smith—probably the most prominent academic exponent of the nationalistic revival of the last decades—as a social community "with shared ancestry myths, histories and cultures, having an association with a specific territory and a sense of solidarity".[113] Thus, when it comes to the definition of the "ethnie", the similarities with the traditional concept of nation are manifest: while the references to the genetic homogeneity are deleted, the cultural elements are nonetheless presented in a form that completely refrains from any implication of subjective acts of will.

Now, taken for granted that the latest revival of the nation is characterized by the centrality of the notion of "ethnos", what is more interesting, here, is to understand how the supporters of this revival get to grips with the challenges that globalization poses to the nationalistic project. Once again, it was Anthony D. Smith who provided the most helpful insights. In his analysis of the persistence of national identities in times of globalization, Smith asserts that the nation state currently faces challenges on a twofold dimension: one external and one internal. In its external dimension, the crisis affects the "military and economic power [of the nation state] in a world of giant transnational companies, military blocs and continental associations linked together by electronic mass communications".[114] The external crisis has itself two aspects: the first deriving from the almost unfettered power of economic global players; the second connected with the development of the new communication technologies. As regards the first point, Smith plays down the threat to national autonomy by simply upholding that "the national economies remain the standard unit of regulation and allocation of resources".[115] Yet, if this may be true for a few global superpowers, it verges on wishful thinking with reference to all other nation states. Moving on to the second external challenge to national identity, i.e., to its ongoing possible erosion as a result of worldwide networks of communication, Smith articulates his counter-arguments, first, by claiming—in a way which is quite usual among many critics of globalization, regardless of whether they are politically progressive, or conservative—that global culture is nothing but the expression of imperialism.[116] Accusing cultural globalism of being imperialistic and oppressive against specific identities does not imply, however, that these identities also have the resources to withstand the challenge.

In his second counter-argument against the thesis of the cultural depletion of nation states through the new communication technologies, Smith focuses, on the contrary, on the advantages that these technologies may provide for those who are engaged in the defence of national identities. In fact, internet-based communication makes the spreading of cultural contents quite easy—and, beyond that, it makes it possible at costs which were unimaginable before, therefore facilitating the safeguard of still existing, albeit marginal traditions, or even enabling to rediscover those identities which have been obfuscated by more powerful narrations.[117] Yet, Smith's most important counter-argument is the third, according to which every human being, in order to develop a robust identity which allows her/him to take well-grounded decisions and to act with responsibility, needs a stable reference to a strong system of values. Furthermore, insofar as these values are shared by a community, they also build the fundament for mutual solidarity. However, the more inclusive a system of values is, the thinner it is—actually too thin to fulfil its essential task. Global culture, in fact—Smith argues—is void, "historically shallow" and "memory-less".[118] As a result, if humans still want to properly implement their social dimension, then they cannot but rely on the strong and homogeneous ethical system of national communities since "the myths, memories, symbols and ceremonies of nationalism provide the sole basis for ... social cohesion and political action".[119]

Finally, focusing on the internal side of the challenge against national identity, Smith ascertains that nation states are threatened by the increasing emergence of subnational identities, whose claims range from the request for more autonomy within the legal and institutional framework of the state, to explicit secession. However, according to Smith, this phenomenon would be far away from demonstrating the growing weakness of the idea of nation. To the contrary, it would rather prove that the nationalist project, in its true meaning, is becoming more and more assertive, to the point that long time oppressed ethnic communities are now strong and self-conscious enough to raise their voices even against the power of the historically rooted, but ethnically inhomogeneous territorial states.[120]

In the end, Smith's arguments can be led back to two main assumptions, both of them quite contestable. The first is that no personal identity is possible without a self-constrained, ethnically based system of values. Against this assumption it has to be pointed out that, if it is true that identity needs ethical references, it is also incontestable that everyone's identity is a rather multi-layered structure with a plurality of references. Limiting these references to just one element does not make our personality stronger, but poorer, more one-sided, less capable of criticism and ultimately less free. The second assumption, which lies at the basis of Smith's position, is that ethnic nationalism, though endangered by globalization, is still strong enough to preserve itself even against the background of an ever more interconnected world. Yet, this assumption may refer to the fact that ethnic identities are still so stable as to shape the self-understanding of many social and political communities. Or it may suggest—instead of, or in addition to the former claim—that ethically based communities, no matter how large or small, are still generally capable of maintaining their independence and defending their interests. And, while the first assertion is empirically confirmed, up to the present days, by the growing number of identity-claiming political movements,[121] the second is highly questionable, even if we admit that the globalization process was characterized from the very beginning by some distortions. In fact, the growth of a global economy and worldwide markets disproportionately benefited the educated elites of the Global North, while creating a new, relatively affluent middle class in the developing countries. On the other hand, however, it lowered the quality of life and the social security of the blue-collar workers of the Western world as well as increased social inequality by concentrating wealth in the hands of the tiny upper layer of the social scale, both nationally and internationally. The dysfunctions of globalization eventually triggered the present "populist backlash",[122] with its sometimes aggressive revival of ethnic nationalism. Furthermore, the globalization boost that had its apex between the end of the twentieth and the beginning of the twenty-first century was not completely unprecedented. We had, in fact, other periods of human history—such as the Roman Empire, the European late Middle Ages, the age of empires and, lastly, the *belle époque* before World War I—in which the exchange of goods was relevant in terms of quantity and economic value, and broad as regards its geographical extension. Yet, all those previous forms of globalization came finally to a more or less abrupt end, giving way to different episodes of particularistic resurgence.[123] In fact, we should recognize that the present phenomenon of globalization comes along with the development of a worldwide institutional and legal framework, as well as with an idea of universally valid human rights and justice, that has no match in human history. Nonetheless, it cannot be ruled out that it might also be rolled back—or even that it is already in the process of being actually rolled back—and replaced by that kind of national identities that make up the horizon of Smith's thinking. Yet, what Smith claimed was more than this: indeed, he argued that a nationalistic revival would eventually put particularistic decision making at the centre of politics again, and that this would bring an advantage not only in terms of collective identity, but also of democracy and justice. In fact, although the "populist backlash" seems capable of threatening cosmopolitanism, it is far from guaranteeing more justice and wealth, while its democratic record is more than worrying. Few doubts can be raised on the necessity of re-adjusting globalization. Nevertheless, if nationalistic self-reliance is one-sidedly re-affirmed, then the wealth of a large part of the world population is destined to be put in danger together with peace, justice and democracy. Instead, if the interests of the citizens in terms of chances for self-realization as well as their due commitment to peace, democracy and justice are taken seriously, then independence must be balanced with interconnection, and identity must go hand in hand with responsibility.

## 2.8 Contemporary Hegemonism and Beyond

Within the horizon of the holistic-particularistic paradigm of order, hegemonic attempts never aspired to establish any kind of worldwide order. Indeed, since the identity of the community is no less based on the awareness of its distinctiveness if compared to other communities, than on the positive construction of common values within the political arena,[124] the world of holistic particularism cannot but be a "pluriverse". As a consequence, holistic-particularistic hegemonism is never global, but is conceived of as limited to vast territories, in which a population lives that is assumed to share the fundamental traits that make it different from any other. In Carl Schmitt's formulation, the hegemonic community was articulated roughly on a continental scale, comprising a dominant nation state and some satellite countries which shared the same racial and cultural background. Due to its openly racist content, Schmitt's idea of the *Großraumordnung* was destined to oblivion after World War II. Nonetheless, in recent times a somehow comparable conception has reappeared, now grounding the hegemonic community on the essentials of a shared civilization and, more specifically, of a common religion (2.8.1). On the other hand, a different kind of hegemonism has also made its entry, more or less at the same time, into the arena of political ideas. It is the concept of a hegemonic international law, in which a supremacy related to the assumption of the superiority of a cultural and economic model tends to sideline the normativity of the laws that govern international interactions. However, in its most radical form, Western cultural hegemonism produces a dialectic movement, somehow paving the way to its own overcoming. Although always ignoring the voices of the "others", it stretches particularism to a global dimension, thus emphasizing that the vision of order, in times of globalized interactions, needs more than just selfishness (2.8.2).

### 2.8.1 The Theory of the Clash of Civilizations

In his book *The Clash of Civilizations*—first published in 1996 after having been anticipated, by an essay with the same title, in 1993—[125] the political scientist Samuel P. Huntington is well aware of the crisis of the nation state. Indeed, it is justified to seriously doubt that this is currently capable of exercising an effective control over the flow of goods, capital, people, technology and ideas, sufficient to maintain a clear distinction between the "internal" and the "external" dimension and to preserve the sovereignty of the individual national community. "State borders, in short – Huntington maintains – have become increasingly permeable".[126] Given the necessity to seek a new horizon, Huntington found it in the concept of "civilization". In his view, this concept would have in essence two advantages: firstly, it would acknowledge the decline of Western domination and the transition to a multipolar and multi-cultural world,[127] and, secondly, it would recognize the increasing influence of the cultural element.[128] Huntington starts from the assumption that these two developments have already been completed and that it is therefore essential to become aware of a paradigmatic transformation in international politics, or of the transition from the conflict between classical nation states to the clash of civilizations.[129]

According to the use made by Huntington, "civilization" is—like "culture"—the "overall way of life of a people",[130] but understood, with respect to "culture", in a wider and more essential dimension. Among the features that distinguish a civilization from the other, Huntington refers to "common objective elements, such as language, history, religion, customs, institutions, and the subjective self-identification of people".[131] In addition, Huntington specifies that there is a significant overlapping between racial differences and the distinction between civilizations. Yet, they are not identical, since "people of the same race can be deeply divided by civilization; people of different races may be united by civilization".[132] Indeed—Huntington claims—"the crucial distinctions among human groups concern their values, beliefs, institutions, and social structures, not their physical size, head shapes, and skin colors".[133] What shapes a civilization, among all its features, is rather the religious dimension:

> To a very large degree, the major civilizations in human history have been closely identified with the world's great religions; and people who share ethnicity and language but differ in religion may slaughter each other, as happened in Lebanon, the former Yugoslavia, and the Subcontinent.[134]

Therefore, if compared to the supporters of the idea of the centrality of the nation, Huntington plays down, on the one hand, the meaning of the racial or ethnic identity, while stressing, on the other, only one element among those that form the cultural heritage, namely religion. In doing so, he puts the feature to the fore which is more suited to aggregate the most individuals and resources on the vastest geographical scale, without any risk of gliding into some form of globalism. Moreover, the concept of "civilization" emphasizes far more than that of "nation"—and even more than that of "ethnos"—the cultural content of collective identities, making them more flexible and suitable for political use. Summing up, the "civilization" represents the widest possible form of human aggregation, beyond the individual state or people, and without hypostatizing the allegedly fictional entity of a universal humanity.

Heavily relying on the theories of Oswald Spengler,[135] Arnold Toynbee[136] and Fernand Braudel,[137] Huntington maintains that it is incorrect to speak of "civilization" in singular, as though there had been only one process of developing a unitary civilization in the whole history of humanity. Rather, we should speak of "civilizations" in plural, thus acknowledging the existence of their plurality and difference.[138] Furthermore, every civilization is assumed to have a sort of lifecycle, with a birth, a growth, a flourishing, a decay and a disintegration.[139] By this assumption, Huntington goes back, to a certain extent, to a premodern, organic understanding of history, according to which no unitary historical progress can be detected, but only many cyclical processes involving all collective actors. Moving on, then, to specify the civilizations that characterize the present time, he identifies eight of them: the Sinic, the Japanese, the Hindu, the Orthodox Russian, the Islamic, the Western—including North America (the United States and Canada, but not Mexico and Central America), the Protestant and Catholic countries of Europe, Australia and New Zealand—the Latin American (which is seen by some scholars as a sub-entity of the Western civilization), and (possibly) the African.[140] Each civilization comprises all kin-countries that share the same fundamental features, tending to organize them around a leading core state, with all other countries forming concentric circles around it. Along the borders that separate distinct civilizations, tensions may arise which can degenerate into open and sometimes also armed conflicts. When the hostility between two neighbouring countries belonging to distinct civilizations threatens to deteriorate into a broader and more devastating war also affecting other actors, the core states generally intervene searching for a compromise that should guarantee the interests of the countries directly involved, but much more those of the civilization as a whole.[141]

By structuring social and political order around the distinguishing features of a common civilization, Huntington develops a conception that attributes to the core states the indisputable status of a hegemonic power among the kin-countries. Furthermore, the reference points for the analysis of international relations—i.e., the different civilizations—are conceived of as entities disposing of large populations, vast territories and relevant resources, and thus far better equipped than nations to face the uncertainties that derive from a globalized competition. Yet, unlike Carl Schmitt as the most relevant supporter of the political philosophy of hegemonism in the first half of the twentieth century, Huntington considers the relations between hegemons with their vassal states not necessarily verging on open war. Rather, what he envisages seems to be a number of temporary solutions to avoid more damaging conflicts which remind of Morgenthau's concept of "accommodation". In times of increasing religious tensions, Huntington's approach seems to be capable of mirroring facts as they are while providing feasible solutions. Nevertheless, this could prove to be too hasty a reaction for at least two reasons. Firstly, if it really happened to be true that identities in international relations constitute themselves increasingly along the lines of religious division, then searching for a compromise between hegemons could turn out to be a mere illusion due to the deep psychological involvement which is determined by religious beliefs and affiliations. Secondly, Huntington shares an assumption with all exponents of the holistic-particularistic paradigm of order, which is far from self-evident or convincing, namely that the social and political entity is—and cannot but be—homogeneous in itself, so that internal distinctions are simply ignored or dismissed as irrelevant. To the contrary, social and political entities are internally highly differentiated—and so are religion-based civilizations too, which are divided, for instance, between fundamentalist and open-minded groups. Bringing the open-minded of any religious belief or cultural affiliation together, while broadening their influence within the communities to which they belong—not sturdily reasserting exclusive identities—nurtures the hope and a realistic chance to establish a more stable framework for global relations.

### 2.8.2 *Particularism Going Global in the Neo-Conservative Approach*

A second hegemonic attempt that has been formulated in the last decades arises from that stream of political thought usually known as neo-conservatism. Highly influential in particular at the juncture of the twentieth and the twenty-first centuries, when the United States hegemonic power reached its broadest expansion, the neo-conservative movement comprises quite a large number of authors, whose positions sometimes differ significantly from one another. Nonetheless, what they all have in common is the conviction that the United States is endowed with some kind of exceptionalism. More concretely, the defence of US exceptionalism is articulated in three steps, following the way of a progressive increase in radicalness and ambition, until the original particularistic intent—which is never completely denied—ends up asserting an idea of global order, thus merging with its opposite and, actually, undermining from within the most essential tenet of the original paradigm.

The first step of the neo-conservative project consists in advocating a hegemonic concept of international law. However, to re-design international law in a hegemonic setting, it is first necessary to challenge the normativity of the current international law system. This is precisely what we can find—in a peculiarly aggressive fashion—in the works of Jeremy A. Rabkin. In Rabkin's view, international law is nothing but an instrument for restraining the well-motivated and legitimate national interests of the United States, as the paladin of the free world, and of all other liberal and democratic nation states. As it was still called "law of nations"—Rabkin argues—international law was largely about war and commerce, and therefore limited in reach and range.[142] Moreover, it was based on reciprocal restraints and did not aim at establishing international institutions as well as, *a fortiori*, at enforcing decisions taken by a nebulous international community. However, in the last decades, international law developed into a much more ambitious and invasive enterprise, thought to give effect to the alleged will of nothing less than humankind itself, with its interests and values. This change of meaning of international law coincided with the establishment of the United Nations as successor to the League of Nations. To some extent, this evolution can be compared to a similar change in domestic law. Just as domestic law moved from a framework designed to guarantee the interaction of free subjects to an instrument for boosting a certain idea of collective values, international law also left the firm domain of state interaction in order to support a vague concept of the common interests of humankind.[143] The consequence has been not only a loss of efficiency, but also a shift in the political meaning of international law. By building institutions which claim to be binding on sovereign nation states, contemporary international law is becoming "a sheer monument to collectivist ideology".[144] That change—Rabkin claims—should pose in itself a problem for liberalism. Yet, an even more serious challenge arises from it: in a world which is characterized by a large number of non-democratic states, binding international institutions can represent a handicap for liberal states and for their actions taken in defence of liberty. From this perspective, arguably identifiable as a problem even for those not beholden to a neo-conservative point of view, Rabkin infers a more far-reaching consequence, namely the rejection of *any* idea of an ethical and political universalism. He adopts this position alongside a radical reaffirmation of the traditional doctrine of unilateral national sovereignty which is generally central to the paradigm of holistic particularism.[145] We see what radical and, ultimately, absurd conclusion can be drawn from Rabkin's theory in his critique of the International Criminal Court (ICC): to his eyes, the ICC serves only as an ingenious expedient for the Germans to "overcome the past, by licensing German judges to try Americans and Israelis for war crimes".[146]

Dismantling the normativity of the multilateral, inclusive and horizontal system of international law opens the way to a reorganization of its legal and political framework, in particular to what has been called the "imperial" conception of international law.[147] Following this hegemonic form of thought and praxis, the dominant superpower exploits the existing norms and reinterprets them in accordance with its most selfish interests; when this proves to be impossible, it withdraws its compliance to the whole or to a part of the international legal system; finally, in a last and more radical attempt, it seeks to replace international law with domestic norms.[148] However, the imperial approach to international law cannot be realized without significant costs. Since the stabilizing effect of consensus is largely eliminated, a minimal order in international interactions can only be guaranteed by a large use of military and economic means—for example through the transfer of resources in order to ensure the favour of local elites. A second cost concerns legitimacy. To the extent that the action of the hegemonic power is no longer framed within the traditional criteria of international legitimacy, consensus can only be established, once again, by recurring to economic transfers—an operation that weighs on the budgets of the "imperial" superpower. Given the enormous burden that comes from it, the exercise of a hegemonic position always tends to overload the resources of a country and, ultimately, to weaken it.[149]

The attack on international law is not an untypical feature of thinkers sharing the holistic-particularistic point of view. What comes in addition, in Rabkin' position, is his assumption of an exceptional role that is—and should be—assigned to the superpower of the liberal world, more specifically to the United States.[150] The second step of the neo-conservatives in their attempt to redesign the features of the holistic-particularistic paradigm coincides, thus, with the defence of the function that is attributed to the American "empire" in shaping world order, even beyond the weak normative framework that is left to an international law turned into a hegemonic instrument. The idea of "empire" as a globalized political and legal regime has been emphatically re-vitalized, in particular, by Deepak Lal. In Lal's view, empires can realize the main goals of social life, namely maintaining peace and securing prosperity, much better than nation states.[151] Furthermore, empires achieve these goals on a significantly larger scale. The rehabilitation of the historical function of empires is then applied to the role played by the United States at the beginning of the twenty-first century. Tearing the "million strings" of international law which aim at tying down the super-power, impeding its free movement as the Lilliputians did with the overwhelming Gulliver, the United States should accept its imperial position along with the duties arising from it. This consists, firstly, in securing global order, and secondly in expanding modernization. While global order guarantees peace on a large scale, modernization is the condition for prosperity.[152] Therefore, Lal's imperial conception globalizes hegemony in a way unknown to the tradition prior to the neo-conservative turn. Indeed, the regime imposed by the hegemonic US superpower is now extended throughout the world, in fact in a form that largely exceeds any other factual imperial attempt of the past as well as any historical ideology of hegemonism. But we find no reference, here, to the universality of the values carried forth by the "empire". The sense of the empire's rule has to be found—Lal argues—in the security and wealth it can deliver all over the world, not in the questionable superiority of its moral and ethical principles.

According to the most radical strand of neo-conservative thought—which represents the third step on the way to a justification of US exceptionalism and to a dialectic turn of particularism—the unique position of the United States is not only due to its economic, cultural and military strength—at least during the period of the "unipolar moment"—[153] but also to its alleged moral leadership. The most committed defender of the superiority of Western values as well as of their global validity has probably been Robert Kagan. Far from being analogous to the despotic superpowers of the past, the United States "is a liberal, progressive society through and through, and to the extent that Americans believe in power, they believe it must be a means of advancing the principles of a liberal civilization and a liberal world order".[154] Precisely here we can find the most radical claim made by the neo-conservative movement, namely that the Western values of freedom, rule of law and respect of human rights are not only to be regarded as superior but also that they must be defended and, if possible, even imposed everywhere in the world. Liberty being a value shared, in principle, by all humans, the United States can reasonably claim to act globally. Furthermore, its intervention in the name of freedom is not a violation of the principle of equal sovereignty but a defence of a fundamental right. From the global validity of liberty, Kagan ultimately draws the legitimacy of the worldwide American predominance:

> modern liberalism cherishes the rights and liberties of the individual and defines progress as the greater protection of these rights and liberties across the globe. In the absence of a sudden democratic and liberal transformation, that goal can be achieved only by compelling tyrannical or barbarous regimes to behave more humanely, sometimes through force.[155]

Earlier variants of hegemonism never bore really global aspirations. Rather, they extended the range of the homogeneous community, aiming to create a hegemonic system in distinct spheres of influence, in order to gather more assets for global competition. Nonetheless, they did not aspire to impose everywhere in the world a coherent set of values. Therefore, hegemony was always limited to a large but not worldwide scale, and thus, there was no global order per se, but only the competition among the enlarged hegemonic communities. Not surprisingly, we find both in Schmitt[156] and in Huntington[157] cautious warnings against the tendency to overestimate the community's values and the ambition to impose them universally. On the contrary, as a consequence of the neo-conservative turn, particularly in its more radical expression, hegemonism has reached an unprecedented worldwide extension. By doing so, one of the most recent strands of holistic particularism explicitly rejects one of its major claims, namely that order can never be global, but is necessarily limited to well-defined, restricted and ethnically or culturally homogeneous communities. Yet, the project of a particularism going global does little, in the end, to contradict the fact that the content of the hegemon's values does not reach beyond the borders of a specific tradition. In fact, the hegemon's extension cannot properly be understood as the result of a really *universal* process because it does not arise from deliberative processes open, in principle, to all well-motivated arguments and contributions. Rather, the assertion of the superiority of Western values is grounded on a unilateral claim, pretending to be self-evident but denying the challenge of a possible falsification. Neo-conservative thought refuses, in general, to engage with the "other" via a deliberative method, potentially involving all concerned subjects. But only such a discourse could lead to universally acceptable results and thus transcend particularistic interests. Consequently, it remains within the tradition of political theory that asserts that order can only be produced by homogeneous communities—with the difference, however, that a single community now claims to extend its idea of order and values on a *global* level. Globalizing its rule and values, the superpower makes itself fit for new challenges. But shaping the rules in a properly inclusive and hence really universal way lies beyond the horizon of the limited neo-conservative outlook.

## 2.9 The Dialectics of Holistic Particularism

Due to a weakening of the US superpower in the last decade, following its overstretching over the previous twenty years, the global vision of the neo-conservatives—in particular of the most radical among them—may belong to the past, giving way again to a more traditional understanding of self-restraining particularism. Indeed, the current state of world dis-order does not seem to be characterized primarily by an imperial globalism underpinned by a sense of moral superiority, but rather by the reaffirmation of national identities, the return of traditional, power-related geopolitics and the crisis of international law.[158] Nonetheless, the emerging of a particularism going global in the shape of the neo-conservative thought tells us that even the most anti-universalistic paradigm of order is struggling to maintain one of its fundamental tenets—namely the assumption that a well-ordered society must be limited in extent—when its supporters, if confronted with the challenges deriving from globalization, do not opt for an only defensive and lastly, if feasible, self-damaging entrenchment. A similar, quite unexpected dialectic characterizes at least two further essentials of the holistic-particularistic paradigm: the claim that only egoistic behaviour is rational, and the assertion that the identity of the self is necessarily rooted in the parochial community. In both cases, analogously to how the discussion unfolded as regards the extension of order, the essential is first developed according to the most strict understanding of the holistic-particularistic paradigm, but is then transformed in the course of the debate—by authors who regarded their theories as being still consistent with the conceptual framework of holistic particularism—into a theoretical construct which is rather poised to pave the way for the overcoming of the traditional, quite narrow-minded interpretation of the paradigm.

### 2.9.1  *Rational Choice Theory*

Since Thucydides, the idea that only a behaviour that gives unchallenged priority to one's selfish payoffs can be correctly considered *rational* has been a constant feature in any variant of holistic particularism. Obviously, the question at stake being about social order, the entity which was thought to take advantage of selfish behaviour was not the individual, but the community. The understanding of rationality as the ability to distinguish egoistic advantage from disadvantage was then taken up by economists and transformed into the theory of rational choice. Deeply influenced by methodological individualism, the assumption of the selfish rationality is applied, here, to individuals, and not to collective entities. However, little more than a decade ago, the theory of rational choice was itself applied for the first time to the analysis of the behaviour of collective entities, so that the concept of the selfish rationality made its way back—so to say—from the individual to the collective level, although the analytical tools were now somehow different and more sophisticated than before due to the intellectual contribution provided by economic science.

The authors who applied the epistemological framework of rational choice—based on the assumption that only selfishness is rational—to legal theory in order to assert the normative limits of international law were Jack L. Goldsmith and Eric A. Posner.[159] Their highly innovative intellectual move has been courageous, influential and, if we consider the broadness of the debate triggered by their work, successful too. Starting with the assumption that every rational actor will prefer the choice that promises to obtain the highest immediate payoffs, and arguing that states, in international relations, always face the possibility of being trapped in a situation comparable to that of the prisoner's dilemma, Goldsmith and Posner maintain that every rationally acting state, given the fact that the behaviour of its counterparts turns out to be unpredictable in the most cases, cannot but pursue its own egoistic interest. Neither customary international law nor treaty law can build a reliable normative framework of shared and effective rules, really able to guarantee the stable proceduralization of conflict solution as well as, in the most favourable cases, cooperation. States thus comply with international law only insofar as this compliance coincides with their immediate and egoistic interests, so that the legal framework of relations among political communities is left with a very modest normative consistency.

The first problem that we meet while applying Goldsmith and Posner's approach to international law impacts directly on their most significant innovation. In fact, it is problematic to extend the rational choice approach, conceived in order to interpret the behaviour of individuals, to collective entities like states, which are themselves composed of a plurality of individuals and social groups with articulated and sometimes diverging interests.[160] The justification that the "billiard ball" approach, considering every single state as a unity, albeit "far from perfect", would be simply "parsimonious"[161]—in the sense that it would allow to usefully reduce the number and complexity of the analysed phenomena in order to concentrate on the most significant among them—cannot really remove the sense of an epistemological shortcoming. Nor can the consideration be convincing that "[both] ordinary language and history suggest that states have agency and thus can be said to make decisions and act on the basis of identifiable goals".[162] Such an understanding seems to be somehow old-fashioned in a world in which state agency is challenged both at the *infra*-state and at the *supra*-state level.

However, even if we accept the rather unconvincing application of the rational choice analytical tools to the action of collective entities, some additional questions arise. To begin with, according to the understanding of rationality proposed by Goldsmith and Posner, actors—in this case states—have predefined preferences which do not change during interaction. To the contrary, evidence shows that preferences shift in the course of interactions.[163] Moreover, the definition of the elements whose evaluation essentially contributes to making a choice rational may be considered short-sighted insofar as it excludes factors like "reputation" and "reciprocity".[164] Yet, three further problems are probably even more relevant—at least from the point of view of the dialectic of the holistic-particularistic paradigm. In fact, Goldsmith and Posner do not distinguish clearly between immediate payoffs and mid- as well as long-term interests. Furthermore, they presuppose that states interact exclusively *vis-à-vis* each other, i.e., they are not embedded in a broader and multipolar context. Finally, state interaction is seen as an individual and unique event, excluding the consideration of any form of iteration. Yet, the application of instrumental rationality may lead to the conclusion that cooperation and solidarity are irrational and that egoism is the most rational choice only if we collocate the actors within an abstract horizon, quite different from that in which they usually act. Indeed, interactions—even those among international actors—happen normally within multilateral contexts and include iteration. From this perspective, the attitude of international actors will be significantly more prone to complying with international law and, generally, less hostile to cooperation since they would take into account possible remuneration or retaliation in the next rounds of interaction.[165] Besides, the actions of international actors are not *bi*polar but *multi*polar, constructing the framework of "collective actions" that help us to understand cooperation.[166] The contexts of multipolar iterative interactions have been described as "international regimes".[167] Within these regimes, international law takes the role of the normative element that decisively contributes to shaping actors' interactions, making them predictable.

Therefore, the application of the analytical tools of rational choice to the interpretation of international order—regardless of whether we consider it justifiable in principle, or not—leads to conclusions which are not consistent with the fundamental assumption of holistic particularism according to which rationality is coincident with the search for egoistic and immediate payoffs. In fact, the benefits of cooperation can be higher if we consider the advantages in a long-term perspective, as well as if the individual community accepts to be part of a stabilizing political and legal framework. Yet, this framework and the possibility that it reliably works on the whole are precisely what the supporters of holistic particularism reject. If taken seriously, rational choice brings us to a domain that is located beyond the borders of the paradigm.

### 2.9.2 Communitarianism

In the history of thought, insistence on the social nature of humans— i.e., on their being necessarily part of a collective structure with specific and historically rooted values—came not only from the conservative side and was not only motivated by the attempt to defend existing hierarchies. Rather, it also had the function of warning against the atomistic and centrifugal forces triggered by one-sided individualism. In this sense, Plato's idea of "justice" was conceived as a bulwark against the destabilizing effects of the Sophistic protoindividualism. Similarly, Hegel's *Sittlichkeit* ("ethical oder") sought to correct the unilateralism of early-stage liberalism, without completely denying its conquests. Political philosophy has recently revitalized the traditional exhortation to cohesion as part of the highly influential *debate between liberals and communitarians*. The dispute was prompted, on the liberal side of the divide—i.e., on the side that gives priority, in principle, to individual freedom over social cohesion—by John Rawls who, at the beginning of the 1970s, published his seminal *Theory of Justice*.[168] Following in the footsteps of historical contractualists like Locke, Rousseau and Kant, Rawls started his analysis by using a conceptual artifice. In particular, he put, at the beginning of any consideration on how a *just* society should be organized, socially unbound individuals whose only feature consists in their transcendental endowments, such as freedom, ability to act rationally and neutrality in their mutual attitudes. In this socially neutral position, individuals ignore what their future fortunes and misfortunes may be: they do not know whether they will have economic, political or social power, whether they will be healthy, or affected by some kind of adversity. Being covered by the "veil of ignorance", they cannot but take any decision on the only basis of purely rational and abstract considerations, while also considering the possibility of meeting the unluckiest case. The result, thus, is a contract agreed upon by all individuals involved, which contains the essential rules ensuring the implementation of rational and shared principles of justice. Given these premises, the most reasonable choice is that the principles of justice, which are to be subscribed by everyone, must safeguard the best possible living conditions even for the less fortunate. In fact, every rational being, in the face of the risk—that cannot be excluded beforehand—to be hit by misfortune, will only be willing to choose the option that guarantees a reasonable protection for everyone. In John Rawls's re-discovery of contract theory, inequality of property and resources can only be justified insofar as also the less privileged—as a result of a Pareto optimal solution—benefit from the situation.[169]

Rawls's revival of methodological individualism and classical contractualism raised a relevant critical reaction. Firstly, it was pointed out that no idea of justice could be established without reference to the values that any actual society has developed during its history, i.e., without taking into account the socially shared representation of what is "good".[170] Going even further, thus at the very root of what they consider to be the deficit of his liberalism, Rawls's critics claimed that the allegedly wrong attempt to define what is "right" without referring to a representation of the "good" arises from an erroneous conception of subjectivity, which would be understood in excessively conjectural terms and without the necessary anchoring to the real life of individuals.[171] Indeed, from the standpoint of the communitarians, what is "good" for a society is not thought to be, primarily, the consequence of the rational exercise of free will by the political actors, but the result of a pre-rational sentiment of belonging, due to common experiences and education as well as to shared values like the ethical heritage of the community. In short, communitarians focus on "the richer [than the purely deontological approach – S.D.] background languages in which we set the basis and point of the moral obligations we acknowledge".[172]

At first glance, it seems to be evident that while liberals tend to adhere to a universalistic understanding of order, communitarians are inclined towards a rather particularistic view of society. Yet, a distinction has to be made, which is quite relevant for the theory of the paradigms of order and how they relate to one another. Communitarianism presents, in fact, two different versions, one of which goes beyond short-sighted particularism. Some communitarians—representing, so to say, the homogeneity-centred or ethnocentric variant of communitarianism—assume that the social bond that holds individuals together can only work if it is grounded on a strenuous and one-sided defence of the values and interests of one's own community—even, and in many cases explicitly, against values and interests of other nations.[173] But others, the *republican* communitarians, embrace a remarkably more open-minded attitude. They do not place the emphasis on pre-reflexive identities—like the exponents of the former strand—but give precedence to participation. In the view of republican communitarians, therefore, social identity does not precede intersubjective interaction, but is *dialogically* constituted in essence.[174] Like all communitarians, they reject the classical liberal vision of society as a sum of atoms, but counter it with a rather conciliatory proposal, namely with the idea of a "liberal holism", where the defence of the values of freedom goes hand in hand with the identification of the individuals with the community to which they belong.[175] Against a merely "negative" concept of freedom,[176] republican communities are assumed to be "animated by a sense of a shared immediate common good",[177] while individuals are bound together by their "common history".[178] However, unlike what is assumed in the ethnocentric variant, the common identity is not rooted in a pre-political dimension, but is only realized through reflexive commitment and the "participation in self-rule as ... the essence of freedom, as part of what must be secured".[179] As a result, in liberal republics, citizens identify themselves with the order of freedom of the communities in which they live, which their ancestors have contributed to create and they help to perpetuate through their daily self-reflexive support.

Whereas the "ethnocentric" communitarianism *à la* MacIntyre, with its rejection of universal morality and its plea for an ethics of public life strictly and exclusively connected to the values of a specific political community, is undoubtedly located within the holistic-particularistic paradigm, the same cannot be said about its "republican" counterpart. Far from supporting a conservative vision of the homogeneity of the political community, authors such as Charles Taylor justifiably emphasize that the values of a liberal society do not arise in the isolated minds of atomized individuals, but within communicative processes which unfold in historically determined societies. In doing so, they put their finger on a real weakness of a one-sided universalism, namely on its tendency to ignore that "people are parochial in their commitments and beliefs".[180] In fact,

> we live, for the most part, among our neighbours, in our home places, with local landscapes, customs, climates, and conventions. Much that is sweetest in life is built among human societies, according to the happenstance of provincial circumstances.[181]

Despite its often radical and disturbing rejection of the recognition of any form of shared universal humanity, this may be the lesson that we can learn from holistic particularism: citizens' rights, democracy, as well as the fundamental sense of justice and commitment to solidarity, were all born within parochial contexts; therefore, if universalism wants to have a chance, it should not try to eradicate parochial identities, but live and flourish along with them by building upon them.

## NOTES

1. Hannah Arendt, *On Revolution*, Viking, New York 1963, at 23.
2. Kallinos, *A Call to Arms Against the Cimmerian Invaders*, in: Willis Barnstone (ed.), *Ancient Greek Lyrics*, Indiana University Press, Bloomington 2010 (1st ed. 1962), at 16 et seq.
3. Barnstone, *Ancient Greek Lyrics*, *supra* note 2, at 16.

4. Tyrtaeus, *Spartan Soldier*, in: Barnstone, *Ancient Greek Lyrics*, supra note 2, at 18 et seq.
5. Barnstone, *Ancient Greek Lyrics*, supra note 2, at 18.
6. Thucydides, *The Peloponnesian War*, in: *Hobbes's Thucydides*, Richard Schlatter ed., Rutgers University Press, New Brunswick (NJ) 1975, Book V, Chapter 84 et seq., at 377 et seq.
7. Ibid., Book V, Chapter 105, at 382.
8. Ibid., Book V, Chapter 113, at 384.
9. Ibid, Book I, Chapter 75 et seq., at 70 et seq.
10. Ibid., Book I, Chapter 76, at 70.
11. Ibid., Book III, Chapter 82, at 222 et seq.
12. Ibid., Book III, Chapter 82, at 223.
13. Plato, *Gorgias*, English translation by Terence Irwin, Oxford University Press, Oxford/New York 1979, 483d, at 57.
14. Plato, *The Republic*, English translation by Tom Griffith, Cambridge University Press, Cambridge/New York 2003, 1st ed. 2000, Book I, 338c, at 15.
15. Plato, *Gorgias*, supra note 13, 488b et seq., at 61 et seq.
16. Ibid., 506c et seq., at 84 et seq.
17. Plato, *The Republic*, supra note 14, Book I, 344d et seq., at 23 et seq.
18. Ibid., Book II, 369b, at 50 et seq.
19. Ibid., Book IV, 433b and 434b et seq., at 127 et seq.
20. Ibid., Book V, 470b, at 171.
21. Ibid., Book V, 469b et seq., at 170 et seq.
22. Aristotle, *Nichomachean Ethics*, English translation by Roger Crisp, Cambridge University Press, Cambridge/New York 2000, Book V, Chapter 5, 1134a, at 90 et seq.
23. Ibid., Book V, Chapter 2, 1130b, at 84.
24. Ibid., Book I, Chapter 7, 1097a, at 10.
25. Ibid., Book I, Chapter 7, 1097a et seq., at 10 et seq.
26. Ibid., Book 10, Chapter 7, 1177a et seq., at 194 et seq.
27. Aristotle, *Politics*, English translation by H. Rackham, Harvard University Press, Cambridge (MA) 1959, Book VII, Chapter 1, 1324a et seq., at 538 et seq.
28. Ibid., Book VII, Chapter 8 et seq., 1328b et seq., at 572 et seq.
29. Ibid., Book I, Chapter 2, 1252b et seq., at 6 et seq.
30. Niccolò Machiavelli, *Discorsi sopra la prima deca di Tito Livio* (1513–1519), Einaudi, Torino 1997, Book I, Chapter 13 (English translation by Ninian Hill Thomson, Kegan Paul, Trench & Co., London 1883, at 70 et seq.).
31. Ibid., Book II, Chapter 2 (Engl.: at 215).
32. Niccolò Machiavelli, *Il Principe* (1513), Einaudi, Torino 1995, Chapter XVII, para. 2 (English translation by James Atkinson, Hackett, Indianapolis 1976, at 271).

33. Ibid., Chapter XIX, para. 2 (Engl.: at 289).
34. Machiavelli, *Discorsi*, supra note 30, Book I, Chapter 6 (Engl.: at 44).
35. Machiavelli, *Il Principe*, supra note 32, Chapter XXV, para. 5 (Engl.: at 365).
36. Machiavelli, *Discorsi*, supra note 30, Book II, Chapter 25 (Engl.: at 307).
37. Machiavelli, *Il Principe*, supra note 32, Chapter III, para. 3 et seq. (Engl.: at 107).
38. Machiavelli, *Discorsi*, supra note 30, Book I, Chapter 2 (Engl.: at 24).
39. Jean Bodin, *Six livres de la république*, Imprimerie de Jean de Tournes, Lyon 1579 (1st ed. 1576), Book I, Chapter VIII, at 85 (English translation by M. J. Tooley, Blackwell, Oxford 1955).
40. Ibid.
41. Ibid., Book I, Chapter VIII, at 92.
42. Ibid., Book I, Chapter VIII, at 91 et seq.
43. Ibid., Book I, Chapter VIII, at 98 et seq.
44. Ibid., Book I, Chapter VIII, at 91 et seq.
45. Heinrich Kipp, *Völkerordnung und Völkerrecht im Mittelater*, Deutsche Glocke, Köln 1950, at 124.
46. Hans Kelsen, *Reine Rechtslehre*, Deuticke, Leipzig/Wien 1934, Chapter IX, 50 (i), at 153.
47. Bodin, *Six livres de la république*, supra note 39, Book I, Chapter I, at 1.
48. Ibid., Book I, Chapter II, at 7.
49. See *infra*, Chapter IV.
50. Robert Filmer, 1680, *Patriarcha, Or the Natural Power of Kings*, Richard Chiswell, London 1680, Chapter I, para. 1.
51. Ibid., Chapter I, para. 10.
52. Ibid., Chapter III, para. 1.
53. Ibid.
54. Ibid., Chapter II, para. 14.
55. René Descartes, *Principia philosophiae* (1644), Elzevir, Amsterdam 1672 (5th ed.), Part I, para. 53.
56. Thomas Hobbes, *Leviathan, or the Matter, Form, and Power of a Commonwealth Ecclesiastical and Civil*, Crooke, London 1651, Chapter I.
57. Ibid., Chapter V.
58. Julien Offray de La Mettrie, *L'homme machine*, Luzac, Leyden 1748.
59. Paul-Henri Dietrich D'Holbach, *Système de la nature*, London 1771.
60. Jeremy Bentham, *Introduction to the Principles of Morals and Legislation* (1789), Athlone, London 1970, Chapter I, para. 1.
61. Nicolas de Condorcet, *Esquisse d'un tableau historique des progrès de l'esprit humain* (1793–1794), Vrin, Paris 1970, "Avant-propos", at 3.

62. Ibid., Chapter X, at 203 et seq.
63. Adam H. Müller, *Die Elemente der Staatskunst* (1809), Fischer, Jena 1922, Book I, Chapter 1, at 3.
64. Johann Gottfried Herder, *Abhandlung über den Ursprung der Sprache*, Reclam, Stuttgart 1997, at 29 et seq., 108 et seq.
65. Ibid., at 129 et seq.
66. Ibid., at 141 et seq.
67. Ibid., at 146 et seq.
68. Müller, *Die Elemente der Staatskunst*, *supra* note 63, Book II, Chapter 10, at 199.
69. Ibid., Book I, Chapter 2, at 28.
70. Ibid., Book I, Chapter 2, at 37.
71. Ibid., Book I, Chapter 5, at 89 et seq.
72. Ibid., Book II, Chapter 10, at 200.
73. Ibid., Book I, Chapter 1, at 7.
74. Ibid., Book I, Chapter 4, at 80; Book II, Chapter 10, at 202 et seq.
75. Martti Koskenniemi, *The Gentle Civilizer of Nation: The Rise and Fall of International Law 1870–1960*, Cambridge University Press, Cambridge/New York 2001.
76. See *infra*, Sect. 4.5.
77. Carl Schmitt, *Über die neuen Aufgaben der Verfassungsgeschichte* (1936), in: Carl Schmitt, *Positionen und Begriffe*, Duncker & Humblot, Berlin 1994 (1st ed. 1940), 261–267, at 265 et seq.
78. Carl Schmitt, *Neutralität und Neutralisierungen* (1939), in: Schmitt, *Positionen und Begriffe*, *supra*, note 77, 309–334, at 333.
79. Carl Schmitt, *Verfassungslehre*, Duncker & Humblot, München/Leipzig 1928, Chapter II, para. 12.I.1., at 125.
80. Carl Schmitt, *Der Begriff des Politischen* (1932), in: Carl Schmitt, *Der Begriff des Politischen. Text von 1932 mit einem Vorwort und drei Corollarien*, Duncker & Humblot, Berlin 1963, 20–78, Chapter 2, at 26 et seq. (English translation by George Schwab, The University of Chicago Press, Chicago/London 2007, at 25 et seq.).
81. Ibid., Chapter 3, at 29 et seq. (Engl.: at 28 et seq.).
82. Ibid., Chapter 2, at 27 et seq. (Engl.: at 26 et seq.).
83. Ibid., Chapter 5, at 46 et seq. (Engl.: at 46 et seq.).
84. Schmitt, *Verfassungslehre*, *supra* note 79, Chapter III, para. 17.II.4.d), at 231 et seq.
85. Schmitt, *Der Begriff des Politischen*, *supra* note 80, Chapter 6, at 54 (Engl.: at 53).
86. Ibid., Chapter 3, at 32 et seq. (Engl.: at 32 et seq.); Chapter 5, at 45 et seq. (Engl.: at 45 et seq.).
87. Carl Schmitt, *Der Nomos der Erde im Völkerrecht des Jus Publicum Europeum*, Greven, Köln 1950, at 25 (English translation by G. L. Ulmen, Telos, New York 2006, at 55).

88. Ibid., at 111 et seq. (Engl.: at 139 et seq.).
89. Ibid., at 285 et seq. (Engl.: at 309 et seq.).
90. Carl Schmitt, *Das politische Problem der Friedenssicherung*, Teubner, Leipzig/Berlin 1934, 2nd ed., at 1.
91. Carl Schmitt, *Die Wendung zum diskriminierenden Kriegsbegriff*, Duncker & Humblot, München 1938, at 45 et seq.; Carl Schmitt, *Das internationale Verbrechen des Angriffskrieges und der Grundsatz "Nullum crimen, nulla poena sine lege"* (1945), Helmut Quaritsch ed., Duncker & Humblot, Berlin 1994.
92. Schmitt, *Der Begriff des Politischen*, supra note 80, Chapter 6, at 54 et seq. (Engl.: at 53 et seq.).
93. Carl Schmitt, *Völkerrechtliche Großraumordnung mit Interventionsverbot für raumfremde Mächte*, Deutscher Rechtsverlag, Berlin/Wien 1939.
94. Francis Fukuyama, *The End of History and the Last Man*, Free Press, New York/London 1992.
95. Hans Morgenthau, *Politics Among Nations: The Struggle for Power and Peace*, Knopf, New York 1954 (1st ed. 1948), at 31.
96. Ibid.
97. Ibid., at 35 and at 244.
98. Ibid., at 471.
99. Ibid., at 470 et seq.
100. Ibid., at 93 et seq.
101. Ibid., at 201 et seq.
102. Ibid., at 505.
103. Ibid., at 220 et seq.
104. Ibid., at 214 et seq.
105. Ibid., at 518 et seq.
106. Scott Burchill, *Realism and Neo-realism*, in: Scott Burchill et al., *Theories of International Relations*, Palgrave Macmillan, Basingstoke/New York 2001 (2nd ed.), at 70 et seq.; Niklas Schörnig, *Neorealismus*, in: Siegfried Schieder, Manuela Spindler (eds.), *Theorien der Internationalen Beziehungen*, Budrich, Opladen 2006, at 65 et seq.
107. Morgenthau, *Politics Among Nations*, supra note 95, at 31.
108. See *infra*, Sect. 2.9.1.
109. Nicholas Greenwood Onuf, *World of Our Making*, University of South Carolina Press, Columbia, South Carolina (SC) 1989; Alexander Wendt, *Anarchy Is What States Make of It: The Social Construction of Power Politics*, in: "International Organization", Vol. 46 (1992), Issue 2, 391–425.
110. Ernest Renan, *Qu'est-ce qu'une nation?* (1882), Presses-Pocket, Paris 1992 (English translation by Ethan Rundell, *What Is a Nation?*, http://ucparis.fr/files/9313/6549/9943/What_is_a_Nation.pdf).

111. Hans Kohn, *Die Idee des Nationalismus. Ursprung und Geschichte bis zur Französischen Revolution*, Fischer, Frankfurt a. M. 1962 (1st ed. 1950); Eugen Lemberg, *Nationalismus*, Rowohlt, Reinbek bei Hamburg 1964; Louis L. Snyder, *Varieties of Nationalism: A Comparative Study*, The Dryden Press, Hinsdale (IL) 1976.
112. Anthony D. Smith, *The Ethnic Origins of Nations*, Blackwell, Oxford 1986.
113. Ibid., at 32.
114. Anthony D. Smith, *Nations and Nationalism in a Global Era*, Polity Press, Cambridge 1995, at 96.
115. Ibid., at 117.
116. Ibid., at 16 et seq.
117. Ibid., at 17 and at 27.
118. Ibid., at 19 et seq.
119. Ibid., at 155.
120. Ibid., at 103 et seq.
121. The Economist, *The New Nationalism*, November 19, 2016.
122. Eric A. Posner, *Liberal Internationalism and the Populist Backlash*, Public Law and Legal Theory Working Paper No. 606, The Law School of the University of Chicago, January 2017.
123. Ibid., at 17.
124. Samuel P. Huntington, *Who Are We? The Challenges to America's National Identity*, Simon & Schuster, New York/London 2004.
125. Samuel P. Huntington, *The Clash of Civilizations*, in: "Foreign Affairs", Vol. 72 (1993), Issue 3, 22–49.
126. Samuel P. Huntington, *The Clash of Civilizations and the Remaking of World Order*, Simon & Schuster, New York 1996.
127. Ibid., at 21 et seq.
128. Ibid., at 36 et seq.
129. Ibid., at 29 et seq.
130. Ibid., at 41.
131. Ibid., at 43.
132. Ibid., at 42.
133. Ibid.
134. Ibid.
135. Oswald Spengler, *Der Untergang des Abendlandes (1919–1922)*, DTV, München 2003.
136. Arnold J. Toynbee, *A Study of History (1934–1954)*, Oxford University Press, London 1963.
137. Fernand Braudel, *Grammaire des civilisations*, Arthaud-Flammarion, Paris 1987.
138. Huntington, *The Clash of Civilizations and the Remaking of World Order*, supra note 126, at 40 et seq.

139. Ibid., at 43 et seq.
140. Ibid., at 45 et seq.
141. Ibid., at 155 et seq.
142. Jeremy A. Rabkin, *Why Sovereignty Matters?*, AEI Press, Washington, DC, 1998, at 24.
143. Ibid., at 28.
144. Ibid., at 95.
145. Jeremy A. Rabkin, *What We Can Learn About Human Dignity from International Law*, in: "Harvard Journal of Law & Public Policy", Vol. 27 (2003–2004), 145–168.
146. Jeremy A. Rabkin, *Worlds Apart on International Justice*, in: "Leiden Journal of International Law", Vol. 15 (2002), 835–857, at 835.
147. Ugo Mattei, *A Theory of Imperial Law: A Study on U.S. Hegemony and the Latin Resistance*, in: "Indiana Journal of Global Legal Studies", Vol. 10 (2003), 383–448; Jean L. Cohen, *Whose Sovereignty? Empire Versus International Law*, in: "Ethics & International Affairs", Vol. 18 (2004), 1–24.
148. Nico Krisch, *Imperial International Law*, Global Law Working Papers 01/04, New York 2004.
149. Ibid.
150. Rabkin, *Why Sovereignty Matters?*, supra note 142, at 100; Rabkin, *Worlds Apart on International Justice*, supra note 146, at 851.
151. Deepak Lal, *In Defense of Empires*, AEI Press, Washington, DC, 2004, at 2. See also: Deepak Lal, *In Praise of Empires: Globalization and Order*, Palgrave Macmillan, Basingstoke/New York 2004.
152. Lal, *In Defense of Empires*, supra note 151, at 35.
153. Charles Krauthammer, *The Unipolar Moment*, in: "Foreign Affairs", Vol. 70 (1990), 23–33.
154. Robert Kagan, *Power and Weakness*, in: "Policy Review", Vol. 113 (June and July 2002), http://www.policyreview.org/jun02/kagan.html, at 7.
155. Robert Kagan, *America's Crisis of Legitimacy*, in "Foreign Affairs", Vol. 83 (2004), 65–87, at 78.
156. Schmitt, *Völkerrechtliche Großraumordnung*, supra note 93.
157. Huntington, *The Clash of Civilizations and the Remaking of World Order*, supra note 126, at 316.
158. Heike Krieger, Georg Nolte, *The International Rule of Law—Rise or Decline?—Points of Departure*, KFG Working Paper Series No. 1, Berlin, October 2016.
159. Jack L. Goldsmith, Eric A. Posner, *The Limits of International Law*, Oxford University Press, Oxford/New York 2005.
160. Andrew Moravcsik, *Taking Preferences Seriously: A Liberal Theory of International Politics*, in: "International Organization", Vol. 51 (1997), Issue 4, 513–553; Anne-Marie Slaughter, *International Law in a World*

*of Liberal States*, in: "European Journal of International Law", Vol. 6 (1995), Issue 6, 503–538; Anne-Marie Slaughter, *A Liberal Theory of International Law*, in: "American Society of International Law", Vol. 94 (2000), 240–248; Anne-Marie Slaughter, *International Law and International Relations*, in: "Collected Courses of the Hague Academy of International Law", Vol. 285, Nijhoff, The Hague 2000, 9–250.
161. Goldsmith/Posner, *The Limits of International Law*, supra note 159, at 6.
162. Ibid., at 5.
163. Nicole Deitelhoff, *Was vom Tage übrig blieb. Inseln der Überzeugung im vermachteten Alltagsgeschäft internationalen Regierens*, in: Peter Niesen, Benjamin Herborth (eds.), *Anarchie der kommunikativen Freiheit*, Suhrkamp, Frankfurt a. M. 2007, at 26; Thomas Risse, *Global Governance und kommunikatives Handeln*, in: Niesen/Herborth, *Anarchie der kommunikativen Freiheit*, supra note clxiii, at 57; Harald Müller, *Internationale Verhandlungen, Argumente und Verständigungshandeln*, in: Niesen/Herborth, *Anarchie der kommunikativen Freiheit*, supra note 163, at 199.
164. Andrew T. Guzman, *How International Law Works: A Rational Choice Theory*, Oxford University Press, Oxford/New York 2008, at 33.
165. Robert O. Keohane, *After Hegemony*, Princeton University Press, Princeton 1984, at 75 et seq.
166. Ibid., at 76 et seq.
167. Ibid., at 78 et seq. and at 85 et seq.
168. John Rawls, *A Theory of Justice* (1971), Harvard University Press, Cambridge (MA), 1999.
169. Ibid., at 57 and 263.
170. Alasdair MacIntyre, *After Virtue*, University of Notre Dame Press, Notre Dame (IN) 1981.
171. Michael Sandel, *Liberalism and the Limits of Justice*, Cambridge University Press, Cambridge 1982.
172. Charles Taylor, *Sources of the Self*, Harvard University Press, Cambridge (MA) 1989, at 3.
173. Alasdair MacIntyre, *Is Patriotism a Virtue?*, "The Lindley Lecture", University of Kansas, Depertment of Philosophy, 1984.
174. Charles Taylor, *The Politics of Recognition*, in: Amy Gutmann (ed.), *Multiculturalism*, Princeton University Press, Princeton (NJ) 1994, at 32 et seq.
175. Charles Taylor, *Cross-Purposes: The Liberal-Communitarian Debate*, in: Nancy L. Rosenblum (ed.), *Liberalism and the Moral Life*, Harvard University Press, Cambridge (MA), 159–182.
176. Charles Taylor, *What's Wrong with Negative Liberty*, in: Charles Taylor, *Philosophy and the Human Sciences*, Philosophical Papers 2, Cambridge University Press, Cambridge 1985, 211–229.

177. Taylor, *Cross-Purposes*, *supra* note 175, at 169.
178. Ibid., at 166.
179. Ibid., at 179.
180. Mortimer N. S. Sellers, *Introduction*, in: Mortimer N. S. Sellers (ed.), *Parochialism, Cosmopolitanism, and the Foundations of International Law*, Cambridge University Press, Cambridge/New York 2012, at 1.
181. Ibid.

CHAPTER 3

# Holistic Universalism as the Second Paradigm of Order

In his *Divina Commedia* (*Divine Comedy*), written at the beginning of the fourteenth century, Dante Alighieri described his imaginary journey through the world of the afterlife. Going through the stages of Inferno, Purgatorio and Paradiso, he gave account of how his soul came increasingly closer to God. In the 33rd Canto of the Paradiso, thus in the last Canto of the whole work, he tried to illustrate the vision of God, which concluded the journey, being its ultimate end. Since human instruments are inevitably insufficient to depict the divine infiniteness, what Dante can express and present to the readers are just some glimpses of God's perfection, like flashes that illuminate the darkness. Yet, a couple of these glimpses are very important to understand how Dante—and, with him, all supporters of the new paradigm that characterized the late antiquity, the whole Middle Ages and beyond—conceived the notion of order. Indeed, since God is the highest perfection, he must also give form to the most perfect order. But let us have Dante speaking in his own verses:

© The Author(s), under exclusive license to Springer Nature Switzerland AG 2021
S. Dellavalle, *Paradigms of Social Order*,
Philosophy, Public Policy, and Transnational Law,
https://doi.org/10.1007/978-3-030-66179-3_3

| | |
|---|---|
| Oh abbondante grazia ond' io presunsi<br>ficcar lo viso per la luce etterna,<br>tanto che la veduta vi consunsi! | O grace abounding, through which I<br>presumed<br>to set my eyes on the Eternal Light<br>so long that I spent all my sight on it! |
| Nel suo profondo vidi che s'interna,<br>legato con amore in un volume,<br>ciò che per l'universo si squaderna: | In its profundity I saw – ingathered<br>and bound by love into one single<br>volume –<br>what, in the universe, seems separate,<br>scattered: |
| sustanze e accidenti e lor costume<br>quasi conflati insieme, per tal modo<br>che ciò ch'i' dico è un semplice lume | substances, accidents, and dispositions<br>as if conjoined – in such a way that<br>what<br>I tell is only rudimentary |
| La forma universal di questo nodo<br>credo ch'i' vidi, perché più di largo,<br>dicendo questo, mi sento ch'i' godo | I think I saw the universal shape<br>which that knot takes; for, speaking<br>this, I feel<br>a joy that is more ample[1] |

In these verses, one of the hints of God's perfection that Dante can perceive refers to the unity of the order of creation. Indeed, by penetrating—though only partially and for a fraction of a second—into the deepest truth of God's uniqueness and unity, the poet can have an intuition of the correspondent and homologous unitary principle that rules the world. In other words, being God the unitary principle of perfection, the world created by him cannot but be a unity too. From this perspective, all phenomena of the world—the "substances, accidents and dispositions"—can be correctly understood as pages or chapters of "one single volume". As a result, we can see the last Canto of the Paradiso as "the poem's ultimate metaphor of unity."[2]

Yet—as we have learned from the authors presented in the previous chapter—the unitary character of order does not rule out that the range of this order could be limited. This possibility, however, is precisely what is excluded in Dante's view. In fact, the order created by the God that Dante is allowed to shortly contemplate at the end of his journey in the afterlife is not only unitary but also explicitly "universal", in the sense that it comprises every aspect and dimension of the universe, without exclusion, discrimination or limitation. Nonetheless, Dante's universalism would hardly be a surprise or something new in the history of ideas, at least if compared to the tenets of the holistic-particularistic paradigm, provided that we restrict the meaning of universalism only to the laws of nature. Put differently, laws of nature have always been regarded as universally valid, so that an idea of universal order that stresses exclusively this point—in the sense of the assumption that God created a well-ordered universe insofar as the physical and biological world is ruled by a unitary set of laws—would not stand for any significant conceptual novelty. Yet, Dante added a decisive element, which is expressed with the utmost clarity in the very last verses of his *Comedy*:

| | |
|---|---|
| A l'alta fantasia qui mancò possa; | Here force failed my high fantasy; but my |
| ma già volgeva il mio disio e'l velle, | desire and will were moved already—like |
| sì come rota ch'igualmente è mossa, | a wheel revolving uniformly—by |
| l'amor che move il sole e l'altre stelle | the Love that moves the sun and the other stars[3] |

The poet left no doubt that the source of all order—from which the movement of the heavenly spheres derives and, hereby, the development of all natural phenomena—has, in his eyes, a *spiritual*, not only a *natural* dimension. Furthermore, this spring of all order is described as "love". Therefore, the source of world order is not regarded as a spiritual motor of material processes, but—since "love" is generally interpreted as the force that creates reconciliation and harmony in the world of human interactions—[4] rather as a spiritual principle that gives form also to moral, ethical and social phenomena. If order is determined by "love", then the well-ordered world should include also the relations based on the use of practical reason—and this should apply on a universal scale.

Summing up, Dante's idea of order is characterized by three most relevant features. Firstly, it is *unitary* in the sense that a system—natural, social or spiritual—can only be seen as well-ordered if it is not allowed that two genetically distinct and substantively diverging norms or rules can be true, right and valid at the same time, while being applied to the same domain. Secondly, it is *holistic* because norms and institutions—both mundane and spiritual—are arranged hierarchically as an organic body under the command of a supreme ruler whose authority has, at the same time, a natural and a supernatural character. Thirdly, it is *universal* insofar as it comprises the whole world: more specifically, it includes the whole humanity if order is about social rules, and even the whole universe in the case that we understand order in its broadest meaning. It is relevant to point out, here, that the two first mentioned features—unity and holism—were already present in the most ancient paradigm of order. On the contrary, the explicit reference to the universalistic character of the well-ordered world testifies that a huge novelty had been introduced—at some time before Dante wrote his *Divine Comedy*—into the way in which order was, or at least *could be*, understood.

Therefore, the first paradigmatic revolution that occurred in the history of the theories of order affected the assumption regarding the extension of the well-ordered society. In fact, whereas in the first paradigm each specific order has always only a limited range and no all-encompassing world order is considered feasible, the concept of natural and spiritual order to which Dante gave probably the highest poetic expression was assumed to include the entire creation and, as a result of this, the totality of human beings as well. However, when Dante wrote his work, the new paradigm of order—that we can define as *holistic universalism*—had already gone through quite a long history. In fact, the paradigmatic revolution from particularism to universalism was initiated, more than one and a half thousand years before Dante, by the Stoic philosophers (3.1). Nonetheless, it was with its further development by the Christian political theology that the holistic-universalistic conception of order became influent. Although the Christian message was addressed, in principle, to all humans, in fact the Christian conception of universality ended up struggling with the limits that inevitably affect all cosmopolitan perspectives based on religious assumptions: religious beliefs can hardly be universalized, not even by force. As a result, on the one hand, the would-be universalism of the Christian community never came to include more than a minority of humankind, and on the other hand, it was generally biased against non-Christians. Furthermore, the Christian theology of the Middle Ages was utterly committed—as it was also its Catholic follow-up—to the philosophical and theological justification of the political status quo, so that they proved to be rather unable to properly understand the good reasons that lied behind the desire for change and to conciliate them with their original conceptual framework. As a result, the most recent Catholic theology—insofar as it can be considered the rightful heir of the Christian theology of the Middle Ages and of the Catholic philosophy of the early Modern Ages, with all their greatnesses and weaknesses—is still caught in an unresolved tension between an alleged universalism that hardly hides the traditional prejudice against the "other" and a sincere attempt to open up to mutual recognition and social change (3.2).

Yet, the link that Christian thinking maintained between the *lex aeterna*, as the God-given universal order, and the natural reason shared by all human beings provided an alternative path beyond the particularistic biases that afflicted—and, partially, still afflict—the doctrine of the

Church. In fact, while the sense of a God-given order contained in the divine law can be recognized only by those who embrace the Christian faith, natural reason is regarded as an endowment of all humans, with the consequence that an order grounded on pure natural reason should be actually able to include the whole humankind. Given these premises, a more convincing universalistic conception of order can be based on nothing else than on what natural reason demands from every rational being, thus detaching it—at least in the intention of its supporters— from any religious assumptions. This is the theoretical foundation of what became known as the theory of *natural law*, which had—and still has— a significant influence on the ways how international law is conceptually justified, from the historical *jus gentium* to the contemporary attempts to "constitutionalize" its legal framework (3.3).

## 3.1 Universal Logos and World Nomos in the Stoic Philosophy

The idea of a global community including all human beings is anything but obvious. Rather, it took quite a long time for human thinking to overcome the long-lasting predominant conviction that only limited societies can be well-ordered and to develop the perspective of some kind of worldwide order. The first glimmer of a universal idea of order can be found in Buddhism. In Buddhist tradition, indeed, the *dharma* can be interpreted—among other possible understandings—as the "natural order of the universe."[5] However, the universal range of the *dharma* goes, first, far beyond the boundaries of the human community, including at least all sentient beings and, possibly, even the non-sentient world. Secondly, to be recognized, the *dharma* requires to complete a path of spiritual enlightenment which, in principle, is open to all members of the human community, but—like all religious experiences—can hardly be expected from each one of them. Therefore, to develop a perspective of cosmopolitan order in the sense of the word which is most common to us, two further steps had to be undertaken: order had to be centred on the human community, and it had to be based on a faculty arguably inherent to all humans, regardless of which spiritual experiences they may have gone through. Both elements were introduced into the history of ideas for the first time by the Stoic philosophy.

In fact, in Western philosophy too, some pre-Socratic thinkers gave us a hint that seems to point towards the overcoming of particularism long before Stoicism.[6] As a first example, we read that according to Democritus "for the wise man the whole earth is open; the universe is the homeland of the noble soul."[7] Furthermore, the Sophist Antiphon asserted that:

> by nature we are all equal, barbarians and Hellenes. It can be seen from what is necessary by nature to all men. Everyone has the opportunity to get it the same way, and in all this neither a barbarian nor a Hellene are different. In fact, we all breathe air through our mouth and nose, and we all eat with our hands.[8]

Finally—and, at least at first glance, most significantly—Heraclitus stated that "all human laws are drawn from the only divine law."[9] Undoubtedly, reconstructing a theory from short fragments is always a risky endeavour. However, even if we admit that this can be reasonably done, the theories that we derive from the quoted passages do not suggest necessarily the overcoming of the particularistic idea of order that characterized the first paradigm. In fact, what we read in the words of Democritus is rather the aristocratic refusal of being considered part of a specific social community—which does not imply that the refined sage would aspire to be seen as a member of an even more crowded and disturbing cosmopolitan community. Much more, he seems to refuse to be member of *any* structured social community, regardless of which extension it might have. As for Antiphon, then, his reference to some kind of universalism comprising the whole humankind is limited to the *physical* features of humans, whereas no assumption is made as regards a global community based on normative contents. Indeed, in the entire history of ideas, no serious doubt has ever been raised about the evident fact that humans have most traits of their natural constitution in common, by which assertion, however, it is not involved that they have to share ethical and legal norms too. At best, it was generally assumed that all human beings have a natural tendency to social life; yet—as we know from Aristotle—the claim that the human being "is by nature a political animal"[10] comes perfectly along with a strict limitation of the community range. In other words, the acknowledgement of the social nature of humans does not say anything about the extension of the well-ordered society. Lastly, even the most ambitious statement—that of Heraclitus—must not necessarily be interpreted in the sense that there is a universally valid ethical and/or legal nomos with which all specific nomoi of the poleis have to comply; it could simply mean, just as well, that no civic law can go against the general, in principle value-free law of divine origin that governs the universe. Indeed, if we consider Heraclitus's pessimism as regards the natural propensity of man to war and his conviction that "war is the father of everything, and its king",[11] it is likely that the general law that runs the universe does not lead, ultimately, to a global well-ordered society, but rather to a global everlasting conflict. Summing up, references to a proto-universalistic idea of order that precedes Stoicism are rare and, on the whole, rather unconvincing. Beyond the surface, they provide further evidences that if we want to find the very moment that conceptually initiated the paradigmatic revolution from particularism to universalism, then we have to look at the most fundamental assumptions developed by the Stoics.

The basic notions of the Stoic philosophy are tightly connected to the political context in which they were developed. In fact, Stoicism grew out of the cultural background of Hellenism and, later, of the Roman Empire, when the singularity of the poleis gave way to the project of a more far-reaching social and political order—even, with Alexander the Great, to the idea of a universal monarchy and, with the Roman Emperors, at least to a political structure that included a large part of the Western civilized world. In this sense, Stoicism is located at the intersection between a philosophy of nature that had long recognized the unity of the natural world and a political thought forced to take note of the transition from the citizenship of the poleis to the creation of broader and potentially universal political units.[12]

The groundbreaking novelty of the Stoic philosophy derives largely from its assumption of a universal order based on a new concept of rationality. In fact, it was with the Stoic philosophy that the idea of a universal rationality including normative contents made its entry into the history of Western culture. Essentially, the Stoic conception of rationality has four dimensions. First, the Stoic philosophy is—more than any other before it—a "philosophy of the logos",[13] in the sense that it is the logos that informs the whole world. In fact, according to the Stoic interpretation logos means not only the logical-gnoseological capacity of the individuals, but also—and above all—the worldwide, all-encompassing and objective reason that governs the universe. Indeed, it was Zeno of Citium, the very founder of the school, who already identified in the divine logos one of the two "principles"—the second being the matter (ὕλη)—which are present in physical nature.[14] In his interpretation, the reason (or logos) is assumed to be more than just a human faculty: rather, it is a substantial force that makes the world in its entirety well-ordered. In a conception in which it is nature as a whole that is ruled by reason, a form of ontologically distinct rationality is assumed which is superior to the human intellect. Therefore, with respect to the world logos, the human intellect is only an imperfect derivation, or the instrument granted to human beings so as to partially penetrate the perfect order of the cosmos.

The second dimension of the Stoic idea of rationality, then, is a direct derivation of the first. Since the *logos* governs the whole world including the entirety of its phenomena, it must be characterized by both material and spiritual components, and it is conceived of as having effect on the domain of theoretical as well as of practical reason. In other words, the logos was regarded as the fundament not only of the laws of the physical matter but also of the rules of the moral, social and political domain. This implies—as the third dimension of the Stoic rationality—a reinterpretation of the concept of *nomos*, which no longer stands to indicate only the law in force in the individual political collectives, but a universal law, or the nomos of the world. Insofar as—contrary to Plato and Aristotle, who maintained that the universality of physical laws was accompanied by the particularity of political ones—the universality of the logos includes in the Stoic philosophy both the physical and the ethical–political reality, the nomos overlaps in its extension, even if not completely in its meaning, with the logos. In fact, both embrace now the entire cosmos, even though the logos describes its overall rational structure, while the nomos identifies its inherent normative content. And, while Zeno of Citium only compared the rational order of the world to that of "a political collectivity governed in the best way,"[15] his successor Chrysippus of Soli went beyond similitude and postulated an essential derivation of the cosmopolitan order from the logos of the world, with the consequence that "the cosmos is the great polis and has only one constitution and one nomos."[16] In a further passage, the same Chrysippus went as far as downright identifying "the universal nomos", despite the ontological differences mentioned above, "with the right reason (ὀρθός λόγος) that permeates everything".[17]

In the second and third dimension of the Stoic concept of rationality lies the fundament of the notion of *natural law*, which was a Stoic creation as well, though destined to have a huge and long success far beyond this philosophical school. It was again Chrysippus who formulated for the first time the concept of a law which is located in nature itself—or in the logos that governs it—and is understandable to every reasonable being. According to that notion, the universal nomos inherently entails an intuitive claim on "what is right and what is wrong", thus "prescribing to those living beings who are political by nature what must be done, and forbidding what is not permitted to do".[18] This idea was then further developed by Cicero, who provided the classic definition of natural law:

> True law is right reason, consonant with nature, spread through all people. It is constant and eternal; it summons to duty by its orders, it deters from crime by its prohibitions. Its orders and prohibitions to good people are never given in vain ...It is wrong to pass laws obviating this law; it is not permitted to abrogate any of it; it cannot be totally repealed. We cannot be released from this law by the senate or the people...[19]

Thus, the idea that there is a nomos anchored directly to a rational, eternal, universal and immutable nature enters in the philosophical analysis of politics and law. To the extent that the rationality on which the concrete norm is based is no longer restricted to a socially, ethnically or politically particularistic order, we have here for the first time, in a still germinal form, a conception according to which any written or customary law has not only a hierarchically higher system of norms above it, but is also required to verify its validity on the basis of the criteria formulated by that system.

The fourth dimension of Stoic rationality regards the relation between the universal nomos and the positive institutional and legal order. In general, within the conceptual framework of the universal nomos and due to the assumption of a universal sociability among humans (οἰκέιωσις), every human being can—and should—be seen as a κόσμου πολίτης, a "citizen of the world". Although the terminus of κόσμου πολίτης was probably used for the first time not by a Stoic philosopher, but already two generations earlier, by the Cynic Diogenes of Sinope,[20] the Stoic conception of universal rationality and nomos laid down the foundation for the further development of the notion of "cosmopolitanism".[21] More concretely, the Stoic approach led to two possible outcomes. The first was already envisaged by Zeno of Citium: it is the project of a *cosmopolis* or of a *civitas maxima* that is assumed to include the whole humankind into a unique institutional framework. Zeno's conception has been developed in his *Politèia*—curiously, and probably not coincidentally, the same title that Plato gave to his main political work, but now turned into a globally-reaching project. Yet, as far as we can say on the basis of what is left of it, Zeno's *Politèia*—far from clearly describing political institutions and a legal framework—remains politically vague and legally underdeveloped.[22] In the end, this global society united by the respect of equal norms and no longer fragmented by frontiers, but nevertheless radically "de-politicized", reminds us more of a community of the sages than of what, centuries later, will be described as the *civitas maxima*.[23] Actually, also Seneca's intention to "view all lands as though they belong to me, and my own as though they belonged to all mankind,"[24] mirrors the appreciable wish of a culturally and socially privileged intellectual to strive for the philosophical acknowledgement of the common roots of all human beings, but can hardly be seen as expressing a recognizable political agenda.

The second institutional outcome of the Stoic idea of global order shines through Cicero's above-mentioned passage: it is the idea of a plurality of individual political and legal orders, each one belonging to a specific polity and characterizing it, which are held together by an overarching set of non-positive norms. According to this approach, the nomoi of the individual, social and political communities are based, at least implicitly, on the universal nomos and take their legitimacy from this. The alternative between those two options—the *cosmopolis*, *civitas maxima* or world state, on the one hand; and a plurality of states under the all-encompassing dome of shared rational principles, on the other—was destined to play a major role well beyond the Stoic philosophy in which both of them had their roots. In this long-lasting success of its political proposals, despite the lack of concreteness of their first formulations, lies one of the most significant achievements of Stoicism.

## 3.2 The Christian-Catholic Conception of Universalism

The Stoic idea of world order was highly innovative. Nevertheless, Stoicism was, in general, rather alien to the world—with its exponents mostly tending to assertively withdraw from the world in the "ivory tower" of knowledge in order to concentrate on their philosophical speculations. Therefore, also the impact of the Stoic vision of the world was—at least initially—quite marginal. What made Stoic cosmopolitanism and the concept of a universal natural reason, as well as the notion of a natural law which is assumed to be based on it, extremely influential on the political and intellectual history of the following centuries was the fact that many of the Stoic ideas—and, in particular, cosmopolitanism and natural law—were adopted by the nascent Christian philosophy. In fact, the universalistic approach of the Stoic philosophy became one of the most distinctive features of Christianity on its way to develop into the leading force of the Western world, not only in spiritual but also in political and legal matters. The role played by the Christian religion in shaping the institutional and legal framework of the Western societies urged Christian thinkers to go beyond merely abstract suggestions and to develop quite sophisticated conceptions of how that framework had to be structured (3.2.2).

As testified by the commandment to the *missio ad gentes*, which implies the duty to spread the Christian Gospel universally, the cosmopolitan vocation of Christendom was unequivocal from the very beginning.[25] The *communitas christiana* was thus conceived of as including, at least potentially, the whole humankind, without any restraint due to the different cultural or ethnic belongings of the individuals. The groundbreaking novelty of Christian universalism—in particular if compared to the previously dominant paradigm—was already very clear to the first major political philosopher of the Christian era, namely Augustine of Hippo. However, we can detect in his work not only the fascinating perspective of a new order of peace but also the shortcomings that arise when this order is supposed to be necessarily based on the worldwide spreading of *one* religious belief (3.2.1). Since it is quite illusionary—and hardly desirable—to assume that one single religious community can get to comprise the whole humanity, the project of a peaceful world order is largely projected into the afterlife, on the one hand, while, on the other, the question of how to deal with those who never embraced the allegedly true religion remains substantially unsettled. In the worst, but quite common case, the attitude towards non-Christian peoples degenerated into a more or less open justification of discrimination or explicit persecution, even among those thinkers, like Vitoria and Suárez, who showed a certain sensitivity for the question (3.2.3).

Along with the biases against non-Christians, the Christian and then Catholic philosophy and theology were affected by a second relevant deficit, consisting in its backward-oriented understanding of politics and society, which led to a substantial refusal of precisely those social and political changes that most characterized the entry into the Modern Ages.

Only few voices were raised against these shortcomings, the most important of which was that of Bartolomé de Las Casas (3.2.4). His plea for the recognition of the "others" and for an idea of political community based on freedom remained for long time an isolated example within the panorama of Catholic thinking. Yet, at the beginning of the second half of the twentieth century, a gust of fresh wind blew away the dust that had settled on the Vatican's ideology. It was the Second Vatican Council that seemed to reconcile—at least temporarily—the Catholic vision of society with the achievements of modernity (3.2.5). After a period of radical restoration (3.2.6), the last developments—both of the "official" and of the "unofficial" theology—reveal a newfound glimpse of hope (3.2.7 and 3.2.8).

### 3.2.1 The Idea of the City of God in Augustine

In the most important political work of early Christianity—namely *De civitate Dei* (*The City of God*), written by Augustine of Hippo probably between 413 and 426 C.E.—the author distinguished between "two cities, or ... two communities of humans."[26] The first community, defined by Augustine as the "earthly city" or the "city of the devil" (*civitas diaboli*), is destined with its inhabitants "to suffer eternal punishment with the devil," while the second—the "heavenly city"—is "predestined to reign eternally with God."[27] The earthly city represents the pagan world, dominated and consumed by particularistic egotism, by the "love of self", by the desire for glory and "passion for domination".[28] This is the society tormented by struggles, "divided against itself by litigations, wars, quarrels, in search of victories that are either life-destroying or short-lived."[29] Here, order is the exception, and peace an improbable and precarious condition. On the other side, there is the Christian city, typified by the message of peace and universal love, "where victory will be stable in eternal and perfect peace."[30]

Augustine's work already showed a strong awareness of the innovative character of the Christian idea of order. In fact, it is not difficult to identify in his words the contiguity between what he defines as the "earthly city" or the *civitas diaboli*, and the most relevant characters of what has been described, in the previous chapter, as the holistic-particularistic paradigm dominant in antiquity. More specifically, the announcement of the dawn of a new conception of order went hand in hand, in Augustine's thought, with a categorical condemnation of the old paradigm. Contrary to the old view of a general disorder due to the dominant and unrestrained greed for power and riches, the Christian message would open up the possibility—which he mistakenly believed to be unknown before the announcement of the Gospel—of establishing a universal order to which all human beings, and not only the citizens of a specific political community, belong. Therefore, what is new if compared to the previous paradigm of order is the assumption regarding the extension of the well-ordered society, which turns from limited to universal. Instead, the conviction that only an organic society can be peaceful and cooperative remains basically unchanged. No doubts are left, in fact, on the organic nature of the order envisaged by Augustine: "order is the distribution which allots things equal and unequal, each to its own place."[31] Given these premises, it is not surprising to find in *De civitate Dei* not only the classical holistic metaphor of the *corpus*,[32] but also an idea of social cohesion in which the same idea of a social division of labour and tasks dominates—not reflexively based on free choices of the individuals, but on the largely authoritative presumption of uncontestable organic and natural predispositions—which has been already highlighted with reference to the classical exponents of holistic thought in antiquity:

> Peace among humans is well-ordered concord; domestic peace is the well-ordered concord between those of the family who rule and those who obey; civil peace is a similar concord among the citizens.[33]

Along with the explicit recognition of the novelty of the Christian conception of order, however, we find in Augustine's work also the first evidences of the shortcomings that inevitably affect an idea of order based on faith. Indeed, since in the light of Augustine's universalism "the peace of the celestial city is the perfectly ordered and harmonious enjoyment of God,"[34] the acceptance of the laws of the God of the Gospel as the warrant of order turns out to be the characteristic and indispensable condition for the realization of the universal peace project of Christianity. Yet, religious faith can be hardly universalized. Surely, this was specifically true with regard to the times of dramatic turmoil in which Augustine wrote his palingenetic political work: whereas the sack of Rome perpetrated by Alaric's Visigoths in 410 C.E. was interpreted by Augustine as a just punishment inflicted on the pagans for their sins and their rejection of the "true" religion,[35] the future of the newly established Christian religion seemed to be no less uncertain. However, there is an even more profound reason why a religion-based universalism is almost impossible to realize. In fact, it is not just a question of time until the supposedly "true" religion becomes really universal—as the most uncompromising supporters of a religion-based universalism, rather in the past than in present times, may have hoped for—nor is it casual that no religion ever attained universal reach. Religion is by far a too personal question, which involves the deepest aspects of the individual personality, for the same kind of involvement to be expected from all members of the human community. Moreover, religious faith generally imposes on its adepts a quite strict understanding of what a "good life" should be, thus building expectations that, once again, considerably vary between the different religious communities and are inevitably difficult to generalize.

The almost inescapable consequence of a concept of universal order in which the worldwide well-ordered society cannot be realistically implemented in this world is that the perspective of order is projected into the afterlife. In fact, the peaceful society imagined by Augustine has nothing in common with a concrete proposal; rather, it has the character of an all-encompassing reconciliation between the progeny of the first sinners and God himself—a reconciliation which is assumed to include the whole creation. As a result, the world in which the true peace is realized can only be the heavenly city, the "eternal Sabbath" or—in other words—the eternal life as a total serenity, harmony and freedom.[36] If peace can only be accomplished under God's reign, but God's kingdom—according to the words of the Gospel of John, which Augustine seems to make wholeheartedly to his own—"is not of this world,"[37] then the universal community of peace attains an utterly counterfactual character. As a matter of principle, there is no contradiction if a strongly normative conception proves to be contrary to facts as they are presently. Rather, developing a perspective *beyond* the present reality makes up a significant part of what a moral or social theory should be, which does not limit itself to mirroring the state of facts. A problem arises, however, when this perspective is set uncompromisingly and one-sidedly *against*—and not *beyond*—the present state of facts, or as a strict contraposition to the society as it is, and not as an evolution of it or as a contradiction that unfolds in it. By doing so, theory gives up definitively the possibility of interacting positively with reality, thus changing from a feasible political project into an explicitly unrealizable utopia.

If universal peace is actually a project for the afterlife, the question remains as to how those who are striving for the city of God should deal with the "earthly city", which is assumed to further exist until the day of the final triumph of Christianity—to be precise, until the day of the Last Judgment. Here is a second deficit to find, not only in Augustine's conception, but in the Christian theory of universal order as a whole. Indeed, Augustine grounded on his assumption of a harsh contraposition between the *civitas Dei* and the *civitas diaboli* a radical theory of the "just war" which was destined to have a huge influence on the later debate. The "earthly city" lives—following Augustine's interpretation—in the "love of self", in selfishness and in the search for the satisfaction of greed, to the point that its citizens do not refrain from violence in order to meet their insane desires.[38] In the *civitas diaboli*, therefore, war is nothing but an attack that one political community wages against another so as to satisfy its unfettered appetite for worldly goods. In this sense, it can only be a "great robbery" and, by its very nature, always an *unjust* war.[39] Political communities, or even empires, created in this way are not destined to last for long: devoured by passions and greed, they fall prey to internal wars after a more or less long, but always unstable truce.[40] Thus—according to Augustine—"the wicked wage war against the wicked", but, because of the "hatred that subsists between the two cities, that of God and that of men", "the good also wage war against the wicked."[41] This latter war— of the citizens of the *civitas Dei* against the inhabitants of the *civitas diaboli*—is assumed to be a *just* war to the extent that it opposes the Christians to the pagans. As a result, according to Augustine's theory, the most relevant condition for a war to be regarded as just seems to be that it is fought by followers of the Christian religion against "infidels": other qualifications are to be ultimately considered of secondary importance. It is almost superfluous to underline that this understanding of "just war" not only lays the foundation of later discriminations against non-Christians, but also amounts to an implicit justification—maybe beyond the intentions of the author—of any crime that has been perpetrated against other religious communities, or against non-believers. As we will see in the following, this original failure of the Christian doctrine was destined to taint profoundly its further developments.

To conclude, although Augustine's political philosophy depicts a universal community based on peace and solidarity, the reality that comes before this vision can be implemented—actually, during the entire evolution of humankind before the Last Judgment—tells a completely different story. Far from being peaceful and cooperative, the real world is afflicted by ongoing conflicts. Nonetheless, Augustine does not reject entirely the possibility that the citizens of the *civitas Dei* make some compromises, in the time before the palingenesis, with what he calls "the peace of Babylon", i.e., with the possibilities of limiting disorder offered by the particularistic society.[42] Yet, this is always the exception and never the rule. Moreover, the outcomes of the "peace of Babylon" are partial and short-lived. In Augustine's doctrine, therefore, as long as the "earthly city" exists, there will be struggle within it because of its intrinsic nature, and struggle between it and the "heavenly city" because of the existential opposition that separates the two kingdoms. As long as we are still waiting for universal peace to be realized in a world in which Christianity will expand to the whole humankind, reality remains inevitably imbued with violence, partially for the reason that the promise of order is postponed to a future that may never come, but also because of that non-inclusiveness, or even of the intrinsic intolerance, which is inescapably related to an idea of order based on faith.

### 3.2.2 The Shaping of Political Universalism

After the Christian religion became politically dominant in the Western world, the question arose on how its universalism could be conveyed into an adequate institutional and legal framework. Two variants of the idea of an ethical, political and legal order of universal scope based on the Christian religion were developed. Initially, it was the plea in favour of a universal monarchy, where the worldwide validity of secular power is justified as the worldly expression of God's universal authority (3.2.2.1). Later, as this project was abandoned not only by the rulers but also by the thinkers, the idea of a highly differentiated and innovative system of laws was developed, in which the unity of the *lex divina* is articulated, within a multilevel setting including natural law and the *jus gentium*, as an all-encompassing dome, thought to comprise and justify all legal systems of the single polities beneath it. In this conception, the relations between independent states should be regulated, in order to improve peace and preserve mutual recognition, on the basis of generally accepted principles derived from God's commands (3.2.2.2).

#### 3.2.2.1 Dante's Apology of the Universal Monarchy

The coronation of Charlemagne as emperor on Christmas day of the year 800 in Rome symbolized the principle of the *unitas ecclesiae*, or the unity of Church and empire, as well as the necessity of the mutual reference of the two supreme powers.[43] The theory and praxis of the correspondence between the supreme spiritual power and the supreme secular power had three most significant implications. The first was that, insofar as the spiritual message of Christendom was assumed to have universal reach, the political power that was supposed to be connected to it had to be universal too. The second implication developed rather into a question, namely on whether one of the two interconnected powers, the spiritual or the secular, had to be considered superior and dominant over the other. The third implication, finally, concerned the legitimacy of earthly power: taken for granted that the last source of legitimacy—from the perspective of the Christian theology, at least until the Reformation—had to be necessarily God, the issue was whether this legitimacy comes directly from God to the secular power, or it is mediated by the Church.

As regards the first point, however, the idea of the universal unity of the empire as a derivation from the metaphysical unity of God proved to be an illusion from the very beginning. In fact, it was already Charlemagne who abandoned the idea of the universal empire exactly at the moment when he recognized the political legitimacy of the Byzantine Empire. Nor did the Emperors of the Ottonian dynasty or their successors claim to revive a universalistic-imperial dream that their most famous and successful predecessor had already dropped.[44] The ideology of the universal *Respublica christiana* gave ultimately rise, in the late Middle Ages, to a large-scale confrontation with the peoples outside the Western Christianity, while inside of it the centrifugal forces increasingly prevailed. Curiously enough, the first major ideological blow against the perspective of a public power with the same universalistic ambition which characterized its spiritual counterpart was delivered by the papacy. Deeply entangled in the fight with the Holy Roman Empire on which power should have primacy, it was the papal authority which officially undermined the political unity of the Western Christianity with the purpose of taking advantage of the internal division and the consequent weakness of the secular power. Indeed, the first justification of the independence of the kings of the newly established territorial states from the emperor came from a pontifical Decretal, with the title *Per Venerabilem*, issued in 1202 by Pope Innocent III—probably the most politically powerful of all popes, not only of the Middle Ages. In this text, we find the explicit phrase "*cum rex ipse superiorem in temporalibus minime recognoscat*" ("since the king himself by no means recognizes a superior power in the temporal domains"), which amounts to a factual acknowledgement of the non-universality of political power. Yet, what had only the form, at first, of a rather cursory recognition of a matter of fact, was shortly afterwards developed into a legal principle by the Bolognese jurist Azo who, taking position on the powers of the King of England, sentenced that *"item quilibet hodie videtur eandem potestatem habere in terra sua, quam imperator, ergo potuit facere quod sibi placet"* ("each one who seems to have, today, the same power in his own land as the emperor, is entitled to do what he likes to").[45] The principle found then its canonic, most renowned and definitive formulation, some decades later, according to which *"rex est imperator in regno suo"* ("the king is the emperor in his own domain")—a phrase that is generally attributed to Baldus de Ubaldi (1327–1400), but was already shaped, in fact, by Bartolus de Saxoferrato (1313–1357).[46]

When not only the perspective of a universalistic public power had definitively proved to be a chimera—which happened quite immediately after the foundation of the Holy Roman Empire—but also the internal political unity of the Western Christianity had broken up long since, giving rise to bitter conflicts, it was Dante Alighieri who delivered, in his *De Monarchia* (*Monarchy*), the probably most pregnant defence of the idea of an all-encompassing secular power of universal reach. In his fascinatingly outdated reflection on the role of the empire and on its relationship with the papacy, Dante begins by defining imperial power as "a single sovereign authority set over all others in time, that is to say over all authorities which operate in those things and over those things which are measured by time."[47] He goes on, then, by asking what is the rationale behind imperial power, or what the justification should be for a political dominion that claims to subject all other forms of worldly power. In order to find such a justification, Dante looks for an element characterized by the property of being common to the whole humanity, making a unity out of the plurality of individuals and communities. This element is identified in a purpose which is assumed to be common to all human beings, consisting—in accordance with the Aristotelian and, then, Thomist tradition—in the full realization of "happiness", i.e., of our highest spiritual potentialities:

> the activity proper to mankind considered as a whole is constantly to actualize the full intellectual potential of humanity, primarily through thought and secondarily through action (as a function and extension of thought).[48]

Yet, while in Aristotle's philosophy the "last end" was attainted through metaphysical speculation, in Thomist theology as well as in Dante it corresponded to the contemplation of God.

Having given the definition of the "last end", the Italian poet specified that it would need the fulfilment of three main conditions in order to be properly achieved. The first condition is the accomplishment of *universal peace* since this is "the best of those things which are ordained for our human happiness."[49] The second condition for "happiness" which, according to Dante, is best attained within the context of universal monarchy is *justice*,[50] while the third is *freedom*.[51] Doubts could be justifiably raised on whether a centralized universal public power—even leaving aside its feasibility—is really the best institutional framework in order to achieve peace, justice and freedom. It is well-known—just to recall a famous example—that Kant, quite to the contrary, regarded universal monarchy as the most significant threat, at least for freedom.[52] However, it has to be recognized that the sensibility at the beginning of the thirteenth century was obviously quite different from that of the end of the eighteenth century: while in the latter case the aim was to protect the citizens' liberty from absolutistic monarchy, at Dante's times the most pressing concern consisted in keeping at bay the many and frequent abuses perpetrated by local warlords and feudal masters in a context of weak central power.

Regardless of whether the assumption that the universal monarchy has to be regarded as the best place to realize peace, justice and freedom is really convincing—or, from our standpoint, rather not—what is striking is that the first reasons given by Dante to support his proposal have an essentially pragmatic nature. In other words, the beginning of his plea is about reasonable solutions, or—to be more precise—about the best way to implement a social and political condition in which human beings can thrive and achieve the most complete self-realization, and not about how the social and political order can be made coherent with ontological, metaphysical and theological presuppositions. Nor did Dante connect, at first, his political vision with the Christian faith. Yet, shortly afterwards, his analysis leaves the field of the pragmatic reasons and moves on to what he actually considered the most decisive argument in favour of the universal monarchy—and this argument has, indeed, an essentially ontological, metaphysical and theological character. From the ontological point of view, Dante relies on Aristotle's authority by claiming that, when an entity tends to a single end, it must be governed by a single principle.

Aristotle's metaphysics also provides the fundament for Dante's holistic-organic as well as strictly hierarchical understanding of the cosmopolitan public power: "when a number of things are ordered to a single end, one of them must guide or direct, and the others be guided or directed".[53] However, it is the theological argument which assumes the most central role. In fact, if we assume that God is one, then the universal monarchy—i.e., a political order which is one, too—must be seen as the most suitable form of human society since it would bring humanity closer to the supreme theological principle. In Dante's words,

> mankind is in a good (indeed, ideal) state when, to the extent that its nature allows, it resembles God. But mankind most closely resembles God when it is most a unity, since the true measure of unity is in him alone; and ... mankind is most a unity when it is drawn together to form a single entity, and this can only come about when it is ruled as one whole by one ruler.[54]

Thus, the unity of humankind becomes, together with the universal political order that governs it, an ontological derivation of the divine unity. The Christian doctrine and, through this, the holistic paradigm define in this way the horizon (and the limits) of Dante's perspective. In fact, according to the foundational principle of the holistic paradigm, the order of totality does not correspond to the sum of the partial orders, but is explicitly superior to it, since—as Dante wrote—"the goodness of the order in a part does not exceed the goodness of the order in the whole, but rather the reverse."[55] Surely, Dante's political thought was sophisticated enough to avoid the short-sighted one-sidedness of a centralized universal monarchy without internal articulation. Rather, his vision resembles some kind of proto-subsidiarity since "this rule or law should be received from him [i.e., from the emperor] by individual rulers, just as the practical intellect, in order to proceed to action, receives the major premise from the theoretical intellect."[56] Dante's cosmopolitan legal and institutional framework is nonetheless far from recognizing the principle of "dual legitimacy"—i.e., a legitimacy of the supranational power which is derived, at the same time, from both the supranational constituency and the plural constituencies of the individual states that, in their sum, constitute the supranational edifice. Nor is that framework limited to a "thin" overall organizational structure with the task of coordinating the interaction among the individual states. Rather, the emperor is seen as the only true political sovereign, endowed with superior and undisputed authority, whereas the subordinated princes only possess a derived sovereignty and a restrained competence to issue orders. "Therefore – Dante reaffirms – it is better for humankind to be ruled by one person than by several, and thus by a monarch who is the only ruler."[57] In conclusion, even if we assume that Dante's conception shows traits of proto-subsidiarity, his understanding of the notion does not represent any challenge to the traditionally hierarchical interpretation of the system of norms and institutions.

Having laid down the main reasons that are assumed to speak in favour of a cosmopolitan public power in form of a universal monarchy, Dante addressed the questions of the legitimacy of that power as well as of its relationship to the spiritual authority. A very influential strand of medieval theology asserted for long time that, God being the only legitimate source of power and Christ having transferred legitimate power on spiritual and mundane matters to his representative on earth, namely the pope, the logical conclusion must be that only those earthly rulers who have been directly or indirectly invested by the pope are to be considered rightful sovereigns. This assumption did not exclude that political powers exist which are located outside the *communitas christiana*—which was simply undeniable—but rather insisted on the non-legitimacy of commands issued by non-Christian rulers, so that any disobedience or even uprising against them had to be regarded as essentially justified. The most radical expression of this theory can be found in the work of Henricus Hostiensis, in which the "infidels" were denied any rightful claim to the exercise of political or jurisdictional power.[58] Moreover, in the case that they would maintain that claim, a "just" war could be fought against them.[59] In a more moderate form, but in the same spirit, the theory of the spiritual origin of all secular power was upheld also by two further leading theologians of the thirteenth century, namely Thomas Aquinas and Sinibaldo Fieschi, who rose to the papal throne under the name of Innocent IV. In particular, Thomas Aquinas conceded that "unbelief ... is not inconsistent with dominion", since earthly rule belongs to the "law of nations, which is human law", whereas "the distinction between believers and unbelievers is of divine right, which does not annul human right."[60] Analogously, Sinibaldo Fieschi admitted that the secular power of non-Christian princes is in principle legitimate, in the sense that it has to be respected and is entitled to make agreements with the representatives of the *communitas christiana*.[61] However, in case of conflict, the legitimacy of the dominion of Christian rulers has to be regarded as higher than that of non-Christian princes, since the Christian God is presumed to be the ultimate ruler of the whole world. Furthermore, for both theologians, the pope possessed not only the highest spiritual power but also the highest temporal authority.[62] As a result, the legitimacy of non-Christian dominion must be considered somehow provisional and normatively subordinated to the preferences of the Christian counterpart.

Against the background of this debate, Dante took quite an original and also, at least partially, innovative position. The rather conservative aspect of his idea regarding the legitimacy of earthly power concerns his conviction that, since there is only one legitimate dominion in the world and this dominion has to be Christian, the question of the possible legitimacy of non-Christian rulers is not even taken into account. On the innovative side, instead, we have his position as regards the relationship between the secular ruler and the papacy: whereas the power of the emperor is seen as deriving "top-down" from God, this derivation is assumed to be direct, i.e., not mediated by the Church. In fact, as Dante concisely stated after a long analysis that fills the whole third book of *De Monarchia*, "it is evident then that the authority of the temporal monarch flows down into him without any intermediary from the Fountainhead of universal authority."[63] Yet, if it should come to a dispute between the two powers, it is the spiritual one that—also according to Dante—has to be granted the upper hand. This priority, however, does not depend on a structural hierarchical inferiority of the emperor, but rather on a general superiority of spiritual on earthly matters "since ... earthly happiness is in some sense ordered towards immortal happiness."[64]

### 3.2.2.2 Francisco Suárez: The Attempt to Reconcile Unity and Diversity in the First Multilevel Conception of Legal Order

Though not necessarily convincing in all its assumptions, Dante's defence of the universal monarchy was remarkably sophisticated. Its main problem, however, was that the very idea of a universal monarchy was irretrievably passé even long before it was brilliantly exposed in *De Monarchia*. Thus, starting with the late Middle Ages, the supporters of holistic universalism found themselves stripped bare of what had been for long time—at least at the abstract level of theory—the institutional and legal framework into which the cosmopolitan vision had to be transferred. As a result, they were faced with the necessity to find a new political project, more specifically one in which the recognition of the plurality of polities, each of them governed by specific rules, could be reconciled with an all-encompassing legal framework in order to guarantee sufficient standards of civilized interaction. Unsurprisingly, since the Western supporters of holistic universalism were firmly rooted in Christian-Catholic belief, that legal framework had to be ultimately based on God's law.

The most intriguing and groundbreaking proposal for a new framework for universalism was delivered by Francisco Suárez, the last and probably most innovative exponent of the Thomist School of Salamanca. In his *De legibus, ac Deo legislatore* of 1612, the normative system is structured in four levels, from the highest and most general—the *lex divina* or *lex aeterna*—to the lowest and most specific—the *lex civilis*—passing through the *lex naturalis* and the *jus gentium*.[65] At the top of the hierarchy is the *lex aeterna* (eternal law), defined as "a rational principle existing in the mind of God."[66] As coinciding with the "divine providence", this law is also called *lex divina* (divine law).[67] Besides the more general meaning of the "divine law" as a rational principle that shapes the world as a whole, Suárez also identified a second semantic value of the same term, according to which it indicates, as *lex positiva divina* (divine positive law), the written norms coming directly from God through the Scriptures.[68] The second meaning of the *lex aeterna*—as divine positive law laid down in the Scriptures—is, according to the Spanish philosopher, the only way in which we can become aware, though quite partially, of the deep-going design that informs the whole creation. Every other law, be it natural or positive, derives from the eternal law, and every norm receives its binding force from it.[69]

Immediately beneath the *lex aeterna* we find the *lex naturalis* (natural law), i.e., "that form of law which dwells within the human mind, in order that the righteous may be distinguished from the evil."[70] Basically, the *lex naturalis* is the dimension of the *lex aeterna* which is accessible to any rational being.[71] Therefore, its contents are more limited than those of the *lex aeterna*; nonetheless, as far as the norms laid down in the *lex naturalis* are concerned, their continuity with what the *lex aeterna* provides for is—in Suárez's view—so evident that he explicitly maintained "that the natural law is truly and properly divine law, of which God is the author."[72] As the rational norm that should guide human action, the natural law "is a unified whole with respect to all human beings and in all places"[73]: it "is binding in conscience"[74] "with respect to all times and every condition of human nature."[75]

A further step from abstraction to concreteness, as well as from the general to the specific level, is represented by the *jus gentium*—the third layer, from above, of Suárez's system of laws. The *jus gentium* is that part of *lex naturalis* which, expressed by shared habits, gives order to human interactions beyond the laws of the single polities. It is identical with the *jus commune*,[76] which is assumed to be shared by all peoples:

> The rational basis ... of this kind of law consists in the fact that the human race, into howsoever many different peoples and kingdoms it may be divided, always preserves a certain unity, not only as a species, but also a moral and political unity (as it were) enjoined by the natural precept of mutual love and mercy; a precept which applies to all, even to strangers of every nation.[77]

The *jus gentium* as the system of norms that establishes universally valid rules in the relations among nations is strictly connected to natural law: indeed, its "precepts ... are conclusions drawn from natural principles, since their appropriate character and moral value are immediately made manifest by the force of natural reflection."[78] However, unlike natural law, the *jus gentium* is not merely a rational norm, but a "human and positive" law,[79] which does not give immediately commands to the conscience, but takes shape in a set of rules which "are established through the customs (*mores*) not of one or two states or provinces, but of all or nearly all nations."[80] Even though it is a human law too, the *jus gentium* is distinguished from the *lex civilis*, i.e., from the norms of the individual polities, insofar as it is not written, but entrusted to the common habits of the nations.

The *lex civilis*—or, rather, the *leges civiles* (civic laws)—makes up the lowest, or the most specific, level of the legal system as a whole. The *lex civilis* is the law that, according to the general principles of the *jus gentium*, organizes the social and political life within the specific context of a single polity. Therefore, since there are many polities, we have to recognize the plurality of the *leges civiles* too. The *lex civilis* is human law: contrary to natural law, it is positive law; and, contrary to the *jus gentium*, it is written law. While the *lex aeterna*, the *lex naturalis* and the *jus gentium* guarantee the universality of order, the *lex civilis* refers to its concretization in the specific context of the individual social and political communities. It is the "particular human law [of individual communities] to which the name of positive human law has been applied, and which is said to be peculiar to any given state (*civitas*), commonwealth (*respublica*) or similar perfect community (*congregatio*)."[81] Due to his acknowledgement of the full legitimacy of the legal orders of the individual communities, Suárez explicitly rejects the perspective of a universal monarchy or, in general, of a world state:

> This power [to make laws of an individual and special nature, laws which we call civil] never existed in one and the same form throughout the whole world of human beings, being rather divided among various communities, according to the establishment and division of these communities themselves.[82]

In other words, "in view of the nature of things – that is to say, according to the natural and ordinary course of human events – there are no civil laws established universally for the whole world and binding upon all human beings."[83] Thus, following Suárez's premises, the plurality of the legal orders of the different social and political communities has to be accepted insofar as it legitimately expresses the intrinsic diversity of the human world.

Contemporary legal theory and political philosophy generally grant Suárez little more than a historical relevance, namely as one of the thinkers who grounded modern international law. Yet, on closer analysis, we must conclude that the inspiration that can be drawn from his work is much broader and more deep-going than commonly assumed. In fact, Suárez's innovative and far-sighted conception of order deserves appreciation for at least five mainly theoretical (and not just historical) reasons. Firstly, he was one of the first modern theorists—though not the very first— who grounded international order on the assumption of the universally shared belonging to humanity. Although two other major philosophers— specifically, Vitoria and Gentili—reintroduced this old Stoic assumption ahead of the Spanish Jesuit, no one could formulate it, either before or after him, in a more pregnant form. Secondly, Suárez created a conceptual framework which went beyond both the idea of a global state and the normative inconsistency which always characterized—and still characterizes—the particularistic paradigm, deeply influencing the further theoretical approach to international law. In particular, his system of laws manages to assert the plurality of the legal orders of individual states without abandoning the idea of a universal normative system. As a result, Suárez made plausible, on the one hand, that cosmopolitan order can be achieved without resorting to the idea of a global monarchy, with its tyrannical threat and lack of feasibility, and, on the other, that the recognition of diversity does not need to degenerate into particularistic lawlessness and disorder. Thirdly, we find in his work the unprecedented elaboration of a system of laws which is multilayered, or multilevel, in essence. In this sense, it represents an interesting anticipation of highly relevant recent developments in the fields of both continental supranational integration and cosmopolitan supra-state organization. Fourthly, Suárez introduced a criterion for the assessment of the validity and legitimacy of state law. Though maintaining its specificity, each level of Suárez's system of laws, from the second downward, is derived from the level above, in the sense that its content, if it has to be accepted as "law", cannot be in contrast to the substance of the higher law. Rather, it has to be seen as the partial application of the contents of the superior level to a different ontological context. As a consequence of the deductive structure of the legal system, no civil law, if it claims to be respected, can contradict rational law or the *jus gentium*. Fifthly, and lastly, Suárez conceived of international order as a system essentially based on law, and not on political institutions. In fact, all layers of his system which guarantee cosmopolitan order—the *lex aeterna*, the *lex naturalis* and the *jus gentium*—are legal constructs, without significant institutional and political background other than the authority of the Roman Church, whereas the possibility of enforcing the law by political power is limited to the lowest level of order, i.e., to the *lex civilis*. As far as this point is concerned, Suárez qualifies as a forerunner of all those theories which, many centuries later, have proposed to build "peace through law". Contrary to these theories, however, in Suárez's vision cosmopolitan law was still not assumed to be laid down in written treaties and lacked whatever judicial system to support it. From this point of view, the progress that has been made—starting from his groundbreaking suggestion—has been significant. Nonetheless, what brings Suárez's conception and some contemporary theories of international law together is not only the courageous conviction as regards the feasibility of a cosmopolitan legal order, but also the underestimation of the importance of politics in shaping world order. In fact, while global order must undoubtedly take the form of cosmopolitan law, the legal order of the world—without political will and institutions to legitimately support it—is doomed to remain a paper tiger.

## 3.2.3 On Discrimination, Persecution and the Defence of the Status Quo, Or: Can Universalism Be Based on Religion?

Christian universalism was flawed from the very beginning by two deficits. The first, which has its roots in Augustine's theory of "just war", consists in the almost irresolvable difficulty in integrating non-Christians into the legal and institutional framework that should guarantee global peace (3.2.3.1). The second refers to the strenuous defence of the political status quo, which resulted in a substantial failure to understand what was going on in the social fabric of the early Modern Ages (3.2.3.2).

### 3.2.3.1 The Subjugation of the "Others"

Despite the early justification of war against the "infidels", the attitude of Christian states against non-Christian peoples was, for long time, rather defensive. Even when they went on the offensive, in particular during the Crusades against the Muslims, due to the strength of the opponent the mutually inflicted violence was—unfortunately for both sides—quite well-balanced. The situation changed when the Christian states began to develop—roughly at the end of the Middle Ages—an increasing scientific, technological, economic and, then, also military superiority. Furthermore, following the Western discovery of the New World, the Christian peoples came into contact with populations which were not capable of resisting their aggressive and expansive pressure.

The first case of a war of aggression waged by Christian on peaceful non-Christian peoples occurred, however, even before the beginning of the European conquest of the New World. It was the Baltic Crusade that—starting in the twelfth century and ending in the early fifteenth century—marked the first step of a wave of extremely violent aggressions and subjugations of "others" carried out by Christians. Indeed, there was some sort of early awareness of the fact that such wars of conquest posed significant moral problems to Christianity, which led to the discussion of the question at the Council of Constance (1414–1418)—yet to the conclusion that, since it was accepted that Christians have a universal rule over the world, a justified war can be waged on those who do not recognize the Christian dominion. Moreover, in the case of resistance the pagans could be justifiably deprived of their goods—even of the individual ones—since these could be rightly regarded as spoils of war.[84] The abandonment of the defensive position, together with the assumption of an unequivocally aggressive approach towards the "infidels", formulated at the Council of Constance, was then confirmed, in the following years, by three major papal bulls: *Rex regum*, issued by Martin V in 1418; *Romanus pontifex* (1436), in which Eugene IV regarded the paganism of the inhabitants of the Canary Islands as a sufficient reason to justify their submission by the Portuguese; and *Romanus pontifex* of Nicholas V (1455), in which the Portuguese again were authorized even to enslave the "infidels".[85]

The question became a matter of contestation anew—but then at a much broader scale—as a consequence of the conquest of the Americas. Although many European countries participated in the brutal race in order to seize as much land as possible, Spain was the only one in which a large debate arose about the moral and theological justifiability of the enterprise. Therefore, we find in the Spanish political and legal philosophy of the sixteenth century, until the beginning of the following century, three different strands: those who unapologetically supported the *conquista*; those—only quite a few—who basically opposed it; and those—including the most relevant thinkers of their generation—who took a differentiated, maybe even ambiguous, position by condemning the excesses of the *conquistadores*, but substantially justifying the endeavour. Starting with the first strand, the philosophers, theologians and jurists who were particularly zealous in delivering a support to the submission of the Native Americans, based their plea on two main arguments: the old Aristotelian thesis of the natural slavery and the universal power allegedly attributed by God to the pope and/or to the emperor. To be precise, however, the first scholar who took up the highly questionable chapter of Aristotle's *Politics*, according to which some human beings are destined by nature to be enslaved because of their intellectual inferiority,[86] was not a Spaniard, but a Scot. Indeed, it was John Major (or Mair) who, in his *Secundum librum sententiarum* of 1510, stated that "it is clear that some men are by nature slaves, others by nature free ... And this has now been demonstrated by experience, wherefore the first person to conquer [the Indians], justly rules over them because they are by nature slaves."[87] A couple of years later, the reference to the alleged natural slavery became the central argument in the fervent defence of the *conquista* by Juan Ginés de Supúlveda, more commonly known as the uncompromising adversary of Bartolomé de Las Casas in the Valladolid debate of 1550 about rights and treatment of the colonized peoples. In fact, the claim that "the barbarians are slaves by nature" builds the first and most important pillar to sustain the subjugation of the *Indios*.[88] Those who are slaves by nature—Sepúlveda argued—should accept the dominion of the "more prudent, powerful and perfect", and, if they do not willingly do so, the superior people have the right to wage war on them. Three further pillars follow: "the nefarious lusts and the great shame of the consumption of human flesh"; the necessity to stop the practice of human sacrifices; and the guarantee of the free preaching of the Gospel.[89]

Surprisingly, Sepúlveda did not refer to the second most influential argument in order to justify the violent subjugation of the Natives, i.e., to the assumption of the God-given universal power of the Church and, as a result of the *translatio imperii* (the transfer of dominion), of the derived earthly power of the emperor over the territories of the New World. As mentioned above (3.2.2.1), the claim that an earthly ruler could only be legitimated by the transfer of power carried out by the pope as the original holder of all authority, spiritual as well as secular, had been formulated by Hostiensis and other theologians in the thirteenth century, obviously with reference to the Old World. Immediately after the discovery of the new territories beyond the Atlantic Ocean, the theory had been reaffirmed and adapted to the New World by the highest moral authority of the *communitas christiana*, namely by the pope Alexander VI with the bull *Inter cetera* (1493). Coherently, the argument of the universal power of the pope and of the emperor built also the bulwark of the first "official" Spanish justification of the *conquista*, issued—as early as roughly a generation before Sepúlveda's interpretation—by the jurist of the Habsburg Crown, Juan López de Palacios Rubios. While Sepúlveda defended the results of a land seizure that had already occurred, Palacios Rubios's intent was to find good reasons for what was going to happen. The outcome of his efforts was one of the most infamous documents of a generally infamous enterprise: the *Requerimiento* (1513), which was an "injunction to capitulate, which was to be read to the Natives before unleashing a 'just' war against them."[90] The starting point of the document was the claim that the pope is, by the will of the one and true God, "Lord and Superior of all the men in the world."[91] Given his authority, the pope was assumed to have conferred the political power over the territory in which the community is located and to which the *Requerimiento* was referred, to the Spanish Crown, as proved by the bull *Inter cetera*. On that basis, the Spanish emperor had to be recognized as the rightful ruler over the said community. For the case that its members did not accept the Spanish dominion and the free preaching of the Gospel, the document threatened with actions that have little to do with the principles of the Christian faith:

with the help of God, we shall powerfully enter into your country, and shall make war against you in all ways and manners that we can, and shall subject you to the yoke and obedience of the Church and of their Highnesses; we shall take you and your wives and your children, and shall make slaves of them, and as such shall sell and dispose of them as their Highnesses may command; and we shall take away your goods, and shall do you all the mischief and damage that we can.[92]

As a kind of additional mockery, the *Requerimiento* closes with the remark that the Natives should only blame themselves for what the Spaniards might carry out following their act of defiance.

Leaving the analysis of the position that openly rejected the legitimacy of the *conquista* for later (3.2.4), we concentrate now on those who tried to stay between the front lines. The best example for this position is given by Francisco de Vitoria. In his *Relectio prior de Indis recenter inventiis* of 1538/39, he first addressed what he called the "illegitimate titles" in favour of the submission of the American aborigines by the Spaniards. The first two "illegitimate titles" dismantled, in fact, the most central arguments of the supporters of the *conquista*, giving therefore a strong philosophical backing to those who regarded the whole enterprise as a pure act of oppression. Indeed, the first "illegitimate title" denies that the emperor is "the lord of the whole world",[93] while the second asserts that the pope "has no spiritual jurisdiction over unbelievers", so that he cannot be "the civil or temporal lord of the whole world" either.[94] Leaving aside the reason presented by Vitoria to justify his position, it has to be pointed out that this is the first time that a major Christian philosopher distanced himself explicitly from the universal claims of both the pope and the emperor, recognizing to the first only spiritual authority over the members of the Christian community and to the second secular authority over a specific and clearly identified territory as well as over its inhabitants. Given the premise contained in the first two titles, the contents of the further five "illegitimate titles" are simply matter of deduction. Thus, if neither the pope nor the emperor are, in principle, the rulers of the world, then the sheer discovery of new territories cannot justify the claim to sovereignty over them (third illegitimate title); the refuse to convert to Christianity cannot give good reasons for waging war on the Natives (fourth Illegitimate title); sins against God's laws cannot be legitimately persecuted (fifth illegitimate title); the Natives cannot be attacked as a consequence of their refusal to acknowledge the king of Spain as their ruler (sixth illegitimate title); and, finally, it cannot be rightly assumed that the Spaniards have been chosen by God to punish the Natives for their sins (seventh illegitimate title).

After having given, with his "illegitimate titles", some glimpses of hope—and sophisticated philosophical backing—to those who questioned the legitimacy of the Spanish enterprise in the New World, however, Vitoria did a U-turn and added eight "legitimate titles" for the *conquista*, significantly one more than the "illegitimate" ones.[95] Once again, the most important argument is at the very beginning. In fact, with the first "legitimate title", he introduced a new concept which was destined to influence deeply the nascent *jus gentium*, i.e., the notion of the "natural society and communication" (*naturalis societas et communicatio*).[96] By the concept of *naturalis societas et communicatio*, it is meant that all human beings build a worldwide society based on their natural capability to communicate and interact with each other. Considering the nature of the concept on which the "legitimate titles" of the *conquista* were based, Vitoria completely refrained—contrary, for instance, to Palacios Rubios— from references to religious or political authorities, and grounded the justification of the land seizure in the New World exclusively on considerations of natural reason. In this sense, his premises are rather on the line with those of Sepúlveda—although with quite different outcomes, since Sepúlveda put natural slavery at the centre, whereas Vitoria did the same with natural communication. Albeit highly promising, the concept of natural society and communication is nonetheless also extremely ambivalent. On the one hand, it is possible to draw consequences from it which are highly forward-oriented even from today's perspective. In particular, Vitoria was probably the most radical defender of the right to migrate in the whole history of political thought. Specifically, he derived from the *naturalis societas et communication* the conclusion that everyone is entitled to travel to the land of her/his choice, where she/he believes that an improvement of her/his life conditions can be achieved, and settle down there, provided that no harm is done to the Natives. Moreover, Vitoria was an early and uncompromising advocate of the *jus soli*[97] and rejected the expulsion of "strangers who have committed no fault,"[98] thus implicitly opposing the practice of refoulement. Finally, he decidedly supported free trade—which, however, clearly served the interests of the Europeans.[99] On the other hand, however, Vitoria's notion of the natural society and communication can also be regarded as a justification of the conquest for at least three reasons. Firstly, the right to travel can only be seen as just if reciprocity is guaranteed; yet, what Europeans could do in the Americas could not be done by Native Americans in Europe. Secondly, insofar as common property was not recognized, the lands of the Natives were simply regarded as *res nullius* and, therefore, rightfully seized.[100] Thirdly, the duty of hospitality was not thought, primarily, to protect the persecuted, but to make the settlement of foreigners rightful. Should the native inhabitants of those territories oppose the entitlements of the newcomers—Vitoria added—these latter are granted the right to wage war on the Natives and subdue them.

While the "illegitimate titles" from the third downwards are strictly deduced from the first two, only one of the "legitimate" ones is explicitly derived from the premise of natural reason contained in the first. This is the case of the fifth "legitimate title", which authorized the Spaniards to intervene in order to overthrow a barbaric tyranny that violates the laws of nature and "brings harm to innocent people". The exact reference, here, is—analogously to the fifth "illegitimate title"—to human sacrifices and cannibalism; yet, contrary to the "illegitimate title", the reason for intervention does not consist in the defence of the laws of God, but of the laws of nature.[101] The sixth title, then, legitimates the intervention of the Spaniards to crush a revolt against their rule, but only after the Natives had willingly accepted the emperor as their king, thus without any presumption of a Spanish a priori rule. This title is also, to some extent, connected to natural law insofar as this is assumed to command obedience to the rightful prince.[102] Four of the remaining titles are, from the point of view of their foundation on natural law, quite ambiguous, since all of them refer, in some form, to the Christian religion, implicitly taking its superiority for granted. In this spirit, the second "legitimate title" should guarantee the free preaching of the Gospel[103]; the third asserts the legitimacy of a war against a local monarch who oppresses the Natives who have converted to Christianity[104]; the fourth provides for the right of the pope to transmit earthly sovereignty over the converted Natives to a Christian ruler, subtracting it from the "barbarian" prince[105]; and the seventh maintains that it is permissible for the Spaniards to intervene in support of the allies, when their cause is just, and to draw out the benefits granted to them by the *jus in bello*.[106] It is almost superfluous to say that no similar guarantee is given for the religion of the Natives, so that an evident bias is established. Moreover, for the case that the Natives should react to the injustice and try to oppose the religious and economic expansion into their territories, Vitoria guarantees to the Spaniards the right to wage a "just war" on them—which turns out to be, in the end, nothing else than a sophisticated validation of the *conquista*. To top the justification of discrimination, Vitoria introduced—as the eighth "legitimate title"—the argument of the "natural slavery" of the Native Americans because of their alleged "defective intelligence".[107]

In conclusion, Vitoria's legacy appears to be extremely ambivalent. In fact, he paved the way to the progressive idea of a *jus gentium* based on the assumption of a universal belonging to humanity. This idea, however, is also deeply biased in favour of the most powerful European countries, so that it remains to be decided whether this bias did not taint the essence of modern international law from its very beginning.[108] Furthermore, Vitoria's conception of natural reason and law, on which a universalistic law of the peoples should be based, shows a problematic mixture of rational arguments and pro-Christian presumptions, so that Vitoria's universalism always risks to degenerate into an apology of the unilateral expansion of Christianity based on economic and military supremacy. Actually, the bias in favour of Christendom can be made consistent with the centrality of natural reason, which characterizes the first and most important of the "legitimate titles", only if we assume what cannot be proved, namely that Christendom should "reasonably" prevail over the other religions because it is the most rational among them all. Precisely this assumption—which remained rather in the background in Vitoria's texts—[109] comes explicitly to the fore in Suárez's work. It is quite a short and specific, but nonetheless significant, passage in which this aspect clearly emerges. The question is about a corollary of the theory of the "just war", namely whether the right to undertake military intervention to protect innocent people from violent practices contrary to natural law is held only by Christian princes, or also by "every sovereign who wishes to defend the law of nature."[110] Here, a difference in treatment also emerges which is substantially similar to what we already know from Vitoria's *Relectio de Indis*: if a people intends to embrace the Christian religion and its non-Christian sovereign wants to prevent it, Christian princes are authorized to intervene in defence of the coreligionists.[111] On the contrary, if a people wants to abandon Christianity, non-Christian sovereigns cannot legitimately grant him their support.[112] Yet, Suárez—contrary to his predecessor Vitoria—based discrimination not on matters of religious exegesis (referring to the explicit universal mandate of Christianity), but on exclusively rational arguments, at least at first glance. In fact, "there is no injury at all in prohibiting the acceptance of a non-Christian belief", since whoever wishes to listen to the Gospel "may be convinced through reason that this is the most credible faith and that it ought to be believed."[113]

### 3.2.3.2 A Backward-Oriented Conception of Political Order

Besides the fact that the Christian-Catholic universalism seems to have discriminated, almost inevitably, against non-Christians, who were factually excluded from the order of peace that, in principle, should comprise all human beings, a second deficit affected the holistic-universalistic paradigm, when it was assumed to be based on the shared belonging to a community of faith. Indeed, its understanding of the legitimacy of political power was so dramatically backward-oriented that the Christian-Catholic holistic universalism ended up being, for long time, one of the most reliable bulwarks of reaction—maybe the most reliable at all—in the Western world. To demonstrate the immunity of early-modern Catholicism against the most advanced political ideas of the time, we can call to testify—once again—the two most sophisticated philosophers of their generation within this strand of political and legal thought: Vitoria and Suárez.

As regards Vitoria, his "top-down" concept of legitimacy is clearly expressed in his *De potestate civili* (*On Civil Power*) of 1528. The wording of the Question I, Article 8, leaves no doubts about his preference for the monarchy:

> I prefer to believe, with all the most honoured and wise peoples of earth, that monarchy is not merely equitable and just, but also of all forms of government the most excellent and convenient to the commonwealth.[114]

Furthermore, in the previous article, he already presented the most important reason for his preference, which is not pragmatic—i.e., it does not primarily refer to the advantages for the commonwealth—but ontological and theological, insofar as it makes reference to the very essence of political power and of its legitimacy. Unambiguously, Vitoria stated there that "public power is of God, and that as such it is just and legitimate. And from this follows … that power of this kind cannot be abolished even by the consensus of men".[115] Therefore, the authority of the prince arises from natural law and, through this, from divine law. As a result, every questioning of it brought about by humans can only rise from the ignorance of the foundations of human society, or from an intentional violation of the fundamental rule that governs the whole of creation. Finally, according to the Christian tradition of the Middle Ages and then to its Catholic continuation, the custodian of the highest law of God is the Church, in particular the pope as Christ's representative on earth. Consequently, on the basis of the principles that the pope is the true interpreter of God's law on earth and that within the *communitas christiana* the secular power is transferred from the pope to the earthly rulers, Vitoria asserted—at least with reference to the Christian states—that a civil law can be cancelled by the pope if it is against the divine law.[116]

Suárez's view is undoubtedly much more nuanced, although the outcome, in the end, is largely the same. The reason for the different starting point of the two authors is that in the century that separated Suárez from Vitoria the theory of popular sovereignty was taken up—in particular by Calvinist thinkers—and made to a powerful political weapon. Théodore de Bèze as one of the so-called Monarchomachs, for example, asserted explicitly in his *Du droit des magistrats sur leur subjects (On the Law of the Magistrates and of Their Subjects)* of 1575 that "not the peoples are created for the magistrates, but, on the contrary, the magistrates for the peoples."[117] Suárez inserted the theory of popular sovereignty in his political and legal philosophy to the extent that he admitted—contrary to Thomas Aquinas or Vitoria—that political power is not bestowed by God directly upon the monarch, but first upon the community.[118] In fact—he maintained—humans "are governed in civil affairs not by revelations, but by natural reason."[119] Furthermore, Suárez specified, quite in accordance with the traditional holistic spirit, that the original power is not transferred to the individuals, and even not to the sum of them—which marks a clear difference to the contractualist theory of state—but to their community *as a whole*:

> the said power resides not in individuals separately considered, nor in the mass or multitude of them collected, as it were, confusedly, in a disorderly manner and without union of the members into one body; thereof, such a political body must be constituted, before power of this sort is to be found in humans ... Once this body is constituted, however, the power in question exists in it, without delay and by force of natural reason.[120]

Thus, it is the social and political community that, in a second step, hands over the power to the monarch. The limitations that the author introduced at this point, even though they do not touch the core of the argument, are nevertheless so deep-going as to nullify much of the innovative quality of his initial position in favour of popular power. Firstly, he gave preference not to the self-organization of the political community, but to the monarchical form of government.[121] Secondly, although the community, as the original holder of political power in the mundane domain, was granted the right—in face of a severe abuse—to depose a king who had become tyrannical, nonetheless the condition that it must meet in order to take this step is so demanding that it nearly amounts to a prohibition. In fact, a king could only be stripped of his power if the *respublica* was "acting as a whole, and in accordance with the public and general deliberations of its political communities (*civitates*) and leading men."[122] Thirdly, Suárez stated that the pope has the "jurisdiction for the correction of kings" and, thus, the authority to remove them. The intervention of the pope is justified both when the faults of the monarchs concern spiritual matters and when their severe errors or tyrannical actions, albeit regarding secular matters, "constitute sins" and, therefore, are a violation of the highest law of nature.[123] Popular sovereignty in Suárez degenerates thus into a woolly principle which, lacking a precise institutional articulation, can only rely, ultimately, on the superior authority of the source from which it derives, i.e., to the *lex divina* according to the interpretation of the Roman pontiff.

### 3.2.4 Bartolomé de Las Casas and the Way Beyond Discrimination

Besides those who openly supported the *conquista* and those who found a more indirect way to ultimately justify it, a clear, powerful and courageous voice was raised against the abuses. It was the voice of Bartolomé de Las Casas. The Dominican friar is mostly known as the rhetorically skilled and morally committed—even though probably not always perfectly accurate—chronicler of the Spanish occupation of the New World, in particular of the Greater Antilles, modern-day Mexico, Central America and Venezuela.[124] In addition to that, however, he has also been a highly innovative political philosopher, at least as regards some aspects of his work. The reason why this part of his legacy is less recognized may depend on a certain deficit of coherence that affects his texts, in particular if taken as a whole. This shortcoming is probably due to the fact that Las Casas's aim always consisted primarily in making a successful case in favour of the strengthening of the rights of Indian peoples—and not in laying down a perfectly consistent system of political and legal theory. The consequence, anyway, is that while some features of his thought are astonishingly progressive—we could say: more than two hundred years ahead of his time—some other positions seem to be clearly backward-oriented.

To start with the probably most conservative claim contained in his texts, it may be quite surprising that the most prominent advocate of the rights of the Natives maintained the rather old-fashioned view that the pope was the ruler of the whole world and that he had the rightful authority, as a consequence of his position as the representative of Christ on earth, to hand over the earthly power to the princes of his choice. As we have seen in the previous Sects. (3.2.2.1 and 3.2.3.1), this view had been firmly stated by Hostiensis roughly three hundred years before Las Casas's time, but, in the meantime, had been already prominently contested by Vitoria, so that it could not be seen any longer as an irrefutable argument. In his *Treinta proposiciones* of 1548, his reference to the bull *Inter cetera*—and, therefore, to one of the most problematic documents of the official Catholic doctrine as regards the understanding of sovereignty and rights in the New World—is, though implicit, nonetheless quite evident.[125] Some interpreters have seen Las Casas's resort to the argument of the *translatio imperii* as the definitive proof that he was, in the end, not far away from the most usual position of the Spanish Scholasticism. In other words, he would share the conviction that the free preaching of the Gospel, as guaranteed by public power being bestowed upon Christian princes, is far more important than any other concern, including the freedom of native peoples and the original rights of the "infidels".[126] Some others have considered this part of Las Casas's work simply as a stage in the evolution of his thought.[127] Finally, the most favourable interpreters have seen Las Casas's concession to the spirit of his time as an especially smart move to guarantee essential rights to the Natives once they had been recognized as rightful subjects of the Spanish Crown on the basis of the *translatio imperii*.[128] In this sense, he would have accepted compromises in the field of theory in order to achieve the best possible results as regards the political praxis.

Quite uncompromising, instead, was his most abstract and systematic work, i.e., the treatise *De regia potestate*, which was probably written between 1555 and his death in 1566, but was first published—remarkably not in Spain, but in Frankfurt—a couple of years later, in 1571. Las Casas's analysis starts, here, from the original freedom of all human beings, as well as from the full availability of all things: "freedom, in fact, is a right which is necessarily inherent to man."[129] This assertion is based on the *rationalis natura* of all humans, namely on the assumption of the basic rationality of all members of the human community. Indeed, according to the traditional canon of the Christian Scholasticism, Las Casas interpreted human rationality as God's gift.[130] Nonetheless, the reference to God remains rather marginal in this work, so that Las Casas's discourse can concentrate almost exclusively on rational arguments.[131] In fact, all fundamental propositions of his political philosophy—as laid down systematically in *De regia potestate* and confirmed in other, more circumstantial texts—are derived from the original freedom and rationality of all humans, the first being the denial of any idea of natural slavery.[132] It follows—as Las Casas explicitly stated in his treatise on *The Remedy against the Depopulation of the West Indies*—that the slavery of the *Indios*, which took shape in the Spanish dominions through the system of the *encomiendas*, was essentially illegitimate.[133] Furthermore, as he added in his text on *The Indians Who Have Been Enslaved*, even if we admitted that the slavery of war should be regarded as a justifiable exception to the assumption of the original freedom of all humans, this argument would not be applicable in the Indies because the conditions for a just war were not given in that case.[134] The second proposition drawn from the foundational idea of universal freedom and rationality of humans is that, since all things are originally free and available to all,[135] the infidels who have acquired them legitimately cannot be deprived of their goods for the mere fact of not being followers of the Christian religion.[136] Thirdly, the natural freedom of the individuals gives rise to the political freedom of peoples: "originally, all human beings were free", which is why "no burden which is not voluntarily accepted can be imposed."[137] Fourthly, since freedom is an essential endowment of all peoples, the infidels have the right to autonomous political power and jurisdiction,[138] with the consequence that, in case this right is violated, they can legitimately oppose resistance. Therefore, the war that the Indians were desperately fighting against the Spaniards at Las Casas's time had to be seen as "absolutely just" (*justísima*).[139] Finally, the people being "the true source of the power of kings", they never gave up their freedom when they voluntarily submitted to public authority by transferring their original entitlements.[140] The limits imposed on the monarch are thus strict and laid down in great detail,[141] so that it can be assured that his action is exclusively directed to the welfare of the people.[142]

Las Casas's thought shows that an idea of order was conceivable which, although still deeply rooted in the Christian-Catholic tradition, was nonetheless capable of overcoming the usual discriminatory biases against the "others" as well as the backward-oriented fixation on absolute political authority. However, in order to achieve his goal, Las Casas had to take two courageous steps which, in their radicality, were quite new in Christian political philosophy. The first led to more emphasis on the natural human rationality than on God's commands, while the second juxtaposed human rationality with individual freedom. Both human rationality and individual freedom were identified as God-given, but Las Casas's argumentation develops almost entirely without resorting to God as their last guarantor. In other words, rationality and freedom as the two pillars of his philosophical construction seem to be able to stand on their own. As a result of this move, he went beyond the Christian-Catholic philosophical tradition of his time in a twofold sense. By switching attention from the *lex divina* to the *lex naturalis* or *rationalis* as the basis of social order, he anticipated to some extent the emancipation of natural law from the dominion of faith that was brought to completion by Protestant thinkers, like Gentile and Grotius, many decades later. And by grounding his entire political system on the essential assumption of the freedom of the individuals, he took the road that led to Locke and Rousseau—one and a half centuries or even more than two hundred years later, respectively. Although Las Casas's influence on those authors is hard to prove, he surely contributed significantly to the creation of the intellectual background that made both the emancipation of natural law and an idea of social and political order grounded on individual freedom possible. On a more general note, it can be concluded that the history of the reception of Las Casas's work confirms that the more innovative a thinker is, the less likely it is that her or his contribution to the progress of knowledge is properly recognized. In fact, to become mainstream, ideas need a favourable context—precisely what Las Casas bitterly missed.

### 3.2.5 *The Inclusion of the "Other" in the Doctrine of the Second Vatican Council*

In Catholic political philosophy, Las Casas remained an isolated personality for almost four hundred years after his death. In the meantime, the Catholic Church—as a result of the Counterreformation and in particular with regard to its top hierarchical level as well as to its official doctrine—became a steadfast defender of all sorts of reactionary social and political ideas. The only exceptions were a certain sensibility for the suffering of the working class, but with an essentially paternalistic understanding of social justice,[143] and the condemnation of the carnage of World War I, yet fundamentally because it opposed Christian nations,[144] while little or no concern was raised on how "uncivilized" peoples were treated. A new light of hope for all those members of the Catholic community who firmly believed in a different role of their Church lit up in the 1960s, with the Second Vatican Council.

The most relevant document issued during the time of the Second Vatican Council with regard to a new understanding of national and international order was the encyclical *Pacem in terris* (*Peace on Earth*), released by Pope John XXIII on the 11th of April 1963. The text is structured in a highly systematic form, being divided—after an introduction dedicated to the "order in the universe" and "in human beings"—[145] into five clearly distinct parts: the first on the "order between men", therefore on individual rights and duties[146]; the second on the "relations between individuals and the public authorities"[147]; the third on the "relations between states"[148]; the fourth on the "relationship of men and of political communities with the world community"[149]; the fifth, finally, containing "pastoral exhortations" on how to behave in the world with reference to the issues dealt with in the previous parts.[150]

Many aspects of the encyclical cannot fail to strike the reader, the first being the structure of the text itself, which reminds us more of a political or even of a constitutional text than of a theological dissertation. Moreover, almost in a Kantian way, the *Pacem in terris* starts by asserting the rights of the individuals—though combining them with non-rights-related duties, which in this form is surely not Kantian—[151] ending, then, by affirming a kind of supra-state, thus cosmopolitan law. A further novelty is the appreciation of democracy in the section dedicated to the internal political relations. In fact, the traditional Christian-Catholic natural law argument is taken up, according to which "representatives of the state have no power to bind men in conscience, unless their own authority is tied to God's authority, and is a participation in it"[152]—which leads to the equally usual position in favour of the right to conscientious objection in front of a political power that is justifiably regarded as opposed to the laws of God.[153] Yet, this argument undergoes, here, an unusual interpretative turn in a democratic sense, since the encyclical explicitly states that "the above teaching is consonant with any genuinely democratic form of government."[154] Quite unsurprisingly, the consistency of Catholic natural law with democracy is not justified by adopting the individualistic conceptual framework of those who maintain that "the will of the individual or the group is the primary and only source of a citizen's rights and duties."[155] Rather, by adopting an approach that is coherent with the holistic doctrine of the Catholic Church, political participation is interpreted as an expression of human dignity, which is placed at the centre of the divine order of the universe.[156] The foundation may be different from the secular and individualistic democratic doctrines; the substance of the conclusions, however, does not differ much from them.

In the sections dedicated to international relations and cosmopolitan law, the thrust is markedly universalistic. Not that this was a new element in the doctrinal tradition of the Catholic Church; nevertheless, innovative aspects are evident on this point either. The argument is in favour of an ordering of relations between all nations which should be inspired by "truth, justice, willing cooperation, and freedom."[157] All four criteria—taken both singularly and together—are explicitly thought to distance the Catholic Church from any kind of colonialism, and, more implicitly, from the support that the official doctrine of the Church gave to it. Indeed, "truth" is understood as the principle that "calls for the elimination of every trace of racial discrimination, and the consequent recognition of the inviolable principle that all states are by nature equal in dignity."[158] Justice, then, means that "states have the right to existence, to self development, and to the means necessary to achieve this,"[159] while "willing cooperation" calls for the states to take "positive steps to pool their material and spiritual resources ... [which] is already happening in our own day in the economic, social, political, educational, health and athletic spheres—and with beneficial results."[160] Finally, freedom implies that "no country has the right to take any action that would constitute an unjust oppression of other countries, or an unwarranted interference in their affairs."[161] Therefore, international relations must be built on the criteria of equal sovereignty, economic support and respect for national resources. But there is a further dimension which goes beyond the mutual relations between national communities, requiring the establishment of a robust supra-state sphere. The first justification for the creation of supra-state institutions relies on the traditional holistic assumption of the belonging of all human beings to the world community, from which also the right to migrate is drawn. Indeed, "the fact that ... [every human being] is a citizen of a particular state does not deprive him of membership in the human family, nor of citizenship in that universal society, the common, world-wide fellowship of men."[162] Yet, along with this ontological assumption, it is the increasing interdependence on a global scale that boosts the need for a well-organized form of supra-state order.[163] While it was once reasonable to hope for the realization of the "universal common good" by resorting to the traditional means of diplomacy and international law treaties,[164] the encyclical maintains that in the second half of the twentieth century "the rulers of individual nations, being all on an equal footing, largely fail in their efforts to achieve [peace and security]",[165] as well as the "recognition, respect, safeguarding and promotion of the rights of the human person".[166] In fact, "this is no reflection on their sincerity and enterprise: it is merely that their authority is not sufficiently influential".[167] Moving on to the question of which institution is more suited to carrying out these tasks, the encyclical makes explicit reference to the United Nations, accompanied by a substantially positive, even if cautious, judgement on the *Universal Declaration of Human Rights*—which marks a further turn in the doctrine of the Catholic Church.[168]

Yet, the probably most innovative and—we may say—almost "revolutionary" aspect of *Pacem in terris* consists in its opening towards other confessions and religions. Although it reaffirms the centrality of the Christian God according to the natural law doctrine of the Roman Church, this centrality is limited to the *theological* and *metaphysical-ontological* dimensions, while on the *practical* level it envisages the cooperation with the "others" in the name of the common interest of the whole humankind. The strategy of opening is divided into three steps. Firstly, the "right to worship God in accordance with the right dictates of ... [one's] own conscience" is emphasized,[169] so that other confessions and religions are acknowledged as having equal dignity, even if not equal theological truth. Secondly, it is asserted that the understanding of the world developed in the encyclical and the exhortations contained therein "take their rise from the very nature of things" and "derive, for the most part, from the consideration of man's natural rights".[170] In other words, they originate from the natural reason that, even if it is derived ontologically from the only true God, it is nevertheless common to all human beings. As a result, the encyclical is unprecedentedly directed not only to the members of the Catholic community but also "to all men of good will". Thirdly, we have the distinction between "error", which has to be severely condemned, and "errant", who must always be recognized in her or his dignity as a human being.[171] Furthermore, who is making theological mistakes in matters of faith can be seen nevertheless, in case that she/he shows "good will", as an ally on the way to peace and justice.

The novelty introduced by *Pacem in terris* does not aim at breaking with the holistic doctrine of the Church. In particular, we find the explicit assertion that "peace on earth ... can never be established, never guaranteed, except by the diligent observance of the divinely established order".[172] Beyond that, other holistic *topoi* are the metaphor of the *corpus*,[173] the theory of the natural sociability of humans[174] and the interpretation of humankind as an enlarged family.[175] Nonetheless, John XXIII's encyclical shows that it is possible to reconcile the traditional holistic tenets with a sincere recognition of the "others" and with the support for democracy and human rights. To do so, it has only to be acknowledged that, while Catholic believers may derive their commitment to a global idea of order from their faith in the Gospel and in the teachings of the Church, the very same commitment can also be achieved by resorting only to natural reason and law, on the basis of which cooperation with non-believers becomes possible. As a result of this assumption, which lies at the very core of *Pacem in terris*, Las Casas's truly universalistic spirit seemed to have pervaded, at last, even the centre of the pontifical authority and, thus, the official moral and political philosophy of the Catholic Church. This hope, however, was not destined to last long.

### 3.2.6 Faith and Logos in the Resumption of Catholic Exceptionalism

The pontificate of John XXIII was followed by a cautious consolidation of its achievements—but already with some concession to the conservatives—[176] by Paul VI. Then, however, after the very short papacy of John Paul I, the reaction came under John Paul II and Benedict XVI. To understand the contents of the return to more traditional positions by the Roman Church between the end of the twentieth and the beginning of the twenty-first century, we have to consider, in particular, an encyclical issued by John Paul II on the 7th of December 1990 and dedicated—as the title *Redemptoris missio* (*The Mission of the Redeemer*) already reveals—to "the permanent validity of the Church's missionary mandate". It might seem strange that a text devoted to the missionary vocation of Christendom—which, by the way, had never been questioned at any moment of its past history—should contain the explanation of the theological, philosophical and ideological restoration that characterized the papacy of John Paul II. Yet, what is interesting in this encyclical are the reasons that are given to justify the duty for all believers to spread the Christian Gospel all over the world, which have significant consequences for the idea of order. More specifically, these justifications are sought not only in the alleged theological superiority of the Christian faith, which is an obvious assumption for all believers, but also in the reaffirmation of an exclusive relationship between the Christian message and human rationality, so that—implicitly, but in some passages also explicitly—a world order of reason could only thrive on the basis of a worldwide triumph of the Christian Gospel. On those premises, it is quite evident that, with the impulse given by John Paul II and Benedict XVI,[177] the Catholic approach to the idea of order returned theologically and philosophically to views not only far behind the innovations introduced by the Second Vatican Council, but even prior to the most advanced contributions of the School of Salamanca between the sixteenth and the seventeenth centuries.

The starting point of the *Redemptoris missio* is the assertion that salvation can only and exclusively come from Jesus Christ.[178] As reaffirmed in the declaration of the Congregation for the Doctrine of the Faith—published on the 6th of August 2000 and signed by Joseph Ratzinger, who followed John Paul II on the papal throne as Benedict XVI, and Tarcisio Bertone—the "salvific event of Jesus Christ" involves a "significance and … value for the human race and its history, which are unique and singular, proper to him alone, exclusive, universal, and absolute."[179] In this regard, one could rightly argue that every religion is founded on the specific faith in a particular salvific event (or in a particular myth). The fact, however, that the accent is focused, here, precisely on this specificity—and not on shared and universal elements, as in the *Pacem in terris*—already represents a relevant change of perspective, if not compared to the farthest past, at least with regard to both the universalistic rationalism of Francisco Suárez and the spirit of the Second Vatican Council. Stressing the uniqueness and universality of the salvific message of Jesus Christ has at least four important consequences for the relations between the Catholic world and the "others", therefore also for the way to conceive international order.

The first consequence consists in the radical confirmation of what is already vaguely expressed in the title of the encyclical, namely the right of the Church to the *missio ad gentes* and its duty to carry out its mission of evangelization towards non-believers: "the Church is the sacrament of salvation for all mankind, and her activity is not limited only to those who accept her message".[180] And, in the same vein: "with the coming of the Saviour Jesus Christ, God has willed that the Church founded by him be the instrument for the salvation of *all* humanity".[181] The corollary that derives from this assumption is that international order in the most appropriate sense of the word—i.e., as a system of relations aiming at peace and cooperation—is possible only to the extent that true salvation has been realized, that is, that the Christian-Catholic faith has reached universal acceptance. Yet, since there is no doubt that this is an unrealizable claim in the real world, the implementation of peace is necessarily postponed, taking up the perspective of Augustine of Hippo, to the time of the triumph of the *civitas Dei*.

The second consequence—closely connected to the first—leads to the apodictic affirmation of the superiority of the Christian-Catholic confession over all other religions. Though stressing that there should be no compulsion to listen to the Catholic message,[182] the encyclical insists on the assumption— which all Catholics are invited to reiterate, especially in the missionary work—that the only true "salvation comes from Christ" and that "*the Church* ... *alone* possesses the fullness of the means of salvation".[183] The issue was further explored in *Dominus Jesus*, in which it is unambiguously stated that "it would be contrary to the faith to consider the Church as *one way* of salvation alongside those constituted by the other religions",[184] since "the distinction between *theological faith* and *belief* in the other religions, must be *firmly held*". In fact, while "faith" is described as "the acceptance in grace of revealed truth," beliefs of other religions are reduced—with a quite explicit sense of superiority—to "that sum of experience and thought that constitutes the human treasury of wisdom and religious aspiration."[185] The unavoidable—and quite disturbing—consequence of this premise is that "the followers of other religions ... [,]*objectively speaking* [,] ... are in a gravely deficient situation in comparison with those who, in the Church, have the fullness of the means of salvation."[186] At this point, the question arises as to the role that the inter-religious dialogue is going to assume. Although its importance is confirmed in the encyclical,[187] it is legitimate to have doubts about its destiny in a context so clearly unbalanced. Nonetheless, *Redemptoris missio* has also been explicitly interpreted as an appeal for the strengthening of the dialogue between the religions. According to this understanding, the recognition of the specific worth of other religions is ensured only to the extent that also the uniqueness of the Christian-Catholic message is underlined. Thus, the consolidation of one's own identity would be the best—if not the only possible—guarantee for the peaceful coexistence with other strong religious identities.[188] This interpretation, however, is based on the very questionable assumption that mutual recognition can be successful between impermeable collective identities—each of them firmly convinced that the other(s) is/are in a serious condition of not only theological but also metaphysical, moral, rational and, finally, existential insufficiency—and that this process of recognition can refrain from the identification of a common rational and moral meta-language. In fact, the possibility and/or the function of the rational and moral meta-language is generally challenged by any kind of religious radicalism, which always tends to see the only possible truth in its own specific revelation and beliefs. However, it is largely unlikely that a social and political community can succeed—in other words, that it can identify and accept common rules and develop acceptable standards of solidarity—merely as the result of the parallel self-affirmation of identities without osmosis and a common ground. Regardless of the theoretical dimensions, historical experiences do not seem to encourage such a hypothesis.

The third consequence of the assertion of the uniqueness and universality of the Christian message, uphold in the *Redemptoris missio*, consists in the affirmation that "any sort of separation between the Word and Jesus Christ is contrary to the Christian faith".[189] Thus, the logos is no longer understood according to the interpretation developed by the Second Scholasticism of the School of Salamanca, and brought to completion in the *Pacem in terris*, namely as a dimension of thought derived from the supposedly revealed truth, but also to a certain extent independent of it as accessible to mere natural reason. On the contrary, the logos is fully identified with the revelation and hereby largely deprived of all its autonomy. By doing so, reason is re-anchored in faith and removed from its vocation as the mediating element between human beings and cultures with different and sometimes contrasting existential projects and identities. The attribution of this vocation to reason, by the way, is one of the features that most distinguish its enlightened and secular thinking, according to which reason is not a belief among others, but the essential basis for a meta-language for the encounter between distinct ideas of the good.[190] What matters, here, is not the question of whether it is possible to separate the logos from Christ from a theological perspective. Even admitting that this is not sustainable from the point of view of the Catholic doctrine, and certainly neither the Spanish Scholasticism nor the *Pacem in terris* went in a different direction, it is still possible to emphasize the presence of different levels, one of which—the level of natural reason—is also accessible to non-believers, therefore providing a solid basis for shared ethical–political projects.

The fourth and last consequence is focused on the revival of the eschatological element. The Church—as the encyclical states—"is a dynamic force in mankind's journey toward the eschatological kingdom".[191] Therefore, "the kingdom of God ... is a reality present in time, but its full realization will arrive only with the completion or fulfillment of history".[192] By projecting towards a distant and unearthly future, the doctrine of the Catholic Church dismisses that the Kingdom of God always overlaps more than marginally with the worldly reality. Far from being open to the global realization of peace, justice and freedom, the real world is interpreted in terms which are profoundly marked by cultural pessimism[193]: gripped by moral decadence, sick with individualism and scientism, worldly society (especially the Western one) cannot find hope in an ethical and political project that involves all humans endowed with good will and reason. In this dark world, the Church must re-define itself as a "creative minority",[194] invested with the task of carrying believers— also with a strategic use of the mass media—[195] towards the transcendent world. The focusing of the *Redemptoris missio* on the dimension beyond reality is nothing but the logical consequence of the tight connection between rationality and revelation. Indeed, since it is assumed that a rational order of the world is only possible on the basis of the acceptance of the doctrine of the Catholic Church, but its universal acceptance is hardly to be expected (or, from the perspective of non-Catholics, to be wished for) in the near or far future, the Catholic believers cannot but prepare for the afterlife. In doing so, the Catholic Church abandons the dimension of mundane rationality, since it does not acknowledge its non-religious and open-to-others specificity—and, with secular rationality, it also gives up the idea of a realizable worldwide order.

### 3.2.7 Towards a "Global Ethic"?

During the three and a half decades of doctrinal restoration and reassertion of Catholic exceptionalism, the task of speaking up in favour of a non-biased religious dialogue and of the full recognition of the "others" was left to dissidents, who, though characterized by high intellectual ambitions, were put to the margins of the official Church—mostly because of their unorthodox positions. Among them, a prominent role has been taken by the theologian Hans Küng and his "Foundation for a Global Ethic".[196] The reasons for a worldwide ethic are identified by Küng in the globalization of economy, technology and media, which brings about also a globalization of the problems.[197] Starting from this consideration and from the need to act that derives from it, two assumptions are formulated that represent the conceptual skeleton of the project for a global ethic. The first assumption is that there cannot be a universal order without a set of generally shared ethical principles. To be universally accepted, this set should not be formulated as a unitary system of norms, but—according to the terminology deliberately chosen by the proponents—as a general "ethic", i.e., a minimal body of "values, fundamental attitudes and criteria", without systematic ambitions or a substantial catalogue of required behaviours.[198] The assertion that the universal order needs an ethical foundation is justified on the basis of the conviction that the political and legal system depends, for its good functioning and for its very existence, on a "consensus on values, norms and responsibility"—a consensus, however, that it is itself unable to create or implement successfully.[199] In other words, politics and law cannot forgo an ethical basis, and it is precisely this ethical basis—not the general political institutions or the overall legal framework—which the project of a global ethos is focused on.

According to the distinction introduced by Max Weber in his speech on *Politik als Beruf* (*Politics as a Vocation*) of 1919,[200] Küng's proposal does not aim at creating an "ethics of conviction" (*Gesinnungsethik*)—namely a set of rules and principles laid down by the moral agent on the basis of her/his personal persuasion as regards what is true and just—but, rather, an "ethics of responsibility" (*Verantwortungsethik*), in which the moral agent is primarily focused on the consequences of her/his actions. Moreover, taking up the interpretation given by Hans Jonas,[201] the emphasis in the definition of "responsibility" is not only put on the consequences of action (and not so much on its motivations) but also on duties, alongside and in some ways even beyond the recognition of rights.[202] In fact, the supporters of the project of a global ethic firmly maintain that the mere insistence on rights, if not accompanied by a comparable attention to duties, only justifies selfish claims and preferences, with the inevitable consequence of accentuating disruptive conflicts rather than preventing them.[203]

The second assumption on which the project for a global ethic is based claims that no universal peace can be achieved if there is no peace between religions.[204] Although it is recognized that religions are profoundly different from each other as regards the metaphysical vision, the theological conception and the practices of worship, and that these differences must be respected and preserved,[205] nevertheless they are also assumed to possess a common substratum of values, which forms a sort of "minimal fundamental consensus" on ethical issues.[206] Therefore, the global ethic should be understood as the minimum standard common to all the most important religious traditions.[207] The fact, then, that the religions are regarded as the best interpreters and spokesmen of common ethical values, although it is admitted that these are accessible even through purely rational means, is explained by their specific ability to reach and change the "hearts" of people: "they can provide what obviously cannot be attained by economic plans, political programs, or legal regulations alone: a change in the inner orientation, the whole mentality, … and a conversion from a false path to a new orientation."[208]

Turning now to the content of the global ethic, or to the concretization of the ethical principles that are believed to be shared by all world religions, the proposal is articulated in a fundamental axiom and four directives. The axiom on which the whole structure of the world ethic rests states the centrality of human dignity and is expressed by the commandment that requires to respect its integrity universally and with absolute priority.[209] The principle of fundamental respect for human dignity is commonly known as the so-called golden rule, the first and fundamental commandment shared by all great religious traditions: "we must treat others as we wish others to treat us".[210] Starting from the essential demand to treat every human being humanely, four directives are elaborated[211]: the first requires the commitment to non-violence and the respect for life, including the protection of the natural environment; the second commands solidarity and a just social order; the third commits to respect for truth and tolerance; the fourth, finally, prescribes that the full and equal dignity of women be recognized (but, interestingly, not equal rights for women and men).

Three aspects of the theory of world ethic should be emphasized: the first regards the relationship between rights and duties; the second is related to the concept of "values"; the third addresses the very nature of what has been described as the "golden rule". As for the first element, it is quite evident that the four directives of the global ethic actually represent a kind of synthesis of a more detailed catalogue of those rights that are generally recognized as universal or, simply, "human". The only significant deviation from the usual canon concerns the already outlined reduction of the equality between women and men to the general concept of "dignity", without spelling out a concrete equality on rights—probably in order to involve all major religions and not only with their most progressive influential exponents. However, in the discourse on global ethic attention is drawn on duties or obligations, rather than on rights— which is not devoid of possible complications. In fact, in the liberal and democratic tradition, duties are only justified as related to corresponding rights. In this sense, I have a duty only to the extent that someone else is assumed to have a right. As a result, no duty has an autonomous non-rights-related basis for legitimation. If this were also the case with regard to Küng's proposal, then no conceptual problem would emerge, since insisting on duties would not add anything more to the usual rights-centred discourse. However, if drawing attention to duties against rights is to be more than just pleonastic, then there must be a source of obligations which is independent of the mutual recognition of entitlements within the community of the free and equal—and this would be clearly at odds with the assumption, which is fundamental for a liberal and democratic society, that the mutual and reflexive self-obligation is the only fundament for the justification of duties[212] and that no self-proclaimed authority or non-reflexive entity can justifiably claim to be the addressee of whatsoever obligations.

The second aspect of the theory of the global ethic that should attract our particular attention is the assertion that all major religious traditions basically share the same core of *values*, which raises the question about the meaning of values. In other words, does the definition of values adopted by Küng correspond to its usual understanding? And can values be understood in a universalistic way, or is a certain set of values necessarily related to a specific idea of the "good life"? What strikes here, once again, is the attempt to divert the focus from the mutual recognition of rights to a different justification of obligations—possibly situated beyond the dimension of rights—namely to the existence of common values. However, the transition from a rights-centred to a values-focused discourse is not without problems, in particular if values are defined as alternative to rights. In fact, rights are articulated in highly formal propositions, which are limited to the justification of claims made by individuals (the rights holders) towards one another as well as towards the community as a whole. The aim is that no member of the society and no public power behaves in such a way as to jeopardize the conditions of individual self-realization, but supports it. Thus, the catalogues of rights do not need to presuppose substantial contents, such as metaphysical or philosophical visions and religious faith, but are characterized by the formulation of what could be defined as the "framework principles" of an interaction between social actors that allows each of them to realize her / his potential in the best way. By defining the general conditions of interaction, the language of rights entails a universal vocation that is not easy to achieve by the values-focused discourse.

In fact, "values" are mostly seen as those principles that distinguish each society in its specificity, defining its characteristic idea of the "good life". Through its particular pool of values, each community shapes the ethical identity that differentiates it from any other. If understood this way, a set of values can hardly be applied to the whole humankind: too different, indeed, are the ideas of the "good life" that have been developed in the distinct cultural traditions. Yet, there is a second, more general way to interpret the notion of "value". Here, "value" represents the ethical internalization of those rules of conduct that guarantee correct social interaction. According to this meaning, the "value" is the result of the transformation of the abstract rule of conduct into a habit and constitutes, therefore, the other side of the rights system. While in the domain of rights the rule of behaviour established in order to protect the correct development of the interaction takes the shape of a formal norm that attributes specific entitlements (and duties) to the individuals, "values" translate the rules into a social ethos internalized by all members of the society (or, at least, by most of them). Usually, the rules of behaviour concern the interaction within a particular community, which is why the values that are connected to this kind of rules draw the picture of a particularistic ethos, as described for the first meaning of the concept of "value". However, when reference is made instead to the global interaction that potentially involves all human beings, "values" can turn out to be the ethical consolidation of that code of conduct that is necessary in order to recognize every other individual as our fellow human endowed with equal dignity. In the context in which rights become human rights, values are transformed into universal values. In conclusion, on the basis of its most widespread reading, the notion of "value" refers to the ethical basis of particular societies and is therefore unsuitable for the use made of it by the proponents of the global ethic. However, if we shift our attention to a broader horizon and, by abandoning the level of particular communities, we see in the "values" the ethical grammar of interaction no longer between members of a specific community, but between human beings as such—i.e., the internalized dimension of what, on the formal level, are human rights—then it is possible to speak of "universal values" and the intent of the supporters of the global ethos becomes plausible.

The third aspect of the theory of global ethic is related to the role played by the golden rule. Basically, the supporters of the project for a global ethic maintain that, first, the golden rule describes the respect for universal humanity which is common to all major religions, and, secondly, that it is essential part of the doctrinal content of each of them. Put differently, the golden rule would be enshrined in the most relevant religious doctrines and result from their overlapping. Thus, following Küng's approach, the members of religious communities who refer the golden rule to their beliefs are not doing so just in order to stress the driving force of their actions, but rather because it is primarily and essentially to be found in religious traditions. However, there is also a different way to understand the golden rule, namely as one of the most relevant elements of natural reason, or—to be more precise—of intersubjective rationality, which is taken into account, to some extent, by all major religions, but is not generated by them or even essentially connected with them. In fact, two arguments speak in favour of the second interpretation. Firstly, there is no evidence that supports that non-believers have a diminished understanding of the golden rule; rather, since it is a command of pure reason, it is to assume that they have a perfect access to it. Secondly, non-doctrinal philosophy is not a belief like any other, but the universal discipline of the exercise of reason, which does not presuppose any revelation or predetermined truth. Now, if we combine these two arguments, we can conclude that the golden rule should be assumed as a product of universal rationality and that, if world religions proclaim it, this depends on the fact that part of their doctrines relies on natural reason. Yet, when we talk about what we owe to every fellow human—regardless of whether we are believers or not—we are using primarily rational arguments, and only secondarily we may refer, if we are members of a religious community, to the proclamation of universal dignity in our tradition. Once again, when it comes to universality faith has to give way to reason.

### 3.2.8 The New Frontier of Catholic Theology

With the beginning of the papacy of Francis in 2013, the Catholic doctrine seems to look again at some of its most advanced achievements. Pope Francis's papacy has been already the subject of intense controversy. While the most progressive activists inside and outside the Church are disappointed by Francis's upholding of the traditional doctrine on matters such as contraception, abortion, LGBT issues, ordination of women and priestly celibacy, and even more deplore his overcautious dealing with allegations of sexual abuse within the Catholic clergy, many conservative Catholics regard him as a danger for the stability, the unity and the authority of the Church. Anyway, although Pope Francis is not expected to dismantle many of the official Catholic precepts—in particular in sexual and gender issues—which might be difficult to understand from a purely rational point of view, nonetheless he has brought the official doctrine of the Church to that point again, where dialogue with other confessions or with non-religious groups in order to address concretely the world problems is possible and fruitful. Obviously, that approach could not but be disturbing to all those who maintain that identity comes first.

In fact, in the history of Catholic thinking—apart from Las Casas's philosophy, which never belonged to the Catholic mainstream—hardly a document can be found which is more forward-looking than Francis's encyclical *Laudato si'* of the 24th of May 2015. The main topic of the encyclical is not social, political and legal order, but the role played by humans in disrupting the ecological balance of the planet, and their duty to change their attitude and to contribute to its reinstatement and preservation. Nonetheless, at least two major elements of the *Laudato si'* remind us directly of the most innovative contents of the rationalist theology of the School of Salamanca and of the Second Vatican Council, going to some extent even beyond them. The first of those elements is that the encyclical is explicitly and repeatedly addressed to all people, thus taking up the spirit of the *Pacem in terris*.[213] Indeed, Francis reaffirms that "the ethical principles capable of being apprehended by reason can always reappear in different guise and find expression in a variety of languages, including religious language".[214] Therefore, since the humankind as a whole is facing an unprecedented ecological challenge which threatens its very existence, "we need a conversation which includes everyone". According to the spirit of human solidarity and to the commands of natural reason, "all of us can cooperate as instruments of God for the care of creation, each according to his or her own culture, experience, involvements and talents".[215]

The second forward-looking element of the *Laudato si'* regards the relationship between scientific knowledge and religious faith. Admittedly, we find in the encyclical some rather traditional tenets of the Catholic understanding (and criticism) of science. Among these are: the rejection of the so-called technocratic paradigm, which is simplistically seen as a means of human dominion over the world[216]; the condemnation of the alleged hubris of subjectivism, regarded as the main source of the relentless exploitation of nature (which it probably is), but not as the fundament of human rights and of the possibility to overcome the ecological disaster through the progress of science as well[217]; an exceedingly simplified view of anthropocentrism[218]; and—besides the largely shareable concern with regard to experiments on human embryos—the unsurprising reassertion of the integrity of human life and moral personality from its very conception.[219] All these elements contribute to reasserting the well-established Christian-Catholic interpretation of society as an organic whole, in which the respect for the natural environment is part of a broader acceptation of the given order and hierarchy of creation.

On the other hand, however, we have in the *Laudato si'* also a very significant and unusual content for an official text of the Catholic doctrine. In fact, it is not only addressed to all people endowed with natural reason and good will but also starts its case for the conservation of the natural environment of our planet by presenting exclusively rational arguments worked out by scientific research.[220] By doing so, Pope Francis testifies a respect for the knowledge that derives from non-ideological and unprejudiced investigation as well as for the independence of science which is probably unprecedented in the history of doctrinal Catholic thinking.[221] No less attention is shown to the dialogue with philosophy.[222] Therefore, the first justifications for an ecological turn accurately listed by Francis can be shared by all members of the human community. Yet, Christian-Catholic believers have—according to Francis—one additional reason to perform this turn, and this derives from the Holy Scripture, more precisely from both the Old and the New Testament. However, it is quite interesting that this second argument is introduced only later in the encyclical.[223] As a result, the believers are confronted with a two-level justification for a behaviour which is respectful of life and ecological balance: the first only resorts to the use of reason and is common to rationally behaving non-believers, while the second—surely the most important for Christians—is based on the Bible and the Gospel. Without diminishing the subjective importance of faith, the Catholic Church seems to be open again for a cooperation with all women and men of good will.

## 3.3 THE UNIVERSALISM OF NATURAL LAW

Besides a long-established tendency to support non-democratic forms of social and political conservatism—only partially and perhaps not definitively rejected by recent encyclicals like *Pacem in terris* and *Laudato si'*—the most significant shortcoming of the Christian-Catholic theory of world order has to be identified in its early connection between the idea of a well-ordered community and the acceptance of the "true" religion. On that basis, the proclaimed universalism could never be really implemented, either in theory or in practice. Consequently, insofar as the Catholic thinking was committed to the idea of a truly universal peace and order, a positive result was to be achieved only by separating the approach of natural reason from faith, and by grounding universalism essentially on the first, with religious arguments being relevant only for believers. This was the lesson that could be drawn—at least in part—from the works of the most innovative thinkers of the Spanish Scholasticism, to be fully developed, then, in the encyclicals *Pacem in terris* and *Laudato si'*.

Given the impossibility to conceive a true universalism by grounding it on faith—and with regard to how a possible solution was sketched by strengthening the reference to the *ratio naturalis*, while keeping it nonetheless beneath the *lex divina*—the question arose whether it would not be easier and more coherent to skip the religious justification entirely, and found universalism only and explicitly on the commands of reason. The first step in this way consisted in emancipating natural reason from religious belief, and natural law from divine law (3.3.1). The hereby established independence of reason led to different theoretical outcomes and to distinct ideas of social and political order (3.3.2). Each of these conceptions, however, had its own flaws. Moreover, a new social and economic context made other understandings of order more attractive. In part because of the deficits of the old theory of natural reason, and in part as a result of the change of social environment, the rationalistic variant of the universalistic paradigm of order fell into a deep crisis, which was destined to last from the mid-eighteenth century until the end of World War II. In the last decades, however, a significant revival of natural law came up, which aimed at overcoming the previous shortcomings, but simply resulted in making the weak spots even more evident (3.3.3). Finally, it must be considered that the theory of natural law and reason—with all its grandness and weakness—has inspired not only an important approach to moral philosophy but also a very influential conception of international law, namely the theory of its constitutionalization (3.3.4).

### 3.3.1 From the Law of God to the Law of Humanity: On the Natural Law Theory from the Middle Ages to the Reformation

The idea of the existence of a natural law became part of the Christian doctrine very early, namely with the letter to the Romans written by Paul the Apostle, also known by his Jewish name of Saul of Tarsus: "for when the Gentiles – Paul wrote – which have not the law, do by nature the things contained in the law, these, having not the law, are a law unto themselves".[224] Yet, it was Thomas Aquinas who introduced a fundamental quality leap in the discussion by clarifying and systematizing the concept of natural law. In particular, his *Summa theologica*, written between 1265 and 1273, laid the fundament of a relationship between the *lex aeterna* and the *lex naturalis* which was destined to influence the reflection on the topic in the following three and a half centuries. Thomas starts specifying, with a simple syllogism, that the law being "nothing else but a dictate of practical reason emanating from the ruler who governs a perfect community" and "the whole community of the universe [being] ... governed by Divine Reason", it derives that "the very idea of the government of things in God the Ruler of the universe has the nature of a law". Moreover, this law must be called eternal because the idea that emanates from the divine reason knows no limits of time.[225] Once the *lex aeterna* has been defined as the law that originates directly from God and governs the world as a whole, the *lex naturalis* is determined as the "the rational creature's participation of the eternal law."[226] The universal capacity of the rational creature to distinguish what is good—and what is evil—according to the law that governs the world, is thus interpreted as the result of the partial accessibility of the eternal law to reason. Precisely because of this faculty, natural reason lays the very fundament of natural law, or, indeed, is to be downright identified with natural law.[227] At this point, a third dimension of law is introduced, i.e., the *lex humana* or *positiva*: in fact, "the human reason needs to proceed" from the "general and indemonstrable principles" of natural law to "the more particular determination of certain matters".[228] These are the positive human laws, which are different in their relatively distinct contexts. In the face of this tension between the *lex naturalis* and the *lex humana*, the *jus gentium* is placed where both overlap. On the one hand, it is indeed in a close genetic relationship with natural law, though not coinciding with this to the extent that it takes, on the other hand, the form of positive law and is therefore more restrictive with regard to its addressees.[229] In other words, the *jus gentium* is part of the *lex humana* since it has a positive character. Thus, it is addressed only to humans and not to all rational creatures like the lex naturalis. However, the *jus gentium* must be included in that set of positive laws which, due to their content, are directly derived from the law of nature and therefore do not represent a mere human artefact. For that reason, all human beings share it and are bound to respect it.

Thomas's most relevant merit—with regard to the definition of law—consists in having identified the conceptual basis of the logical, ontological and hierarchical relationship which connects and distinguishes the different categories of law. The premise is that law "denotes a kind of plan directing acts towards an end". Thomas added to this general definition the hierarchical-genetic principle that, when a plurality of layers is involved in directing the action, the subordinate level becomes active only in the presence of an impulse sent by the layer above, so that ultimately, if we proceed upward in the chain of causality, everything depends on the so-called *primum mobile*. This is what happens in the government of human communities as well as of the entire universe, where "the eternal law is the plan of government in the Chief Governor" and "all the plans of government in the inferior governors must be derived from the eternal law". Given those premises, the conclusion is that "all laws, in so far as they partake of right reason, are derived from the eternal law".[230] As a consequence, natural law is not granted a self-relying foundation, so that, when we speak of the obligations deriving from natural reason, we are constantly referred to the divine law and, then, to the precepts of revealed religion. More precisely, in Thomas's interpretation, the lack of ontological and epistemological autonomy of natural law in its relationship with divine law is characterized by four elements. The first is the ontological derivation and dependence of the *lex naturalis* from the *lex aeterna* in the sense that natural law cannot have any content which is not already contained in God's commands. As a result, natural law is not allowed to prescribe, permit or prohibit actions if the wording of the divine law is interpreted by those who are in charge of the true doctrine as not including such prescriptions, permissions or prohibitions. The second element consists in the epistemological inferiority of the *lex naturalis* insofar as its contents are assumed to be only a small part of the all-encompassing order of the world which is provided for by divine law. The third element, then, is the limited application of the concept of rationality. Indeed, following Thomas, rationality is only a human category which cannot describe properly how God's will operates. Put differently, we call "rational"—using our own very limited understanding of the world—what in fact is the free will of the Creator. Thus, our concept of reason is not applicable to the work of God, who—however rational the creation may be in our eyes—is not assumed to be bound by any rule. The last element is the presumption of the essential unity of the system of knowledge that governs the use of the theoretical and practical reason. Consequently, there is no plurality (or, simply, duplicity) of cognitive organons, with the consequence that reason has essentially the task of assisting in the discovery of the highest truth. That happens, by the way, even in case that the specific methodology of rational inquiry is partially recognized, since its organon is always regarded as something auxiliary to the interpretation of God's will and, therefore, as inferior to theological disputes to which it is intended to give its support.

Thomas's interpretation of natural law deeply influenced all major thinkers of the Western world until the beginning of the seventeenth century. Yet, during this period, two changes were introduced, the second of which finally led to the definitive acknowledgement of the full autonomy of natural law on the basis of pure reason. But let us start with the less deep-going modification of accent, which was the product of the Spanish Scholasticism. Here, the element on which the conceptual evolution was focused is what has been defined above as the third element of Thomas's theory of natural law, namely the limitation of rationality as a purely *human* category. It was Vitoria who began to wonder whether God as well as his actions should be regarded as inherently rational (or, insofar as ultimately free, at least as rationally directed). Vitoria's position is extremely ambiguous, though, if not even contradictory. On the one hand, in full agreement with Thomas, he stated that "natural law ... has no force except for the fact that it was established by divine authority. Otherwise it would not be mandatory [...] since an obligation cannot exist except from a higher instance."[231] Indeed, Vitoria went as far as saying that if God did not exist, no action could be declared reprehensible in the moral sense, so that a parricide would not be different from the killing of a human being by a beast.[232] In other passages, however, he maintained that murder is not bad because it is forbidden, but it is forbidden because it is bad.[233] In this sense, God seems to be connected to a rational content that is in some measure objective, even though always identical to his will. Thus, Vitoria's contribution fits into a process which, albeit in the continuity of tradition, aimed to identify a more solid rational basis for natural law. Yet, he got stuck somewhere along the way. In fact, the most advanced novelties introduced by Vitoria must be sought in other aspects of his thought. First, we have the unequivocal affirmation that human laws are to be considered binding only if they correspond to public interest and are in harmony with hierarchically superior laws: "in many cases – Vitoria clarifies – divine law binds where human law does not".[234] We can deduce from this statement the existence of a suprapositive norm which goes beyond positive state law and on which a human rights policy can be founded—not necessarily in a fideistic or natural law perspective. Secondly, in Vitoria's work, the concept of "right" (*jus*) is no longer understood in a merely objective sense, i.e., as a derivation from what is *justum* or objectively rightful, but in a subjective sense,[235] as an "entitlement that belongs to someone according to the laws".[236]

The transition from the assumption that, in accordance with Thomas's interpretation, "natural law is rational because God wants it" to the assertion that "natural law is rational because God, its creator, is rational" was accomplished by Francisco Suárez, the most rationalist of all Catholic theologians of the early Modern Ages—except for Las Casas. Most certainly, Suárez overcame Vitoria's ambiguity insofar as he firmly attested the overlapping of rationality and divine will:

> the free acts of God ... are ruled by the divine reason as by a natural law of God Himself. The proof of this statement is that God always acts according to the right reason, not the reason of another, but His own; and therefore, the rectitude of the free acts of God's will is measured by the judgment of His own intellect.[237]

Although Suárez's system of laws and his distinction between *lex divina*, *lex naturalis*, *jus gentium* and *lex civilis*[238] takes up, by and large, Thomas's doctrine and definitions, his theory is characterized by three major improvements if compared with his predecessor's. Firstly, albeit in the same spirit, Suárez's presentation is clearer and more differentiated. Secondly, since the source of all laws, namely God, is the essence of rationality, the whole system is thought primarily from the rational perspective, while religious arguments play a surely not marginal, but at least less decisive role. Thirdly, Suárez explicitly accepts what in Thomas's time was still unacceptable, at least officially, namely that order has to be conceived of—and made possible—in a context of religious and political plurality, in which, even it is assumed that the Catholic faith has no match with regard to the truth content, natural law becomes the most viable theoretical instrument to figure out a realizable order of peace. However, Suárez's assertion according to which "the divine order is rational" is necessarily integrated by the corresponding and reverse assumption that "the rational order is divine". In fact, he openly stated that "the eternal law involves not a necessary, but a free act of God".[239] As a result, also in this most advanced theory of natural law developed by influential Catholic philosophers before Jacques Maritain[240] and the Second Vatican Council, the law of reason remains a law ultimately given by God. Therefore, it is still the legal order based on the essential tenets of a specific religion and is subject to the inevitable limit of all fideistic approaches, namely to the risk of excluding or disadvantaging the "others", the "infidels" who do not recognize the superiority of the Christian God.

Yet, what really mattered in order to affirm the autonomy of natural law was not the assumption that "God is identical with rationality", but rather that "natural law is rational in and of itself", i.e., it has its own argumentative method as well as its own logical and ontological foundation, being no longer depending for its content on deductions from the divine law. Taking this decisive step was made possible by a historical event which, at first glance, seems to have little to do with the empowerment of natural reason. This event was the Protestant Reformation. Indeed, according to the Catholic theology, natural reason has the capacity to reach the most essential elements of the divine law—or, at least, to deliver an essential contribution in order to attain them. As a result, it was on the universal scope of God's law and on the osmosis between this and natural reason that the project of a worldwide order was grounded. On the contrary, Protestant theologians generally assumed, following Martin Luther's interpretation,[241] that original sin made humans unfit to understand the plans of God by means of reason, so that the way of directly deriving the fundament of a just social order from God's will was shut down. The first implication was the establishment of the principle that only faith can bring humans, as natural-born sinners, nearer to God's commands. A second implication, however, concerns directly how reason was understood. Following Luther's most unfavourable interpretation, reason was seen as the "Devil's greatest whore".[242] Yet, the Protestant thought—in particular in its Calvinist variant—developed also a different, quite less adverse or even well-disposed attitude towards rationalism.[243] No divergence is given with regard to the conviction that God is approachable exclusively through grace and faith. On that basis, nonetheless, the rationalist strand of Protestant thought—building rather on Calvin's than on Luther's doctrine—also admitted that reason, being excluded from the religious context, could emancipate from the control by the Church and improve with less restraint in its application to secular matters. By taking this stance, Protestant thinkers did not introduce, like the School of Salamanca, a change in the third assumption made by Thomas Aquinas as regards the relationship between natural law and divine law—namely with reference to the status of rationality as either an exclusive quality of humans, or of God as well—but in his fourth postulation, i.e., there would be only *one* organon, both rational and fideistic, for the true knowledge of the world. Instead, Protestant philosophers maintained that there are *two* distinct organons: one, based on faith and theological doctrine, for the knowledge of the religious truth; the other, based on reason, for the description and explanation of earthly matters. Thus, natural reason—in order to properly accomplish its task—must develop a specific methodology to discover its own truth, independently of what God's plans may be and of how the religious doctrine may interpret them.

On that basis, thanks to the contribution made by the Reformation, the way was opened for natural law to become a pure law of reason. Once established that natural reason has its own organon with the purpose of discovering the laws of the earthly world, the other elements of Thomas's definition of natural law in its relationship to the divine law became rather secondary. Indeed, it can still be assumed, from a religious perspective, that natural law has been created—as everything else—by God, but, since we cannot understand God's will by means of reason, that kind of derivation is ultimately irrelevant for rational knowledge. Moreover, even if it is accepted that divine law is broader and more profound than the cognition that is attained through reason, only the latter is significant for the human knowledge of earthly matters. And, finally, since we cannot know

God's plans, the question whether God is rational or not is simply out of our reach.

Along with the affirmation of the autonomy of human reason, a further aspect of Calvinist Protestantism should be pointed out as decisive for the development of the modern idea of social, political and legal order. It is the fact that Calvin—distinguishing his doctrine, also in this case, from Lutheranism—laid great emphasis on the self-organization of the new Church, which developed according to the covenant pattern of the Old Testament. Therefore, the Calvinist tradition paid considerable attention, already at an early stage, to the political self-regulation of the religious community. The consequence was that politicians and philosophers influenced by the Calvinist doctrine massively contributed to pave the way to some of the more ambitious and forward-looking developments of modern political thought, such as the secularization of political power and its "bottom-up" legitimization by means of foundational contracts and parliamentarism.[244] On the contrary, Lutheran theology, which basically followed the theory of the two kingdoms, did not exert for quite a long time a significant influence on the modern reorganization of political power. Later, when scholars who were brought up in a predominantly Lutheran environment took finally up some progressive political ideas, they did it in a rather moderate form, mostly under the influence of the enlightenment and often at the price of heavy conflicts with the religious hierarchy.

The first author who elaborated on the groundbreaking innovation introduced by the Reformation was Alberico Gentili. In his *De jure belli* of 1589, he took up the traditional Scholastic distinction between *jus divinum*, *jus naturale* and *jus humanum*. As regards the definition of the layers of the legal system, it is to be noted, first, that his preference for the use of *jus*—and not of *lex* as in most Scholastic texts—is substantially meaningless since *jus* and *lex* were used indifferently until Hobbes established the two different definitions which are still in use, namely *jus* as a subjective right and *lex* as an objective obligation. Secondly, Gentili considered the *jus humanum* as identical with the *jus gentium*, thus leaving aside the *jus civile* as the law of the single polities, for the simple reason that he only focused his research on the rules of interaction between states, and not on the domestic legal system. Although Gentili's terminological choice remains in the tradition, the same cannot be said, however, with regard to his definition of the main concepts.[245] In his interpretation, indeed, the *jus gentium* is still part of the *jus divinum*—but, significantly, just a "small part", a *particula*, which "God left us after our sin". Nevertheless, we can see the "light in the great darkness", even though—Gentili added—"because of the error, the bad custom, the obstinacy and other affections due to darkness, we are often unable to recognize it". In order to identify the hidden truth that "lies in the deep", he relied on the testimony of those authors who, through the centuries, have unanimously confirmed that "the *jus gentium* is the law used by all human peoples, which was established by natural reason among all human beings and is observed by everyone equally; this is the natural law (*jus naturae*)". In other words, we have access to the *jus gentium* no longer by deducing it from the *jus divinum*, but because we can see it as part of the *jus naturae*, the contents of which we are able to conceive by means of natural reason.

Gentili's approach has two important consequences. With regard to the methodology of knowledge, it marks an important step on the path towards the emancipation of legal doctrine and political science from the subjection to theology, while maintaining the idea of a worldwide order that characterized the religiously-based universalism. With reference to the contents, Gentili's perspective raises the question of where the ontological and epistemological basis of the common rules of interaction, enshrined in natural law, should be located after the foundational role of the *jus divinum* has been dismissed. His first suggestion refers—as said above—to the common wisdom of classic authors. Yet, this kind of answer only elicits a second issue, concerning the reason why the classic authors should have developed convergent positions on the rules of worldwide interaction between peoples. Gentili's solution contoured—though only in a germinal shape—what was destined to become the classical *topos* of non-religiously-based holistic universalism with reference to the ontological and epistemological fundament of a worldwide order: "listen to the truth – he wrote – that the whole world is one body, and that all human beings are the limbs of that body, and that the world is a home and a commonwealth".[246] Therefore, the world in general and the humankind in particular constitute a *corpus* with *one* set of rules which is based, since the parts of a body have to work together in order to survive, on a shared feeling of belonging and organic solidarity.

Gentili's intuition of the common destiny of humanity was flawed by a substantial lack of coherence. Indeed, the metaphor of the "body" was applied sometimes to the whole world, sometimes to the humankind in its entirety and sometimes exclusively to individual political communities. Moreover, in this last meaning, the argument of the necessary defence of the social and political body's integrity was used in order to justify preemptive wars on grounds of utility (*utilis defensio*).[247] This aspect of Gentili's philosophy was surely due to the influence that Machiavelli had on him and was explicitly directed against the threat posed by the Turks to Christian countries and by the Spaniards to the Protestants communities.[248] Yet, since one-sided utility is hardly a reason for actions in a world that should have shared rules, Gentili's *De jure belli* happens to be trapped in a fundamental contradiction between the general spirit of universalism, in which it was written as an attempt to discover the principles of a non-religious world order, and the particularistic thrust of some of its passages. Anyway, both novelties introduced by Gentili—the decoupling of natural law from divine law, and the reference to the community of humankind as the ontological and epistemological fundament of universalism—were to be taken up slightly more than thirty-five years later and brought to higher consistency by the most important among the thinkers who founded modern international law, namely Hugo Grotius.[249]

In his *De Jure Belli ac Pacis*, published for the first time in 1625, Grotius defines natural law as "the rule and dictate of right reason, showing the moral deformity or moral necessity there is in any act, according to its suitableness or unsuitableness to a reasonable nature".[250] More specifically, a behaviour is good or bad not because God has commanded or forbidden it, but vice versa, God commands or forbids a behaviour as this is intrinsically good or bad. In this sense, the moral quality of an action is equally independent of the will of God as is the mathematical rule by which two and two cannot but make four.[251] Thus, Grotius completed the process begun by Gentili by definitively breaking the bonds that, following the Scholastic doctrine, made of natural law a recognizable derivation of the *lex divina*. According to his interpretation, natural law has to be seen as a secular and universal authority, since it possesses an independent validity claim and can be grasped without any reference to allegedly superior laws of a transcendent nature.[252] However, the decoupling of natural law from the God's eternal law also brought about a by-product which had been already addressed by Gentili, i.e., the loss of a solid basement for the construction of the normative edifice according to the commands of reason. In other words, from the ontological perspective, which is the entity from which the rules of natural law are to be developed? In the previous interpretation, it was God himself and his creation, but now? And, from the epistemological point of view, how can the truth content of natural law be guaranteed if the previous guarantor—once again, God himself—is dismissed? There are two possible solutions according to Grotius, the first of which is "more subtle and abstract", while the second is "more popular". Following the first solution, which is a so-called a priori demonstration, the correspondence of an action or omission to the commands of natural law is verified on the basis of its compliance with the "reasonable and sociable nature" of humans, so that natural law is ontologically and epistemologically founded on an assumption regarding human nature. In accordance with the second solution—the a posteriori proof that had already been adopted by Gentili—the correspondence between a certain action or omission and natural law is based on the exegetical reconstruction of what "is generally believed to be so [i.e., a command of natural law] by most or, at least, by the most civilized nations".[253]

The first way, i.e., the a priori proof, is doubtlessly the most ambitious. To provide this kind of proof, Grotius took up the Stoic theory of the twofold dimension of human nature. The first, which is common also to non-human animals, corresponds to the instinct of self-preservation: "the first duty of every one [of every living being] [is] to preserve himself in his natural state, to seek after those things which are agreeable to nature, and to avert those which are repugnant". The second dimension, which is essentially human—according to both the Stoics and Grotius, but probably not to our present sensibility and scientific knowledge[254]—consists in a "desire of society, that is, a certain inclination to live with those of [… the same] kind, not in any manner whatever, but peacefully, and in a community regulated according to the best of [… human] understanding".[255] In Grotius's understanding, this sort of natural "sociability" is what constitutes the basis of the organic belonging of each individual, first, to a specific polity and then to the international community. The law of the individual polity "arises from consent", the research of which is triggered by the instinct of sociability and not, like in the individualistic paradigm, by the interest in protecting the fundamental rights of the person.[256] On the other hand, "as the laws of each state respect the benefit of that state, so amongst all or most states there might be, and in fact there are, some laws agreed on by common consent, which respect the advantage not of one body in particular, but of all in general".[257] Thus, as the instinct of sociability urges human beings to come together and form a specific community, the very same driving force also leads states to adopt common norms and to respect them.

Nonetheless, an idea of international order which is grounded on the belief in the universal sociability of humans has to meet the challenge deriving from the empirical perception of the many acts of selfishness, aggression, violence and worse that characterize human interaction no less than the tendency to build social bonds. In other words, if unsocial behaviour is no less a trait of human nature than sociability, how reliable is a theory that takes into account only the latter and ignores the former? Grotius was aware of the problem to the extent that he introduced four arguments to strengthen the structure of his conceptual edifice. The first—and weakest—strategy consists in the threat of punishment for those who violate the rules. However, for social cohesion to prevail, there must be an a priori agreement on the necessity of rules, which justifies their establishment and guarantees their respect even if there is a reasonable opportunity to escape the penalty. Grotius's second argument underlines that the violation of laws—by individuals as well as states—in view of an immediate advantage may undermine the possibility of a relatively stable peace in the future, thus jeopardizing the achievement of a greater mid- or long-term advantage.[258] This justification is interesting because it is independent of any one-sided assumption as regards the anthropological nature of humans and their alleged tendency to sociability. Insofar as it presupposes only a rational ability to evaluate advantages and disadvantages, it seems to anticipate—to some extent—the rational foundation of natural law according to Hobbes as the initiator of the individualistic paradigm in its political version. This element, however, remains isolated in Grotius's overall argumentation and is not further developed. The third strategy relies on the presupposition that "justice brings peace to the conscience; injustice, racks and torments"—[259] from a disenchanted point of view more a wish than an observation. Indeed, even if we admitted that Grotius's hopeful consideration can be justified on the psychological level for a good part of humanity, nevertheless it would be difficult to establish a universally binding legal system on it. It is not by chance, thus, that Grotius moves on, still in the same paragraph, to a fourth strategy, that is, to the appeal to God who, as the "patron" of justice and the "enemy" of the wrongdoers, is invoked to ensure the fulfilment of the norms of natural law in the afterlife, but in many cases already in this world. By appealing to God, however, he returns precisely to that kind of religious justification that he had rejected in his initial definition.

Ultimately, none of the strategies put in place by Grotius to corroborate the a priori foundation of natural law is robust and convincing enough to accomplish the assigned task. As a result, there was no other way left for him but to finally opt for the a posteriori demonstration, so as to prove the factual existence of a *jus naturale* as a substrate of the *jus gentium* through authoritative witnesses. In fact, this was the privileged way for Grotius to deal with the various issues addressed in his work. Indeed, he explicitly recognized the centrality of historical testimony in its methodology: for the study of the law of nations, "eminent historians are of excellent use to us".[260] In conclusion, the re-interpretation of natural law in non-religious terms by Grotius represents an essential attempt at the dawn of modern legal and political thought. However, it remains unaccomplished, first of all, because of the substantial failure to find a consistent rational basis to the still holistic idea of an organic community now comprising all humans. Faced with these difficulties, Grotius went so far as to return to the divine guarantee of universal order, erasing hereby the most groundbreaking element of his philosophy. The second reason is that the prevailing method in Grotius's work, i.e., the citation and discussion of historical and cultural testimonies—which was extremely erudite in his case—belonged to a time which was drawing to a close.[261] Under these premises, it is not surprising that the later development of the natural law theory—at least in its theoretically most significant version—abandoned Grotius's organic vision and scholarly attitude, putting at the centre rather sceptical considerations of the most immediate forces that drive the individuals as the first and essential social actors and resorting to a methodology more characteristic of natural sciences than of historical research or legal doctrine. A courageous witness to the crisis of an entire era of political thought and an influential thinker who was able to address the issue of a universalism without religious prejudice, Grotius left it to others to propose more innovative and consistent solutions.

### 3.3.2 *Human Sociability and the Law of Nations*

Whereas Gentili and Grotius directly addressed in their writings the question of the relationship between natural law and divine law and formulated the reasons why the former should be emancipated from the latter, other authors took this emancipation for granted and elaborated well-structured and influential theories on social, political and legal order on its basis. In their works, we can see a thread of development of the rationalist variant of holistic universalism: from the cosmopolitan federalism of Johannes Althusius (3.3.2.1) to Samuel Pufendorf's idea that natural law can shape social order largely on its own (3.3.2.2), and then back to a more institutionalized form of the well-ordered society with Christian Wolff's *civitas maxima* (3.3.2.3). Each one of their visions has its own merits: no other author was more courageous than Althusius in conceiving a worldwide bottom-up idea of political power; Pufendorf's account of the different levels at which natural law can be applied to societal organization was unprecedented; and, finally, Wolff's very idea of an all-encompassing *civitas maxima* based on law is in itself one of the most daring and forward-looking achievements of the century of enlightenment and paved the way, to some extent, to Kant's vision of a cosmopolitan peace. However, each of them had also quite relevant shortcomings. More specifically, the ontological and epistemological fundament of their theories—namely the assumption of a general human tendency to sociability and, with the exception of Pufendorf, the familistic theory of society—was generally shaky. Thus, all of the three authors are examples of how fascinating political theory can be; yet, if we want to have a robust conceptual background for the implementation of the most advanced aspects of their theories, we have ultimately to look beyond their horizon.

*3.3.2.1 Johannes Althusius: Sociability and Universal Federalism*
The first author who conceived a universalistic system of political theory almost exclusively grounded on reason—even before the publication of Grotius's *De jure belli ac pacis*—was Johannes Althusius.[262] At the very beginning of his *Politica Methodice Digesta*, which was first published in 1603, he specified what the issue and the purpose of politics are:

> Politics is the art of associating humans for the purpose of establishing, cultivating, and conserving social life among them. Whence it is called 'symbiotics'.[263]

The social and political community is a "symbiosis" in the sense that its members live together in a spirit of solidarity, and is a *consociatio* because they do so on the basis of a covenant. Within the symbiosis, they share what is useful to the implementation of a good life, more specifically "things, services and common rights".[264] Yet, which is the reason why humans build a *consociatio*, an association among them? Althusius justified this tendency by resorting to their fundamental weakness. In fact, the goal of politics is the creation of a "holy, just, comfortable, and happy symbiosis". Nonetheless, at the time of birth, every human being is very far from reaching that goal. Rather, she or he is "destitute of all help, naked and defenceless, as if having lost all goods in a shipwreck".[265] As a result, human beings must seek the help of fellow humans simply to enhance their chances of survival, even before they try to improve, through a common effort, their life condition.

The first and most essential association is the family which is made of individuals "covenanting among themselves to communicate whatever is necessary and useful for organizing and living in private life".[266] A number of broader and more complex social unities are situated above the family, namely the "kinship" (*consociatio propinquorum*), the "collegium", which is an association of individuals united by the same interests, profession or way of life, the city, the province, and the "universal association" (*consociation universalis*) or "realm" (*regnum*). For a better understanding of the similarities and the differences between these associations, Althusius introduced two distinctions. The first is between natural and civil associations: the former, which include family and kinship, are characterized by the bond being based on affection or parentage; on the contrary, the latter, which comprise all other associations, are derived from free decisions which are not depending on feelings of attraction or belonging, but are related to questions concerning the organization of society at large. Althusius's second distinction is between private and public *consociationes*: while private associations only concentrate on the priorities of those who constitute them and are represented by them, public associations aim at "establishing an inclusive political power".[267] Despite the well-articulated differentiation of social forms, the natural family is defined as the "primary" association from which "all others derivate", since "without this primary association others are able neither to arise nor to endure".[268] Furthermore, Althusius states that the "public association exists when many private associations are linked together". In fact, "human society develops from private to public association by the definite steps and progressions of small societies".[269]

Thus, it is surely correct to say that his philosophy is essentially consistent with the familistic understanding of society.[270] However, as it is evident from the two distinctions, Althusius does not extend—like Bodin—the structure of the family to the analysis of the whole society in order to justify absolutism as the most natural form of public power. Quite to the contrary—and coherently with the Calvinist tradition of the self-organization of the community—he used the argument of the natural sociability of humans, and of their immediate need to unite in society because of their weakness, to give reasons for the creation of associations characterized by a bottom-up establishment of political power. "The people – he wrote – or the associated members of the realm have the power (*potestas*) of establishing this right of the realm and of binding themselves to it".[271] Therefore, "this right of the realm, or right of sovereignty (*majestas*), does not belong to the individual members, but to all members joined together and to the entire associated body of the realm".[272] Significantly, following Althusius, every association, from the smallest to the largest, is institutionalized by a covenant (*pactum*) insofar as "the symbiotes pledge themselves each to the other, by explicit or tacit agreement, to mutual communication of whatever is useful and necessary for the harmonious exercise of social life".[273] In other words, in order to exist, every *consociatio* must be grounded on the consent of its members, so that Althusius's organic interpretation of society does not justify—like in most exponents of the familistic theory of his time—the allegedly natural imbalance of power, but rather the original right of the community to constitute every kind of private and public authority. In this sense, he went the opposite way if compared to Bodin: while the defender of absolutism moved from the family to the state in order to establish also at the political level that kind of unrestrained power that traditionally distinguished the patriarchal authority, Althusius expanded to the family the necessity of an agreement between the members. Yet, while in civil associations consent is explicit and reflexive, in the case of natural communities it cannot but be implicit and spontaneous.

If the bottom-up understanding of political power is the first most characterizing and innovative element of Althusius's political theory, the second is the federalist structure of universalism. Indeed, the question of the extension of order appears, in Althusius's work, only indirectly. His attention, in fact, is more focused on the foundations of sovereign power than on the nature and feasibility of the *jus gentium*. Nonetheless, to the extent that the *summa potestas* is denied to the individual monarchs, his philosophy regards international order at least as a viable possibility.[274] Ultimately and at all stages of what he considered the rational institutionalization of political life, Althusius's purpose consisted in safeguarding the sovereignty of the "body of a universal association" (*corpus consociationis universalis*) as the rightful holder of authority according to divine and natural law.[275] While this approach negates, on the one hand, the legitimacy of a sovereignty *legibus soluta*, it does not set limits, on the other, to the extension of the *regnum*. Starting from the smallest natural community, political and legal self-organization proceeds—at least potentially—to frame the society until the most inclusive global level is achieved.

Despite its progressive attitude, Althusius's relationship to religion remains nevertheless ambiguous. Indeed, he emphasized to "have returned all merely theological, juridical, and philosophical elements to their proper places".[276] A true follower of the Calvinist doctrine, he could not but concede that human reason is unable to perform the deduction of human law from divine law. It follows that universal communication, which cannot be rationally deduced from the *lex aeterna*, must find a merely rational basis, without reference to theology. Quite in contrast to that, however, when he referred to the suprapositive law, he explicitly mentioned not only natural, but also divine law (*jus naturale et divinum*)—as if they were *one* body of laws. Furthermore, he explicitly asserted that "the right of the realm is twofold: it pertains both to the welfare of the soul and to the care of the body",[277] and reiterated that "if anyone would take [... the precepts of the Decalogue] out of politics, he would destroy it".[278] In a similar way to what will happen to Grotius a couple of decades later, he ultimately refrained from leading the secularization of politics to its last consequences.

### 3.3.2.2 Samuel Pufendorf: The Law of Nations as Pure Natural Law

Almost seventy years after the first edition of Althusius's most relevant contribution to the theory of political order, Samuel Pufendorf published his *De Jure Naturae et Gentium*, which was destined to mark a further major step in the history of holistic universalism. The first salient feature of Pufendorf's work if compared with his predecessor is that he begins his analysis of the forms of human society by describing the state of nature. This is not the "most perfect condition ultimately intended by nature as most suited for [... humans], but one into which we conceive [... them] placed by the mere fact of [... their] birth".[279] Focusing on the state of nature allows Pufendorf to identify the most essential traits of human condition and predispositions, which are taken, then, as the basis for a more scientifically founded understanding of society in all its features. With reference to this aspect, he follows the methodology of political philosophy introduced, thirty years earlier, by Thomas Hobbes. However, the similarities end with this initial assumption and—partially— with the rationalistic and analytic style of the argumentation, although this latter is much more traditionally filled with erudition in Pufendorf than in Hobbes. In fact, as regards the contents, throughout the whole work of the German Counselor of state no author has been targeted with more criticism than the British inventor of modern contractualism. A major difference emerges quite soon since it refers to the very conception of the state of nature which is, according to Pufendorf, a basically peaceful condition. On this point, therefore, his conception is nearer—at least at first glance—to Locke's vision of the original human condition. Yet, there is a significant divergence which is related to the reasons why humans should leave the state of nature. While following Locke it is mainly the fear that the original peaceful life could turn into a state of robbery, private retaliation and, ultimately, war, in Pufendorf's work, it is the indigence of non-socialized humans, or the necessity of a division of labour in order to improve their life conditions.[280] The first evidence, thus, is the natural weakness of humans:

> Besides this love of and eagerness to preserve himself by all means, we also find in man an extreme weakness and a natural neediness. Hence, if we were to conceive him as abandoned to himself in this world without any assistance from other men, his life could seem to have been given him as a punishment.[281]

The acknowledgement of the human fragility and limitedness leads, in a second step, to the necessity to move from the state of nature to a social bond built on division of labour and solidarity:

> Indeed, societies were introduced into the human race at the very beginning not in order to prevent a natural state from existing, but because humankind could otherwise not be increased and preserved.[282]

Both elements—human weakness and the necessity to establish social bonds—merge into the third essential characteristic of humankind, namely its sociability, which is described by Pufendorf as that "kind of disposition whereby a man is understood to be joined to every other man by ties of benevolence, peace, and charity, and therefore by a mutual obligation".[283] Though formulated in a slightly different way, we have here essentially the same argument that we already found in Althusius's work. As it is known, the foundation of society on the sociable tendency that derives from the recognition of our own inadequateness is a *topos* of holistic thought from Plato on—with reference to its particularistic variant—and starting with the Stoics as regards its universalistic understanding. Since Pufendorf made this *topos* to one of the main tenets of his political philosophy and—along with that—put a specific accent on duties as though they would be independent of rights,[284] we can reasonably maintain that his most adequate place in the history of ideas is to be sought—despite some concessions made to the methodology of inquiry inaugurated by Hobbes—among the exponents of the holistic interpretation of order.

Although sharing basically the same ideas on human nature, on why humans should build a society, and on the potential extension of this society—thus also advocating, on the whole, the same paradigm of order—Althusius and Pufendorf are divided, apart from the introduction of the fiction of the state of nature by the latter, by four further aspects. The first of these further differences—and the second in general—is related to the role attributed to the family. Indeed, Pufendorf maintained that "civil states [are] made up of lesser societies"[285] and even assumed that political sovereignty has its foundation in the authority of the husband over the wife.[286] Nonetheless, he broke with the tradition of the familistic understanding of society in a twofold sense. On the one hand, he introduced the natural society of the family not at the beginning of his enquiry, but only at a relatively advanced stage of it. In fact, although the family is presented as the first form of societal relation, its analysis is placed after what he called "the humankind's faculty over things",[287] which can be easily interpreted as a concession to that kind of individualism that was becoming the predominant pattern of social order. On the other hand, in no passage of his *De Jure Naturae et Gentium*, we can find the assumption that political society as a whole is the result of the merging of many families. Rather, if one considers how Pufendorf presented the origin of the state, the most evident impression is that it seems to be created not as an expansion of precisely the same driving force that led to the establishment of the family, but out of a specific necessity, in which the general tendency to sociability—which is present in both cases—is integrated and counterbalanced by the need "to surround themselves with defences against the evils threatening man from man".[288]

The third difference between Pufendorf and Althusius is that the reference to God—or, rather, to the Holy Scripture—is even more marginalized. In particular, no mention is made of God's commandments as the framework in which also the rules of society should be laid down. Instead, since law must be promulgated by some agent and natural law has not been created by humans, then there must be a God who is the author and guarantor of natural law.[289] In this sense, the mention of God in Pufendorf's political theory does not come into play with reference to the positive contents of the divine commands, but only as a kind of ontological foundation of rationality. The fourth distinctive element is that the consent that is required to legitimate political power is not critical and reflexive, but rather limited to the acknowledgement of the rationale that is inherent to the existing social and political relations. Indeed, "rules ... can exist ... only if they are recognized, understood, and accepted by those subject to them".[290] This is what Pufendorf defined as "the tacit intervention in the formation of states".[291] The fifth—and last—difference is that international order does not develop, as it was following Althusius, from self-conscious decisions taken by the members of the universal commonwealth, nor is it construed through essentially political institutions. Quite to the opposite, Pufendorf's *jus gentium* is exclusively natural law, confirmed by the implicit consent of the (allegedly civilized) peoples, but without any transposition into written law and lacking a consistent support by a political and legal framework.[292]

In conclusion, Pufendorf significantly contributed to the modernization of the holistic-universalistic paradigm of order, in particular by further secularizing its assumptions, by abandoning the familistic interpretation of society, as well as by strengthening the methodology and systematizing the presentation of the matter. However, he marked also a certain kind of regression. Indeed, his interpretation of consent was much less politically corrosive of the status quo and much more quietist than that of some of his Calvinist predecessors. Moreover, his idea of founding international order exclusively on the unwritten and non-political rules of natural law ultimately proved to be of little use when it came to the transition from the lofty spaces of abstract reason to the concrete implementation of an order of peace.

*3.3.2.3 Christian Wolff: The Apotheosis of the Civitas Maxima*
Pufendorf has been the most outstanding example of the crisis of the *jus gentium* after the breaking down of the two pillars that supported it in the philosophy of Scholasticism. Having acknowledged that first the emperor and then the pope could not justifiably claim to possess

universal authority, international order was doomed to be devoid of any institutional framework, be it political or legal. The only possible consequence was that it had to be based solely on the commands of the law of reason—which is precisely the idea that Pufendorf brought to completion. Two generations later, it was the task of Christian Wolff to reassert that the *jus gentium*—and international order—must be different from, and more specific than, the mere prescriptions of natural law.[293] Indeed, although Pufendorf introduced into his work treaties as a component of the *jus gentium*, he limited their significance to the extent that they were supposed only to settle rather marginal bilateral disputes or to fix, in most cases, the contents that were already implicit in natural law.[294] To the contrary, Wolff distinguished precisely between four different kinds of *jus* which constitute, if taken as a whole, the body of international law.[295] These kinds of law are, first, the natural or necessary law of nations (*jus gentium naturale vel necessarium*), which is "nothing except the law of nature applied to nations".[296] Secondly, we have the "voluntary law of nations" (*jus gentium volontarium*), which is the law of nations that is assumed to derive from their will, on the basis of natural law, and to be valid vis-à-vis the whole community of states. In this sense, it is comparable to state law, which is analogously drawn from the same source of natural law, but with reference to the body of laws of the individual political community.[297] The third component of the *jus gentium* is treaty or "stipulative law" (*jus gentium pacititium*), i.e., the law that "arises from stipulations entered into between different nations" in order to settle their specific issues.[298] The last element of *jus gentium* is the customary international law (*jus gentium consuetudinarium*), which "has been brought in by long usage and observed as law" and is presumed to be based on a tacit agreement.[299] While the first component of the *jus gentium* is suprapositive, the further three are explicitly positive law, and it is evident that they build the bulk of what had to be regarded, following Wolff, as the *corpus* of international law.

In fact, according to Wolff—and on this point there is no difference between his conception and those of the Scholastic philosophers, as well as of Grotius, Althusius or Pufendorf—natural law makes up the foundation of any kind of positive law. However, this means only that no positive law is legitimate if it is in conflict with natural law, but not that positive law should be seen as nothing but a transcription of natural law. We see, here, a clear shifting of accent, if compared to Pufendorf, from the almost absolute centrality of natural law to more attention to the positive dimension of norms, almost to some kind of early positivism. Indeed,

> far be it from you to think – Wolff wrote – that ... there is no need of our discussing in detail the law of nations. For the principles of the law of nature are one thing, but the application of them to nations another, and this produces a certain diversity in that which is inferred, insofar as the nature of a nation is not the same as human nature.[300]

To some extent, thus, Wolff brought the idea of universalistic order away from the supremacy of natural law and back to its former stage in which—during the time of medieval and Catholic Scholasticism—the norms of natural law were supposed to be supported by a robust legal framework, first centred on the empire and on the papacy, and then, after the power of the empire had collapsed, at least on the moral and legal authority of the pope. Yet, in Wolff's world, no universal authority is reasonably assumed to exist, or even to be a desirable perspective. Therefore, the positive framework that should implement world order has, first, essentially a *legal* character and, secondly, is created and realized on the basis of *consent*[301] by *morally equal* nations, which are like "individual free persons living in a state of nature".[302] Indeed, according to Wolff, the most fundamental command of natural law with regard to international order is that "all nations are equal the one to the other" in the same way in which individuals are morally and legally equal in the single political community.[303] As a result, he understood the *jus gentium* "as the law between states as legal persons".[304]

In Wolff's perspective, the morally and legally equal states come together to build a community based on legal norms which he defines as the *civitas maxima*. The concept of the *civitas maxima*—or of the "supreme state", as it is often translated—is, along with the turn to legal positivism, the second major achievement of Wolff's political philosophy.[305] With regard to this concept, to the development of which Wolff gave his decisive contribution,[306] the questions arise, firstly, as to how the community of states is established, and, secondly, how it can take legitimate decisions. The first question can be best answered if we keep in mind that the *civitas maxima* is made up of equal and originally sovereign states,[307] so that a treaty between them can only be legitimate if founded on a general agreement of all involved polities. However, as it is impossible to expect that all nations gather together in a single place to stipulate the agreement, the foundational treaty of the *civitas maxima* must be fictitious.[308] In other words, we have to reasonably assume that a community of all nations has been built on natural law and on their common consent—or at least on the consent of those nations which, in accordance with the usual discrimination, are deemed "civilized".[309] Yet, an agreement that is only fictitious is a rather weak fundament for a community: since it lacks a legal document, it must rely on something different, i.e., on an ontological foundation that justifies the presumption that the agreement, though not positively stipulated, should nonetheless be regarded as existent and binding. Basically, this is the problem that all supporters of suprapositive law have to address and solve. Wolff's first reference is, as we have already seen, natural law. But what is the content of natural law which should substantiate the presumption that all nations must come together? At this point, Wolff introduced the usual argument of the rationalistic variant of holistic universalism, namely the universal sociability of humans.[310] However, he made here also a step backwards in the history of political philosophy: in order to make his case for universal association more powerful, he added the idea—in his time already quite old-fashioned—of the familistic origin of all political institutions.[311]

Summing up, Wolff's idea of a worldwide order arose as a compromise between three elements: the most traditional *topos* of holistic universalism in its rationalistic variant—i.e., the assumption of the universal sociability of humans—; a rather conservative setback, such as the revival of the familistic theory of society; and the requests arising from the intellectual atmosphere of the century of enlightenment, to which the substantial abandonment of erudition and, in general, the methodology of his work belong. Nevertheless, the result is hardly convincing. Especially the project of the *civitas maxima* turns out to be rather thin: indeed, the option for legal positivism as the core of social order is half-hearted and the contents of the universal agreement are so meagre that more effort is dedicated by Wolff to the discussion of the justifications of war and to the *jus in bello* than to the conditions that should guarantee peace.[312] But it is with reference to the foundation of universalism that the proposed solution is not only particularly unsatisfying today, but was already a kind of cul-de-sac during Wolff's lifetime: in times of rising individualism, the appeal to a universal solidarity founded on an allegedly natural sentiment of social belonging seemed—and seems—to be wishful thinking. In fact, for the whole seventeenth century as well as for the following centuries, the main task of the supporters of the idea of a worldwide order was to reconcile it with the priority of individual rights and freedom, and not to back it with a one-sided anthropology. On the other hand, when faced with the return of holistic particularism in the shape of an aggressive nationalism during the eighteenth century and the first half of the nineteenth century, an optimistic anthropology that hoped for the rule of reason and humanity seemed to be for long time on the losing side.

### 3.3.3  The New Natural Law

The period after World War II was characterized, however, by a sudden and strong revival of natural law. This is not surprising insofar as both concurring paradigms which had dominated the way in which social, political and legal order was understood between the second half of the eighteenth century and the beginning of the twentieth century— i.e., holistic particularism and individualistic universalism—had fallen into a deep crisis. As regards the first, it had been held responsible, with good reasons, for the horrors of two world wars, while the second—in particular because of its non-value-based and individualistic attitude as well as of its unrestrained and maybe too optimistic trust in the power of (legal) norms—had proved uncapable of stopping the breakdown of Western civilization in the first half of the twentieth century.[313] As the result of the decadence of the competing paradigms, holistic universalism came to the fore again since it seemed to provide a more objective and unshakable foundation for civilization and humanity. The most significant philosophical movement that was born from the attempt to rediscover natural law was the Grisez School, so named because of Germain Grisez, its founder and one of its most outstanding exponents. The New Natural Law movement—which comprised, along with Grisez, other significant thinkers, mainly exponents of the conservative wing of the anglophone Catholic Church, like John Finnis, Joseph Boyle and Robert P. George— has essentially tried to restate natural law in a way that should overcome its shortcomings and overrule the previous criticism against it.[314]

The first step for a consolidation of the theory of natural law was the rejection of naturalistic fallacy. We speak of "naturalistic fallacy" when a theory of action attempts to deduct an "ought" (*Sollen*) from an "is" (*Sein*), or claims the correctness of *immediately* deriving the content of a decision concerning the use of practical reason from evidences regarding the outside world. On that basis, resolutions concerning the use of practical reason would originate almost directly or "naturally" from a true knowledge of the objective reality, without any necessity to stress the specificity of practical reasoning. In the field of ethics, this approach is considered unacceptable to the extent that, if it is true that we need a knowledge as accurate as possible of the objective reality in order to take a justifiable decision, on the other hand that knowledge is hardly ever so univocal that no problems of choice would arise. Furthermore, even if the evidence is unequivocal, the very nature of objective knowledge does not relieve practical reason from its proper task of opting for one hypothesis of action or another. In other words, there is a logical gap between knowledge and action that should be acknowledged and properly taken into account. The option in favour of a certain action can be justified, then, by resorting to quite different criteria—for instance, prudential or deontological claims—but all of them are characteristic of practical reasoning anyway.

The historical doctrine of natural law was strongly suspected of naturalistic fallacy due to the close relationship established between the *jus* and the objective truth of a nature understood as part of the creation. The exponents of New Natural Law acknowledge that a moral theory cannot be based directly on some form of ontology, but also deny that the reference to the naturalistic fallacy could be justifiably applied to their approach.[315] Indeed, whereas the exponents of the Grisez School reject the idea that moral norms can be drawn from an "is" or an external objective entity conceived in naturalistic terms, a similar deduction becomes possible "if the *is* expresses a truth about a reality which embodies a moral norm".[316] In other words, if the "is" or the outside non-subjective entity includes an ethical dimension—as it was, just to give two examples, in the metaphysics of Aristotle and Hegel—then it will be possible to deduce norms concerning the use of practical reason from it, without falling into naturalistic fallacy. In this case, according to the interpretation of New Natural Law, the "is" is not conceived in the same terms in which natural sciences understand the outside world, namely as a measurable, simply objective and value-free entity. However, even if we admitted that it is possible, in such a way, to circumvent the shortcoming of naturalistic fallacy, the essential problem at its basis would persist nonetheless. The foundation of morals on the findings of natural sciences, which is targeted by the criticism against naturalistic fallacy, is in fact only one variant of a broader conception, which we could define as a *substantialist* understanding of the use of practical reason. According to this view, it is always the access to a *substantial and objective truth*—regardless of whether this substance is defined in naturalistic, ontological-metaphysical or religious terms—that validates the practical choice. Therefore, it is not the knowing subject that draws from herself or himself—or from his relationship with other subjects—the rational justification of his actions; rather, it is the knowledge of an external and objective truth that should lead us to the right decision. If the alleged objective truth is not understood in naturalistic terms, then the above-described fallacy may be avoided. What is not overcome hereby, yet, are the general problems of every kind of ethical substantialism, in particular its difficulty in being supported by evidence and the idiosyncratic character of the choice of the principles on which every action (or omission) should be based.

Even though New Natural Law should be assumed to become a "theory of practical reasonableness" in which nature is actually "hidden",[317] it is nevertheless imbued with substantialism—just as it is affected with all the problems that usually come along with it. This aspect becomes quite evident when the core questions are addressed of how to define an ethically right action and of which content it should have. Following the definition given by Grisez, Boyle and Finnis, "moral truths direct free choices towards actions which tend to satisfy natural desires".[318] That means that human action, if properly guided, must be oriented towards the satisfaction of desires that are assumed to be natural, and therefore true. In other words, human action is morally right when desires possess the specific quality of a "true" naturalness. Yet, not all our desires have such a quality. The decision with regard to which desires are "truly" natural is articulated in two steps. The first consists in a simple refusal to regress indefinitely in the search for the motivations of action. In fact, when we decide to act, we justify this choice by indicating a good that we want to achieve by performing the action. Not always, however, the indicated good truly represents the ultimate reason for our action: in many cases, it is rather an intermediate step, which refers to the pursuit of an even more important good. The regress to infinity can be interrupted only by postulating the existence of "basic goods", namely of goods that "are known as ultimate rational grounds … for proposing actions to be done for certain benefits".[319] Hence, "basic goods" are characterized by the fact of being absolutely *fundamental* and by needing no other reason to justify an action: they are ends in themselves and not instruments to achieve something else. However, the choice of the "basic goods" cannot only be motivated by the need to avoid infinite regress. There must be something more—which makes up the second step of the search for the ultimate goods—namely the identification of a substantial criterion that can explain why the search must stop at one specific good, and not at another. The Grisez School essentially indicates seven basic goods[320]: (a) the protection of life and its transmission; (b) knowledge and aesthetic experience; (c) excellence in work; (d) harmony between and among individuals and groups of people; (e) harmony between the different dimensions of the Self; (f) harmony between the dimensions of the Self and the actions that are performed; and (g) harmony with the more-than-human source of meaning and values.

It is almost superfluous to emphasize the deficits of this list. First of all, it is not clear why "basic goods" should be just these: others could be added, or we could search for even more essential ones.[321] For instance, why should human activity not aim at attaining freedom? Or at realizing justice? And why should harmony be more "basic" than individual self-affirmation? The supporters of New Natural Law preempted this criticism by asserting that "basic goods" would be self-evident. Yet, this assertion is itself far from self-evident.[322] Indeed, the exponents of the Grisez School do not simply identify some inescapable qualities of human (and, to some extent, even not only human) experience, such as the use of reason, which already comes into play at the very moment that we ask ourselves whether we are capable of rational thinking; or the capacity to feel pain and pleasure, which belongs to the most essential endowments of all complex living beings; or, finally, the faculty to interact with our fellow humans and with some non-human animals. All these features are highly general and abstract, so that no specific content of human action and interaction is implied; in fact, the authors who abide by an only transcendental definition of the essentials of human action and interaction assume that more specific contents of that action and interaction can only develop as a result of the concrete display of its general and abstract features. To the contrary, the exponents of the Grisez School go a long step further insofar as they fix the presupposed contents of human nature in a way that is much more substantial than it could be expected from the definition of a transcendental a priori principle. For instance, the whole wealth of knowledge and aesthetic experience, to the extent that it is transmitted as a specific "cultural heritage",[323] is something quite different from the very *capacity* to know and feel. Moreover, the assumption of an all-encompassing harmony, that should only be detected and preserved, is no less clearly distinct from the transcendental disposition to intersubjective communication. Finally, compliance with some kind of transcendent source of meaning is definitely at odds with any form of reflexive thinking. As a result, the philosophy of New Natural Law identifies, as the fundament of ethics, a conception of human nature and the good life that is to a significant extent predefined and, in general, hardly deducible even from the already broadly interpreted axioms laid down as the starting point of the analysis. In fact, a being that essentially aims at living in harmony with God and the world is a much more substantial image of what should be desirable than the abstract idea that humans are purely rational and sensitive creatures.

However, if the vision of the essence of humanity and of the good life is significantly thicker than generally shareable transcendental assumptions, then the moral theory of the New Natural Law movement ends up being basically a principled stance in favour of a certain metaphysical understanding of the human condition, actually lacking proper foundation. Thus, it is not really surprising that, faced with the difficulty to find an adequate justification for the substantial contents of its moral theory, the exponents of the New Natural Law movement ultimately re-propose the most classic solution which has been developed by the holistic-universalistic paradigm of order to substantiate its idea of the well-ordered society, namely they resort to theological arguments and to God. According to Finnis—as it was already for the Stoics—human life only finds true meaning in the divine order of the cosmos.[324] Thus, in the perspective of the Grisez School, God carries out the function as the guarantor for the ultimate ontological justification of ethical principles or as the "transcendent source of meaning and value",[325] and—more generally—as the metaphysical reason for "the *is* of what is *but need not be*".[326] By reintroducing the cosmological-ontological evidence of the existence of God, the Grisez School brings the philosophical–theological discussion exactly back to the point where it was before Kant's criticism in the *Kritik der reinen Vernunft* (*Critique of Pure Reason*).[327] Yet, there is no reason to believe that Kant's arguments are less justified today than at the time when they were published. Therefore, what Hans Kelsen claimed with reference to the natural law theorists until the beginning of the twentieth century[328] is confirmed also by the more recent exponents of this philosophical strand, namely that natural law theory, if it is not to collapse, must rely on a transcendent power.[329] On the basis of the evidence collected in more than two thousand years of history, this result seems to be inescapable with regard to the substantialist-ontological variant of natural law, whereas this criticism cannot apply to those forms of suprapositive normative systems—such as Kant's philosophy and the communicative paradigm—that only refer to transcendental preconditions of knowledge and action.

The reference to God's authority is an essential component of one strand of holistic universalism and a kind of argumentative last resort for the other. Therefore, it comes as no surprise that it is also referred to in the works of the Grisez School. Nor do they fail to include some hints to the second, no less fundamental justification of holistic universalism, i.e., the assumption of the existence of a universal community comprising all human beings. In fact, since it is claimed that basic goods are incommensurable with each other, so that no hierarchy can be established among them, it follows that, if there is conflict, only an arbitrary decision could tip the scales in some direction. Or, if we want to avoid the trap of arbitrary decision-making, it is necessary to refer to a good the content of which is part of all of them and the superiority of which should be immediately visible.[330] If we look at the list of basic goods identified by the Grisez School, we see that "harmony" is mentioned with regard to as many as four of the goods indicated. Even though it is not explicitly stated by the authors, it seems evident that "harmony" is the only value that can take on the task of being the overlapping element that brings together and clarifies all basic goods. Many evidences of this are disseminated by the authors of the Grisez School throughout their analysis. Not only harmony in human relations is unequivocally defined as a good,[331] but moral truth is also conceived of as the highest possible degree of achievement of all basic goods by all human beings.[332] This kind of achievement corresponds ultimately to the morally appropriate self-fulfilment of human beings in both their qualities, i.e., as individuals and as *members of a community*:

> So, although integral human fulfillment is an unrealizable ideal, there is a sense in which it can be considered the morally true ultimate natural end of persons, both as individuals and in community.[333]

On the other hand, the bad and immoral will is largely identified with a selfish attitude.[334] And, finally, the list of basic goods can be justified, once the shaky theological-metaphysical foundation has been ascertained, also through the reference to a hypothetical consensus of all human societies—in fact one more hint about an all-encompassing harmony and a classic *topos* of a large part of the tradition of natural law.[335]

The definition of the highest good as a common good to all human beings gives necessarily rise to the idea of the universal community of humans, understood as the highest possible synthesis of ethical worth and social order based on reason: "is not such a perfect community – Grisez, Boyle and Finnis ask – the ultimate natural end of all human persons and communities?"[336] However, the community of all communities—which is defined by the authors of the Grisez School as an "ideal"—[337] is not, in their view, something to be built up as the result of a non-prejudiced and postmetaphysical exchange of arguments, based on the faith in human capacity to find rational and inclusive solutions. Rather, it is conceived of as a matter of fact, as an already existing ontological reality, grounded on the "true" nature of human beings, which is only to be discovered and fulfilled. Because, according to the theory of New Natural Law, the ideal condition of a global harmony is ultimately justified by resorting to metaphysics, its exponents' option in favour of global order depends, in the end, on the assumption that a "worldwide human community exists which shares essential values and interests". Yet, precisely such an assumption is characterized by a highly uncertain truth content. Nonetheless, before I focus on the criticism against the deficits of this approach, which has been an essential pillar of holistic universalism as a whole, it must be remembered that it has also been used as a fundamental justification of the option for global order by one of the most influential recent strands of international law scholarship, i.e., by the supporters of the so-called theory of the constitutionalization of international law. Before criticism is addressed, it is thus appropriate to concentrate briefly on this ambitious transfer of the idea of a worldwide human community grounded on a supposedly self-evident assumption from the philosophical level to the more practical domain of legal theory.

### 3.3.4 The Constitutionalization of International Law

The idea that the international community possesses a kind of constitution *sui generis* was introduced into the debate by Alfred Verdross. The starting point of Verdross's considerations is to be found in his criticism of some aspects of Kelsen's conception of the legal system. Although Verdross largely endorsed Kelsen's monistic approach as well as the priority assigned to international law within the hierarchical legal system,[338] he was sceptical about the content that Kelsen gave to the concept of *Grundnorm*. Verdross substantially accepted the idea of the

*Grundnorm* as the basis of a unitary and hierarchically organized legal system,[339] but rejected its formalistic interpretation as it had been elaborated by the doctrine of legal positivism: a merely formalistic principle can justify the formal validity of the legal norms as an "ought", a *Sein-Sollendes*, but cannot give us any arguments about its "objective validity". Indeed, Kelsen's positivistic *Grundnorm*, which is originally empty, is eventually filled with nothing more than the effectiveness of power. In order to avoid swinging between empty formalism and crude power, which can account for our factual respect for the law but not for the reasons why this respect should be seen as *legitimate and just*, Verdross claimed that the *Grundnorm* needs to be traced back to objective values.[340] The *Grundnorm* should be identified, therefore, with an objective principle that pre-exists individuals as well as their political and legal institutions, i.e., with an idea of a cosmic order as it had been conceived by the legal philosophy of natural law.[341]

In Verdross's interpretation, the reference to the *corpus universale* of humankind is actually a corollary of a broader pantheistic conception of cosmic order as the basis of moral and legal norms—a conception originally inspired by Plato's[342] and Hegel's[343] metaphysics. In the decades following the publication of Verdross's seminal work, the authors who supported the possibility and desirability of the constitutionalization of international law[344] progressively cleared their proposal from the pantheistic elements of Verdross's conception while still maintaining an at least implicit resort to natural law as the fundamental criterion for the objective validity of the legal system and as the justification of an international law aiming at cooperation and solidarity. Furthermore, they have attached more importance again to the role played by individual states within the general context of the legally organized international community. Finally, they have specified the contents of what is assumed to be the "common law of mankind",[345] i.e., of that part of international law which, regardless of whether treaty or customary law, is regarded as "constitutionalized" to the extent that it is expected to be valid not only for the parties involved vis-à-vis, but for the whole humankind. With reference to this latter aspect, after World War II the legal dimension of the "constitution of humankind" was established in particular through the discipline of the obligations *erga omnes*, on the basis either of the UN Charter or of the theory of *jus cogens*. According to Christian Tomuschat, one of the major exponents of the theory of the constitutionalization of international law, supra-state international law is considered to be "constitutional" insofar as it takes on three main features of historical constitutionalism. The first aspect is the centrality of the individuals and of their rights.[346] The second feature is the increasing inclusion into international law treaties of references to values, like democracy and the rule of law, which should serve as a foundation for a well-ordered international community.[347] The third element is the establishment of a germinal division of powers within the system of international organization, whereas the focus is concentrated in particular on the creation of an ever more powerful international judicial power.[348] A more formal approach to the constitutionalization of international law underlines rather the function of the UN Charter at the top of the hierarchy of the legal instruments of international law.[349]

As regards the recognition of the role of individual states within the "constitutionalized" international community, following Tomuschat, states must be still regarded as the most important actors of international law,[350] although—contrary to what the pre-Kelsenian tradition of international law scholarship claimed—further subjects, such as suprastate institutions, international organizations, courts and, last but not least, individuals and NGOs, have also to be recognized as autonomous agents.[351] Yet, a state has a legitimate claim to exercise its public power only if it respects the international legal framework and guarantees peace and security.[352] The third characteristic of the contemporary theory of the constitutionalization of international law—as mentioned above—is the rejection of Verdross's original metaphysical and pantheistic assumptions with regard to the content of the *Grundnorm* as the founding element of the global validity of international law. Though unquestionably justified, this rejection also had the consequence of leaving the assumption of a universal community of humankind once again as the main—if not the only—pillar to support the entire legal system with international law at its top. Indeed, Tomuschat defines the international community as "an ensemble of rules, procedures and mechanisms designed to protect collective interests of humankind, based on a perception of commonly shared values".[353] Against this background, international law—or, at least, the most general part of it—is the legal expression of the activity of the international community and the most striking evidence of its existence. In other words, international law arises as the formalization of shared values as well as of the rules that guarantee the protection of common interests:

> like a people – Tomuschat claims – which through the process of establishing its political constitution reaches agreement on a set of basic values

which should determine the general course of the common journey into the future, the nations of the world, too, need a set of shared values in order for them to be classified as an international community.[354]

However, unlike the constitutional rules of individual states, the common values enshrined in international law are not essentially the result of deliberative and inclusive processes, but are, rather, already present *in re* as an objective fact of reason. The rational observer simply has to recognize them, international law has to assume and formalize them, and international adjudication has to make them effective. The international community, therefore, is not something which is yet to be created—like, for instance, in the perspective of the communicative paradigm—but is a previously existing ontological reality, characterized by common values and interests.[355] From this point of view, having assumed access to a kind of ontological truth, it is not surprising that the exponents of the theory of the international community dedicate little interest to deliberative processes due to determinate common rules as well as to the conditions of legitimacy of such rules, and prefer to concentrate on the role of international tribunals as the interpreters and executors of an objective principle of justice.

Serious criticism has been raised against the theory of the constitutionalization of international law. In fact, the alleged division of powers within the system of international organization is at best incomplete since the UN Security Council holds both the legislative and the executive competences. Moreover, the UN Charter is far from having the same hierarchical position generally recognized to constitutions in national systems and the authority of supra-state international law is often contested. Lastly, the rule of law is constantly threatened by the display of power.[356] Besides these critiques, however, the most significant deficit is related to the assertion that "a universal human community exists which shares fundamental interests and values". Since this assumption builds the backbone of the holistic-universalistic paradigm of order from its very beginning, it is now time—at the end of the analysis of this paradigm—to raise the question of the truth content of such a claim. In assessing its ontological and epistemological quality, it has to be pointed out, first, that the proposition cannot correspond to any kind of *analytic judgement* because the assertions that such a community exists, as well as that any such community shares values and interests, are not originally contained in the subject of the proposition. Thus, the proposition must be a *synthetic judgement*, aimed at reaching some knowledge of the world on which the whole *corpus juris* of a constitutionalized global order is ultimately based. Furthermore, the judgement is a priori because it aims at building assertions that are necessary and universally valid. Yet, from a post-metaphysical approach, a synthetic a priori judgement—i.e., a proposition that makes an assertion of necessary and universal validity and claims to improve our knowledge of the world—can be acceptable only if it is based on empirical evidence about phenomena. Furthermore, the proposition, relying upon empirical evidence, must be falsifiable, i.e., it must be open to correction as a consequence of new empirical data about phenomena which may be incompatible with the previous assertion. Yet, the assertion that "a universal human community exists which shares fundamental interests and values" does not satisfy either of the above-mentioned consistency conditions. Indeed, empirical evidence of such a universal human community is rather controversial—the realistic assumption of a permanent struggle for survival between human communities reveals significant evidence to the contrary—and the assertion, not being based on empirical evidence, cannot be falsified either. On these terms, the argument for the existence of a universal human community turns out to be the result of the quasi-metaphysical ontologization of a transcendental capacity with which all humans are endowed, namely the faculty to interact communicatively with each other. In other words, the theory of the international community seems to draw from the transcendental capacity to interact and to search for consensus in a communicative way a presumed ontological fact that actually lacks proper evidence. From a post-metaphysical perspective, the universal human community is something to be created and a task to be accomplished, not a reality to be simply discovered. The existence of the transcendental capacity of universal communication gives us the hope necessary to succeed in the ambitious purpose of construing a universal community of all human beings; an ontological certainty is, nonetheless, out of our reach.

In conclusion, the most essential pillar on which the whole construction of holistic universalism is based seems to be of poor ontological and epistemological quality. Surely, we are living in a time in which the hope for a global order of justice and freedom under the rule of an inclusive legal system is hampered by a lot more—and more powerful—obstacles than just epistemological inconsistency. Yet, as we have already seen, paradigms come and go, so that the hope is not out of this world that one day in the future the idea that humans can come together in order to rationally address the problems that they all share will come to the fore again and become once more the most urgent goal of the political agenda. And for that time we need an intellectually sound justification. Indeed, ideas require surely much more than a robust truth content to be implemented, but, if they do not have truth in themselves, they will never develop into good realities.

## NOTES

1. Dante Alighieri, *Divina Commedia* (1306–1321), "Paradiso", Canto XXXIII, Petrocchi Edition, Columbia University Libraries, New York (NY) 2017, https://digitaldante.columbia.edu/dante/divine-comedy/paradiso/paradiso-33/, 82–93 (English translation by Allen Mandelbaum and Henry Wadsworth Longfellow).
2. Teodolinda Barolini, *"Paradiso 33: Invisible Ink"*, Commento Baroliniano, Digital Dante, Columbia University Libraries, New York (NY) 2017, https://digitaldante.columbia.edu/dante/divine-comedy/paradiso/paradiso-33/.
3. Dante, *Divina Commedia*, *supra* note i, "Paradiso", Canto XXXIII, 142–145.
4. Plato, *Symposium*, Benjamin Jowett trans., Cambridge University Press, Cambridge/New York 1980, 189d et seq.
5. Rebecca Redwood French, Mark A. Nathan (eds.), *Buddhism and Law*, Cambridge University Press, Cambridge/New York 2014, at 4.
6. Otfried Höffe, *Demokratie im Zeitalter der Globalisierung*, Beck, München 2002 (1st ed. 1999), at 234 (English translation by Dirk Haubrich and Michael Ludwig: *Democracy in an Age of Globalization*, Springer, Dordrecht 2007, at 162); Ernst-Wolfgang Böckenförde, *Geschichte der Rechts- und Staatsphilosophie. Antike und Mittelalter*, Mohr Siebeck, Tübingen 2002, at 40 et seq.
7. Hermann Diels, Walther Kranz (eds.), *Die Fragmente der Vorsokratiker*, Weidmannsche Buchhandlung 1958 (1st ed. 1903), 68 B 247.
8. Ibid., 87 B 44.
9. Ibid., 22 B 114.
10. Aristotle, *Politics*, H. Rackham trans., Harvard University Press, Cambridge (MA) 1959, Book I, Chapter 1, 1253a et seq., at 8 et seq.
11. Diels/Kranz, *Die Fragmente der Vorsokratiker*, *supra* note 7, 22 B 53.
12. Peter Coulmas, *Weltbürger. Geschichte einer Menschheitssehnsucht*, Rowohlt, Reinbek 1990, at 113 et seq.
13. Böckenförde, *Geschichte der Rechts- und Staatsphilosophie. Antike und Mittelalter*, *supra* note 6, at 132.

14. Johannes von Arnim, *Stoicorum veterum fragmenta*, Teubneri, Lipsiae 1903–1905, Vol. I, at 85.
15. Ibid., Vol. I, at 98.
16. Ibid., Vol. III, at 323.
17. Ibid., Vol. III, at 4.
18. Ibid., Vol. III, at 314.
19. Marcus Tullius Cicero, *De re publica* (51 B.C.E.), Book III, para. 33, at 71 (English translation by James E. G. Zetzel, Cambridge University Press, Cambridge/New York 1999).
20. Diogenes Laertius, *Vitae philosophorum*, Clarendon, Oxford 1964, Book VI, at 63.
21. Martha C. Nussbaum, *Kant and Stoic Cosmopolitanism*, in: "The Journal of Political Philosophy", Vol. 5 (1997), 1–25.
22. Arnim, *Stoicorum veterum fragmenta*, *supra* note 14, Vol. I, at 259 et seq.
23. Böckenförde, *Geschichte der Rechts- und Staatsphilosophie. Antike und Mittelalter*, *supra* note 6, at 141 et seq.
24. Lucius Annaeus Seneca, *De vita beata*, Book XX (English translation by Aubrey Stewart, Bell, London 1900).
25. *The Holy Bible, New Testament*, Matthew, Chapter 28, para. 19; Acts, Chapter 2.
26. Aurelius Augustinus, *De civitate Dei* (413–426), Moretus, Antverpiae 1600, Book XV, Chapter 1 (English translation by Philip Schaff, The Christian Literature Publishing Co., New York 1890, at 284).
27. Ibid.
28. Ibid., Book XIV, Chapter 28 (Engl.: at 282 et seq.).
29. Ibid., Book XV, Chapter 4 (Engl.: at 286).
30. Ibid. (Engl.: at 286).
31. Ibid., Book XIX, Chapter 13 (Engl.: at 409).
32. Ibid.
33. Ibid.
34. Ibid.
35. Ibid., Book I, Chapter 1 et seq. (Engl.: at 1 et seq.).
36. Ibid., Book XXII, Chapter 30 (Engl.: at 509 et seq.).
37. *The Holy Bible, New Testament*, John, Chapter 18, para. 36.
38. Augustinus, *De civitate Dei*, *supra* note 26, Book XIV, Chapter 28 (Engl.: at 282 et seq.).
39. Ibid., Book IV, Chapter 6 (Engl.: at 67).
40. Ibid., Book XV, Chapter 4 (Engl.: at 286).
41. Ibid., Book XV, Chapter 5 (Engl.: at 287).
42. Ibid., Book XIX, Chapter 26 (Engl.: at 419).
43. Wilhelm Grewe, *Epochen der Völkerrechtsgeschichte*, Nomos, Baden-Baden 1984, at 60.

44. Ibid., at 61.
45. Azo, *Die Quaestiones des Azo*, Ernst Landsberg ed., Mohr-Siebeck, Freiburg 1888, at 87.
46. Jean Rivière, *Sur l'origine del la formule juridique: "Rex imperator in regno suo"*, in: "Revue des Sciences Religieuses", Vol. 4 (1924), 580–586.
47. Dante Alighieri, *De Monarchia* (1310–1314), in: Dante Alighieri, *Opere minori*, Vol. II, Utet, Torino 1986, Book I, Chapter II (English translation by Prue Shaw, in: Dante Alighieri, *Monarchy*, Cambridge University Press, Cambridge/New York 1996, at 4).
48. Ibid., Book I, Chapter IV (Engl.: at 8).
49. Ibid.
50. Ibid., Book I, Chapter XI (Engl.: at 15 et seq.).
51. Ibid., Book I, Chapter XII (Engl.: at 19 et seq.).
52. Immanuel Kant, *Zum ewigen Frieden. Ein philosophischer Entwurf*, in: Immanuel Kant, *Werkausgabe*, Wilhelm Weischedel ed., Suhrkamp, Frankfurt a. M. 1977, Vol. IX, 193–251, at 225 et seq. (English translation by H. B. Nisbet: *Perpetual Peace: A Philosophical Sketch*, in: Immanuel Kant, *Political Writings*, Cambridge University Press, Cambridge/New York 1991, 93–130, at 113 et seq.).
53. Dante, *De Monarchia*, supra note 47, Book I, Chapter V (Engl.: at 9).
54. Ibid., Book I, Chapter VIII (Engl.: at 13).
55. Ibid., Book I, Chapter VI (Engl.: at 11).
56. Ibid., Book I, Chapter XIV (Engl.: at 25).
57. Ibid.
58. Henricus Hostiensis, *Summa Aurea* (1250–1261), Servanius, Lugduni 1556.
59. Ernest Nys, *Les origines du droit international*, Castaigne, Bruxelles 1894, at 144.
60. Thomas Aquinas, *Summa theologica* [1265–1273], W. Benton-Encyclopedia Britannica, Chicago 1980, Part II, Section II, Question 12, Article 2.
61. Sinibaldo Fieschi, *Apparatus super quinque lib[ris] decr[etalium] et super decretalibus* (ca. 1245), Lugduni 1535 (1st ed. 1477).
62. Thomas Aquinas, *Political Writings*, R. W. Dyson ed., Cambridge University press, Cambridge/New York 2004, at 278; Fieschi, *Apparatus*, supra note lxi, Book II, Chapter II, para. 2.
63. Dante, *De Monarchia*, supra note 47, Book III, Chapter XVI (Engl.: at 93).
64. Ibid. (Engl.: at 94).
65. Francisco Suárez, *De legibus, ac Deo legislatore* (1612), in: Francisco Suárez, *Selections from three Works*, Clarendon Press, Oxford 1944, 1–646.

66. Ibid., Book I, Chapter III, para. 6, at 39.
67. Ibid., at 39 et seq.
68. Ibid., Book I, Chapter III, para. 14, at 45.
69. Ibid., Book II, Chapter IV, para. 4, at 172 et seq.
70. Ibid., Book I, Chapter III, para. 9, at 42.
71. Ibid., Book II, Chapter V, at 178 et seq.
72. Ibid., Book II, Chapter VI, para. 13, at 198.
73. Ibid., Book II, Chapter VIII, para. 5, at 220.
74. Ibid., Book II, Chapter IX, para. 2, at 224.
75. Ibid., Book II, Chapter VIII, para. 8, at 222.
76. Ibid., Book III, [Introduction], para. 2, at 361 et seq.
77. Ibid., Book II, Chapter XIX, para. 9, at 348.
78. Ibid., Book II, Chapter XX, para. 2, at 352.
79. Ibid., Book II, Chapter XIX, para. 3, at 343 et seq.
80. Ibid., Book II, Chapter XIX, para. 6, at 345.
81. Ibid., Book III, [Introduction], para. 2, at 361 et seq.
82. Ibid., Book III, Chapter II, para. 6, at 376.
83. Ibid., Book III, Chapter IV, para. 7, at 387.
84. Jörg Fisch, *Die europäische Expansion und das Völkerrecht. Die Auseinandersetzungen um den Status der überseeischen Gebiete vom 15. Jahrhundert bis zur Gegenwart*, Steiner, Stuttgart 1984, at 196 et seq.
85. Ibid., at 207.
86. Aristotle, *Politics*, H. Rackham trans., Harvard University Press, Cambridge (MA) 1959, Book I, Chapter 2, 1253b et seq., at 12 et seq.
87. Quoted from Joseph E. Capizzi, *The Children of God: Natural Slavery in the Thought of Aquinas and Vitoria*, in: "Theological Studies", Vol. 63 (2002), 31–52, at 34. See also: Fisch, *Die europäische Expansion und das Völkerrecht*, supra note 84, at 227.
88. Juan Ginés de Sepúlveda, *De justis belli causis apud indos* (1544–1545), Fondo de Cultura economica, Mexico 1941, at 152.
89. Ibid., at 154.
90. Fisch, *Die europäische Expansion und das Völkerrecht*, supra note 84, at 228.
91. Juan López de Palacios Rubios, *El Requerimiento* (1513), https://en.wikipedia.org/wiki/Requeriminto#Requerimiento_translation.
92. Ibid.
93. Francisco de Vitoria, *De Indis et De Jure Belli Relectiones*, Oceana, New York/London 1964, Section II, Chapter 1 et seq.
94. Ibid., Section II, Chapter 3 et seq.
95. Ibid., Section III.
96. Ibid., Section III, Chapter 1.
97. Ibid., Section III, Chapter 5.

98. Ibid., Section III, Chapter 1.
99. Ibid., Section III, Chapter 3.
100. Ibid., Section III, Chapter 4.
101. Ibid., Section III, Chapter 15.
102. Ibid., Section III, Chapter 16.
103. Ibid., Section III, Chapter 9.
104. Section III, Chapter 13.
105. Ibid., Section III, Chapter 14.
106. Ibid., Section III, Chapter 17.
107. Ibid., Section III, Chapter 18.
108. Antony Anghie, *Imperialism, Sovereignty and the Making of International Law*, Cambridge University Press, Cambridge/New York 2005.
109. However, a quite unequivocal reference is made in: Vitoria, *De Indis*, supra note 93, Section III, Chapter 9.
110. Francisco Suárez, *De Triplici Virtute Theologica, Fide, Spe & Charitate* (1621), Disputation XIII, Section V, Chapter 5, in: Suárez, *Selections from three Works*, supra note 65, at 826.
111. Ibid., Disputation XVIII, Section II, Chapter 8, at 755 et seq.
112. Ibid, Disputation XIII, Section V, Chapter 7, at 826.
113. Ibid, Disputation XIII, Section V, Chapter 7, at 827.
114. Francisco de Vitoria, *Relectio de potestate civili* (1528), Question 1, Article 8, § 11, in: Francisco de Vitoria, *Political Writings*, Anthony Padgen and Jeremy Lawrance eds., Cambridge University Press, Cambridge/New York 2012, 1–44, at 20.
115. Ibid., Question 1, Article 7, § 10, at 18.
116. Francisco de Vitoria, *Relectio de potestate ecclesiae prior* (*On the Power of the Church*—1532), in: Vitoria, *Political Writings*, supra note 114, 45–108, at 45.
117. Théodore de Bèze, *Du droit des magistrats sur leur subjects* (1575), EDHIS, Paris 1977, at 13.
118. Suárez, *De legibus*, supra note 65, Book III, Chapter I, para. 4, at 365 et seq.; Book III, Chapter III, para. 2, at 378.
119. Ibid., Book III, Chapter IV, para. 2, at 383 et seq.
120. Ibid., Book III, Chapter III, para. 6, at 379 et seq.
121. Ibid., Book III, Chapter IV, para. 1, at 382 et seq.
122. Francisco Suárez, *Defensio fidei catholicae et apostolicae adversus Anglicanae sectae errores* (1613), in: Suárez, *Selections from three Works*, supra note 65, Book VI, Chapter IV, para. 15, at 718.
123. Ibid., Book VI, Chapter IV, para. 16, at 719.
124. Bartolomé de Las Casas, *Brévisima relación de la destrucción de las Indias* (1552), in: Bartolomé de Las Casas, *Colección de las Obras*, Vol. I, Rosa, Paris 1822, at 101 et seq. (English translation: *A Brief Account of the Destruction of the Indies*, Hewson, London 1689, https://www.gutenberg.org/cache/epub/20321/pg20321-images.html).

125. Bartolomé da Las Casas, *Treinta proposiciones* (1548), in: Las Casas, *Colección de las Obras*, *supra* note 124, Vol. I, at 372 et seq.
126. Fisch, *Die europäische Expansion und das Völkerrecht*, *supra* note 84, at 232 et seq.
127. Böckenförde, *Geschichte der Rechts- und Staatsphilosophie. Antike und Mittelalter*, *supra* note 6, at 350 et seq.
128. Mariano Delgado, 1996, *Universalmonarchie, translatio imperii und Volkssouveränität bei Las Casas*, in: Bartolomé de Las Casas, *Werkauswahl*, Mariano Delgado ed., Schöningh, Paderborn 1996, Vol. 3/1, at 164.
129. Bartolomé de Las Casas, *Sobre la Potestad Soberana de los Reyes* (*De imperatoria seu regia potestate*) (1971), in: Las Casas, *Colección de las Obras*, *supra* note 124, Vol. II, para. 1, at 56.
130. Ibid.
131. Aside from the reference to rationality as God's gift in para. 1, we have also a mention of the *jus natural et divinum* (natural and divine law) in para. 13 (ibid., at 81).
132. Ibid., para. 1, at 56.
133. Bartolomé de Las Casas, *Remedio contra las despoblacion de las Indias Occidentales* (1552), in: Las Casas, *Colección de las Obras*, *supra* note 124, Vol. I, Chapter VIII, at 290.
134. Bartolomé de Las Casas, *Sobre la libertad de los Indios, que se hallaban reducidos á la clase de esclavos* (1552), in: Las Casas, *Colección de las Obras*, *supra* note 124, Vol. II, art. 1, at 3 et seq..
135. Las Casas, *Sobre la Potestad Soberana de los Reyes*, *supra* note 129, para. 2, at 58 et seq.
136. Bartolomé de Las Casas, *Tratado de las Doce Dudas* (1564), in: Las Casas, *Colección de las Obras*, *supra* note 124, at 194 et seq.
137. Las Casas, *Sobre la Potestad Soberana de los Reyes*, *supra* note 129, para. 4, at 63.
138. Las Casas, *Tratado de las Doce Dudas*, *supra* note 136, at 202 et seq.
139. Ibid., at 246.
140. Las Casas, *Sobre la Potestad Soberana de los Reyes*, *supra* note 129, para. 4, at 64.
141. Ibid., para. 5 et seq., at 66 et seq.
142. Bertolomé de Las Casas, *Principia quaedam ex quibus procedendum est in disputatione ad manifestandam et defendendam iustitiam indorum* (1552), German trans. in: trad. ted. in Las Casas, *Werkauswahl*, *supra* note 128, Vol. 3/1, at 52.
143. Leo XIII, *Rerum novarum. Encyclical on Capital and Labor*, 15 May 1891, https://w2.vatican.va/content/leo-xiii/en/encyclicals/documents/hf_l-xiii_enc_15051891_rerum-novarum.html.

144. Benedict XV, *Ad Beatissimi Apostolorum*, 1 November 1914, https://www.ewtn.com/library/ENCYC/B15ADBEA.HTM.
145. John XXIII, *Pacen in Terris*, 11 April 1963, https://w2.vatican.va/content/john-xxiii/en/encyclicals/documents/hf_j-xxiii_enc_11041963_pacem.html, para. 2 et seq.
146. Ibid., para.8 et seq.
147. Ibid., para. 46 et seq.
148. Ibid., para. 80 et seq.
149. Ibid., para. 130 et seq.
150. Ibid., para. 146 et seq.
151. See: *infra*, Sect. 3.2.7.
152. John XXIII, *Pacen in Terris*, *supra* note 145, para. 49.
153. Ibid., para. 51.
154. Ibid., para. 52.
155. Ibid., para. 78.
156. Ibid., para. 79.
157. Ibid., para. 80.
158. Ibid., para. 86.
159. Ibid., para. 92.
160. Ibid., para. 98.
161. Ibid., para. 120.
162. Ibid., para. 25.
163. Ibid., para. 130.
164. Ibid., para. 133.
165. Ibid., para. 134.
166. Ibid., para. 139.
167. Ibid., para. 134.
168. Ibid., para. 142 et seq.
169. Ibid., para. 14.
170. Ibid., para. 157.
171. Ibid., para. 158.
172. Ibid., para. 1.
173. Ibid., para. 89 and 145, where the Latin original version speaks of "membra viva".
174. Ibid., para. 23 and 31.
175. Ibid., para. 97 et seq., 117, 132 and 145.
176. See, for example, the encyclical *Humanae vitae* (*Of Human Life*) of the 25 of July 1968, in which Paul VI prohibited almost all forms of artificial contraception (https://w2.vatican.va/content/paul-vi/en/encyclicals/documents/hf_p-vi_enc_25071968_humanae-vitae.html).
177. Joseph Ratzinger who later became pope by the name of Benedict XVI, is assumed to have significantly contributed to the drafting of *Redemptoris missio* in his then quality as the appointed Prefect of the Congregation for the Doctrine of the Faith.

178. John Paul II, *Redemptoris missio*, 7 December 1990, https://w2.vat ican.va/content/john-paul-ii/en/encyclicals/documents/hf_jp-ii_enc_ 07121990_redemptoris-missio.html, Chapter I, para. 5.
179. Joseph Ratzinger, Tarcisio Bertone, *Dominus Jesus*, https://www.vat ican.va/roman_curia/congregations/cfaith/documents/rc_con_cfaith_ doc_20000806_dominus-iesus_en.html, Chapter III, para. 15.
180. John Paul II, *Redemptoris missio*, supra n. 178, Chapter II, para. 20.
181. Ratzinger/Bertone, *Dominus Jesus*, supra n. 179, Chapter VI, para. 22.
182. John Paul II, *Redemptoris missio*, supra n. 178, Chapter IV, para. 39.
183. Ibid., Chapter V, para. 55.
184. Ratzinger/Bertone, *Dominus Jesus*, supra n. 179, Chapter VI, para. 21.
185. Ibid., Chapter I, para. 7.
186. Ibid., Chapter VI, para. 22.
187. John Paul II, *Redemptoris missio*, supra n. 178, Chapter V, para. 55.
188. Joseph H. H. Weiler, *A Christian Europe? Europe and Christianity: Rules of Commitment*, in: "European View", Vol. 6 (2007), 143–150.
189. John Paul II, *Redemptoris missio*, supra n. 178, Chapter I, para. 6.
190. Joseph Ratzinger has explicitly criticized the enlightened concept of reason. See: Joseph Ratzinger, *L'Europa nella crisi delle culture*, in: "Il Regno-Documenti", 9/2005, 214–219. On reason and law in the thought of Benedict XVI, see: Marta Cartabia, Andrea Simoncini (eds.), *Pope Benedict XVI's Legal Thought: A Dialogue on the Foundation of Law*, Cambridge University Press, Cambridge/New York 2015.
191. John Paul II, *Redemptoris missio*, supra n. 178, Chapter II, para. 20.
192. Ratzinger/Bertone, *Dominus Jesus*, supra n. 179, Chapter V, para. 18.
193. Significantly, Ratzinger refers to Spengler and Toynbee. See: Joseph Ratzinger, *L'Occidente che fu e quello che sarà*, in: "Il Foglio", 14 April 2004, at 4.
194. Ibid.
195. John Paul II, *Redemptoris missio*, supra n. 178, Chapter IV, para. 37.
196. Hans Küng, *Projekt Weltethos*, Piper, München 1990.
197. Hans Küng, *Menschen-Rechte und Menschen-Verantwortlichkeiten*, in: Hans Küng (ed.), *Dokumentation zum Weltethos*, Piper, München 2002, 139–149, at 142.
198. Ibid.
199. Ibid., at 148.
200. Max Weber, *Politik als Beruf* (1919), Reclam, Stuttgart 1992; English: *Politics as a Vocation*, in: Max Weber, *The Vocation Lectures*, ed. by David Owen and Tracy b. Strong, translated by Rodney Livingstone, Hackett, Indianapolis (IN)/Cambridge 2004, 32–94.
201. Hans Jonas, *Das Prinzip Verantwortung. Versuch einer Ethik für die technologische Zivilisation*, Suhrkamp, Frankfurt a. M. 1984, 1st ed. 1979 (English translation: *The Imperative of Responsibility*, University of Chicago Press, Chicago 1984).

202. Hans Küng, *Zur Problematik von Welpolitik, Weltstaat und Weltethos*, in: Stefan Gosepath, Jean-Christophe Merle (eds.), *Weltrepublik. Globalisierung und Demokratie*, Beck, München 2002, 122–133.
203. Küng, *Menschen-Rechte und Menschen-Verantwortlichkeiten*, supra n. 197, at 144 et seq.
204. Hans Küng, *Geschichte, Sinn und Methode der Erklärung zu einem Weltethos*, in: Küng, *Dokumentation zum Weltethos*, supra n. 197, 37–67, at 38.
205. Parliament of the World' Religions, *Declaration toward a Global Ethic*, 3 September 1993, https://parliamentofreligions.org/pwr_resources/_includes/FCKcontent/File/TowardsAGlobalEthic.pdf, at 6.
206. Ibid., at 3.
207. Küng, *Menschen-Rechte und Menschen-Verantwortlichkeiten*, supra n. 197, at 140.
208. Parliament of the World' Religions, *Declaration toward a Global Ethic*, supra n. 205, at 6.
209. Ibid., at 5 et seq.
210. Ibid., at 2.
211. Ibid., at 7 et seq.
212. Certainly, the moral and legal community must be conceived in a way that makes the inclusion of those human (or even non-human) individuals who share the common destiny, but are—for whatever reason—unable to express their needs and preferences in a propositional way.
213. Francis, *Luadato si'*, 24 May 2015, https://w2.vatican.va/content/francesco/en/encyclicals/documents/papa-francesco_20150524_enciclica-laudato-si.html, para. 3.
214. Ibid., para. 199.
215. Ibid., para. 14.
216. Ibid., para. 106.
217. Ibid.
218. Ibid., para. 115.
219. Ibid., para. 136.
220. Ibid., para. 17 et seq.
221. Ibid., para. 61.
222. Ibid., para. 63.
223. Ibid., para. 62 et seq.
224. *The Holy Bible, New Testament*, Romans, Chapter 2, para. 14.
225. Thomas Aquinas, *Summa theological*, supra n. 60, Part II, Section I, Question 91, Article 1.
226. Ibid., Part II, Section I, Question 91, Article 2.
227. Ibid., Part II, Section I, Question 94, Article 4.
228. Ibid., Part II, Section I, Question 91, Article 3.

229. Ibid., Part II, Section I, Question 95, Article 4; Part II, Section II, Question 57, Article 3.
230. Ibid., Part II, Section I, Question 93, Article 3.
231. Francisco de Vitoria, *De potestate papae et concilii* (1534), in: Francisco De Vitoria, *Relecciones Teológicas*, Librería Religiosa Hernández, Madrid 1917, Vol. II, 36–93, at 38.
232. Francisco de Vitoria, *De eo, ad quod tenetur homo, cum primum venit ad usum rationis* (1535), in: Francisco de Vitoria, *Vorlesungen*, Kohlhammer, Stuttgart (1997), Vol. II, at 158 et seq.
233. Francisco de Vitoria, *Relectio de homicidio* (1530), in: Vitoria, *Relecciones Teológicas*, supra n. 231, Vol. II, 190–236, at 198 et seq.
234. Francisco de Vitoria, *Relectio de potestate civili* (1528), in: Vitoria, *Relecciones Teológicas*, supra n. 231, Vol. II, 1–35, at 24.
235. Böckenförde, *Geschichte der Rechts- und Staatsphilosophie. Antike und Mittelalter*, supra note 6, at 326 et seq.
236. Francisco de Vitoria, *Comentarios a la Secunda secundae de Santo Tomás*, Vicente Beltrán de Heredia ed., Salamanca 1932 et seq., Part II, Section II, Question 62, Article 1, n. 5.
237. Suárez, *De legibus*, supra note 65, Book II, Chapter II, para. 3, at 152 et seq.
238. See: *supra* Sect. 3.2.2.2.
239. Suárez, *De legibus*, supra note 65, Book II, Chapter III, para. 3, at 162.
240. Jacques Maritain, *Man and the State*, Chicago University Press, Chicago 1951.
241. Martin Luther, *Disputatio de homine*, in: Gerhard Eberling, *Lutherstudien*, Tübingen, Mohr Siebeck, 1989, Vol. 2.
242. Martin Luther, *Werke. Kritische Gesamtausgabe*, Boehlaus, Weimar 1914, Vol. 51, at 126, Line 7 et seq.
243. Jean Calvin, *Institutio christianae religionis*, Genevae 1559.
244. Michael Walzer, *The Revolution of the Saints*, Harvard University Press, Cambridge (MA) 1982.
245. Alberico Gentili, *De Jure Belli Libri Tres* (1589), Typographeo Clarendoniano, Oxonii (Oxford) 1877, Book I, Chapter I, at 6 (English: Clarendon Press, Oxford 1933).
246. Ibid., Book I, Chapter XV, at 64.
247. Ibid., Book I, Chapter XIV, at 57 et seq.
248. Ibid., Book I, Chapter XIV, at 61.
249. See: Stefan Kadelbach, *Hugo Grotius: On the Conquest of Utopia by Systematic Reasoning*, in: Stefan Kadelbach, Thomas Kleinlein, David Roth-Isigkeit (eds.), *System, Order, and International Law*, Oxford University Press, Oxford/New York 2017, 134–159.
250. Hugo Grotius, *De Jure Belli ac Pacis* (1625), Book I, Chapter I, para. X.1 (English: *The Rights of War and Peace*, Richard Tuck ed., Liberty Fund, Indianapolis 2005, at 150 et seq.).

3 HOLISTIC UNIVERSALISM AS THE SECOND PARADIGM ... 193

251. Ibid., Book I, Chapter I, para. X.5 (English: at 156).
252. James Brown Scott, *Introduction*, in: Hugo Grotius, *De Jure Belli ac Pacis*, William S. Hein & Co., Buffalo (NY) 1995, Vol. II, IX–XLIII.
253. Grotius, *De Jure Belli ac Pacis*, *supra* n. 250, Book I, Chapter I, para. XII (English: at 159).
254. Indeed, Grotius himself admitted that also non-human animals have a social tendency, though imperfect (ibid., *Prolegomena*, para. VII, at 82 et seq.).
255. Ibid., *Prolegomena*, para. VI (English: at 79 et seq.).
256. Ibid., *Prolegomena*, para. XVII (English: at 93).
257. Ibid., *Prolegomena*, para. XVIII (English: at 94).
258. Ibid., *Prolegomena*, para. XIX (English: at 94 et seq.).
259. Ibid., *Prolegomena*, para. XXI (English: at 96).
260. Ibid., Book I, Chapter I, para. XIV (English: at 163).
261. Norberto Bobbio, *Il modello giusnaturalistico*, in: Norberto Bobbio, Michelangelo Bovero, *Società e stato nella filosofia politica moderna*, Il Saggiatore, Milano 1979, 15–109, at 21 et seq.
262. On Althusius's political thought, see: Daniel J. Elazar, *Althusius' Grand Design for a Federal Commonwealth*, in: Johannes Althusius, *Politica*, Frederick S. Carney ed., Liberty Fund, Indianapolis 1995, XXXV–XLVI; Thomas O. Hueglin, *Althusius: Back to the Future*, in: Kadelbach/Kleinlein/Roth-Isigkeit, *System, Order, and International Law*, *supra* n. ccxlix, 115–133.
263. Johannes Althusius, *Politica Methodice Digesta* (1603), Chapter I, para. 1 (English transl. of the 1614 ed.: Althusius, *Politica*, *supra* n. 262, at 17).
264. Ibid., Chapter I, para. 7 (English: at 19).
265. Ibid., Chapter I, para. 1 (English: at 17).
266. Ibid., Chapter II, para. 3 (English: at 27).
267. Ibid., Chapter V, para. 1 (English: at 39).
268. Ibid., Chapter II, para. 2 (English: at 27).
269. Ibid., Chapter V, para. 1 (English: at 39).
270. Bobbio, *Il modello giusnaturalistico*, *supra* n. 261, at 42.
271. Althusius, *Politica*, *supra* n. 263, Chapter IX, para. 16 (English: at 70).
272. Ibid., Chapter IX, para. 18 (English: at 70).
273. Ibid., Chapter I, para. 2 (English: at 17).
274. Heinrich Kipp, *Völkerordnung und Völkerrecht im Mittelater*, Deutsche Glocke, Köln 1950, at 124.
275. Althusius, *Politica*, *supra* n. 263, Chapter IX, para. 22 (English: at 72).
276. Ibid., Preface to the Third Edition (1614) (English: at 11).
277. Ibid., Chapter IX, para. 28 (English: at 74).
278. Ibid., Preface to the Third Edition (1614) (English: at 11).

279. Samuel Pufendorf, *De jure naturae et gentium libri octo* (1672), complete English translation by Basil Kennet, Lichfield et al., Oxford 1703, Book II, Chapter II, para. I; partial English translation by Michael J. Seidler, in: Samuel Pufendorf, *The Political Writings*, Craig L. Carr ed., Oxford University Press, Oxford/New York 1994, at 140 [the quotations are taken from the edition of 1994].
280. Ibid., Book II, Chapter III, para. XIV (English: at 151).
281. Ibid.
282. Ibid., Book II, Chapter II, para. VII (English: at 145).
283. Ibid., Book II, Chapter III, para. XV (English: at 152).
284. Samuel Pufendorf, *De officio hominis et civis libri duo* (1673), Oxford University Press, New York 1927.
285. Pufendorf, *De jure naturae et gentium*, supra n. 279, Book VI, Chapter I, para. I (English: at 198).
286. Ibid., Book VI, Chapter I, para. XI (English: at 199).
287. Ibid., Book IV (English: at 174 et seq.).
288. Ibid., Book VII, Chapter I, para. VII (English: at 206).
289. Ibid., Book I, Chapter VI (English: at 119 et seq.).
290. Craig L. Carr, *Introduction*, in: Pufendorf, *The Political Writings*, supra n. 279, 3–21, at 11.
291. Pufendorf, *De jure naturae et gentium*, supra n. 279, Book VII, Chapter II, para. X (English: at 214).
292. Ibid., Book VIII, Chapter VI et seq. (English: at 257 et seq.).
293. On Wolff's relevance in the history of the philosophy of international law, see: Thomas Kleinlein, *Christian Wolff: System as an Episode?*, in: Kadelbach/Kleinlein/Roth-Isigkeit, *System, Order, and International Law*, supra n. 249, 216–239.
294. Pufendorf, *De jure naturae et gentium*, supra n. 279, Book VIII, Chapter IX, para. I et seq. (English: at 261 et seq.).
295. Christian Wolff, *Institutiones Juris Naturae et Gentium* (1754), Officina Rengeriana, Halae Madgeburgicae 1754, Pars IV, § 1088 et seq., at 679 et seq.
296. Christian Wolff, *Jus Gentium Methodo Scientifica Pertractatum* (1764), Prolegomena, § 3 (English transl. by Joseph H. Drake, Clarendon, Oxford 1934, Vol. II, at 9).
297. Ibid., Prolegomena, § 22 (English: at 18).
298. Ibid., Prolegomena, § 23 (English: at 18).
299. Ibid., Prolegomena, § 24 (English: at 18).
300. Ibid., Prolegomena, § 3 (English: at 9).
301. Ibid., Prolegomena, § 19 et seq. (English: at 16 et seq.).
302. Ibid., Prolegomena, § 16 (English: at 15).
303. Ibid., Prolegomena, § 16 (English: at 15).
304. Kleinlein, *Christian Wolff: System as an Episode?*, supra n. 293, at 232.

305. Wolff, *Institutiones Juris Naturae et Gentium, supra* n. 295, Pars IV, § 1090 et seq., at 680 et seq.
306. Francis Cheneval, *Philosophie in weltbürgerlicher Absicht. Über die Entstehung und die philosophischen Grundlagen des supranationalen und kosmopolitischen Denkens der Moderne*, Schwabe, Basel 2002, at 132 et seq..
307. Wolff, *Institutiones Juris Naturae et Gentium, supra* n. 295, Pars IV, § 1140 et seq., at 710 et seq.
308. Wolff, *Jus Gentium Methodo Scientifica Pertractatum, supra* n. 296, Prolegomena, § 20 et seq. (English: at 16 et seq.).
309. Ibid., Prolegomena, § 20 (English: at 17).
310. Wolff, *Institutiones Juris Naturae et Gentium, supra* n. 295, Pars IV, § 1090, at 680 et seq.
311. Ibid., Pars III, Sectio II, § 972 et seq., at 597 et seq.
312. Ibid., Pars III, § 1169 et seq., at 729 et seq.
313. See: Gustav Radbruch, *Gesetzliches Unrecht und übergesetzliches Recht* (1946), Nomos, Baden-Baden 2002.
314. See: Robert P. George, *In Defense of Natural Law*, Clarendon Press, Oxford 1999.
315. Nigel Biggar, Rufus Black (eds.), *The Revival of Natural Law*, Ashgate, Aldershot 2000, at 2 et seq.
316. Germain Grisez, Joseph Boyle, John Finnis, *Practical Principles, Moral Truth, and Ultimate Ends*, in: "The American Journal of Jurisprudence", Vol. 32 (1987), 99–151, at 102.
317. Pauline C. Westerman, *The Disintegration of Natural Law Theory: Aquinas to Finnis*, Brill, Leiden 1998, at 253 et seq.
318. Grisez/Boyle/Finnis, *Practical Principles, Moral Truth, and Ultimate Ends, supra* n. 316, at 101.
319. Ibid., at 106.
320. Ibid., at 106 et seq.
321. Timothy Chappell, *Natural Law Revived: Natural Law Theory and Contemporary Moral Philosophy*, in: Biggar/Black, *The Revival of Natural Law, supra* n. cccxv, 29–52, at 37 et seq.
322. Westerman, *The Disintegration of Natural Law Theory, supra* n. 317, at 257 et seq.
323. Grisez/Boyle/Finnis, *Practical Principles, Moral Truth, and Ultimate Ends, supra* n. 316, at 107.
324. John Finnis, *Natural Law and Natural Rights*, Clarendon Press, London 1980, at 376.
325. Grisez/Boyle/Finnis, *Practical Principles, Moral Truth, and Ultimate Ends, supra* n. 316, at 141.
326. Ibid. See also: Finnis, *Natural Law and Natural Rights, supra* n. 324, at 386 et seq.

327. Immanuel Kant, *Kritik der reinen Vernunft* (1781), in: Kant, *Werkausgabe*, supra n. 52, Vol. III–IV, Vol. II, at 529 et seq. (English translation by Paul Guyer and Allen Wood, Cambridge University Press, Cambridge/New York 1998, at 563).
328. See: Viktor Cathrein, *Recht, Naturrecht und positives Recht*, 2nd ed., Herdersche Verlagshandlung, Freiburg 1909; Viktor Cathrein, *Die Grundlage des Völkerrechts*, Herdersche Verlagshandlung, Freiburg 1918, Viktor Cathrein, *Moralphilosophie*, 6. Aufl., Vier Quellen Verlag, Berlin 1924.
329. Hans Kelsen, *Die Grundlage der Naturrechtslehre*, in: "Österreichische Zeitschrift für Öffentliches Recht", Vol. XIII (1963), 1–37 (English translation in: John Finnis (ed.), *Natural Law*, Dartmouth, Aldershot 1991, Vol. I, 125–153).
330. Westerman, *The Disintegration of Natural Law Theory*, supra n. 317, at 272 et seq., 282 et seq.
331. Grisez/Boyle/Finnis, *Practical Principles, Moral Truth, and Ultimate Ends*, supra n. 316, at 101, 108.
332. Ibid., at 128.
333. Ibid., at 133.
334. Ibid., at 123 et seq., 145 et seq.
335. Chappell, *Natural Law Revived*, supra n. 321, at 41.
336. Grisez/Boyle/Finnis, *Practical Principles, Moral Truth, and Ultimate Ends*, supra n. 316, at 131.
337. Ibid.
338. Alfred Verdross, *Die Verfassung der Völkerrechtsgemeinschaft*, Springer, Wien/Berlin 1926, at 33 et seq.
339. Ibid., at 12.
340. Ibid., at 23.
341. Ibid., at 22, 32.
342. Ibid., at 32.
343. Ibid., at 2 et seq.
344. See: Hermann Mosler, *The International Society as a Legal Community*, Sijthoff & Noorfhoff, Alphen aan den Rijn 1980; Bruno Simma, *From Bilateralism to Community Interest in International Law*, in: "Collected Courses of The Hague Academy of International Law", Vol. 250/VI, Nijhoff, The Hague 1994, at 217 et seq.; Ronald St. John Macdonald, *The International Community as a Legal Community*, in: Ronald St. John Macdonald, Douglas M. Johnston (eds.), *Towards World Constitutionalism. Issues in the Legal Ordering of the World Community*, Nijhoff, Leiden 2005, at 853 et seq.
345. C. Wilfred Jenks, *The Common Law of Mankind*, Praeger, New York 1958.

346. Christian Tomuschat. *International Law: Ensuring the Survival of Mankind on the Eve of a New Century*, in: "Collected Courses of The Hague Academy of International Law", vol. 281, Nijhoff, The Hague 1999, at 23 et seq.
347. Ibid., at 28 et seq., 63 et seq.
348. Ibid., at 305 et seq.
349. Bardo Fassbender, *Rediscovering a Forgotten Constitution*, in: Jeffrey L. Dunoff, Joel P. Trachtmann (eds.), *Ruling the World?*, Cambridge University Press, Cambridge/New York 2009, 133–147.
350. Tomuschat. *International Law: Ensuring the Survival of Mankind on the Eve of a New Century*, supra n. 346, at 161.
351. Ibid., at 23.
352. Ibid., at 94 et seq.
353. Ibid., at 88.
354. Ibid., at 78.
355. Mehrdad Payandeh, *Internationales Gemeinschaftsrecht*, Springer, Heidelberg/New York 2010.
356. Andreas L. Paulus, *The International Legal System as a Constitution*, in: Dunoff/Trachtmann, *Ruling the World?*, supra n. 349, 69–109.

CHAPTER 4

# Universalistic Individualism as the Third Paradigm of Order

In Shakespeare's *Hamlet*, which was written between 1599 and 1602, the protagonist—a meditative young man, rather averse to impulsive action—finds himself involved in a story which bears all the traits of a perfect tragedy, and finally leads him to an almost inescapable doom. More concretely, he repeatedly gets some clues that his father, the former king, may have been murdered by his uncle Claudius, who then hastily married his mother Gertrude to become the new king. Interestingly, among many differences, there are some remarkable resemblances with the story that lies at the basis of Aeschylus's *Oresteia*, which was first performed in 458 B.C.E., thus more than two thousand years before Shakespeare's work. In both cases, we have a young man of noble origin who is confronted with the assassination of his father—a matter of fact in the Greek tragedy, and a possible, or likely, course of events in the Elizabethan drama—and, then, with his assumed duty to restore justice, or to execute revenge. However, the way in which the respective protagonists of the tragedies, Orestes and Hamlet, get to their decision and justify their action is significantly diverging. One could say that this is simply obvious, considering the huge interval of time that separates the two works. Yet, the divergences also underline the specific novelty of the understanding of the world that lies behind *Hamlet* and the entire *opus* of Shakespeare,

© The Author(s), under exclusive license to Springer Nature
Switzerland AG 2021
S. Dellavalle, *Paradigms of Social Order*,
Philosophy, Public Policy, and Transnational Law,
https://doi.org/10.1007/978-3-030-66179-3_4

contouring the characteristics of a new paradigm of order, namely the *individualistic* paradigm of Modern Ages.

Basically, Hamlet has to deal with two main questions: first, how can he be sure that his father has been assassinated and that Claudius is the murderer? And, secondly, what should he do if the suspicion turned out to be true? In the *Oresteia* the first question does not need to be posed since it seems to be generally known that Orestes's father, Agamemnon, had been killed by his wife—Orestes's mother Clytemnestra. In any case, the facts were perfectly known from the very beginning to the hero himself, who had to flee in order to save his life, just to get back, ten years later, to impose justice or to take vengeance. However, we know conditions of uncertainty as regards questions of guilt and the attribution of responsibility for negative events—often for plagues—from other ancient Greek tragedies, for instance from Sophocles's *Oedipus Tyrannus*. In Sophocles's tragedy Oedipus is confronted with the task—which he has as the king of Thebes—of ridding his city of the disease that is killing its inhabitants. The whole drama develops along the line of Oedipus's search for the truth—until he discovers that he himself was the unaware perpetrator of the crimes for which the gods were punishing Thebes with the disease. In his despair, he pierces his eyes, leaves his city—which was doomed to be the site of more tragedies in the following years, with Oedipus's cursed and unlucky progeny as their victims and perpetrators—only to live the rest of his life as a beggar. The path towards the discovery of the crime that infected the city—namely that Oedipus killed his father Laius and married his mother Jocasta—is marked by many interviews that the protagonist has with a number of characters, from which the events slowly emerge, with great dramatic mastery, as they happened. However, the interviews are not really what enables the characters of the tragedy and the readers to unveil the truth. Rather, they help to interpret it correctly. In fact, the truth about what happened has already found a linguistic form—though a quite obscure one—or, in other words, it has already been expressed through linguistic utterances in the guise of the four prophecies that are introduced, one by one, at the turning points of the unfolding action. First, we have Creon, Oedipus's brother-in-law, who refers that the oracle at Delphi has stated that Thebes, to get rid of the plague, has to punish the murders of Laius.[1] Much more important is, secondly, Tiresias's testimony who explicitly accuses Oedipus of being the curse of his city, with the result that Tiresias himself is expelled from Thebes.[2] Yet, Tiresias gives no evidences for his assertions, grounding them only on his fame as a prophet endowed with a privileged access to the truth. Then, a third prophecy is reported—uttered, once again, by the oracle at Delphi—which was given to Laius many years before the events at the centre of the tragedy, according to which Laius himself was destined to be killed by his own son.[3] The fourth prophecy, finally, was spoken by the Delphic oracle to Oedipus, announcing that he would kill his father and generate with his mother a cursed progeny.[4] At first, these prophecies seem to be counterfactual since Oedipus grew up in Corinth in the belief that he was the son of the local king. When he heard that he was going to be the murderer of his father, he left Corinth so as to make the crime impossible, regardless of what the Delphic oracle had said. Furthermore, in the meantime the king of Corinth had died of natural causes. Thus, how could Oedipus have committed parricide? However, it is revealed that he had killed a grey-haired man, who had provoked him at a crossroads, before he came to Thebes—and this man turns out to be, in the end, no other than Laius himself, the former king of Thebes. But, how could Laius be Oedipus's father, if the child that seemed to be destined to become his murder had been immediately killed after the unlucky prophecy had been revealed? The fact was that the child had not been killed by the servant who had to perform this criminal task, but was given into custody, reaching Corinth in the end. Putting the pieces of the puzzle together and with the help of the testimonies, Oedipus's destiny becomes clear as well as the truth.

Summing up, the ancient Greek tragedy presents a three-level understanding of knowledge: we have, first, the objective truth in the world outside; secondly, this truth is captured by more-than-human utterances, which enshrine a content that is, at the same time, objective and divine, but also prepared to be received and understood by human ears and brains; thirdly, there is the action of the knowing subject who primarily has to interpret correctly the more-than-human utterances. As a consequence, we—as knowing subjects—do not have to construe the objective truth on the basis of evidences; rather, we have only to open the shrine of truth that already exists before our eyes. Two elements are decisive in this context: we have unlimited access to the objective truth, if we only decode it correctly, since there is no discontinuity between the three levels of knowledge, and not the knowing subject, but the outside object, is the epistemological barycentre. Completely different is the perspective in Shakespeare's *Hamlet*. Here, the hints of truth are not served in the form of divine prophecies, but shine through the vision of the ghost of

Hamlet's father.[5] Although these visions are not experienced exclusively by the protagonist of the tragedy, but are shared with other characters, nonetheless visions as such described by Shakespeare are highly subjective and can also be interpreted as (collective) hallucinations or as the result of a sick state of mind. In fact, for a great part of the drama Hamlet behaves in a quite erratic way, maybe because of the distress caused by the events that unfold before his eyes, maybe as a kind of disguise in order to conceal his vengeful intentions. In fact—as Polonius, the sycophantic lord in the service of Claudius, suspects—"though this be madness, yet there is method in't".[6] Anyway, regardless of these aspects, the vision of the ghost and what he is assumed to say are by no means comparable to the ancient prophecies since they do not contain an incontestable truth, but are rather quite impalpable clues that should help put the knowing subject on the right path. Furthermore, as regards the gathering of evidence, this is much more relevant in the story of Hamlet than in the ancient Greek tragedy. Hamlet even goes so far as to stage a theatrical performance in which the murder of his father is reproduced in the way he believes it happened, so as to observe Claudius's reaction: "I'll observe his looks – Hamlet says – I'll tent him to the quick. If a but blench, I know my course".[7] It is no exaggeration to say that this is a kind of experiment in order to collect evidence to support—or to reject—the initial hypothesis. Indeed, the observation of Claudius's reaction is assumed to be more relevant for the decision to be taken than the ghost's obscure and uncertain accusation, since Hamlet is expecting to "have grounds more relative than this" from his theatrical experiment.[8] Basically, we have here an anticipation of what will be established as the scientific method, transferred, in this case, from the field of natural sciences to that of social relations.

Substantially, in Shakespeare's modern tragedy the truth about the outside world is not already contained in—and expressed through—authoritative propositions uttered by an entity which, being both material and spiritual, is assumed to mediate between the reality and the knowing subject. Rather, it is the knowing subject her- or himself, without any other help but that deriving from her/his capacity to think, that reconstructs the truth by means of the pieces of evidence she/he can gather. So much for the theory of knowledge—or for the understanding of the use of theoretical reason—which is implicitly contained in Shakespeare's *Hamlet*. But, if we move on, now, to the theory of action—or to the use of practical reason—the picture is substantially the same. To better understand the novelty of the early modern approach, let us go back again to the ancient Greek tragedy—this time, as mentioned at the beginning, to Aeschylus's *Oresteia*, in which a comparable case of murder and revenge is presented. In both tragedies one of the most relevant questions is: How does the protagonist of the tragedy—Orestes in the one case, Hamlet in the other—justify the assassination of a close relative, with the further consequence of plunging the polity into a deep political crisis? Orestes is utterly committed to accomplishing his revenge by killing Clytemnestra as well as her former lover and new husband Aegisthos during the whole course of action: "the deed must still be done".[9] He shows only one moment of weakness and uncertainty when Clytemnestra, realizing that Orestes has come to kill her, implores him to spare her for the sake of the bond that once united mother and son: "wait, my son! Have pity, child, upon this breast at which many times while you slept you sucked with toothless gums the milk that nourished you".[10] At the sight of his desperate mother, Orestes's vengeful hand stops, and he asks his friend Pylades: "what shall I do? Shall I spare my mother out of pity?"[11] But his friend's answer is unequivocal: "What then will become in the future of Loxias' oracles declared at Pytho, and of our sworn pact? Count all men your enemies rather than the gods".[12] Therefore, there is a divine will that Orestes has to execute which states that the political law represented by the father is situated above the bonds of love embodied by the mother. Under these premises, the human agent acts rightfully only to the extent that she/he pursues what has been established by the gods. Once again, Hamlet's condition is completely different. He has no divine law to accomplish, but can only try to restore justice on the basis of his fallible judgement. Indeed, his father's ghost called for revenge: "let not the royal bed of Denmark be a couch for luxury and damned incest".[13] But the ghost talks to Hamlet alone, and no one else can hear him, so that his request could also be nothing else but the product of the prince's fantasy. As a result, Hamlet is full of doubts about what to do, as it is masterly expressed in his most famous monologue: "to be, or not to be".[14] In the end, what is true and right has its unique fundament in the rational capacity of the individual and can only be found out through her/his act of thinking, "for there is nothing either good or bad but thinking makes it so".[15] The turn to *individualism* in epistemology and ethics has been, if not completed, at least powerfully anticipated by Shakespeare, and the paradigmatic revolution from the priority of the *holon*—of the whole that takes form in divine and natural law—to the centrality of the individual, first outlined in poetry, had to be formulated, then, in a coherent theory of knowledge and action. This has been the main task of the philosophy of the seventeenth and eighteenth centuries.

"Something is rotten in the state of Denmark": this is what Marcellus, one of the soldiers, states in Shakespeare's tragedy.[16] But something was rotten in the epistemology of the late Middle Ages too, since the former unquestioned assumption of an osmosis between the knowing subject and the outside reality could not be regarded as convincing any longer due to the huge social, political, economic and religious upheaval that marked the beginning of the Modern Era. However, the mere subjectivistic destruction of the old order could not be the solution. Indeed, in Shakespeare's drama the contestable truth of the knowing subject finds its only place in Hamlet's mind and deeds since no one shares it during the course of action. It is not by chance that Hamlet's solitary fight for justice ended up with the loss of many human lives and the collapse of the most important institutions of the state. If a new order based on the centrality of the individuals was to be built, this could consistently happen only on one condition, namely that criteria were formulated according to which the knowledge and the justifications of action, elaborated by the knowing subject without resorting to a pre-subjective outer fundament, could be *universally* recognized, nonetheless, as *true*. It was René Descartes who took up this challenge by developing a theory of knowledge that was based on two elements: the very *individual* capacity of questioning generally established theories and of creating new ones by means of the unprejudiced, purely rational thinking of the knowing subject, on the one hand, and the identification of a method for ensuring that those theories were *universally accepted as true*, on the other (Sect. 4.1).

Only a few years later, Thomas Hobbes extended the *individualistic paradigm*, which was destined to become the distinctive pattern of modern philosophy, from the theory of knowledge to political philosophy (Sect. 4.2). The second *paradigmatic revolution* in the theories of order was hereby initiated. This time, the dimension of order involved was not its extension—as in the first paradigmatic revolution—but its ontological fundament. In particular, the second paradigmatic revolution in the theories of order overturned the former hierarchy between community and individuals. Within the former paradigms the whole of the community was presumed to be in any sense superior to the sum of its members, no matter how far the extension of the social and political community was assumed to reach, in other words whether it was particularistic or universalistic. Following the second paradigmatic revolution, instead, the centre of social order was put in the rights, interests and rational capacity of the individuals, and authority was only justified if it aimed at the protection of individual rights and interests. To underline the individualistic character of the foundation of public power, the establishment of political and legal institutions endowed with authority was regarded, in the strand of modern political philosophy that began with Hobbes, as the result of a *contract*—mostly of fictitious nature—among those who were willing to come together in order to form a "body politic". Differences among the supporters of the modern contract theory of state—or contractualism— emerge, however, if we consider the extent of competences attributed to public power. This depends, ultimately, on how many rights were assumed to be necessarily transferred to the sovereign authority by the individuals, as their original rights holders, at the moment of the creation of the *societas civilis*. This is the point at which Hobbes, curiously enough, turned from a supporter of the original rights endowment of all individuals, to an advocate of absolutism, as he is generally known—quite to his unjustified detriment. In his pessimistic vision, indeed, social and political order can only be safeguarded if individuals give up almost all their entitlements—with the only exceptions of the right to life and to a rather marginal space of negative freedom—handing them over to the newly established Leviathan.

Hobbes's political thought is characterized, therefore, by an internal contradiction: on the one hand, it advocates the creation of a public power with almost unlimited competences, while its establishment is justified, on the other, by the reflexive will of the members of the community. By grounding power on consent and, thus, through a "bottom-up" or ascending procedure, he distanced himself explicitly from the traditional "top-down" or descending legitimation of power. After the contradictory outcome of Hobbes's political philosophy, the highly innovative potentiality of the contract theory of state contained in its "bottom-up" conception of political legitimacy was accomplished by two variants of contractualism, destined to become powerful ideologies in the following centuries. The main difference between them—and in comparison with Hobbes—is located in the distinct way in which the individual rights are transferred from their original holders to the public power, especially as regards how many rights are transferred. In the first of these variants—John Locke's *liberalism*—the transfer of rights is minimal since public power has the only task of ensuring compliance with the law, so that inter-individual transactions can develop peacefully (Sect. 4.3.1). In

Jean-Jacques Rousseau's *radical-democratic* idea of the "social contract", instead, *all* natural rights are alienated—in an even more uncompromising manner than in Hobbes—yet not to the Leviathan-like monarch, but back to the citizens themselves, who have constituted the sovereign political community expressed by the *volonté générale* (Sect. 4.3.2).

Once the second paradigmatic revolution had established a new fundament for social order and, hereby, the priority of the individuals over the holistic community, the question arose on the first dimension of the paradigms of order, i.e., on the extension of the well-ordered society. In other words, how far could the individualistic order of society reach? Was it assumed to stop at the borders of the single polity, or was it thought to include, in principle, the whole humanity? Indeed, at least at the beginning, the contract theory of state was conceived as an instrument for the new foundation of political power and for its legitimation under the conditions of the modern centrality of individuals. Thus, interest in international order was initially marginal and, insofar as international law and relations were addressed, scepticism was the prevailing attitude. Regardless of the early indifference of its exponents towards global order, the individualistic paradigm was *universalistic* in its essence. In fact, according to the individualistic paradigm, human beings are regarded as endowed with socially non-situated rights, interests and reason, so that they are considered in principle universally equal. Being these socially non-situated individuals the barycentre of the political and legal community, no reasonable justification can be given why this community should be shaped following the limits of ethnic, cultural, linguistic, historic or religious identities. As a result, due to its conceptual premises the individualistic paradigm cannot but be universalistic. It was only with Immanuel Kant, however, that the paradigm came to develop its full potentialities. In particular, Kant introduced for the first time a tripartition of public law, in which the third part—going from the most specific to the most general and inclusive—is what he unequivocally defined as "cosmopolitan law". Furthermore, universal peace was regarded by Kant not only as a political necessity but also as a moral duty. Nevertheless, when it came to the formulation of a concrete proposal, Kant swung undecided between opposing options: the "world republic" (*Weltrepublik*) and the "confederation of peoples" (*Völkerbund*). The lack of an implementable option did not come by chance: having developed the idea of cosmopolitan order at the price of a radical decontextualization of the individuals,

Kant's groundbreaking intuition was lastly doomed to remain abstract (Sect. 4.4).

Kant's difficulty in proposing a clear-cut solution for the institutional shape of a universalistic idea of social, political and legal order—or of world constitutionalism—is just an example of the complexity of holding together the achievements of national constitutionalism and the project of universalism. Little more than a century after Kant, Hans Kelsen suggested resolving the conflict by cutting the Gordian knot. More specifically, he developed the uncompromising idea of a radically monist legal system, in which international law—in the sense of a supra-state law—was put, for the first time in the history of legal theory, at the apex of the hierarchy of norms. As a result, state law—even constitutional law—was authorized to govern social interaction only within the framework established by international law (Sect. 4.5). In doing so, Kelsen prevented any kind of conflict between national and international norms since supremacy was always recognized to the latter. In this sense, his legal philosophy can be regarded as the apotheosis of cosmopolitanism. Nonetheless, his ambitious goal was achieved at high cost. First, Kelsen's monism firmly rejected any kind of legal pluralism as it was based on the assumption that conflicting norms grounded in different legal systems can never justifiably claim validity if contemporarily applied to the same matter. In his view, only the establishment and acknowledgement of hierarchy can put an end to the conflict. Secondly, Kelsen's world order has explicitly and exclusively a *legal* dimension, without any significant involvement of political institutions. Thus, the interpretation of norms by the international courts seems to be more important, to guarantee global order and peace, than democratic legitimacy and political dialogue.

Kant's *Weltrepublik* and Kelsen's legally shaped *civitas maxima* are probably the intellectually highest and most radical achievements of universalistic thought in its whole history. Yet, if the uncompromising nature of these visions is the source of their fascinating greatness, it also makes up a great part of their tragic dimension. Indeed, universalistic individualism—in particular in the way in which it was elaborated by its most courageous exponents—is affected by many and significant shortcomings: mentalism, excessive abstraction, inflexible hierarchy among different dimensions of knowledge and action, as well as among institutions and norms, and rejection of pluralism. Ultimately, these problems are rooted in the deficits that hit the subjectivistic epistemology from Descartes to Kant and finally triggered the postmodern criticism. And the flaws of the subjectivistic theory of knowledge were then transposed to the universalistic-individualistic paradigm of order: just as the knowing subject was believed to hold, in her/his individuality, the keys of the shrines of true knowledge and right action, the all-encompassing *civitas maxima*—in its unity and uniqueness as well—was assumed to shape the world as a whole unitary system. In front of these problems, it is not surprising that the legacy of the highest achievements of universalistic individualism has been mostly preserved in a different paradigmatic context, in which they could be combined—in communicative and, partially, postmodern perspective—with more flexibility, intersubjectivity and a post-unitary approach. Nonetheless, there have been also attempts to revitalize the idea of the *Weltrepublik* in the contemporary context of globalization (Sect. 4.6).

## 4.1 The Individualistic Turn in the Western Theory of Knowledge

At the dawn of the Modern Era three significant phenomena emerged in the Western world which were destined to have a significant impact on almost every aspect of social and cultural life, including the predominant theories of knowledge and action as well as, in a second step, the paradigms of order. First, impressive economic transformations gave a leading role to social actors that did not exist before or were placed in a subordinate position. The growing of a mercantile class with massive economic resources and an ever-increasing self-confidence overturned the existing system of values. Under the new circumstances, social and political ideas were not required to find for the individuals an organic position in the totality of social relations or in the whole cosmos any longer, but to give space precisely to what had been previously concealed or ignored, i.e., private interests and needs as expressions of the free individuality. The empowerment of the individuals generally happened independently of the given order of the *holon* and, in the most extreme cases, even against it. The struggle for independence in the Netherlands, the seventeenth-century revolutions in England and the creation of colonies with advanced constitutional arrangement in North America are among the most significant political consequences of this epochal change.[17] Secondly, the Reformation broke the unity of the Church and contributed to dissolving the relative political homogeneity of the Western world, hereby "accelerating the tendency towards the increase and consolidation of the power of the local monarchies" as well as towards the secularization of temporal power.[18] Moreover, the Protestant theology introduced the free interpretation of the Scripture, according to which every believer, with the help of the divine grace, is in principle able to understand its content correctly, without the official mediation of the clergy. Quite evidently, this move amounted to a further step towards the emancipation of the individuals from the established authority. Thirdly, the idea of an all-encompassing institutional and political structure in the form of the Holy Roman Empire came factually to its end, which gave way to the formation and rapid consolidation of territorial states at the service of dynastic, economic and social interests that were difficult to reconcile with the idea of an organic totality. Each of these developments contributed, in its own way, to undermining the idea of a universal order as something which is regarded as antecedent and superior to the singular elements of which it is made. Furthermore, these singular elements—individuals, religious confessions, political views, territorial identities, economic interests, social groups—were granted previously unknown possibilities of self-development and expression. The necessity to cope with the new circumstances, in all their nuances, and the drive to recognize the emerging interests, identities and priorities, as well as their plurality, led to an enormous conceptual revolution: for the first time in history, the idea of the *holon* that is assumed to include all individualities in itself was to be replaced by the conception according to which it is individuality itself, with its set of rights and interests, that is at the centre of the world.

Summing up, the phenomena that took place at the beginning of Modern Ages paved the way to the strengthening of the *individual* dimension and to a massive weakening of its holistic counterpart, up to the disappearing of the latter, at least in the forms that were known before the earthquake that ushered in the new era. From the point of view of the history of philosophical thought, the first victim of the new situation was the conviction that the world of nature and society can be adequately understood by deducing the categories for its interpretation from the hypostasis of a totality in which rationality is equivalent to the knowledge enshrined in tradition. It was precisely on this assumption that Scholasticism had founded its majestic systematic constructions. And it is against the holistic understanding of the world, supported by unquestioned tradition, that criticism arose, starting roughly in the first half of the seventeenth century. At first cautiously expressed, it grew then increasingly open and courageous. Faced with the rising amount of empirical data made available by scientific and technological progress, the most forward-looking scholars did not hesitate to make the difficulty of inserting them into the conceptual framework of the Aristotelian-scholastic metaphysics explicit. Galileo Galilei emphasized for example, in his *Dialogue Concerning the Two Chief World Systems*, the "absurdity of [... the] Peripatetic's reply; who, as a counter to sensible experience, adduced no experiment or argument of Aristotle's, but just the authority of his bare *ipse dixit*".[19] To explain the world and what we can know of it, it is no longer sufficient to recall the authority of tradition and the universal order that this seemed to express and preserve. The life of Galileo and the trial that the Church held against him show how dangerous this kind of stance was for one's personal safety. But what is interesting here is another, eminently epistemic danger, which arose from the rejection of the old philosophical system. Indeed, the Aristotelian-scholastic metaphysics had created a set of conceptual tools which had guaranteed for long time, at least in the eyes of the vast majority of the members of the scientific and social community, that two fundamental goals were achieved, namely that knowledge was recognized as true and that social order was generally perceived as legitimate and just. As for the epistemological dimension, insofar as the old certainties were shaken, it was necessary to identify a new conceptual and methodological fundament capable of giving theoretical solidity to the newly acquired evidences about the outside world and truth content to the scientific propositions elaborated on them. With reference to the justification of a just and legitimate social order, the question revolves around the conditions for a re-foundation of the political community on a new legitimacy basis.

The attempt to re-found knowledge on a ground that no longer referred to the interpretation of the divine law or to the lessons that can be drawn from the most consolidated philosophical wisdom makes up the main content of the philosophical work of René Descartes—and the solution elaborated by him marked one of the major achievements of nascent modernity. For Descartes the starting point also consisted in the critical overcoming of what had been handed over by the tradition as an incontestable truth:

> as for the opinions which up to that time I had embraced – he wrote in his seminal *Discours de la Méthode* –, I thought that I could not do better than resolve at once to sweep them wholly away, that I might afterwards

be in a position to admit either others more correct, or even perhaps the same when they had undergone the scrutiny of reason.[20]

But once the iconoclastic turn was accepted, there could no longer be certainty in the domain of knowledge, and truth could no longer be distinguished from dream or illusion—unless it was possible to identify a new and more consistent rational foundation.[21] To do this, Descartes was guided by the rules of his new method, which maintain that: (a) what is not clear and distinct to reason should not be accepted as true; (b) problems, to better solve them, should be divided into their parts; (c) knowledge should be reconstructed by starting from the simplest objects; (d) finally, "enumerations [should be made] so complete, and reviews so general, that [... one] might be assured that nothing was omitted".[22] To re-found knowledge, therefore, it is indispensable to make out an original nucleus that is simple, clear and distinct. This original nucleus, in Descartes's conception, cannot but be identical with the thinking subject.[23] Indeed, what remains, solid as a rock even in the most unsettling uncertainty, is the evidence of my existence as a thinking subject, whose activity does not cease even when producing false results:

> Thinking? Here I find the answer: it is the activity of thinking that, alone, cannot be separated from me. I am, I exist; that is certain. But for how long? Of course, as long as I am thinking.[24]

To reconstruct the theory of knowledge, however, it was not only necessary to create a new method according to which the knowing subject could elaborate rational and empiric evidences. An inescapable further pillar was, in fact, the formulation of a credible epistemological postulate which could assure that the cognitive elaborations of the single knowing subject would bring about results that would be universally shared and recognized as true. In other words, we know, now, that knowledge has to be based on the mental activity of the individual and not on tradition and authority, but what can make us sure that the products of that activity are true (in the sense that they correspond to the outer reality) and universally acceptable (in the sense that every rational being agrees on their truth content)? To address this question, Descartes opted for a solution which leads him, in the end, to a circular argumentation. In fact, he entrusted the guarantee of the truth of knowledge to none less than God, since, as he said, "God is not a deceiver".[25] Otherwise, the idea of

God is itself formed in the mind of the knowing subject,[26] who thinks of him as the absolute perfection, therefore as an existing being—God would not be perfect and complete if he did not exist—and as the guarantor of all truth.[27] In the end, if the guarantee of the truth content of the subjective knowledge should lie in God, but God is known through the mental activity of the subject, then the way goes from the subject to God, and back—which is the typical structure of a circular argumentation. As a consequence of the impracticability of the argument, the only assurance that the outcomes of the knowing subject's mental activity are universally recognized as having a truth content is the postulation that every human being endowed with reason, insofar as she/he applies the correct method of research, will inevitably achieve the same results.

From the rational activity of the thinking subject—and only from this—is the construction of a new knowledge to start, which is finally impermeable to the attacks of scepticism. Having made the matrix of knowledge coincide with the subject's thinking activity represents the great innovation of Descartes: the building of human knowledge was no longer grounded on objective metaphysical truths, which the individual had to discover outside her-/himself, but on her/his own subjectivity. With this epochal step, Descartes delivered the keys of knowledge to the individual—and inaugurated a new era in the history of human thought.

## 4.2 Thomas Hobbes's Contractualist Theory of State

The gnoseological turn in favour of subjectivism was followed, only a few years later, by a parallel development in the field of political theory. Its first advocate was Thomas Hobbes, the author who performed what has been called the "Copernican revolution" in political thought, or the transition from an Aristotelian holistic model for the understanding of social reality, to the interpretation of the *societas civilis* as the result of an agreement between free individuals.[28] In fact, Hobbes's theory of knowledge was significantly different from that of Descartes. While the latter assumed an ontological dualism between the knowing subject as the *res cogitans* (mental substance), and the outside world as the *res extensa* (physical matter), Hobbes took a substantially materialistic stance, according to which the mind of the knowing subject, too, is ultimately made of physical matter and the content of knowledge is exclusively constituted by the mental elaboration of external inputs. Nonetheless, for both authors knowledge is essentially based on the activity of the subject, who has a more or less complete access to the truth—or to what is assumed to be the truth—not by simply mirroring it from the world outside, but by forming true propositions in her/his mind. Thus, if the epistemology of both Descartes and Hobbes was subjectivistic, this same centrality of the individual was extended by the English philosopher to the domain of social and political relations.

Hobbes introduced two fundamental clarifications in the first paragraphs of *De Cive* (*On the Citizen*), published in 1642. In the first—at the very beginning of the treatise—he asserted that "the faculties of human nature may be reduced to four kinds: physical force, experience, reason, passion".[29] This simple empirical ascertainment should build the basis for the entire following inquiry. In the second clarification the author openly dismissed the Aristotelian theory of the natural sociability of humans: "this axiom, though very widely accepted, is nevertheless false; the error proceeds from a superficial view of human nature".[30] The first clarification is the starting point from which the methodological intent of the whole work originates, namely that political philosophy must be based exclusively on rational considerations. At this point, the question inevitably arises as to how Hobbes understood the meaning of reason. Far from regarding the *ratio humana* as somehow related to the knowledge of the divine law, or even deriving—no matter whether directly or indirectly—from it, Hobbes gave the notion a strictly secular interpretation. Having specified—in empiristic, if not even materialistic terms—that natural law "is a certain right reason, which (since it is no less part of human nature than any other faculty or passion of the mind) is also said to be natural",[31] he concluded that the "right reason" corresponds to the "act of reasoning, that is, [to] a man's own true reasoning about actions of his which may conduce to his advantage or other men's loss".[32] In other words, reason allows us, through calculations consisting in adding and/or subtracting the advantages and disadvantages deriving from our behaviour, to identify with high reliability the consequences of our actions for our chances of survival and self-realization. To carry out this operation correctly, reason should not be guided by authority, but based on experience. The rational evaluation of experience generates the truth content of knowledge, in general, and of science in particular: "intending not to take any principle upon trust [in authority], but only to put men in mind of what they know already, or may know by their own experience, I hope to err the less [if compared to my predecessors]".[33] Given the definition of "right reason", it is not surprising that Hobbes's arguing method marked a clear-cut turning point in comparison with the tradition.[34] Indeed, he abandoned both the historical investigation of facts as well as the argumentative method of Scholasticism—and, in general, of legal thought—relying on the reference to and the interpretation of recognized sources which are deemed capable of substantiating the exposed thesis. In his view, what is relevant is not the historical origin of the phenomena, or the justification that the doctrine may give, but their rational causes and the evidence-based inquiry that unveils them. Thus, he grounded a kind of "physics of politics",[35] i.e., an approach to social and political phenomena which shared the essential methodological assumptions with the leading science of his time, namely physics, and in particular mechanics. It is no coincidence that Hobbes began all three of his most relevant political treatises—the *Elements of Law*; the *Elementorum Philosophiae*, of which the *De Cive* is the third part; and the *Leviathan*—with a presentation of the physical nature of human experience, to indicate without any ambiguity that it is precisely in the latter that the social and political life of humans is rooted, whereas only the application of a rigorous scientific method can help us to better understand it.

Along with the turn in the methodological approach, Hobbes's second innovation concerned—as mentioned above—his break with the traditional idea of the natural human sociability. At the logical—but not historical—origin of social life there are not the "natural" belonging of humans to society, their spontaneous inclination to cooperation because of their weakness, or the consideration that everyone of us is born within a constituted relational structure. Rather, if we consider human nature with its drives from an unprejudiced and scientific point of view—Hobbes claimed—we see that humans are originally moved by selfish feelings of self-preservation and self-realization. The condition in which no society is given and every human being struggles on her/his own for her/his survival is called by Hobbes *status naturae*, or "state of nature". He used the fiction of the "state of nature" not to explain how human sociality really originated, but rather to better clarify the condition of human beings outside or before socialization. Indeed, he knew perfectly that every human being is always born into some kind of community, so that society always preexists individuality. And in fact—he clarified—we never see a general state of nature expanded all over the world, nor should we locate it at the beginning of history. Rather, a real situation which resembles to some extent the state of nature is given where the only social bond is the family or the tribe—which is not seen by Hobbes as the first stage of sociability, but as a deficient status—or, above all, when the political power disintegrates into civil war.[36] In Hobbes's understanding, therefore, putting humans into the state of nature is a fundamental mind game in order to analytically understand the essential driving forces of human action and what the establishment of society is for. The first element that he worked out was that humans, in the state of nature, are necessarily deprived of the social bonds of dependence: thus, if we want to start from that fiction to better understand the rationale of political power, then we must admit that the primary factor of political life is not constituted by the existing community, but by the *individuals*, with their original endowment of rational capacities, interests and rights. Secondly, individuals in their primal state are *equal*, where equality refers both to the unanimously shared desire to impose on others, and to the fragility that makes each person vulnerable to the attack of anyone else.[37] Not only do all of them desire the same things,[38] but they all also have the right to appropriate them, or at least to try to do so, since the *jus omnium in omnia*—the "right of all to all things"—is the logical consequence of a state in which individuals live, side by side, in a situation which is prior to the establishment of social rules and hierarchies.[39] It follows, as an inevitable consequence, that the *status naturae* is a state of war and that in this *bellum omnium contra omnes*—the "war of all against all"—[40]the life of every human being can only be "solitary, poor, nasty, brutish, and short".[41]

It is at this point that the laws of nature come into play. In the state of nature there can be no justice because there is no political power or positive law. The only existing right is the *jus naturale* that guarantees every single individual to resort to every means available to preserve her/his natural existence, i.e., life. The result, however, is exactly the opposite of what the *jus naturale* should assure to everyone, namely the safety of life: precisely because of the right of everyone over all things, individual existence becomes insecure and miserable. The exit from the dead end presupposes the passage from the priority of the *jus* to the *lex*. Hobbes was the first thinker to distinguish clearly between the two concepts: while the former protects the natural right of everyone, the second specifies their obligations. And, since at this point of the analysis individuals are still trapped in the state of nature, the *lex* is obviously a *lex naturalis*, thus not a positive, but a merely rational law, primarily aiming at safeguarding the most essential good of humans. More precisely,

> a law of nature, *lex naturalis*, is a precept, or general rule, found out by reason, by which a man is forbidden to do that which is destructive of his life, or taketh away the means of preserving the same, and to omit that by which he thinketh it may be best preserved.[42]

Therefore, in the condition of the state of nature, the first and fundamental law of nature cannot but prescribe "to seek peace and follow it".[43] In other words, given the general situation of insecurity and danger generated by the *bellum omnium contra omnes*, the first precept of right reason must necessarily order us to get out of it, creating peaceful and stable relations. Yet, this is only possible—and here the second law of nature comes into play—if every human is "willing, when others are so too, ... to lay down this right to all things; and be contented with so much liberty against other men as he would allow other men against himself".[44] The conditions are hereby set for the individuals to abandon the *status naturae* and enter the *societas civilis*, i.e., for them to constitute a social and political community and to become part of it. However, in order for this transition to the social state to effectively achieve its goal, namely the preservation of peace, it is not enough for the individuals to respect the stipulated agreements: indeed, as Hobbes wrote, "covenants, without the sword, are but words".[45] Rather—as a further step commanded by the third law of nature—all individuals have to transfer their rights to a sovereign power, invested with the monopoly of the use of force and the task of safeguarding the life and economic activity of those who, at this point, have become subjects:

> This submission of all their wills to the will of one man or of one assembly comes about – Hobbes specified – when each of them obligates himself, by an agreement with each of the rest, not to resist the will of the man or assembly to which he has submitted himself. ... This is called Union.[46]

Thus, through a single agreement—a contract in the form of a covenant, or a *pactum unionis*—individuals establish at the same time stable social relations, and a strong public power, or, in Hobbes's words, a "commonwealth" or *civitas*.

It is almost impossible to overestimate the extraordinary change of perspective introduced by Hobbes into political thought. In open contrast to premodern holism, what has been called the "Hobbesian model" turned the previous paradigms upside down.[47] In particular, five aspects stand out. First, individuals are no longer included within "natural" political constraints, but are originally *free*. Being independent of organic social hierarchies, they are—secondly—also originally *equal*. Thirdly, the family is not the basis of the political community since they fulfil clearly distinguished social functions: well-ordered reproduction of the community in the first case, shared safety and wealth in the second. Fourthly, state power has a *contractual* and not a naturalistic origin. Fifthly, given that the contract is a "voluntary act",[48] the legitimacy of political authority is due to *consent* and is not grounded simply on force or tradition. Tracing all the novelties back to their central core, we can say that while in the previous paradigms the individuals were organically at the service of society, the latter is now seen as an instrument aimed at satisfying the needs of individuals and at protecting their essential rights. While before Hobbes's turn individuals were planets revolving around a star represented by the established authority, starting from the fundamental elements of his thought makes it possible to think of authority as a satellite attracted in the orbit of human rights.

## 4.3 Individual Rights and State Power

Hobbes has been regarded by many influential thinkers as one of the fiercest advocates—if not the fiercest at all—of absolute public power. It should be sufficient, as an example, to remember the interest for his work that Carl Schmitt showed throughout his whole life.[49] Surely, some elements speak in favour of this interpretation. In Hobbes's view, in fact, to protect the established social and political order the individuals have to transfer almost all their original rights to the authority that exercises public power. They retain only the right to take the preservation of their lives into their hands in case that the public power does not accomplish its task, and—very partially—to safeguard an essential space of negative freedom. Within that space, individuals can pursue those activities that help them achieve "happiness", but only insofar as such actions do not jeopardize the overall order of peace.[50] It follows that Hobbes' contractualism is characterized by the passage from the condition of free individuals to that of subjects deprived of almost all rights: by agreeing to the *pactum unionis*, the freedom of individuals in the *status naturae* goes through a process of voluntary quasi-annihilation, which vests the sovereign authority with virtually unlimited powers. However, the conservative or reactionary sympathy for Hobbes is a rather recent phenomenon: when they had to rely on an advocate for absolutism, his contemporaries generally preferred to choose rather traditional thinkers like Filmer. This mistrust, indeed, was not accidental: Why should the supporters of absolutism put their case in the hands of a philosopher who had first claimed that all humans are originally free and equal? As a result, the future of political contractualism was neither in the conservative nor in the reactionary strand of political thought, but rather on the opposite side, in the liberal and democratic theories of society and state. It was John Locke and Jean-Jacques Rousseau, respectively, who took credit for making the groundbreaking intuition of contractualism fruitful for the political ideas of the centuries to come.

### 4.3.1 John Locke's Liberalism

John Locke's idea of the well-ordered society significantly diverges from Hobbes's on two essential points: the individuals should retain most of their entitlements after the establishment of the *societas civilis*, and the competences of the state—quite in the spirit that will characterize *liberalism* throughout its whole history—should be reduced to the minimum indispensable to guarantee social order and individual safety. However, these differences root ultimately in a third disagreement, which is located at the starting point of their respective inquiries, namely in a quite differing conception of the *status naturae*. This is in Locke, as well as in Hobbes, the (largely hypothetical) living condition of individuals who are, before the creation of public power, all free and equal.[51] Nonetheless, for the author of the *Two Treatises on Government* human beings are not essentially moved by the instinct, or by the interest, to dominate their fellow humans in order to prevent any risks for their own safety. Indeed,

> the state of nature has a law of nature to govern it, which obliges every one: and reason, which is that law, teaches all mankind, who will but consult it, that being all equal and independent, no one ought to harm another in his life, health, liberty, or possessions ... .[52]

Therefore the *status naturae* is, at least at its outset, a peaceful state, in which humans can pursue their interests in quiet coexistence and cooperation. Locke distinguished it explicitly from the state of war:

> here we have the plain difference between the state of nature and the state of war, which, however some men have confounded, are as far distant as a state of peace, good-will, mutual assistance and preservation, and a state of enmity, malice, violence, and mutual destruction, are one from another.[53]

However, this condition of benevolence and collaboration can easily be disturbed: it is sufficient that an individual makes an attempt on the life of a fellow human, or that she/he attacks the safety, freedom or property of another individual—which can never be excluded in principle—and the latter, in the absence of a superior authority to protect her/him, will be forced to defend her-/himself by resorting to private violence. Therefore, the situation can at any moment, everywhere and suddenly degenerate into a state of war, in which none of the rights of the individuals are safeguarded any longer. To prevent such a development—unalike as regards the premises, but similar in the results to Hobbes's conception—it is indispensable to leave the state of nature and constitute a public power endowed with authority. Thus, the primary function of public power is to ensure that the breach of natural law rules by an individual does not degenerate into a war of all against all. This happens when a public authority is instated which exercises justice and guarantees that the fundamental rights of all are generally respected. Locke summarizes the reasons and purposes of the transition from the state of nature to the *societas civilis* in the following passage:

> If man in the state of nature be so free as has been said; if he be absolute lord of his own person and possessions, equal to the greatest, and subject to nobody, why will he part with his freedom, why will he give up this empire, and subject himself to the dominion and control of any other power? To which it is obvious to answer, that though in the state of nature he hath such a right, yet the enjoyment of it is very uncertain, and constantly exposed to the invasion of others; for all being kings as much as he, every man his equal, and the greater part no strict observers of equity and justice, the enjoyment of the property he has in this state is very unsafe, very unsecure. This makes him willing to quit a condition, which, however free, is full of fears and continual dangers: and it is not without reason that he seeks out, and is willing to join in society with others, who are already

united, or have a mind to unite, for the mutual preservation of their lives, liberties, and estates, which I call by the general name property.[54]

In short, the state's most fundamental task is the protection of the potentially peaceful life of all citizens as well as of their essentially economic interactions. Locke's understanding of the state of nature—by far less grim than that of his predecessor and, actually, rather optimistic— and the reasons consequentially given for the birth of society serve, as mentioned above, as justifications for the further aspects that differentiate his conception of political order from that of the founder of modern contractualism. Firstly, the hypothesis of the establishment of an absolute monarchy is explicitly rejected since we do not need a Leviathan to keep fundamentally nonviolent citizens at bay.[55] Secondly, in the transition to the *societas civilis* individuals, being rather prone to cooperation, only need to give up a minimal part of their rights, basically only the prerogative of taking the law into their own hands. As a result, the protection of general security is the main task of the public authority established by the social contract. Furthermore, the legislature—as the supreme expression of the largely unrestricted freedom and sovereignty of the citizens—is defined as the supreme power,[56] which is invested with the authority to specify by law the competences of the other powers.[57] It is "established, by consent, in the commonwealth"[58] and placed— "in well-ordered commonwealths, where the good of the whole is so considered, as it ought"—exclusively in the hands of the assembly of the representatives of the citizens, namely of the parliament.[59] Thus, the specificity of Locke's liberal theory of public power culminates, on the one hand, in a substantial limitation of its prerogatives, which are restricted to the guarantee of peaceful interaction, and, on the other, in a powerful case for the attribution of institutional supremacy to the parliamentary representation of the citizens.

### 4.3.2  Jean-Jacques Rousseau's Democratic "Social Contract"

In Locke's liberalism the main task of the commonwealth consisted in safeguarding private property, which would be at stake if its defence—as in the state of nature—were put in the hands of any individual owner.[60] Not so in Jean-Jacques Rousseau's work. Here, the "conception of the historical development of humanity is not dyadic – state of nature and *societas civilis* – as for the previous exponents of contractualism, where the first condition is essentially negative and the second positive, but

## 4 UNIVERSALISTIC INDIVIDUALISM AS THE THIRD PARADIGM... 221

triadic – state of nature, civil society, and republic founded on the social contract – where the negative moment, which is the second, is placed between two positive conditions".[61] According to Rousseau, the state of nature, although certainly not characterized by prosperity, is nevertheless a largely peaceful and relatively happy state, in which humans are "without industry, without speech, without any fixed residence, [... without any] social tie", but also "without war, [...] without any need of [... their] fellows, as well as without any desire of hurting them".[62] In this sense, he took up the Enlightenment's typical understanding of history as progress; yet, he also introduced—consciously or not—an element derived from the Jewish-Christian tradition. In his political theory, in fact, the progress is not uninterrupted, but, after a period of relative happiness comparable, to some extent, to the Garden Eden, a steep decline is assumed to happen, as after the original sin, just to achieve in the end a condition which is regarded as more accomplished than the original one.

The true state of war did not begin, according to Rousseau, in the *status naturae*, but at a later time, after humans, driven by their "faculty of improvement", developed the first forms of technique.[63] By enhancing their ability to control their own existence, individuals—and, in particular, the most successful ones—also increased their desire to take control of the lives of the fellow humans. In other words, technological and cultural development introduced the differences between humans and created the conditions for an unequal and conflict-ridden society. The path from the condition of humble equality to a more affluent, but unjust social reality was marked by two main turning points, which consolidated inequality: the introduction of private property and the origin of political power and law. On both of them Rousseau's judgement was peremptorily negative. The creation of a system of private property as the first turning point of a misled process of civilization went hand in hand with the foundation of "civil society" (*société civile*), whereby the innocence of the state of nature was abandoned.[64] With the second, then, a political constitution of society was established, with binding norms and powerful institutions. These were actually destined to consolidate the inequality among humans, especially among the rich and the poor, according to the unjust condition that had been created through the first turning point. Here are Rousseau's words in this regard:

> when estates increased so much in number and in extent as to take in whole countries and touch each other, it became impossible for one man to aggrandize himself but at the expense of some other; at the same time, the

supernumerary inhabitants, who were too weak or too indolent to make such acquisitions in their turn, impoverished without having lost anything ..., were obliged to receive or force their subsistence from the hands of the rich. ... The rich on their side scarcely began to taste the pleasure of commanding, when they preferred it to every other; and ... they no longer thought of anything but subduing and enslaving their neighbors ... Destitute of valid reasons to justify, and sufficient forces to defend himself, ... the rich man ... at last conceived the most thought-out project that ever entered the human mind: this was to employ in his favor the very forces that attacked him, to make allies of his enemies, to inspire them with other maxims, and make them adopt other institutions as favorable to his pretensions, as the law of nature was unfavorable to them.[65]

From this fraudulent pact "which, historically, has given rise to the state",[66] a political order was born which had, as its sole purpose, the legal consolidation of a status quo dominated by injustice. This was the condition described by Rousseau in the famous opening of his *Du contrat social* (*The Social Contract*): "man was born free, and everywhere he is in chains".[67] The solution, following Rousseau, is the "social contract". This covenant among all members of the social and political community is thought to overcome both the humbleness of the state of nature and the injustice of the civil society. At the same time, however, it should reinstate the condition of freedom and human dignity which characterized the original condition of humankind, and it should maintain the conquests of a more comfortable life that were achieved by the constitution of the civil society. Rousseau's political programme aimed at reconstructing at the political level the equality of all members of the community that was lost at the social level as a result of diverging economic performances and opportunities. In fact, whereas the political dimension commands absolute and general equality, the economic domain allows the development of a certain degree of inequality. It is interesting, in this sense, that Rousseau criticized the unlimited expansion of private property, which can jeopardize social cohesion and may be seen as the root of many of the worst social pathologies. Yet, he never condemned the system of private property as such. On the contrary, he explicitly conceded that private property should be officially recognized and protected,[68] albeit only under the condition that it is maintained under the supremacy of the political dimension through the stipulation of the "social contract" and that the amount of the individual possessions does not reach a level which would be incompatible with political equality and the good functioning of a democratic system.[69]

Rousseau's idea of the consensual constitution of a sovereign social body composed of all individuals in conditions of political equality laid down the conceptual cornerstone of all models of democracy that have been developed ever since. However, his radical variant was not without a potentially threatening dark side. In fact, in his understanding of how the democratic public power should be created, *all* original rights of the citizens—without any exception—had to be alienated. To that extent, Rousseau was even more uncompromising than the notoriously authoritarian Hobbes. Yet, in a somehow more citizen-friendly manner, the transfer did not take place towards a Leviathan-like monarch, but back to the citizens themselves, then united to form a political community expressed by the *volonté générale*. Nonetheless, as a consequence of both the complete alienation of individual rights and an insufficient establishment of institutions with the task of counterbalancing such transfer, the sovereign authority of the *volonté générale* ended up neglecting the effective protection of the concrete individuality of citizens. It is no coincidence that Rousseau defined the members of the community founded on the "social contract" not only as "*citoyens*" but also—in particular in their relation to public power—as "*sujets*", deeming it acceptable that they were even "forced to be free".[70] It was only after the integration of its foundational idea with two elements taken from the liberal tradition—i.e., a robust division of powers and a constitutional protection of individual rights—that democracy, as the best guarantee for justice and positive citizens' freedom, could be conciliated with the no less essential principle of individual liberty.

## 4.4 The Universalistic Turn of Contractualism and the Cosmopolitan Order in Immanuel Kant

Despite the differences between the concrete proposals, the general traits of the idea of order developed by the most influential exponents of the individualistic paradigm of the Modern Era remain essentially the same: a society can be considered well-ordered if it is not only peaceful and cooperation-oriented but also based on institutions of contractual origin and aimed at safeguarding both the fundamental rights of individuals and their personal self-realization. Once the *nature* of order outlined by the basic categories of the individualistic paradigm has thus been clarified, it is still to be seen what its *extension* is, or, in other words, whether such an idea of order is applicable beyond the borders of each single polity. In general, for a long time the political philosophers of contractualism showed little interest in the questions related to international order. This reluctance is insofar understandable as the focus of their analysis was on how public power could be re-founded as well as better legitimated—and the barycentre of public power was doubtlessly located within each single state. Moreover, to the extent that they addressed the topic nonetheless, their stance was at least sceptical, if not worse. Therefore, at first glance, the new paradigm centred on the individual rights seems to be ill suited to preserve the aspiration to a cosmopolitan order that characterized the *jus gentium* elaborated in the intellectual context of holistic universalism. Starting with Hobbes again, in his work there are only few references to the relations between states. Here is how he summarized the question:

> Concerning the offices of one sovereign to another, which are comprehended in that law which is commonly called the law of nations, I need not say anything in this place, because the law of nations and the law of nature is the same thing. And every sovereign hath the same right in procuring the safety of his people, that any particular man can have in procuring the safety of his own body. And the same law that dictateth to men that have no civil government what they ought to do, and what to avoid in regard of one another, dictateth the same to Commonwealths; that is, to the consciences of sovereign princes and sovereign assemblies; there being no court of natural justice, but in the conscience only, where not man, but God reigneth … .[71]

Starting from the analogy between international law and natural law, as well as from the inherently belligerent character of the latter, it follows almost necessarily that relations between states closely resemble those between hostile individuals in the condition preceding the establishment of the commonwealth.[72] Furthermore, the need to "defend [the members of the community] from the invasion of foreigners" was seen as one of the reasons that lead to the establishment of a "common power".[73] Finally, the unquestionable and absolute power to decide about peace and war was assigned—according to a tradition hostile to the institution of binding international norms—to the sovereign of every single polity.[74]

In the same vein was the political philosophy of Baruch Spinoza—a further exponent of modern contractualism, who also claimed that the commonwealth is established on the basis of consent.[75] In his *Tractatus Politicus* (*Political Treatise*), written between 1675 and 1676, but published posthumously in 1677, he claimed indeed that "the sovereign's right is nothing other than the right of Nature itself",[76] so that "two commonwealths are by nature enemies".[77] Spinoza went even further by formulating an explicit tribute to the principle of the *raison d'état* and by asserting that "every commonwealth has full right to break a treaty whenever it wishes, and it cannot be said to act treacherously or perfidiously in breaking faith" since "each of the allied commonwealths retains the right to consult its own interests".[78] This assertion, in fact, should not come as a surprise since in Spinoza's political theory the original agreement—unlike in most other modern contractualists—does not aim essentially at preserving individual rights, or at least some of them, but at maximizing "power over Nature".[79] On the whole, Spinoza's theory represents the undisguised negation of the very idea of a binding international order—a position that a staunch supporter of particularism could hardly express in more crude terms than in the following passage of Spinoza's *Tractatus Theologico-Politicus* (*Theological-Political Treatise*):

> Allies are the men of two states who, to avoid being exposed to the hazards of war or to gain some other advantage, pledge themselves to abstain from mutual aggression and to afford each other aid when occasion demands, each state still retaining its independence. This contract will remain in force for as long as its basis – namely, the consideration of danger or advantage – persists; for nobody makes a contract, or is bound to abide by an agreement, except through hope of some good or apprehension of some evil. If the basis is removed, the agreement becomes void of itself ... .[80]

Locke's considerations on the topic may be less drastic in their formulation; yet, ultimately, they share the same spirit. Indeed, the *Treatises* also contain the reference to the *topos* of the parallel between the states (or between the princes who govern them) in their mutual relations and the individuals in the state of nature.[81] The analogy is justified by resorting to the common—but nonetheless fallacious—assumption that "the whole community is one body in the state of nature, in respect of all other states of persons out of its community".[82]

However, the rejection of universalism by the philosophers who laid down the fundaments of modern contractualism is in contrast with their most fundamental epistemological assumptions. In fact, modern rationalism understood individuals in the most abstract and general way, namely not as entities characterized by a specific language and culture, a distinct history, a particular lifestyle, etc., but as non-situated rational holders of rights and interests. Individuals, understood this way, were then seen as the founders and the essential elements of the social and political community. Yet, under these premises, how could the well-ordered social and political community be justifiably limited in its extension to the single territorial polity?.

The first opening-up of the individualistic paradigm to a perspective of order beyond the single community can be found in the work of William Penn. In his *Essay towards the Present and Future Peace of Europe* of 1693, he claimed—in line with the foundational tenet of contractualism—that, even though the origin of political power is "patrimonial", its "most natural and human" form is "that of consent, for that binds freely … when men hold their liberty by true obedience to rules of their own making".[83] After specifying that, Penn extended the principle of consent—beyond the scope of his predecessors—to the establishment of peace among the states too.[84] In doing so, he applied for the first time the conceptual framework of individualistic contractualism to the solution of the problem of supra-state order.[85] Doubtlessly, his project contains highly innovative aspects—in particular, the idea of a supranational system provided with enforcement powers[86] and ruled by a "general Diet, Estates, or Parliament", characterized by a qualified majority voting system,[87] according to which each state was assumed to have a number of votes depending on its economic strength.[88] However, the radius of the well-ordered international community did not reach beyond the borders of Europe. Moreover, although Penn admitted the Turks to the Diet,[89] he nevertheless identified in the peace among Christians the first evident benefit of the agreement,[90] and a further advantage in the strengthening of the defence against the Ottoman Empire, in the event that this would oppose the peace covenant.[91] In conclusion, the founder of Quakerism overcame the statist restriction of the first versions of contractualism, but outlined a model that is better suited, as already clarified in the title of Penn's work, to forms of regional or continental integration—with some interesting anticipations of institutional solutions which would be implemented, much later, in the European Union—than to the project of a truly cosmopolitan order of peace. To this purpose, the proposed project is, on the one hand, institutionally too ambitious and "thick", while being quite exclusive on the other: in fact, one of the most significant justifications for the establishment of peace among European nations is the potential menace deriving from a non-included geopolitical counterpart.

A similar geographic restriction of the well-ordered international community can also be found in another step towards a universalistic approach made by an exponent of the modern contract theory of state, namely in Rousseau's *Projet de paix perpétuelle* (*Plan for Perpetual Peace*), written between 1754 and 1756, and then published in 1761.[92] In this text Rousseau commented on the peace project of the Abbé de Saint-Pierre, one of the most influential contributions to the debate on the conditions for the establishment of a lasting peace during the century of enlightenment.[93] Aligning his position to that of his predecessors Penn and Saint-Pierre, the philosopher of Geneva seems not to have found anything to complain about the spatial and cultural limits of pacification. Moreover, addressing the causes of war, he severely criticized, in his *Second Discourse*, the condition of "political bodies" which, "remaining in a state of nature among themselves, soon experienced the inconveniencies that had obliged individuals to quit it".[94] Yet, he did not even consider the possibility of applying to the international realm the same kind of social contract which was assumed to remove injustice from the internal domain of the political community. In fact, individuals never feature as subjects of international law, leaving the states—once again because of the pernicious analogy between individual persons and individual states—as the only agents in the field beyond the single statist communities. On the other hand, however, Rousseau could hardly assume that the holders of an unjust internal public power would freely accept to constrain, through a mutual covenant, their right to go to war in order to increase their undeserved privileges. On that unfavourable basis, the solution could only be the imposition of a social contract in every single political community, assuming that peace beyond its borders would also be guaranteed—almost automatically—by more legitimate and just governments within the internal domain.

Finally, the cosmopolitan vocation of the individualistic paradigm was explicitly and completely recognized by Immanuel Kant. If compared to the works of his predecessors, Kant's political philosophy introduced two major novelties which can also be interpreted as original syntheses of the most ambitious approaches that had been developed until his time. First, he combined for the first time the methodological individualism of modern thought with the idea of a universally well-ordered society, which had been rather the product of the holistic paradigm. In other words, he recognized that worldwide order does not need to be grounded on some kind of predetermined social *holon*, no matter whether religiously or rationally justified; to have a cosmopolitan society aiming at peaceful cooperation, we only have to rely—according to Kant—on the rational capacity of every human being. As an unprecedented corollary of this assumption, individuals are identified as subjects of international law and a part of the public *corpus juris* is unequivocally dedicated to protect their rights beyond the borders of the state of which they are citizens. Kant's second novelty merged Rousseau's sensibility for the necessity of a just and legitimate political system within every single polity with the awareness that cosmopolitan order cannot be guaranteed only by internal reforms and political adjustments, so that the constitution of each single state is republican,[95] but requires specific institutional and legal solutions at the supra-state level.

Like all modern contractualists who opted in favour of the individualistic paradigm, Kant started the construction of his political theory by presupposing an original state of nature, from which humans can get out by stipulating a contract to establish the social and political community.[96] He left no doubts as regards the fictional character of the *status naturae*, nor did the original contract correspond, in his view, to any real historical event since he was rather keen on believing that public power had its origin in the use of brute force.[97] Nonetheless, he was also firmly convinced that the idea of a fictitious contract created the conceptual background for a better understanding of the conditions according to which the authority of the institutions exercising public power can be regarded as legitimate and justified.[98] As regards the human situation in the state of nature, Kant largely took up Hobbes's pessimistic view, interpreting the fictitious original condition basically as a state of endemic and ongoing war[99] since the human being—he added—is nothing but a "warped wood" (*krummes Holz*).[100] Analogous to Hobbes is also the mechanistic conception of the state, seen as an "automaton" (*Automat*) which, thanks to internal equilibrium, is able to guarantee stability and adequate correspondence to the goals established by the contract.[101] Yet, Kant defined the aim of the establishment of society in a significantly different way if compared to his English predecessor. The difference between Hobbes and Kant can be traced back, ultimately, to their quite diverging understandings of rationality. Since the conduct of individuals and communities is assumed by both to be essentially based on rational considerations, those quite distinct—if not opposite—understandings of rationality also have a relevant impact on what they considered, respectively, as the ultimate goal of practical life.

As for the general concept of rationality, Kant shared with all contractualists—and, thus, with Hobbes too—the conviction that the transition to society is a command of reason; yet, rationality is understood by Kant not in a selfishly-strategic, but in a transcendental way. This means that every human being implements the commands of reason only insofar as she/he contributes to the creation of a condition in which *all* her/his fellow humans also live in a way that can be justifiably seen as the realization of the very same commands. In other words, it cannot be enough—if we want to act rationally—that everyone carves out a space for her/himself, while being indifferent to what might happen to the others. On the contrary, the command of reason is only fulfilled if everyone is involved and her/his self-realization is secured. As a result, rational self-realization can only be *inclusive*—and even *universalistic*—insofar as it should comprise every single member of the community. As powerfully expressed in the first formulation of Kant's categorical imperative—"act only according to that maxim whereby you can at the same time will that it should become a universal law"—[102] universalistic inclusion is the first outcome of Kant's transcendental understanding of rationality, an essential element of his theory on the right use of practical reason, and a no less fundamental component of the just society that should be built on the basis of that understanding.

Moving on to discover the contents of right action, we have to turn to the second formulation of Kant's categorical imperative:

> Act in such a way that you treat humanity, whether in your own person or in the person of any other, never merely as a means to an end, but always at the same time as an end.[103]

With this famous sentence, Kant identified the *humanitarian* nucleus of the "golden rule" as the second outcome of his understanding of rationality and as a further element that characterizes the correctly understood idea of the moral self-realization of the individual, on the one hand, and of the just society on the other. Without the most absolute respect for humanity neither a moral life can be accomplished, nor a morally justifiable society can be established.

The third formulation of the categorical imperative—namely the idea that "the will could ... regard itself as giving in its maxims universal laws"[104]—leads us to the last element of right action and just society according to Kant. Once again, it is about the meaning of individual self-realization. Provided that the self-realization of the individual represented for both Hobbes and Kant the ultimate goal of action, the differences are nonetheless striking. In Hobbes's work the peaceful society created by the contract was essentially thought to secure life and property of the individuals who had joined it. Thus, its aim consisted in safeguarding the necessary room for that kind of negative liberty that is implemented through the self-centred maximization of payoffs. The worth of private self-realization is surely recognized by Kant as well, but his idea of the right action has also a much more important and ambitious dimension, which depends, once again, on his non-strategic concept of rationality. In accordance with the third formulation of the categorical imperative, human beings do not act rationally if they only maximize their payoffs, but exclusively to the condition that they follow the commands that they have given to themselves. *Autonomy* is therefore—together with universalism and humanity—the third cornerstone of Kant's theory on the right use of practical reason and an essential component of what should be understood as the rational individual self-realization. And, since reason is a common gift of all human beings and the commands are inherently rational, the autonomy of everyone of us is only implemented insofar as the autonomy of *all* is enacted.

By stressing the concept of autonomy, Kant departed from Hobbes to lean, instead, on Rousseau. Indeed, the philosophical inspirer of the French Revolution had already claimed that the overcoming of the state of nature for the creation of a democratic and peaceful society did not lead to the loss of freedom, but rather to the accomplishment of its most noble interpretation, i.e., to the autonomy of the political community:

> we must clearly distinguish natural liberty, which is limited only by the powers of the individual, from civil liberty, which is limited by the general will ... . We might also add to the advantages of the civil state moral freedom, which alone enables man to be truly master of himself; for the impulse of mere appetite is slavery, while obedience to a self-prescribed law is freedom.[105]

Thus, following Rousseau, the satisfaction of instincts is not freedom, but, indeed, subjugation of the individuals to their compulsions. On the contrary, only the political community based on the social contract can implement the true form of freedom, which consists in following the laws that we have given ourselves. In the same way as Rousseau, Kant also considered autonomy as one of the basic elements of moral life, according to the principle that "the laws to which [… the individual] is subject are only those of his own giving, though at the same time they are universal".[106] Furthermore, autonomy was also regarded by Kant as an essential component of the well-ordered society, more specifically of legitimate public power.[107] In the transition from Rousseau to Kant, however, the factors were reversed. According to Rousseau the main achievement was political self-government, and its corollary—which is basically guaranteed through the social context created by a just society—was moral autonomy. For Kant, vice versa, the primary purpose of the foundation of society was the moral improvement of the individual, which implied the establishment of a regime of political autonomy. Moreover, when it comes to the concrete definition of political autonomy, Kant identified it with a strong legislature as the institutional expression of the autonomy of the citizens:

> The legislative authority can belong only to the united will of the people. For since all right is to proceed from it, it *cannot* do anyone wrong by its law. Now, when someone makes arrangements about *another*, it is always possible for him to do the other wrong; but he can never do wrong in what he decides upon with regard to himself (for *volenti non fit iniuria*). Therefore only the concurring and united will of all, insofar as each decides the same thing for all and all for each, and so only the general united will of the people, can be legislative.[108]

Doubtlessly, this is one of the most impressive pleas for the self-government of the citizens in the whole history of human thought. However, in explicit contrast with the radical-democratic preferences of the author of the *Social Contract*, legislative power in Kant's political thought has to be adequately softened and counterbalanced, quite in Montesquieu's tradition, by the executive and judicial powers.

Universality, humanity and autonomy are therefore the most essential elements of Kant's theory on the correct use of practical reason. As regards autonomy, we have already seen what it means with reference to the moral and political dimension, namely that a moral agent, to be autonomous, has to follow only the laws she/he has given her-/himself, thus becoming independent from any external influence or authority. Turning our attention, now, on the other two components—humanity and universality—it is also quite evident how they can be translated into a moral rule. According to Kant's interpretation, every human being has to put every fellow human, on a mutual basis and without any geographic, cultural, ethnic, religious or whatsoever restriction, at the centre of her/his efforts. Moreover, those efforts should be understood in a deontological way, i.e., as duties—therefore, not as a matter of prudential choice—since, given the transcendental premises of Kant's philosophy, the respect for the human dignity of all is the only rationally justifiable behaviour. Acting in accordance with moral duties may be sometimes difficult; yet, this matter of fact does not diminish the rational value of Kant's argument since moral action, in his view, has an inherently counterfactual aspect: we have to strive for morality and believe that this approach is basically successful and universally shared; otherwise, society would disintegrate. The question, however, is more complicated if the implementation of universality and humanity is also assumed to take shape in an institutional design, in which the counterfactual driving forces of individual action must give way to a concrete political and legal architecture. Put differently, a place must be found in which the political and legal system implements universality and humanity.

The universal defence of humanity is no new idea in the history of political thought. Indeed, it has already been detected, in a previous chapter, as an essential element of the holistic-universalistic paradigm of order. However, at that stage, it was shaped as a result either of the divine or of the rational law, thus without a clearly identifiable positive legal content. The only partial exception was represented by Christian Wolff, whose *civitas maxima*—though legally shaped—was made of sovereign states and not of individuals, so that the interests of the latter could merely be taken into account in an indirect way. Against this background, one of the most important achievements of Kant's legal and political philosophy was precisely the identification of a part of the *corpus juris* with the specific task of defending human dignity—i.e., the dignity of each single individual—on a universal scale, whereas this part of the *corpus juris* was established as *positive and human law*. Traditionally, positive public law had always been divided in two parts: state law and international law. Kant was the first author to introduce a tripartition of public law, in which the third part—going from the most specific to the most general and inclusive—was unequivocally defined as "cosmopolitan law" (*jus cosmopoliticum*):

> But any legal constitution, as far as the persons who live under it are concerned, will conform to one of the three following types: a) a constitution based on the civil rights of individuals within a nation (*jus civitatis*); b) a constitution based on the international rights of states in their relationships with one another (*jus gentium*); c) a constitution based on cosmopolitan right, insofar as individuals and states, coexisting in an external relationship of mutual influences, may be regarded as citizens of a universal state of humankind [*allgemeiner Menschenstaat*] (*jus cosmopoliticum*).[109]

Beside the law *of the state*—as the first part of his system of public law—and the law *between states*—or *international law* as the second part of it—cosmopolitan law included principles and rules that govern the interactions between human beings as such, regardless of their nationality or citizenship. Thus, by introducing the *jus cosmopoliticum*, Kant achieved two results, impacting, respectively, on the traditional understandings of individualism and universalism. First, as regards individualism, he granted its foundational principle, namely the centrality of individuals, an unprecedented worldwide and all-encompassing scope, since—as he explicitly stated—"what man ought to do by the laws of his freedom" applies "in all three areas of public law, in state law as well as in international and cosmopolitan law".[110] Secondly, with reference to universalism, he overcame the usual approach according to which cosmopolitan entitlements were seen as being intrinsically commands of natural law, and not as positive law—even though, in his time, only in the perspective *de lege ferenda*. Unequivocally, he maintained on this point that the "rational idea of a peaceful, even if not friendly, thoroughgoing community of all nations on the earth ... is not a philanthropic (ethical) principle, but a principle having to do with law".[111] If compared with the novelty of Kant's position, it may be surprising how "thin" the rights contained in his *jus cosmopoliticum* are. In fact, they were restricted to nothing more than pure "hospitality", i.e., to the entitlement not to be treated as an enemy while being—by choice or necessity—in a foreign country, whereas no right of settlement is acknowledged and the specific condition of persecuted foreigners is not addressed.[112] Surely, Kant's time was not ripe for an exhaustive catalogue of human rights, which were generally included, at the end of the eighteenth century, under citizens' rights—and he cannot be made responsible for this. Nevertheless, other authors before him, like Vitoria, went further in the recognition of what is owed to every human being.[113] This can be partially explained by the fact that Catholic authors were more prone to limit the authority of the state in front of the rights of the members of the *communitas christiana*, while Kant tried to find a more equilibrate balance between the two instances. Yet, the thinness of his *jus cosmopoliticum* may also be seen as the hint of a more profound conceptual problem that affects the individualistic paradigm as a whole and on which I will come back in short.

If there is something that threatens the universal respect for human dignity, this has always been—and always will be—war. Therefore, following Kant as well as all other supporters of universalism, building and preserving peace is the first and most compelling command of reason, which must be translated not only into an individual moral duty and into a system of legal norms, but also into an adequate institutional framework. From the perspective of the moral driving force of the individual, it is the "moral-practical reason" itself that "pronounces in us its irresistible veto: there is to be no war, neither war between me and you in the state of nature, nor war between us as states".[114] Furthermore, on the political side, the overcoming of war is regarded by Kant as the most relevant goal that has to be achieved through the transition from the state of nature to the *societas civilis*; indeed,

> establishing universal and lasting peace constitutes not merely a part of the doctrine of right (*Rechtslehre*), but rather the entire final end of the doctrine of right within the limits of reason alone; for the condition of peace is the only condition in which what is mine and what is yours are secured under laws for a multitude of humans living in proximity to one another.[115]

Since war is the most severe obstacle to moral development,[116] Kant consistently put the creation of a stable condition of peace as the ultimate end of the whole historical development of humanity.[117] However, since the command to build and preserve peace does not address only the moral conscience of the individual but has also a political component, the question must be raised of which institutional structure would be best suited to that end. Kant presented in his texts two diverging—if not downright opposite—solutions. The first consisted in the creation of a "world republic" (*Weltrepublik*), i.e., of a global statist edifice, largely centralized and governed by binding norms, in which the individual sovereign states would eventually dissolve. The second, on the contrary, aimed at the foundation of a free "federation"—according to Kant's language, but it would be probably better to say "confederation"—of sovereign states, or peoples (*Völkerbund*).

The *Weltrepublik* is presented as a "positive idea" and "true *in thesi*".[118] In addition, Kant explicitly praised it with the following words:

> There is only one rational way in which states coexisting with other states can emerge from the lawless condition of pure warfare. Just like individual human beings, they must renounce their savage and lawless freedom, adapt themselves to public coercive laws, and thus form a state of peoples (*Völkerstaat*) (*civitas gentium*), which would necessarily continue to grow until it embraced all the peoples of the earth.[119]

Given the tenor of this passage, there can be little doubt that this is the solution that Kant considered to be preferable under the aspect of the guarantee of peace and for the moral progress of humanity. In fact, only an order built on binding norms can consistently avoid the permanent danger of conflict that derives from self-reliant and unrestrained multiple sovereignties with just temporarily converging interests. Nevertheless, some important considerations speak, in Kant's view, against such a hypothesis, up to the point of making it impracticable. The first problem is identified with the risks for freedom that would be created by the establishment of a universal government. More precisely, the menace would be even more evident if the universal government took the shape of a "universal monarchy"—actually, the only possibility that Kant considered—i.e., of a hegemonic government which, starting from the power of a single state, ends up spreading globally. It is plain, here, that Kant had in mind historical examples of global hegemonic attempts which, precisely because of their claim to settle all differences, had degenerated into "the most fearful despotism",[120] that is to say into a "soulless despotism".[121] However, it is curious—and, as I will show later, also illustrative of a shortcoming in Kant's philosophy—that he did not even consider that some kind of *Weltrepublik* could also originate in a federalist way, i.e., from an agreement between peers, and have a decentralized structure.

The second objection to the idea of a global legal and institutional structure refers to the necessity of maintaining the plurality of the cultural identities of peoples, from which the ineludible plurality of states would also derive.[122] Only as members of the *Völkerbund* would peoples preserve their linguistic and religious identity alongside their freedom. Also in this case, however, Kant's argument is not convincing to the extent that he failed, once again, to take a multilayered organization of global order into consideration and to distinguish between cultural and political identity.[123] Finally, the third criticism against the *Weltrepublik* pointed at its factual impracticality since a political structure of global dimension would have difficulty in imposing the law in every single part of its domain.[124] Moreover—and here the tone of Kant seems to become regretful—the single sovereign states would do everything in their power to boycott the creation of a *Völkerstaat*, so that the only remaining feasible solution would be to accept, in the end, the *Völkerbund* as the "negative surrogate" of the *Weltrepublik*.[125] The main characteristic of the *Völkerbund*, if compared to the *Weltrepublik*, is that it does not imply the subjugation of states to "public laws and to a coercive power which enforces them".[126] Therefore, the *Völkerbund* is not primarily at the service of a steady order of global scope, but of the freedom of each individual state in its own interest. Peace thus represents, in this perspective, the secondary consequence of an attitude aimed, above all, at safeguarding the particular benefit of every single political community. On the basis of these premises, it does not come as a surprise that the confederation of states is assumed to apply the principle of non-interference.[127] Ultimately, success and endurance of the *Völkerbund* depend on the free decisions of its members, which can at any time and for any reason resolve to dissolve it.[128]

In such a precarious situation, in which the *Weltrepublik* seemed to be unattainable (or even not desirable) and the *Völkerbund* did not give any guarantee, Kant ultimately entrusted his hope for a peaceful future not so much to politics and law, but rather to morals and a teleological conception of history and nature. Thus, he appealed to the duty of every human being to act in such a way as to favour the moral progress of humanity.[129] Although he claimed that some historical evidence of the progress towards peace and humanity would be detectable—whereby an explicit reference to the French Revolution was made—[130]he also firmly maintained that moral action towards those ends is simply a duty, which does not need to be corroborated or confirmed by factual success. In fact, what Kant called the "fact" of practical reason[131] is mere expression of the transcendental faculties of the subject and proves to be refractory (or indifferent) to any translation into institutional or legal procedures. The same is true for the teleological conception of history[132] and nature,[133] which, as a product of the subjective judgement aimed at consolidating the moral attitude of the individual, is nothing but a surrogate—one could maliciously say: a consoling surrogate—of a really binding order of universal peace. In the absence of such an order, only the moral duty founded on the subject and a non-evidence-based conviction that history and nature have a goal are presumed to reassure us—in a quite partial form—that perpetual peace is going to be achieved[134] and that the republican constitution in all states will be realized. Indeed, in a context of largely unrestrained sovereign states, the transition to a republican constitution in every state would be the only guarantee that international agreements are respected.[135]

In the end, Kant outlined two solutions for a worldwide order of peace which are not only different but seem also to be—at first glance—irreconcilable: the one is maybe feasible, but does not bring about a reliable condition of peace; the other would solve the problem, but is out of reach and, to some extent, weighted down by other deficits. The result cannot but be a conceptual stalemate. However, was it inevitable for Kant to remain stuck in this contradiction? In fact, the arguments in favour or against both solutions are undeniably strong. Nonetheless, was a compromise between cosmopolitan order and particular political identities really impossible? Or, put differently, why was Kant incapable of figuring out a construction in which a cosmopolitan institutional and legal structure— but not a world state—was entrusted with the safeguard of world peace and fundamental human rights, while the single states maintained all other competencies? The most spontaneous answer could be that Kant's times were not ripe, yet, for that idea. This answer, nevertheless, would just trigger a further question: Why were those times not ripe? Has this perhaps something to do with a deep-going shortcoming of Kant's fundamental philosophical assumptions, or even with the basic tenets of the individualistic paradigm of order? Indeed, we can find in Kant's theory of world order at least four conceptual deficits or mistakes, which appear to indicate that the roots of the stalemate between *Weltrepublik* and *Völkerbund* lie at a deeper level.

The first of those deficits or mistakes refers to Kant's unwavering identification of the notion of "constitution", in its range of application, with that of "state".[136] The theoretical and factual overlapping of the two concepts, which he arguably derived from Rousseau's concept of popular sovereignty, not only made impossible to regard forms of social, political and legal order beyond the state as constitutional, but also unveils his strongly unitary and statist understanding of public power. The same centralist and statist attitude emerges also with reference to the second shortcoming of Kant's political theory, namely his conceiving of sovereignty as essentially undivided, whereby he, once again under the influence of the French republican tradition, overlooked the most recent developments of American federalism.[137] The unitary character of identity is outlined also in the third inadequacy, which is related to the missing distinction between cultural and political identity, with the consequence that it seems to be impossible, in Kant's view, that a plurality of cultural identities coexist within one political entity. But the most revealing shortcoming of Kant's political philosophy is the fourth, i.e., the irreflexive analogy between the transition of the individuals from the state of nature to the *societas civilis*, as a single political community, and the passage from the condition of permanent conflict between the communities thus established—i.e., the states[138]—to the supra-state order of peace.[139] The analogy is hardly convincing, already from the point of view of its pure internal logic, since it puts on the same level—with an intent which is not only metaphorical, but explicitly genetic and normative—two deeply different realities: in the first case individuals, and in the second collective entities, namely states, composed of a high number of precisely those individuals. In fact, the equivalence between individuals and states is a widely spread *topos* of political thought: just to mention a couple of examples, we already came across it in a former chapter[140] and, in this one, while analysing the political philosophy of Hobbes, Locke and Rousseau. Its popularity, however, does not make the argument any better. Indeed, if we can arguably assume the unity of intent of single individuals as physical persons, the same cannot be done with collective entities which are made of many individuals and social groups with diverging priorities. For that reason, subjects interacting in international relations, maybe seeking an agreement in order to guarantee peace, must be perceived—if the observer wants to avoid an evident fallacy—at both levels: as individual states entrusted with public power, and as single persons, endowed with rights and interests, which ultimately constitute those states. Kant's incapacity to distinguish between the two levels may account for the thinness of the rights guaranteed by his *jus cosmopoliticum*.

The interesting question, now, is why Kant made this mistake. Is this just a marginal deficit of his grand philosophical project, or is it the clue of a problem affecting the universalistic-individualistic paradigm as a whole?

Some elements speak for the second option. Indeed, all supporters of the individualistic paradigm—from Descartes and Hobbes to Kant and beyond—conceive of the individual, as both a knowing and an acting subject, in terms of an entity which is presumed to be unquestionably self-reliant, utterly solipsistic in its self-referentiality, and more isolated and focused on her-/himself than immersed in a network of relations. In other words, the individual of the theoretical and practical paradigm of modernity is a monad endowed with reason and rights, which, precisely because of her/his self-reliant nature, is believed to precede the dimension of intersubjectivity both epistemologically and axiologically. More specifically, the monadic subjectivity of modern philosophy is distinguished by three features: internal unity, self-referential hierarchy of epistemological categories and moral norms, and solipsism. Internal unity refers to the assumption that all elements that make up the theoretical and practical experience of the individual have to be consistent with each other in order to be true and just: self-contradictions or internal conflicts are only pathologies to be healed and are not accepted as healthy driving forces of personal and social development. As the second component of modern subjectivity, self-referential hierarchy means that in both the theoretical and the moral experience some components have to dominate over others: the abstract categories of theoretical reason must transform the multifaceted and sometimes chaotic experience into a well-structured system of knowledge, and moral commands have to control instinctual compulsions. Finally, solipsism indicates that intersubjective interaction is not assumed to be needed in order to achieve truth and to distinguish right from wrong: everyone of us is presumed to be able to reach the best possible results of the use of reason all alone.

Among the three (problematic) elements of modern subjectivity, the first—i.e., its unitary character—is the most important in order to understand the shortcomings of Kant's political philosophy. In fact, on the basis of the firm assumption of the unitary character of subjectivity, it becomes impossible to attribute to the individual any kind of multidimensional identities, multiple memberships, or different levels of integration corresponding to distinct qualities of social relations. Given those premises, we can realize why Kant rejected the distinction between constitution and state, which would create a variable geometry of cosmopolitan constitutionalism while breaking the unity of the constitutional system. The same bias in favour of unity prevented him from taking the idea of divided sovereignty seriously, or from figuring out the potentiality of the distinction between cultural heritage and political belongingness, once again with the possibility of variable geometries. But, above all, the rigid unity of subjectivity explains the analogy between individuals and states as well as the contradiction between *Weltrepublik* and *Völkerbund*. The monadic individual, not being able to shatter her/his unity, can only join other individuals with identical characteristics to establish, by means of one single act, a collective entity which takes over the very same features of the entities by which it was created. Therefore, the *societas civilis* is nothing but a collective individual that derives its competences from the rights alienated by the citizens. This process is perfectly described by Rousseau:

> Each of us puts in common his person and all his power under the supreme direction of the general will; and in return each member becomes an indivisible part of the whole. Right away, in place of the particular individuality of each contracting party, this act of association produces a moral and collective body, composed of as many members as the assembly has voices, and which receives from this same act its unity, its common self (*moi*), its life, and its will.[141]

Likewise, for collective individuals there is no other prospect than agreeing to constitute, in their turn, a global body—no less unitary, but larger than the single states—according to an ascending process that always reproduces at the higher level the same features that characterized the lower stage. The ontological depletion of the lower stage by the upper one is destined, however, to provoke increasing resistance the further one moves away from the lifeworld of the individuals, and to lead, as we have seen in Kant, to the failure of the project of world order in the shape of a *Weltrepublik*. Thus, according to the most fundamental assumptions of the individualistic paradigm, the social and political agents—no matter whether as small as the single individual or as huge as the *Weltrepublik*—cannot but be unitary and self-reliant entities, which are refractory to any form of variable geometry of memberships. As a result of this essential tenet, any coexistence between different forms and levels of supra-state order is ruled out: either we opt for a global megastate, or for a precarious confederation of sovereign nation states. The conceptual framework of traditional individualism allows no third option, i.e., no combination of binding global order and respect for national identities, although it would be much needed. To make such a combination even only thinkable, however, a new paradigm had first to be developed.

## 4.5 HANS KELSEN AND THE PRIORITY OF INTERNATIONAL LAW

Hans Kelsen's legal philosophy can be regarded, at the same time, as the apotheosis of the universalistic-individualistic paradigm of order, and as its breaking point. On the one hand, he carried the essential tenets of the paradigm to their most unequivocal and radical consequences, while making, on the other, their deficits more explicit than any other author before him. As regards the radicalization of the paradigmatic approach, six aspects deserve particular attention: his utterly *antimetaphysical epistemology*, his conception of the *state*, his understanding of the notion of *people*, his quite revolutionary ideas on the taxonomy of the different political systems and the *justification of democracy* resulting from it, the predominance of *international law as the apex of the pyramid of legal norms*, and the uncompromisingly *unitary conception of the legal system*.

With reference to the rejection of metaphysics in the theory of knowledge, there can be no doubt that this is a feature that has characterized the epistemology of the individualistic paradigm throughout its entire development. The claim that knowledge, in order to be true, must be supported by evidence appears in the work of Descartes and Hobbes, at the very beginning of the paradigmatic evolution, to eventually find its completion in Kant's *Kritik der reinen Vernunft* (*Critique of Pure Reason*). Yet, precisely Kant, who is generally regarded as having put a tombstone on classical metaphysics, is the target of Kelsen's antimetaphysical criticism. The premise is that Kelsen—as the most consistent advocate of legal positivism—wanted to establish legal theory as a "pure doctrine", or as a self-reliant science, with legal norms as its material and legal categories as the logical instruments capable of structuring that material to form a coherent system and of interpreting it. Just as every established science—be it biology or physics, or even sociology or psychology—has its own object to analyse by employing its own epistemological organon, without resorting to any external notion or to moral, theological or philosophical arguments, legal theory should also reject any kind of reference to predetermined and extra-legal assumptions, if it aims at being acknowledged as a discipline that applies a scientific method.[142] According to Kelsen, while Kant's theory of knowledge overcomes metaphysics in the field of theoretical reason, his political and legal thought—i.e., his practical philosophy—would betray his own methodological premises as a theoretical epistemologist. More concretely, Kelsen claimed that Kant's concept of positive law would have been based on a metaphysical foundation since it still presupposed the reference to natural law and, thus, to some kind of "objective" truth. As a result, his political and legal philosophy would conflict with that ethical plurality which is essential in contemporary society, jeopardizing the possibility of conceiving the law as the formal mediation of different conceptions of the good.[143] In fact, Kant is quite explicit about the link between law and extra-legal discourses, in particular moral principles:

> In contrast to laws of nature, the laws of freedom are called *moral* laws. As directed merely to external actions and their conformity to law they are called *juridical* laws; but if they also require that they (the laws) themselves be the determining grounds of actions, they are *ethical* laws, and then one says that conformity with juridical laws is the *legality* of an action and conformity with ethical laws is its *morality*.[144]

As it has been already pointed out above, morals and law are both interpreted as aiming at the realization of *autonomy* as the condition in which human beings—who are at the same time moral and political subjects—give themselves the rules that they ought to follow. Nevertheless, Kant's morals can hardly be seen as "metaphysical" in the traditional sense of the word, since morality, in his conception, does not resort to an "objective" truth which is assumed to be rooted in God's will or in nature, being situated, therefore, beyond and above the critical reflexion of individuals. Rather, Kant's moral principles build a *transcendental* foundation for peaceful and cooperative human interaction: insofar as they express the fundamental rules that humans give themselves so as to live with each other in peace and solidarity, they are not objective and substantial, but *subjective* and *formal*. Furthermore, in Kant's approach the connection between law and morals guarantees three essential functions: (a) a criterion for the validity of the law (a law that violates the principle of autonomy can be effective and in force, but cannot claim to be endowed with full normative validity); (b) a conceptual basis for criticism of the existing law, as a precondition for further development of the legal system (on the basis of the principle of autonomy it is justifiable to criticize a law that violates this principle and to engage for its improvement); (c) a definition of the social function of the law (a law endowed with full normativity takes up the function of guaranteeing autonomy in social and political interactions).

At this point, the questions arise whether, first, a legal system is really conceivable that refrains—as claimed by Kelsen and legal positivism in general—from any extra-legal reference, and, secondly, whether such a system can accomplish on its own the same functions that, in Kant's philosophy, are attributed to the conjunction of law and morality. To answer the first question, a premise has to be made. According to Kelsen's "pure theory of law", the legal system is made up of hypothetical propositions—without any resorting to social realities or ethical principles[145]— the validity of which is guaranteed exclusively by the fact that their production follows the rules established by a higher norm. Therefore, in the formal pyramid of legal positivism the validity of any proposition is founded on the validity of a norm situated at a hierarchically higher level. Yet, the logic of such a conception inescapably leads to an infinite regress, so that Kelsen—in order to avoid a conceptual shortcoming that would undermine his whole construction—created a borderline concept of legal theory, namely the *Grundnorm* or "basic norm".[146] According to the hierarchical understanding of the legal system, we have at its top a set of positive legal propositions which serve as the foundation of the whole structure, so that all other norms are grounded on them and justified by them. Within the national legal system this set is identified with the constitution, while at the most inclusive global level the same function is taken up by the fundamental norms of international law. However, to be valid, all these positive legal propositions should be based themselves on another, even more essential norm. This is precisely the point at which the *Grundnorm* is introduced to put an end to the regress and to accomplish the task of supporting the whole system. Yet, if the *Grundnorm* is to be successful in bringing the regress to a halt, it must be of a different kind if compared to the other norms; otherwise, it would also be subject to the same necessity of further justification that characterizes all norms. This is the reason why the *Grundnorm* is described by Kelsen as non-positive, or—more precisely—as a pre-positive and "presupposed" (*vorausgesetzt*) principle which guarantees the validity of all positive legal propositions. Under these premises, the *Grundnorm* may actually incorporate any content: the only quality that is essential to the pre-positive principle of the whole legal system is its effectiveness.

In conclusion, the *Grundnorm* ends up assuming the same role as the morals in Kant's political and legal philosophy insofar as it provides the kind of validation to the system of legal norms that this is not able to give itself autonomously. Furthermore, as far as the autonomy of the law is concerned, Kelsen's solution is not, in the end, better than the one proposed by his predecessor since the *Grundnorm* is no less extra-legal than Kant's morality. This evidence cast a shadow on the scientific project of legal positivism as a whole, in particular on its claim that the epistemological content of the law should and could rest exclusively on the law itself. H. L. A. Hart, as the most prominent positivist after Kelsen, tried to overcome the gridlock by rejecting the explicitly foundational and thus still substantial, if not even metaphysical, concept of the *Grundnorm* and by substituting it with the more formal notion of the "rule of recognition".[147] In Hart's theory, the foundation of the legal system is itself a content-free and quite essential acknowledgement of the validity of a legal system, which is assumed to be internal to the latter and not a pre-legal postulation. Nevertheless, the "rule of recognition" consists itself, ultimately, in identifying a self-imposed obligation, the acceptance of which is based on extra-legal conditions. As a result, Hart's revised positivism shares with Kelsen's conception the same flaws that seem to affect every positivist understanding of the legal system: first, the legal system cannot refrain from references to extra-legal circumstances; and, secondly, due to the extra-legal conditions on which it is based, legal positivism meets with an irreflexive and normatively unrestrained social and political power. This way, the normativity of the law is largely—and dangerously—reduced to value-free compliance. This is also the reason why—coming now to the question referred to above—the *Grundnorm* and the "rule of recognition" are not only as extra-legal as the reference to moral principles, but also largely incapable of taking up the same regulative function. Indeed, they guarantee far less than Kant's morals—or than any other similar solution—an adequate standard for the normativity of the law, nor do they propose a rational criterion for its further development.

The second aspect of Kelsen's radicalization of some of the most relevant tenets of the individualistic paradigm concerns the concept of *state*. Kelsen joined the previous exponents of the individualistic paradigm in rejecting the understanding of the state as a living body, or as a *corpus*, which was distinctive of holism, in general, and of political romanticism in particular. Indeed, he stated explicitly that the state is not a "metalegal entity, ... a kind of macro-anthropos endowed with full power", or "a social organism ... which is the precondition of law and, at the same time, ... a legal entity that presupposes the law as it is subject to this, as well as obliged and authorized by it".[148] In other words, the state does not create the law with a pre-legal act of will, based, for instance, on the alleged identity of the nation or of a religiously cohesive social group. Nor does it presuppose the law as the foundation of its legitimacy, in the sense of a *Rechtsstaat*, or of a state based on the "rule of law", the task of which is identified entirely with the implementation of legal procedures, substantially aiming at the protection of formally constituted fundamental rights. Rather—and this is the point in which Kelsen's legal philosophy went beyond the usual contents of the individualistic paradigm—the state simply and radically coincides with the law, meeting both in the function of guaranteeing a well-ordered space for the unfolding of human interactions.[149] The clue to the individualistic background of Kelsen's idea of the state, therefore, is that this is not understood as a metaphysical entity, but as an institutional structure, which is insofar "artificial" as it has been created by humans,[150] and completely overlaps with law since both have the task of guaranteeing a well-ordered human behaviour.[151] Indeed, to the extent that interactions proceed in an orderly manner, individuals enjoy the highest possible chance of self-realization. In his conception of the state, however, Kelsen is insofar more radical than any of his predecessors as he completely ignores—or even utterly denies—that the state, being not only law but also politics, might develop a specific sense of identity among its citizens which is value-oriented as well as distinctive to the extent that it cannot be adequately explained only by recurring to the formal rules of interaction.

A similar constellation reappears also with reference to the third individualistic element in Kelsen's legal theory, namely his conception of the "people". Far from being a homogeneous reality, the population of a political community is divided through national, religious and economic differences, being, according to sociological analysis, "more a bundle of groups than a coherent, homogeneous mass".[152] Once the internal plurality of every social and political community is acknowledged, the reaction should not consist, according to his view, in attempting to create a substantial homogeneity, i.e., in removing the differences, but—quite in accordance with the individualistic canon—in shaping a space in which social diversity can coexist. This is precisely the function taken up by a non-ontological notion of the "people". To accomplish the task of guaranteeing peace and order in a diverse society, the concept of "people" should be seen as a purely legal construct, which fosters formal unity on the basis of the law in a context where economic, ethnic and religious conflicts loom. Thus, the unity of the people is not a reality that can be found in social and political life, nor is some kind of substantial unity to be established through political measures. Rather, according to Kelsen, it is a postulate, based only on the unitary and internally coherent character of the legal system which the individuals and groups being part of the hereby constituted "people" acknowledge as legitimately shaping their behaviour. The element of cohesion must therefore be sought exclusively in the neutral and formal dimension of the law:

> it is a fiction when the unity, which the state legal order fashions out of the multiplicity of human actions, poses as a "popular body" by calling itself the "People." It creates the illusion that individuals belong to the People with their whole being, when in actuality they only belong to it through certain actions which are either commanded or prohibited by the political order.[153]

No less illusory is the idea of the existence of a "common interest" of all members of the supposed "organic community", to which Kelsen pragmatically opposed the thesis that, "if the will of society is not to be the expression of the interests of one group alone, that will must be the result of a compromise between opposing interests".[154] In short, following this interpretation the "people" is nothing more than a legal fiction that gives unity to the plurality of individuals. The resulting problem, however, is similar to what has been worked out for the concept of "state": to the extent that the "people" is interpreted as a merely formal concept, no attention is paid to the shaping of specific values that, without being in contrast with cosmopolitan purposes, might develop within a parochial political context due to the higher intensity of internal interactions.

The fourth individualistic element in Kelsen's theory is related to his highly innovative taxonomy of the political systems. Aristotle had introduced in his political theory the influential and long-lasting distinction between three types of public power: monarchy as the rule by a single person; aristocracy as the rule by the few; and democracy as the rule by the many.[155] The key factor, here, was the number of people who hold public power. This kind of *quantitative* focus on the number of power-bearing social actors was replaced by Kelsen through a *qualitative* criterion.[156] According to his new perspective, there are two ideal forms of state power that differ in the way in which the legal system of the state is created and justified: more specifically, either from top to bottom, or from bottom to top. In the first case—the case of "autocracy"—public power is given from above and the governed subjects are largely excluded from decision-making. In the second case—the case of democracy—power rises from the bottom up, or, to be more precise, it comes from the governed and is entrusted by the individual members of the political community to those chosen by them to exercise authority.[157] Not only has this dichotomy simplified the discussion of legitimacy by introducing a clear criterion for distinction; in addition to that, Kelsen also introduced an explicit normative dimension. In a society in which a given and passively accepted view of the good life no longer exists, the only source of legitimacy for power lies with those who must follow the rules. Indeed,

> those who only rely on earthly truth and only allow human knowledge to direct social policy can justify the coercion, which the realization of that policy inevitably requires, in no other way than with the assent of at least the majority of those who are supposed to benefit from the coercive order.[158]

Thus, even though Kelsen admitted that every legal system which is effective—i.e., is characterized by sufficient compliance with norms by those living in the territory where the system is applied—should be regarded as valid, nonetheless he left no doubts on his preference for democracy. In fact, if the political and legal order has to guarantee that the interests of each individual find the best possible satisfaction without thereby damaging the interests of others and thus endangering social cohesion, then it is evident that the best political regime has to be the one in which individuals take part in the formulation of those norms that make civil life possible. It follows, on the other side, that the autocratic regimes will be considered as substantially incapable of guaranteeing the stability of the political and civil order: by marginalizing the subjects from the formulation of the rules to which they are subject, they cultivate dissatisfaction and, ultimately, the germs of revolt.[159]

However, Kelsen's appreciation of democracy is essentially value-free. Indeed, the ascending legitimation of public power is not corresponding, in his view, to a moral or ethical superiority, in the sense that it would implement at the political level the best possible form of human interaction—since it is based on mutual recognition—or a better idea of the good—because it allows more cohesion and self-realization. Rather, his preference for democracy is on a pragmatic basis as the democratic regime with its formal rules—the majority principle, for instance, or the respect for minority rights—would allow taking compromise decisions and operationalizing conflicts through peaceful procedures, thus making a society work which is characterized by a potentially disruptive heterogeneity of economic, cultural and religious identities. However, this should happen—according to Kelsen—without attributing to democracy any kind of ethical value, i.e., without the democratic rules being transformed into a habit which is interiorized by those who exercise them and is perceived as an essential element of the "good life". To be pursued, democracy does not need—Kelsen claimed—to be seen as "good"; it is enough that it is interpreted as useful. Since the democratic rules are only understood as a "method for the creation of a social order",[160] Kelsen's concept of democracy can be defined as *formal*, as opposed to a more *substantial* notion according to which democratic interaction would create ethical values that specify the identity of the community and its idea of the "good life".

An exclusively "formal" concept of democracy, however, is insofar problematic as it fails to adequately address the so-called paradox of the free rider. In other words, it does not give a convincing answer to the hypothetical situation that is created, in a democracy, when one or more of the agents agree(s) to the compromise without accepting responsibility. Thus, the compromise is virtually signed, but only with the tacit reserve of violating it as soon as a superior personal advantage should arise. The difficulty in sanctioning the attitude of the free rider in the formal conception of democracy results from the circumstance that the pursuit of the individual interest makes up the only justification for action.[161] In fact, it is questionable whether it is possible, in Kelsen's case, to speak of a normative horizon of democracy at all. Basically, criticism arises from the consideration that no social structure can function without shared values being internalized. This unresolved problem of the formal doctrine of democracy can be convincingly addressed by resorting to rational-discursive categories.[162] According to the communicative paradigm, democratic discourse is in fact the political manifestation of a rational interaction which goes beyond the instrumental research of individual advantage.[163] Reference is made, here, to those forms of discourse based on the criteria of openness to all rationally motivated contributions, of non-coercion and non-violence in the mutual relations, and on the commitment to accept the best argument. Given these premises, the participants in the exchange of arguments are expected to engage in the sincere attempt to reach a solution to the issue at the centre of the discourse. In this context, however, the most important point is that the solution, from the perspective of the discourse theory, is not seen as a compromise, but as a truth—always to be regarded, of course, as falsifiable—and as a shared value. In this sense, communicative action as the linguistic and philosophical fundament of democracy is assumed *to create values* in the course of the interaction—and in particular those values that the members of the social and political community are willing to recognize as their own.

The fifth aspect of Kelsen's radicalization of the contents of the universalistic-individualistic paradigm of order refers to his interpretation of the relation between state law and international law, in particular to the uncompromising priority that he gave to the latter. The reason for his choice can be drawn from his analysis of the contraposition between dualism and monism.[164] Kelsen's starting point is what he asserted to be a paradox: paradoxical indeed is the claim put forward by the supporters of nationalism, according to which a nation state pretends to be sovereign though acknowledging the validity of international law. In fact—Kelsen maintained—the condition of sovereignty is realized when no superior power is recognized, so that the individual agent's capability to act is not limited by any heterarchic authority.[165] Yet, international law—if taken seriously—imposes precisely such a limitation.[166] For that reason, either the nation state is not sovereign, or international law has little, if any, normative quality. Kelsen detected three possible ways to solve the paradox—the first relying on a dualistic conception of the legal system, the second and third based on its monistic interpretation. The dualistic solution assumes that two different legal systems—the national and the international—coexist, the first one providing rules for the domestic realm, the second one for the relations between states. According to this perspective, each system has its own basis of legitimacy and is unchallenged in its area of competence.[167] The problem, following Kelsen, is that in this case we would possibly have two diverging norms, derived from two different legal systems, both effective and legitimate, which simultaneously apply to the same matter. Kelsen refused this possibility and pointed out, unambiguously, that the simultaneous validity of two diverging norms would lead to a contradiction that would jeopardize the normative quality of the entire legal system.[168] Therefore, in his view the existence of a plurality of norms—i.e., the presence of more than one rule applicable at the same time to the same legal field—is completely inacceptable: a pathology of disorder that should be avoided, or, if already present, healed as soon as possible.

Having established that dualism would lead to systematic and irresolvable conflicts between norms and should thus be rejected—an assumption which turns out to be hardly tenable in our time, due to the necessity to cope with the proliferation of different legal regimes—Kelsen moved on to consider the further solutions to the question of the relation between state law and international law. Both are grounded on a monistic conception of the legal system, i.e., on the assumption that domestic and international law have one and the same foundation for validity and legitimacy. The difference is that in the first case domestic public law prevails on international law, whereas in the second international law is placed at the top of the pyramid of legal norms. According to the first definition of monism, international law is conceived of as a part of domestic public law, and thus, following a well-established tradition, as "external state law".[169] Therefore, it is among the competences of the sovereign individual state to specify the scope of international legal norms. The curious—and even quite absurd—consequence of this modus operandi is that, given the fact that we have a large number of individual states, if international law were depending for the specification of its normative range on sovereign decisions taken by each of those single states, then we would also have as many different international law systems as we have sovereign states—with the consequence that no binding international law would exist. No less incongruous is the circumstance that, since international law norms provide for the mutual recognition of states as equal actors in the international arena, exactly this mutual acknowledgement, which is fundamental for the very functioning of the international system, would have to rely upon the free and arbitrary will of each individual state. The result would be that the recognition of every state as equal actor of international law would lie in the hands of every other single state, as well as that each individual state would decide on the international recognition of all other states—a confusing condition, which is illogical, on the one hand, and surely does not contribute to stability in international relations on the other.[170]

Thus, the only solution to the problem consists indeed, if we follow Kelsen and accept his conceptual presuppositions, in the preference for the monistic structure of the entire legal system, but turned upside down as against the former option, i.e., with international law at the apex of the pyramid. According to this understanding, domestic public law would act as the executor of the fundamental principles and norms of international law within a limited territory, towards a specific group of individuals—the citizens of the state, or other individuals dwelling in this territory—and within the range of competences attributed to the state by international norms.[171] Kelsen openly admitted that such a construction of the legal system would mark the end of any serious pretension of sovereignty by the single states.[172] In doing so, he made his rejection of the conception of international law that dominated between 1870 and World War I explicit, namely that a partially "tamed" sovereignty—at least with reference to the relations among "civilized" nations—could lead to a balance between "moderate nationalism" and "liberal internationalism".[173] In the view of the most progressive international lawyers of the 1920s—a multifaceted group of which Kelsen became one of the most influential exponents—the carnage of World War I had laid the definitive tombstone on that vision, so that new and more courageous solutions were regarded as necessary. In particular, against the background of the initial optimism about the prospects of the League of Nations as the fundamental and unprecedented instrument "for a more peaceful world order",[174] the most innovative international lawyers of the time—and Kelsen among them—advocated to abandon the centrality of sovereignty as well as the idea that the international order had to be based on the "self-obligation" of individual nation states, in favour of a robust and uncompromising universalism, to be extended far beyond the borders of the "civilized nations".[175]

Thanks to Kelsen's contribution, some of the most central *topoi* of international law have been placed in a new light. For instance, individuals have been advanced to essential subjects of international law not only on a philosophical basis—as Kant had already done before Kelsen—but within the context of a sound and ambitious legal theory. As a result, they remain indirectly objects of rights and obligations (mediated by states), but also become direct holders of rights and direct recipients of obligations.[176] Kelsen did not openly draw from this assumption the request to abolish the principle of collective responsibility—which he assumed to remain necessarily part of international law as long as this will have the characteristics of a "primitive law"—[177] Humanities Press, Atlantic Hi but claimed nonetheless that collective responsibility should be integrated through the notion of individual accountability for acts corresponding to violations of international law.[178] Furthermore, the traditional instruments of sanction available to international law—i.e., retaliation and war—were also considered "primitive" since they do not target those responsible for the crime, but an entire population[179] and, secondly, because the authority which is in charge of clarifying whether there has actually been a violation of the rules and who is responsible for it is insufficiently specified.[180] Albeit cautiously, Kelsen did not exclude completely the legitimacy of the use of such instruments—again because of the "primitiveness" of international law—in particular when conditions are given which make the application of more valid alternatives impossible.[181] However, he strongly advocated the establishment of a supra-state criminal jurisdiction with the task of implementing individual sanctions for the breech of the rules of international order.[182] Finally, although states were assumed to remain the central actors of international law, they were understood by Kelsen merely as the "organs of the international legal order",[183] i.e., as those institutions of public law that were designed to implement the norms established by precisely that order. By diminishing the role of the state within the context of international law, Kelsen's theory exposes that shortcoming again that has been already mentioned above, namely the tendency to underestimate the function of the individual political community in forging a specific identity among its members, which—in the case of democratic regimes—also guarantees mutual recognition, freedom and justice.

The intellectual plan of Kelsen's monism was to merge all dimensions of public law together into a "grand unified theory".[184] This leads us to his sixth—and last—radicalization of universalistic individualism, i.e., to his thoroughly unitary conception of order. As it has been shown in the sections above, the individualistic paradigm was leaning towards a unitary idea of order from its very beginning due to the monadic self-reliance of the subject as the central element of its epistemology and moral philosophy. This reverberated first on the idea that statist order had to be unitary as well, and was then strengthened by Kant who extended the unitary character of the statist order to the cosmopolitan level through the *Weltrepublik*. Yet, although the framework created by Kant introduced cosmopolitan law at the top of his tripartite system of public law, a certain dialectic between the state level and its supra-state counterpart was still conceivable since no rigid hierarchy between the two layers was established. On the contrary, in Kelsen's perspective even the slightest glimmer of such a dialectic was extinguished under the all-encompassing dome of the unitary system of laws. Kelsen's uncompromisingly unitary conception of the legal order was the result of the twofold aim that defines, on the whole, his intellectual endeavour: the justification of monism, on the one hand, and the transformation of the legal discourse into a self-relying science, with a theoretical foundation and a strict methodological approach which aspired to be nothing short of the achievements of natural sciences, on the other. To realize both aims, Kelsen needed a robust conceptual basis, i.e., an epistemological organon which could give unity and consistence to the whole construction—and, quite early in his intellectual biography, he believed to have found it in the neo-Kantian theory of knowledge.[185] Neo-Kantianism—in particular as it was developed by Hermann Cohen—[186] maintained that any knowledge, in order to be true and self-coherent, has to be based on an epistemological a priori concept. As a result—Kelsen added—insofar as law has to be regarded itself as an object of scientific knowledge, it must be grounded on an a priori concept too, actually on the *Grundnorm*, which guarantees the unity as well as the cognitive and normative content of the whole system. However, precisely this structure of the legal system, based on a single a priori conceptual assumption to assure internal self-coherence and universality, is not only the probably most outstanding achievement of Kelsen's legal theory, but also one of its most significant shortcomings. In fact, Kelsen's idea of legal order is essentially characterized by two elements: first, the strictly hierarchical and rigid structure of a globally unified legal system, grounded as a whole on only one, utterly undifferentiated epistemological fundament, and, secondly, his harsh refusal of legal pluralism, condemned as a source of confusion and disorder, which he derived from his philosophical premises. Yet, both of them are severely unsuited to properly face the challenges with which the legal praxis and the concept of law are confronted at the beginning of the twenty-first century. In a context of increasingly complex interactions, the multiple facets of law can hardly be correctly understood and further developed if forced to fit into a traditional pyramidal hierarchy of norms.

No doubt can be raised on the outstanding intellectual courage and originality of Kelsen's conception, even if we put it within the context of the most forward-oriented strand of international law of his time.[187] His turn from an international law conceived as subordinated to domestic law to the assertion of its pre-eminence, based on an exceptionally ambitious conceptual framework, is one of the most fascinating innovations ever formulated in the field of legal thinking. Nevertheless, it is not without problems. These have been already cursorily referred to during the analysis of Kelsen's thought; yet, it may be useful to briefly recall them altogether at this closing point. First, his radically unitary and hierarchical understanding of the legal system sealed off the road to any kind of acceptance of legal pluralism as well as to the idea that conflict solution might no less rely on the dialogue between diverging interpretations and different systems of adjudication than on the determination of which norm is superior. It must be underlined, here, that the pluralism rejected by Kelsen is not the ethical, religious, ideological, political or philosophical pluralism, but only the legal and institutional pluralism, i.e., the acknowledgement that the presence, within the same territory, of a plurality of non-hierarchically organized institutions vested with political authority may be seen, under certain circumstances, as an added value. However, his strict preference for unity and normative hierarchy may prove fatal for a theory in times of legal differentiation and hierarchical indeterminacy. Secondly, under the all-encompassing dome of the cosmopolitan order no room is left for the recognition of the function played by the ethical identity of the single social and political community. In fact, even though it must be acknowledged that this kind of identity has been the source of many international conflicts, nonetheless it has also been, in many cases, the guarantee for social cohesion and democratic self-determination. As a result, it is probably better to aim at some sort of dialectic between the identities of the single polities and cosmopolitan order, than at the subordination of the former under the latter. Thirdly, it is surely a significant achievement that Kelsen underlined, like no other thinker before him, the centrality of the law in shaping cosmopolitan order: without a legal system vested with sufficient authority, every promise of peace and respect for human rights remains void. Yet, law alone cannot be enough if it is not accompanied by the establishment of political institutions: only these, indeed, can provide the indispensable legitimacy and participation.

## 4.6 The World Federal Republic as the Only Possibility for Cosmopolitan Order

All paradigms that have been considered so far share a unitary understanding of order. None of them, however, is as uncompromising on this point as universalistic individualism. Indeed, even though the exponents of holistic particularism insist on the homogeneity of the internal order of each single social and political community, all communities, if taken together, present a significant number of different understandings of order, so that we could say that holistic particularism justifies a pluralism of non-pluralist orders. On the other hand, holistic universalism allows an amount of internal differentiation, although under the all-encompassing dome of a unitary idea of the "just order", which is unconceivable for the supporters of universalistic individualism. Therefore, precisely because the concept of order of the paradigm of modernity is so hierarchically and consistently structured, it is also quite ill-suited to cope with the requirements of the post-national constellation or, to be more precise, with the forms of supranational, transnational and international integration that emerged after World War II and, even more, after the fall of the iron curtain. The consequence was that, while the most relevant contents of the universalistic-individualistic conception of order—namely that order, to be normatively acceptable, has to put the individuals at the centre of a cosmopolitan project of freedom and justice—were destined to be further developed in a different paradigmatic context (basically, within the communicative paradigm), we can hardly find important authors who committed themselves to the core assumption of universalistic individualism, i.e., that only a largely centralized cosmopolitan *civitas maxima* could guarantee a just order. One of the few exceptions—and probably the most interesting of all—is the political philosophy of Otfried Höffe.

Against the trend towards pluralism, Höffe emphasizes that only a "world republic" (*Weltrepublik*) can provide peace and the respect of human rights. This is even more true—he claims—in times of globalization, in which nation states are threatened with the loss of their "conditions of agency", i.e., of their capacity to act autonomously in order to pursue their interests, because of the growing interconnection as well as of the disparity of the agents' resources and power.[188] This is to a great extent the situation that had been postulated by the early contractualists with reference to the state of nature—and, like them, Höffe also proposes the solution of an agreement for the establishment of a society, albeit in his case of a society made of nation states. Two remarks should be made with reference to Höffe's understanding of the fictitious contract that should mark the transition from the state of nature to a society committed to peace and to the protection of fundamental rights. First, although he explicitly refers to Kant's political philosophy as his main inspiration, his understanding of the social contract recalls rather Hobbes's variant. In fact, its aim seems to be more the guarantee of sufficient room for individual self-realization, and therefore of *negative* freedom, than the establishment of the *positive* freedom that is implemented through individual and collective autonomy as well as through political participation and self-determination. Mutual recognition in the political realm is, under these premises, only an instrument to achieve individual payoffs, not an end in itself, nor the highest goal that can be achieved through the use of practical reason.[189] Secondly, Höffe's view of the original contract goes—at least with regard to one aspect—even further back than to its modern re-interpretation by Hobbes. Unlike the English founder of the contractualism of the Modern Ages, the German philosopher does not see the contract as a single act, a *pactum unionis* that, at the same time, creates the civil society and establishes public power, but—similarly to the medieval contract theory—as a two-step procedure: a *pactum societatis* for the transition from the state of nature to the civil society, and a *pactum subjectionis* which found the state institutions. Yet, it was a significant achievement of modern political philosophy to rule out that society can exist without public power, but also that public power can be set up independently of that founding act of original and universal mutual recognition between free and equal.

The *pactum societatis* and the *pactum subjectionis* are two steps that refer, in the end, to only *one* transition from the pre-social state to the political community. Nonetheless, following Höffe, national and international order is based on three clearly separate contractual transitions: the contract among the fellow citizens to establish the individual social and political community;[190] the contract among the single political communities to create the rules and institutions of international order; and the contract among all human beings to legitimate—from the cosmopolitan perspective and from the bottom up—those same rules and institutions.[191] In no other author belonging to the contractualist tradition—at least not before Höffe—is a similar tripartition of the original contract to be found in a comparable explicit outline. Early contractualists only took the first contract with reference to the foundation of the individual community into consideration, while radical cosmopolitans maintained, along the lines of Kelsen, that only the rules and institutions of the *civitas maxima* created by the third type of contract mattered. Only Kant was able to anticipate, to a certain extent, the threefold nature of the contract establishing social and political order in his conception of public law, but ultimately failed, as it has been showed above, to provide a coherent and sound institutional solution. This said, it is unquestionable that Höffe's theory marks a significant step forward in the history of contractualism. In particular, it has to be underlined that stressing that global order must be based on two contracts *at the same time*—i.e., on both latter contracts: the contract between states and the contract between individuals on a cosmopolitan scale—overcomes the gridlock that affected Kant's institutional proposal. In other words, it has not to be either the *Weltrepublik* or the *Völkerbund*, but it is the *Weltrepublik* itself that has to be partially grounded on a *Völkerbund*, so that individual states still maintain a significant role in providing legitimacy to the project of a worldwide order of peace, freedom and justice.

Höffe's forward-looking intuition seems to be poised to guarantee a more dynamic and internally differentiated understanding of global order, so that the project of a perpetual peace might be revitalized so as to cope with an ever more interconnected, but also plural world of rules and institutions. Then, however, the promising view is almost entirely obfuscated by the author's insistence on a largely centralized concept of the cosmopolitan institutions. Indeed, although far from being a kind of global Leviathan,[192] Höffe's *Weltrepublik*—quite surprisingly if we consider his premises—is in any sense a *statist* construction. In particular, it is not conceived of as an overarching legal and institutional structure, based on a complex system of reciprocal "checks and balances", of "weak" and yet authoritative powers, of normative priorities not founded on an undisputed sovereignty, of intertwined forms of legitimation not secondarily rooted in the democratic processes of the national or supranational units that constitute it. Rather, it is a real state, even if sui generis. Several elements can be referred to in support of the thesis that Höffe still sticks to a quite traditional and state-centred view of social and political order. The first is what Höffe defines as "the universal precept of a legal order and a state".[193] More specifically, this means that "in order to realize justice, a state under the rule of law, as the embodiment of public powers, must be established".[194] In other words, an order of freedom, justice and respect of human rights could only be implemented—according to Höffe—by resorting to largely traditional statist institutions. Secondly, Höffe goes so far as to speak of a worldwide "*Staatsvolk*" ("nation", or, literally, "people of the state") or of a "*(Welt-)Volk*" ("global nation")—rather surprising concepts if applied to the global constellation. Thirdly, even though he advocates a large application of the principle of subsidiarity,[195] the structure of the global federal state that should provide worldwide order is unequivocally unitary, vertical and hierarchical:

The subsidiary structure of responsibilities, strengthened by the principles of democracy and federalism, produces a vertical separation of powers. The world republic is organized bottom-up, not vice versa, and distinguishes itself through a layered structure of statehood.[196]

Finally, Höffe elaborates a virtual design of the institutions of the *Weltrepublik* he argues for along the lines of the template offered by the German federalism and the supranational public power of the European Union.[197]

In conclusion, Höffe's attempt to adapt Kant's *Weltrepublik*—and thus one of the most ambitious political concepts of the paradigm of modernity—to the challenges of the twenty-first century stops halfway. On the one hand, he acknowledges that the institutional structure that should provide order has to be more internally differentiated, so as to comprise more than just one layer. On the other hand, however, he still maintains that the different layers are in a hierarchical relationship to one another, so that no real dialectic can unfold between them. In the end, he simply bypasses the question whether establishing a "universal state" is really the only way to achieve a just and peaceful order at international level. In fact, some quite convincing arguments—not only by referring to what is feasible but also to what is desirable—underpin rather the opposite, non-statist view, namely that a "global and complementary supra-state order" can carry out many of the functions identified by Höffe, without causing all the irritations connected with the prospect of a *Weltrepublik*.[198] Yet, conceiving order in a post-statist constellation requires the development of a post-unitary theoretical framework, and then the overcoming of the grand tradition of universalistic individualism.

## Notes

1. Sophocles, *Oedipus Tyrannus* (429 B.C.E.), line 87 et seq. (English translation by Richard Jebb, Cambridge University Press, Cambridge 1887).
2. Ibid., line 328 et seq.
3. Ibid., line 707 et seq.
4. Ibid., line 785 et seq.
5. William Shakespeare, *Hamlet* (1599–1602), in: William Shakespeare, *The Complete Works*, Stanley Wells and Gary Taylor eds., Oxford University Press, Oxford/New York 2005, 681–718, Act 1, Scene 1, 4 and 5, at 683 et seq.
6. Ibid., Act 2, Scene 2, line 207 et seq.

7. Ibid., Act 2, Scene 2, line 598 et seq.
8. Ibid., Act 2, Scene 2, line 605 et seq.
9. Aeschilus, *Choephori* (*Libation Bearers*) (458 B.C.E.), line 298 (English translation by Herbert Weir Smyth, Harvard University Press, Cambridge (MA) 1926).
10. Ibid., line 896 et seq.
11. Ibid., line 899.
12. Ibid., line 900 et seq.
13. Shakespeare, *Hamlet*, supra note 5, Act 1, Scene 5, line 82 et seq.
14. Ibid., Act 3, Scene 1, line 58 et seq.
15. Ibid., Act 2, Scene 2, line 251 et seq.
16. Ibid., Act 1, Scene 5, line 67.
17. Georg Jellinek, *Allgemeine Staatslehre*, Haering, Berlin 1900, at 471 et seq.
18. Luis Weckmann, *El Pensamiento Político Medieval y las Bases para un Nuevo Derecho Internacional*, Universidad Nacional Autonoma de Mexico 1950, at 277.
19. Galileo Galilei, *Dialogo sopra i due massimi sistemi del mondo, tolemaico e copernicano* (1632), Seconda Giornata (English translation by Stillman Drake: *Dialogue Concerning the Two Chief World Systems*, University of California Press, Berkeley/Los Angeles 1967, at 108).
20. René Descartes, *Discours de la Méthode* (1637), Reclam, Stuttgart 2001, Part 2, Chapter 2, at 30 (English translation by John Veitch, Project Gutenberg, http://www.gutenberg.org/ebooks/59).
21. René Descartes, *Meditationes de Prima Philosophia* (1641), Reclam, Stuttgart 1986, First Meditation, at 62 et seq. (English translation by John Cottingham: *Meditations on First Philosophy*, Cambridge University Press, Cambridge/New York 1996, at 12).
22. Descartes, *Discours de la Méthode*, supra note 20, Part 2, Chapter 7-9, at 38 et seq.
23. Descartes, *Meditationes*, supra note 21, Second Meditation, at 76 et seq. (English: at 16 et seq.).
24. Ibid., Second Meditation, at 82 (English: at 18).
25. Ibid., Sixth Meditation, at 192 (English: at 55).
26. Ibid., Third Meditation, at 134 (English: at 35).
27. Ibid., Fourth Meditation, at 140 (English: at 37 et seq.).
28. Norberto Bobbio, *L'età dei diritti*, Einaudi, Torino 1990, at 45 et seq., 121 et seq.
29. Thomas Hobbes, *Elementa philosophica de Cive* (1642), Johan. Jac. Flick 1782, Part I, Chapter I, para. 1, at 2 (English translation by Richard Tuck and Michael Silverthorne: *On the Citizen*, Cambridge University Press, Cambridge/New York 1998, at 21).
30. Ibid., Part I, Chapter I, para. 2, at 3 (English: at 22).

31. Ibid., Part I, Chapter II, para. 1, at 22 (English: at 33).
32. Ibid.
33. Thomas Hobbes, *The Elements of Law, Natural and Politic* (1640), in: Deborah Baumgold (ed.), *Three Text Edition of Thomas Hobbes's Political Theory*, Part I, Chapter 1, para. 2, at 3.
34. Norberto Bobbio, *Il modello giusnaturalistico*, in: Norberto Bobbio, Michelangelo Bovero, *Società e stato nella filosofia politica moderna*, Il Saggiatore, Milano 1979, 15–109, at 17 et seq.
35. Hans Schelkshorn, 2003, *Thomas Hobbes' Ethik des Friedens*, in: Norbert Brieskorn, Markus Riedenauer (eds.), *Suche nach Frieden: Politische Ethik in der Frühen Neuzeit*, Kohlhammer, Stuttgart 2003, 217–253, at 217.
36. Thomas Hobbes, *Leviathan, or the Matter, Form, and Power of a Commonwealth Ecclesiastical and Civil* (1651), Clarendon Press, Oxford 1929, Chapter XIII, at 95 et seq.
37. Hobbes, *De Cive*, supra note 29, Part I, Chapter I, para. 3, at 9 et seq. (English: at 25 et seq.).
38. Ibid., Part I, Chapter I, para. 6, at 11 (English: at 27).
39. Ibid., Part I, Chapter I, para. 10, at 13 et seq. (English: at 28 et seq.).
40. Ibid., Part I, Chapter I, para. 12, at 16 et seq. (English: at 29 et seq.); Hobbes, *Leviathan*, supra note 36, Chapter XIII et seq., at 92 et seq.
41. Hobbes, *Leviathan*, supra note 36, Chapter XIII, at 95.
42. Ibid., Chapter XIV, at 99.
43. Ibid., Chapter XIV, at 100.
44. Ibid.
45. Ibid., Chapter XVII, at 128.
46. Hobbes, *De Cive*, supra note 29, Part II, Chapter V, para. 7, at 88 (English: at 72).
47. Bobbio, *Il modello giusnaturalistico*, supra note 34, at 34 et seq.
48. Hobbes, *Leviathan*, supra note 36, Chapter XIV, at 101.
49. John P. McCormick, *Teaching in Vain: Carl Schmitt, Thomas Hobbes, and the Theory of the Sovereign State*, in: Jens Meierhenrich, Oliver Simons (eds.), *The Oxford Handbook of Carl Schmitt*, Oxford University Press, Oxford/New York 2016, 269–290.
50. Hobbes, *De Cive*, supra note 29, Part II, Chapter XIII, at 217 et seq. (English: at 142 et seq.); Hobbes, *Leviathan*, supra note 36, Chapter XVII, at 128 et seq.
51. John Locke, *Two Treatises on Government* (1690), Yale University Press, New Haven/London 2003, Book II, Chapter II, para. 4, at 101.
52. Ibid., Book II, Chapter II, para. 6, at 102.
53. Ibid., Book II, Chapter III, para. 19, at 108.
54. Ibid., Book II, Chapter IX, para. 123, at 154 et seq.
55. Ibid., Book II, Chapter VII, para. 90 et seq., at 138 et seq.
56. Ibid., Book II, Chapter XI, para. 134, at 158 et seq.

57. Ibid., Book II, Chapter XIII, para. 150, at 167.
58. Ibid., Book II, Chapter IV, para. 22, at 110.
59. Ibid., Book II, Chapter XII, para. 143, at 164.
60. Ibid., Book II, Chapter IX, para. 124 et seq., at 155 et seq.
61. Bobbio, *Il modello giusnaturalistico*, supra note 34, at 54.
62. Jean-Jacques Rousseau, *Discours sur l'origine et les fondements de l'inégalité parmi les hommes* (1755), Meiner, Hamburg 1983, 61–268, at 182 (English translation: *Discourse on the Origins and Foundations of Inequality Among Mankind*, in: Jean-Jacques Rousseau, *The Social Contract and the First and Second Discourses*, Susan Dunn ed., Yale University Press, New Haven/London 2002, 69–148, at 110 et seq.).
63. Ibid., at 106 et seq. (English: at 96 et seq.).
64. Ibid., at 190 et seq. (English: at 113 et seq.).
65. Ibid., at 222, 224 (English: at 123 et seq.).
66. Bobbio, *Il modello giusnaturalistico*, supra note 34, at 62.
67. Jean-Jacques Rousseau, *Du contract social, ou principes du droit politique* (1762), Garnier-Flammarion, Paris 1966, Book I, Chapter I, at 41 (English translation: *The Social Contract*, in: Rousseau, *The Social Contract and the First and Second Discourses*, supra n. 62, 149–254, at 156).
68. Ibid., BooK I, Chapter IX, at 56 et seq. (English: at 167 et seq.).
69. Ibid., Book III, Chapter IV, at 107 et seq. (English, at 201).
70. Ibid., Book I, Chapter VII, at 54 (English: at 166).
71. Hobbes, *Leviathan*, supra note 36, Chapter XXX, at 273.
72. Ibid., Chapter XIII, at 92 et seq.
73. Ibid., Chapter XVII, at 131.
74. Ibid., Chapter XVIII, at 133 et seq.
75. Benedictus de [Baruch] Spinoza, *Tractatus Politicus* (1677), Chapter 2, para. 13 (English translation by Samuel Shirley, in: Spinoza, *Complete Works*, Michael L. Morgan ed., Hackett, Indianapolis 2002, 676–754, at 686).
76. Ibid., Chapter 3, para. 11 (English: at 694).
77. Ibid., Chapter 3, para. 13 (English: at 694).
78. Ibid., Chapter 3, para. 14 (English: at 694 et seq.).
79. Ibid., Chapter 2, para. 13 (English: at 686).
80. Benedictus de Spinoza, *Tractatus Theologico-Politicus* (1670), Chapter 16 (English translation in: Spinoza, *Complete Works*, supra note 75, 383–583, at 532).
81. Locke, *Two Treatises*, supra note 51, Book II, Chapter II, para. 14, at 106; Book II, Chapter XVI, para. 183, at 182. See: Francis Cheneval, *Philosophie in weltbürgerlicher Absicht. Über die Entstehung und die philosophischen Grundlagen des supranationalen und kosmopolitischen Denkens der Moderne*, Schwabe, Basel 2002, at 295 et seq.

82. Locke, *Two Treatises*, supra note 51, Book II, Chapter XII, para. 145, at 165.
83. William Penn, *An Essay towards the Present and Future Peace of Europe* (1693), in: William Penn, *The Political Writings*, Liberty Fund, Indianapolis 2002, 401–419, Section III, at 404 et seq.
84. Ibid., Section IV, at 406.
85. Melvin B. Endy Jr., *William Penn's Essay on the Present and Future Peace of Europe: the Proposal of a Political Pacifist*, in: Brieskorn/ Riedenauer, *Suche nach Frieden*, supra note 35, 373–405, at 394.
86. Penn, *An Essay towards the Present and Future Peace of Europe*, supra note 83, Section IV, at 406.
87. Ibid., Section VIII, at 410.
88. Ibid., Section VII, at 408 et seq.
89. Ibid., Section VII, at 409.
90. Ibid., Section X, at 413 et seq.
91. Ibid., Section X, at 415 et seq.
92. Jean-Jacques Rousseau, *Projet de paix perpétuelle*, in: Jean-Jacques Rousseau, *Collection complète des œuvres*, Genève 1780–1789, Vol. XII (English translation By Christopher Kelly and Judith Bush, in: Jean-Jacques Rousseau, *The Plan for Perpetual Peace, On the Government of Poland, and Other Writings on History and Politics*, Christopher Kelly ed., University Press of New England, Hanover/London 2005, at 25 et seq.).
93. Charles-Irénée Castel Abbé de Saint-Pierre, *Projet pour rendre la paix perpétuelle en Europe* (1712), Schouten, Utrecht 1713.
94. Rousseau, *Discours sur l'origine et les fondements de l'inégalité parmi les hommes*, supra note 62, at 230 (English: at 126).
95. Immanuel Kant, *Zum ewigen Frieden. Ein philosophischer Entwurf*, in: Immanuel Kant, *Werkausgabe*, Wilhelm Weischedel ed., Suhrkamp, Frankfurt a. M. 1977, Vol. XI, 193–251, at 204 et seq. (English translation by H. B. Nisbet: *Perpetual Peace: A Philosophical Sketch*, in: Immanuel Kant, *Political Writings*, Cambridge University Press, Cambridge/New York 1991, 93–130, at 99 et seq.).
96. Immanuel Kant, *Über den Gemeinspruch: Das mag in der Theorie richtig sein, taugt aber nicht für die Praxis* (1793), in: Kant, *Werkausgabe*, supra note 95, Vol. XI, 125–172, at 151 et seq. (English translation by H. B. Nisbet: *On the Common Saying: 'This May be True in Theory, but It Does not Apply in Practice*, in: Kant, *Political Writings*, supra note 95, 61–92, at 77 et seq.).
97. Kant, *Zum ewigen Frieden*, supra note 95, at 230 et seq. (English: at 115 et seq.).
98. Kant, *Über den Gemeinspruch*, supra note 96, at 153 et seq. (English: at 79 et seq.).

99. Kant, *Zum ewigen Frieden, supra* note 95, at 203 (English: at 98).
100. Immanuel Kant, *Idee zu einer allgemeinen Geschichte in weltbürgerlicher Absicht* (1784), in Kant, *Werkausgabe, supra* note 95, Vol. XI, 31–50, at 41 (English translation by H. B. Nisbet: *Idea for a Universal History with a Cosmopolitan Purpose*, in: Kant, *Political Writings, supra* note 95, 41–53, at 46).
101. Ibid., at 43 (English: at 48).
102. Immanuel Kant, *Grundlegung zur Metaphysik der Sitten* (1785), in: Kant, *Werkausgabe, supra* note 95, Vol. VII, 9–102, at 51 (English translation by Thomas Kingsmill Abbott: *Fundamental Principles of the Metaphysic of Morals*, in: Immanuel Kant, *Critique of Practical reason and Other Works*, Longmans, Green and Co., London/New York 1898, 1–84, at 38).
103. Ibid., at 61 (English: at 47).
104. Ibid., at 67 (English: at 52).
105. Rousseau, *Du contract social, supra* note 67, Book I, Chapter VIII, at 55 et seq. (English: at 167).
106. Kant, *Grundlegung zur Metaphysik der Sitten, supra* note 102, at 65 (English: at 51).
107. Kant, *Zum ewigen Frieden, supra* note 95, at 204 (English: at 99); Immanuel Kant, *Der Streit der Fakultäten* (1798), in: Kant, *Werkausgabe, supra* note 95, Vol. XI, 263–393, Part II, Chapter 8, at 364 (English translation by Mary J. Gregor: *The Conflict of the Faculties*, Abaris Books, New York 1979, at 163).
108. Immanuel Kant, *Die Metaphysik der Sitten* (1797), in: Kant, *Werkausgabe, supra* note 95, Vol. VIII, 309–634, Part I/II, § 46, at 432 (English translation by Mary J. Gregor: *The Metaphysics of Morals*, Cambridge University Press, Cambridge/New York 1991, at 125). The same concept can be found also in: Kant, *Über den Gemeinspruch, supra* note 96, at 150 et seq. (English: at 77 et seq.).
109. Kant, *Zum ewigen Frieden, supra* note 95, at 203 (English: at 98 et seq.). See also: Kant, *Die Metaphysik der Sitten, supra* note 108, Part I/II, § 62, at 475 et seq. (English: at 158 et seq.).
110. Kant, Zum ewigen Frieden, supra note 95, at 223 (English: at 112).
111. Kant, *Die Metaphysik der Sitten, supra* note 108, Part I/II, § 62, at 475 (English: at 158).
112. Kant, *Zum ewigen Frieden, supra* note 95, at 213 (English: at 105 et seq.); Kant, *Die Metaphysik der Sitten, supra* note 108, Part I/II, § 62, at 475 et seq. (English: at 158 et seq.).
113. See the rights recognized by Vitoria on the basis of the *naturalis societas et communicatio* (*supra*, Sect. 3.2.3.1).
114. Kant, *Die Metaphysik der Sitten, supra* note 108, Part I/II, at 478 (English: at 160).

115. Ibid., Part I/II, at 479 (English: at 161).
116. Kant, *Der Streit der Fakultäten*, supra note 107, Chapter 10, at 367 (English: at 169).
117. Kant, *Idee zu einer allgemeinen Geschichte*, supra note 100, at 41 et seq. (English: at 47 et seq.).
118. Kant, *Zum ewigen Frieden*, supra note 95, at 212 et seq. (English: at 105).
119. Ibid., at 212 (English: at 105).
120. Kant, *Über den Gemeinspruch*, supra note 96, at 169 (English: at 90).
121. Kant, *Zum ewigen Frieden*, supra note 95, at 225 (English: at 113).
122. Ibid., at 225 et seq. (English: at 113 et seq.).
123. Ibid., at 209 (English: at 102).
124. Kant, *Die Metaphysik der Sitten*, supra note 108, Part I/II, § 61, at 474 et seq. (English: at 156 et seq.).
125. Kant, *Zum ewigen Frieden*, supra note 95, at 212 (English: at 105).
126. Ibid., at 211 (English: at 104).
127. Ibid., at 199 (English: at 96).
128. Kant, *Die Metaphysik der Sitten*, supra note 108, Part I/II, § 54, at 467 (English: at 151); Part I/II, § 61, at 475 (English: at 156 et seq.).
129. Kant, *Über den Gemeinspruch*, supra note 96, at 167 (English: at 88 et seq.).
130. Ibid., at 168 (English: at 89); Kant, *Der Streit der Fakultäten*, supra note 107, Chapter 6, at 357 et seq. (English: at 153 et seq.).
131. Immanuel Kant, *Kritik der praktischen Vernunft* (1788), in: Kant, *Werkausgabe*, supra note 95, Vol. VII, 105–302, Part I, Book I/I, § 7, at 142 (English translation by Thomas Kingsmill Abbott: *Critique of Practical reason*, in: Kant, *Critique of Practical reason and Other Works*, supra note 102, 85–262, at 120).
132. Kant, *Über den Gemeinspruch*, supra note 96, at 171 (English: at 91); Kant, *Zum ewigen Frieden*, supra note 95, at 217 (English: at 108).
133. Immanuel Kant, *Kritik der Urteilskraft* (1790), in: Kant, *Werkausgabe*, supra note 95, Vol. X, Part II, § 61, at 305 et seq. (English translation by James Creed Meredith: *Critique of Judgement*, Nicholas Walker ed., Oxford University Press, Oxford/New York 2007, at 187 et seq.); Kant, *Zum ewigen Frieden*, supra note 95, at 224 (English: at 113)..
134. Kant, *Die Metaphysik der Sitten*, supra note 108, Part I/II, § 61, at 474 (English: at 156).
135. Kant, *Über den Gemeinspruch*, supra note 96, at 170 (English: at 90 et seq.); Kant, *Zum ewigen Frieden*, supra note 95, at 204 et seq. (English: at 99 et seq.).
136. Jürgen Habermas, *Eine politische Verfassung für eine pluralistische Weltgesellschaft*, in: "Kritische Justiz", Vol. 38 (2005), 222–247, at 224 (English: *A Political Constitution for the Pluralist World Society*, in:

"Anales de la Cátedra Francisco Suarez", Vol. 39 (2005), 121–132, at 122).
137. Ibid.
138. Kant, *Zum ewigen Frieden*, supra note 95, at 208 et seq. (English: at 102).
139. Kant, *Idee zu einer allgemeinen Geschichte*, supra note 100, at 44 (English: at 49); Kant, *Über den Gemeinspruch*, supra note 96, at 169, 171 et seq. (English: at 90 et seq.); Kant, *Zum ewigen Frieden*, supra note 95, at 212 (English: at 104 et seq.); Kant, *Die Metaphysik der Sitten*, supra note 108, Part I/II, § 54, at 467 (English: at 151).
140. See: *supra*, Sect. 2.9.1.
141. Rousseau, *Du contract social*, supra note 67, Book I, Chapter VI, at 51 et seq. (English: at 164).
142. Hans Kelsen, *Reine Rechtslehre. Einleitung in die rechtswissenschaftliche Problematik*, Deuticke, Leipzig/Wien 1934 (English translation from the Second German Edition of 1960 by Max Knight, University of California Press, Berkeley/Los Angeles 1967).
143. Hans Kelsen, *Die philosophischen Grundlagen der Naturrechtslehre und des Rechtspositivismus*, Pan-Verlag Rolf Heise, Berlin-Charlottenburg 1928.
144. Kant, *Die Metaphysik der Sitten*, supra note 108, at 318 (English: at 42).
145. Kelsen, *Reine Rechtslehre*, supra note 142, at 21 et seq.
146. Ibid., at 67 et seq. (English: at 193 et seq.); Hans Kelsen, *General Theory of Law and State*, Harvard University Press, Cambridge (MA) 1949 (1st ed. 1945), at 115 et seq.
147. H. L. A. Hart, *The Concept of Law*, Clarendon Press, Oxford 1994 (1sr ed. 1961), at 91 et seq.
148. Kelsen, *Reine Rechtslehre*, supra note 142, at 116.
149. Hans Kelsen, *Gott und Staat* (1923), in: Hans Kelsen, *Staat und Naturrecht. Aufsätze zur Ideologiekritik*, Ernst Topitsch ed., Fink, München 1989 (1st ed.. 1964), 29–55, at 54.
150. Hans Kelsen, *Die Idee des Naturrechts* (1928), in: Kelsen, *Staat und Naturrecht*, supra note 149, 73–113, at 77.
151. Kelsen, *Reine Rechtslehre*, supra note 142, at 117.
152. Hans Kelsen, *Vom Wesen und Wert der Demokratie*, Mohr, Tübingen 1929 (2nd ed.), at 15 (English translation by Brian Graf, Nadia Urbinati and Carlo Invernizzi Accetti eds., Rowman & Littlefield, Lanham 2013, at 36).
153. Ibid.
154. Ibid., at 22 (English: at 40).
155. Aristotle, *Politics*, H. Rackham trans., Harvard University Press, Cambridge (MA) 1959, Book III, Chapter 4, 1278b et seq., at 199 et seq.

156. Mario Dogliani, *Introduzione al diritto costituzionale*, Il Mulino, Bologna 1994, at 115 et seq.
157. Kelsen, *General Theory of Law and State*, supra note 146, at 283.
158. Kelsen, *Vom Wesen und Wert der Demokratie*, supra note 152, at 102 et seq. (English: at 104).
159. Ibid., at 64 and 98 et seq. (English: at 74 et seq. and 101 et seq.).
160. Ibid., at 94 (English: at 98).
161. Karl-Otto Apel, *Die Konflikte unserer Zeit und das Erfordernis einer ethisch-politischen Grundorientierung*, in: Karl-Otto Apel, *Diskurs und Verantwortung. Das Problem des Übergangs zur postkonventionellen Moral*, Suhrkamp, Frankfurt a. M. 1990, 15–41, at 26 et seq.; Karl-Otto Apel, *Die Situation des Menschen als ethisches Problem*, in: Apel, *Diskurs und Verantwortung*, supra n. 161, 42–68, at 55 et seq. (English translation in: Karl-Otto Apel, *Selected Essays*, Eduardo Mendieta ed., Humanities Press, Atlantic Highlands (NJ) 1996, 174–191, at 181 et seq.); Karl-Otto Apel, *Das Anliegen des anglo-amerikanischen "Kommunitarismus"in der Sicht der Diskursethik. Worin liegen die "kommunitären" Bedingungen der Möglichkeit einer post-konventionellen Identität der Vernunftperson?*, in Micha Brumlik, Hauke Brunkhorst (eds.), *Gemeinschaft und Gerechtigkeit*, Fischer, Frankfurt a. M. 1993, 149–172, at 152 et seq.
162. See: *infra*, Chapter 8.
163. Jürgen Habermas, *Faktizität und Geltung. Beiträge zur Diskurstheorie des Rechts und des demokratischen Rechtsstaats*, Suhrkamp, Frankfurt a. M. 1992, at 352 et seq. (English translation by William Rehg: *Between Facts and Norms: Contributions to a Discourse Theory of Law and Democracy*, The MIT Press, Cambridge (MA), 1996 (2$^{nd}$ ed.), at 290 et seq.).
164. Kelsen, *Reine Rechtslehre*, supra note 142, at 136 et seq. (English: at 332 et seq.).
165. Hans Kelsen, *Das Problem der Souveränität und die Theorie des Völkerrechts* (1920), Scientia, Aalen 1981, at 12.
166. Ibid., at 40.
167. Ibid., at 102.
168. Kelsen, *General Theory of Law and State*, supra note 146, at 363.
169. Kelsen, *Reine Rechtslehre*, supra note 142, at 139 et seq. (English: at 333 et seq.).
170. Ibid., at 142 et seq.
171. Ibid., at 147 et seq. (English: at 336 et seq.); Hans Kelsen, *Peace through Law*, University of North Carolina Press, Chapel Hill, 1944, at 35.
172. Kelsen, *Reine Rechtslehre*, supra note 142, at 142 and 153.
173. Martti Koskenniemi, *The Gentle Civilizer of Nation: The Rise and fall of International Law 1870–1960*, Cambridge University Press, Cambridge/New York 2001, at 4.

174. Jochen von Bernstorff, Thomas Dunlap, *The Public International Law Theory of Hans Kelsen*, Cambridge University Press, Cambridge/New York 2010, at 7.
175. Ibid.
176. Kelsen, *General Theory of Law and State*, supra note 146, at 343 et seq.
177. Hans Kelsen, *Law and Peace in International Relations* (1942), Hein, Buffalo (NY) 1997, at 96 et seq.
178. Kelsen, *Peace through Law*, supra note 171, at 11 et seq. and 71 et seq.
179. Kelsen, *Reine Rechtslehre*, supra note 142, at 131 et seq. (English: at 323 et seq.).
180. Kelsen, *Law and Peace in International Relations*, supra note 177, at 47 et seq.
181. Ibid., at 34 et seq.; Kelsen, *General Theory of Law and State*, supra note 146, at 331 et seq.
182. Kelsen, *Peace through Law*, supra note 171, at 11 et seq. and 71 et seq.
183. Kelsen, *General Theory of Law and State*, supra note 146, at 351.
184. François Rigaux, *Hans Kelsen on International Law*, in: "European Journal of International Law", Vol. 9 (1998), 325–343, at 326.
185. Stanley L. Paulson, *The Neo-Kantian Dimension of Kelsen's Pure Theory of Law*, in: "Oxford Journal of Legal Studies", Vol. 12 (1992), 311–332; Stefan Hammer, *A Neo-Kantian Theory of Legal Knowledge in Kelsen's Pure Theory of Law*, in: Stanley L. Paulson and Bonnie Litschewski Paulson (eds.), *Normativity and Norms*, Oxford University Press, Oxford/New York 2007 (1st ed. 1999), 177–194.
186. See: Hermann Cohen, *Kants Theorie der Erfahrung*, Dümmler, Berlin 1871; Hermann Cohen, *Logik der reinen Erkenntnis*, Cassirer, Berlin 1902.
187. See: Hauhe Brunkhorst, *Critique of Dualism: Hans Kelsen and the Twentieth Century Revolution in International Law*, in: "Constellations", Vol. 18 (2011), 496–512.
188. Otfried Höffe, *Demokratie im Zeitalter der Globalisierung*, Beck, München 2002 (1st ed. 1999), at 55 et seq. (English translation by Dirk Haubrich and Michael Ludwig: *Democracy in an Age of Globalization*, Springer, Dordrecht 2007, at 32 et seq.).
189. Jürgen Habermas, *Die nachholende Revolution*, Suhrkamp, Frankfurt a. M. 1990, at 71 et seq.
190. Höffe, *Demokratie im Zeitalter der Globalisierung*, supra note 188, at 53 et seq. (English: at 30 et seq.).
191. Ibid., at 308 et seq. (English: at 218 et seq.).
192. Ibid., at 315 et seq. (English: at 223 et seq.).
193. Ibid., at 25 (English: at 9).
194. Ibid., at 102 (English: at 66).
195. Ibid., at 317 et seq. (English: at 225 et seq.).

196. Ibid., at 425 (English: at 307).
197. Ibid., at 310 et seq. (English: at 219 et seq.).
198. Heinhard Steiger, *Brauchen wir eine Weltrepublik?*, in: "Der Staat", Vol. 42 (2003), 249–266; Georg Lohmann, *Menschenrechte und "globales Recht"*, in: Stefan Gosepath, Jean-Christophe Merle (eds.), *Weltrepublik. Globalisierung und Demokratie*, Beck, München, 2002, 52–62.

CHAPTER 5

# The Failed Paradigmatic Revolution: Particularistic Individualism, or the Spontaneous Order of Transnational Economic Actors, as a Possible Fourth Paradigm of Order

All paradigms that have been analysed so far are characterized by the assumption that order must be *public* and *reflexive*. In other words, the well-ordered community has to share, firstly, a common idea of the "good life" and some fundamental social goals; secondly, the members of the community have to be sufficiently aware of this preference. As a result, the values or, more modestly, the rules of interaction on which social life is grounded are presumed to be consciously known and, to some extent, even interiorized by the members of the community, who are not expected to follow them only passively or to prioritize selfish interests. The inescapability of those conditions is evident as regards both holistic particularism and holistic universalism, irrespective of the opposite options with reference to the extension of the well-ordered community. No matter whether individuals are conceived of as belonging to the polis, the enlarged family, the nation, to an ethnically or religiously distinctive group, or to the universal humankind, they are supposed to know the values of the community in which they live, to support them and to give them priority over their own interests. Yet, even according to the supporters of the individualistic paradigm, who started from the assumption that the interests of the individuals are originally superior to those of the society, peaceful social interaction is possible only on the condition that the individuals give up their selfishness and reflexively agree on a common foundation of social and political life. Indeed, all authors of modern contractualism from Hobbes to Kant share the conviction that, if individuals refused any compromise and insisted on their personal and unilateral advantage, the only possible outcome would be the disintegration of society and ensuing chaos. Yet, is it really impossible to develop a consistent pattern of order that is generated *spontaneously* and *irreflexively* from the interaction of individuals who only pursue their egoistic payoffs? Must general interest always be deliberate? Or can it also emerge from the actions of agents who do not aim, at any moment of their endeavours, at achieving a common ethical ground or a shared benefit?

In the language of the metatheory of social order, this approach would correspond to a new paradigm, which would be, at the same time, *individualistic* since it puts the interests of the individuals at the centre, and *particularistic* because those interests are the only conscious horizon of human activity. As regards this aspect, it has to be pointed out that the concept of particularism does not refer here—unlike in the first paradigm of order—to the distinctiveness of a social structure that is, nonetheless, a *public body* or a *community*. Insofar as a social structure is typified by the existence of a public dimension, it must have internal common values, even if it is assumed that these values cannot reach beyond the borders of the single community. On the contrary, what is *particularistic* in the paradigm which makes up the content of this chapter is a plurality of exclusively *private* agents, with the only ambition to be successful in their mutual competition and, thus, without any shared goal or common ethical ground. Put differently, order is merely given within the radius of action of every private agent, while beyond this the only rules that have to be established are those which secure the smooth unfolding of the interactions between the competitors. No attempt is made, thus, at creating shared values as well as an encompassing and inclusive order of cooperation and solidarity.

Yet, even if we admitted that this kind of a minimalistic idea of a general order exclusively based on the interactions of private agents is in abstract conceivable, to become a paradigm it would have also to find convincing advocates, coherent elaborations and a favourable intellectual context. Among the authors taken into account in the previous chapters, the one who came closest to accepting such a scenario was John Locke, who admitted that the state of nature is essentially based on economic transactions and that it is a peaceful condition, albeit not necessarily cooperative or cohesive. Nonetheless, even Locke regarded the original state of humans as too instable, so that it had to be left, whereas every thinker before him and nearly all of them who followed after him were, for a long time, significantly more sceptical as regards the possibility of a spontaneous order of private economic actors. Given the predominant distrust of the perspective of securing order without establishing public power and shared values, it is not surprising that the publication in 1723 of a book by an until then little known English author of Dutch origin triggered great indignation. This book was *The Fable of the Bees: Or Private Vices, Public Benefits* by Bernard de Mandeville. The edition of 1723 was in fact the expanded reissue of a book which had been already released in 1714, and was followed by an even larger version in two volumes in 1728—which is actually the form in which *The Fable of the Bees* went down as a seminal work in the history of thought. The core element of Mandeville's book is a short poem, entitled *The Grumbling Hive, or Knaves Turn'd Honest*, which appeared in 1705 and achieved a modest success. Around the nucleus of the poem, the author added several detailed explanatory notes and an essay in 1714, and then a growing number of further texts on quite delicate issues concerning public ethics and social policy in the following editions. However, the essential content of his view was already clear in the poem. The story, in form of a fable, is about

> A spacious hive well stock'd with bees,
> That liv'd in luxury and ease;
> And yet as fam'd for laws and arms,
> As yielding large and early swarms;
> Was counted the great nursery
> Of science and industry.
> No bees had better government,
> More fickleness, or less content:
> They were not slaves to tyranny,
> Nor rul'd by wild democracy;
> But kings, that could not wrong, because
> Their power was circumscrib'd by laws.[1]

The beehive is compared to human society, since "these insects liv'd like men, and all our actions they perform'd in small".[2] But why is this beehive so successful? Because—Mandeville answered—"millions [are] endeavouring to supply each other's lust and vanity".[3] In other words, every member of the community of bees is exclusively pursuing her/his own benefit, without any respect for whatever idea of the common good. Nonetheless, precisely this relentless selfishness is assumed by Mandeville to be the reason of the thriving of the beehive since it fuels the development of the economy in all its forms as well as the progress of technology and knowledge. Therefore, it was only because "virtue ... made friends with vice",[4] that "every part was full of vice, yet the whole mass a paradise".[5] More in detail, Mandeville described the condition of the beehive with the following words:

> The root of evil, avarice,
> That dam'd ill-natur'd baneful vice,
> Was slave to prodigality,
> That noble sin; whilst luxury
> Employ'd a million of the poor,
> And odious pride a million more:
> Envy itself, and vanity,
> Were ministers of industry;
> Their darling folly, fickleness,
> In diet, furniture, and dress,
> That strange ridic'lous vice, was made
> The very wheel that turn'd the trade.[6]

Although the hive was wealthy and, as a whole, rather happy, some moralists began grumbling and complaining about the moral decay of their community, finally appealing to the gods so as to get rid of vice. Unfortunately for the destiny of the beehive, Jove followed up on their call by transforming the community into a model of honesty. However, when the members of the community started to behave virtuously and to prefer frugality and the common good to luxury and personal benefits, the hive also began to wither: without the stimulus of selfishness and lavishness, the society became more egalitarian, but also poorer. As a result, many bees were forced to leave the hive, and the remaining ones were fiercely attacked by foes. The few who survived finally gave up any hope of restoring the previous comfortable life: "they flew into a hollow tree, blest with content and honesty".[7] The moral that Mandeville drew from the fable is as simple as disturbing if compared to the usual understanding of what a good community should look like:

Then leave complaints: Fool only strive
To make a great an honest hive.
...
Fraud, luxury, and pride must live,
While we the benefits receive.[8]

Mandeville's work contains a rather modest idea of order for two main reasons. First, and more generally, his moral fable is not about the *best* way for humans to live together. Rather, it is a caveat to keep in mind a very simple principle, the ignorance of which would bring severe damages, namely that wealth is impossible without vice.[9] Thus, if a society wants to enjoy comfort, it should "learn more patiently to submit to those inconveniences, which no government upon earth can remedy".[10] Secondly, Mandeville did not conceive of social order as a condition in which interactions necessarily unfold to the advantage of *all* those who belong to the "well-ordered society". In other words, even though the benefits of distinct social groups may differ in size, according to the most ambitious definition of order, a society is assumed to be "well-ordered" only in case that no individual ends up being worse off, as a consequence of the rules of interaction that characterize this society, than in any other realistic hypothesis. Therefore, even if agent A has double as much an advantage from the social rules than agent B, at least it should be guaranteed that agent B has more comfortable life conditions than under any other social code of interaction. On the contrary, precisely this guarantee is not clearly addressed by Mandeville. In his industrious society, in order to increase wealth, "the poor should remain poor".[11] Indeed,

Yet, it was thought, the sword she [justice] bore
Check'd but the desp'rate and the poor;
That, urg'd by mere necessity,
Were ty'd up to the wretched tree
For crimes, which not desev'd that fate,
But to secure the rich and great.[12]

In a kind of proto-utilitarian spirit, Mandeville only considered the benefit for the whole society, calculated on the basis of the total sum of advantages and disadvantages for the single individuals and social groups. As a result, while the payoffs for the wealthy are evident, as it is clearly stated in the passage quoted above, the benefits that the less well-off would draw from the societal condition are rather called into question or, at best, they are only admitted if compared to former and significantly poorer stages of social development.[13] For that reason, it is quite clear that Mandeville's understanding of "public benefits" is quite different from that developed by authors—actually by all thinkers taken into consideration in this research—who prioritize an idea of order as a cohesive cooperation to the advantage of all members of the community. Thus, if his concept of "benefit" has been widely criticized, this is because "we want our benefits to be of a different kind".[14]

Regardless of the limits of Mandeville's overall conception, his work is nevertheless important from the perspective of a metatheory of social order because it provides some arguments in favour of the possibility of establishing a further paradigm of order. Completely unknown to his contemporaries—which explains the animosity of the criticism against Mandeville's work—as well as to any other author considered so far, the new paradigm is assumed to be based on the idea that order can be generated through the interactions of private actors, without any involvement of public power. Among the different interactions between private actors, some are traditionally regarded as distinguished by a rather limited scope. This is the case as regards family issues regulated by private law, which—although highly relevant for the physical and intellectual reproduction of society—impact in each single case only on a small number of individuals. The idea that family issues do not have relevance for social order in general, as long as the reproduction of society is secured, is surely old-fashioned, or simply wrong. Nonetheless, it must be acknowledged that, for the most part of the history of political thought, the divide between family and civil society has marked the border between what is matter of interest for only a few individuals and what concerns the whole society. On the contrary, some non-familiar interactions between private actors have been mostly regarded as having a general scope and affecting more or less directly the society as a whole. This is what makes up the *economic* sphere: insofar as they are related to the production and exchange of goods and these are not only at the service of the survival of the family, economic interactions are expressed by commercial transactions, i.e., by *trade*. Thus, the evaluation of the social significance of trade has played a pivotal role in paving the way to a possible third paradigmatic revolution, namely to the establishment of *particularistic individualism* as the fourth paradigm of order.

In the history of political and economic thought three distinct theories of trade have been developed—the doctrine of the "universal economy" in antiquity, the Lex mercatoria in the Middle Ages, and the theory of free trade between the second half of the eighteenth century and the first half of the nineteenth century—which seem to contour three chronologically quite distant attempts to trigger a paradigmatic revolution by establishing a new paradigm of order. However, to be considered firmly established, the new *particularistic-individualistic paradigm of order* should consistently display four features at the same time: firstly, individual payoffs should make up the only horizon for the justification of action; secondly, no reflexively shared value should be introduced as the ultimate goal of personal action; thirdly, no public dimension should serve as the guarantee that private interactions unfolds smoothly; fourthly, the self-organization of private actors should constitute a self-relying and encompassing system of social order, and not only a functional subsystem at the service of a higher situated concept of the well-ordered society. For one reason or another, none of the historical theories of trade presents all these characters together. As a result, we cannot but conclude that none of them realized the paradigmatic revolution that would have led to a really new pattern of social order. On the basis of what these theories have conceived and achieved, the implementation of a fourth paradigm of order is largely incomplete and the third paradigmatic revolution must be seen as a failed one. To make it succeed, a more profound paradigmatic upheaval and a new conceptual organon were needed.[15]

## 5.1 Trade as Instrument of World Order

Though separated in time by more than one thousand years, the first two theories of trade that have been elaborated in the history of ideas—the first in the Hellenistic period and during the Roman Empire; the second at the beginning of the second millennium C.E.—have two important traits in common. Firstly, both theories are strongly committed to emancipate trade from the harsh criticism that had been raised against it, respectively, by the great philosophers of classical antiquity and by early Christian thinkers. Secondly, trade is seen in both cases as an activity which has its deepest justification in contributing to the overall balance of the world. As a result of the most profound meaning that is attributed to trade, according to which the economic activity of the individuals is assumed to make sense only to the extent that it supports the homeostasis of the *holon*, both theories remain within the conceptual horizon of one of the already established paradigms of order, namely of holistic universalism, without being able or willing to implement any real paradigmatic revolution.

### 5.1.1 The Hellenist Doctrine of the Universal Economy

In Greek-Roman antiquity, trade was initially regarded with scepticism.[16] Early authors saw it as a threat to economic self-sufficiency, political stability and social cohesion. Aristotle, for instance, condemned commercial activity if its sole purpose was profit, although he valued some of its practical advantages like, for example, the import of food or timber for shipbuilding.[17] Plato was even more resolute and, in the name of the self-sufficiency of the *polis*, rejected both the idea of importing unnecessary goods, and the export of merchandise that could be useful to the community.[18] In the Greek *polis*, political activity was the central focus, and consequently, trade and commerce were pushed to the periphery of daily civic life.[19] In a world where the interests of the individual were seen as ancillary to the interests of the wider community, the individual pursuit of profit was regarded as a moral failure and a threat to common values. Therefore, trade was largely left to foreign merchants. This attitude also shaped the era of the Roman Republic, as indicated by Cicero's disdain of trade in *De officiis*:

> Trade, if it is on a small scale, is to be considered vulgar; but if wholesale and on a large scale, importing large quantities from all parts of the world and distributing to many without misrepresentation, it is not to be greatly disparaged.[20]

Several decades later, however, a fundamental change occurred. Writing about the sea and, indirectly, about seaborne trade, Plutarch adopts an indisputably positive approach to commerce:

> So that it may be said, this element united and perfected our manner of living, which before was wild and unsociable, correcting it by mutual assistance, and creating community of friendship by reciprocal exchanges of one good turn for another. And as Heraclitus said, If there were no sun, it would be perpetual night; so may we say, If there were no sea, man would be the most savage and shameless of all creatures. But the sea brought the vine from India into Greece, and out of Greece transmitted the use of corn to foreign parts; from Phoenicia translated the knowledge

of letters, the memorials that prevent oblivion; furnished the world with wine and fruit, and prevented the greatest part of mankind from being illiterate and void of education.[21]

A few years earlier, Seneca had already said that the wind "has given all nations communications with each other and brought together peoples separated by geography".[22] Both Plutarch and Seneca regarded the elements that favoured the exchange of goods as divine providence, as they did not threaten social interaction, but enhanced development and growth instead. The goal was no longer to protect the homogeneity of a single political entity, but to globally realize the potentialities of the organic whole, the *holon*.

The transitional period from the culture of self-contained city-states in ancient Greece to the cosmopolitanism of the Hellenistic and Roman imperial world witnessed for the first time what was to be called the "doctrine of universal economy".[23] The idea of a universal economy is characterized by four features[24]: firstly, the conviction that all resources are unequally distributed; secondly, the emphasis on the benefits generated by the exchange of goods through trade; thirdly, the stoic-cosmopolitan belief in the universal sociability that unites all human beings; and, finally, the faith in divine providence to balance out the inequalities in the distribution of resources since it is God's will that humans cooperate peacefully. The most accurate description has been provided by Philo of Alexandria:

> For all created things are assigned as a loan to all from God, and He has made none of these particular things complete in itself, so that it should have no need at all of another. Thus through the desire to obtain what it needs, it must perforce approach that which can supply its need, and this approach must be mutual and reciprocal. Thus through reciprocity and combination, even as a lyre is formed of unlike notes, God meant that they should come to fellowship and concord and form a single harmony, and that an universal give and take should govern them, and lead up to the consummation of the whole world.[25]

If we consider the four above-mentioned criteria that have to be met for a new particularistic-individualistic paradigm of social order to be regarded as established, it is quite evident that none of the goals has been consistently accomplished by the "doctrine of universal economy". Far from being the only horizon for the justification of action, individual payoffs may play a significant role as a personal driving force, but when it comes to determining the reasons why a certain action should be considered right and just, the reference is to the function that this action may have in securing the well-ordered redistribution of resources in the world and, therefore, in maintaining or recreating its internal balance or homeostasis. Furthermore, no doubt can be raised that the internal balance of the whole world is assumed—by the supporters of the "doctrine of universal economy"—to represent a common good and a shared value. No attention is given, then, to the question whether the economic transactions among private actors have to rely, in order to work properly, on the support given by some kind of public power. Therefore, the functional self-reliance of the "universal economy" remains highly uncertain. Finally, even if the "universal economy" seems to span all over the known world, thus freeing the interaction between economic actors from subordination to the interests of individual political communities, nonetheless the system of economic transaction is not considered a goal in itself, but rather a tool—and not the most important one—to fully realize the potentialities of the *holon*. In this sense, it is nothing more than an instrument for the stabilization of worldwide order, or—instead of being a new paradigm of order—only a corollary within the conceptual construction of holistic universalism.

### 5.1.2 The Lex Mercatoria of the Middle Ages

Though putting the preservation of the *holon* at the centre of its conception of order, the "doctrine of universal economy" supported nonetheless a certain degree of freedom of action by individual actors on the global market. Thus, it contained centrifugal elements that barely fitted into the idea of a strictly hierarchical and organic society. This was the first reason why it was firmly condemned by the early Church Fathers.[26] Moreover, during the crises pervading late antiquity and the early Middle Ages, individuals were encouraged to focus on the afterlife and to subordinate their secular interests to it—which ultimately contrasted with the mission envisaged by the "doctrine of universal economy". The scepticism of early Christian philosophy towards the perspective of conceding some freedom to economic actors was expressed with the highest systematic clarity by Thomas Aquinas. Assessing the value of private property—and therefore, indirectly, also the possibility of using it to promote individual preferences in a contest of self-relying economic transactions—he recognized indeed private property as a necessary social and legal institution,[27] but only if it served to consolidate and guarantee the status of the possessor within a static understanding of society as a predetermined *holon*.[28] Only with the shift to the Modern Ages Protestant thinkers eventually acknowledged individual property as an essential instrument for the self-realization of those who had the merit of acquiring it,[29] and Christian-Catholic philosophers delivered a moderately positive assessment of trade.[30] Yet, trade had already expanded in the High Middle Ages, so that the issue of a transnational economy as a factor for growth and welfare increasingly gained importance. The revival of trading activities and merchants' ability to self-organization was closely linked to the development of a legal system called *Lex mercatoria*. Unlike the "doctrine of universal economy", which had been essentially a philosophical theory, the Lex mercatoria was a legal system, thus adding the dimension of the law to the perspective of a transnational paradigm of order based on the spontaneous self-organization of private agents with reference to their economic transactions.

Referring to Harold Berman, Emily Kadens provides a widely shared interpretation of this system, defining it as "a coherent, European-wide body of general commercial law, driven by merchants, and more or less universally accepted and formalized into well-known and well-established customs during the period from 1050 to 1150".[31] When it comes to the details, however, the opinions of the scholars are divided. In general, they agree that the Lex mercatoria originated in the Middle Ages as a body of laws to regulate commercial transactions, that many of its norms relied on Roman trade law, and that its fundamental aim consisted in avoiding discrimination of foreign merchants in transnational economic relations. Precisely because of this last feature, some of its provisions were deduced from the Roman *jus gentium*.[32] Controversial are, nevertheless, the exact influence of the ancient legal doctrine,[33] the comparability of medieval Lex mercatoria with contemporary trade law, the uniformity of Lex mercatoria in different territories of application, and its independence from political power.[34] The last point is particularly interesting because it indicates that a consistent public sphere is indispensable for the establishment of a stable regime among private actors. And what applied in the Middle Ages with their weak public authorities can hardly be considered obsolete with reference to contemporary societies, characterized as they are by large and influential public administrations.

The Lex mercatoria was essentially a *corpus juris* of practical relevance. Among the few texts that contain an attempt to outline not only the rules but also the philosophy behind the praxis of this legal system, the most significant is probably *Consuetudo vel Lex Mercatoria*, written by the English merchant Gerard de Malynes in 1622 and then republished many times in the subsequent decades. In his philosophical introduction to the legal rules of the Lex mercatoria, Malynes first defined the activities of the trader as the "buying and selling of commodities, or by way of permutation of wares both at home and abroad in foreign parts".[35] He then examined when and why this social role was able to develop. Like the ancient exponents of the "universal economy", Malynes indentified the originally unequal distribution of goods as the basis for the justification of the merchant's role. Indeed, the trader's main function was assumed to consist in compensating the initial inequality.[36] Malynes ascribed the causes of the inequality to the non-homogeneous distribution of natural resources. As a second cause, he added their processing through human activity, thus emphasizing the role of the individual contribution to the accumulation of wealth more strongly than ancient theories did. According to Malynes, the main goal of commercial activity should not be seen in the pursuit of individual success. Rather, commerce is the consequence of the natural division of labour which arises from the social nature of man, who was created by God as a "social creature".[37] As such, the human being is not assumed to be able to live well on its own. When people come together to form a society, they divide the labour among themselves according to their abilities. Since each of them possesses certain goods in abundance while lacking others, they need a trader to create an equilibrium between abundance and scarcity.

Apart from an accentuated emphasis on the essential contribution of human activity to the production of goods—which was surely the consequence of the stronger economic dynamism of Modern Ages and of the increasing importance that was given to individual creativity if compared to the rather static idea of society that characterized the antiquity and the Middle Ages—the conceptual horizon of Malynes is largely consistent with the ancient conceptions of the "universal economy". Economic activity, namely, is assumed to remain integrated into an organic context, aiming to preserve the homeostasis of the whole. Individual priorities cannot lead to global order and are still embedded in a God-given metaphysical cosmos. This does not exclude the fact that the merchants of the Greek and Roman era, of the medieval age and of the early modern period might have been guided, from the point of view of their personal preferences, by egoistic interests. Yet, in all theoretical reflections elaborated—at least until the beginning of the seventeenth century—to clarify the significance of trade for social life, economic activities were embedded into a broader context of human sociality. This was thought to weaken and bring under control their individualistic, centrifugal and potentially subversive tendencies, because they had to adapt themselves to a general idea of the *holon*. Therefore, also the approach formulated by the theorists of the early Lex mercatoria is conceptually far away from the centrality of a self-reliant and egoistic economic rationality that would distinguish a coherent particularistic-individualistic paradigm of order.

## 5.2 The Free Trade Theory

At the beginning of the seventeenth century economic activities still served the organic equilibrium of the whole. By the end of the eighteenth century, however, the focus had shifted to private interests. This transformation was possible because during that time a new awareness emerged concerning the specificity of individuality and the impossibility to reduce it to the organic whole. In the area of economic theory it was especially Adam Smith who stressed this new position. His *Inquiry into the Nature and Causes of the Wealth of Nations*, first published in 1776, turned the traditional hierarchy between public and private interests upside down. He argued that it was not the economic failure of private actors but the sheer inefficiency and wastefulness of public administrations that impoverished the nations:

> such are the people who compose a numerous and splendid court, a great ecclesiastical establishment, great fleets and armies, who in time of peace produce nothing, and in time of war acquire nothing which can compensate the expence of maintaining them.[38]

The best guarantee for growth and prosperity, therefore, is not provided by the activities of the public sector but by "the uniform, constant, and uninterrupted effort of every man to better his condition .... It is this effort, protected by law and allowed by liberty to exert itself in the manner that is most advantageous, which has maintained the progress of England towards opulence and improvement in almost all former times, and which, it is to be hoped, will do so in all future times".[39] For the first time the self-interest of individuals was regarded as the basis of general wealth, with self-interest being neither reflexively oriented to the ultimate priority of common good, nor being substantially dignified and mitigated—like in Hobbes's contract theory—by the aim of establishing public power and political institutions. Moreover, Smith introduced a new criterion to evaluate economic policy: while for the previous authors—who were generally influenced by mercantilism—national wealth is well protected when the key sectors are sheltered against competition from outside, his only criterion to measure wealth is the real value of gross domestic product, regardless of how it is earned.[40]

Smith's redefinition of the relationship between private interest and public dimension as well as his post-mercantilist understanding of national wealth were the fundaments for his theory of free trade. In order to generate maximum wealth, merchant activities must not be constrained by public restrictions like high customs duties or import bans.[41] A protectionist policy is damaging for society as a whole since it brings advantages only to the industries that profit from it:

> That this monopoly of the home-market frequently gives great encouragement to that particular species of industry which enjoys it, and frequently turns towards that employment a greater share of both the labour and stock of the society than would otherwise have gone to it, cannot be doubted. But whether it tends either to increase the general industry of the society, or to give it the most advantageous direction, is not, perhaps, altogether so "evident".[42]

Indeed, statist dirigisme can only direct the use of capital, but it cannot increase its profitability:

> No regulation of commerce can increase the quantity of industry in any society beyond what its capital can maintain. It can only divert a part of it into a direction _. into which it might not otherwise have gone; and it is by no means certain that this artificial direction is likely to be more advantageous to the society than that into which it would have gone of its own accord.[43]

To take advantage of the productivity of capital as effectively as possible, it is necessary to use it for activities that promise the greatest return on investment. In Smith's view, these conditions are met if the holders of private capital are free to decide where and how to invest it: in fact, "every individual ... can, in his local situation, judge much better than any statesman or lawgiver can do for him".[44] Consequently, the intervention of the public power in the regulation of trade, not being able to exploit capital in an optimal way, is without effect in the most favourable case, or—in the less favourable cases—it brings harm to society. Furthermore, the abolition of trade restrictions would strengthen the positive effect of the international division of labour since not all goods can be produced with the same profit in each country. On the contrary, some offer the best conditions for the competitive realization of certain products, others guarantee maximum profit in other areas: "the natural advantages which one country has over another in producing particular commodities – Smith maintained – are sometimes so great, that it is acknowledged by all the world to be in vain to struggle with them".[45]

Unlike in contract theory or in the communicative understanding of order, according to Smith public interest is not assumed to be determined reflexively. In other words, it does not derive from self-conscious rational processes or intersubjective communication aiming to reach a shared basis—or, in the most ambitious theories, even consensus—for the solution of theoretical and practical questions as well as for the establishment of essential social values. On the contrary, it is the selfish pursuit of private interests that affects society most favourably. The mechanism for the creation of public welfare takes on the form of an almost "natural" law, arising spontaneously as a result of the legally regulated interaction of individuals, particularly of economic actors, who concentrate exclusively on the egoistic maximization of their profits. In Smith's famous conception it is the "invisible hand" that, like a kind of secular providence, leads to the best social development, beyond any rational attempt individuals might undertake and with better results than they can knowingly achieve:

> by directing that industry in such a manner as its produce may be of the greatest value, he [every individual] intends only his own gain, and he is in this, as in many other cases, led by an invisible hand to promote an end which was no part of his intention. Nor is it always the worse for the society that it was no part of it. By pursuing his own interest he frequently promotes that of the society more effectually than when he really intends to promote it.[46]

The "invisible hand" best ensures both the growth of the economies of single nation states and the overall equilibrium between nations:

Hereafter, perhaps, the natives of those countries may grow stronger, or those of Europe may grow weaker, and the inhabitants of all the different quarters of the world may arrive at that equality of courage and force which, by inspiring mutual fear, can alone overawe the injustice of independent nations into some sort of respect for the rights of one another. But nothing seems more likely to establish this equality of force than that mutual communication of knowledge and of all sorts of improvements which an extensive commerce from all countries to all countries naturally, or rather necessarily, carries along with it.[47]

Summing up, it seems quite evident that Smith introduced—far more resolutely than his predecessors—a new perspective on the form, composition and possible scope of social order. For the first time, he developed a conception which coherently relies on the priority of individual interests. These are presumed to produce a global equilibrium independent of public norms and institutions. Furthermore, the intervention of public power is not seen as an indispensable support, but rather as a hampering factor. Yet, is the free interaction of economic actors pursuing their selfish interests really a goal in itself, on which Smith's general idea of a worldwide economic order is grounded? Or is it, more exactly, only an instrument—even if probably the most important one—for a different and higher purpose? And did Smith consistently assume that no shared values are necessary for social interactions to develop smoothly? As regards these points, Smith's vision lacks the ultimate consequence. If we take his work as a whole, in fact, the main goal of the pursuit of private interests is not private but collective welfare. Moreover, welfare is not understood in global terms but from the perspective of the primacy of the nation. Indeed, as Smith pointed out in his *Theory of Moral Sentiments* of 1759:

> The love of our own country seems not to be derived from the love of mankind. The former sentiment is altogether independent of the latter, and seems sometimes even to dispose us to act inconsistently with it. [...] We do not love our country merely as a part of the great society of mankind: we love it for its own sake, and independently of any such consideration.[48]

Then he projects patriotism onto the idea of economic prosperity:

> France may contain, perhaps, near three times the number of inhabitants which Great Britain contains. In the great society of mankind, therefore, the prosperity of France should appear to be an object of much greater

importance than that of Great Britain. The British subject, however, who, upon that account, should prefer upon all occasions the prosperity of the former to that of the latter country, would not be thought a good citizen of Great Britain.[49]

The love for one's own country should never be accompanied—according to Smith—by disrespect, jealousy or even hatred against other nations. Nevertheless, the wealth of one's own nation should be regarded as the vanishing point and the essential criterion of right action, so that also free trade eventually serves this crucial goal. To point out the supreme role of national welfare—to which the pursuit of private interests is but a subordinated means—Smith explicitly addresses the wealth of *nations* in the title of his most famous book. Moreover, while discussing the objects of political economy in the *Wealth of Nations*, he specified that they consist in identifying, through the application of a scientific method, not only the instruments "to provide a plentiful revenue or subsistence for the people, or more properly to enable them to provide such a revenue or subsistence for themselves", but also those that are necessary "to supply the state or commonwealth with a revenue sufficient for the public services".[50] Thus, Smith considered public services—albeit only a few of them—indispensable for the market system to be well-functioning, for the economy to successfully grow and for the whole society to be well-ordered.[51] Among the services that should be delivered by the public authority are defence, justice, education,[52] a moderately progressive taxation system—thought to relieve poverty, but only in the sense of enabling the poor to fully participate in the market transactions[53]—and some other provisions that, in general, cannot profitably be delivered by the markets.[54] As a result, Smith's theory of free trade cannot be considered a consistent basis for a new paradigm of order only centred on the spontaneous interaction of private actors for three reasons. Firstly, the call for free trade is eventually connected to national preferences, so that individual payoffs have ultimately to comply with national interests. Secondly, the state is still granted a significant role in securing that society is well-ordered. Thirdly, the initial subversion of the traditional hierarchy between public and private makes way for a moderate restoration, in which the dimension of common benefits is largely independent of mechanisms of political legitimation and rather bears quasi-natural features.

The idea that the free interaction of participants in market transactions is beneficial, first and foremost, to the national wealth was quite a *topos* among the most important economists who wrote in the first half of the nineteenth century. While Thomas Malthus's radical plea for an import tax on cereals, and therefore for protectionism,[55] remained the exception among English economists of that period, the advocacy of free trade—and thus, of the right to pursue individual economic interests—is nevertheless generally justified by evoking its contribution to the prosperity of the nation. As David Ricardo wrote in his work *On the Principles of Political Economy and Taxation* of 1817:

> Under a system of perfectly free commerce, each country naturally devotes its capital and labour to such employments as are most beneficial to each. The pursuit of individual advantage is admirably connected with the universal good of the whole. By stimulating industry, by regarding ingenuity, and by using most efficaciously the peculiar powers bestowed by nature, it distributes labour most effectively and most economically, while, by increasing the general mass of production, it diffuses general benefit, and binds together by one common tie of interest and intercourse the universal society of nations throughout the civilized world.[56]

John Stuart Mill further pursued this contention. As for the indirect advantages of free trade, he enumerated the benefits society can draw from it at the national level, such as the improvement of the productive processes, the increased division of labour, a better use of technology and the stimulation of entrepreneurship.[57] At the same time, he pointed out the importance of transnational economic activity for the creation of a cosmopolitan society:

> Finally, commerce first taught nations to see with good will the wealth and prosperity of one another. Before, the patriot, unless sufficiently advanced in culture to feel the world his country, wished all countries weak, poor, and ill-governed, but his own: he now sees in their wealth and progress a direct source of wealth and progress to his own country. It is commerce which is rapidly rendering war obsolete, by strengthening and multiplying the personal interests which are in natural opposition to it. And it may be said without exaggeration that the great extent and rapid increase of international trade, in being the principal guarantee of the peace of the world, is the great permanent security for the uninterrupted progress of the ideas, the institutions, and the character of the human race.[58]

Smith, Ricardo and Mill saw the interest of the nation as an intermediary between the economic priorities of individuals and a global order that serves all humanity. On the one hand, economic activity not only generates personal wealth but also overall welfare for the entire country; on the other hand, peaceful coexistence is in everyone's best interest, because the nation's wealth depends on the freedom of transnational economic interaction. We can assume, however, that the strong promotion of the harmonious interplay between the pursuit of individual interests, the prosperity of the nation and international peace by English economists was the consequence of Great Britain's economic and geopolitical predominance at the time. Accordingly, free trade met with much more scepticism in economically less developed countries such as France,[59] Germany[60] or the United States.[61] Indeed, the most important economists of these countries retained a rather traditional understanding of the relationship between private and public interests. As a consequence, they still thought it necessary to restrain the pursuit of private interests for the sake of the nation's public welfare and did not consider the latter the result of free transnational economic interaction.[62] Thus, not even in its "golden era" between the middle of the eighteenth century and the middle of the nineteenth century the idea of free trade could evolve into a coherent theory of a global order of private actors: generally rejected by non-British economists, it was still not free of contradictions and reservations in its country of origin. From the mid-nineteenth century until World War II, the emerging nationalism reinforced the idea that the pursuit of private interests was only valuable if it served the common interest of the nation. Therefore, in the course of a growing engagement of public powers in economic priority-setting, decisions and processes, the theory of free trade had to make room for public interventionism.

In conclusion, to delineate an autonomous paradigm of order, the classical economic theories—from the "doctrine of the universal economy" to the liberal theory of free trade, passing through the Lex mercatoria of the late Middle Ages—should have formulated a consistent idea of social interaction grounded on a specific and distinct ontological basis, i.e., on the self-regulating economic transactions of private actors on a global scale, without resorting to reflexively shared values or to any kind of support by the public power. Yet, none of these theories proved to be capable of implementing consistently a new paradigm of order. Both the "doctrine of universal economy" and the medieval Lex mercatoria did not ultimately place individual interests at the centre of the system, but still saw them in the light of the predominance of common values, quite in the spirit that typified the old holistic-universalistic paradigm. On the other hand, the free trade theory emancipated indeed the private agents, but only because their free entrepreneurship seemed to be the best way to strengthen the territorial state and the national community—in line with the tradition of a benevolent national particularism. Furthermore, the function of public power was never explicitly and completely set aside. Therefore, the regime of private interactions was never really autonomous, but always at the service of rather traditional concepts of the well-ordered society. After a long period in which the very idea of a pattern of social order only relying on the transnational interactions of private interests was radically marginalized, a new—and this time successful—attempt to consolidate the particularistic-individualistic paradigm finally emerged with the globalization of markets at the end of the twentieth century.

## NOTES

1. Bernard Mandeville, *The Fable of the Bees* (1728), Irwin Primer ed., Capricorn Books, New York 1962, at 27, line 1 et seq.
2. Ibid., at 27, line 13 et seq.
3. Ibid., at 28, line 33 et seq.
4. Ibid., at 31, line 163 and 166.
5. Ibid., at 31, line 155 et seq.
6. Ibid., at 31, line 177 et seq.
7. Ibid., at 38, line 407 et seq.
8. Ibid., at 38, line 409 et seq. and 415 et seq.
9. Ibid., at 22.
10. Ibid., at 23.
11. Irwin Primer, *Introduction*, in: Mandeville, *The Fable of the Bees*, *supra* note 1, 1–17, at 14.
12. Mandeville, *The Fable of the Bees*, *supra* note 1, at 31, line 149 et seq.
13. Ibid., at 32, line 201 et seq.
14. Primer, *Introduction*, *supra* note 11, at 9.
15. See *infra*, Sect. 6.3.
16. Douglas A. Irwin, *Against the Tide*, Princeton University Press, Princeton 1996, at 11 et seq.
17. Aristotle, *Politics*, H. Rackham trans., Harvard University Press, Cambridge (MA) 1959, Book VII, Chapter 6, 1327a, at 562 et seq.
18. Plato, *Nomoi—Laws*, R. G. Bury ed., Heinemann, London 1926, Book VIII, 847b et seq., at 183 et seq.

19. Irwin, *Against the Tide*, *supra* note 16, at 12.
20. Marcus Tullius Cicero, *De officiis* (44 B.C.E.), English translation by Walter Miller, Heinemann, London 1928 (1st ed. 1913), Book I, Chapter XLII, at 154 et seq.
21. Plutarch, *Morals*, William W. Goodwin ed., Little, Brown, and Company, Boston 1878, Vol. V, Chapter: *Whether Water or Fire Be Most Useful*, at 333 et seq.
22. Lucius Annaeus Seneca, *Naturales Quaestiones* (62–65), English translation by Harry M. Hine, University of Chicago Press, Chicago/London 2010, Book V, Chapter 18.4, at 83.
23. Irwin, *Against the Tide*, *supra* note 16, at 15 et seq.
24. Jacob Viner, *The Role of the Providence in the Social Order*, Princeton University Press, Princeton 1976, at 27 et seq.
25. Philo Judaeus, *On the Cherubim*, in: Philo, *Works*, English translation by F. H. Colson and G. H. Whitaker, Harvard University Press, Cambridge (MA)/London 1994 (1st ed. 1929), Vol. II, 3–85, Chapter XXXI, at 72 et seq.
26. Irwin, *Against the Tide*, *supra* note 16, at 17 et seq.
27. Thomas Aquinas, *Summa theologica* [1265–1273], W. Benton-Encyclopedia Britannica, Chicago 1980, Part II, Section II, Question 66, Article 2.
28. Ibid., Part II, Section II, Question 32, Article 6.
29. Hugo Grotius, *De Jure Belli ac Pacis* (1625), Book II, Chapter II (English: *The Rights of War and Peace*, Richard Tuck ed., Liberty Fund, Indianapolis 2005, at 420 et seq.).
30. Irwin, *Against the Tide*, *supra* note 16, at 21.
31. Emily Kadens, *Order within Law, Variety within Custom: The Character of the Medieval Merchant Law*, in: "Chicago Journal of International Law", Vol. 5 (2004–2005), 39–65, at 40. See Harold J. Berman, *Law and Revolution: The Formation of Western Legal Tradition*, Harvard University Press, Cambridge (MA) 1983, at 333, 340 et seq.
32. Richard A. Epstein, *Reflections on the Historical Origins and Economic Structure of the Law Merchant*, in: "Chicago Journal of International Law", Vol. 5 (2004–2005), 1–20.
33. Charles Jr. Donahue, *Medieval and Early Modern Lex mercatoria: An Attempt at the probatio diabolica*, in: "Chicago Journal of International Law", Vol. 5 (2004–2005), 21–37.
34. Kadens, *Order within Law*, *supra* note 31.
35. Gerard de Malynes, *Consuetudo, vel, Lex Mercatoria, or, the Ancient Law-Merchant* (1622), Redmayne, London 1685, at 4.
36. Ibid., at 2.
37. Ibid.

38. Adam Smith, *An Inquiry into the Nature and Causes of the Wealth of Nations* (1776), R. H. Campbell, H. S. Skinner and W. B. Todd eds., Oxford University Press, Oxford/New York 1976, Vol. I, Book II, Chapter III, at 342.
39. Ibid., Vol. I, Book II, Chapter III, at 343, 345.
40. Irwin, *Against the Tide*, supra note 16, at 75 et seq.
41. Smith, *An Inquiry into the Nature and Causes of the Wealth of Nations*, supra note 38, Vol. I and II, Book IV.
42. Ibid., Vol. I, Book IV, Chapter II, at 453.
43. Ibid.
44. Ibid., Vol. I, Book IV, Chapter II, at 456.
45. Ibid., Vol. I, Book IV, Chapter II, at 458.
46. Ibid., Vol. I, Book IV, Chapter II, at 456.
47. Ibid., Vol. II, Book IV, Chapter VII, Part 3, at 626 et seq.
48. Adam Smith, *The Theory of Moral Sentiments* (1759), Ryan Patrick Hanley ed., Penguin Books, London 2009, Part VI, Section II, Chapter II, at 271.
49. Ibid.
50. Smith, *An Inquiry into the Nature and Causes of the Wealth of Nations*, supra note 38, Vol. I, Book IV, "Introduction", at 428.
51. Amartya Sen, *Introduction*, in: Smith, *The Theory of Moral Sentiments*, supra note 48, VII–XXVI, at XIII et seq.
52. Smith, *An Inquiry into the Nature and Causes of the Wealth of Nations*, supra note 38, Vol. II, Book V, at 689 et seq.
53. Ibid., Vol. II, Book V, Chapter I, Article I, at 725.
54. R. H. Campbell, A. S. Skinner, *General Introduction*, in: Smith, *An Inquiry into the Nature and Causes of the Wealth of Nations*, supra note 38, Vol. I, 1–60, at 34 et seq.
55. Irwin, *Against the Tide*, supra note 16, at 94 et seq. See Thomas Malthus, *The Grounds of an Opinion on the Policy of Restricting the Importation of Foreign Corn*, Murray, London 1815.
56. David Ricardo, *On the Principles of Political Economy and Taxation* (1817), Batoche Books, Kitchener 2001, at 89.
57. John Stuart Mill, *Principles of Political Economy* (1848), Longmans, Green & Co., London/New York/Toronto 1936, Book III, Chapter XVII, at 574.
58. Ibid., Book III, Chapter XVII, at 582.
59. Antoine-Augustin Cournot, *Recherches sur les principes mathématiques de la théorie des richesses*, Rivière, Paris 1838.
60. Friedrich List, *Das nationale System der politischen Ökonomie* (1841), Akademie-Verlag, Berlin 1982.
61. Henry Carey, *Principles of Political Economy*, Carey, Lea & Blanchard, Philadelphia 1837–1840.
62. Irwin, *Against the Tide*, supra note 16, at 98.

CHAPTER 6

# The Post-unitary Paradigms of Order I: Systems Theory and the New Lex Mercatoria

Since the beginning of Western thought, social, political and legal order has always been conceived of as depending on the unity, internal coherence, reliable hierarchy and often also homogeneity of the community which was envisaged as the primary basis for social interaction. Therefore, regardless of its extension—it could be as small as the Greek *polis*, or as large as the Roman Empire, as exclusive as the nation state, or as inclusive as the cosmopolitan *civitas maxima*—and of its holistic or individualistic ontological foundation, the community regarded as the foundation of well-ordered social relations had always to be characterized by a pyramidal structure of political institutions and legal norms. The simultaneous presence of different normative and institutional orders within the same territory, thus, was not welcomed as the establishment and recognition of diversity, but rather condemned as sheer *dis*-order. In other words, according to the *unitary* idea of order, an institutional structure and a body of norms were considered "well-ordered" only if organized as a coherent and hierarchical unity, as a pyramid in which conflicts between different institutions and norms had to be resolved by defining which institution or norm, respectively, has priority over the conflicting one. In the last decades, however, a new approach to the understanding of legal and political order has been developed, in which the plurality of norms and institutions within the same territory and regulating the same matter is not denounced as a pathology any longer, but is accepted as a fact, on the one hand, and as a desirable perspective on the other. This quite recent and still ongoing process corresponds to a third paradigmatic revolution in the theories of order. This involves what has been described as the third element—along with the claims concerning the extension of order and its ontological basis—of a paradigm of order, namely the assertion about the unitary or non-unitary character of a well-ordered society. The paradigmatic revolution from a unitary to a post-unitary idea of order has paved the way for an approach in which the well-ordered society can also be seen as a polyarchic and horizontally interconnected structure that reminds more of a network than of a pyramid. In this social, political and legal configuration of interrelated decision-makers, conflicts of institutions and norms are not a dangerous threat to order; rather, they can be operationalized in discursive procedures aiming at reaching a shared objective and not at establishing—or re-establishing—hierarchy.

It is interesting to observe that the third paradigmatic revolution introduces a novelty also with reference to the first two features of order, namely extension and ontological basis. Indeed, in a supposedly well-ordered society which is organized in a unitary form the alternatives as regards, respectively, order extension and its ontological basis can only be conceived as dichotomous. Put differently, either is the society that is assumed to be well-ordered also limited in its extension and composition, or it is cosmopolitan in its dimension and inclusiveness. In the same spirit, either is the well-ordered society centred on the superiority of the community over the individuals, or it gives priority to the individual rights over the homogeneity of the *holon*. To the contrary, a well-ordered society that is organized in form of a plurality of interconnected and non-strictly-hierarchical institutions and norms can be universal and particular at the same time, insofar as it extends far beyond the borders of the single community, but recognizes the inescapability and value of the sub-universal institutionalizations of order. Moreover, it can be holistic as well as individualistic since it implies, in the multilayered and plural complexity of its overall structure, both the recognition of the specific identity of the social groups as well as of the sense of belongingness created by them, and the individual striving towards self-realization—or at least, as in systems theory, the concomitant connections of each individual with many different social subsystems. Summing up, the acknowledgement of plurality as a value makes possible to conceive of the well-ordered society, at the same time, as universalistic *but also* particularistic, and as holistic *but also* individualistic.

Three approaches can be singled out in this still unfolding process of transition from the unitary to the post-unitary conception of order: the first, namely systems theory, makes up the content of this chapter, while the next chapters address, respectively, postmodern thinking and the communicative paradigm. Each of these approaches—which correspond to different forms of criticism against the concept of rationality that dominated modern philosophy—is not only characterized by a specific understanding of the practical and theoretical use of reason but also lays the ground for a particular notion of post-unitary legal order: the idea of the existence of a multiplicity of self-reliant, albeit not mutually indifferent, legal systems in the first case, legal pluralism in the second, and cosmopolitan constitutionalism in the third. Systems theory, which conceives of global society in form of a plurality of self-relying subsystems (Sect. 6.1), addresses the contemporary phenomenon of the fragmentation and globalization of law with a sophisticated conceptual organon (Sect. 6.2). Moreover, it makes possible to re-propose—now on a substantially more robust theoretical basis—the idea of an autonomous legal system as a non-public framework for the self-organization of the worldwide economic transactions by private actors. Under these premises, the particularistic-individualistic paradigm of order, which—as it has been shown in Chapter 5—had never been convincingly laid down in the classical theories of trade between the antiquity and the first half of the twentieth century, was finally brought to completion as a corollary of the post-unitary conception of order introduced by systems theory (Sect. 6.3). Systems theory has proven to possess a high potential for drawing insight and knowledge from its method if applied to the analysis of complex societies. Nonetheless, both the fundamental assumptions of its theoretical organon and the application of some of them to the revitalization of the Lex mercatoria raise questions that remain, so far, unanswered (Sect. 6.3).

## 6.1 Niklas Luhmann and the Plurality of Systemic Rationalities

Fritz Lang's film *Metropolis*, released in 1927, is probably the most impressive visual representation of the triumph of modern systemic rationality—and of the losses that it may imply. The city designed by Lang with unprecedented visionary intensity is a rationalistic dystopia, run by huge machines which work according to their internal, functionalistic logic, thus enslaving the workers and disregarding their most basic needs. Lang went so far as to display, in his movie, a machine that takes the features of a human being, hinting at the possibility that a misled rationalization of society could restlessly colonize the minds and bodies of humans. In the end, the systemic rationality proves to be self-destroying, so that a new beginning based on a renewed social contract and on a rationality at the service of human needs is made possible.

Lang's film has been widely criticized because of its rather cheap final consolatory and conciliatory message. Nonetheless, the vision of a throughout rationalized society, in which the meaning of rationality is reduced to the most efficient accomplishment of ethically unquestioned functions, cannot but deeply and lastingly impress the spectator. Furthermore, even though we cannot expect from a work of art the analytical accuracy and the conceptual coherence of a sociological essay, it touches with unusual creativity the question of the specificity of modern rationality, namely its value-free functionalism and its neutralization of the human lifeworld. Far away from having been seduced by the muses of art, it was Max Weber who explored—only a couple of years before Lang released *Metropolis*, and from a surely less critical viewpoint—the characteristics of the modern functionalistic rationality. Among the many topics addressed in his *Wirtschaft und Gesellschaft* (*Economy and Society*) of 1922, a prominent position is taken by his analysis of the modern transformation of how legitimate political power is understood. Beside the "traditional" and the "charismatic" forms of political power—the first bearing the traits of a mythological and religious origin, the second focusing on personal leadership—a third ideal type is identified, which is called by Weber "rational".[1] This is characterized by three factors: an effective legal system in order to regulate social relations and to give predictability to interactions; an efficient bureaucracy with hierarchical structure; and the presumption that the holders of power and, in general, the members of the bureaucratic apparatus are endowed with better skills and superior knowledge. Unlike the others, the third form of legitimate political power belongs explicitly and exclusively to modern society and is strictly connected with the development of the bureaucratic-administrative state. Modern society, which has been informed by functionalist rationality in all its dimensions, is compared by Weber to a "machine". The bureaucratic modern state, which has been "cut loose from vocational-ethical attitudes", has become a "rationally operating machine"[2]:

> An inanimate machine is mind objectified. Only this provides it with the power to force men into its service and to dominate their everyday working life as completely as is actually the case in the factory. Objectified intelligence is also that animated machine, the bureaucratic organization, with its specialization of trained skills, its division of jurisdiction, its rules and hierarchical relations of authority.[3]

Yet, Weber did not look at the development of the bureaucratic machine of the modern state, which is assumed to be capable of transforming human beings from autonomous and self-relying entities into cogs of the system, without a sense of unease due to the loss that modern functionalist rationality may bring about:

> How can one possibly save any remnants of "individualist" freedom in any sense? After all, it is a gross self-deception to believe that without the achievements of the age of the Rights of Man any one of us, including the most conservative, can go on living his life.[4]

Talcott Parsons, who played a central role in making Max Weber known to the English-speaking audience, introduced a new element into the concept of functionalist social rationality, namely the idea that societies must differentiate into *subsystems* so as to perform the functions that are required from them.[5] While this may be true for all societies, it is even more evident for the most complex among them, which are expected to carry out a great number of functions. It is within the social subsystems that the "value-patterns" and the behaviour roles are consolidated into systemic conventions. These take the form of normative orientations of action which must be taken up by the individuals so that their behaviour is made consistent with social expectations.[6] It is unquestionable that role expectations bring relevant constraints on individuals as regards their options for action. Nonetheless, we cannot detect in Parsons's analysis that sense of discomfort and worry that still shone through in some passages of Weber's inquiry into the distinctive features of functionalist rationality. Since society can only continue to exist if individuals take on specific behaviour roles, so that their actions can be directed towards fundamental social functions, no room is left for regret about the limitation of individual freedom.[7]

Both Weber's analysis of bureaucratic rationality and Parsons's inquiry into the fundamentals of systems theory take a functionalist viewpoint while highlighting the mechanisms of society. In principle, their theoretical tools can be used to underpin any of the traditional conceptions of order. Therefore, functionalist and systemic categories are suitable to be applied to the study of well-ordered societies no matter according to which paradigm of order these are shaped in other respects. As a result, a holistic-particularistic society can be approached with functionalist instruments when it comes to the investigation of its operating modus, while the same categories are liable to be consistently employed in the analysis of the institutions of the holistic-universalistic *civitas maxima* or of the universalistic-individualistic cosmopolis as well. It was Niklas Luhmann who transformed the sociological approach of functionalist rationality from an indistinctively applicable tool to the basis for an original and accomplished paradigm of order which bears the features, moreover, of a post-unitary conception of the well-ordered society.

Indeed, if compared to Parsons's model of systems theory Luhmann's variant is characterized by the introduction of four innovative aspects. First, Parsons's analysis is primarily focused on *individual action*; only in a second step—as a result of the acquisition of value-patterns and role expectations—the many options of individual action are rationally scrutinized and reduced to those models of behaviour that are in conformity with the functional requirements of the subsystem in which the individual is acting.[8] Thus, the individuals and their capacity of action build the centre of his conception, while the systemic rules—though acknowledged as the only modi operandi through which individuals can be socialized—take second place. On the contrary, Luhmann focuses his attention from the very beginning on the forms of *systemic communication*, while variants of individual action with their driving forces are implicitly regarded as irrelevant for a scientifically-based sociological research. A second difference then arises from this first divergence: individuals with their biological, psychological, ethical and motivational endowment are the main material of Parsons's sociology and the essential content of which social interactions are made according to his approach. In Luhmann's view, instead, individuals are only taken into account as biological and psychical systems and therefore—since sociology exclusively concentrates on social systems—excluded from the sociological research. Thirdly, Parsons admits that society is divided into subsystems, but this division seems to be largely porous, so that the subsystems are, at least to some extent, internally interconnected to one another. In contrast, Luhmann's subsystems are strictly self-relying and hermetically closed against each other. Finally, Parsons's subsystems are seen as essentially related to some form of national society, while Luhmann's subsystems, precisely because of their self-reliance, are regarded as having the tendency to expand into the postnational constellation. It is on the basis of the last two divergences that we can arguably speak, with reference to Luhmann's systems theory, of the creation of a truly *new paradigm of order*. In fact, unlike the former paradigms, Luhmann's idea of order is essentially plural because of the many self-reliant subsystems; and, unlike the more flexible approaches of his predecessors, it does not provide an analytical tool for the inquiry into the mechanisms of whatsoever pattern of social order, but a vision of order that contains a specific claim—and a new one if compared to the former conceptions—as regards all three aspects that qualify a paradigm of order, namely extension, ontological basis and unitary/non-unitary character of the well-ordered society.

Though Luhmann's sociological theory is huge both in scope and complexity, it is possible—with a dash of audacity—to lead it back to only eight main assumptions. First, Luhmann distinguished social systems from other categories of systems—for instance, psychic, biological or technical systems.[9] The specific characteristic of social systems consists in operationalizing "communication". In other words, the transmission and elaboration of information represent the essential operation that distinguishes society as a system[10]: communication is therefore "the operation that produces and reproduces society".[11] Secondly, according to Luhmann what we can scientifically describe as "society" is not—as it has been mainly conceived—a group of individuals, but a sum of communicative operations connected to each other. The distinction becomes clear, here, between the concept of communication in Luhmann's systems theory and its notion in Habermas's philosophy:

> Intersubjectivity – Luhmann claimed – has neither always been given nor can it be produced (which would presuppose that one can establish whether it has been attained or not). What is decisive instead is that communication continues – howsoever the consciousness required for the purpose is persuaded to join in. It can never be ascertained in communication whether consciousness systems are "authentically" involved or are only contributing what is necessary for continuation.[12]

In the theory of intersubjectivity, the individual, having a potentially universal language, guarantees the communicative and normative unity of society beyond the fragmentation of the interaction that inevitably distinguishes the plural and polyarchic constellation. To the contrary, Luhmann's approach recognizes indeed that "persons"—i.e., in his language, individualized psychic systems—are indispensable for social systems to work. In fact, "persons cannot emerge and continue to exist without social systems, nor can social systems without persons".[13] Nonetheless, Luhmann's sociology regards the individuals as *external* to the communication system properly understood, so that, if related to the communication system that makes up the society as a whole, they are nothing but part of the "environment". Moreover, Luhmann maintains that normative contents of social interaction can neither be scientifically described—which is not surprising in a theory that claims to be rigorously value-free—nor are they necessary, in principle, for a society to work properly.

Thirdly, following Luhmann society is a system (or meta-system) that consists of different (sub-)systems. As a result, "the theory of society is the theory of the comprehensive social system that encompasses all other social systems".[14] Since society as a whole must perform a significant number of functions so that it can continue to exist, each specialized subsystem has the task of delivering precisely one of those essential functions. The more specialized a system is, the better the quality of its functional performance will be. Therefore, subsystemic differentiation is an inescapable condition for that rationalization process that makes a society more efficient. As a result, Luhmann's theory of society eschews any reference to an overarching rationality that, starting from the transcendental capacities of the individuals, would purport to encompass all forms of social interaction. No universal reason—subjective or intersubjective—is here envisaged, either at the descriptive or at the prescriptive level. To the contrary, Luhmann maintains that many rationalities can be observed by the social scientist, each of them characterizing the way of functioning of one specific social subsystem. In other words, while we do not detect—according to Luhmann's systems theory—any extra-systemic rational processes, we observe the implementation of different rational processes that, within the manifold functional subsystems of society, guarantee that these subsystems deliver the performances for which they have developed and that are necessary for the continuity and the further improvement—in the sense of higher efficiency—of the whole society.

The fourth assumption of Luhmann's social theory arises from a question: namely, how can a system—or, rather, the persons (in the vocabulary of systems theory, the psychic and biological systems) that are involved in the elaboration of information within a specific subsystem—recognize that an input should be operationalized precisely in that social context? In other words, how can we understand that an information is part of the communication that characterizes a certain social subsystem? To answer this question, Luhmann assumes that every subsystem is distinguished by "a binary code that is unique to itself".[15] The subsystem of the law, for example, adopts the code "legal/illegal" (*Recht/Unrecht*),[16] while the scientific subsystem applies the code "true/false" (*wahr/unwahr*), and so on. These codes allow to operationalize information in a way that is useful to the single subsystem to properly carry out its functions. Moreover, the functional rationality of the subsystems, which is expressed through their specific operational codes, ensures a higher predictability of human experience and behaviour. Finally, they make possible to sort out those inputs that do not fit into the code and, therefore, would be of no use or even harmful to the systemic functioning. For instance, considerations about love or art have nothing to do with law and should thus be excluded from the legal discourse. All information that does not fit into the subsystem, being therefore expelled from the intra-systemic operations as a result of the scrutiny carried out through the binary code mechanism, is regarded as belonging to the external "environment" (*Umwelt*).[17] As regards the distinction between "system" and "environment", while the system is "a context of factually enacted operations which, since they are social operations, must be forms of communication",[18] "environment" means everything that surrounds the system, not sharing the specificity of the function and the operational code.

Fifthly, following an inspiration coming from the notion of system that was elaborated with reference to biological entities by Humberto Maturana and Francisco Varela,[19] Luhmann asserts that also social systems are *autopoietic*:

> Autopoietic systems are systems that themselves produce not only their structures but also the elements of which they consist in the network of these same elements.[20]

Like living organisms, social systems are assumed to reproduce themselves and to continually develop on the basis of their internal processes. In other words, the operations of any system originate from other, functionally similar operations of the same system, and in turn produce operations of the same type. With reference to social systems, this means that communication originates from communication and produces communication.[21] Sixthly, to be properly autopoietic, systems need to be "operationally closed" against the environment, i.e., against other systems:

> If we describe society as a system, it follows from the general theory of autopoietic systems that it must be an operationally closed one. At the level of the system's own operations there is no ingress to the environment, and environmental systems are just as little able to take part in the autopoietic processes of an operationally closed system.[22]

Put differently, if all systems—and, thus, also social subsystems—are self-reliant, then no agent who is acting as an element of one specific subsystem can operate within another subsystem in the same capacity, nor communication generated within a social subsystem can directly flow into another subsystem, thereby immediately influencing its operational chain.[23]

Seventhly, the fact that Luhmann's theory of systems presupposes their "operational closure" (*operative Geschlossenheit* or *operative Schließung*), therefore ruling out "causal relations between the system and the environment",[24] does not mean that there is no interdependence between the system and the environment. Yet, how can "the system of society – Luhmann asks – organize its relationship with the environment if it maintains no contact with this environment and has only its own referential capacity at its disposition?"[25] The answer is that each system interacts with the environment through so-called "structural couplings" (*strukturelle Kopplungen*). Given the premises that: (a) no suprasystemic agent can act within a subsystem; (b) no systemically rational chains of causality go beyond the borders of the single system; and (c) that the direct operationalization of information outside its original subsystem can only lead to a loss of functional efficiency, systems are nonetheless able to react to changes in external systems which are relevant to their operations. Concretely, they can do so by correcting their own modus operandi. Thereby they adapt their operations to external solicitations, without having to presuppose—at least according to Luhmann—that external operations directly affect the internal chain of cause and effect. Luhmann makes the example of the interaction between consciousness systems and communication systems: the operations of the former never come directly into the latter, and vice versa. However, each system captures what happens in the other to the extent that it influences the accomplishment of its specific function. In other words, they are "irritated" (*Irritation*)— or even "disturbed" (*Störung*) or "perturbed" (*Perturbation*)—[26] with the consequence of mutually adapting their operations:

> consciousness systems and communication systems are adapted to one another to allow them to function in unobtrusive coordination.[27]

Since the categories of subjective rationality—or, to put it differently, the categories that are traditionally assumed to be at the basis of the individual use of practical reason and of the justification of action—are not regarded by systems theorists as objects of a serious sociological research, the ex ante tuning of subsystems should happen without any implication of individual awareness or reflexivity. The solution reminds us, to some extent, of Leibniz's metaphysics, in which the self-reliant monads harmonize to realize the allegedly "best of all possible worlds" without any conscious participation of the individuals to the implementation of the ambitious plan. Leibniz's conviction was grounded on a providential ontology. In systems theory, which cannot resort to metaphysical assumptions and claims to deliver a methodologically sound descriptive research, the systemic tuning must have a "basis in reality", which is explained as an ongoing evolutionary parallelism.[28] In other words, what we perceive and describe as an ex ante tuning is nothing other than the result of a long process of internal operations, irritations due to external stresses, and reciprocal adaptations. In conclusion, in Luhmann's theory of society "the concept of structural coupling explains that, although systems are completely self-determined, they develop by and large in a direction tolerated by the environment".[29] The almost organicist component that shines through the idea of the parallel development of systems reveals how much Luhmann's systems theory owes to biological sciences.

The eight—and last—assumption refers to the extension of subsystems. On this point, Luhmann maintains that "the consequence of defining society as the comprehensive social system is that there can be only one system of society for all connective communication".[30] Indeed, when a subsystem—as a result of functional rationality—has become self-reliant on the basis of its specific function and of the binary code according to which it carries out its operations, it necessarily tends to expand to all those contexts which function with the same code and carry out homologous operations. This kind of expansion increases significantly the efficiency of the subsystem, since the more information are gathered and operationalized, the better they can be used with a view to improving the subsystemic output. Given these premises, the limitation of the subsystemic activities to an only national dimension would not only be difficult in general, but downright harmful to the interests of that very same national society.

On the basis of these eight fundamental assumptions, systems theory unquestionably confirms its qualification as a new paradigm of order. If compared to the paradigms analysed so far, as mentioned earlier, it is the first theory of society that endorses an explicitly post-unitary idea of order. Furthermore, it overcomes the traditional dichotomy between particularism and universalism: in fact, since society is interpreted as being made of a plurality of subsystems and no universal rationality is assumed to exist, order is necessarily particularistic; on the other hand, because every subsystem tends to expand worldwide, also an element of cosmopolitanism is nevertheless present. Nor is the second well-established dichotomy between holism and individualism easily applicable to systems theory: while the self-contained character of subsystems suggests the presence of a robust remainder of holism, the fact that individuals—or: individualized psychic and biological systems—are never correlated to only one social subsystem reminds us rather of that flexibility of belongingness that has been usually attributed to the individualistic understanding of society.

## 6.2 THE LAW OF GLOBALIZATION AND FRAGMENTATION

Law is one of the subsystems into which society differentiates. Luhmann left no doubts about the autopoietic character of the legal subsystem: "only the law itself – he claimed – can say what law is".[31] More explicitly, every legal norm is produced on the basis of other norms that share the same systemic code and is in turn destined to shape the production of further legal norms. As regards the function taken on by the legal subsystem, Luhmann first denies that it consists in guaranteeing social integration since it would not be possible to prove that the law provides the neutralization and peaceful settlement of conflicts.[32] Regardless of any further consideration, this position seems to be inspired by Luhmann's strong aversion towards the idea of conflict as the driving force of social development that inspires the intersubjective theory of society. Instead, from his socially rather conservative standpoint, the law would take up the "function of the stabilization of normative expectations by regulating how they are generalized in relation to their temporal, factual, and social dimensions".[33] In fact, it often happens that social communication "is not sufficient in itself": in case that it does not find the right expression or praxis in its operations, expectations are generated which extend into the future and become part of the subsystemic communication itself. On this basis, the law has the task of stabilizing the legitimate expectations by defining and, at the same time, containing them.[34] Translated into a more mundane vocabulary, that means that every social subsystem produces expectances or claims as a result of the carrying out of its functions. In order to prevent the disruptive effects that this could have on the functionality of the subsystem, the expectances are expressed in the form of norms specifying what can legitimately be expected for the present and for the future, and the claims based on these norms are processed in formal procedures following the principles laid down by law. To carry out its function, the law does not need to be correlated with extra-legal values of justice or legitimacy; it simply has to operate with its own code, with its "schematic control" which allows to separate, in an ethically, politically and morally neutral form, what is in conformity with the law from its violation.[35]

Elaborating on Luhmann's definition of the function of the law as a social subsystem as well as on two further assumptions ascribed by systems theory to all social systems, namely their tendencies to internal differentiation and globalization, Gunther Teubner and Andreas Fischer-Lescano have provided an accomplished and sophisticated analysis of the features of the legal system under the conditions of its worldwide expansion and fragmentation. Starting with the transition to "global law", Teubner highlights four distinctive features of the process.[36] First, the *boundaries* of the global law system, increasingly independent of national territories, invisibly follow the outlines of specialist circles, professional bodies and social networks. Secondly, *regulation* by public institutions, especially through legislative assemblies, loses significance: "global law is produced – Teubner claims – in self-organized processes of 'structural coupling' of law with ongoing globalized processes of a highly specialized and technical nature".[37] Thirdly, while state law, due to the constitutional processes in liberal and democratic societies, has developed in relative *distance* from social interests, global law remains in a state of diffuse but strong interdependence with the respective specialized social areas. As a result, there is a pervasive and obtrusive presence of organized interests. Fourthly, for nation states the *unity* of the law is a symbol of their identity and a criterion for justice—at least within national boundaries. In contrast, from a global perspective it would constitute a threat. At present, the primary concern should be to ensure sufficient diversity of legal sources within globally standardized law.

Along with the globalization of law Teubner and Fischer-Lescano also underline its increasing "fragmentation". The phenomenon of legal pluralism is the "expression of deep-seated contradictions which concern society as a whole and exist between colliding sectors of world society".[38] This evolution becomes particularly evident when looking at the growing number of international courts with sectoral competences. Teubner and Fischer-Lescano focus on six outstanding characteristics of "fragmented law", which partially overlap in their content with the above-mentioned features of "global law".[39] Firstly, the globalization of social systems accompanies the consolidation of *particular rationalities*. To give shape to the different social subsystems and to stabilize their rationality, the law differentiates itself as well. Therefore, global law is fragmented as a consequence of the fact that specialized legal regimes have to follow different rationalities in order to accomplish their task. Secondly, during the time of classic public international law, cleavages in the global legal system largely coincided with the borders of nation states. In addition to these collisions, today conflicts arise from a *transversal thematic-functional differentiation*. Therefore, insofar as the interferences between sectoral rationalities belonging to different social subsystems result in collisions, legal regimes—as "an epiphenomenon of the deeper multi-dimensional fragmentation of global society itself"—also tend to conflict with one another.[40] Thirdly, according to the traditional conception of legal regimes based on the nation state, the "peripheries" of the legal system, especially private contracts, were always related to its "centre", namely to constitutional law. In contemporary law such a clear relationship between "centre" and "periphery" can no longer be ascertained, with the consequence that individual branches have developed into "self-contained regimes". Fourthly, in constitutional states the unity of law was generated by the constitution. Since in the constellation of a fragmented legal system this kind of unity must be regarded as definitively lost, the only solution in case of conflict is to resort to some forms of "inter-legality", i.e., to connections largely independent of hierarchical layers. Fifthly, as a result of fragmentation, *autonomous private regimes* develop, consolidating the idea that a global private law regime can guarantee peaceful and effective human interaction at least in its own area of regulation without resorting to the public sphere. Sixthly, self-contained regimes transform into "auto-constitutional regimes", triggering a fundamental change in the concept of "constitution".

Summing up, from the fact that world society divides up into self-referential subsystems in which specific law regimes apply, collisions result which constitute conflicts both between different rationalities of autopoietic systems and between different legal regimes.[41] These collisions cannot be resolved by a comprehensive legal system. Conflict resolution can only be achieved through mechanisms of horizontal coordination, by "reciprocal observation, anticipatory adaptation, cooperation, trust, self-commitment, reliability, negotiations, and lasting relationship contexts".[42] As a consequence of this development, the *hierarchical* legal system becomes "*heterarchical law*"—or also "polyarchic law"—i.e., "law which is limited to establish a loose connection between fragmented legal regimes".[43] Correspondingly, expectations are low with regard to the social role of law:

> Realistically there is only the chance to contain, through their legal "formalization," the self-destructive tendencies that may arise from collisions between different rationalities. [...] If things work out, [the law] will translate a – limited – part of these rationality conflicts into the *quaestio juris*, hereby constituting a forum for their peaceful settlement. But even in this case the law does not function as a superior coordinating authority; rather, it could already be considered a success if the law could provide legal guarantees for mutual autonomy against totalizing tendencies and the unilateral overpowering of social fragments. Confronted with the potential threats arising from social fragmentation, the law will have to restrict itself to the narrow tasks of delivering compensation for mutual harms and keeping damages to human and natural environments under control.[44]

Notwithstanding the humility that "heterarchical law" necessarily brings into the way in which the function of law and the work of jurists are understood if compared with more traditional hierarchical conceptions, systems theorists explicitly claim that the fragmentation of law is not the result of an irrational disorder, but expression of the manifold order of plural rationalities.[45] By doing so, they underline the novelty of their approach and implicitly qualify it as a post-unitary paradigm of order.

### 6.3 THE LEX MERCATORIA OF SYSTEMS THEORY

Following the approach of functionalist rationality that informs systems theory, society differentiates into many social subsystems in order to increase its efficiency in accomplishing its most fundamental tasks. Law is one of those social subsystems. Since the task of law consists in stabilizing the normative expectations that arise from the social subsystems, the legal subsystem goes itself through a process of internal differentiation to the extent that as many self-reliant legal regimes develop as there are social subsystems in need of stabilization. As a consequence of this process, each specialized legal regime takes on the specific rationality of the subsystem to which it applies. Thus, insofar as the law has the function to guarantee the internal order of different social subsystems, the law itself loses its unity and develops into distinct legal subsystems, each of them characterized by the rationality, expressed in legal terms, that underlies the implementation of the subsystemic functions.

A further functional subsystem consists of the economy, the interpretation of which by the leading systems theorists focuses—following, indeed, a trend in economics—more on the exchange of goods and on financial transactions than on the conditions of production and on criteria for a just provision of those goods.[46] Since the economic subsystem also needs to be ruled by norms, a branch of the legal system has turned into an autonomous body of laws especially dedicated to this task. The legal subsystem that regulates economic interactions has global scope—like all social systems—and is essentially made of private law provisions. As a result, the diagnosis of the globalization and fragmentation of law leads to the thesis that the *private law regime* is strengthened at the global level. This thesis is important from the viewpoint of the history of ideas, because it claims for the first time that there could be a social order without institutional or normative reference to a comprehensive public sphere, to a general interest or to an idea of the common good.

One of the most fully developed global private law regimes—together with the Lex digitalis of the internet—is the Lex mercatoria of the globalized economy.[47] Thus, the private law regime which focuses on the global regulation of economic transactions takes up not only the medieval definition but also the very idea of a self-organization of economic agents, without any intervention or guarantee by the public power. Yet, the old theory is revived on the basis of a substantially different and more solid theoretical background. In doing so, the project of a particularistic-individualistic paradigm of order—the realization of which previously failed—[48] is finally accomplished, although not as the outcome of a specific paradigmatic revolution, but rather as the byproduct of the transition to a pluralist pattern of order in form of systems theory. In fact, each of the three historic theories of a global order of private actors ultimately situated private law interactions within an overriding context of general interests. In the universal economy of antiquity and in the Lex mercatoria of the Middle Ages, no priority is accorded to private interests. Even within the modern theory of free trade, economic activity remained subordinate to the wealth of the nation. Therefore, the autonomy of the private law dimension vis-à-vis the public law dimension was always conditional. Be it embodied in the homeostasis of the whole or in the wealth of the nation, there was always an idea of the common good which established the primacy of public law norms and institutions in case of conflict. This is not the case in the contemporary Lex mercatoria, according to which private interests are explicitly recognized as the only relevant factor. The independence of the dimension of legally structured private interactions is achieved through two conceptual innovations, both provided by the pluralist organon of systems theory. First, while previous theories permanently fought about whether the private or the public dimension was hierarchically superior—with the result that the latter always won— the Lex mercatoria of systems theory does not try to reverse the usual hierarchy, but simply establishes the self-sufficiency of the globalized private law regime. Thus, the theorists of the new Lex mercatoria do not claim its superiority to public law, but limit themselves to maintain that the private law regime has to be recognized as something clearly different from the public domain and, therefore, as conceptually, normatively and hierarchically independent from any kind of public authority. Secondly, the private law regime does not aim at establishing an all-encompassing global order, but is rather restricted to the regulation of only one field; this explicit limitation in scope, however, is turned into an advantage in terms of self-reliance insofar as any external interference is excluded from the domain made up by the normative self-organization of private actors.

The idea, developed by the contemporary theorists of the Lex mercatoria, that the field of economic transaction with their normative regulation has to be seen as an autonomous social subsystem is quite a unique case in the intellectual panorama of the recent economic theory. Indeed, we have other attempts to reconstruct the contemporary Lex mercatoria—for instance, from a strictly positivistic perspective—but they limit themselves, in general, to a doctrinal collection of norms, lacking a more ambitious and profound theoretical background.[49] On the other hand, the authors who gave a solid conceptual foundation to the revival of economic liberalism in the second half of the twentieth century, although no less critical of anything that might have the semblance of a superiority of the public domain or of an affirmation of "public interests", never went as far as system theory in asserting the self-sufficiency of the system of economic interactions with its normative regulation. Friedrich Hayek, for example—one of the most influential inspirers of twentieth century's neoliberalism—endorsed indeed a "negative" concept of freedom as "the absence of coercion", while coercion was defined as the situation in which "one man's actions are made to serve another man's will, not for his own but for the other's purpose".[50] Moreover, he strongly pleaded for a restriction of state intervention to the least possible,[51] so that interactions can be spontaneous and "voluntary" to the greatest feasible extent.[52] Yet, the rules that, albeit only few in number, were nonetheless recognized as necessary to make a society well-ordered, were generally assumed to be of statist origin.[53] As a result, he never regarded the economic sphere as self-supporting and, to the extent that he considered the possibility of a worldwide order, he maintained that this should be based on an "interstate federalism" with great economic freedom and minimal public governance.[54]

Largely in the same vein, Milton Friedman not only defended the free market but also admitted "the need for government ... as a forum for determining the 'rules of the game' and as an umpire to interpret and enforce the rules decided on".[55] Furthermore, international trade agreements were essentially understood as arrangements between states—once again without any reference to some kind of self-sufficiency of international economic agents.[56] Beside the "liberal market economy", which was mainly defended by English-speaking economists, the second leading strand of liberal economic theory in the second half of the twentieth century was the so-called coordinated market economy—commonly known as "ordoliberalism"—which was developed by German scholars.[57] Yet, while the supporters of neoliberalism were strongly committed to the reduction of the intervention of public power to a minimum, their continental counterpart candidly supported from the very outset the idea that economic interactions among private agents can only develop properly—and with the highest advantage for the whole society—if they are set in an ordering political and legal framework that those agents cannot autonomously put in place.[58]

By claiming its self-reliance, the Lex mercatoria of systems theory introduces two fundamental innovations, both contributing to the dissolution of the traditional link between law and the state.[59] First, exclusively private institutions (such as contracts and associations) allegedly produce valid law without authorization and control by the state. Secondly—and largely as a consequence of the first assumption—the Lex mercatoria, once relieved from statist supremacy, is supposed to be also valid outside nation states. But, if the Lex mercatoria is to be, at the same time, self-reliant—i.e., not depending on public power—*and* valid, then it should be proved as capable of self-validation. That means, however, that good arguments should be found against both classical theory and prevailing contemporary theory, according to which a private law contract has no validity in and of itself, but is only valid due to public law. The probably most sophisticated doctrinal justification of why private law cannot be regarded as self-sufficient has been laid down by Friedrich Carl von Savigny in his seminal work, *System des heutigen Römischen Rechts* of 1840—one of the foundational texts of the doctrine of continental civil law. Although his interest was concentrated mainly on private law, so that he surely cannot be suspected of partisanship in favour of public law, he nonetheless maintained that private law cannot be founded only on itself, but always needs the fundamental support of public law and authority. Besides the consideration that private law shall always find its deeper sense within the context of the higher interest of the *Volk*[60]—which is, so to speak, a *völkisch* version of the same argument that we have already seen developed in Adam Smith's texts—according to Savigny private law depends on public law for three specifically *juridical* functions which it cannot accomplish by itself.[61] The first is the nomopoiesis: private law is created through public law procedures. The second is the establishment of civil law procedures against the fortuity of interactions between private actors. The third, lastly, is the establishment of criminal law to punish the breach of private agreements when this is assumed to have consequences for the legal order of the whole community. The consequence that we can draw from Savigny's considerations is that private law, to be valid and effective, always needs a solid public law system to be established above it.

According to Teubner, the legal subsystem of the Lex mercatoria—or, rather, the agents involved in it—has deployed three different but simultaneous strategies to secure its self-validation.[62] Following Savigny, the first problem of the self-validation of private law consists in the lack of an internal private-law set of norms with the aim of specifying the procedures for the production of secondary norms. As a result, to produce private law norms, the system of private law has generally resorted to public law. The answer to this problem by the autonomous system of private law has been the establishment of an *internal hierarchy of norms*, i.e., a primary system of non-public-law-based and spontaneous norms as a legal basis for the generation of secondary norms. The second deficit of a presumably self-reliant system of private law is the apparent contingency and uniqueness of every single private law agreement between private agents which—according to the traditional doctrine—makes the intervention of public power necessary in order to guarantee predictable and consistent procedures. The reaction resorts in this case to what Teubner calls a *"temporalization"* of contingency. This means, concretely, that the single contract between private actors is superseded by iterated processes in which a standardization of rules occurs insofar as the contract both refers to the past and projects into the future. The third shortcoming is related to the system of private law's presumed incapacity to enforce by itself the respect of its own rules, so that the public authority has to assist by establishing criminal law. The response, here, is *externalization*: the system of private law and property "externalizes the fatal self-validation of contract by referring conditions of validity and future conflicts to external 'non-contractual' institutions which are nevertheless 'contractual,' since they are a sheer internal product of the contract itself".[63] In other words, the private law system provides institutions with arbitration functions that monitor the validity and execution of norms. Although these arbitral bodies are created by means of private law, they overcome the spontaneous private law dimension because of their institutional nature.

Against this background, the recent understanding of Lex mercatoria based on systems theory paves the way for an innovative interpretation of the normative regulation of transnational private actor interactions. The Lex mercatoria of systems theory for the first time coherently detaches the private law regime from any axiological priority of reflexively formulated common interests and from any public institution aiming to implement these interests. Accordingly, the private law subsystem which globally regulates the interactions between non-public actors and their interests operates exclusively according to its own rationality and is not subordinated to any other legal or institutional dimension. From the operations regulated by the global private law subsystem, a general advantage can indeed arise. However, this advantage—like the effect produced by the "invisible hand" of classic liberal economic theory—is a quasi-natural result and not the outcome of reflexive deliberative processes. For the comprehension of such processes, systems theory simply lacks the organon, namely the idea of an intersubjective rationality overarching the functional systems and independent of them.

## 6.4 Supra-Systemic Rationality and the Inescapability of the Public Realm

Many questions arise with reference to both the conceptual organon of system theory, in general, and its application to the new Lex mercatoria. The former concerns the relation between systems theory and postmodern thinking (a), the assumed self-referentiality of social systems and the forms of interconnections between subsystems (b), the obliteration of the normative dimension from human rationality (c), the realization of justice (d), and the redefinition of the concept of constitution (e). On the other hand, it is questionable whether the theory of the Lex mercatoria can really keep its promises of autonomy and normative consistency (f).

(a) According to Luhmann, systems theory does not confirm the passage from modernity to some form of postmodernity.[64] Rather, he assumed that the last decades have seen the advance of precisely those aspects of rationality which are generally described as specifically modern. On the other hand, Teubner underlines the conceptual proximity between systems theory and postmodern thought, at least with reference to the legal system.[65] This apparent contradiction can be resolved by referring to the respective positions of the two approaches within the panorama of the theories of national and international order. The element that unites them—and explains the parallelism of some analyses—consists in their common emphasis on the fragmentation of order and in their positive view about that. Nonetheless, this proximity between systems theory and postmodern thought, though significant, should not lead us to overshadow the equally important differences. To better understand the distinction between the paradigm of systemic plurality and that of postmodern deconstruction of order, it is useful to examine the different attitudes of the two conceptual patterns as regards the modern concept of subjectivity. As far as the theory of systems is concerned, it has been pointed out that the notion of system presents many analogies with the modern concept of subject.[66] Not unlike the mental processes of the subject, the systemic operations are also pervaded by a coherent rationality and a solid internal order. What is lacking of modern subjectivity, in systems theory, is the critical potentiality that emerges from self-consciousness which, in modern thinking, still allowed to attain a partial detachment from systemic rationality. On the contrary, following the logic of social systems alone makes it difficult to identify spaces for criticism and ultimately cancels the possibility of a universalistic morality. Even more distant from systemic rationality is—as mentioned above—the intersubjective evolution of the traditional subjectivistic patterns of knowledge. Therefore, while some aspects of modern subjectivity are incorporated into systems theory, some others—in particular, the reflexive and self-critical dimension—are simply deleted. Different—and in some ways opposite—is the way in which postmodern thought departs from modernity. To be frontally attacked, here, is the claim to objective rationality—which is still present in systems theory, though multiplied into a plurality of idiosyncratic functional solutions—while precisely those elements that are most alien to systems theory, namely the hyperreflexive subjectivity and the non-systemic individuality, become central. As a consequence, although the attack of postmodern thought against modernity seems to be more virulent, it nevertheless maintains its promise of emancipation largely intact. Not so systems theory which, while remaining closer to the strong rationality concept of modernity, empties it nonetheless of its essential prescriptive moment.

(b) The assumption that social systems display self-referentiality, or "operational closure", is central to systems theory. If insisting on the self-reliance of systems only aimed at increasing the sensitiveness to the specificity of the language that characterizes communication within every single social system and to the necessity to translate the information coming from outside into that language in order to secure its adequate operationalization, there would be no reason to disagree. Yet, the "operational closure" of systems theory is a much more wide-ranging and ambitious concept, which goes as far as to deny that any external information has a direct impact on the operational chain within a system—provided that the system is made capable of working properly—and that no external agent can influence internal processes by being involved into the flow of processed information. Therefore, systems are presumed to internally perceive only a kind of disturbance. Yet, this far-reaching assumption poses at least three significant epistemological problems.

First, from the point of view of empirical knowledge, it has been claimed on the basis of case studies that communication flows largely *between* subsystems—in particular between legal subsystems—and not only *within* them, as well as that legal actors, while performing their actions, follow rules that are drawn from disparate systemic logics, put together on the basis of their individual preferences and purposes.[67]

Secondly, at a more abstract level, it is not clear how systems can interact with one another if they lack a common language and their respective rationalities are incommensurable. Biological systems, for example—quite the original blueprint for Luhmann's theory of the "operational closure" of social systems—though undoubtedly self-reliant, can interact with each other only because they share indeed an interaction language, largely based on biochemical stimuli. In fact, it remains quite mysterious how a social system could react properly to external stimuli, by correctly deciphering them and translating them into its own language, if no common language is identified or, a fortiori, if ruling out such a possibility is an essential component of the theory. It is rather to assume that the probable outcome of an indistinct irritation would only be chaos. Nor are "structural couplings" a convincing corollary since they boldly presuppose a kind of anticipated and unproven harmony on the only ground that the tenet of the absolute self-reliance of systems should not be shaken, no matter what it might cost in terms of the multiplication of nebulous concepts. Here however, like in any other scientific context, Ockham's razor should be applied, according to which "entities must not be multiplied beyond necessity", and the easiest solution should be sought.

Thirdly, the entity that could play an intermediary role between social systems—as well as between systems and the lifeworld—is the individual with her/his action (or the intersubjective contexts with their different forms of interaction). This was still the conceptual solution envisaged by Talcott Parsons before Luhmann's turn towards a systems theory explicitly rejecting any hint of individuality or intersubjectivity. It has been said above that Luhmann had the merit of transforming systems theory into an innovative and comprehensive paradigm of order. He did that, however, at the high cost of deleting the conceptual structure that significantly contributed to understand systemic interaction and allowed to conceive of social experience as a coherent—even though differentiated—unity.

(c) Subjectivity and intersubjectivity—the first in modern thinking in general, the second in contemporary philosophy—not only provide an indispensable support for the most easy-to-understand and conceptually parsimonious explanation of social interaction; they also account for that kind of non-systemic rationality which is the driving force of innovation and social improvement. Deleting traditional subjectivity and contemporary intersubjectivity implies, therefore, also rejecting non-systemic, overarching rationality and, with it, a great part of the normative content of modern thought. Indeed, the approach of Luhmann's version of systems theory leads to deficits when it comes to the interpretation of norms that cannot adequately be understood merely in functionalistic terms or are deemed to possess universal validity. This holds true especially for human rights norms. To systematically collocate and conceptually explain the specific quality of these norms appears difficult from the perspective of the functionally restriction and the operational closure of subsystems.

Indeed, it is no surprise that, with regard to human rights norms, even a firm supporter of the systems theory approach like Andreas Fischer-Lescano has tried to conceptualize a "universal law" (*Weltrecht*) or a "global-constitution" (*Globalverfassung*) as formal expressions of a comprehensive *lex humana* centred around the protection of fundamental rights.[68] In Fischer-Lescano's interpretation, we have a "global civic society" (*globale Zivilgesellschaft*),[69] in which normative requests are articulated; these are then legally recognized by recurring to the so-called global remedies. The problem, from the point of view of systems theory, is that the *lex humana* elaborated by the *globale Zivilgesellschaft*—as the author himself admits—emerges from the spontaneous domain of the global political system,[70] but is formalized through heterarchical procedures within the legal system. It follows that the *Weltrecht*, in form of the *Globalverfassung*, is indeed a legal system, but "politically supported".[71] At this point, however, the question arises whether such a strong osmosis is still compatible with the founding principle of Luhmann's systems theory, i.e., with the axiom of the mutual closure of the systems. A similar breach of orthodoxy, outlining an implicit dialectic between systems and the vital world, also transpires in Teubner's work, particularly in his proposal to contrast "anonymous communication matrices", on the one hand, with "people" or "individuals" on the other.[72] As a result, it seems that, when it comes to normatively significant questions, some of the most essential principles of systems theory in its most uncompromising form—such as the operational closure with the following non-interconnection of systems, as well as the exclusion of the concept of "individuality"—have to give way to far-reaching exceptions.

(d) The idea of systemic differentiation—if not corrected by the supra-systemic rationality of the lifeworld—runs the risk of being excessively exposed to the socially asymmetric rationale of markets and power. The difficulty in bypassing this intrinsic closeness clearly emerges in the redefinition of the concept of justice provided by systems theorists. Indeed, the realization of justice has always been considered one of the most important tasks to be accomplished by public power. Following a post-traditional social philosophy, a "just society" is generally assumed to be characterized by the fact that its members jointly accept public law rules in a condition of mutual recognition. Under that premise, inequality is only permitted insofar as it is commonly regarded as necessary—in the sense of a Pareto-superior option—for the benefit and welfare of the entire polity. As a result, if public power loses its leading function in expressing the common interests of the whole society, justice becomes a distant and almost unattainable perspective as well. Moreover, insofar as justice is not properly realized, the usual assumption is that it is the task of individuals—be they understood on the basis of subjectivistic or intersubjectivistic categories, yet always relying on a non-merely-systemic rationality—to push for the overcoming of the contradiction between their needs and the performances of the system(s). However, if no individuality is believed to exist and only systemic rationality is regarded as detectable by social science, the question arises on how justice could ever be implemented and improved in a less-than-perfect world.

Luhmann was explicitly critical against the "critical-emancipatory" strand of systems theory and its tendency to include questions of social justice into its analytical framework.[73] Instead, Teubner recognizes the problem and proposes to settle it by relocating the justice issue.[74] In his view, justice is not a task to be implemented by an overarching public power with its primacy over functional subsystems and grounded on an allegedly supra-systemic rationality; rather, it is a "contingency formula" directly embedded into the operational logic of the self-referential subsystems. Thus, the necessity to stabilize normative expectations would stimulate the subsystems to continuously transcend their own rational boundaries from the inside.[75] However, given the assumption of the "operational closure" of the subsystems, it remains unclear where the rationality principle that is supposed to transcend the operational routine could originate from. If rationality is only and always systemic and contextual, it is difficult even to conceive of the transcendence of a given reality and praxis. And if transcendence is supposed to be based on an extra-systemic rationality, the epistemological assumption that subsystems are self-referential is at stake.

To illustrate the problem, it may be useful to give a concrete example. According to systems theory, the economy is the "social mechanism" that "combines a stable supply in the future with distributive processes always focused on the present".[76] Since every economic agent tends to take possession of the greatest possible quantity of goods in the present, their availability is likely to progressively decrease. The only way to guarantee supply in the future is by identifying a code—the specific code of the economy—that allows a sufficient long-range balance. In the economy this code is identified by Luhmann in "payment/non-payment":

> The unit act of the economy is the payment. Payments have all the characteristics of an autopoietic system: they are possible as a result of other payments and, in the recursive nexus of economic autopoiesis, they make no other sense than making further payments possible.[77]

It is easy to see that this code—as well as the rationality that is assumed to be inherent to the economy—is completely indifferent to the question of social justice. To the extent that external irritations affect the subsystem, this will only optimize the operationalization of information following its own code, therefore securing the highest possible financial profitability of the goods to be sold, possibly at the expense of human rights or of the environment. In fact, the impact that the optimization of systemic processes may have on the level of human rights protection, or on the environment, is no question that can be addressed with reference to systemic rationality for the simple reason that the system is presumed to be incapable of elaborating such an information. As a result, triggering a process of self-correction can only be achieved by integrating the internal processes through an external input directly affecting the rationality that leads the operational chain, while initiating the correction is a task for the social entity that expresses the claims of an overarching and supra-systemic rationality.

(e) The normative limits that characterize the idea of self-referential private law regimes become even more apparent if we consider the reasons for the polemic that supporters of systems theory raise against a possible "re-politicization" of structures of social order essentially based on agreements among private actors to pursue private interests.[78] The proposal to overcome fragmented private law regimes by "political" means actually aims at creating a renewed social and normative unity under the primacy of the "public" dimension. In state law, this priority is expressed by the primacy of the constitution. By contrast, systems theorists argue that the claim of the nation state to give a "constitution" to the whole of society belongs to the past.[79] Allegedly, this development can neither be compensated by pursuing international or supranational constitutionalization, nor by establishing institutions of "global domestic policy". At best, the "constitutionalization of international law" would only lead to the globalization of the political system; however, this would not have any direct impact on any of the other systems.[80] Therefore, on the one hand it is unlikely that the nation state will be able to bring the sectoral subsystems back to the previous internal constitutional unit, nor is such a backwards-oriented development desirable; on the other hand, the traditional constitutional model, centred on the domain of the public sphere, is hardly applicable to the highly differentiated contexts of postnational integration. The consequence—and a groundbreaking alternative to the theoretical and practical stalemate—would consist, according to Teubner, in the consolidation of "global civil constitutions".[81] From the point of view of systems theory, the establishment of "civil constitutions" does not only aim at consolidating the self-referentiality of private law regimes like the Lex mercatoria but also at generally reshaping the relationship between the "public" and the "private" domain. In the present state of "policontextuality",[82] claims traditionally operationalized by public law institutions are transferred into specific contexts of "civil constitutions". Therefore, ethical, social and political questions, traditionally the substance of the discussions within the "public fora", are not cancelled from the agenda of social communication as a consequence of overcoming the dichotomy between public and private. Rather, these questions are left to the communication occurring within specialized social subsystems and thus emancipated from the paternalistic control usually exercised by the welfare state as the successor of the historical *Policeystaat*.

The reduction of the entire public dimension to the illiberal practices of the *Policeystaat* is the first problem that arises from the application of the concept of constitution to spontaneous legal regimes regulating exclusively private interactions. Indeed, the public sphere is far from simply being an expression of authoritarian aspirations. Rather, it provides the context in which *spontaneous* interaction becomes *reflexive*, thus enabling a discourse on shared priorities based on argumentation and going beyond the mere agreement on casually overlapping private interests. Furthermore, the authoritarian and paternalistic interpretation of public interest constitutes only one strand within the history of state theory—admittedly a mighty one, but by far not the most convincing. For many hundreds of years, this understanding has been opposed by a liberal and democratic conception of a public domain which arises—as contract theory or, more recently, democracy theories in the tradition of Kelsen or Habermas show—from the reflexive interaction of individuals in order to protect (and not to oppress) their common rights and interests. Thirdly, the public sphere, in particular in its democratic interpretation, was conceived to neutralize, at least partially, the social and economic power inevitably rooted in the interactions among private actors. For that reason, abolishing the specificity of the public domain would always also risk to destroy the political bulwark of equality as the normatively inescapable counterpart of a world of social and economical inequalities. Lastly, a "constitution" that is solely "civil", and therefore based on private law, runs the risk of losing the essential reference to the legitimation generated by political representation. Yet, it is precisely this aspect that does not only account for the political character of the constitution but also for its specific *public* dimension. Deprived of its political and public range, the "constitution" would shrink to a simple set of rules regulating the further production of norms.[83] By doing so, however, the private law system would only retain some of the typical characteristics of a "constitutional" framework, namely a certain gradation of different levels of law, the functional relation of the legal system to a specific social system, and the distinction between a formally organized and a spontaneous sector. Nonetheless, these characteristics barely appear adequate—at least in the tradition of liberal constitutionalism—to interpret the private law system as a "constitution" in the full sense of the word.

(f) We can move on, now, to the unresolved questions that concern, more specifically, the application of systems theory to the consolidation of a new Lex mercatoria for the globalization era and to the reformulation of the particularistic-individualistic paradigm of order. With reference to this point, it has to be underlined, first, that the strategies developed by private law regimes in order to guarantee their autonomous validity without resorting to public norms and institutions, namely hierarchization, temporalization and externalization, do not address the fundamental question lying beneath the paradox of the self-validation of private law. There are indeed good reasons in favour of the traditional view that a norm, to be valid, must be something more than just the formal expression of the agreement between two or more individuals. Rather, it must incorporate a general normative framework established by means of public law and expressing common interests and values of the society, so that the rules through which certain behaviours are forbidden, allowed or prescribed can be regarded as the "grammar" of civil life. In detail, the private contract deals with matters of particular interest to a few, but in its fundamental principles, i.e., in the overall normative framework in which its specificity is placed, it has to be validated by the society as a whole. By employing strategies exclusively based on private law, regardless of their effectiveness, the lex mercatoria system neither aims at building any link to a common set of social interests and values, nor does it demonstrate to possess the conceptual tools to do so.

Secondly, from a more technical point of view, it has been argued that the efforts to codify the Lex mercatoria that were initiated by some of its advocates in order to consolidate its autonomy actually undermine its goal. These efforts have been concretized in unified codes, projects and principles, like "Unidroit, the Cornell Common Core Project, the Lando Commission Principles of European Contract Law, the various ICC formulations and, finally, general lists of principles formulated by prominent scholars in the area of lex mercatoria such as Berthold Goldman, Lord Mustill, and ... Klaus Peter Berger".[84] This is because these efforts necessarily involve political and social actors not belonging to the system, thus jeopardizing the private law regime's self-referentiality. Moreover, by becoming an integral part of private international law through this "creeping codification", the Lex mercatoria eventually ends up sharing the complex relationship that divides and at the same time binds *private* international law and its *public* counterpart.

Thirdly, the irreplaceable function of public law reemerges in the recurring request for a stronger political guide to the phenomena of economic globalization.[85] Indeed, no thriving of transnational economic interaction is possible without guaranteeing favourable framework conditions, the establishment of which goes beyond the competences and possibilities of private agents.[86] Moreover, the globalization of markets raises fundamental ethical problems that involve the protection of fundamental human rights on a worldwide scale and require a bottom-up process of empowerment of the stakeholders—quite a typical task for the public dimension of human interaction.[87] Indeed, the development of half-autonomous private law regimes may enhance the diversity of society, but when it comes to the defence of fundamental values such as peace, freedom and justice, the sphere in which shared goals are inclusively discussed and reflexively determined—in other words, the public sphere—must remain the normative barycentre of a social and political community.

## NOTES

1. Max Weber, *Wirtschaft und Gesellschaft*, Mohr, Tübingen 1922, at 124 (English translation by Ephraim Fischoff et al.: *Economy and Society*, Guenther Roth and Klaus Wittich eds., University of California Press, Berkeley/Los Angeles/London 1978, at 215).
2. Jürgen Habermas, *Theorie des kommunikativen Handelns*, Suhrkamp, Frankfurt a. M. 1981, Vol. II, at 454 (English translation by Thomas McCarthy: *The Theory of Communicative Action*, Beacon Press, Boston 1987 (3rd ed.), Vol. II, at 307).
3. Max Weber, *Wirtschaft und Gesellschaft*, Johannes Winckelmann ed., Kiepenheuer & Witsch, Köln 1964, at 1060 (English: Weber, *Economy and Society*, supra note 1, at 1402); quoted in: Habermas, *Theorie des kommunikativen Handelns*, supra n. 2, Vol. II, at 454 et seq. (English: Vol. II, at 307).
4. Weber, *Economy and Society*, supra note 1, at 1403.
5. Talcott Parsons, *The Social System* (1951), Collier-MacMillan, London 1964, at 68 et seq.
6. Ibid., at 11.
7. Ibid., at 30 et seq.
8. Ibid., at 6 et seq.

9. Gralf-Peter Calliess, *Systemtheorie*, in: Sonja Buckel, Ralph Christensen, Andreas Fischer-Lescano (eds.), *Neue Theorien des Rechts*, Lucius & Lucius, Stuttgart 2006, 57–75, at 58; Karl-Ludwig Kunz, Martino Mona, *Rechtsphilosophie, Rechtstheorie, Rechtssoziologie*, Haupt, Bern/Stuttgart/Wien 2006, at 210.
10. Calliess, *Systemtheorie*, *supra* note 9, at 58 et seq.
11. Niklas Luhmann, *Die Gesellschaft der Gesellschaft*, Suhrkamp, Frankfurt a. M. 1997, Vol. I, at 70 (English translation by Rhodes Barrette: *Theory of Society*, Stanford University Press, Stanford (CA) 2012, Vol. I, at 35).
12. Ibid., Vol. II, at 874 (English: Vol. II, at 172).
13. Niklas Luhmann, *Soziale Systeme. Grundriß einer allgemeinen Theorie*, Suhrkamp, Frankfurt a. M. 1984, at 92 (English translation by John Bednarz, Jr., and Dirk Baecker: *Social Systems*, Stanford University Press, Stanford (CA) 1995, at 59).
14. Luhmann, *Die Gesellschaft der Gesellschaft*, *supra* note 11, Vol. I, at 78 (English: Vol. I, at 40).
15. Richard Nobles and David Schiff, *Introduction*, in: Niklas Luhmann, *Law as a Social System*, Fatima Kastner et al. eds., Oxford University Press, Oxford/London 2004, 1–52, at 9.
16. Niklas Luhmann, *Das Recht der Gesellschaft*, Suhrkamp, Frankfurt a. M. 1993, at 66 et seq. (English: *Law as a Social System*, *supra* n. 15, at 98 et seq.).
17. Luhmann, *Die Gesellschaft der Gesellschaft*, *supra* note 11, Vol. I, at 60 et seq. (English: Vol. I, at 28 et seq.).
18. Luhmann, *Das Recht der Gesellschaft*, *supra* note 16, at 40 et seq. (English: at 78).
19. Humberto R. Maturana, Francisco J. Varela, *Autopoiesis and Cognition: The Realization of the Living*, Reidel, Dordrecht 1980.
20. Luhmann, *Die Gesellschaft der Gesellschaft*, *supra* note 11, Vol. I, at 65 (English: Vol. I, at 32).
21. Ibid., at 95 (English: at 51).
22. Ibid., at 92 (English: at 49).
23. Luhmann, *Das Recht der Gesellschaft*, *supra* note 16, at 40 et seq. (English: at 78 et seq.).
24. Ibid., at 44 (English: at 80).
25. Luhmann, *Die Gesellschaft der Gesellschaft*, *supra* note 11, Vol. I, at 100 (English: Vol. I, at 54).
26. Ibid., Vol. I, at 118 (English: Vol. I, at 66).
27. Ibid., Vol. I, at 106 (English: Vol. I, at 58).
28. Ibid., Vol. I, at 102 (English: Vol. I, at 56).
29. Ibid., Vol. I, at 118 (English: Vol. I, at 66).
30. Ibid., Vol. I, at 145 (English: Vol. I, at 83).

31. Luhmann, *Das Recht der Gesellschaft*, supra note 16, at 50 (English: at 85).
32. Ibid., at 126 (English: at 143).
33. Ibid., at 131 (English: at 148).
34. Ibid., at 125 (English: at 142).
35. Ibid., at 60 (English: at 93).
36. Gunther Teubner, "*Global Bukowina*": *Legal Pluralism in the World Society*, in: Gunther Teubner (ed.), *Global Law Without a State*, Dartmouth, Aldershot 1997, 3–28, at 7 et seq.
37. Ibid., at 8.
38. Andreas Fischer-Lescano, Gunther Teubner, *Fragmentierung des Weltrechts: Vernetzung globaler Regimes statt etatistischer Rechtseinheit*, in: Mathias Albert, Rudolf Stichweh (eds.), *Weltstaat und Weltstaatlichkeit. Beobachtungen globaler politischer Strukturbildung*, Verlag für Sozialwissenschaften, Wiesbaden 2007, 37–61, at 40.
39. Ibid., at 50 et seq.
40. Ibid.
41. Andreas Fischer-Lescano, Gunther Teubner, *Regime-Collisions: The Vain Search for Legal Unity in the Fragmentation of Global Law*, in: "Michigan Journal of International Law", Vol. 25 (2004), 999–1046; Andreas Fischer-Lescano, Gunther Teubner, *Regimekollisionen. Zur Fragmentierung des globalen Rechts*, Suhrkamp, Frankfurt a. M. 2006.
42. Fischer-Lescano/Teubner, *Fragmentierung des Weltrechts*, supra note 38, at 52.
43. Ibid., at 51.
44. Ibid., at 54.
45. Gunther Teubner, *Privatregimes: Neo-Spontanes Recht und duale Sozialverfassungen in der Weltgesellschaft?* in: Dieter Simon, Manfred Weiss (eds.), *Zur Autonomie des Individuums*, Nomos, Baden-Baden 2000, 437–453; Gunter Teubner, *Globale Zivilverfassungen: Alternativen zur staatszentrierten Verfassungstheorie*, in: "Zeitschrift für ausländisches öffentliches Recht und Völkerrecht", Vol. 63 (2003), 1–28; Gunther Teubner, *Constitutional Fragments: Societal Constitutionalism in Globalization*, Oxford University Press, Oxford/New York 2012.
46. Niklas Luhmann, *Die Wirtschaft der Gesellschaft*, Suhrkamp, Frankfurt a. M. 1988.
47. Fischer-Lescano/Teubner, *Fragmentierung des Weltrechts*, supra note 38, at 47.
48. See Chapter 5.
49. See Stefan Langer, *Grundlagen einer internationalen Wirtschaftsverfassung. Strukturprinzipien, Typik und Perspektiven anhand von Europäischer Union und Welthandelsorganisation*, Beck, München 1995; Hercules Booysen, *Principles of International Trade Law as a Monistic System*, Interlegal, Pretoria 2003.

50. F. A. Hayek, *The Constitution of Liberty* (1960), University of Chicago Press, Chicago/London 2011, at 209.
51. F. A. Hayek, *Individualism and Economic Order* (1948), University of Chicago Press, Chicago/London 1958, at 16 et seq.
52. Hayek, *The Constitution of Liberty*, supra note 50, at 203.
53. Ibid., at 71 et seq.; Hayek, *Individualism and Economic Order*, supra note 51, at 22.
54. Ibid., at 269 et seq.
55. Milton Friedman, *Capitalism and Freedom* (1962), University of Chicago, Chicago/London 2002, at 15.
56. Ibid., at 56 et seq.
57. Peter A. Hall, David Soskice, *Varieties of Capitalism*, Oxford University Press, Oxford/New York 2001.
58. Walter Eucken, *Die Grundlagen der Nationalökonomie* (1939), Springer, Heidelberg 1959, at 240 et seq. (English translation by T. W. Hutchison: *The Foundations of Economics*, Springer, Berlin/Heidelberg 1992, 1st ed. 1950, at 313).
59. Teubner, "*Global Bukowina*", supra note 36, at 10 et seq.
60. Friedrich Carl von Savigny, *System des heutigen Römischen Rechts*, Bei Veit und Comp., Berlin 1840, Book I, Chapter I, Section IX, at 21 et seq. (English translation by William Holloway: *System of Modern Roman Law*, Higginbotham, Madras 1867, at 17 et seq.).
61. Ibid., at 24 et seq. (English: at 19 et seq.).
62. Teubner, "*Global Bukowina*", supra note 36, at 16 et seq.
63. Ibid., at 16.
64. Luhmann, *Die Gesellschaft der Gesellschaft*, supra note 11, Vol. II, at 1143 (English: Vol. II, at 345).
65. Gunther Teubner, *Des Königs viele Leiber: Die Selbstdekonstruktion der Hierarchie des Rechts*, in: Hauke Brunkhorst, Matthias Kettner (eds.), *Globalisierung und Demokratie. Wirtschaft, Recht, Medien*, Suhrkamp, Frankfurt a. M. 2000, 240–273.
66. Jürgen Habermas, *Der philosophische Diskurs der Moderne*, Suhrkamp, Frankfurt a. M. 1991 (1st ed. 1985), at 426 et seq. (English translation by Frederick Lawrence: *The Philosophical Discourse of Modernity*, Polity Press, Cambridge 1987, at 368 et seq.).
67. Nico Krisch, *Beyond Constitutionalism*, Oxford University Press, Oxford/New York 2010, at 232.
68. Andreas Fischer-Lescano, *Globalverfassung: Verfassung der Weltgesellschaft*, in: "Archiv für Rechts- und Sozialphilosophie", Vol. 88 (2002), 349–378; Andreas Fischer-Lescano, *Globalverfassung: Die Geltungsbegründung der Menschenrechte*, Velbrück Wissenschaft, Weilerswist 2005.
69. Fischer-Lescano, *Globalverfassung: Die Geltungsbegründung der Menschenrechte*, supra note 68, at 30.

70. Fischer-Lescano, *Globalverfassung: Verfassung der Weltgesellschaft*, supra note 68, at 367 et seq.
71. Fischer-Lescano, *Globalverfassung: Die Geltungsbegründung der Menschenrechte*, supra note 68, at 271.
72. Gunther Teubner, *Die anonyme Matrix*, in: Winfried Brugger, Ulfried Neumann, Stephan Kirste (eds.), *Rechtsphilosophie im 21. Jahrhundert*, Suhrkamp, Frankfurt a. M. 2008, 440–472.
73. Niklas Luhmann, *Einige Probleme mit "reflexivem Recht"*, in: "Zeitschrift für Rechtssoziologie", Vol. 6 (1985), 1–18.
74. Gunther Teubner, *Selbstsubversive Gerechtigkeit. Kontingenz- oder Tranzendenzformel des Rechts?* in: "Zeitschrift für Rechtssoziologie", Vol. 29 (2008), 9–36.
75. See also Gunther Teubner, *Quod omnes tangit. Transnationale Verfassungen ohne Demokratie?* in: "Der Staat", Vol. 57 (2018), 1–24.
76. Niklas Luhmann, *Die Wirtschaft der Gesellschaft*, Suhrkamp, Frankfurt a. M. 1988, at 64.
77. Ibid., at 52.
78. Fischer-Lescano/Teubner, *Fragmentierung des Weltrechts*, supra note 38, at 38 et seq.
79. Gunther Teubner, *Globale Zivilverfassungen: Alternativen zur staatszentrierten Verfassungstheorie*, in: "Zeitschrift für ausländisches öffentliches Recht und Völkerrecht", Vol. 63 (2003), 1–28.
80. Ibid., at 12 et seq.
81. Ibid., at 6 et seq.; Gunther Teubner, *Constitutional Fragments: Societal Constitutionalism and Globalization*, Oxford University Press, Oxford/New York 2012.
82. Gunther Teubner, *State Policies in Private Law? A Comment on Hanoch Dagan*, in: "The American Journal of Comparative Law", Vol. 56 (2008), 835–843.
83. Teubner, *Globale Zivilverfassungen*, supra note 79, at 13 et seq.
84. Celia Wasserstein Fassberg, *Lex Mercatoria – Hoist with Its Own Petard?* in: "Chicago Journal of International Law", Vol. 5 (2004–2005), 67–82, at 69. See also Berthold Goldman, *The Applicable Law: General Principles of Law—The Lex Mercatoria*, in: Julian D. M. Lew (ed.), *Contemporary Problems in International Arbitration*, Queen Mary College, London 1986, 113 et seq.; Rt. Hon. Lord Justice Mustill, *The New Lex Mercatoria: The First Twenty-Five Years*, in: Maarten Bos (ed.), *Liber Amicorum for the Rt. Hon. Lord Wilberforce*, Clarendon, Oxford 1987, at 149 et seq.; Klaus Peter Berger, *The Creeping Codification of the New Lex Mercatoria*, Kluwer, Alphen aan den Rijn 2010 (2nd ed.).
85. Christian Tietje, *Global Governance and Inter-Agency Co-operation in International Economic Law*, in: "Journal of World Trade", Vol. 36 (2002), 501–515.

86. Pierre Marc Johnson, *Creating Sustainable Global Governance*, in: John J. Kirton, Joseph P. Daniels, Andreas Freytag (eds.), *Guiding Global Order*, Ashgate, Aldershot 2001, 245–280.
87. James Tully, Jeffrey L. Dunoff, Anthony F. Lang Jr., Mattias Kumm, Antje Wiener, *Introducing Global Integral Constitutionalism*, in: "Global Constitutionalism", Vol. 5 (2016), 1–15.

CHAPTER 7

# The Post-unitary Paradigms of Order II: From Modernity to Post-modernity

In 1927, Joseph Roth—an Austrian-Jewish journalist and writer—published a short novel with the title *Die Flucht ohne Ende* (*Flight Without End*). It is hard to find a better expression of the feelings of loss and disorientation that affect an individual in the face of the collapse of the established order than in this brilliantly written fictional report of the peregrinations of a young man at the end of World War I. In the eyes of Franz Tunda—the protagonist of Roth's novel and, to some extent, his alter ego—the established order, which gave him a robust cognitive and ethical framework, was identical with the Austro-Hungarian Empire, whose end he experienced in Siberia, after escaping a camp for prisoners of war of the Russian army. From this moment on, the course of his life—though thrilling and interesting for most external observers—seems to lose any internal coherence and meaningful purpose. Every stage is a disappointment and a reason for seeking something else. He is involved in the Russian civil war and fights for the Red Army, but ultimately rejects the Communist ideology and its oppressive discipline. He marries a young woman named Alja, only to desert her shortly afterwards. Instead, during his restless journey, Tunda has love affairs with other women, but, although no one of them lacks some sort of fascination, nothing lasting grows from these encounters and no enduring solace is given to his tormented soul. He visits his brother in Western Germany, only

© The Author(s), under exclusive license to Springer Nature Switzerland AG 2021
S. Dellavalle, *Paradigms of Social Order*,
Philosophy, Public Policy, and Transnational Law,
https://doi.org/10.1007/978-3-030-66179-3_7

to discover that they have nothing to talk about. He lives in different places—from Irkutsk in Siberia to Vienna and from Berlin to Paris—but he does not settle down in any of them. At the end of the novel, Tunda is stranded in Paris and broke, but has the chance to get back to Irkutsk to live with his wife Alja and the old friend Baranowicz. Yet, he is undecided and does not know what to do: in fact, he prefers living in the decay of a poor Paris housing, looking back in nostalgia at his experiences and at the promises of happiness enshrined in them, than taking his life back in his hands. The final sentences of the novel are among the most desperate one may find in world literature: "he had no occupation, no desire, no hope, no ambition, and not even any self-love. No one in the whole world was as superfluous as he".[1]

Surely, Roth's novel is open to quite different interpretations, but, without forcing the issue too much, it is possible to see in the way in which Franz Tunda looks at the Austro-Hungarian Empire and at the social stability that was guaranteed by the old status quo, a cypher of the relationship between the individual and the paradigms of order until the beginning of the twentieth century. Indeed, irrespective of which one of the traditional paradigms was predominant in a certain period of time, the identification of the individual with its main tenets was unquestioned. This cannot be surprising because, within the context of the unitary paradigms of order, individuals had no choice as regards the cognitive and normative frame that gave shape to their lives. Simply, they had no alternatives since a unitary organon of categories dictated the criteria for true knowledge and a no less self-coherent set of moral principles was thought to steer practical reason towards right action. In the same vein—at least according to Tunda's (and Roth's) approach— the Austro-Hungarian Empire provided to all its subjects, regardless of their ethnic, cultural, linguistic and religious differences, an encompassing political and legal framework for the organization of predictable interactions and a meaningful life. Therefore, the end of the unity of the Austro-Hungarian political community also foreshadows and artistically symbolizes the collapse of the unitary conception of order, leaving the members of the community to an unpredictable destiny. Surely, the overcoming of the unitary view of order also implies that new adventures can be dared and new opportunities seized. Yet, Franz Tunda seems not to care about all of this: in his world, when order is lost, only emptiness remains, and a desperate attempt to restore what has gone forever.

If we assume that Roth's *Flight Without End* is a metaphor for the transition from a unitary idea of order to the post-unitary social universe of innumerable options, cognitive and normative uncertainty and contradictory strivings, we have also to acknowledge that this transition is regarded by the Austrian-Jewish novelist with a high degree of scepticism. Substantially, Tunda wishes the old order back, or at least another, but no less consistent form of social predictability and overall coherence. In the end, we see in the report of Tunda's adventures almost exclusively the death of the old world, but are not made capable of glimpsing the birth of a new one. The presentation of the new age takes instead a much more assertive form in another novel, published by Milan Kundera in 1984—during the golden age of the meanwhile well-established postmodern thinking—with the much telling title *The Unbearable Lightness of Being*.

Kundera's story develops between the second half of the 1960s and the following decade and is mainly set in that part of then Czechoslovakia which presently builds the Czech Republic and—to a lesser extent—in Switzerland. Thus, the events unfold from shortly before the beginning of the Prague Spring—i.e., the attempt to give to the Czechoslovakian Communist regime a more "human" face, which began in January 1968—to the restoration of totalitarian practices following the intervention of the military forces of the then Warsaw Pact, under the leadership of the Soviet Union, in August of the same year. Four main figures are at the centre of the stage: Tomas, a brilliant Czech surgeon who ends up being a window washer and a truck driver in a collective farm; Tereza, Tomas's girlfriend, a sensitive young woman and a talented photographer who in the end prefers a quiet life, on the same farm in which also Tomas works, to avoid too many political compromises with the Communist regime; Sabina, a paintress from Prague and Tomas's occasional mistress; and Franz, a Swiss professor and idealist. According to the author, the "being"—as expressed in the lives of the protagonists as well as of every other human being—is inevitably "light" because it is essentially contextual while lacking any kind of inherent truth. Indeed, Kundera claims,

> human life occurs only once, and the reason we cannot determine which of our decisions are good and which bad is that in a given situation we can make only one decision; we are not granted a second, third or fourth life in which to compare various decisions.[2]

Since none of our deeds is destined to last or stand the test of repetition and time, all of them are doomed to lack substantial truth. It may be useful, at this point, to compare Kundera's approach with the sense of life that emerges from a novel written only one year after *The Unbearable Lightness of Being*, but imbued with an almost opposite spirit, namely John Irving's *The Cider House Rules*.[3] Although Irving's novel does not assert the existence of ontologically objective values and truths either, it maintains—faithful, as regards this point, to the modern tradition of Kantian morals and to what will be presented, in the next chapter, as the communicative understanding of the use of practical reason—that, in order to live a dignified and meaningful life, we have to be "of some use" to our fellow humans. This assumption means that our actions should be directed towards a universal purpose and that this commitment has to shape our lives. Surely, there is no ontological guarantee that the universal intention really corresponds to a universal result, but at least we have to make subjectively that postulation. Otherwise, social life would lose a great part of its sense. It is not by chance that Irving, though expressing some restraint in the notes to his novel,[4] endorses in the end the favourite prayer of his grandmother:

> Oh Lord, support us all the day long, until the shadows lengthen and the evening comes, and the busy world is hushed, and the fever of life is over, and our work is done.[5]

It is not an exaggeration to say that Kundera's view is nearly the opposite—and exemplifies the shifting of the weltanschauung from "modern" to "postmodern". In fact, against the background of the "lightness of being", human life has no missions to accomplish: "missions are stupid – Tomas says to Tereza –. I have no mission. No one has. And it's a terrific relief to realize you're free, free of all missions".[6] When we believe to have a mission, we fall prey to *kitsch*,[7] namely to a somehow tasteless and almost ridiculous overestimation of the scope of our lives and actions—like good-hearted Franz, who participates in a march on Cambodia to advocate the respect of human right in that land, ravaged by famine and political oppression, just to end up being killed in a rather trivial attempt to rob him.[8] Furthermore, there is—according to Kundera—no substantial difference between opposite ideologies.[9] Finally, because of the heterogenesis of ends, we can never be sure of the real effects of our actions: Tereza, for example, takes photos to document the Russian oppression of the Czech people after the invasion on the 21st of August 1968, only to discover, years later, that the documentation had been used by the intelligence of the Communist state to identify the resisters.

Modern subjectivity and contemporary intersubjectivity base the confidence in the existence of a sufficient coherence between individual commitments and the effect of actions on the reasonable assumption—rooted in mental or communicative processes—that we have access to some kind of truth content. On the contrary, according to Kundera's postmodern view, since truth—be it ontological, transcendental, or intersubjective—is utterly unattainable, individuals themselves cannot aspire to having any internal coherence. Rather, they only seem to react to a hardly understandable environment. Against this background, political engagement is an illusion; instead, the noblest goal that we can realistically achieve consists in trying to live our lives in the most decent way, without having any assurance that the effects of our acts will correspond to our intentions. The most reliable human capacity, that should lead us to a life in decency, is not reason, but empathy.[10] However, empathy does not justify binding duties, but rather uncompelling and quite casual generosity. As a matter of fact, Tomas harbours sweet feelings of empathy towards Tereza, which does not deter him, however, from his womanizing attitude and thus from inflicting pain and humiliation to his faithful long-time partner.

Works of art have a significant advantage—along with some disadvantages—towards philosophical, political and legal theory: they are not required to deliver explicit arguments and can therefore maintain an undertone of ambiguity. It is hardly questionable that most readers of Kundera's novel will feel most attached to Tereza—the least postmodern of all its figures. Yet, also Sabina seems to suffer under the "unbearable lightness of being".[11] Social sciences do not enjoy this blessing: they have to present straightforward arguments. As a result, the new understanding of order, that made its reluctant appearance in Roth's work and re-emerged—much more consistently—in Kundera's novel has to be translated into unambiguous assertions and an affirmative theory of order (or into a consistent criticism of its traditional understanding). The first step was made by the postmodern turn of a significant part of twentieth century's philosophical research, which delivered substantial arguments to some assumptions that also characterize Kundera's novel, such as the rejection of universal truths, the contextuality of meaning, the scepticism about order and the dissolution of the unity of individual experience into a plurality of dimensions (7.1). Since the philosophical novelties were introduced before Kundera wrote his work, it can be assumed that, in this case, literature follows philosophical research—though introducing some intriguing ambiguities—and not vice versa. The ball went then to political, social and legal theory, which confronted the modern idea of order (7.2), sometimes searching for ways to allow for individual self-realization within the postmodern context of plurality (7.3). Interestingly, we find here too—like in Kundera's "lightness of being"—an approach according to which human solidarity is not based on universal obligations, but on contextual empathy (7.3.4). While it is hardly questionable that postmodernism introduced a much-needed introspection into the flaws of modern thinking, some problems arise nonetheless from its conceptual organon, in particular—if we take into specific account the fields of political and legal theory—with reference to the watering down of concepts like legitimacy and normativity (7.4).

## 7.1 The Philosophical Foundations of Post-modernism

The knowing subject was the fundament on which the building of modern philosophy, both in its theoretical and practical dimension, was erected. Indeed, as for the theoretical use of reason, the correct unfolding of the mental processes of the subject was assumed to guarantee that utterances regarding the objective world outside were *true*—in the sense that they exactly describe or understand the object—and *universally accepted*. Within the strand of the rather sceptical empiricism from Hobbes to Kant, there was no pretension that the subjective knowledge of the world would be exhaustive since much of the objective reality was presumed to remain largely unknown to our senses and reason. Nonetheless, our subject-based knowledge was regarded as the most profound and vast knowledge that we are enabled to achieve on the basis of our limited capacities. Furthermore, even if our capacities were recognized as restricted, what we know of the world—provided that this was attained through the application of strict and shared procedures—was seen as a sufficient basis for the establishment of a robust and universally acknowledged science. Much more optimistic was the view of the idealist philosophers—such as, for example, Hegel—who were convinced that subjective knowledge can disclose, in principle, the whole universe. What was common to both strands, however, was the belief that the centre of knowledge was the subject and not the object outside. It was not by chance, in fact, that in all philosophical systems developed during the centuries of the dominion of the individualistic paradigm—roughly from the seventeenth to the early twentieth centuries—the presentation always began, no matter whether the authors were influenced by empiricism or by idealism, by analysing the mental processes of the knowing subject and not by describing the object outside. Not much different was the question with reference to the use of practical reason. Analogously, it was up to the subject to elaborate the contents of right action on the basis of an adequate implementation of rational principles.

Modern subjectivity realized its potentialities in the fields of theoretical and practical reason thanks to three specific characteristics: internal unity, self-referential hierarchy and cognitive solipsism. The quality of internal unity refers to the circumstance that both the knowledge of the world and individual actions had to be organized—in order to be, respectively, true or right—as a coherent structure or as a totality of self-consistent claims regarding facts or deeds. In other words, knowledge was not allowed to be unsystematic or rhapsodic and the course of individual actions had to follow a stringent path. The internal coherence that should result from the use of the theoretical and practical reason is reflected by the unitary character of the modern subjectivity, which is generally represented as an undivided monad. In this perspective, conflicts are mostly directed towards the world outside and, inasmuch as they occur between different dimensions of the monad, they have to be resolved by re-establishing hierarchical relations. Precisely the resort to hierarchy constitutes the second characteristic of modern subjectivity. According to modern philosophy, the path to knowledge must undergo a severe organization of the data derived from experience through abstract and hierarchically superior categories. In the course of this process, sensory experiences are depurated from any contingent or existential content and are made available for generalizing procedures; in other words, they are transformed into abstract description of facts or laws of nature, often expressed through mathematical formulas. In the same vein, higher moral norms have to take control of lower instinct within the horizon of practical philosophy. The subjectivistic hierarchy of cognitive instruments and moral norms is then insofar self-referential as the supreme authority in both the theoretical and the practical dimensions is located within the knowing subject and not outside of it, like in the paradigms before the individualistic turn. This claim does not rule out that the individuals can come together to build scientific, moral or political communities, united by shared knowledge, common assumptions as regards the principles of action, or a mutual recognition of legal norms and institutions. Yet, the establishment of these communities does not happen *during* the decision-making-processes of the individuals, but *after* every single individual has come to the same results *on his or her own*. This consideration leads us to the third and last main characteristic of modern subjectivity, namely solipsism. Indeed, according to modern individualistic thinking, the knowledge of the world does not emerge from intersubjective exchanges of arguments, but from the individual subsumption of data into proper categories. Of course, if all individuals apply the same categories, and they apply the categories in the correct way, the results will be the same and a community of knowledge can be built. Nevertheless, the fact remains that the whole process is viewed from an exclusively mentalistic perspective and no social aspect is taken into account.[12] The same can also be said with reference to moral norms as the product of a purely individualistic use of reason—as proposed by Kant—[13] or to laws or political institutions as created by an abstract contract.[14]

The doctrine of subjectivism—with its three main assumptions of the internal unity, self-referential hierarchy and cognitive solipsism of the knowing and acting subject—dominated Western philosophy for many centuries, until at the beginning of the twentieth century its main tenets began to be questioned. The first assumption to come under attack was solipsism (7.1.1), then followed by the idea that the subject is to be regarded as a unity in itself and that its internal hierarchy should be seen as the best guarantee for truth and rightness (7.1.2). Since the new philosophical strand concentrated its criticism on the *modern* idea of the knowing and acting subject, it went down in history as *postmodernism*.

### 7.1.1 Discovering Contextuality

In Western philosophy the knowing and acting subjects were considered, for long time, the masters of their life. Within the practical dimension, the implication was that the subjects were expected to create the moral, legal and political norms of the world in which they lived. In short, we were assumed to be the architects of our time. This view was systematically contested for the first time by Martin Heidegger in his *Sein und Zeit* (*Being and Time*) of 1927. His first step, in this work, consisted in stripping the knowing subject of modern Western philosophy from its absoluteness and from its pretension to shape the world in the image of its abstract categories: "the being of the person – he wrote – cannot consist in being a subject of rational acts that have a certain lawfulness".[15] By doing so, Heidegger led the individuals back to their "Da-sein", namely to their real existence, and away from the sideral heights of the abstract subjectivity. This earthing of the subject was, in fact, nothing really new in Western philosophy since, after the almost unrestricted apotheosis of subjectivism in Hegel's philosophy, other authors—such as Søren Kierkegaard[16] and Arthur Schopenhauer[17]—already drew attention on the limits of abstract thought and highlighted the concrete dimensions of human life. What Heidegger added, inter alia, was the transformation of the analysis of the existential horizon of life into a post-rationalist ontology—hardly a great achievement for a strand of thinking which aspired to focus again on the conflicts of life while moving away from hypostasizing conceptualizations. A second element introduced by Heidegger, however, is more important for our analysis. Pushed down from the pedestal of its presumed absoluteness and traced back to its real existence, individuality is identified by Heidegger as essentially "temporal" (*zeitlich*).[18] This means that, whereas Hegel's subject receives a historical existence as a result of its immersion in the concreteness of the world, according to Heidegger the individuality is not "already 'objectively present' beforehand, and then at times gets 'into a history'".[19] Rather, "only because Da-sein is historical in its being, are anything like circumstances, events, and destinies ontologically possible".[20] In this sense, the subject is not the master of its time any longer, but only a part of it.

From Heidegger's turn two consequences are derived, the first quite disturbing, the second, on the contrary, potentially groundbreaking. The disturbing element in his philosophy is related to the critical function against the status quo that was always implicitly or explicitly present in the concept of the subject in modern Western thinking—or, more precisely, to the loss of this function in Heidegger's germinal postmodernism. Indeed, first, inasmuch as the individuals were presumed to be the masters of their time, no status quo had to be accepted for the mere reason of its existence, but had to be justified—and, if necessary, changed—as a result of individual judgement and action. Secondly, insofar as the subject was put to some extent above history and since the main instrument of the subject was reason, it was assumed that the individuals maintain a certain distance from the reality in which they happen to live and that this distance is measured by the arguments of reason. In other words, since we are not stuck within a specific historical context, but we can observe it from above, we are also enabled to use our reason to criticize it and to conceive of possible alternatives. All these privileges are lost in Heidegger's perspective. In his view, indeed, individuals essentially belong to a certain community and cannot refrain from it if not through a radical and ultimately antisocial self-isolation.[21] Moreover, the rational instruments that enabled individuals to distance themselves from the rules of that community are dismantled. Consequently, social and political criticism becomes a chimera or even a form of betrayal. As a consequence, Heidegger's support for National Socialism and his rootedness in a vernacular and essentially anti-cosmopolitan cultural tradition might not have been pure coincidences. On the other hand—coming now to the potentially groundbreaking element of Heidegger's philosophy—his thought contributed to question the myth of the self-reliance of the knowing and acting subject, opening the gate for an intersubjective understanding of all social processes. However—as we will see in the last chapter—intersubjectivity does not need to come at the cost of the rejection of modern rationalism's achievements.

Moving on, now, to the theoretical or epistemological dimension of subjectivistic solipsism, it must be kept in mind, first, that during the whole history of philosophy the meaning of an utterance was considered depending on its truth content, and that this truth content was determined by the interaction between the knowing subject and the object outside. In other words, the historically predominant attitude was the assumption that utterances have a meaning essentially because they refer to an external—i.e., non-linguistic—object and that this relationship between the elements of language and the non-linguistic world accounts for the truth content of the language. Before the paradigmatic revolution towards individualism, the guarantee of the truth content was located in the object, whereas the subject had basically to take up and reflect the external truth content. Some distinctions from a strict "objectivistic" theory of truth had been already introduced in the late Middle Ages—for instance, through the "nominalist" interpretation of universal or abstract concepts in the work of William of Ockham.[22] Yet, it was with the transition to the Modern Ages that the epistemological centre was moved inside the individuals, who had to shape knowledge on the basis of their categories. Nonetheless, until the middle of the twentieth century no philosopher, scientist or linguist ever claimed that the meaning of utterances is independent of the external object, or that sentences can have a sense and be correctly understood without having any objective truth content. This dramatic and highly unsettling move was made by Ludwig Wittgenstein with his *Philosophische Untersuchungen* (*Philosophical Investigations*), written in the 1940s and published in 1953. It is remarkable that Wittgenstein with this work not only introduced a huge novelty in the field of the theory of knowledge and of language but also profoundly changed his own previous position. While in his *Tractatus Logico-Philosophicus*[23] he still maintained a rather traditional theory of meaning, according to which the truth content of an utterance is necessarily related to an object, in his later work he claimed, for the first time in the history of thought, that we can understand each other through our linguistic communication by just relying on linguistic habits and without resorting to any assumption of a more-than-contextual truth content of our utterances. In doing so, Wittgenstein abandoned the well-established idea that mutual understanding is based on a twofold pillar: first, the rational structure that would underlie all forms of communication, and, secondly, the link of this structure to "facts" of the world.[24] Instead, he decided to turn his attention to concrete languages. Here the meaning of a term can no longer be logically reconstructed by searching for its relationship with an object or with the state of an object, nor can one purport to define such meaning in a coherent and univocal way. On the contrary, in common languages what matters most is the "use" (*Gebrauch*) that the speaker makes of the term: "the meaning of a word – Wittgenstein said concisely and unequivocally – is its use in the language".[25] This also means that each term can have different meanings. Wittgenstein exemplifies this fundamental aspect by referring to the semantic denotation of "seeing": "only do not think you knew in advance what the '*state* of seeing' means here! Let the use *teach* you the meaning".[26] The prevalence of use in determining the meaning of words implies that language is no longer seen as a logical structure that reflects the cognitive abilities of each individual, enabling her/him to communicate with other beings who are also equipped with the same tool. On the contrary, it is now born in *communication*, it does not *lead* to it; and it develops *among* individuals, not *within* each of them.

Wittgenstein's radical idea of a language devoid of objective references and, thus, without falsifiable truth content never became mainstream among philosophers of language and epistemologists. Rather, in order to avoid a cognitive scepticism that would prove disruptive, in particular for natural sciences, and to prevent a moral neutralism that would permanently weaken the normative content of human sciences, the post-Wittgensteinian philosophy of language and theory of knowledge were rather committed to mend the rift and to bridge the gap between language and objective reality again.[27] However, the view that there is no universal and rational truth, but only a plurality of contextual and communicatively shared narrations proved to be highly influential on the contemporary theories of order, in particular by strongly supporting the post-unitary turn.

### 7.1.2 Beyond Modern Subjectivism

In the whole history of thinking, the establishment of order—generally linked to some form of rationality—was always regarded as a positive development, as the beginning of knowledge and social life and, therefore, as opposed to the darkness of ignorance and chaos. With the transition to Modern Ages, subjectivity was then elevated to the status of the most essential creator and guarantor of order. In particular, subjectivity was identified—not secondarily because of its connection to order and hierarchy with respect to the "lower" forms of experience—with a desirable progress of reason and with an advancement of human beings towards better living conditions and towards emancipation from a nature experienced as hostile. In the epistemological field, the positive evaluation of order implied the distinction between "true" knowledge, which was assumed to be based on the rational structuring of evidences, and narrations devoid of truth content, which did not meet the strict criteria laid down by modern science. In political theory, the apotheosis of order in the image of the subjective macro-anthropos—with its claim on internal unity and hierarchy—led to the creation of the modern notion of sovereignty and to its central relevance until the present time.[28] Similarly to what happened in the social and political sphere, the dominance of the subjectivist categories was also reaffirmed in the ethical and psychological dimensions of the individual personality. The geometric visualization of passions and instincts, and therefore their control by the cognitive functions of the mind, represented one of the most ambitious projects of modernity. In the "Preface" to the fifth Part of his *Ethica Ordine Geometrico Demonstrata* (*Ethics*) of 1677, Spinoza expressed this programme with outstanding clarity:

In this part ... I shall be dealing with the power of reason, pointing out the degree of control reason has over the emotions, and then what is freedom of mind, of blessedness, from which we shall see how much to be preferred is the life of the wise human being to the life of the ignorant human being.[29]

Nor has the hierarchy decisively changed since the discovery of the subconscious at the beginning of the twentieth century. Indeed, classical psychoanalysis seemed to shake, at first sight, the previous solidity of the mental structure based on the prioritization of rational order over instinct insofar as the instinctual dimension was considered unsuitable to be fully "tamed". In fact, the subconscious constantly keeps the rational sphere of subjectivity under siege, generating what Sigmund Freud called the "discontents" of civilization.[30] However, far from upholding the idea that order should be rejected in favour of some form of instinct-oriented behaviour, the founder of psychoanalysis himself maintained that the "id", representing the instinctual impulses, has to be contained first by external authorities and then by their internalization in the shape of the "super-ego". Precisely the control of the "id" through the "super-ego" makes—in Freud's interpretation—the constitution of the rational ego possible and should thus be considered a synonym of progress and an unavoidable condition for the development of civilization.[31]

The overturning of the traditionally positive view of order and of the contribution given to its establishment by the modern notion of subjectivity was essentially initiated by the philosophical work of Michel Foucault. While Heidegger and Wittgenstein may be considered, to some extents, the most relevant forerunners of postmodernism, Foucault consciously chose modern subjectivism as the explicit target of his criticism. As a result, he has to be regarded as the first outspoken exponent of postmodernism and arguably its most innovative and influential representative so far. Foucault did not question the relationship between the constitution of subjectivity and modernity; rather, he reversed the evaluation of this relationship, transforming it from positive—as it usually was—to negative. More concretely, in his interpretation the creation of the subject—far from freeing the individuals from the chains of ignorance and need—corresponds to a process of "objectification", through which human beings in all their dimensions are converted into handy tools of power.[32] This occurs at various levels: first, by imposing rules and constraints—which match with the categories of subjectivity of modern philosophy—to humans as speaking beings through grammar, philology and linguistics:

> I presume – Foucault asserted in his inaugural lecture at the Collège de France on the 2$^{nd}$ of December 1970 – that in every society the production of discourse is at once controlled, selected and organized by a certain number of procedures whose role is to ward off its powers and dangers, to gain mastery over its chance events, to evade its ponderous, formidable materiality.[33]

Furthermore—he specifies shortly after—the control of discourse is closely linked to the creation of the concept of the knowing subject or "founding subject" in the sense of the Cartesian *cogito*: "the idea of the founding subject is a way of eliding the reality of discourse".[34] Secondly, the establishment of modern subjectivity affects human physicality, not least sexuality as one of its strongest drives. The process does not result in a mere repression of instincts, but rather in their regulation through practices that make them productive and discourses that transform the *scientia sexualis* into an "objective" discipline.[35] Corporeity is therefore not simply repressed, but is inserted into a conceptual horizon that puts chains on it in the precise moment in which it conceptualizes it by means of a "scientific" discourse. Thirdly, by regulating bodies and minds, the notion of the "founding subject" provides the tools for the ordering of experience. On the basis of that assumption, Foucault shows how sciences such as linguistics, the taxonomy of living beings and natural history, not least the economy itself, arise from the need to submit previous forms of knowledge, which were not seen as sufficiently "exact", to a stricter methodological discipline. By doing so, the dimension of experience enshrined in those "non-scientific" forms of knowledge is sacrificed on the altar of the rigid canon of a simplified rationality focused on "subjectivity".[36] Once the canon of the well-ordered, epistemologically correct and productive subjectivity had been defined, it became also possible to identify deviant behaviours, so as to finally neutralize and expunge them.[37]

In Foucault's work, the criticism against modern subjectivity goes hand in hand with a redefinition of power. In his view, indeed, power does not essentially emanate from a public institution, namely from the state, nor does it originate from the unequal distribution of economic resources as the result of the accumulation of capital. Rather, it is decentralized and widespread. In concrete terms, it expresses itself in a myriad of canons of speech and behaviour, of forms of interaction and exchange, of ways of living and thinking, to the point of forming an omnipresent network:

> power comes from below; that is, there is no binary and all-encompassing opposition between rulers and ruled at the root of power relations, and serving as a general matrix – no such duality extending from the top down and reacting on more and more limited groups to the very depths of the social body. One must suppose rather that the manifold relationships of force that take shape and come into play in the machinery of production, in families, limited groups, and institutions, are the basis for wide-ranging effects of cleavage that run through the social body as a whole.[38]

Faced with the rejection of subjectivity as an instance of selective order, on the one hand, and with power as an intrusive network of social control, the task of a postmodern enlightenment consists, following Foucault, in identifying the moment of discontinuity: "the history ... is not that of continuity at the service of a founding subjective spirit, but a series of contingently connected discourse strata".[39] We are dealing with discontinuities not only between the different epochs in the history of thought, but also within each of them. Against the illusion of a homogeneous and coherent order, at least within each single paradigm, Foucault's "archeology" of knowledge shows the plurality of discursive strategies.[40] In particular, "the essential aim of archeology consists in the de-struction of philosophical-subjectivistic and scientific-humanistic concepts and theories – not least because these prevent an adequate vision of science, history and experience".[41] However, Foucault's scientific enterprise has not only an epistemological intent: the destructuring of the presumed rational order is proposed not only to better understand the history of thought but also to free the real individuals from the oppressive hierarchy of subjectivity. Thus, the process of destructuring has two targets, the first being the presumably coherent order of knowledge and society, while the second is the unity of subjectivity with the aim of gaining room for the self-realization of individuals. Destructuring modern subjectivity becomes therefore an essential step on the way to a new form of Enlightenment. According to Foucault's approach, clarifying the limits of rational theories and denying their wrongly assumed universal validity, completes the project of the Enlightenment to the extent that it emancipates the real individuals from the limitations which, produced on a philosophical, scientific and social level, went along with the idea of the subject.[42] With specific reference to the archaeological work, Foucault summed up the core content of the postmodern reinterpretation of knowledge with the following words:

> In the proposed analysis, instead of referring back to the synthesis or the unifying function of a subject, the various enunciative modalities manifest his dispersion. ... Thus conceived, discourse is not the majestically unfolding manifestation of a thinking, knowing, speaking subject, but, on the contrary, a totality, in which the dispersion of the subject and his discontinuity with himself may be determined. It is a space of exteriority in which a network of distinct sites is deployed. I showed earlier that it was neither by 'words' nor by 'things' that the regulation of the objects proper to a discursive formation should be defined; similarly, it must now be recognized that it is neither by recourse to a transcendental subject nor by recourse to a psychological subjectivity that the regulation of its enunciations should be defined.[43]

## 7.2 Order as Oppression

The philosophical criticism of modern subjectivity led, with reference to the theories of order, to four results, which partially complement each other and partially represent alternatives that exclude one another. (a) True knowledge and convincing justifications for action cannot be attained by the knowing subject in a solipsistic way, but need to be developed within intersubjective contexts. (b) Order must not necessarily be unitary; on the contrary, we can conceive of a well-ordered society which is made of a network-like interconnection of different normative and institutional systems. (c) Order does not unavoidably stand for a society characterized by justice and freedom; rather, it can arguably be seen as an instrument of oppression and as an obstacle for individual self-realization. (d) Individual self-fulfilment can be best achieved within the context of a plurality of normative and institutional systems, without whatsoever prioritization of any of them. Result (b) is shared by all post-unitary paradigms of order and result (a) brings together the postmodern theories and the communicative paradigm. Instead, results (c) and (d) represent two opposite ways to put the lessons of postmodernism in place, whereas they are not taken up by the other two post-unitary paradigms of order, namely systems theory and the communicative paradigm, which maintain a more traditional view as regards the positive features of order. With reference to the specifically postmodern theories of order, we thus have two contrasting options: on the one hand, those theories that basically *reject* order, either per se, or at least as an expression of patriarchy or Western domination; and, on the other, those views which see in the *multiplications* of orders—in plural and without hierarchical relations to one another—the best chances for personal gratification and social reasonableness. Once said that, let us start with those conceptions that frontally attack order, without paying much attention on whether it is understood in singular or plural.

### 7.2.1 Against Empire

According to Michael Hardt and Antonio Negri's interpretation, postmodern order can be described as a new form of "empire".[44] They list four arguments to underpin their assumption. First, Hardt and Negri remark that in the last decades of the twentieth century—they published *Empire* in 2000—world order has become less and less *inter-national* and increasingly *global*. To the extent that power is transferred from the national to the supra-state sphere,[45] an "imperial notion of right" crystallizes.[46] In this context, but far beyond the limits of formal law, a new type of order is being created, "defined by its virtuality, its dynamism, its functional inconclusiveness".[47] A second indication of the genetic change of the idea of order consists in the globalization of capitalist production.[48] A third factor is identified by Hardt and Negri in the resurgence of the idea of just war.[49] Here the two authors, despite their clearly neo-communist political affiliation, use an argument that explicitly refers to Carl Schmitt[50]: inasmuch as the contemporary global order is presented as an expression of universal values, "humanitarian" military interventionism is purified from its true nature of action in defence of material and particular interests and unduly transformed into a police action in order to punish the "criminals".[51] The peculiarly Schmittian character of Hardt and Negri's position unequivocally emerges from the fact that the two authors do not limit themselves to criticizing the more radical doctrine of unilateral military interventionism—as it has been advocated, for instance, by some American Neocons—but also distance themselves from the "right to intervention" in the form enshrined in the *Charter of the United Nations*.[52] In their interpretation, every imposition of a cosmopolitan law can only be a more or less elegantly masked form of imperial oppression. The fourth—and last—indication regarding the revival of imperial power emerges from the hegemony that the "empire" exercises over legal practices: normativity, sanction and repression now have their roots in a discipline in which there is a "relative (but effective) coincidence of the new functioning of domestic law and supranational law".[53] In other words, the consolidation of imperial power requires a regulatory continuity between national and international law, cancelling their doctrinal and factual specificity: in a "global" world, the only possible law is the "domestic" law of the empire.

Hardt and Negri's postmodern concept of "empire" has quite different connotations from how the word has been used to describe both its traditional and historical realizations—such as the Roman or the British Empires—and the US empire of the second half of the twentieth and the beginning of the twenty-first century, as it has been defended by some Neocons.[54] The uniqueness of the postmodern empire is essentially related to how power is understood in its sphere of influence. On this point, Hardt and Negri heavily borrow from Foucault's analysis. In particular, they apply to the imperial power Foucault's definition of *biopower*. By "biopower" Hardt and Negri mean—in the same way as Foucault did before them—a power "that regulates social life from its interior, following it, interpreting it, absorbing it, and rearticulating it".[55] Biopower, thus, is a form of power that insinuates itself in all the folds of life, not by *commanding* compliant behaviours, but by *shaping* forms of life, production, reproduction and consumption which are entirely in line with the systemic requirements:

> Power is thus expressed as a control that extends throughout the depths of the consciousnesses and bodies of the population – and at the same time across the entirety of social relations.[56]

The second characteristic of imperial power also draws from Foucault's lesson, but goes then a step further by introducing a distinction that was highlighted for the first time by Gilles Deleuze.[57] In Hardt and Negri's interpretation, imperial power is linked, in today's reality, to the transition from the "disciplinary society" to the "society of control". The concept of "disciplinary society" (*société disciplinaire*) was created by Foucault in his book *Surveiller et punir* (*Discipline and Punish*) of 1975[58] and is identified by Hardt and Negri as "that society in which social command is constructed through a diffuse network of *dispositifs* or apparatuses that produce and regulate customs, habits, and productive practices".[59] In such a social and ideological structure, the holders of power are clearly identifiable, as are the social groups that lack it and are induced, through a precise and identifiable authoritative hierarchy, to obey and carry out the reproductive practices of the power. The situation in a "society of control"—according to the notion that was brought into the debate by Deleuze—is quite different. Here, "the mechanisms of command become ever more 'democratic', ever more immanent to the social field, distributed throughout the brains and bodies of the citizens".[60] Therefore, "the behaviours of social integration and exclusion ... are thus increasingly interiorized within the subjects themselves. Power is now exercised through machines that directly organize the brains (in communication systems, information networks, etc.) and bodies (in welfare systems, monitored activities, etc.)".[61] In short, while in the "disciplinary society" actions that are consistent with the tendency of power to consolidate and increase are imposed bottom-down by those who hold that power, in the "society of control" it is the individuals themselves who freely display behaviours in line with the systemic requirements of power, without any need for authoritative commands.

A further postmodern element in Hardt and Negri's notion of empire is to be found in their emphasis on the non-centralized and therefore— with reference to the categories of modern subjectivism—*post-subjective* nature of global order. From the very beginning of their analysis, the two authors distanced themselves from "the idea that order is dictated by a single power and a single centre of rationality *transcendent* to global forces, guiding the various phases of historical development according to its conscious and all-seeing plan".[62] In particular, Hardt and Negri refuse to give credit to the widespread belief that there is a coincidence between the contemporary "empire" and the power exercised by the United States. More specifically—as argued by Hardt and Negri in *Commonwealth* of 2009, the third part of the trilogy that began with *Empire* and went on with *Multitude* of 2004—the attempt of the United States "to establish the unilateral control ... over global affairs" after the attacks on the World Trade Center and the Pentagon on the 11th of September 2001 "has been all but aborted".[63] The result is a power whose ramifications are everywhere and nowhere since its heart and brain are not in the offices of governments, but in the minds and bodies of all of us. It is in this all-encompassing network that everything is assumed to flow into the "empire", from our daily actions as consumers and producers to the policies of the hegemonic nations and their satellites, from the initiatives of intergovernmental and supranational organizations to humanitarian interventions and NGOs.

Still in 2009 Hardt and Negri described the current situation of world affairs in terms of their theory of imperial power, namely as "a complex network of global norms, structures, and authorities, which is partial, incomplete, and in some respects fragile but nonetheless real and effective".[64] Nonetheless, in times in which the influence of nation states seems to strengthen again, it is appropriate to ask whether Hardt and Negri's diagnosis of a diffuse world dis-order of postnational networks at the service of capital is still viable. Moreover, even if one were prone to admit the persistence of the postmodern empire—which, for my part, I am not—some further questions would emerge. Especially, if imperial power insinuates itself in every corner of our bodies and minds, to the extent that "the imperial machine ... demonstrates that [the] ... external standpoint no longer exists",[65] where is the room for resistance to develop? And, furthermore, which is the rationality of the alternative political and social project, if the only rationality that seems to exist is enslaved to the system-internal logics? The two authors indirectly answer to the first question by claiming that imperial power, though omnipresent, is actually unable to resolve the issues of peace and justice, so that it is destined to remain intrinsically unstable.[66] However, when it comes to the analysis of the social movements that should stand for the alternative, their discourse—though covering a significant part of the trilogy—becomes quite indistinct. The requests—such as a universal income for all and a general right to reappropriation—might be ambitious, but are also unsupported by any reasonable consideration on how they could be implemented.[67] In addition, the social groups that should usher in a new era form a rather inhomogeneous ensemble made of "a potentially infinite number of classes ... based not only on economic differences but also on those of race, ethnicity, geography, gender, sexuality, and other factors".[68] Yet, being united by the hardships of an undeniable condition of injustice does not imply per se a unity of intents and a clarity of perspective. Moreover, the reference to common goods—be they natural or social—as the values at the basis of the new "commonwealth",[69] though quite justifiable in principle, ultimately goes lost in the mist of political rhetoric, while lacking a stringent analysis of what those goods are and how they could concretely be protected. Finally, as regards the means of the transition from imperial power to the new "commonwealth", the only clear claim made by the authors is that it must be a revolution.[70] Instead, they do not take a definite position either on whether this process should be guided by a vanguard or be spontaneous, or on the peaceful or necessarily violent character of the social change.[71]

Concluding, whereas it is undeniable that the present world order is largely—even if not uniquely—defined by injustice and oppression, Hardt and Negri's focusing on the negative dimension of order ultimately blurs the sight of alternatives. In other words, if order is absolutely negative, then every kind of negation of it—no matter of which kind: "frontal assault, ... sabotage, withdrawal from collaboration, countercultural practices, and generalizes disobedience"—[72]becomes, without any need for further justification, an appropriate step towards a better future. In the end, within the horizon of absolute negation, no reasonable defence of social and political alternatives is required.

### 7.2.2 The Third World Approach to International Law

In his manifesto for a Third World Approach to International Law (TWAIL), Bhupinder S. Chimni criticizes the present world order, as it is enshrined in International law, in a no less severe way than Hardt and Negri. Yet, the difference—which is destined to have significant consequences as regards the formulation of alternative proposals—is that, while the target of Hardt and Negri's criticism is "order" in itself inasmuch as it is based on biopolitical processes of self-reproduction of power, Chimni points the finger at a specific kind of order, namely *Western* order. Consequently, the concept of order is not dismissed as a whole; rather, a different type of order is not only possible but also desirable, provided it is purged from its current First World biases. Whereas Chimni's initial scepticism against order and his critical look at the Western tradition are implicitly, but arguably rooted in postmodern thinking, the propositional part of his analysis and, in particular, the dialectic move that leads his discourse from the negation of the present, flawed situation to the description of a better one, is unquestionably derived from the Marxist approach to social criticism.

Moving on to the contents of the manifesto, Chimni starts by addressing the question whether it makes any sense to speak of a Third World in the current situation and due to the huge differences among the countries that are generally subsumed under that label. His answer is insofar affirmative as it is possible to identify a number of nations which are "bound and united" by the "structures and processes of global capitalism", which ultimately are the same "structures and processes that produced colonialism and have now spawned neo-colonialism" in the era of globalization.[73] The mechanism of neo-colonialism pinpointed by Chimni refers, in part, to legal systems established to secure economic and financial transactions to the advantage of the most powerful countries. This first dimension of neo-colonialism includes the internationalization of property rights,[74] trade law,[75] supra-state control of national currencies,[76] the Lex mercatoria,[77] and the internationalization of the labour market.[78] The second group of measures aims at the creation of a post-national jurisdiction with the purpose of weakening the sovereignty of national adjudications, and comprises extra-territorial jurisdiction—i.e., the cases in which a state claims to have judicial authority even with respect to non-nationals and as regards actions carried out outside its territory—as well as international tribunals hierarchically located above domestic courts.[79] The third set of neo-colonial instruments is made of those normative frameworks and concrete actions through which international organizations and powerful states attempt to impose a political and moral model of society on the individual nations. Imposing democracy[80] and human rights,[81] as well as a certain idea of good governance,[82] belongs to this category.

Whereas Chimni is surely right in highlighting the imbalance of power that has characterized all developments triggered by globalization, an important distinction should nonetheless be made. On the one hand, indeed, we have measures that weaken the sovereignty of the less powerful countries essentially in order to better allow the particularistic maximization of payoffs either by private actors or by the hegemonic nations. This is the case of the instruments that have been inserted in the first above-mentioned category. On the other hand, however, the second and third sets of measures maintain the commitment to a universalistic understanding of order. As a matter of fact, it is at least questionable to put democracy, human rights and international courts on the same level as the Lex mercatoria or the internationalization of property rights, which have the explicit task of protecting one-sided interests, not common goods, and where shared advantage come possibly into play only as the result of some kind of "invisible hand"—in many cases, of an extremely *invisible* hand. Yet, universalistic measures aiming at the safeguard of common goods such as democratic participation, the rule of law and essential human rights—if they were not only to be the deceitful disguise of particularistic egoism—must be really inclusive, in the sense that they have to take into account the voices of all those involved. It is at this point that the fundamental contribution of the TWAIL emerges according to Chimni. Through "non-violent means" which exclude "all manner of dogmatic thinking and undemocratic practices",[83] Third World social and political actors should push for an agenda that takes into due account the requests of the less powerful countries.

The practices of Third World actors imply, above all, a strenuous resistance against neo-colonialism. In the view of the TWAIL, however, the actions aiming at negating the given order do not exhaust the TWAIL's political programme and—in contrast to Hardt and Negri' position—do not even make up the main part of it. If it is clear that, in Chimni's perspective, present order is profoundly flawed, no doubt can be raised on the fact either that it can and should be amended largely from within, and not simply rejected and substituted, from outside, with something completely different—no matter how obscure and indefinite in its contents. Following the critical approach of the TWAIL, therefore, the essential structures of international law should be maintained, but with some fundamental changes.[84] The first step consists in increasing transparency and accountability of international institutions as an initial measure to "push forward the global democracy agenda".[85] Secondly, accountability should be also required from transnational corporations, for instance by firmly demanding the adoption of codes of conduct that include the protection of human rights as well as by adopting boycott of goods and by making use of shareholders rights in case of corporations which do not abide by those standards. Thirdly, sovereignty should be reconceived as referring to peoples and not to states. Fourthly, the language of human rights has to be used to protect the most vulnerable as well as to guarantee the mobility of human bodies. Fifthly, sustainable development must be put to the fore. Sixthly, and lastly, international law should comprise provisions to protect monetary sovereignty. Basically, from the perspective of the TWAIL, international order can live up to its cosmopolitan expectations only to the condition that it gives up its particularistic biases and embrace a truly inclusive approach.

### 7.2.3  Feminist Theory

The way in which feminist theory addresses the questions of domestic and international order and its limits has much in common with the TWAIL. In both cases, in particular, the traditional idea of order is criticized because of its biases and replaced by a different understanding of the "well-ordered society", which has to include the perspectives of discriminated social groups. While from the point of view of the TWAIL the perspective that has to be introduced into a discourse about a non-curtailed and, thus, truly universalistic cosmopolitan order is the one that emerges from the Third World, for the feminist theory it is the standpoint of women that has to be taken into due account.

Yet, which are the characteristics of the patriarchal or male-dominated idea of order? And, then, how can women's claims be brought into play, and with which result? To clarify the first question, Catharine MacKinnon—in her highly influential book *Toward a Feminist Theory of the State* of 1989—first distinguishes between sex and gender.[86] The existence of the two sexes is simply a fact of nature—and so are their biological differences too. However, what counts in the social discourse is not that much the biological identity of the sexes—which, on the contrary, is generally rather downplayed or even concealed—but the gender distinction. Gender is a social creation which—on the basis of a natural distinction, but going much further than this, and essentially in a direction unrelated to nature—shapes the identities of women and men with reference to specific roles that they should take in society. With little evidence—or no evidence at all—rooted in biological facts, men are assumed to be power-oriented, self-controlled, sexually active, as well as better at mathematics and, in general, at natural sciences, while women are regarded as submissive and nurturing, thus better suited to caring professions. On that basis, social roles and power are distributed beforehand according to a generalization in which the premises (the natural differences) have little or nothing to do with the conclusions (the attribution of social functions). MacKinnon synthesizes her analysis with the following words:

> In … [the] mainstream epistemologically liberal approach, the sexes are by nature biologically different, therefore socially properly differentiated for some purposes. Upon this natural, immutable, inherent, essential, just, and wonderful differentiation, society and law are thought to have erected some arbitrary, irrational, confining, and distorting distinction.[87]

Forced to always play their cards from a socially weak position, women are given only two possibilities: either they claim the right to be treated like men—i.e., to receive the same social recognition and to be granted the same chances, but thus concealing the specific needs that they may have as *women*—or they ask for protection as the "weaker sex". In both cases, they end up accepting some form of social disadvantage. Those two alternatives—between being treated "like a man" and being protected "as a non-man"—also shape the way in which law against discrimination is conceived and transformed into another brick in the edifice that supports male dominance. In fact, the principle of "sameness" of antidiscrimination law is nothing but a deception insofar as it purports to regard women as the "same" as men without taking into consideration two major factors.[88] First, since the social point of reference is the male gender as well as the often discriminatory power exercised by it, women might have been disadvantaged in their professional careers or in their lives in general. For instance, when a leading position has to be awarded, it is hypocritical to expect from most women the same achievements that might be submitted by men given the huge obstacles that they are likely to meet during their whole lives. Secondly, real differences—like, for example, pregnancy—are simply ignored, although they undeniably introduce inequalities and constraints.[89] In short, "from a feminist perspective, male supremacist jurisprudence erects qualities valued from the male point of view as standards for the proper and actual relation between life and law".[90] The presumption of "sameness" is also what has led to what Hilary Charlesworth calls the "incoherence critique" against feminist theory.[91] According to the criticism expressed by Fernando Teson,[92] the underrepresentation of women in most institutions cannot be considered a form of injustice inasmuch as the principle of democracy is respected and women are not formally restricted from having access to those positions. In this sense, formal democracy should prevail over real equality. However—Charlesworth counters—"formal equality ... offers equality when women and men are in the same position, but it fails to address the underlying causes of sex discrimination".[93] In other words, *formal* equality degenerates into pure deception if the *real* conditions for making use of the opportunities are not put in place.

Following MacKinnon's analysis, in liberal jurisprudence "male forms of power over women are affirmatively embodied as individual rights in law".[94] For instance, women's exploitation which is carried out through pornography is legally protected through the reference to the freedom of speech.[95] Yet, what can be concretely done against the male predominance enshrined in the system of abstract individual rights? Simply, women should raise their voices and express their needs, i.e., the claims that derive from their specific sexual identity. An essential step in this process consists in women taking back the control over their bodies, for example through a redefinition of sexual consent and its negation, namely rape, as well as through a strong defence of the right to abortion.[96] As a result, MacKinnon's alternative jurisprudence inspired by feminism does not aim essentially at laying down a new catalogue of rights—yet, one that is no less fixed than the traditional liberal one—with the intent of inserting women's standpoint into it. Rather—and at this point we can clearly see the influence of postmodernism—she wants to foster an ongoing process of social contestation of the dominant rules. According to the essentially critical and non-systematic approach of postmodernism, MacKinnon is not primarily interested in delivering a static feminist theory of individual rights, but in identifying the ever-changing lines of rupture in which change can be introduced.

While MacKinnon focuses on constitutional law, Charlesworth turns one's attention to international law—with widely comparable results. Indeed, international law is biased, no less than constitutional law, by an inherent predominance of male interests—and, once again in the spirit of postmodernism, the first stage of Charlesworth's investigation aims at de-structuring the status quo:

> feminist analysis of international law involves searching for the silences of the discipline. It means examining the structure and the substance of the international legal system to see how women are incorporated into it.[97]

The results of the inquiry are disillusioning: women are excluded from most economic, religious, political and military systems of power at the international level. Consequently, women's needs are an almost completely blind spot in the theory and practice of international law and relations. In the same vein as in MacKinnon's work, Charlesworth's conclusion is that women should claim more space in international law and relations and that their requests have to gain momentum in theory and praxis. For example, fundamental rights are traditionally protected essentially in the public sphere, in the sense that the state should protect the individuals from harm done by itself or within areas regulated by it. Yet, a large part of the violence against women does not happen in the public, but in the private domain. As a consequence, a feminist theory of human rights must commit to overcoming the usual public/private divide and ask for the full implementation of individual rights also in the context of family life. Once again, however, the outcome of the process of women's inclusion is not defined in all details, but large room is left to the social, political and cultural contestations—or struggles for recognition—that might develop in the near and far future. In a last remark, Charlesworth cautions against any form of "feminist essentialism", i.e., against the idea that women have universally and unhistorically the same inherent qualities and needs, while calling for a multicultural dialogue in search of overlapping areas.[98] This last consideration makes clear how much some strands of feminist critique have in common with the idea of cultural and legal pluralism, to which we now turn our attention.

## 7.3 The Break of Unitary Order as a Chance for Individual Self-realization

In the first track of their *Meddle* album of 1971, the British rock band Pink Floyd seems to take up the epistemological programme of postmodernism. After a famous intro with a rousing double bass line, a heavily distorted voice pronounces the sentence: "One of these days I am going to cut you into little pieces". This is precisely what postmodernism wanted to do with modern subjectivity: to cut it into little pieces. However, whereas the voice of the music track counterbalances the rather energizing atmosphere of the track with an undoubtedly menacing undertone, thus expressing the ambiguity of the situation, no negative feeling is left in postmodern thinking: de-structuring the strong subjectivity of modern philosophy is the unavoidable condition for freedom and self-realization of the concrete individualities and social groups. Made free from the aspiration to an all-encompassing totality, the self-realization of the distinct components of society—be they individuals or social groups—take various forms, which correspond to the different theories of social order that may be considered inspired by this branch of postmodernism.

### 7.3.1 Legal Pluralism

Postmodern philosophy disaggregated the unitary edifice of modern knowledge by asserting that there is not only *one* truth, to be universally recognized, but a *plurality of truths*, each of them related to a specific context of interaction. This assumption made its entry into legal theory through the introduction of the notion and the praxis of *legal pluralism*. The novelty introduced by the approach of legal pluralism into legal theory is underlined by Nico Krisch. In his passionate and eloquent plea, pluralism is presented as a "break",[99] thus—in epistemological terms— as a paradigmatic revolution which overcomes the old-fashioned idea of the unity of the legal system,[100] paving the way to the acknowledgement of diversity.[101] National constitutionalism is criticized because it "not only fails to include but also fails to deliver".[102] As regards the first issue, "domestic constitutionalism, which places the national community at the centre of the legal and political universe [...] cannot reflect [the] broader constituency" that "goes well beyond the national community": therefore, "on transboundary issues, it remains underinclusive".[103] And, referring to the second point, "domestic constitutionalism [...] would require us to withdraw from, rather than extend, effective postnational decision-making structures in order to safeguard control by domestic political processes".[104] Criticism is then broadened to comprehend cosmopolitan or postnational constitutionalism as well, insofar as it is accused "to provide continuity with the domestic constitutionalist tradition by construing an overarching legal framework that determines the relationships of the different levels of law and the distribution of power among their institutions".[105] On contrast, pluralism is adaptable and enables us to adopt a highly flexible system of checks and balances which can fit into the postnational legal system with its heterarchical character.[106] Last but not least, legal pluralism not only defines a theoretical instrument able to describe the present state of the art but also depicts what can be regarded as a normatively attractive perspective.[107]

By welcoming the coexistence of distinct and non-hierarchically connected legal systems in a sphere that comprises the domestic as well as the international domain, the theory of legal pluralism also acknowledges that these postnational legal systems interact and even overlap with one another. More concretely, "using pluralism, we can conceive of a legal system as both autonomous and permeable; outside norms (both state and nonstate) affect the system but do not dominate it fully".[108] This creates a new phenomenon, which Paul Schiff Berman defines as "jurisdictional hybridity",[109] i.e., a plurality of normative spaces in which norms from different sources—all claiming to be valid and applicable at the same time and to the same cases—contend with one another for priority. Within the context of jurisdictional hybridity, no resort to hierarchy is possible in order to clarify the respective rank of norms, so that the outcome must be seen as the always contestable result of an open-end exchange of arguments. Berman refers to four examples of the phenomenon, the first of which are the "state versus state conflicts of norms".[110] Unlike the traditional jurisdictional disputes between states, contemporary interstate conflicts—due to globalization and to the development of the cyberspace—have a much broader and more deep-going mutual impact on internal forms of interaction and regulation. The problems related to the territorial reach of free speech regulations—as shown by the cases referring to the removal of contents from the internet—demonstrate that solutions cannot easily be found by drawing boundaries between legal systems, but require an innovative approach that mutually takes the position of the counterpart into due account. The second example is the "state versus international conflicts of norms", where the international dimension—as in the case of the International Court of Justice (ICJ) or, even more, of the European Court of Human Rights (ECHR)—is understood in a way that "may have impact on various entities within a nation state", so that "the international forums can provide a source of alternative norms that people then use as leverage in their local settings".[111] Thirdly, Berman introduces the "nation states versus substate conflicts of norms", in which tensions between regional unities and the central state—in particular in fields such as environmental regulation, foreign affairs and immigration—are characterized by an increasing assertiveness of the former, even to the point of bypassing the latter.[112] The last form of jurisdictional hybridity referred to by Berman are the "state versus nonstate conflicts of norms",[113] which seem to blur—arguably for the first time in modern Western legal history—the well-established distinction between formal laws and non-formal social norms.[114]

### 7.3.2 Neo-Liberalism in the Theory of International Relations and in International Law

According to postmodern thinking, the de-construction of the unity of modern subjectivity and its disaggregation into a plurality of partial orders makes possible for the real individuals to find their specific opportunity for self-realization. In the doctrine of legal pluralism, this chance is implemented to a large extent in what we can call a "communitarian" way.

In other words—and with the only exception of the reference to the international community, in which individual belonging is never exclusive—self-realization happens through some kind of *organic* relationship between the individual and a certain normative community. Against this background, the enhancement of opportunities for self-realization depends on the fact that a much larger number of such communities are recognized in their self-reliance and dignity than before. The novelty of the approach is particularly evident if we consider the revaluation of non-statist communities as point of reference for individual identity and normative belonging. Yet, even if we take into account rather traditional political communities—such as states or substate units—the chances for self-realization are implemented *within* the normative communities and as the result of the multiplication of their number, and not in the space *between* the normative communities and, thus, in the possibility for the individuals to choose to which they want to adhere or even in the option to adhere to more than just one of them. This second alternative takes shape in a further strand of political and legal theory influenced by postmodernism, namely in the *neo-liberal* theory of international relations and international law.

Within the doctrine of international relations, the "liberal" strand, as its supporters call it—or "neo-liberal" strand, as we should rather define it, due to the differences if compared to Locke's and John Stuart Mill's classical approaches—is opposed to the powerful school of realism.[115] Its main target of criticism is the so-called billiard ball conception of the state, according to which states have to be conceived of as closed units. Two central assumptions are made on that basis. First, neither international relations nor international law can or should look into the internal social and institutional mechanisms of the state; rather, they must take it as a unity, which is presumed to be exhaustively represented by its executive power. Secondly, states interact with one another as separate units, without any overlapping or interweaving of social or institutional structures. The point, here, is not to utterly deny that some kind of overlapping or interweaving might happen under certain circumstances, but simply to say that these phenomena are not relevant enough for political and legal theory or for praxis to be taken into serious consideration. The position of neo-liberalism on those points—as it has been developed by Andrew Moravcsik[116] and Anne-Marie Slaughter—is quite the contrary. Far from being irrelevant in the international arena, the way in which a state is internally organized has a deep impact on the decisions that it takes vis-à-vis the outside world. Thus, it is important for political and legal research to pay more attention to how the internal structures of the different polities—be these structures social, political, institutional, economic, legal or cultural—interact with one another beyond the borders of the single state. For this purpose, the state must be "disaggregated",[117] which impacts in particular on its most outstanding characteristic, namely sovereignty. Indeed, the "disaggregated" sovereignty loses its traditional meaning, which "would shift from autonomy from outside interference to the capacity to participate in transgovernmental networks of all types".[118] This capacity pertains to all executive-administrative, judicial and legislative bodies which, in a neo-liberal perspective, are liberated from the rigid obligation to respect the priorities of the institutional hierarchy.

In the neo-liberal understanding of international law and relations, the state, while continuing to play an important role,[119] gives up the function of the primary actor in the international system in favour of "individuals and groups acting in domestic and transnational civil society".[120] According to Slaughter's "bottom-up" view of the political phenomenon, actions carried out by individual states are not the expression of their ideological and institutional unity. Nor do they provide evidence for that unity. Rather, the individual states' activities are to be seen as the results of the conflicts of interests that are displayed by those individuals and groups that make up the respective domestic civil societies. Slaughter's neo-liberal theory is therefore different from traditional international law for two main reasons: first, it overcomes the idea of individual states as the only—or, at least, as by far the most important—actors of international law and relations; secondly, it identifies the reason for their conflicts not, as usual, in an unbalance of power, but in the inhomogeneity of the interests, respectively, dominant in their societies.[121] Consequently, whereas the striving for dominance by individual states has always an element of uncompromising absoluteness, a composition of the diverging interests becomes much easier to achieve peacefully if the states are disaggregated and we can take the bottom-up perspective—obviously on condition that in every state those forces and interests prevail that, in a classically liberal perspective, aim at building up synergies well beyond national borders. Consistently with the neo-liberal focus on a transnational civil society, Slaughter explicitly justifies humanitarian interventions, at least under certain circumstances.

Instead of being exclusively made of treaties stipulated between states, neo-liberal international law is expected to be created—at least in part—directly "from below", i.e., immediately by individuals and social groups. Slaughter explicitly states that "international law [...] identifies multiple bodies of rules, norms and processes that contribute to international order, beginning with voluntary codes of conduct adopted by individuals and corporate actors operating in transnational society".[122] In other words, these same actors—whose autonomy of action is itself the result of the disaggregation of the traditional states, being therefore located outside and beyond the statist unitary and hierarchical structure—have rightly begun to create by means of contracts a significant part of the new *corpus juris* of international law. Interestingly, they are assumed to do so in a way which is independent of and parallel to the actions of governments. Consistently with the liberal legacy, Slaughter entrusts the function of founding a relevant proportion of the rules of the new *corpus juris* of international law to the private law instrument of contract—with one difference, however: while in classical contractualism the founding contract is essentially brought into play in order to establish a public law which is adequately legitimated by the citizens, the neo-liberal perspective aims at overthrowing the historical predominance of the public sphere over the private.

This aspect clearly emerges when it comes to the description of the three levels of the neo-liberal system of international law.[123] Indeed, at the first level—which comprises the Lex mercatoria as one of its most important components—we have precisely those private actors, more specifically companies, that give themselves a set of rules to regulate their interaction in the transnational context. As a confirmation of the tendency to reverse the usual hierarchy of public and private, this level seems to be the most relevant in Slaughter's view: "from the perspective of a liberal theory of international relations, [these sources of law] ... may be the most important and effective ..., since they directly regulate the primary actors in the international system without intermediation".[124] The second layer of international law according to the neo-liberal approach is made of regulations stipulated at the transnational—or, rather, transgovernmental—level by executive agencies. These are established by states, operate through the interaction of their administrative organs and are largely independent of ex post parliamentary control. As a result, their soft law mechanisms do not generally need to be ratified following the internal procedures of each single state, but count as regulatory benchmarks to be respected so as to avoid being sidelined in transnational interactions. The third and last level consists of "the traditional sources of public international law – treaties and customary law".[125]

It is important to outline, at this point, that the neo-liberal project has a descriptive and a prescriptive moment at the same time. In other words, it aims at a more accurate description—if compared with the "billiard ball" theories—of what is really happening in the field of international law and relations. Yet, at the same time, it also claims that the new state of things has a significant normative advantage. Indeed, if we assume individual freedom as the most essential moral and social value, Slaughter's "new world order" emancipates individuals and social groups from the constraints of statist control, enabling them to better implement their priorities. Furthermore, her bottom-up reconstruction of the system of international law is based on the conviction that most international problems have national roots, in the sense that they originate from an imbalance in the internal relations between the state and some economic-social groups—characterized by the dominance of the former over the latter—or directly from the preference accorded by the political power to those interests which are more difficult to reconcile with peaceful transnational interactions. War, ecological crises, oppression, poverty—and, we could add, terrorism and pandemics—are assumed to arise not from civil society, which tends to a peaceful coexistence, but from the delusion of omnipotence that captures the holders of a private interest when they think to be capable of making it coincide with the public good, so that it can be supported by the use of public power. Therefore, the primary task of a neo-liberal theory of international law consists in reshaping national institutions to the advantage of civil society, considering this as the best guarantee for peace, security and cooperation.[126] Nonetheless, the responsibilities of individual states should not be downplayed. Accordingly, Slaughter rejects the idea that individual states should be submitted to some form of cosmopolitan order:

> recognizing the state as still at least the primary actor in the international system, but conceiving of it in terms of its relationship with its citizens, … means focusing rules and remedies at the national rather than the international level, or at the international level as supplemental to the national level.[127]

Consequently, she pleads for a "universal jurisdiction", founded on a synergy with national courts and on the maximum possible guarantee of access of individuals to international courts, rather than for an international jurisdiction with its claim of hierarchical and normative superiority. Even in the field of international criminal law, she insists on the necessity to acknowledge the primary jurisdiction of the national courts, supported and only exceptionally integrated or replaced by international courts. The overall picture that emerges is that of an integrated system, which leaves the maximum space to national civil societies, submitted in the first instance to an internal jurisdiction—though compatible with international standards—and only in a secondly step to international tribunals, to which a complementary function is reserved.

### 7.3.3 Global Governance

As mentioned in the previous section, the second stage of the neoliberal system of international law consists, according to its advocates, in a network of international organizations, composed of representatives of national governments, but largely independent from domestic hierarchies in their decision-making processes.[128] Because it is generally assumed that global processes like labour and financial markets, migration, ecological crises, terrorism, organized crime, technological and scientific innovation, exploitation of natural resources, pandemics, etc., cannot be managed by domestic powers and need international coordination, the network of international organizations is what should constitute the basis for a global governance capable of properly meeting the challenges. In Slaughter's view, the public dimension of global governance is deeply interwoven with the self-regulation of private actors, so that the line that should separate the two spheres is not perfectly clear-cut. Other advocates of global governance, instead, focus unequivocally on its *public* dimension, which is expressed, in particular, by International Public Authorities (IPA).[129] In this case, the "publicness" of the policies that lie at the basis of global governance is assumed to be guaranteed by the fact that IPAs are expected to pursue shared interests and the common good.[130] Here, however, the question arises about the definition of the common good and the ways of its realization. Although the theorists of IPA also refer to substantial criteria like freedom or the rule of law, the most relevant feature to ensure the "publicness" of the IPA policies is lastly just formal, namely the very fact that IPAs are endowed with a public mandate, derived from public power, to act for the common good.[131]

The circular argument referring to the alleged publicness of global governance calls to mind the related issue regarding its legitimacy. In general, its theorists hardly pay any serious attention to full-fledged democratic procedures of legitimation of international organizations. Rather, they tend to circumvent the question by digging out some less demanding alternatives. The first resorts to the rule of law which would inform and control the procedures of global governance. In fact, transnational governance triggers the development of what has been defined as "global administrative law"[132] which—not unlike the task of administrative law in the domestic realm—establishes the legal framework for the measures that transnational executive organizations take in order to guarantee the control of relevant phenomena, while preventing them, at the same time, from overstepping their competences.[133] It has also been argued that a certain degree of accountability, which can be achieved through global administrative law, is actually the only affective way to convincingly address the legitimacy deficit in the transnational realm.[134] A second strategy involves the introduction of a higher transparency of the decision-making processes of international organizations. Indeed, insofar as documents are made accessible to the stakeholders, a discussion can be triggered on which are the best policies in order to address transnational issues in the most successful and legitimate way.[135] More transparency builds therefore the basis for the third element of the global governance programme for the increase of legitimacy, namely the informal and diffuse involvement of the transnational civil society.[136] The members of the transnational civil society can then close the circle of the proposed measures by activating the guarantees provided by global administrative law.

Taken together, thus, the alternatives to the traditional understanding of democratic legitimacy build a coherent unity which, nonetheless, lacks a substantial feature of the non-curtailed view of democratic legitimation. The difference is that, while in traditional democratic processes it is made sure that all individuals involved can really participate in the decision-making processes, postmodern deliberation keeps the gate open to participation, but does not take any concrete measure to guarantee this to happen. For instance, what is the legitimacy gain if all documents can formally be accessed, but not every individual involved knows it and many do not have the means to access? Surely, alternative methods to ensure legitimacy are increasingly important in a complex world, but they cannot adequately replace the old democratic principle according to which only *volenti non fit iniuria*. In other words, only a measure supported by the real possibility of participation of all those involved and by the consent of at least a majority of them is properly legitimated. Instead, without a truly democratic counterbalance, the alternative proposals end up backing—to some extent, in disguise—the idea that the backbone of global governance's legitimacy is ultimately to be sought in an irreflexive and lastly passive acceptance of its measures. This approach can be traced back to Max Weber's idea of the "rational" legitimacy of public power.[137] Along with the "traditional" and the "charismatic", the "rational" form of legitimacy is one of the three variants in which public power is assumed to be justified in the eyes of those who have to abide by its rules. As already mentioned above in Sect. 6.1, according to Weber, "rational" legitimacy is typical for the modern state and has three main characteristics: an effective legal system to regulate social interactions; an efficient and hierarchical bureaucracy; and, finally, the assumption that the holders of power and, in general, the members of the bureaucratic apparatus have superior skills and knowledge than the common citizens. These are the core contents of what can be defined as a *technocratic* understanding of public power.

Implicitly leaning on Weber's analysis, Fritz Wilhelm Scharpf introduced in 1999 the distinction between the "input-oriented legitimacy" and the "output-oriented legitimacy".[138] The first refers to the participation of the citizens in the creation of the norms that govern their lives, corresponding therefore to what Abraham Lincoln defined as "government by the people". In contrast, the second form of legitimacy addresses a largely passive acceptance of authority, due mainly to the belief that this acts in the common interest, thus accomplishing what has been called—again by Lincoln—"government for the people". While the first understanding insists on the active involvement of the governed, the second focuses on their tacit consent, at least as long as the measures taken by the authorities are perceived as beneficial to the self-realization of individuals in the sphere of their negative freedom as well as to the improvement of their living conditions. In conclusion, global governance is erected on two pillars, which are strictly interwoven with one another: a technocratic conception of public power, and a post-democratic or output-oriented vision of legitimacy. Given these premises, it is not surprising that the concept of "government", which—at least in the democratic tradition—implies participation, is substituted by "governance", which rather suggests that social life should be regulated by those who are presumed—wrongly, in most cases—to know best.

### 7.3.4 Legal Formalism

A crucial aspect of postmodern philosophy consists in claiming that utterances do not have any object-related or inherent truth content, but exclusively derive their meaning from the context in which they are used. This assertion can have two different interpretations. According to the first—and less radical—the claim means that no *universal* truth is identifiable, but only *contextual* truths, depending on the limited community of interpreters. This is how postmodern epistemology made its entry into legal theory through the doctrine of legal pluralism. The second—and more far-going—interpretation denies even the possibility of a contextual truth, making the meaning of utterances a matter of primarily individual choices.[139] The second approach, which arguably goes even beyond the intentions of the later Wittgenstein and is probably derived—at least indirectly—from Foucault's uncompromising critical attitude, has been introduced into legal theory by Martti Koskenniemi. Undoubtedly, the results of his inquiry are quite destructive for the epistemological content of the law. Indeed, his analysis unveils what he calls the "substantive indeterminacy" of law,[140] in particular of international law. This happens by leading the international law discourse back to couples of concepts, or to "binary oppositions",[141] which appear to be—at least at first glance—opposites, so that just one of them should be presumed to be correctly applied in a specific situation. Thus, given the opposite couple of legal concept A–B and given that they should be employed to the state of affairs X, if it can be justified to apply A, then the application of B to X should be regarded as false. Resorting to one of the examples proposed by Koskenniemi, the principles of self-determination and of *uti possidetis* build such a "binary opposition", in which the application of one principle should exclude the use of the other. Yet, the reduction of the international law discourse to such a seemingly well-ordered linguistic structure turns out to be an illusion, according to Koskenniemi's interpretation, for two main reasons. First, the concepts forming "binary oppositions", although assumed to rule out overlapping applications, are in fact, from the semantic perspective, no less mutually dependent on each other than mutually exclusive. Going back to the former example, as Koskenniemi claims, "self-government is only possible within a fixed territory; and the authority of existing power can only be justified by reference to some idea of self-government".[142]

The second reason for the indeterminacy of international law discourse does not refer to the meaning of its concepts in their relationship to each other but rather to their role, as concepts, in connection to the world outside. The explanation of this question requires some general considerations on the relationship between the law, more specifically international law, and the field of human interaction for the regulation of which it is conceived, in this case the interactions in the international arena. According to Koskenniemi, international law argumentations aim at the same time at two contrasting goals: "concreteness" and "normativity". By "concreteness" it is meant that the law has "to be verifiable, or justifiable, independently of what anyone might think that the law *should* be".[143] Thus, a proposition of the international law discourse is regarded as "concrete" if it does not just take into account but thoroughly reflects the real conditions of the actors' interactions within the international arena. On the other hand, "normativity" means that the law "is to be applicable even against a state (or other legal subject) which *opposed* its application to itself".[144] In other words, it belongs to the concept of law, and of international law as well, that it may—and in many cases should—oppose the preferences of the involved actors. The problem is that these two essential aims of international law—or, we could say, of law in general—namely concreteness and normativity do not just oppose each other, which is quite self-evident, but also always imply each other. Indeed, every norm, rule or principle, as well as every argument of international law has to be "concrete" so as to be *effective*. However, if its "concreteness" turned out to be nothing more than the formal expression—and justification—of the real conditions of power, then the language of international law would lose that counter-factual dimension which is essential to the very concept of the law, becoming a mere *apology* of the existing state of social and political interactions and a defence of the injustice that may grow out of it. On the other hand, if the legal discourse only insists, in order to maintain its "normativity", on its opposition to reality, largely ignoring how this can have a relevant impact on the law, it degenerates into what Koskenniemi calls a sheer *utopia*. Therefore, in order to be "concrete" the international law discourse always runs the risk of being apologetic— and, in order not to lose its "normativity", it is structurally in danger of becoming utopian.

The indeterminacy of law, thus, is the result of a twofold contradiction: the first one depends on the mutual reference of (allegedly) opposite concepts; and the second one is due to the inherent attitude of the international law discourse, which swings between apology and utopia. As regards the second contradiction, it could also be admitted that it is part of the most essential social function of the law, the norms of which *must be counter-factual* so as to bring about order in spontaneous and therefore rather disordered social interactions, and at the same time *cannot ignore the conditions of reality* so as to avoid ineffectiveness and, thus, uselessness. Yet, the way that contemplates the admission of the inescapability of tensions between legal discourse and reality is not the one chosen by Koskenniemi. Nor does he consider the missing "objectivism" of the international law discourse amendable through a reform of its epistemology and its better adaptation to the world outside. Indeed, according to Koskenniemi's epistemology, the legal discourse is evidently lacking proper truth content; yet, this deficit cannot be resolved by an improvement of the theoretical organon of the legal discourse simply because no universal rationality can be found in that world of social interaction either, to which the law should give rules. Not just the language of the law, thus, is devoid of truth content, but our knowledge in general—according to Koskenniemi's approach—does not lead to any proposition of universal validity.

The consequence of Koskenniemi's epistemological scepticism is that the legal discourse can only be a question of "interpretation", for which we cannot claim any solid rational foundation that could make it acceptable for every reasonable human being.[145] The criticism of the universalistic claim of the legal discourse in general, and of the international law discourse in particular, does not lead however to sheer nihilism. Indeed, Koskenniemi does not reject the idea that some experiences may occur which are not characterized by mere contingency but, on the contrary, assume a kind of universal scope.[146] From the postmodern standpoint, however, this unassuming universality is not based on abstract ontological, moral or epistemological principles, but is derived from the concrete experience of vulnerability shared by all individuals. According to Koskenniemi, artistic expression is probably the most suitable way to give voice to the universal scope of a humanity made of concrete human beings.[147] But legal discourse can also play a role in accomplishing this task. In fact, due to its *formalism*,[148] the law makes possible that, "engaging in legal discourse, persons recognize each other as carriers of rights and duties" which "belong to every member of the community *in that position*". Through the law—Koskenniemi adds—"what otherwise would be a mere private violation, a wrong done to *me*, a violation of *my interest*, is transformed... into a violation against *everyone in my position*, a matter of concern for the political community itself".[149] The formalism to which Koskenniemi refers is of course something quite different from the formal rationalism of modern philosophy, as it has been developed in particular by Kant.[150] Rather, it is a "culture of formalism ... that builds on formal arguments that are available to all under conditions of equality".[151] When they apply the "culture of formalism", the actors of international law, in particular lawyers [and] decision makers, "take a momentary distance from their preferences and ... enter a terrain where these preferences should be justified, instead of taken for granted, by reference to standards that are independent from their particular positions or interests".[152] Among the consequences are "limits to the exercise of power" and the "message ... that those who are in position of strength must be accountable and that those who are weak must be heard and protected".[153] The discourse based on legal formalism involves "professional men and women" who, by engaging "in an argument about what is lawful and what is not, ... are engaged in a politics that imagines the possibility of a community overriding particular alliances and preferences and allowing a meaningful distinction between lawful constraint and the application of naked power".[154]

In line with Koskenniemi's interpretation, the law has no truth content because no universal rationality can be presumed. Nevertheless, we can assume a non-ontological, non-moral and non-epistemological universalism that originates from legal formalism. Against this background, Koskenniemi formulates his conclusive claim: the law, as a result of the fact that it does not refer any longer to a universal rationality, becomes a formal instrument that can be used for quite different purposes. The question on which goal should be pursued by resorting to the formal means of the law actually depends on the personal decision made by the legal professional, so that, in the end, "international law is what international lawyers make of it".[155] Without universal rationality, no universal obligation to freedom, justice, democracy, or to any other value can be objectively justified; only personal preferences can guide legal professionals to commit themselves to these goals. Koskenniemi's epistemological relativism, however, does not end in political indifference or cynicism. Yet, his dedication to the defence of human rights does not rely on reasons of universal validity, but is presented as an unpretentious, though firm, personal and political decision. In fact, Koskenniemi points out that "political views can be held without having to believe in their objectivity and that they can be discussed without having to assume that in the end everybody should agree".[156] Even if we give up—following Koskenniemi's approach—the formulation of a universally valid "method", the "commitment to the whole, to peace and world order" remains.[157] But, insofar as this commitment is now understood as an individual decision and not as a rational principle presumed to be universally valid, law itself, which according to the traditional understanding was thought to be the formal and effective expression of a universal rationality and of a shared truth, cannot but re-modulate and actually reduce its ambitions. Far from being the synthesis of a uniform and compelling normativity, it is now rather a practical instrument for the solution of problems, or "a *practice* of attempting to reach the most acceptable solution in the particular circumstances of the case".[158]

Concluding, Koskenniemi's relativism in epistemological matters and decisionism in political questions leads to the result that the defence of human rights—or of any other value—is not a universal moral duty the accomplishment of which can be demanded from every human being, but a task that committed people take on because of their specific sensibility—or *empathy*—towards the suffering of their fellow humans. As regards the profession of the lawyer, Koskenniemi's approach eventually leads to a plea in favour of the role of legal advisers, who skilfully use the instruments put at their disposal by the formalism of the law in order to suggest solutions for the achievement of what they consider to be "a better society".[159]

## 7.4 THE DECLINE OF NORMATIVITY AND LEGITIMACY

The postmodern turn highlighted—essentially for the first time in the Western history of thinking—that order is not necessarily synonymous to the best possible organization of society, but can imply, at least under certain circumstances, oppression and limitation of individual self-realization. As a result of this unprecedented awareness, authors influenced by postmodernism developed different alternative strategies. Some reacted to the dangers deriving from an oppressive order by basically ennobling any kind of attack on the established well-ordered society, therefore possibly dignifying rebellious tendencies even in the absence of a clear-cut alternative societal project. Others spotted new chances for the freedom of individuals and social groups in the spaces that were opened as a consequence of the disaggregation of statist power and its substitution through private-public networks. Others again identified the chances for self-realization exclusively within those contexts of negative freedom that are assumed to flourish under the benevolent aegis of a technocratic governance. A fourth strand, then, interpreted the freedom resulting from the postmodern revaluation of pluralism essentially as the possibility to emancipate self-referential normative communities from the all-encompassing idea of well-ordered society, no matter whether this society was identified with the individual state or with the cosmopolis. A fifth variant, finally, utterly dismissed any claim to truth content that might be raised by epistemological communities, thus regarding the justification of action as a question only pertaining to individual preferences.

All these variants have their specific merits—but each of them has its deficits too. First, welcoming the destruction of the present order without figuring out an alternative beforehand, thus leaving the development of new rules exclusively to the social processes that are assumed to carry out the change, does not take into due consideration that order—even if far from perfect—guarantees the predictability of social interactions. Indeed, revolutionary theories before the postmodern turn always contraposed a new—and better—conception of order against the older one. On the contrary, some strands of postmodernism dignify in an unprecedented way the view that the current system of order can be simply dismantled without giving much of a thought to what may happen afterwards. Yet, the chaos that might ensue from a de-structuring of current forms of interactions without having any perspective of a proper replacement can hardly be seen as a promise of better living conditions. Secondly, claiming that freedom is enhanced through the recognition of self-enclosed normative communities, which are made independent of an encompassing rationality, wrongly assumes that individual liberty increases at the same pace as the acknowledgement of collective identity. Instead, the two elements build two largely independent variables, whose development is in many cases inversely proportional. In other words, personal freedom can be hampered by a condition of strong belongingness to a normative community that, insofar as it is self-enclosed, also makes very difficult—if not impossible—for individuals to follow their priorities. Even diversity may be damaged by this attitude because, while pluralism *among* communities may be encouraged, pluralism *within* each single community is often restricted. Thirdly, while according to the individualistic paradigm of modernity legitimacy must be based on the consent of those impacted by the measures taken by the public power, the postmodern concept of technocratic governance seems to rediscover the acquiescent acceptance of the purported competence of rulers who unjustifiably assume to possess epistemic superiority. Fourthly, a similar argument can be made as regards the normativity of rules: following modern criteria, the reference to a firmly established public power made sure that laws were considered distinguished from—and superior to—any other kind of norms. On the contrary, the watering down of normativity standards, introduced by postmodern thinking as a result of the disaggregation of public power and of its intertwining with private interests, runs the risk of putting voluntary and casual codes of conduct in the same class as legitimate and binding parliamentary laws. Fifthly, the claim that linguistic propositions have, at best, a contextual truth content or no truth content at all is linguistically, philosophically and logically hardly sustainable. Accordingly, legal argumentation cannot be reduced to a skilful management of rhetorical instruments in order to force through personal preferences, but has to take objective circumstances as well as logical consistency very seriously.

These critiques do not imply that no important lessons are to be drawn from postmodern thinking. First and foremost, its arguments in favour of an uncompromising and radical form of normative pluralism rule out a simple return to the past: even in case that the re-establishment of some form of an all-encompassing normative structure is envisaged—like in the communicative paradigm of order—this can be pursued only to the condition of a high degree of internal diversity and of a post-traditional and non-hierarchical relationship between the whole and its parts. Moreover, the dark sides and the biases of the old-fashioned concept of order have been pitilessly revealed, so that—once again—an idea of order that aspires to mend the ruptures without appearing backwards-oriented cannot ignore that a just order must include the requests of those, like women and non-Western fellow humans, who have been neglected for too long.

## NOTES

1. Joseph Roth, *Die Flucht ohne Ende*, in: Joseph Roth, *Die Rebellion. Frühe Romane*, Aufbau-Verlag, Berlin/Weimar 1984, 309–428, at 428 (English translation by David Le Vay and Beatrice Musgrave: *Flight Without End*, Peter Owen, London 1977, at 144).
2. Milan Kundera, *Nesmesitná lehkost byti*, 1984 (English translation by Michael Henry Heim: *The Unbearable Lightness of Being*, Faber & Faber, London 1984, at 216).
3. John Irving, *The Cider House Rules* (1985), Ballantine Books, New York 1993.
4. Ibid., at 594 et seq.
5. Ibid., at 219.
6. Kundera, *Nesmesitná lehkost byti*, *supra* note 2 (English: at 305).
7. Ibid. (English: at 242 and seq.).
8. Ibid. (English: at 251 and seq.).
9. Ibid. (English: at 250).
10. Ibid. (English: at 271 et seq.).
11. Ibid. (English: at 118).
12. The concept of "paradigm" at the centre of this research assumes an intersubjective—i.e., a non-solipsistic—understanding of the development of knowledge. See Sect. 1.2.
13. See Sect. 4.4.
14. See Sects. 4.2 and 4.3.
15. Martin Heidegger, *Sein und Zeit* (1927), Niemeyer, Tübingen 1986, § 10, at 47 (English translation by Joan Stambaugh: *Being and Time*, State University of New York Press, 1996, at 44).
16. Søren Kierkegaard, *Enten – Eller* (1843) (English translation of Volume I by David F. Swenson and Lillian M. Swenson: *Either/Or. Volume One*, Humphrey Milford, Oxford University Press, London 1944; English translation of Volume II by Walter Lowrie: *Either/Or. Volume Two*, Humphrey Milford, Oxford University Press, London 1944).
17. Arthur Schopenhauer, *Die Welt als Wille und Vorstellung* (1844; 1st ed. 1818), Diogenes, Zürich 1977 (English translation by E. F. J. Payne: *The World as Will and Representation*, Dover, New York (NY) 1969).
18. Heidegger, *Sein und Zeit*, *supra* note 15, § 45 et seq., at 231 et seq., and § 72, at 372 et seq. (English: at 213 et seq., and at 341 et seq.).
19. Ibid., § 73, at 379 (English: at 347).
20. Ibid. (English: at 347 et seq.).
21. Ibid., § 54 et seq., at 267 et seq. (English: at 247 et seq.).
22. William of Ockham, *Opera philosophica et theologica*, ed. by Gedeon Gál et al., The Franciscan Institute, St. Bonaventure, Allegany (NY) 1967–1988. On nominalism, see: Gonzalo Rodriguez-Pereyra, *Nominalism*

*in Metaphysics*, in: *The Stanford Encyclopedia of Philosophy* (Fall 2011 Edition), Edward N. Zalta (ed.), available at http://plato.stanford.edu/archives/fall2011/entries/nominalism-metaphysics/, accessed 24 March 2020.
23. Ludwig Wittgenstein, *Tractatus Logico-Philosophicus* (1921), in: Ludwig Wittgenstein, *Werkausgabe*, Vol. 1, Suhrkamp, Frankfurt a. M. 1984, 7–85 (English translation by D. F. Pears and B. F. McGuinness, Routledge, London/New York 1961).
24. Ibid., 1.1. et seq., at 11 (English: at 5).
25. Ludwig Wittgenstein, *Philosophische Untersuchungen* [1953], in: Ludwig Wittgenstein, *Werkausgabe*, *supra* note 23, Vol. 1, 225–580, No. 43, at 262 (English translation by G. E. M. Anscombe: *Philosophical Investigations*, Blackwell, Oxford 1958, 1st ed. 1953, at 20).
26. Ibid., at 550 (English: at 212).
27. Donald Davidson, *Problems of Rationality*, Clarendon, Oxford 2004; Donald Davidson, *Subjective, Intersubjective, Objective*, Clarendon, Oxford 2001; Robert Brandom, *Making It Explicit*, Harvard University Press, Cambridge (MA) 1998 (1st ed. 1994); Jürgen Habermas, *Vorstudien und Ergänzungen zur Theorie des kommunikativen Handelns*, Suhrkamp, Frankfurt a. M. 1984 (English translation by Barbara Fultner: *On the Pragmatics of Social Interaction*, The MIT Press, Cambridge (MA) 2001); Jürgen Habermas, *Nachmetaphysisches Denken*, Suhrkamp, Frankfurt a. M. 1988 (English translation by William Mark Hohengarten: *Postmetaphysical Thinking*, The MIT Press, Cambridge (MA) 1992); Jürgen Habermas, *Wahrheit und Rechtfertigung*, Suhrkamp, Frankfurt a. M. 2004, 1st ed. 1999 (English translation by Barbara Fultner: *Truth and Justification*, The MIT Press, Cambridge (MA).
28. See Sect. 2.2.2.
29. Benedictus de [Baruch] Spinoza, *Ethica ordine geometrico demonstrata* (1677), in: Benedictus de [Baruch] Spinoza, *Opera*, Carl Gebhardt ed., Winters, Heidelberg 1924), Vol. 2 (English translation by Samuel Shirley, in: Spinoza, *Complete Works*, Michael L. Morgan ed., Hackett, Indianapolis 2002, 213–382, at 363).
30. Sigmund Freud, *Das Unbehagen in der Kultur* (1930), in: Sigmund Freud, 1974, *Kulturtheoretische Schriften*, Fischer, Frankfurt a. M. 1974, 191–270 (English translation by James Strachey: *Civilization and Its Discontents*, Norton & Company, New York 1962).
31. Sigmund Freud, *Das Ich und das Es* (1923), in: Sigmund Freud, 1992, *Das Ich und das Es. Metapsychologische Schriften*, Fischer, Frankfurt a. M. 1992, 251–295 (English translation by Joan Riviere and James Strachey: *The Ego and the Id*, Norton & Company, New York 1960).

32. Michel Foucault, *The Subject and Power*, in: Hubert L. Dreyfus and Paul Rabinow (eds.), *Michel Foucault: Beyond Structuralism and Hermeneutics*, Chicago University Press, Chicago 1983 (1st ed. 1982), 208–226.
33. Michel Foucault, *L'ordre du discours* (1970), Gallimard, Paris 1971, at 10 (English translation in: Robert Young (ed.), *Untying the Text: A Post-Structuralist Reader*, Routledge & Kegal Paul, Boston/London/Henley 1981, 48–78, at 52).
34. Ibid., at 49 (English: at 65).
35. Michel Foucault, *Histoire de la sexualité, I: La volonté de savoir*, Gallimard, Paris 1976 (English translation by Robert Hurley: *The History of Sexuality. Volume I: An Introduction*, Pantheon Books, New York 1978).
36. Michel Foucault, *Les mots et les choses*, Gallimard, Paris 1966 (English translation: *The Order of Things: An Archaeology of the Human Sciences*, Routledge, London/New York 2002, 1st ed. 1989).
37. Michel Foucault, *Histoire de la folie à l'âge classique*, Gallimard, Paris 1961 (English translation by Jonathan Murphy and Jean Khalfa: *History of Madness*, Routledge, London/New York 2006); Michel Foucault, *Surveiller et punir*, Gallimard, Paris 1975 (English translation by Alan Sheridan: *Discipline and Punish: The Birth of the Prison*, Vintage Books, New York 1995, 1st ed. 1977).
38. Foucault, *Histoire de la sexualité*, *supra* note 35, at 124 (English: at 94).
39. Manfred Frank, *Was ist Neostrukturalismus?*, Suhrkamp, Frankfurt a. M. 1984 (1st ed. 1983), at 220.
40. Michel Foucault, *L'archéologie du savoir*, Gallimard, Paris 1969, at 175 et seq. (English translation: *The Archaeology of Knowledge*, Routledge 2002, 1st ed. 1972, at 150 et seq.).
41. Hans Herbert Kögler, *Michel Foucault*, Metzler, Stuttgart/Weimar 1994, at 44.
42. Ibid., at 7.
43. Foucault, *L'archéologie du savoir*, *supra* note 40, at 74 (English: at 60 et seq.).
44. Michael Hardt and Antonio Negri, *Empire*, Harvard University Press, Cambridge (MA) 2000, at 3 et seq.
45. I use the term "supra-state" although Hardt and Negri employ, in their book, the word "supranational". The reason is that, to avoid confusion, I prefer to leave "supranational" for the description of forms of integration at the continental level, such as the European Union, whereas what is meant, here, is the global spreading of a legal system *sui generis*. "Supra-state" only indicates that the global system of laws is located beyond the nation states, without any positive ethical or political qualification. Precisely this kind of positive qualification is generally included, on the contrary, in the reference to "cosmopolitanism".
46. Hardt/Negri, *Empire*, *supra* note 44, at 10.

47. Ibid., at 41.
48. Ibid., at 8 et seq.
49. Ibid., at 12 et seq.
50. Ibid., at 16.
51. Ibid., at 34 et seq.
52. Ibid., at 18.
53. Ibid., at 16.
54. See Sect. 2.8.2.
55. Hardt/Negri, *Empire*, supra note 44, at 23 et seq.
56. Ibid., at 24.
57. Gilles Deleuze, *Postscript on the Societies of Control* (1992), in: "October", Vol. 59 (1992), 3–7, available at http://www.jstor.org/stable/778828, accessed 2 April 2020.
58. Foucault, *Surveiller et punir*, supra note 37, at 195 et seq. (English: at 193 et seq.).
59. Hardt/Negri, *Empire*, supra note 44, at 23.
60. Ibid., at 23.
61. Ibid.
62. Ibid., at 3.
63. Michael Hardt and Antonio Negri, *Commonwealth*, The Belknap Press of Harvard University Press, Cambridge (MA) 2009, at 209.
64. Ibid., at 223.
65. Hardt/Negri, *Empire*, supra note 44, at 34.
66. Ibid., at 20.
67. Ibid., at 393 et seq.
68. Michael Hardt and Antonio Negri, *Multitude*, The Penguin Press, New York 2004, at 103.
69. Hardt/Negri, *Commonwealth*, supra note 63, at VIII.
70. Ibid., at 361 et seq.
71. Ibid., at 367 et seq.
72. Ibid., at 368.
73. Bhupinder S. Chimni, *Third World Approaches to International Law: A Manifesto*, in: "International Community Law Review", Vol. 8 (2006), 3–27, at 4.
74. Ibid., at 8 et seq.
75. Ibid., at 10.
76. Ibid., at 10 et seq.
77. Ibid., at 13.
78. Ibid., at 11 et seq.
79. Ibid., at 12 et seq.
80. Ibid., at 8.
81. Ibid., at 11 and 16 et seq.
82. Ibid., at 16.

83. Ibid., at 21.
84. Ibid., at 23 et seq.
85. Ibid., at 23.
86. Catharine A. MacKinnon, *Toward a Feminist Theory of the State*, Harvard University Press, Cambridge (MA) 1991 (1st ed. 1989), at 215 et seq.
87. Ibid., at 218.
88. Ibid., at 221.
89. Ibid., at 222.
90. Ibid., at 238.
91. Hilary Charlesworth, *Feminists Critiques of International Law and Their Critics*, in: "Third World Legal Studies", Vol. 13 (1995), 1–16, at 5 et seq.
92. Fernando Teson, *Feminism and International Law: A Reply*, in: "Virginia Journal of International Law", Vol. 33 (1993), 647–684.
93. Charlesworth, *Feminists Critiques of International Law and Their Critics*, supra note 91, at 8.
94. MacKinnon, *Toward a Feminist Theory of the State*, supra note 86, at 244.
95. Ibid., at 247.
96. Ibid., at 246.
97. Charlesworth, *Feminists Critiques of International Law and Their Critics*, supra note 91, at 1.
98. Ibid., at 9.
99. Nico Krisch, *Beyond Constitutionalism*, Oxford University Press, Oxford/New York 2010, at 16, 23 and 68.
100. Ibid., at 305.
101. Ibid., at 303.
102. Ibid., at 21.
103. Ibid.
104. Ibid.
105. Ibid., at 23.
106. Ibid., at 78.
107. Ibid., at 103.
108. Paul Schiff Berman, *Global Legal Pluralism*, Cambridge University Press, Cambridge/New York 2012, at 25.
109. Ibid., at 23 et seq.
110. Ibid., at 27 et seq.
111. Ibid., at 36 et seq.
112. Ibid., at 37 et seq.
113. Ibid., at 41 et seq.
114. H. Patrick Glenn, *Legal Traditions of the World*, Oxford University Press, Oxford/New York 2010, at 61 et seq.
115. See Sect. 2.6.

116. Andrew Moravcsik, *Taking Preferences Seriously: A Liberal Theory of International Politics*, in "International Organization", Vol. 51 (1997), 513–553.
117. Anne-Marie Slaughter, *A New World Order*, Princeton University Press, Princeton/Oxford 2004, at 12 et seq.
118. Ibid., at 34.
119. Anne-Marie Slaughter, *International Law and International Relations*, "Collected Courses of The Hague Academy of International Law", Vol. 285, Nijhoff, The Hague 2000, 9–250, at 41.
120. Anne-Marie Slaughter, *International Law in a World of Liberal States*, in: "European Journal of International Law", Vol. 6 (1995), 503–538, at 508.
121. Slaughter, *International Law and International Relations*, supra note 119, at 42.
122. Anne-Marie Slaughter, *A Liberal Theory of International Law*, in: "American Society of International Law", Vol. 94 (2000), 240–248, at 242.
123. Ibid.
124. Ibid., at 245.
125. Ibid.
126. Ibid., at 245 et seq.
127. Ibid., at 248.
128. Slaughter, *A New World Order*, supra note 117, at 36 et seq.
129. Armin von Bogdandy, Philipp Dann, and Matthias Goldmann, *Developing the Publicness of Public International Law: Towards a Legal Framework for Global Governance Activities*, in: "German Law Journal", Vol. 9 (2008), 1375–1400.
130. Armin von Bogdandy, Matthias Goldmann, and Ingo Venzke, *From Public International Law to International Public Law: Translating World Public Opinion into International Public Authority*, in: "European Journal of International Law", Vol. 28 (2017), 115–145, at 134.
131. Ibid., at 138 et seq.
132. Benedict Kingsbury, Nico Krisch, and Richard B. Stewart, *The Emergence of Global Administrative Law*, in "Law and Contemporary Problems", Vol. 68 (2005), 15–61.
133. Eyal Benvenisti, *The Law of Global Governance*, Hague Academy of International Law, The Hague 2014.
134. Nico Krisch, *Global Administrative Law and the Constitutional Ambition*, in: Petra Dobner and Martin Loughlin (eds.), *The Twilight of Constitutionalism*, Oxford University Press, Oxford/New York 2010, 245–266.
135. Slaughter, *A New World Order*, supra note 117, at 235 et seq.
136. Ibid., at 239 et seq.

137. Max Weber, *Wirtschaft und Gesellschaft*, Mohr, Tübingen 1922, at 122 et seq. (English translation ed. by Guenther Roth and Claus Wittich: *Economy and Society*, University of California Press, Berkeley 1978, at 212 et seq.).
138. Scharpf Fritz Wilhelm, *Governing in Europe: Effective and Democratic?* Oxford University Press, Oxford/New York 1999.
139. This claim does not imply that individuals do not try to convince their communication partners of the validity of their assertions, but only presupposes that they cannot rely, in their endeavour, on any kind of previously assumed truth, be it universal or even only contextual.
140. Martti Koskenniemi, *The Politics of International Law*, Hart, Oxford/Portland 2011, at 298.
141. Ibid.
142. Quoted by Emmanuelle Jouannet, *A Critical Introduction*, in: Koskenniemi, *The Politics of International Law*, supra note 140, at 8.
143. Martti Koskenniemi, *From Apology to Utopia: The Structure of International Legal Argument*, Cambridge University Press, Cambridge/New York 2005, at 513.
144. Ibid.
145. Ibid., at 478.
146. Martti Koskenniemi, *International Law in Europe Between Tradition and Renewal*, in: "European Journal of International Law", Vol. 16 (2005), 113–124, at 119 et seq.
147. Ibid., at 120.
148. Martti Koskenniemi, *The Gentle Civilizer of Nation: The Rise and Fall of International Law 1870–1960*, Cambridge University Press, Cambridge/New York 2001, at 500 et seq.
149. Martti Koskenniemi, *International Law and Hegemony: A Reconfiguration*, in: "Cambridge Review of International Affairs", Vol. 17 (2004), 197–218, at 214.
150. Koskenniemi, *The Gentle Civilizer of* Nation, supra note 148, at 500.
151. Ibid., at 501.
152. Ibid.
153. Ibid., at 502.
154. Ibid.
155. Koskenniemi, *From Apology to Utopia*, supra note 143, at 615.
156. Ibid., at 536.
157. Ibid., at 556.
158. Ibid., at 544.
159. Ibid., at 553.

CHAPTER 8

# The Post-unitary Paradigms of Order III: The Communicative Paradigm

Ingmar Bergman's film *The Seventh Seal* of 1957 tells the story of a Swedish knight, called Antonius Block, who returns to his country with his squire Jöns after ten years spent on a disillusioning crusade. The journey to the Holy Land did not meet the expectations, especially those of the profoundly spiritual knight. As Jöns puts it:

> For ten years we sat in the Holy Land and let snakes bite us, flies sting us, wild animals eat us, heathens butcher us, the wine poison us, the women give us lice, the lice devour us, the fevers rot us, all for the Glory of God. Our crusade was such madness that only a real idealist could have thought it up.[1]

No certainty of faith and no spirituality could be found in what had been assumed to be the most sacred place. However, what they find after returning to their country is no less scary since the land is ravaged by the plague. As it is described in the *Book of Revelation*, in a passage which is read at the beginning and towards the end of the movie, after "the Lamb broke the seventh seal, there was silence in heaven"[2]: the final doom of the earth is soundlessly echoed by the silence of God. And, as God did not reveal himself in the Holy Land, so does he seem not to provide any consolation to his creatures, in words or deeds, in the waste country hit by the plague.

© The Author(s), under exclusive license to Springer Nature
Switzerland AG 2021
S. Dellavalle, *Paradigms of Social Order*,
Philosophy, Public Policy, and Transnational Law,
https://doi.org/10.1007/978-3-030-66179-3_8

The people that Bergman introduces to us during the course of the highly symbolic and fascinating filmic journey react in very different ways to the existential threat. Some of them try to overcome fear and uncertainty by resorting to a kind of religious fanaticism. According to the description of a painter, whom Jöns meets in a church while he is painting a *Danse macabre*,

> the remarkable thing is that the poor creatures think the pestilence is the Lord's punishment. Mobs of people who call themselves Slaves of sin are swarming over the country, flagellating themselves and others, all for the glory of God.

As a result of the fanatic religious attitude, those who live for whatever reason at the margins of the religious community, are likely to be persecuted. In Bergman's film, the destiny of the outcasts is depicted through the tragic and frightening end of an innocent young woman who "is believed to have caused the pestilence with which we are affected": after being wrongly accused of witchcraft and summarily condemned, she is burned at the stake—and neither Block nor Jöns can do anything to stop this brutal act of injustice. The only support they are able to give is to partially ease the suffering of the victim through the administration of a potion. A second group of individuals build a mob to reinforce one another in their common prejudices and egoistic convictions—"I suppose a person should look after his house and try to enjoy life as long as he can", a farmer says—and to draw strength from the violent exclusion of those who are regarded as strangers. This is what happens to Jof, an actor who barely escapes lynching in an inn where the "decent" members of the community (farmers, merchants and the like) are gathered to freely express their rather "indecent" attitudes. Others convey an insofar even more unconstrainted selfishness, as they do not search for the encouragement of a group, but pursue their advantage by embracing the ideology and by implementing the behaviours that seem to be most profitable at a given moment. The best example in *The Seventh Seal* is Raval who— being convinced that "each of us has to save his own skin; it's as simple as that"—is first a preacher, when the crusade is declared and being religiously fervent guarantees the best social position, just to become later a thief, when the social breakdown due to the plague weakens all ideological certainties.

The most interesting and differentiated reactions to the existential threat are those displayed by the two protagonists of the movie, Block and his squire Jöns. Beginning by the squire, he is undoubtedly a cynic:

> One moment you're bright and lively, the next you're crawling with worms. Fate is a terrible villain and you, my friend, its poor victim.

However, he does not only "grin at Death, mock the Lord, laugh at himself and leer at the girls"; he is also capable of remarkable empathy and uses his physical strength to save, first, a young woman from a sexual assault, and then Jof—as mentioned above—from the violence of the mob. The knight Block builds the counterpart to Jöns and the centrepiece of the whole story. Although he is perfectly aware that "faith is a torment; ... it is like loving someone who is out there in the darkness but never appears, no matter how loudly you call", he does not give up searching for a truthful meaning of life because "no one can live in the face of death, knowing that all is nothingness". Right at the beginning of the film, Block meets a sinister figure, who turns out to be Death who came to take the knight with him. In a bid to win time, Block challenges Death to a chess match: in case of victory, he will be released; yet, he will stay alive, in any case, as long as he avoids defeat. He actually knows that he is doomed to ultimately lose the challenge, but he needs the borrowed time to find a sense for his life:

> My life has been a futile pursuit, a wandering, a great deal of talk without meaning. I feel no bitterness or self-reproach because the lives of most people are very much like this. But I will use my reprieve for one meaningful deed.

Death checkmates Block in the end, out of mastery and cheating, but in the meantime his defeated opponent has found what he sought: he distracts the sinister master for a moment, so that Jof, his wife Mia and their little son Mikael can escape Death's gaze and his plans to take them with him. Block and his wife, Jöns and the girl he saved from the assault, as well as some other minor figures, are taken by the hand by Death, to dance with him a *Danse macabre* that marks the end of their lives. Yet, the young family—which represents, in Bergman's eyes, the most positive social community and the one which mostly deserves being rescued—can keep on living, at least for a while, their simple but love-filled lives.

It is quite easy to find in Bergman's characters the existential transpositions of the different understandings of the world that have been presented in the previous chapters as the *paradigms of order*. First, we have the religious holism, that claims to pursue the truth, but cruelly persecutes the infidels. Secondly, the scene at the inn reminds us of a particularistic community which is no less united through the fear and the hatred of the aliens than through common values. Raval, then, personifies a particularistic individualism that rejects any idea of the common good. Jöns, on the other hand, represents the postmodern denial of any kind of universal truth; nonetheless, he proves to be capable of a high degree of concrete empathy, even if randomly exercised. Finally, Antonius Block is the modern human being, who "wants knowledge", but has always searched for it in a rather solipsistic way:

> Through my indifference to my fellow men, I have isolated myself from their company. Now I live in a world of phantoms. I am imprisoned in my dreams and fantasies.

Yet, he learns during the journey that the real value, the only one which is worth living for, is not an abstract deity or the solipsistic knowledge of the world, but an interaction between human beings which is based on mutual respect and recognition. While taking a humble meal with the young family, he says to Mia:

> Everything I've said seems meaningless and unreal while I sit here with you and your husband. How unimportant it all becomes suddenly. ... I'll try to remember what we have talked about. I'll carry this memory. ... And it will be an adequate sign – it will be enough for me.

*The Seventh Seal* is a profoundly touching work of art which gives voice to a longing for solidarity, arguably harboured in the human heart from the very beginning of our species—and maybe shared beyond the biological barriers. Nonetheless, Bergman's view is remarkably new, in particular if we consider his beautiful screenplay as a contribution to the philosophy of human existence. Søren Kierkegaard indeed, who deeply influenced Bergman's understanding of life, still saw the Absolute as the highest moment of the existential self-awareness, without any significant reference to intersubjectivity. Deeply disappointed by the impossibility to find a consistent meaning of life either in the pleasure of the senses or in the ethical life of the family, the tormented human being turns to God as the only choice that can be made in an *absolute* way, i.e., without depending on any external circumstance:

> He repents himself back into himself, back into the family, ... until he finds himself in God. Only on these terms can he choose himself, and he wants no others, for only thus can he absolutely choose himself.[3]

On the contrary, Bergman chooses intersubjectivity and mutual recognition as the conditions that can give to human life its most appropriate meaning, marking an important milestone in the history of thought. The question at this point, however, is whether this understanding of life can be transferred into an idea of social, political and legal order as well. The aim of this chapter is to explore this possibility, starting with some anticipations of the concept of intersubjectivity in the nineteenth century (8.1) and with the formulation of a discursive theory of politics in the first decades of the twentieth century (8.2), until a comprehensive idea of the intersubjective communication as the fundament of a correct use of the theoretical and practical reason is developed towards the end of the twentieth century (8.3, 8.4). Some final considerations on the political and existential dimensions of the communicative paradigm conclude the research (8.5).

## 8.1 From Subjectivity to Intersubjectivity—and Back?

One of the most characterizing elements of the communicative paradigm of order is to be found in the transition from subjectivity to intersubjectivity. In other words, while modern philosophy was centred around the subject for all the fundamental functions related to the use of theoretical and practical reason, the same central position is attributed—according to the communicative paradigm—to intersubjectivity, i.e., to the idea that the justifications for true knowledge and right action have to be sought in the interactions among individuals and not in the mental processes of each one of them. Two essential components of the communicative paradigm of intersubjectivity were anticipated by two of the most outstanding thinkers of the nineteenth century, namely Georg Wilhelm Friedrich Hegel (8.1.1) and Karl Marx (8.1.2). More specifically, Hegel contended that social order is neither essentially given—as it was assumed in the holistic paradigms—nor the product of solipsistic decisions—like in the individualistic conception of order—but the outcome of social interactions and conflicts. For his part, Marx highlighted the conflict between intersubjective social interactions, based on mutual recognition, and the systemic rationality of capital profit. Both authors introduced these innovations in their early writings, but failed to develop them in their later works. Rather, they neutralized the novelties, either by consistently rejecting the intersubjective approach in favour of a different understanding of social philosophy, or by relegating it to a quite marginal position within an encompassing system which was towered by a substantial return to subjectivism. Hegel, who chose the latter way, viewed the struggle for recognition—in his mature system—only as a stage, and by far not the more important, on the journey of the subjectivistic idea (or of the all-encompassing subject, which is in the end the only real protagonist of his late philosophy) to its self-deployment. Marx instead, who opted for the first solution, simply substituted the idea that social progress arises from the conflict between lifeworld and systemic rationality with a deterministic understanding, according to which the improvement of human life is essentially due to what happens in the material world of capitalist production and to its laws. This way, intersubjectivity and—with it—the basis for the transition to a communicative pattern of order was lost from the horizon of political and social philosophy for more than a century. When intersubjectivity became a central concept of political philosophy again—this time as a result of an accomplished paradigmatic revolution and as a component of a consistently new pattern of order—Hegel and Marx's legacy was only one, quite important, but rather distant inspiration.

### 8.1.1 *The Struggle for Recognition and the Hypostasis of Subjectivity in Georg Wilhelm Friedrich Hegel*

Georg Wilhelm Friedrich Hegel was the first thinker for whom modernity explicitly needed "self-critical reassurance",[4] in the sense that philosophical modernity had not only to be emphatically affirmed, but critically assessed and possibly improved. In his works, the solution to the "problem of modernity" is not simply sought by reinstating premodern visions, but by developing original proposals, capable of overcoming the deficits of modern individualism while maintaining its most relevant conquests.[5] From the early texts written in the last period spent in Tübingen (1792/1793) and during the stay in Bern (1793/1796), it is clear how Hegel considered the emancipation of the individuals from the ethical bond of the community as the main reason for the social and political crisis of his time.[6] In this first phase of his thinking, however, his counter-proposal did not go beyond the rather backward-oriented idea of a reabsorption—and substantial cancellation—of individuality within the framework of the collective *holon*, which took the form of an ethical community forged on what he called "popular religion" (*Volksreligion*).[7] Hegel's early ideal of a community of values, with which the individuals were expected to wholeheartedly identify themselves, so that the tensions of modern social fragmentation could be overcome, was largely shaped on the basis of a substantialism of Aristotelian derivation. In fact, according to Aristotle's political philosophy, the polity—to be strong and stable— had to be constituted as an objective and substantial entity with its own specific worth, and not as the sum of the individuals that form it or of their interactions. Later—in particular during the first phase of Hegel's stay in Jena (1801/1803)—the community of values was referred to as the "people" (*Volk*), which was regarded as the highest realization of the "absolute ethical life".[8]

Aristotle's influence on Hegel's thought, though undoubtedly strong, has probably been overestimated for a long time.[9] Indeed, quite early in Hegel's philosophical development we may find elements clearly at odds with Aristotle's uncompromising anti-individualistic substantialism. More specifically, Hegel had already begun during his Frankfurt years (1797/1800) to recognize an increasingly positive value to subjectivity—in potential contradiction with his ongoing political preference for a holistic understanding of order. The revaluation of subjectivity was initially expressed in the concept of "life" (*Leben*) of his Frankfurt writings[10] and then made explicit in the notion of "spirit" (*Geist*), which was already anticipated in the same Frankfurt works[11] and later developed in his Jena lectures of 1803/1804.[12] The acknowledgement of the central importance of subjectivity was finally made complete and unequivocal in the Jena Lectures of 1805/1806, in which Hegel stated that individuality represents the "higher principle of the modern era, a principle unknown to Plato and the ancients".[13] At this point, Hegel was faced with a difficult task, namely with the reconciliation of the role that modern individuality, with its inevitable centrifugal thrusts, was taking on in his philosophical system, with his unchanged conviction that the order of theoretical knowledge as well as of practical and political reason could not be achieved but through a centripetal force capable of "overcoming" (*aufheben*) particularistic tensions. While attempting to give a valid answer to this question—which made up a significant part of his philosophical effort—Hegel developed a conception of reflective intersubjectivity, which is unprecedented in the history of thought. A vision of society took shape, here, in which order was not generated from the immediate identification of the individuals with the values of the community (as in classical holism as well as in his early writings), from decisions that each individual takes on the basis of her/his solipsistic mental processes (as in contractualism), or by the providential harmony that would derive from the pursuit of selfish ends (as in the free trade theory), but from the interactions—and also from the conflicts—between individuals and groups. This extraordinarily innovative vision was already sketched in the description that Hegel gave of the concept of "life" in Frankfurt, but came to completion in the different presentations of the "struggle for recognition" (*Kampf um Anerkennung*) in his Jena texts and lectures, from the *System of Ethical Life* (*System der Sittlichkeit*) of 1802/1803[14] to the *Phenomenology of Spirit* (*Phänomenologie des Geistes*) of 1807,[15] passing through the even richer elaborations in the lectures of 1803/1804[16] and, above all, of 1805/1806.[17]

It is important to underline, at this point, that the idea of *reflective intersubjectivity*—created by Hegel in Frankfurt and Jena—is significantly different from that of an *immediate intersubjectivity*, which characterizes the holistic paradigm of order, in general, as well as his earliest writings from his time in Bern. Indeed, while the former originates from social conflicts and their solution, the latter refers to a non-critical identification of the individuals with their community. Although Hegel's introduction of reflexive intersubjectivity did not properly fit into the existent patterns of order and therefore represented a real opening towards a new paradigm, he did not draw all the possible systematic consequences. As a result, his description of the "struggle for recognition" remained an anticipation of an understanding of social order which was destined to become a full-fledged paradigm only towards the end of the following century. In fact, for the idea of the "struggle for recognition" to actually act as a prototype of the interaction from which the social order is reflexively born, it was necessary that the latter maintained at all levels the original intersubjective matrix. In other words, the communicative dimension of social action had to remain evident also in the institutions in which the conflict is channelled and provisionally recomposed. Basically, the dynamic of social interactions and conflicts should never be replaced by static institutions or dimensions of experience, assumed to embody an unchangeable truth. However, it is precisely this aspect that is missing in Hegel's thinking, even in those Jena years in which he came closest to the formulation of an intersubjective and communicative theory of social order. Indeed, the dynamics of intersubjective sociality are always surpassed—in the different attempts that he made to elaborate a philosophical system between 1802 and 1807—by a higher sphere that is no longer intersubjective, but rather the expression of a monologic reality of more or less abstract character, in which the interactions between individuals and groups are quietened by means of their substantial removal. Such is the "absolute ethical life" of the *Volk*, which—at the end of the social and philosophical development described in the *System of Ethical Life* of the first period in Jena—replaced the intersubjective dimension of social interaction, as articulated in the "struggle for recognition", with an immediate unity of individuals and community. An analogous role is played by the "absolute spirit", which was sketched for the first time in the lectures of 1805/1806[18] and then presented in its almost final form in the immediately following *Phenomenology of Spirit*, which marked the apex and at the same time the end of the philosophical reflections of the Jena years.[19] However, while in the *System of Ethical Life* dynamic social interactions are put to an end through the superimposition of a substantially conflict-free political community, in the later Jena works the definitive reconciliation of conflicts happens in the unpolitical spheres of the "absolute subjectivity", i.e., in art, religion and philosophy.

The culmination of the system, in which the intersubjective thrust had to be extinguished, was no longer shaped—starting with the latest works of Hegel's period in Jena—on the basis of a substantialist ontology, but of a subjectivistic gnoseology that bore substantially modern traits, even if reinterpreted with great originality. Precisely in this subjectivistic and, at the same time, post-individualistic gnoseology lies the specificity and originality of Hegel's mature idealism, from the years spent in Nuremberg (1808/1816) and Heidelberg (1816/1818) until its full realization in the Berlin period (1818/1831). Based on the elaboration of a very innovative logic,[20] Hegel built a system focused on the idea of an absolute and universal subjectivity, in which the unity between thought and reality should be realized and individual subjectivities sublimated. In a system thus conceived, which has in the *Enzyklopädie der philosophischen Wissenschaften* (*Encyclopedia of the Philosophical Sciences*) its most complete—even if perhaps not the most fascinating—expression, the space left to the "struggle for recognition" is, at best, marginal.[21] Reconciliation, in fact, does not need to be created by social interaction and intersubjective communication, but is already predetermined by the gnoseological and ontological unity of the absolute subjectivity.

The idea of a macro-subject that integrates and reconciles the manifold articulations of reality in a sort of pre-established order imbues every aspect of Hegel's mature philosophy, including his political theory. In Hegel's *Grundlinien der Philosophie des Rechts* (*Philosophy of Right*) of 1821, the "state" is the most accomplished implementation of absolute subjectivity in the social world, which "overcomes" individual particularities without annihilating them.[22] The result is a synthetic construction, where the holism of the overall system[23] goes along with many elements that derive from the philosophical tradition of methodological individualism. Among these elements are, for instance, the argumentative incipit on the different meanings of the concept of freedom,[24] the space granted to the realization of individual interests,[25] the structure of the chapter on the legal system with the central role played by notions such as "person" and "personality",[26] and the overall use of subjectivistic categories for the analysis of statist institutions.[27] Hegel's holism is thus shrouded in subjectivistic elements, which outlines not only a singular syncretism but also the probably most formidable effort to overcome the classic dichotomies until the beginning of the twentieth century. Nonetheless, the application of the categories of absolute subjectivity to the "state" is directly responsible for Hegel's insensitivity to the importance of explicitly legitimating political order "from below". In fact, where the intersubjective dynamic is removed, the order of statist institutions is necessarily something predetermined, thus not the result of "ascending" processes, but the implementation of a "descending" authority.

A similar ambiguity is also found in Hegel's approach to international law and relations. He did not radically deny the possibility—even the reality—of a universal order (as did all the classic advocates of particularism), but shifted its fulcrum from international law to history. In other words, to the extent that there is order beyond states, this does not coincide with the legal system that binds them—in Hegel's opinion, in a quite precarious way—but with the progress of a rational history that exceeds the particular interests of individual political communities. Indeed, he contended that "the spirit of the world (*Weltgeist*) exercises its right – and its right is the highest right of all – over these finite spirits [of the individuals states] in the history of the world, which is the world's court of justice".[28]

In conclusion, there are three main innovations introduced by Hegel's philosophy with reference to the development of a general theory of social order. To start with, he was the first among all great thinkers to elaborate a conception of order which is difficult to lead back to the traditional dichotomies of holism/individualism and particularism/universalism. More concretely, his political thinking undoubtedly contains many elements of holistic derivation, in particular as regards the most deep-going ontological foundations of order. Nonetheless, the individual dimension—except for the writings of the Tübingen and Bern periods—is never radically deleted. Rather, the author's efforts always focused on a viable way to integrate it into the overall structure of order, so that it could be maintained to some degree without eliciting the most disruptive centrifugal tendencies that might derive from an unconstrained self-realization of subjectivity. On the other hand, it is undeniable that Hegel distanced himself from the universalistic idea of order, both—explicitly—in his Kantian individualistic version,[29] and—more implicitly—in his holistic form referring to the *communitas humana*.[30] However, it is equally evident that Hegel did not support particularism either, since he unequivocally rejected the idea that the defence of selfish interest constitutes the only rationality detectable in the world of international relations. A further innovative element consisted in highlighting the intersubjective dimension of sociality which is conveyed by the conflicting dynamics of the "struggle for recognition". Although it never made it to the top of Hegel's system, to eventually retreat and make room for an increasing "subjectivistic restoration", the intersubjectivity of the "struggle for recognition" is arguably the most important conceptual bridge built by Hegel towards the formulation of a communicative paradigm of order.

Finally, it is possible to detect in Hegel's thought not only the anticipation of an intersubjective conception of social life but also the germinal idea of a fully communicative intersubjectivity, albeit largely hidden under the dominance of the subjectivistic categories. This aspect emerges in Hegel's analysis of the notion of "spirit" (*Geist*) and, in particular, of "freedom" as its "essence" (*Wesen*).[31] In his interpretation, the freedom of the "spirit" includes three different dimensions. The first is what is called "subjective freedom", in which the individuals tend to self-fulfilment in the private domain. The second is the "objective freedom", in which freedom is realized in the institutions of public power, or—as Hegel preferred to say—of the "ethical life". Although "public" freedom is, for Hegel, superior to its "private" counterpart, "objective freedom" can only be considered fully realized if it allows a sufficient degree of individual self-realization.[32] Beyond these two dimensions, however, there is a third—which is, in fact, the most interesting in the context of a search for the communicative perspective in Hegel's thought. This third dimension is what he defines as the "absolute freedom", i.e., the condition in which the individuals consider themselves fully "reconciled" with the outside world, or "being at one with oneself in the otherness" (*Bei-sich-selbst-sein im Anderssein*).[33] In the *Phenomenology of Spirit*, Hegel severely criticized the uncompromising political realization of this idea of freedom through the palingenetic fervour of the French Revolution,[34] only to take it up later—quite in disguise—in the section on "absolute knowledge", i.e., in the unpolitical spheres of art, religion and philosophy. Yet, since in the late work of the Jena period no realization of political freedom is envisaged, a strong tension still remains between our highest aspiration and the realm of social and political interactions. This tension seems to disappear, at first glance, in the mature works, in which political freedom finds a "realistic" implementation in the ethical life of the state. Yet, even in the texts and lectures from the time in Berlin, "absolute freedom" was not really put to the sidelines. For instance, Hegel spoke in his *Aesthetics* of the ongoing human search for the "region of a higher, more substantial, truth, in which all oppositions and contradictions can find their final resolution, and freedom its full satisfaction".[35] Moreover, the *Encyclopedia* also testifies, although in a drier form, the insufficiency of objective freedom as it is materialized in the ethical state.[36] Therefore, starting from Jena, Hegel never fully abandoned the idea that our supreme freedom can only come about in the context of a psychologically and socially satisfying reconciliation with the others. Undoubtedly this conception is imbued, in Hegel, with subjectivity insofar as it is only implemented in the spheres in which individuals are assumed to abandon the social and political world in order to find peace—each one for him- or herself—in artistic, religious or philosophical contemplation. Inasmuch as the "being at one with oneself in the otherness" is confined to the realm of the "absolute spirit", the social and political spillovers appear to be almost non-existing. Nonetheless, it would be short-sighted not to see in the idea of "absolute freedom" the image, albeit a little distorted, of a communication that is fully successful as it is based on mutual recognition and on the overcoming of the instrumental approach in our relations with others. The question is, now, how to grant this idea a social and political dimension again.

### 8.1.2 Karl Marx: From the Overcoming of Alienation to the Necessary Dynamics of Historical Evolution

In the *Deutsche Ideologie* (*The German Ideology*), a collection of texts partially co-written with Friedrich Engels in 1845/1846, Karl Marx gave the most precise, though concise, description of what he assumed to be the best form of society:

> in communist society, where nobody has one exclusive sphere of activity but each can become accomplished in any branch he wishes, society regulates the general production and thus makes it possible for me to do one thing today and another tomorrow, to hunt in the morning, fish in the afternoon, rear cattle in the evening, criticise after dinner, just as I have a mind, without ever becoming hunter, fisherman, shepherd or critic.[37]

Thus, in the communist society every human being has a fair chance to self-realization. Furthermore, the attribution of the tasks whose accomplishment is deemed necessary for the smooth functioning of the social fabric seems to happen on the basis of a frictionless mutual compliance. Undoubtedly, Marx and Engels's understanding of the organization of the well-ordered society bears some questionable traits of a quasi-natural community, or of a pre-reflexive form of social interaction, in which tasks are taken on by individuals not depending on reasonable justifications, but on self-evident predisposition and unjustifiable preferences. It is almost superfluous to say that such an approach always runs the risk of hiding inequalities of power beneath the veil of an unquestioned identification with the society as a whole. However, what is most interesting, here, is the idea of the *wrong* social order against which Marx and Engels's proposal is conceived. Indeed, in Marx and Engels's as well as in our times, society is not characterized by individual self-realization within the context of a communitarian way of life, but rather by significant constraints:

> for as soon as the division of labour comes into being, each man has a particular, exclusive sphere of activity, which is forced upon him and from

which he cannot escape. He is a hunter, a fisherman, a shepherd, or a critical critic, and must remain so if he does not want to lose his means of livelihood ...[38]

Therefore, we can identify in the *Deutsche Ideologie* the germinal distinction between two forms of societal organization: the one typified by division of labour and systemic constrictions; the other by the unconstrained unfolding of the lifeworld interactions. It is important to anticipate, at this point, that the contraposition between systemic rationality and the lifeworld was destined to become, almost one and a half centuries after Marx and Engels's analysis, one of the distinctive features of the communicative paradigm. Significantly, Marx and Engels introduced in their description of the well-ordered society two further elements of the communicative lifeworld of the social philosophy of the twentieth century, namely, first, the assumption that the reproduction of human society—far from being an exclusively natural phenomenon—is essentially mediated by intersubjective interactions, and, secondly, that these interactions are shaped by language.[39]

The division of labour, however, is not the only—and not even the most important—reason why individuals are subject to constraints. In fact, in the well-ordered society the division of labour can be organized with mutual consent and without any limitation of individual freedom. What makes the division of labour detrimental to individual self-realization is its conjunction with the private ownership and control of the means of production. Insofar as the means for the production of the goods that are necessary for the society to exist and thrive— among which are commodities, energy, machines, and even food—are in the hands of a few private individuals, the large majority of the population is forced to accept the conditions of life and work that are dictated by the minority of owners. This situation has been described by Marx in his *Ökonomisch-philosophische Manuskripte* (*Economic and Philosophic Manuscripts*) of 1844, more specifically in his "theory of alienation". According to his analysis, which heavily relies on some aspects of Hegel's philosophy, humans transfer part of themselves—more precisely, part of their strength, their ideas, their aspirations, etc.—into the outside world through their work. This process is called "objectification" (*Vergegenständlichung*) or "alienation" (*Entäußerung*), insofar as the workers use their *subjective* energy for the production of something "alien", which stands as an external *object* in front of them. In Marx's words, this fact expresses merely that the object which labour produces – labour's product – confronts the worker as something alien, as a power independent of the producer. The product of labour is labour which has been congealed in an object, which has become material: it is the objectification of labour.[40]

In principle, "objectification" or "alienation" is what always happens when human beings transform the outside world according to their plans—and must be seen as one of their most outstanding capacities. This simple fact, that originated at the very beginning of human history, takes however a very bad turn under the conditions given by the private ownership of the means of production. Under those circumstances, workers cannot realize themselves through their labour, but are forced to produce following the preferences of the owners. Otherwise, they would not even dispose of the most essential instruments of production—land, seeds, machines, commodities, energy, etc.—and would necessarily end up starving. Under the rule of the private ownership of the means of production, positive "objectification" becomes negative "estrangement" (*Entfremdung*), since the product of the individual work stands in front of the workers as the realization of someone else's priorities and, thus, as something in which they cannot recognize themselves any longer. Indeed,

> the more the worker spends himself, the more powerful the estranged objective world becomes, which he creates against himself, the poorer he himself – his inner world – becomes, the less this belongs to him as his own … The alienation of the worker in his product means not only that his labour becomes an object, an external existence, but that it exists outside him, independently, as something estranged to him, and that it becomes a power on its own confronting him; it means that the life which he has conferred on the object confronts him as something hostile and estranged.[41]

According to Marx, the "estrangement" of labour is characterized by four aspects. The first and most essential is that the product of labour—as already mentioned—is perceived as hostile by the workers, or at least as not belonging to them. The second refers to the act of production or to the activity of the workers:

> labour … does not belong to the essential being of the worker; … in his work, therefore, he does not affirm himself but denies himself, does

not feel content but unhappy, does not develop freely his physical and mental energy, but mortifies his body and ruins his mind ... His labour is therefore not voluntary, but coerced; it is *forced labour* (*Zwangsarbeit*). It is therefore not the satisfaction of a need; it is merely a means to satisfy needs external to it. Its alien character emerges clearly in the fact that as soon as no physical or other compulsion exists, labour is shunned like the plague.[42]

Thirdly, humans are estranged from the natural predisposition of their species. Indeed, humans naturally tend to regard their action on the natural environment as the field of their societal self-realization. On the contrary, under the condition of "estranged labour", they are forced to see their most noble feature as the simple instrument to secure the physical survival of the individual.[43] It is evident, here, that Marx—quite like Hegel—did not have a great respect for the strength and beauty of the untouched nature, which may be disturbing in times of a deep and dangerous ecological crisis. Yet, if we limit Marx's interpretation to the assumption that in a wrongly ordered society the potential creativity of labour is reduced to a frustrating means to avoid poverty, social exclusion and even starvation, then his critical remark maintains a kernel of truth. The fourth and last consequence of "estranged labour" is to find in the "estrangement of human being from human being", i.e., in the destruction of the lifeworld, or of the context of a peaceful and cooperative interaction among humans.[44]

At this point, the question has to be addressed as to why those who have financial resources (i.e., the capital) at their disposal (in other words, the capitalists) should be interested in investing them in buying means of production so that other individuals, who do not possess similar resources, can work with them. In general, it is to assume that the capitalists will only be keen to invest their capitals if they reasonably expect to get a sufficient advantage—to be more precise, to draw enough financial benefits—out of the investment. While quoting Adam Smith, Marx contended in his *Ökonomisch-philosophische Manuskripte* that "the capitalist ... would have no interest in employing the workers, unless he expected from the sale of their work something more than is necessary to replace the stock advanced by him as wages".[45] By stressing the relation between wages and profit, Marx seems to already assume in his text of 1844 that the increase of the invested capital—i.e., the capital accumulation—is not drawn from the means of production themselves, but from the workers who use them under the control of their owners. This theory—generally known as the theory of the "surplus value" (*Mehrwert*)—was then developed in much greater detail and consistency in the first volume of *Das Kapital* (*Capital*), first published in 1867. To understand the question, it is necessary, first, to see the components of which the invested capital is composed. Following Marx, the capital (C) is substantially made of two parts: the *constant* capital (c), which is "the sum of money ... laid down in means of production";[46] and the variable capital (v), which is "the sum of money ... expended on labour-power (*Arbeitskraft*)".[47] However, the final product of the labour process—ready to be sold to possible buyers—has a value (C') that is higher than the original investment (C). Therefore, during the production process the value of the originally invested capital increases to a certain extent, depending on the social conditions of the production process, which accounts for the interest of the capital owners in investing their money. This is what is defined as the "surplus value". Yet, where does the "surplus value" as the difference between the invested capital and the final value of the product (C'–C) come from? According to Marx, it cannot derive from the constant capital (c), the amount of which is simply transferred from the original investment to the final product, so that no accumulation of capital can be drawn from the allocation of financial resources in means of production.[48] It is only the labour-power, instead, that provides the "surplus value" of the final product. Indeed, workers naturally and inevitably produce more value than what is necessary to buy their "labour-power", which actually corresponds to their *capacity* to work and is covered—with reference to the investment of capital—by the means that guarantee the reproduction of that capacity, often at the lowest level possible. As Marx wrote in the *Capital*:

> the property ... which labour-power in action, living labour, possesses of preserving value, at the same time that it adds it, is a gift of nature which costs the worker nothing, but is very advantageous to the capitalist since it preserves the existing value of his capital.[49]

Thus, even though within a much more sophisticated analytical context, it can be reasonably argued that Marx maintained in his later work the convictions firstly expressed in the *Ökonomisch-philosophische Manuskripte*, namely that the creative power that workers express through their activity is a kind of natural gift, that this gift is the only possibility to add value to the resources originally allocated in the production process, and, finally, that under the condition of the private ownership of the means of production, this gift is taken from the workers and from their well-deserved aspiration to improve their living conditions and the surrounding environment, just to fuel the wish of the capitalists to increase their private resources. Basically, Marx assumed that no added value can derive from technological innovation. I will come back to this point in short. Regardless of whether this assumption is correct or not, it is anyway essential to underline—within the context of an analysis on the paradigms of order—that the subtraction of value from the work of some individuals to the exclusive private advantage of some capital owners, be it the only source of surplus value or not, represents a relevant problem that cannot be left untouched from the perspective of what we can reasonably consider a well-ordered society. Indeed, as Marx explicitly claimed in 1844, in the capitalist society "the increase of wealth is ... identical with the increase of poverty and slavery".[50] On the contrary, "the positive overcoming of private property ... is ... the positive overcoming of all estrangement – that is to say, the return of human beings ... to their *human*, i.e., *social* mode of existence".[51] The social and political condition characterized by the "positive overcoming of private property, as human self-estrangement, and therefore ... [by] the real appropriation of the human essence by and for the human being" is what Marx called "communism".[52]

According to the communicative paradigm of the twentieth century, the world of systemic constraint and the lifeworld of free and reflexive interactions coexist one against the other in an ongoing tension. Within this context, it is not even desirable that the rationality of the lifeworld completely replaces systemic rationality because such a development would possibly bring about significant disruption as regards the most efficient accomplishment of societal functions. Yet, communicative rationality can aspire at gaining ground against the counterpart, so that consensus-oriented and constraint-free interactions are granted enough space to qualify the social fabric as a community of free and equal. This is not the perspective taken by Marx (and Engels), however. From their viewpoint, the "estranged" society and its "communist" alternative are two opposite conception of the world: the *whole* society is either organized following the first model, or according to the second. *Tertium non datur.* As a result, for the human beings to be free, the society of the consensus-oriented interaction has to take over for the presently predominant system of exploitation. Yet, how can this happen? With reference to this question, we can detect a significant—and quite problematic—evolution in Marx's thought. In a similar way to Hegel, he opened up a perspective in the writings of his youth, which was later shut down almost completely. Not only in the *Ökonomisch-philosophische Manuskripte*, but also in the *Manifest of the Kommunistischen Partei (Manifesto of the Communist Party)* of 1848—which Marx wrote together with Engels—the transition from the "estranged" to the "communist society" is the result of "class struggles",[53] whose outcome is rather determined by those who have "nothing to lose but their chains" while having "a world to win",[54] than by some kind of deterministic law of the economy. Whereas Marx and Engels wrote in the *Manifesto* that "the victory of the proletariat [is] … inevitable",[55] this sentence only refers to the increasing strength of the working class and reminds more of an appeal to political action, rather than being the depiction of a quasi-natural law of social development.

The conceptual horizon is quite different in the third volume of Marx's *Capital*, which was posthumously published in 1893. Here, the overcoming of the unjust society based on exploitation is not triggered by the challenge posed by the commitment to justice of those who experience solidarity in their day-to-day lives, but by internal processes of the capitalist production. These processes are presented in the chapter about the "law of the tendential fall of the rate of profit". In short, this highly contested theory can be explained as follows.[56] To cope with the huge competition within the capitalist environment, each investor has to employ more constant capital (c), i.e., he/she has to buy more technologies, machines, raw materials, etc., in order to increase the productivity of labour, thus making the product unit cheaper and easier to sell. Yet, given that the only part of the total capital (C) that brings profit is the variable capital (v) with its surplus value (s), inasmuch as the proportion of the constant capital—c related to C—is growing, the rate of profit (s divided by $C = s/C$) is destined to decrease. In other words, if the rate of surplus value (s divided by $v = s/v$) is stable, the lower the percentage of v with reference to C is, the more decreasing $s/C$ will be. Because the capitalists generally react to the fall of profit by investing even more financial resources in constant capital, a vicious circle is triggered, to the detriment of the whole system. Marx mentioned some interventions which can slow down the fall of the profit rate, such as a more intense exploitation of labour through the prolongation of the working day and the intensification of labour, the reduction of wages, the cheapening of raw materials, technologies and machines, as well as the growing recourse to foreign trade.[57] However, each one of these measures only increases the social crisis that affects the capitalist system, leading to an inevitable contradiction between a growing overproduction of goods and the lowering of the living standards of a large part of the population. From this contradiction—Marx concluded his analysis—does a structural crisis emerge, which eventually leads to the collapse of capitalism and its substitution through a more humane form of production.[58]

From the point of view of economic theory, the most obvious criticism that can be raised against Marx's "law of the tendential fall of the profit rate" refers to his assumption that the rate of surplus value $(s/v)$ is not essentially influenced by the investment of additional constant capital $(c)$ in technological improvements. Despite the fact that the third volume of the *Capital* has a rather uncertain philological status since it was prepared by Engels on the basis of Marx's notes, the theory of the fall of the profit rate is substantially consistent with the idea, already expressed in the philologically much more solid first volume of the same work, according to which the labour-power is the only source of surplus value. On the contrary, if we admit that technological innovation may enhance the creation of value per working hour without any deterioration of the living conditions of the workers, then it becomes possible that capitalism be socially improved, so that no radical change of economic regime is necessary to make society more humane. In this sense, social improvement can be regarded as the result of the tension between two different rationalities, and not as the palingenetic transition from an utterly wrong world to a perfectly just one. Furthermore, in Marx's later works this transition is not triggered by a moral and political vision rooted in constraint-free forms of interaction, as opposed to the systemic rationality of capitalist production, but is the almost necessary consequence of internal processes of the economic system. This way, however, the community of unconstrained communication is caught in an unresolvable contradiction: though being presented as necessary and anything but a regulative idea, it remains conceptually indistinct and so far away that it is not surprising that it could never be realized.

## 8.2 The Intersubjectivity of Political Life

During the course of its history, political philosophy developed two main understandings of the social and political community which, albeit opposite in their intentions and priorities, nevertheless shared a common shortcoming. The first approach—identifiable with the holistic paradigm of order—focused on the irreflexive overlapping of individual interests and community's priorities, whereas the latter were granted precedence. On the contrary, the second strand—referring to the individualistic paradigm of order—concentrated on individual entitlements, while considering the public sphere nothing more than the suitable guarantee of their implementation. What both missed, however, was the dialogical dimension of the political life of the community, namely the fact that a healthy political life, which shapes the identity of a well-ordered polity, is neither essentially made up of pledges of allegiance to the unity of the whole, nor can it be demoted to the sheer defence of negative freedom or to electoral processes. Rather, what makes the political realm so special is a fine and complex texture of intersubjective exchanges of arguments. After having been neglected for such a long time, the social and dialogical essence of politics was eventually put to the fore—after World War I and II, respectively—in the works of John Dewey and Hannah Arendt.

### 8.2.1 *The Social and Democratic Dimension of Individual Freedom in John Dewey's Pragmatism*

In John Dewey's thought, the idea of social and political order is strictly related to his theory of cognition. Analysing what is assumed to be the "best way of thinking"—or, in other words, considering the conditions for *true* cognition—he pointed out, first, that in all situations in which our mind is working, we can rightly maintain that we are thinking. However, thinking in general is not tantamount as true cognition. In fact, our thoughts can unfold in the form of a "stream of consciousness" in which the single elements are not related to one another in a consistent way and the "mental streams ... are ... idle and chaotic".[59] Or they can refer to the impalpable world of "things not directly perceived".[60] To avoid these shortcomings—and, therefore, in order to have a truth content—thinking must be "reflective", which means that it has to be qualified through three distinct characteristics. The first is that thinking should not simply consist of a "sequence of ideas", the components of which are logically independent of one another. Rather, "reflection involves ... a *con*-sequence", i.e., it must be based on a set of concepts, in which each one of them finds its justification in another notion or evidence and represents, in turn, the presupposition for further notions: "the successive portions of a reflective thought – Dewey maintained – grow out of one another and support one another; they do not come and go in a medley".[61] The second condition for "reflective thinking" is that it should be based on a careful inquiry, i.e., an "examination, inspection, exploration ... [and] analysis ... of all attainable consideration which will define and clarify the problem in hand".[62] In other words—as Dewey wrote in *How We Think*, first published in 1933—reflective thought is constituted by the "active, persistent, and careful consideration of any belief or supposed form of knowledge in the light of the grounds that support it".[63] The third feature of reflective thinking is that it inevitably aims at a conclusion, i.e., at figuring out an evidence-based solution for a problem of social life.[64]

While the idea that true knowledge must be grounded on consistent thinking and evidence-based analysis—namely the two first conditions for Dewey's reflective thought—seems to be drawn from the typical canon of the subjective gnoseology from Descartes to Kant, the third characteristic, i.e., the conclusion-oriented methodology, makes already clear that the background against which he wanted to situate his philosophy was a remarkably different one. The novelty of Dewey's approach becomes evident if we move from the consideration of the components of "reflective thinking" to the analysis of its stages. In his *Democracy and Education* of 1915, he identified five steps that, taken together, make up what can be reasonably defined as "reflective experience"[65]: (a) "perplexity, confusion, doubt" in front of any problem that may affect whatsoever field of social life; (b) a "conjectural anticipation", i.e., a hypothesis regarding causes and dimensions of the problem as well as a possible solution; (c) a "careful survey", corresponding to the above-mentioned inquiry; (d) a "consequent elaboration of the tentative hypothesis", i.e., its assessment on the basis of the evidences collected in the survey; and, finally, (e) a "plan of action", grounded on the initial hypothesis and substantiated by evidence, to be "applied to the existing state of affairs" and suggesting a feasible solution to the problem from which the whole process started. What is remarkable, here, is that in Dewey's thought research begins with a problem and not with the perspective of a grand design of the world—or of a part of it—and does not end up creating all-encompassing and highly abstract theories, but delivering the most reasonable answer to that problem. Indeed, "demand for the solution of a perplexity is the steadying and guiding factor in the entire process of reflection".[66] As a result, research essentially consists in *problem-solving*—which accounts for the fact that his philosophy was labelled as *pragmatism* (in the sense that it should aim at finding pragmatic responses), *instrumentalism* (since it searches for instruments to tackle problems), or *experimentalism* (because the hypothesis must be proved on facts).

Dewey's pragmatism rests on a strong criticism not only of the philosophy of antiquity and of the Middle Ages but also of modern individualism and subjectivism, which simply "continued the older tradition of a Reason that creates and constitutes the world, but combined it with the notion that this Reason operates through the human mind".[67] He described the contrast between the old understanding of philosophy and its pragmatist turn at the transition from the nineteenth to the twentieth centuries with the following words:

> the social philosopher, dwelling in the region of his concepts, 'solves' problems by showing the relationship of ideas, instead of helping men solve problems in the concrete by supplying them hypotheses to be used and tested in projects of reform.[68]

Pragmatic research does not only deliver a powerful instrument for addressing problems of any kind but also finally acknowledges the most relevant failure of modern philosophy, namely its understanding of the individual as a solipsistic monad. In fact, while aiming at the solution of questions that may arise from whatsoever form of societal interaction, research takes into due account that individuals are social beings and not—like the isolated knowing subject of modern thought—neutral observers of the world. According to Dewey, however, the most deep-going error of the individualistic paradigm of the use of theoretical and practical reason is to be found in the fact that "the individual ... [was] regarded as something *given*, as something already there".[69] Consequently, societal institutions were assumed to be established, in a quite static way, around the unchangeable characteristics of the individuals. On the contrary, we should recognize—along with the philosophical research after the pragmatist turn—that "social arrangements, laws, institutions ... are means for creating individuals".[70] The importance attributed by Dewey to institutions because of their capacity to forge human beings, in particular with reference to their aptitude to correctly address problems, explains both his strong and ongoing interest in education[71] and his considerations as regards how society should be politically shaped so as to guarantee the best approach to problem-solving.

Dewey was adamant about his preference: only a democratic society based on the free exchange of arguments can create the intellectual and political horizon for a successful problem-solving approach. The reason for his choice is twofold. First, in order to find out the best solution, the research must be free, i.e., the political constitution must guarantee that every member of the society can unconstrainedly accomplish the full process of problem-solving. However, secondly and more importantly, the best solution can only be worked out on the basis of "free intercourse and communication of experience".[72] In other words, the different solutions, elaborated by the single individuals, have to be confronted with one another and mutually assessed in a process of exchange of arguments, which is only to be realized in a democratic environment. In fact, "ideas and knowledge" are not "functions of a mind or consciousness originated in individuals by means of isolated contact with objects"; rather, "knowledge is a function of association and communication".[73] Yet, Dewey's conviction that democracy creates the best context for addressing social problems relies on an even deeper assumption, which leads the argument well beyond merely practical considerations. It is freedom itself, indeed, that is essentially social.[74] As he wrote in *the Public and Its Problems* of 1927,

> fraternity is another name for the consciously appreciated goods which accrue from an association in which all share, and which give direction to the conduct of each. Liberty is that secure release and fulfilment of personal potentialities which take place only in rich and manifold association with others: the power to be an individualized self making a distinctive contribution and enjoying in its own way the fruits of association. Equality denotes the unhampered share which each individual member of the community has in the consequences of associated action.[75]

Being freedom realized only within a social context, democracy—inasmuch as it aspires to be the "idea of community life itself",[76] i.e., the best possible political implementation of the well-ordered society—has to be decidedly more than just suffrage.[77] Only counting the votes of the parties that compete in an election—Dewey claimed—"has nothing in common with the procedure of organized cooperative inquiry which has won the triumphs of science in the field of physical nature".[78] To live up to its justified expectations, a democratic community has to be reflexively intersubjective, i.e., it must be grounded on the open exchange of arguments. Against this background, conflicts can be brought out "into the open where their special claims can be seen and appraised, where they can be discussed and judged in the light of more inclusive interests than are represented by either of them separately".[79]

### 8.2.2 Hannah Arendt's Theory of Political Action

In her book *The Human Condition* of 1958, Hannah Arendt distinguished—according to the ancient Greek tradition—between the *contemplative* and the *active* life (*vita activa*). From the way in which she presents this distinction, it becomes evident at first glance that she wanted to distance herself from the approach that prevailed in late antiquity—to be precise, starting with Plato—and was then reinforced by the Christian thought. In fact, while Plato and his disciples as well as the Christian philosophers privileged the contemplation of the truth as the highest goal that a human can achieve, Arendt was explicitly committed to a rediscovery of the meaning and function of the "active life". In her interpretation, the *vita activa* is composed of three distinct activities: labour, work and action. Labour corresponds to the biological processes that are necessary to the reproduction of the human body.[80] Work provides the "artificial world of things" around us,[81] which are distinct from the natural environment and are characterized by the external "durability ... [that is] needed for the establishment of property".[82] It is action, however, the only component of the human condition that directly develops between humans, without any intermediation through natural or artificial objects. Although Arendt never used in her work the concept of intersubjectivity, it is quite clear that what accounts for the outstanding position of action among the dimensions of the active life is, according to her interpretation, precisely the fact that it necessarily unfolds as an *interaction between human beings*, and not between an individual and her/his internal (bodily) or external (material) objectivity. Indeed, "all human activities are conditioned by the fact that men live together, but it is only action that cannot even be imagined outside the society of men".[83]

Arendt not only made clear that action is inherently related to "plurality"—or to intersubjectivity, as we could say instead—but also that "this plurality is specifically *the* condition ... of all political life".[84] However, politics has a much broader meaning in Arendt's interpretation than we usually assume. Indeed, it is much more than the space in which different interests can find their balance, distinct visions of society can compete, or opposite identities struggle for dominance and mutual marginalization, if not annihilation. Rather, it is the context in which the members of the community *directly* discuss with one another—largely beyond the intervention of any kind of organization—about the best way to manage common concerns. Thus, the essential element is not the topic around which the interaction develops—namely the management of the common goods, regardless of how hugely antithetic the determination of these goods may be—but the *way* in which the interaction develops, namely through eminently *discursive* means. In other words, what is important, in Arendt's view, is not to be found in the specification of the identity of the political community, in the clarification of the goods that should be protected, or in the formal rules that govern the political sphere, but rather in the informal dialogue among the citizens. This is what made up the exceptionality of the ancient polis. In fact, Arendt did not leave any doubt about her conviction that the Greek polis is to be regarded as the unsurpassed realization of her ideal of "action". It is in the Greek polis, indeed, that the βίος πολιτικός (*bíos politikós*)—namely the "political life" as the condition most suited to the human being as a ζῷον πολιτικόν (*zóon politikón*), or a "political animal"—comes to completion.

However—Arendt maintained—there is a far-reaching misunderstanding in the way in which we interpret the notion of the *zóon politikón*.[85] In fact, the concept was usually translated into Latin as *animal sociale* (social animal) and, following this tradition, we are used to say that human beings are animals with a social disposition. Yet, being "social" is not the same as being "political". Relying on an old Stoic assumption, Arendt claimed that society essentially emerges from the necessity to cooperate, which results from the weakness of humans if compared to other living beings. Consequently, society is assumed to serve the individual interest to survive and to enjoy the best possible living conditions. On the contrary, the political sphere arises from the reflexive will of the members of the community to discuss how common concerns should be addressed. Like in Marx's early texts, we have here a contraposition between the realm of functional constraints and the dimension of unconstrained interactions. The difference—quite evidently—is that, while in Marx the realm of unconstrained interactions is essentially realized through a form of production that overcomes private property, according to Arendt the lack of constraints characterizes a dimension which has explicitly nothing to do with the world of production. Nonetheless, the two conceptions share a further common element beyond the general distinction between the two opposite realms of functional constraint, on the one hand, and human self-realization through unconstrained interactions, on the other. Indeed, whereas in the communicative paradigm the two dimensions dialectically interact, in both Marx's and Arendt's views they are diametrically opposed and drastically exclude one another. In Marx, however, the contraposition of the two realms is diachronic—i.e., they are supposed to follow one another in time—while in Arendt it is synchronic—i.e., the two dimensions are co-present in time, even though they do not overlap. In fact, in the Greek polis the political dimension could only develop its potentialities because it was clearly separated from the οἰκία (*oikía*), namely from the household and its economy.[86]

We can consistently argue—against Arendt's approach—that the ancient Greek political dimension bought its independence at the high cost of the neutralization of what was regarded as a purely private domain and, thus, of the exclusion of those who were assumed to exclusively belong to that domain, namely women and slaves, along with non-citizens. It is almost superfluous to say that this is not a price that we are still ready to pay. As a result, politics must include into the discussion all questions that impact on any kind of social interaction and all individuals involved. Yet, what was essential to Arendt was surely not to ennoble the shortcomings of the ancient polis, but to underline that politics—regardless of the specific conditions and shortcomings of its implementation—has to be understood as a dialogical interaction among citizens within a context of plurality. Two further considerations are introduced to support this fundamental assumption. First, the political dimension is coessential with language as well as with a conception of the *logos* as the rationality that underpins the subjective exchange of arguments and not—like in the rationalist philosophy that began with the Stoics—as the objective rationality that governs the whole world.[87] Secondly, politics consists in convincing and not in imposing decisions:

> to be political, to live in a *polis*, meant that everything was decided through words and persuasion and not through force and violence. In Greek self-understanding, to force people by violence, to command rather than persuade, were prepolitical ways to deal with people characteristic of life outside the *polis*, of home and family life, where the household head

ruled with uncontested, despotic powers, or of life in the barbarian empires of Asia, whose despotism was frequently likened to the organization of the household.[88]

Once said that the Greek polis, according to Arendt, has been the perfect realization of the political dimension, her analysis can also be read as a plea in favour of a civic republicanism as similar as possible to the ancient model. Consequently, the question as to which factors decisively contributed to the decline of the Greek polis is also important in order to identify the elements that might endanger present forms of civic republicanism. Two major factors proved decisive for the decline of the ancient polis. The first was the increasing colonization of the public domain through private agents and interests.[89] During this process, "the private care for private property … [was transformed] into a public concern".[90] As a result,

> society … assumed the disguise of an organization of property-owners who, instead of claiming access to the public realm because of their wealth, demanded protection from it for the accumulation of more wealth.[91]

If the first threat to civic republicanism with a healthy public sphere is private property and wealth, the second is power. It was already Plato who proposed to overcome the self-organization of the citizens of the polis by assigning the guidance of the community to philosopher kings who—as he explained in the allegory of the cave—[92]were supposed to have a privileged access to the truth and, thus, to know better than the commoners which measures should bring them safety and prosperity.[93] A firm leadership based on an allegedly superior knowledge gives the illusion to escape from the "frailty of human affairs" that is perfectly expressed through the open-ended discourse which unfolds in the political sphere. Actually—Arendt claimed—"the greater part of political philosophy since Plato could easily be interpreted as various attempts to find theoretical foundations and practical ways for an escape from politics altogether".[94] While the political discourse is inherently horizontal, the concept of rule of a great part of political philosophy is based on the idea that humans "can lawfully and politically live together only when some are entitled to command and the others forced to obey".[95] Yet, focusing on rule and not on dialogue leads political theory to a slippery slope. Indeed, as Arendt already explained in *The Origins of Totalitarianism*, published a couple of years before *The Human Condition*, when the community of citizens degenerates into an amorphous mass to be ruled by some kind of allegedly far-seeing elites, democracy inevitably gives way to the surge of authoritarian regimes.[96]

## 8.3 The Rationality of Communication

In the 1960s, Karl-Otto Apel and Jürgen Habermas—the most prominent exponents of the second phase of the Frankfurt School—began to elaborate a communicative understanding of rationality that was destined to have a deep and broad influence in many fields, from the theory of knowledge to the various dimensions of social, political and legal philosophy.

### 8.3.1 The Theory of Language

According to the early advocates of the communicative paradigm, human communication essentially unfolds through language. Therefore, the first step that we take in order to specify the contents of the paradigm must necessarily focus on their contribution to the question as to how human language works, i.e., on the conditions under which our linguistic utterances can lead to mutual understanding. As already mentioned in the previous chapter, Wittgenstein's contextual turn in the philosophy of language detached the theory of meaning from necessary references to external objects.[97] In other words, we are allegedly able to understand the significance of an utterance because we rely on the linguistic context that we share with other humans, while facts, actions or things are ultimately shaped by the linguistic interaction itself. This approach has an upside and a downside. The discovery and proper evaluation of the intersubjective dimension in the determination of the truth content of a proposition belong to the former, whereas the risk of promoting cognitive scepticism and intellectual arbitrariness—due to the lack of a non-subjectivist and reference-based framework—is to be regarded as a significant shortcoming. As a result, a large part of the efforts made by philosophers of language in the last decades was dedicated to the reconstruction of a non-sceptical truth theory. Just to single out two of the most interesting recent attempts in this direction, let us shortly focus on Donald Davidson's neo-empiricism and Robert Brandom's inferential philosophy of language.

Davidson's answer to the sceptical drift in the theory of knowledge as a result of the Wittgensteinian "turn" essentially renews the tradition of the empiricist theory of meaning. The loss of reference to the concrete object within the post-ontological and post-mentalistic understanding of language is countered by Davidson through the return to a kind of "objectivism" that bears the distinctive traits of a pre-intersubjective, if not even of a pre-subjective epistemology. So as to reach his goal, he pursues a twofold strategy. First, he distances himself from Descartes' subjectivism by asserting that doubt itself is an idea of the truth which is based on a *natural* knowledge of the reality and of its objects.[98] By this reference to the possibility of a pre-reflexive knowledge of reality Davidson takes a position that, due to the alleged spontaneous and natural osmosis—which he calls "holism"—between our cognizance and the world outside, clearly recalls essential elements of the pre-Cartesian epistemology. Coherently, Davidson goes so far as to say that, precisely as a result of this alleged quasi-natural osmosis, empiric knowledge would not need any epistemological justification.[99] Yet, Davidson recognizes—rather from a methodological than from an ontological or hermeneutic standpoint—that the process of cognizance does not happen solipsistically, but is socially mediated through the communication between the speaker and the interpret.[100] Here he develops his second strategy for the consolidation of an epistemological return to objectivism by working out a theory of communication that can be considered insofar "pre-intersubjective" as communication is assumed to function even without a normatively significant mutual recognition, or an interpretation of society as a communicative community. From the perspective of Davidson's theory, the interaction of speaker and interpret does not aim at the exchange of arguments, or at the implementation of the normative foundations of social life. Rather, it concentrates—in a kind of triangle modus—on the comparison of the reactions to the stimuli that the external object can produce on both participants in the interaction. Linguistic communication results in mutual understanding if the linguistic reaction to the stimuli happens in a way that can be clearly interpreted by the counterpart.[101] The comparability and, therefore, also the interpretability of the individual reactions are ensured by the fact that all participants in the linguistic interaction are innately embedded in a "common language".[102] Davidson extends his neo-objectivistic understanding of truth in language also to propositions addressing moral or ethical questions. From his perspective, ethical values are insofar "objective" as they are regarded as *given* in a quasi-natural way within the social group of reference of the speaker.[103] In this sense, the social substrate of ethical convictions plays, with regard to the ethical discourse, the same role taken by the "objective" external world within the theoretical discourse. By presuming that ethical values have a quasi-natural basis in social convictions, however, we deny the possibility that values have universal validity—since social convictions may vary from time to time and from place to place. Furthermore, we basically give up on the chance of determining a criterion for validity which could stand as a fundament for the scrutiny of currently predominant values.

Davidson rescues the truth content of language and avoids the risk of a sceptical drift, which is implied in the contextual linguistics developed by Wittgenstein, by shifting attention once again onto the external object. The result is attained, however, at the high cost of rejecting the normatively unreduced, properly intersubjective dimension of language as exchange of arguments. On the contrary, Robert Brandom's aim consists in maintaining the truth content of language while situating it within an unequivocally intersubjective setting. By doing this, he intends to make "explicit" the "implicit" rules of an inferential semantics, characterized by the exchange of reasons and arguments through the linguistic communication.[104] In fact, only an idea of communication as an exchange of arguments takes full account of the novelty introduced by the "linguistic turn". However, if the first hurdle, the Scylla consisting in the danger of wiping out the social dimension of communication by concentrating only on the external object, has been successfully passed by conceiving a truly intersubjective communication theory, a second threat is yet to be mastered, namely the Charybdis of the rejection of what has been defined as the "truth's claim to universality" (*Universalitätsanspruch der Wahrheit*).[105] Without this further step, we would fall back into that kind of Wittgensteinian epistemological scepticism the deficits of which have been highlighted by contemporary language theory. Brandom meets this second challenge by construing an epistemological continuum between "facts", "concepts" and "true claims".[106] Since "concepts" are articulated in an inferential modus—that means, are not regarded as mere representation of objects, but always in the context of propositions based on arguments—they build the theoretical bridge that brings "facts" and "true claims" together. Indeed, both "facts" referring to external objects, as well as "true claims" concerning these same objects, are structured as "concepts" and therefore inferentially. As a result, an ontological overlapping is assumed to exist between the "facts" of the world and our assertions expressing truth claims as regards the same objects of the world: "facts are just true claims", is Brandom's lapidary statement.[107] The outcome of this overlaying of "facts" and "true claims" consists, first, in a theory of knowledge that avoids scepticism by including into the discourse references to concrete objects, although always conceived of in an inferential way, and secondly in a kind of neo-idealistic understanding of communication,[108] clearly influenced by Brandom's innovative revival of Hegel's epistemology.[109] Although remarkably different in its epistemological premises, Brandom's inferential semantics also leads, when applied to questions concerning the use of practical reason, to conclusions which are quite similar to those drawn by Davidson from his objectivistic theory of language. In particular, Brandom widens the ontological overlapping between "facts", "concepts" and "true claims" also to the "norms", going thus beyond theoretical reason and reaching the field of practical reason as well. From his point of view, moral and ethical norms share the same status as descriptive propositions with truth claim: all of them—"norms" as well as "truth claims"—make the rules "explicit" which have their objective fundament in the "facts" of the world.[110]

Summing up, the neo-empiricist strand of the philosophy of language marginalizes the intersubjective dimension, consisting in the exchange of arguments, that characterizes the theoretical and practical use of reason in all its variants. On the other hand, both neo-empiricism and Brandom's inferential semantics regard rules derived from the use of practical reason as something *given*, an "object" or "fact" of the world that communication, if it is to achieve its goal, cannot but accept. Hereby, however, communication turns out to lack the *constructive* dimension that characterizes the use of practical reason. Indeed, by proposing arguments for mutual consideration, moral and ethical discourses do not only take reality into account but also build a dimension that can, in a counter-factual move, transcend actuality and pave the way for the realm of the "yet to come". The exponents of the communicative paradigm counter both these shortcomings—as well as the gnoseological scepticism against which neo-empiricism and inferential semantics were developed—by making two far-going assumptions. The first—directed against the contextualist theory of meaning—is that linguistic communication, so as to work, has to be regarded as always having a truth content. In other words, if we assumed that the utterances of our counterpart in the linguistic interaction are devoid of any content that we can interpret as "true"—i.e., as having a meaning that we can share—we would not engage in any serious interaction with this actor, with the consequence that the interaction would promptly come to an end without results and the communication, as an exchange of meaningful utterances, would actually not take place at all. The second assumption—against both neo-empiricism and inferential semantics—is that, for a proposition to have an evidence-based truth content within an intersubjective setting, the participants in the dialogical interaction have to mutually presuppose that: (a) from an *objective* perspective, the assertions are *true* (in the sense that the propositions refer to real situations or facts); (b) from a *subjective* perspective, the speakers act *truthfully* (in the sense that they are committed to fair-minded purposes and are sincerely persuaded that their assertions meet the conditions for truth); (c) from an *intersubjective* perspective, the speakers interact according to the principles of *rightness* (in the sense that they accept that their assertions have to meet the criteria for a general and mutual acknowledgement by all participants in the communication).[111] From this standpoint, in regard to (a), communication preserves the reference to the external object, which, however, does not constitute—like in the objectivistic theory of language—the only criterion for truth, nor it is conceived in idealistic terms like in Brandom's semantics. Moreover, (c) guarantees the inferential character of a communication made of exchange of arguments. Lastly, (b) and (c) stand for the inherent normativity of the interaction. On the whole, communication understood in this form maintains the claims for a universal validity, but without any resort to ontological or metaphysical presumptions.

Substantially, communicative rationality assumes that communication, in order to function, i.e., if linguistic utterances are to achieve the intended result, has to aim at reaching a consensus among the participants. Doubtlessly, this is a far-going—and possibly quite controversial—presupposition, against which at least three conditions can be brought to mind, in which propositions are apparently uttered not to achieve consensus, but to push through one-sided individual priorities. These conditions happen when linguistic interactions express strategic thinking, a command, or even a menace. While commanding or threatening phrases—such as, respectively, "I command you to do A", or "if you do not do A, I will do you harm"—do not need further explications, strategic linguistic interactions have to be understood as the cases in which individuals already have their fixed priorities and interact with fellow humans only to find out the best way to mobilize the most useful resources to achieve their egoistic, i.e., not mutually shared goals. When confronted with these evidently non-consensual interactions, the theorists of the communicative paradigm nonetheless maintain that also a strategic intention, a command or a menace can only be successful if they live "parasitically off normal linguistic usage, for … [they] only function if at least the one side involved presumes that language is being used in order to reach mutual understanding".[112] In other words, I can exclusively reach my purposes through strategic bargaining, commands or threats under the condition that the counterpart presumes that there is still a kernel of truth in my action, namely that I am not only cheating, my commands are not only in my selfish interest, or that, if the counterpart complies with the threatening request, further harm will be avoided. Otherwise, she/he will simply ignore my utterances and I would be forced to switch from linguistic interaction to open physical violence. Indeed,

> this derivative status [of non-consensual linguistic interactions] points to the intimal logic of linguistic communication; language remains effective in its action-coordinating capacity to the extent that it imposes specific constraints on the purposive activities of the actors.[113]

Although linguistic interaction, if successful, always presupposes an implicit consensus-oriented approach, it has to be kept in mind that—according to the presuppositions of the communicative paradigm—we can only speak of a full-fledged implementation of all potentialities of communicative rationality with reference to the circumstances in which the consensus-oriented attitude becomes explicit.

### 8.3.2  *Gnoseology*

The understanding of language that characterizes the communicative paradigm leads to the fundamental assumption that only the mutual recognition of the validity of claims can lead the use of reason to justifiable results. The outcomes of the application of this tenet to the theoretical use of reason—namely to gnoseology or to the theory of the *true* knowledge of facts of the outside world, to be clearly distinguished from the justification of *right* actions as the field of practical reason—were, at first, an uncompromising criticism of the correspondence theory of truth and the formulation of a radical consensus approach to gnoseological truth claims. In his text on *Wahrheitstheorien* (*Truth Theories*) of 1972—which, most interestingly, was never published in English—Habermas points at the idea that an assertion, in order to be recognized as true, must have a *correspondence* to some object or fact in the outside world. Against this quite usual interpretation, he contended that truth essentially depends on "arguments" and not on the "evidence of experiences". In fact—he specified—"the idea of truth can only be unfolded with reference to the discursive confirmation of validity claims", since "truth is not an attribute of information, but of assertions".[114]

Habermas's consensus theory of truth has the unquestionable merit of highlighting the social mediation which is inevitably part of the allegedly objective knowledge of the world—with results comparable, to some extent, to Kuhn's detachment from the mainstream epistemology.[115] However, the one-sided focusing on the social dimension of the search for truth—which seems to inspire at least the incipit of Habermas's above-mentioned essay—can bring about counterintuitive or even absurd outcomes. In fact, it is quite incontestable that there was no consensus on the heliocentric theory of the then known cosmos at the beginning of the seventeenth century, which led to Galilei's trial. But does that mean that the heliocentric theory was not true at that time as it is recognized as true today? Or, moving forwards to our times, does the fact that climate change is contested by some or that there is little awareness of the man-made sixth mass extinction that presently affects the living world imply that the evidences regarding both phenomena are not to be considered "true"? To meet this quite evident shortcoming, Habermas introduced two elements that counterbalance the intersubjective content of his truth theory and mitigate its most implausible outcomes. The first, with which he already concluded his essay of 1972, specifies that the discursive interaction—insofar as it is expected to produce true outcomes—should be characterized by some normative conditions that qualify it as an "ideal speech situation". In particular, true results can only be achieved if all participants in the discursive interaction are free from constraints and enabled to unrestrictedly submit their interpretations, claims and criticism.[116] This clarification prevents, in fact, the deficit that may derive from an unbalance of power within the context of the exchange of arguments. Since there is no doubt that Galilei's trail was indeed as far away from an "ideal speech situation" as possible, it is not surprising that its outcome proved to be untrue.

Yet, further problems still persist after Habermas's early introduction of this caveat. First, the speech situation that is assumed to bring about theoretical truth is described as "ideal". Does this mean that "real" speech situations only produce untrue outcomes? Such a presumption does not seem to be plausible, though. Rather, we have to postulate that the rules of a power-neutralized and free exchange of arguments not only build a kind of regulative idea that lies in the background of all meaningful communications, but are also to be recognized as the inescapable conditions for the theoretical use of reason through linguistic interaction to bring about *true* results. Put differently, if the linguistic interaction is affected by a relevant imbalance of power or the exchange of arguments suffers from significant constraints, we have to assume that its outcomes are not reliable as regards their truth content. The second problem that still lingers after specifying the *intersubjective* conditions for a meaningful communication is that no mention to *objective* evidences has been made so far to qualify utterances as having truth content. Yet, in particular when the discourse is about an adequate fundament for a scientifically based knowledge of the world, deleting any reference to the object weights heavily on the credibility of the results. Habermas reacted to this problem—in an essay of 1996—by adding a non-intersubjective criterion to the conditions for the recognition of the validity of truth claims:

> Reaching understanding cannot function unless the participants refer to a single objective world, thereby stabilizing the intersubjectively shared public space with which everything that is merely subjective can be contrasted. This supposition of an objective world that is independent of our descriptions fulfils a functional requirement of our processes of cooperation and communication.[117]

In the end, the communicative understanding of "truth", as the outcome of the theoretical use of reason, overlaps almost completely with the communicative approach to the meaning of language: like the reference to outside objects and the mutual recognition among the participants in the exchange of arguments account for linguistic interaction to work, the very same elements also guarantee—inasmuch as they are rigorously applied—that searching for truth is not a meaningless endeavour.

### 8.3.3 *The Communicative Use of Practical Reason*

Although the inquiry into the epistemological conditions for true knowledge plays an important role in the works of the advocates of the communicative paradigm, their attention was doubtlessly more attracted by the different uses of practical reason, i.e., by the criteria for the justification of *right action*. As regards this dimension, it has to be specified, in the first place, that the communicative theory of action is a variant of what is generally known as the cognitive understanding of morals, which implies that the direction of action does not derive from idiosyncratic and thus unjustifiable preferences, but grows from rational arguments and from the critical analysis of evidences. Consequently, it is not surprising that the rules that govern action are ultimately the same, once again, that lie at the basis of language and theoretical knowledge.[118] In fact, following the communicative approach, actions can be regarded as morally justifiable—i.e., they can be seen as "just"—if they correspond to the consensus achieved within the communication community on the basis of the exchange of arguments with reference to the moral problem in question.[119] The community, hereby established through communication processes relying on intersubjective recognition, can be identified—from both the moral and the political-legal points of view—as a community of free and equal individuals. Indeed, from the moral perspective, it is the community that comprises those who freely and mutually recognize each other some essential rights, whereby they also assume corresponding obligations. From the political and legal standpoint, those rights—insofar as they are of public relevance to the life of the community—are then transformed into written and enforceable entitlements.

The idea that action has to be justified against the background of the general consensus of the community as a whole could mistakenly suggest that, according to the communicative paradigm, the only right action is the one that complies with the mainstream values. To avoid this misunderstanding, Apel introduced the distinction between the *real* and the *ideal* communication communities.[120] While the former describes the factual social context in which arguments are exchanged, the latter indicates the most inclusive composition of the communication community, beyond the limitations of the real social contexts. Indeed, as Apel pointed out,

> anyone who engages in argument automatically presupposes two things: first, a *real communication community* whose member he has himself

become through a process of socialization, and second, an *ideal communication community* that would basically be capable of adequately understanding the meaning of his argument and judging their truth in a definitive manner.[121]

Analogously to Habermas's "ideal speech situation", the "ideal communication community" is characterized by an open and free exchange of arguments, in which social power is largely neutralized, as well as by mutual recognition. Furthermore, it strictly follows the principle of the best argument while assessing the results of the discourse. In order to avoid demoting the practical use of reason to a mere exercise of egoistic strategic thinking, we have to anticipate the universalistic rules of the ideal communication community in our day-to-day discursive praxis. Only by doing so the discourse on the practical use of reason can live up to its intrinsic aspiration to move from selfishness to generally shared conclusions. Indeed, when we present an argument during a discussion, we always assume that all participants in the discussion can make this argument their own. Otherwise, we would not engage in any kind of discussion. Although we have to respect the real communication community as the forum in which morally and ethically relevant questions are addressed, we must ultimately refer to the ideal communication community to find out reasonable criteria for the justification of action. Put differently, we are justified to take action in conformity with the best rational argument, as potentially developed in the ideal community, even though this action is not supported by the consensus of the real community or, at least, by the majority of its members. This clarification nullifies the objection that, according to the discourse theory of the use of practical reason, the mainstream values—as those which arguably dominate the debate within the real communication community—would show the way for the justification of action. It also raises the question, however, on which would then be the difference between the communicative understanding of the practical use of reason and Kantian mentalism: in the end, it seems that in both cases, at least at first glance, the final decision on what to do is put in the hands of the rational individual. The analogy, yet, is more apparent than real: while following the mentalist approach individuals have only to prove the reasonableness of their actions before the internal forum of their conscience, the discourse theory always requires the real engagement with other participants in the discourse as well as the anticipation of the claims of all possible fellow rational beings. Those claims have then to be peremptorily taken into due consideration and included into the final decision. This clause definitely rules out that decisions are justifiably taken which cannot be reversed by later consensus or better arguments.

In addition, the distinction between the real and the ideal communication communities fulfils a second important function. Indeed, the idea that the communication community corresponds to the community of the free and equal, in the sense that it is built by reasonable beings who freely recognize rights and corresponding duties to each other, presupposes that its members are perfectly aware of their capacities and able to enter a discursive interaction. But what happens, in this case, to all those beings—human as well as non-humans—who are intuitively rights holders and objects or addressees (even if not necessarily subjects or bearers) of obligations? This condition is common to a number of categories of (real or potential) rights holders: children, elderly affected by dementia, mentally impaired people, future or past generations, sentient beings in particular, and living beings in general. Are they to be excluded from the moral and legal community because they are not capable of participating in the dialogue about the justification of actions? The answer is self-evidently negative—with more or less justifiable doubts as regards past and future generations as well as sentient and living beings. Nonetheless, the question on how these categories of passive moral beings can be taken on board of the vessel of practical reason, although they cannot meet the criteria for moral agency that have characterized the definition of the moral community in the Modern Ages, is far from trivial. A relatively easy solution can be still found with reference to children, who are expected to become full members of the self-aware moral community in the future, and to elderly affected by dementia, who were part of that community in the past. In the same vein, mentally impaired people also belong to the self-reflexive community of the rights holders and duties bearers—though incapacitated to consciously exercise those duties—because, in the name of the *imago hominis*, it is to assume that they would fulfil moral duties if only their destine had been more generous. The question becomes more intricate if we consider past and future generations: here, we have not to deal with presently existing individuals, but with people who are not among us any longer, or are not yet among us (and might never come to a real existence). Not to mention the condition of non-human sentient beings or of the living environment, where the issue of the relationship between moral agency and rights is even harder to address. Nonetheless, including past and future generations into the moral and legal community is important because of the respect that we owe to the cultural gifts of the past as well as—maybe even more—because of the intuitively well-deserved chance of those who will live after us to have a destiny not worse than ours. Furthermore, a growing sensibility for the non-human world admonishes us to take the necessary steps for its adequate protection.

To circumvent the difficulty, it has been suggested to abandon the idea of the self-reflexive community of rights holders and duties bearers and to switch to the use of the concept of *responsibility* for the passive categories of moral objects.[122] Indeed, responsibility better conveys the one-sidedness of the situation—yet, at the cost of presupposing the existence of a privileged observer, who should be able to determine the *objective* claims of the rights holders beyond their *subjective* awareness. In this sense, the rights holders who lack actual agency are explicitly identified as *objects* (and not as *subjects*) of rights. The always problematic postulation of an observer endowed with a privileged point of view, however, is precisely what the idea of the self-reflexivity of the moral and legal community justifiably aims at avoiding. In fact, following the old principle that *volenti non fit injuria*, who should know better than the involved individuals themselves what is in their interest? The introduction of the ideal communication community allows to untie the knot by maintaining the self-reflexive community of the free and equal as the essential reference point for the determination of rights and duties while, at the same time, expanding its composition so as to include some of the above-mentioned categories of objects of rights. As regards past and future generations, it suffices to rationally figure out their arguable claims and to take them into due account during the process of decision-making. Although the members of past and future generations cannot directly take part in the discourse about moral and legal rights and duties, we can reasonably imagine what their request would be, if put in the present situation, because of the analogies that inevitably bind all human beings. The argument of analogy, instead, is more difficult to apply when it comes to non-human animals. In their case, we cannot simply presuppose a similarity of claims because of the interspecific barrier. Does a non-human animal have an interest to live? Or to be free? It is problematic for us to presume what they need because we cannot take on their position. Furthermore, there may be differences between species. There is at least one element, however, that we have in common with many non-human animals: the capacity to feel pain and to suffer. On the basis of this consideration, non-human animals can be included into the moral and legal community, at least in a non-reciprocal condition of moral patients and rights holders.[123] Yet, this inclusion has necessarily to presuppose the partial redefinition of the epistemological fundament of the communication community, which should not be confined to the level of the exchange of rational arguments. Rather, to include sentient beings and also expand the range and meaning of communication, the exchange of rational arguments should be seen as the instrument to mutually avoid pain and suffering. On the contrary, no possibility is given to bring non-individual beings, such as the ecosystem or the world of living creatures as a whole, in the communication community. Their safeguard can nevertheless be justified as a duty towards those individuals whose right is recognized to enjoy the beauty of the world and decent living conditions also in the near and far future.

In conclusion, by slightly modifying the accentuation of the communication community, it is possible to include in the moral and legal community also those addressees of obligations who seemed to have to rely on the exercise of responsibility—and not on the fulfilment of duties—because of their apparent extraneity to the reason-and-autonomy-based pact of the free and equal. Thus, the conceptual instruments put at our disposal by the communicative paradigm allow us to address some of the most intriguing moral questions of our time—in particular, they make it possible to extend moral and legal rights to new categories of human as well as non-human beings—without giving up two of the most important tenets of modern moral theory, namely the focus of the practical use of reason on the self-reflexive community of the free and equal, and the idea that moral obligations are binding duties and not the result of the application of the much more flexible notion of responsibility.

### 8.3.4 Systems and Lifeworld

According to the fundamentals of the communicative paradigm, social subsystems with their functional rationalities are an indispensable factor for the society to accomplish its tasks. But, contrary to the assumption of the systems theorists,[124] systemic rationalities are not reason's last word since, opposite to them, we can detect the unfolding of the processes of communicative rationality.[125] This conceptual contraposition implies four dimensions. Firstly, it is assumed that individuals with their preferences, specific rational processes and actions are still to be considered a significant component of sociological analysis. Secondly, the rationality expressed by individual actions is—at least partially—different from the systemic rationalities. Thirdly, in opposition to modern individualism and mentalism, individual rationality is essentially intersubjective, i.e., it develops through processes of interaction. Fourthly, the intersubjective rationality builds in part a reality which is explicitly contraposed to systemic constraints, namely the so-called *lifeworld*, but in part also permeates the subsystems through the fact that system-conformed actions are ultimately performed by no one else than those individuals who are also the bearers of communicative rationality.

Within the lifeworld—i.e., in the social contexts that are not explicitly dominated by systemic rationality—individual interactions mainly occur according to two different modalities. As already mentioned in a former section while presenting the communicative dimension of language, we speak of a *communicatively* rational behaviour when individuals aim at achieving consensus about goals and means of their action, whereas we assume that they are applying a *strategically* rational behaviour when they have already specified their idiosyncratic or even selfish goals before entering into a dialogue. In this second case, they exchange assertions— also by cheating one another into disadvantageous dealing—only in order to find the way to one-sidedly acquire as many resources as possible so as to reach the previously fixed purpose. Following Apel and Habermas's interpretation, a communicative background must always be presupposed, even in the case of the most deceiving linguistic interaction, since otherwise—i.e., if it were clear from the outset that the counterpart is cheating—no one would engage in dialogue. The same forms of rationality come into play when individuals are confronted with the functional logic of subsystems (for instance, with the public administration, the manufacturing industry and the industrial relations, the financial sector, the health system, and so on). Since the functional logic of each subsystem is fixed, the individuals can display their strategic reason so as to get the best personal advantage out of it. On the other hand, individuals cannot refrain from applying communicative rationality, more or less consciously, when they interact with fellow humans. Thus, because social subsystems are not made of machines, but of interacting individuals, communicative action cannot be ruled out from their mechanisms of functioning, but is a no less intrinsic part of them than their original functional logic. The result is an ongoing tension not only between the lifeworld and the functional subsystems but also, within the functional subsystems themselves, between the exercise of a consensus-oriented dialogue and the imposition of system-internal constraints. Contrary to Marx's understanding, this twofold tension is not going to be overcome by a deep-going social and political change any time soon, but is to be considered an unavoidable trait of complex and highly developed societies. If subsystemic specialization disappeared, the performances in accomplishing social tasks would dramatically decrease, and if dialogic rationality were condemned to die out, social life would mummify. Rather than a palingenetic revolution, the tensions between subsystemic rationalities and the lifeworld generate a number of "struggles for recognition", which steadily redefine the line of demarcation between the two social contexts and—much in Hegel's vein—work out innovative forms of social integration, according to the newly developed sensibilities and claims.[126]

### 8.3.5 Plurality and the Unity of Rationality

In a previous chapter, it has been argued that modern subjectivity was characterized by three main elements—internal unity, self-referential hierarchy and cognitive solipsism—which were tantamount to as many deficits when it came to dealing with pluralism and the recognition of social, political, cultural and legal diversity.[127] Postmodern thinking had the merit of putting conceptual instruments at disposal that made it possible to go beyond those shortcomings and to finally welcome diversity, but at the cost of weakening legitimacy and normativity. The communicative paradigm has taken up the difficult task of putting together again some of those pieces that have resulted from the postmodern iconoclastic destruction of the modern picture of order, while guaranteeing a no less far-going acknowledgement of diversity. In this sense, the communicative paradigm aims at redefining modernity through the introduction of some elements derived from postmodernism.[128] Similarly, it takes a critical stand towards systems theory and its exclusive focusing on a variety of value-neutral rationalities.

As regards the overcoming of subjectivistic solipsism as one of the deficiencies of modern thinking, the communicative paradigm of order does not reject the legacy of individualism as radically as the other post-unitary paradigms of order. Rather, it maintains one of its most essential tenets, namely the idea that the core of the social bond consists of the individuals with their endowment of reason and interests, and not of a predetermined vision of the common good, of self-reproducing functional systems, or of particularistic narrations. However, in contrast to modern individualism—and also to Kant whose philosophy of universalistic rationalism is seen by the exponents of discourse theory as a direct inspiration—it does not assume that true or right results of the use, respectively, of theoretical and practical reason can be achieved on the basis of solipsistic mental processes. In other words, it is not the individual alone who can find out what is true and just according to a correct use of her/his own rational capacities. Instead, the search for truth and justice is the task of intersubjective procedures of communication consisting in the exchange of arguments within the context of mutual recognition.

With reference to the question of how to deal with internal unity, a distinction has to be made between the unity of knowledge and action, on the one hand, and the unity of society on the other. Concerning the first dimension, it is quite evident that the communicative paradigm abandons the approach taken by both systems theory and postmodernism, to ultimately return to a modified form of internal coherence of the use of theoretical and practical reason. Indeed, systems theory factually deletes the analysis of morally relevant decisions from the field of rational research—since we always act following systemic constraints—and considers the implementation of systemic rationalities the only scientifically detectable form of the use of reason. For its part, postmodernism dissolves rationality into a multiplicity of idiosyncratic and often mutually incompatible narrations. On the contrary, the communicative understanding of rationality—as explained in the former sections—still sticks to the more traditional idea that there is *one* rationality that imbues all forms of knowledge and action. However, the communicative rationality is understood as being in essence dialogical—and not monologic. The problem becomes more complex, however, when we move from the claim to unity in knowledge and action to the world of social organization. Here, indeed, the reassertion of the unity of rationality is intertwined with a no less strong position in favour of social, political and legal pluralism. Indeed, analogously to systems theory and postmodernism, the exponents of the communicative paradigm unequivocally welcome the coexistence of a plurality of social systems, political institutions and legal regimes, which are not connected to one another by strictly hierarchical relations. On the other hand, they do not give up on the claim to an overarching order. Yet, if the all-encompassing coherence of rules and institutions is not guaranteed by the imposition of hierarchy, like in the paradigms of order before the pluralist revolution, what should keep the different dimensions of social order together? The most immediate answer refers, once again, to the fact that the implementation of communicative rationality spans over the whole range of social institutions. In other words, inasmuch as the functioning of any kind of social institution is realized through the use of practical reason and the display of practical reason always follows certain principles, the consequence necessarily is that all social institutions are brought together by the same procedures for the implementation of right action.

However, at this point the question still remains on how communicative rationality can be transferred into institutional patterns, or, put differently, on which kind of institutional arrangements should be put in place for the communicative rationality to unfold. As Jan Klabbers claims, we have to identify "something which helps keep the system together".[129] Basically, two different solutions can be singled out: multilevel or multi-layered constitutionalism, and the dialogue between courts. By "multilevel constitutionalism" we understand an institutional and legal system that comprises many layers of organization—from the national (or even the subnational) to the cosmopolitan, passing through the federal and/or the supranational levels—each of them characterized by its own constitutional form, whereas they complement each other and are intertwined with one another. Since the most inclusive level has a cosmopolitan range, the institutional realization of the communicative paradigm can be seen as a variant of global constitutionalism. Yet, contrary to other interpretations,[130] the cosmopolitan constitutionalism of communicative rationality is much less hierarchical and adjudication-based, as well as much more political and keener to acknowledge the importance of diversity. With reference to hierarchy—the third factor that, together with internal unity and solipsism, characterized modern thinking—communicative cosmopolitan constitutionalism clearly distinguishes itself from other forms of cosmopolitanism. Indeed, even if we assume, following the premises of global constitutionalism, that "a constitutional world order is one which has a centre of authority",[131] it has nonetheless to be recognized that this "authority" is not one issuing binding decisions through top-down processes, but one that always attempts to make cosmopolitan order concrete through horizontal interactions, open contestation and dialogue. To the extent that communicative cosmopolitan constitutionalism concedes that some institutional and legal frameworks may be superior to others, this superiority always relies on greater inclusiveness or on the higher availability of legitimacy resources. In other words, global institutions are normatively superior to national ones insofar as they represent the interests of a higher number of individuals; however, the two levels cannot—and should not—settle their conflicts by referring to hierarchy (which is virtually non-existent in that context), but by entering into a mutually respectful dialogue. Moreover, public law institutions and legal systems, being democratically legitimated, are to be regarded as normatively superior to their private counterparts. Yet, against the background of communicative constitutionalism with its multilevel structure, a specific form of democratic legitimation has to be developed.[132]

The rejection of bottom-down hierarchy reverberates on the relations between courts as the second element that "keeps the system together". Among other phenomena, the transition to the pluralist idea of order also implies the presence of a number of horizontally coexisting legal systems which overlap with one another, while not being hierarchically bound to one another. This new situation accounts for both the increase of legal conflicts and the impossibility to resolve them by resorting to the usual procedure, namely by clarifying which norm is superior. As an answer to the issue thereby raised, there has been a surge of the dialogue between courts of distinct legal regimes—or, as it has been specified, of the "engagement with foreign precedents", since the courts' actions are in many cases one-sided and do not imply any interaction with the counterpart.[133] The category comprises both the cases in which a domestic court (in most cases a constitutional court) refers to a decision taken by a foreign court (generally, also a constitutional court), and the situations in which—giving a broad meaning to the definition of "foreign"—a domestic court vertically interacts with a supranational court such as the European Court of Justice (ECJ) or the European Court of Human Rights (ECtHR). Regarded by some as a limited and rather marginal phenomenon[134] while utterly praised by others as a fundamental step towards a cosmopolitan jurisprudence[135] and as a significant contribution "to enhance democracy and inclusion",[136] transnational activities of courts are undeniably growing in numbers and becoming increasingly influential. In a few cases, the otherwise informal interaction between courts has been developed into a formalized procedure by establishing mechanisms of consultation and dialogue, as provided for by Art. 39 of the Constitution of the Republic of South Africa—as regards the collaboration between constitutional courts—and by Art. 267 of the Treaty on the Functioning of the European Union (TFEU) with reference to the interactions between domestic and supranational levels.

Since the dialogue between courts is a phenomenon that has been triggered, in general, by the transition to pluralism and by the problems generated by the new idea of order, it is not surprising that it unfolds according to three different rationales, each of them corresponding to the specific understanding of rationality of one of the post-unitary paradigms of order. The first approach to the dialogue between courts takes up the epistemology of systems theory, regardless of whether explicitly or implicitly. It applies if "foreign precedents" are only taken into account with the purpose of adapting the internal operations of one's own legal system to the challenges coming from outside so as to maintain its original functional rationality. In this sense, law-making happens "through mutual irritation, observation and reflexivity of autonomous legal orders",[137] and the rationality of the external system is only interesting insofar as it impacts on the internal procedures. Instead, if the logic that inspires the interaction originates from postmodern thinking, the main aim of the dialogue will be the establishment of positive comity and tolerance, finally leading to a broad acknowledgement of foreign judgements.[138] In this case, the rationality of the external system is fully recognized as having the same value, although it is also considered incommensurably different since no overarching and all-encompassing rationality is assumed to be possible. Precisely this kind of assumption that an overarching rationality is both arguably identifiable and desirable imbues the third understanding of the rationale of judicial interaction. Indeed, if the epistemological background is the communicative paradigm of order, the goal of transnational interaction arguably consists in the implementation of the normative contents of intersubjective rationality. Because an all-encompassing rationality is presumed to exist, its correct application through horizontal dialogue is likely to lead to consistent solutions of conflicts. Analogously to what has already been said above with reference to the communicative understanding of the institutional setting of multilevel constitutionalism, no implementation of top-down hierarchies is accepted in the interaction between courts either. Nonetheless, the communicative paradigm recognizes, once again, the relative normative superiority of certain legal regimes, in particular when their internal contents—as in the case of human rights law—more reliably embody the principles of communicative rationality.[139]

### 8.3.6 Communication in the Political and Legal Dimension

Following the individualistic paradigm, the foundation of all fundamental and human rights has to be located in the guarantee of individual agency, namely in the capacity of the individuals to make free choices. To avoid any unjustified limitation of this capacity, public power should refrain—as much as possible—from interfering with the sphere of individual negative freedom, i.e., with the contexts in which individuals pursue their self-realization. As a result, the most fundamental category of rights comprises the civil rights, namely those rights which are best guaranteed if public power remains silent, according to the principle *libertas silentium legis* (liberty depends on the silence of the law). From this perspective, political rights come second, being only developed for the institutional safeguard of negative freedom, especially through elections and parliamentary assemblies. On the contrary, the communicative paradigm reverses the well-established hierarchy, putting the political rights at the centre of the stage. This change of priority is not surprising if we consider the inherently intersubjective attitude of the communicative paradigm. Taking up an idea that had already been formulated by Hannah Arendt and John Dewey, Habermas clearly contends that the interaction between the members of a community—based on mutual recognition and aiming at finding shared solutions for common questions—is the centrepiece of social life. As a consequence, it is the political rights, here, that must have precedence over all other categories of rights because they create the conditions for precisely that kind of intersubjective action that should allow to address common problems through the display of communicative behaviours.[140] Coherently, civil rights have to take the second place as those entitlements that safeguard the freedom to develop robust individual personalities with clearly defined interests and priorities, thus adequately enabled to politically interact with one another.

Five corollaries can be derived from the general understanding of politics according to the communicative paradigm. The first is that democracy alone has to be considered a legitimate form of government since it is the only one that corresponds to the principle of communicative action, transforming its most fundamental tenets into a set of positive norms for the self-organization and self-determination of the community.[141] While democracy for communitarians is the political expression of a pre-existing system of values which takes form as "popular sovereignty" and for liberals it is a value-free mechanism for working out compromises on contested issues, the exponents of the communicative paradigm regard the democratic form of government as neutral and intrinsically value-laden at the same time.[142] Neutral, indeed, are the procedures of the decision-making processes insofar as they do not rule out any argument for the simple reason that it is assumed to infringe on a predetermined set of deeply rooted beliefs. Yet, these same procedures also represent a value inasmuch as they allow to create an ethical habit as the result of precisely that exchange of arguments. In other words, an open democratic debate establishes the ethically relevant personal conviction that the free political debate is a good worth being protected and, in a second step, forms a specific, albeit always falsifiable, idea of the good life as the product of the argumentative interaction. Secondly, against a certain tradition of political theory—particularly well-established in the English-speaking world—Habermas maintains the central importance of social rights as those "basic rights to the provision of living conditions that are socially, technologically, and ecologically safeguarded, insofar as the current circumstances make this necessary if citizens are to have equal opportunities to utilize … [their] rights".[143] Thus, if the chance of real individuals to make use of their political and civil rights is to be taken seriously, then a basic quality of the individual living conditions has to be guaranteed. Indeed, it is difficult to imagine that hungry human beings without a shelter or adequate health care can be committed citizens or effectively exercise their freedom rights.

Thirdly, no recognition is given, instead, to "collective rights", namely to rights that are attributed to collective entities—more specifically to social groups—and not to individuals.[144] The set of rights that have been interpreted as "collective" by some authors[145] and, meanwhile, also by some constitutional traditions,[146] comprises social goods so essential as health care, cultural, linguistic and religious identity, a healthy environment, a territory, financial rewards from the exploitation of natural resources as well as, in general, the right of a community to exist. From the standpoint of the communicative paradigm, the problem of this theory is that the communities to which rights are granted are regarded as compact and homogeneous unities, basically without internal tensions and contradictions. Furthermore, individuals are considered members of those communities for the simple—and ethically unqualified—reason that they have been born and socialized in their midst. From this matter of fact, it is then deduced that they have to share the allegedly uncontested community values. Against those assumptions, however, cultural, religious and ethnic communities are by far not as uniform as the advocates of collective rights tend to postulate. On the contrary, internal conflicts are anything but uncommon, whereas they generally unfold precisely because one or more individuals do not comply with the rules of the social group—which, moreover, also decisively contests the presumption that individuals are mostly willing to irreflexively identify themselves with their communities. Finally, if some essential rights like health care and a healthy environment are attributed to the social group, does it imply that the individuals who leave the social group of reference are to be deprived of protection? Indeed, a certain number of activities, such as speaking a certain language or worshipping according to a religious tradition, can only be performed together with other individuals, Yet, to guarantee that this happens, no collective rights must be introduced: following the communicative paradigm, it suffices that such entitlements—for instance, to enjoy a financial reward from the exploitation of natural resources or of traditional knowledge—are recognized to the individuals, who can then join to build a community, if they want, to make use of their prerogatives.

Fourthly, communicative democracy does not limit itself to the guarantee of free participation to election, but includes the uninterrupted activity and contribution of the civil society.[147] It is in the civil society, indeed, that the processes of interaction through the exchange of arguments in order to address shared problems unfold in the first place, while the electoral moment must rather be seen as the formal moment that crystallizes, from time to time, the results of that process. Yet, it is precisely that formalization that makes it possible to take decisions. In fact, common issues must find an answer—even if mostly only one that can be falsified by further evidence and modified by new decisions—which contrasts with the ongoing character of the debates within the civil society. As a solution to this contradiction, the formalized political mechanisms—as they are displayed through legislature and executive—are capable of making clear and binding choices on the basis of a still frame of the civil society. In case that this still frame is not actual any longer and, thus, the decisions taken by parliament and government are losing legitimacy, it is the task not only of the parliamentary minority but also of the civil society itself to provide a critical counterbalance. To allow the civil movements to make their voices be peacefully heard between elections, it is important that adequate instruments, such as referenda, are established.

The fifth—and last—corollary states that constitutional adjudication should only serve the purpose of protecting the conditions for the development of social and political relations based on mutual recognition.[148] In contrast to the theories according to which the constitution enshrines absolute values that constitutional courts have to shield, even against the democratic will of the public opinion,[149] the communicative theory of politics understands constitutional provisions in a procedural way, namely as the rules that make a peaceful and effective social interaction possible. Coherently, constitutional adjudication is largely restricted to the safeguard of those rules, without adding to them a substantial ethical content. The task comprises, in the first place, the defence of the formal conditions that enable citizens to social and political participation through a peaceful exchange of arguments. In a more substantial vein, however, in case that the legislature and/or the executive take decisions that impact on particularly sensitive goods and could therefore be detrimental to the life of the community, the communicative self-restriction does not preclude that constitutional courts suspend the implementation of those decisions and require an enhanced parliamentary and social majority.

## 8.4 The Conception of Order According to the Communicative Paradigm

In accordance with the fundamental assumption of the communicative paradigm, society is made up of a *variety of intersubjective relations*, which shape *different forms of interaction*.[150] As already mentioned in the previous sections, the first distinction that should be made is between strategic (or pragmatic) and properly communicative interactions. The first kind of interactions happens when individuals act within contexts dominated by functional systemic rationalities—i.e., when they aim at obtaining the most advantageous performances from the functions carried out by social subsystems—or when they interact, even outside functional subsystems, simply in order to achieve one-sidedly fixed priorities. On the contrary, properly communicative interactions develop when individuals exchange arguments, on the basis of mutual recognition, to work out shared answers to common issues. Yet, within the broad category of communicative interactions, too, we have to make some distinctions, which have a direct impact on the idea of national and international order formulated by the exponents of the communicative paradigm. Indeed, the *lifeworld* of discourses aiming at achieving consensus also displays distinct dimensions, corresponding to the diversity of our communicative needs—and each interaction has the task of developing one of those dimensions. More specifically, in the broad context of society essentially three consensus-oriented forms of communication occur, which have not only different purposes—each of them related to the specific communicative need that the interaction is apt to satisfy—but also distinct contents.

A first category of communicative interactions comprises discourses focusing on the clarification of the existential condition of the individuals involved, on their cultural identity or religious beliefs.[151] This kind of discourses cannot qualify as *political* because, even if all of us may be involved in some variant of them, the answers that are proposed in order to define the existential, cultural or religious identities of the individuals involved are not—and cannot—be shared by all members of the society. Indeed, common responses to the question about "who we are" cut across the social fabric, building communication communities which, even if utterly influential and important for the enhancement of our existential self-awareness, never overlap with the society in its entirety. As a result, the definition of sovereignty—which is insofar essentially political as it necessarily involves all members of the *polis*—should not be mingled with questions concerning cultural or religious identity.

On the contrary, *political* interaction affects *all* individuals being part of the social fabric, regardless of how broad this fabric is, and therefore impacts on the notion of sovereignty. Every kind of interaction needs rules in order to make communication well-ordered, i.e., peaceful, cooperative and effective. Yet, the rules that govern the political sphere—unlike those that lie at the basis of the communication about "who we are"—are positive and binding *laws*; furthermore, insofar as the norms regulate matters of common concern, the *corpus juris* that comprises them is referred to as *public law*. Basically, rules are binding in the political community because they have to be followed by each one of its members. However, according to a postmetaphysical understating of society, in which no authority is recognized that disguises its power-based authority under the veil of tradition or religion, the binding rules of the political community, to be legitimate, have to be confirmed by the community through processes of democratic participation. Two forms of political interaction can be identified, both of them focusing on the question about "how we should respond to the questions of common concern". The first type of political interaction—and second category of communicative interaction taken in its entirety—refers to discourses addressing the organization of public life within a limited territory and with reference to the community of individuals living in that territory or to those individuals who, even though not living there, maintain nevertheless a special relationship to the territory and to its community. This is what we call a *national political community*, which is here understood as a "nation of citizens", thus being devoid of any ethnic connotation.[152] The questions addressed in the national political discourse should not touch on beliefs or on the existential search for the meaning of individual life. Rather, in order to include into the discourse all citizens of the national political community, the questions must have a rather practical content, being limited to issues like the distribution of resources, the organization of the social subsystems and the form of government. Consequently, the identity forged by the common interaction concerning the question on "how to respond to questions of common concern within the borders of a limited political community" is not substantive, in the sense that it does not aim at touching on a deep existential dimension. Rather, it is formal inasmuch as it is centred around the interiorization of the rules of political communication. Within the formal framework of political rules, each existential, cultural or religious community can find its proper space to thrive and cultivate its interests.

The second form of political interaction—and third category of communicative interaction as a whole—refers to the fact that individuals also meet and interact with each other outside the borders of single states, regardless of their belonging to a specific political community. This level of interaction is also governed by law, more precisely by the *corpus juris* of *cosmopolitan* law, consisting of those principles and rules that guarantee a peaceful and cooperative interaction between humans within the most general context of communication, namely beyond the condition of being citizens of an individual state. Embedded in these rules and principles is the fundamental recognition that we owe to every human being as the consequence of the universal capacity to communicate. The discourse of cosmopolitan interaction—shaped by cosmopolitan law—addresses the question on "how to respond to questions of common concern to the whole humankind". In their systematics of public law, the exponents of the communicative paradigm of order—and most explicitly Jürgen Habermas—take up Kant's tripartition,[153] but reinterpret it from an intersubjective perspective.[154] Along the path of their groundbreaking predecessor, domestic public law regulates, at the first level, the interactions between citizens of each single political community as well as between these citizens and the institutions of the same polity. The use of communicative reason and the application of its normative prerequisites guarantee, here, that decisions are taken through deliberative processes based on the reflexive involvement of the citizens. Thus, legitimate sovereignty—according to the communicative paradigm—necessarily takes a "bottom-up" form. At the second level, international public law addresses the relations between citizens of different political communities insofar as they are primarily regarded as citizens of the state; therefore, the relations between individuals which are here the object of regulation are processed through the form of relations between states. Lastly, at the third level, cosmopolitan law is applied to the direct interactions between individuals from different states as well as between individuals and the states of which they are not citizens.

Against the background of the communicative understanding of national, international and cosmopolitan order as a whole, two further aspects should be highlighted, the first regarding the relation between *national and international solidarity*, the second referring to the *democratic legitimation of the cosmopolitan institutional and legal setting*. As regards solidarity in the multilevel setting, it must be kept in mind that, following the communicative paradigm, every one of us participates in a number of different interactions, while maintaining his or her personal and distinctive integrity. This assumption implies a significant novelty as regards the relation between the national and the cosmopolitan communities. Indeed, according to the unitary paradigms of order, individuals are always seen *either* as belonging to a limited and particularistic polity, *or* as being essentially part of the worldwide community of humankind. Instead, if we consider the issue from the viewpoint of the communicative paradigm, each individual is—at the same time and without irresolvable contradictions—a citizen of a specific national society *and* a member of the universal community of humankind. Therefore, as citizens of a national community, the individuals take part in decision-making-processes that foster domestic interests. But, since they are also members of the global communication community, domestic decisions must be weighed against the obligations that we have towards our fellow humans on a global scale. Imbuing all dimensions of social life, communicative rationality provides the organon to deal with the frictions that may arise from the twofold loyalties on the basis of mutual recognition and according to the principle of the best argument. Against this background, the traditional tension between universalism (namely the idea that we belong to a cosmopolitan community of humankind) and particularism (i.e., the conviction that we are essentially part of a limited, mostly national community) is no longer to be regarded as an inescapable contradiction. To the contrary, it is consistent to be universalists as fellow humans, and particularists as fellow citizens. Moreover, we can accept to have stronger and more deep-going duties towards the members of our political community—or, with the words of Thomas Nagel, an "associative obligation" towards "those with whom we stand in a strong political relation"[155]—without denying hereby our commitment towards global citizenship.[156] The only condition that must be met—admittedly, one that requires a lot of sensitivity—is to distinguish clearly between the issues of citizenship and the discourse which defines them, on the one hand, and discourses and practices aiming at the worldwide protection of human rights on the other.

On the basis of this readjustment of the conceptual framework, we can address the fundamental question about the justifiable specific rights of citizens that make them different from aliens. Indeed, no doubts can be raised on the fact that being born within a specific political and social community is completely accidental, so that no difference should be made, on this account, between citizens and non-citizens. Yet, the consequences of the accidental fact of being born in a certain country are by far not as ethically neutral as the fact itself. In particular, although our initial belonging may be fortuitous, the circumstance of being raised within the horizon of values of a specific society makes us—more or less consciously—members of precisely *that* community. The condition of particular belonging has two dimensions, the first of which consists in the participation in the *political* interaction with the purpose of determining the way how common concerns are addressed. Surely, in traditional societies this participation is rather passive, whereas within a democratic institutional framework the contribution by the individuals is expected to be active and reflexive. In any case, the specific way to address political questions that characterizes a particular society necessarily requires, in order to survive, a support—an implicit one, at least—by the citizens (or the subjects). And, since the problems addressed by political means are, case by case, the questions of a specific society, the individuals involved in the political discourse cannot but be the members of *that* society— and no one else. On the basis of this involvement, we can justify the exclusive political rights of citizens. Furthermore, given that democratic institutions require—and allow—a higher level of participation, it is even more important for democracies to clarify who is entitled to be politically involved, and who is not: due to the connection between democratic self-governance and territorial representation, we have to assume that territorial closure is essential for democratic legitimacy.[157]

Political rights, however, are not the only ones which only belong to citizens; some *social* rights may be exclusive as well. In fact, the accidental circumstance of being born into a society transforms individuals into members of a social bond. Within this bond we may expect more solidarity than from outside—for the simple reason that we are willing to guarantee the same level of solidarity to the other members—and we are disposed to a more substantial redistribution of resources. Certainly, the safeguard of social rights and the benefits that can be derived from them are hugely different from one country to the other. But inequalities, insofar as they are not depending on past or present external interventions leading to exploitation, are generally based on a kind of *social contract* that distinguishes a specific society from any other. In other words, how many resources are spent on health care, social security or education of the disadvantaged, builds upon the specific agreement between distinct social groups and interests in that particular society, as well as on what every citizen was and is disposed to give for the common welfare. The balance between social groups—always endangered by selfish interests— and the quality of the provisions may be easily endangered by a dramatic influx of migrants who never contributed to the charges deriving from the agreement. An unrestricted right to immigration would put all immigrants in the condition of being full members of the hosting society, with the entire endowment of political and social rights. Hence, given that political rights and some social rights are owned only by citizens, we are justifiably entitled to deny unlimited entry to non-citizens. However, we have also to take into account that individuals who have been born into an authoritarian or unjust society are not responsible for their fate. The answer cannot consist, nevertheless, in opening indistinctively all gates of the democratic and more affluent societies but, first, in putting pressure on the governments of the First World in order to avoid misguided and unjust policies of social and environmental exploitation. Furthermore, support has to be given to generous programmes for the development of the living conditions in the countries of origin of the would-be immigrants. In addition to these measures, however, a sustainable number of immigrants should be allowed to enter the First World countries on a yearly basis. As regards this last point, the one-sided preference for the admission of skilled and well-educated individuals is morally justifiable only under the condition that their immigration can be of benefit for both the immigrants themselves and the society they are leaving. Otherwise, more fair-minded criteria should be preferred.

Moving on, now, to the question of the adequate legitimation of the cosmopolitan institutional and legal setting, it has to be pointed out, in the first place, that since the cosmopolitan dimension is no less political than the national—albeit evidently different from it—an exclusively *moral* justification of decisions cannot be considered sufficient. Indeed, moral discourses refer to actions whose justification is regarded as universally valid and whose implementation is seen as a duty, regardless of the existence of a political and legal framework. In other words, moral obligations are not discussed within institutionalized public fora and do not have laws that make them binding. On the contrary, cosmopolitanism is characterized by a clearly defined institutional and legal framework—basically, international organizations and their legal regimes—in which common concerns can be discussed and legally binding measures are taken. Because the cosmopolitan dimension is therefore essentially *political*, the decisions adopted by its institutions—analogously to what can be claimed for the national level—are legitimate only if those on whom the measures are assumed to impact, are also involved in the decision-making process. In short, the legitimation of the decisions issued at the cosmopolitan level has to be *democratic*. However, it must be conceded that the political dimension of cosmopolitanism displays a significant difference from its national counterpart: albeit both are thought to address common concerns, in the latter case the number of individuals involved by those concerns and the territorial range of their impact are limited, while in cosmopolitanism no limitation is given and the concerns are essentially universal—a characteristic, by the way, that the cosmopolitan dimension shares with the moral discourse. Concretely, cosmopolitan order is based on two pillars: a thin layer of international organizations—largely comprised of institutions under the aegis of a reformed UN—with the limited task to protect peace and fundamental human rights,[158] and the nation states which make up the international community. However, in contrast with the present situation and with any kind of technocratic idea of governance, *both* pillars should be endowed with adequate democratic legitimation. This implies—on the side of the whole of the international organization—a serious effort towards the parliamentarization of as many institutions of the international community as possible,[159] and on the other hand a no less heartfelt commitment to the development of democracy inside the individual states. Yet, this system of so-called dual democracy[160], which is already made difficult by the universal extent of the institutional and legal framework, is then even more severely hampered by the undemocratic nature of many national regimes. Indeed, it is hard to imagine how the institutions of the international community can be shaped in a more democratic way if a significant number of member states violate the most fundamental democratic rules. Under these circumstances, the role of the democratic representation of the worldwide community of citizens may provisionally and putatively be taken on by a permanent assembly of NGOs, characterized by precise deliberative rules and unequivocally endowed with the right to be heard. The fact that political cosmopolitanism shares the universalistic attitude with moral discourses is, here, of advantage: indeed, moral discourses can provide an additional justification to decisions taken on the rather thin basis of an incomplete democratic legitimation.

## 8.5 The Perspective of a Cosmopolitan Order of Freedom and Justice in Difficult Times

The normative content of the communicative paradigm is—in accordance with Kant's theory of morals—explicitly counterfactual. This means that it does not aim at depicting the reality, but at contraposing to the social and political conditions, as they are, an alternative perspective and rational answers to the issues raised by those same conditions. Such an assumption does not imply, however, that communicative interaction represents a world apart whose realization would imply a chiliastic turn. More in Hegel's than in Kant's vein, two factors are introduced to reconnect the normative aspiration to the reality. First, intersubjective communication based on mutual recognition is not a chimaera inasmuch as it is already *anticipated* in some interpersonal, social and political contexts. In other words, it may not be expanded to all forms of communication, but we can experience it in some favourable circumstances. The consequence is not that we should assume that communicative interaction will someday shine through every social relation: in fact, functional rationality is ineludible—and rightly so—while strategic action is destined to remain part of our life. Thus, the tension between facts and norms will shape our destiny for the foreseeable future. The point is only that we have to acknowledge that norms are also facts to some extent, or, even if a significant part of them is intrinsically counterfactual, some elements can paradoxically become factual as well. Secondly, the answers to social and political problems based on the communicative understanding of reason should not be distant dreams, but must have the character of *feasible proposals*.

In times of increasing national selfishness, in which democracies are on the retreat and—amidst of their many traditional fallacies—appear to lose even their most valuable focus, the assertion that a cosmopolitan order of freedom and justice is a feasible proposal seems to be extremely daring, if not downright out of touch with the world. Faced with the contemporary hardship, the most immediate answer that could be given from the point of view of communicative rationality is that, even if some solutions might presently be unfashionable, they nevertheless maintain their truth content as long as they enshrine the arguably most reasonable positions. Even if this consideration may be generally true, we also have to admit that it is of rather limited practical help, if any. Rather, we should courageously address the question of how we can deal, from the standpoint of the communicative rationality, with a world that seems at times to be light-years away from it. To this purpose, the distinction between the real and the ideal communication community can, once again, come to the aid. Let us assume that the present international community—with all its failures and shortcomings, violations of human rights and power displays—takes the role of the real communication community, while a world of peace, freedom and justice represents its ideal counterpart. No doubt can be raised on the sheer fact that it is the real communication community the one in which we have to act, which means that it is the nation states as they are, with their selfishness and cunnings, that build the framework of international agreements. In other words, it may be arguably advisable to make arrangements even with tyrannical regimes, if it is to avoid greater damage and suffering. Indeed, the principle of responsibility prescribes that, under certain circumstances, we are allowed to decide not to protect right holders—at least not immediately and without compromise—from the harm that is currently done to them, in case that an intervention might produce even more misery.[161]

Obviously, it is always difficult to quantify the respective suffering and, therefore, to decide about the right moment for an intervention. To make two examples, the refrain from military action against the Nazi regime in 1938, in order to save the lives of tens of thousands of innocent soldiers, arguably led in the end to the loss of many more human lives under unspeakable circumstances—and was therefore a miscalculation of the respective real and possible damages as well as a political and moral failure. On the contrary, a rather cautious attitude during the Cold War—with the remarkable and unsettling exceptions of what has been done through proxy wars and the active support of brutal, but staunchly pro-Western dictatorships—ultimately led the liberal world to prevail without direct confrontations. Thus, it can be seen as a morally and politically justifiable approach, irrespective of how the Western world forfeited its moral advantage, in the aftermath of the victory, because of its irresponsible carelessness towards questions of justice and mutual recognition on the international scale. However, if responsibility commands—regardless of all intrinsic difficulties—to cautiously weigh advantages and disadvantages before moving on to action, it is also unquestionable that this command only holds true, from the standpoint of the communicative paradigm, under the condition that we always keep in mind the perspective of the ideal communication community. In other words, arrangements within the real communication community—i.e., the real community of states—are only justified if they can reasonably be interpreted as steps towards the implementation of the ideal communication community, namely of an international community based on peace, freedom, justice and the respect of human rights. Furthermore, the essential contents of human rights should never be explicitly denied by our actions or omissions. To act in a morally justifiable way—as Apel put it—we have to progressively realize the ideal communication community in the real communication community.[162]

In conclusion, I would like to draw attention to an element of the communicative paradigm which is not social, political or moral, but essentially *existential*. In his *Eros and Civilization*, Herbert Marcuse wrote:

> The philosophy which epitomizes the antagonistic relation between subject and object also retains the image of their reconciliation. The restless labour of the transcending subject terminates in the ultimate unity of subject and object: the idea of "being-in-and-for-itself," existing in its own fulfilment. The Logos of gratification contradicts the Logos of alienation: the effort to harmonize the two animates the inner history of Western metaphysics.[163]

According to his interpretation, most of the major works of Western philosophy present an intellectual journey ending with a stage—which is assumed to be the highest development of human spirit—characterized by a condition in which individuals find their solace while being "at one" with the world. While the prototype of this attitude is probably to locate in the Indian philosophy, namely in the notion of Nirvana, it was Hegel who delivered the most powerful and fascinating adaptation of that everlasting longing to the conditions of Western thinking. In fact, subjective reason, or the logos, is assumed not only to dominate the outside object but also to end up being one with it. This condition of final reconciliation does not only express the illimited gnoseological penetration of the object and the ethical conviction of being part of a well-ordered society; rather, it also includes the feeling of comfort driven by the certainty—or at least the hope—of having found a way to overcome alienation and estrangement. In the Indian Nirvana, the sentiment of reconciliation between the individual and the outside world is realized through the awareness of the unity of the whole universe, once passions have been silenced. On the other hand, Hegel's spirit depicts reconciliation as a triumph of a subjectivity which has abandoned the world of intersubjective relations and has turned in upon itself. The communicative paradigm goes beyond both of these perspectives (as well as beyond both their shortcomings) insofar as it sketches the fundamentals of a thinking in which reconciliation is explicitly rooted in real social interactions—always as a background to make them meaningful, and sometimes as a tangible experience.

Towards the end of his monumental *St. Matthew Passion*, Johann Sebastian Bach inserted a chorale, whose text—written by Picander—reads:

| | |
|---|---|
| Wenn ich einmal soll scheiden, | When once I must depart, |
| So scheide nicht von mir! | Do not depart from me! |
| Wenn ich den Tod soll leiden, | When I must suffer death, |
| So tritt Du dann herfür! | Then stand Thou by me! |

Though a prayer addressed to God, these verses can be interpreted as an appeal to our fellow humans as well: when faced with the mystery of life and death, we hope that our struggling may be eased through empathy and solidarity. Bach's oratorio, which was composed in 1727, proves that the hope and the longing for intersubjective recognition is nothing new in the history of human spirit. It is also to assume that the works of art may have expressed that hope and longing with a heartfelt impact hardly attainable by philosophical research. Nonetheless, credit must be given to the advocates of the communicative paradigm for having explicitly shaped the deep existential aspiration to that "being at one with oneself in the otherness"—already pointed out by Hegel—in terms of relationships between mutually sympathetic individuals and for having enriched this aspiration with a conceptual framework that encompasses the social, political and legal world, potentially going even far beyond this. Indeed, while in the social, political and legal context the right order is the order of rules legitimated through reflexive consensus, in the existential world the very same order is the order of love.

## Notes

1. Ingmar Bergman, *The Seventh Seal: The Screenplay*, available at https://www.imsdb.com/scripts/Seventh-Seal,-The.html, accessed 10 September 2020.
2. *The Holy Bible, The New Testament*, Book of Revelation, Chapter 8, para. 1.
3. Søren Kierkegaard, *Enten – Eller* (1843) (English translation of Volume II by Walter Lowrie: *Either/Or. Volume Two*, Humphrey Milford, Oxford University Press, London 1944, at 181 et seq.).
4. Jürgen Habermas, *Der philosophische Diskurs der Moderne*, Suhrkamp, Frankfurt a. M. 1988, 1st ed. 1985, at 65 (English translation by Frederick Lawrence: *The Philosophical Discourse of Modernity*, Polity Press, Cambridge 1990, 1st ed. 1987, at 51).
5. Sergio Dellavalle, *Freiheit und Intersubjektivität*, Akademie Verlag, Berlin 1998.
6. Georg Wilhelm Friedrich Hegel, *Frühe Schriften I* (1792–1796), Friedhelm Nicolin and Gisela Schüler eds., in: Georg Wilhelm Friedrich Hegel, *Gesammelte Werke*, Meiner, Hamburg 1968 et seq., Volume 1, at 368 et seq.; Georg Wilhelm Friedrich Hegel, *Frühe Schriften*, in: Georg Wilhelm Friedrich Hegel, *Werke in zwanzig Bänden*, Eva Moldenhauer and Karl Markus Michel eds., Suhrkamp, Frankfurt a. M. 1970, Volume 1, at 205 et seq. (partial English translation by T. M. Knox: *On Christianity*, Harper & Brothers, New York 1948, at 151 et seq.).
7. Hegel, *Frühe Schriften I*, supra note 6, at 83 et seq.; Hegel, *Frühe Schriften*, supra note 6, at 9 et seq.
8. Georg Wilhelm Friedrich Hegel, *Ueber die wissenschaftlichen Behandlungsarten des Naturrechts, seine Stelle in der praktischen Philosophie, und sein Verhältniß zu den positiven Rechtswissenschaften* (1802–1803),

in: Hegel, *Gesammelte Werke*, *supra* note 6, Volume 4: *Jenaer kritische Schriften*, Hartmut Buchner and Otto Pöggeler eds., 417–485, at 449 et seq.; also in: Hegel, *Werke in zwanzig Bänden*, *supra* note 6, Volume 2: *Jenaer Schriften 1801–1807*, 434–530, at 480 et seq.; Georg Wilhelm Friedrich Hegel, *System der Sittlichkeit* (1802–1803), in: Georg Wilhelm Friedrich Hegel, *Schriften zur Politik und Rechtsphilosophie*, Georg Lasson ed., Meiner, Leipzig 1923, 413–499, at 460 et seq. (English translation by H. S. Harris and T. M. Knox in: *System of Ethical Life and First Philosophy of Spirit*, State University of New York Press, Albany 1979, 97–177).

9. Steven B. Smith, *Hegel's Critique of Liberalism*, University of Chicago press, Chicago 1989; Allen W. Wood, *Hegel's Ethical Thought*, Cambridge University Press, Cambridge/New York 1990; Michael O. Hardimon, *Hegel's Social Philosophy: The Project of Reconciliation*, Cambridge University Press, Cambridge/New York 1994.

10. Georg Wilhelm Friedrich Hegel, *Frühe Schriften* [aus der Frankfurter Zeit] (1797–1800), in: Hegel, *Frühe Schriften*, *supra* note 6, 237–448, at 341 et seq., 419 et seq. (English translation in: *On Christianity*, *supra* note 6, at 224 et seq., 309 et seq.).

11. Ibid., at 372 et seq., 421 et seq. (English: at 224 et seq., 309 et seq.).

12. Georg Wilhelm Friedrich Hegel, *Jenaer Systementwürfe I* (1803–1804), Klaus Düsing and Heinz Kimmerle eds., in: *Gesammelte Werke*, *supra* note 6, Volume 6, at 266 et seq. (English translation by H. S. Harris and T. M. Knox in: *System of Ethical Life and First Philosophy of Spirit*, *supra* note 8, 187–250, at 205 et seq.).

13. Georg Wilhelm Friedrich Hegel, *Jenaer Systementwürfe III* (1805–1806), Rolf-Peter Horstmann ed., in: Hegel, *Gesammelte Werke*, *supra* note 6, Volume 8, at 263 (English translation by Leo Rauch: *Hegel and the Human Spirit*, Wayne State University Press, Detroit 1983, at 160).

14. Hegel, *System der Sittlichkeit*, *supra* note 8, at 451 et seq. (English: at 116 et seq.).

15. Georg Wilhelm Friedrich Hegel, *Phänomenologie des Geistes* (1807), in: Hegel, *Werke in zwanzig Bänden*, *supra* note 6, Volume 3, at 145 et seq. (English translation by Terry Pinkard: *The Phenomenology of Spirit*, Cambridge University Press, Cambridge/New York 2018, at 108 et seq.).

16. Hegel, *Jenaer Systementwürfe I*, *supra* note 12, at 307 et seq. (English: at 236 et seq.).

17. Hegel, *Jenaer Systementwürfe III*, *supra* note 13, at 214 et seq. (English: at 110 et seq.).

18. Ibid., at 277 et seq. (English: at 173 et seq.).

19. Hegel, *Phänomenologie des Geistes*, supra note 15, at 575 et seq. (English: at 454 et seq.). In the *Phenomenology of Spirit*, however, the "absolute spirit" is still defined as the "absolute knowing".
20. Georg Wilhelm Friedrich Hegel, *Wissenschaft der Logik* (1812–1816), in: Hegel, *Werke in zwanzig Bänden*, supra note 6, Volume 5 and Volume 6, insbesondere: Volume 6, at 243 et seq. (English translation by George Di Giovanni, Cambridge University Press, Cambridge/New York 2010, at 507 et seq.
21. Georg Wilhelm Friedrich Hegel, *Enzyklopädie der philosophischen Wissenschaften im Grundrisse* (1830), Wolfgang Bonsiepen and Hans-Christian Lucas eds., in: Hegel, *Gesammelte Werke*, supra note 6, Volume 20; also in: Hegel, *Werke in zwanzig Bänden*, supra note 6, Volume 10, Ludwig Boumann ed. (1845), § 430 et seq., at 219 et seq. (English translation by William Wallace: *Encyclopaedia of the Philosophical Sciences*, Part 3, Clarendon Press, Oxford 1971).
22. Georg Wilhelm Friedrich Hegel, *Grundlinien der Philosophie des Rechts* (1821), in: Hegel, *Werke in zwanzig Bänden*, supra note 6, Volume 7, § 268, at 413 (English translation by S. W. Dyde: *Philosophy of Right*, George Bell, London, 1896).
23. Ibid., § 258, at 399 et seq.
24. Ibid., § 4 et seq., at 46 et seq.
25. Ibid., § 182 et seq., at 339 et seq.
26. Ibid., § 35 et seq., at 93 et seq.
27. Hegel, *Enzyklopädie*, in: *Werke in zwanzig Bänden*, supra note 21, § 535 et seq., at 330 et seq.
28. Hegel, *Grundlinien der Philosophie des Rechts*, supra note 22, § 340, at 503.
29. Ibid., § 333, at 500.
30. Georg Wilhelm Friedrich Hegel, *Vorlesungen über Naturrecht und Staatswissenschaft. Nachgeschrieben von P. Wannenmann* (1817–1818), C. Becker et al. eds., Meiner, Hamburg 1983., § 162, at 253; Hegel, *Grundlinien der Philosophie des Rechts*, supra note 22, § 194, at 350; Georg Wilhelm Friedrich Hegel, *Vorlesungen über die Philosophie der Weltgeschichte. Berlin 1822/23. Nachschriften von Karl Gustav Julius von Griesheim, Heinrich Gustav Hotho und Friedrich Carl Hermann Victor von Kehler* (1822–1823), Karl Heinz Ilting, Karl Brehmer and Hoo Nam Seelmann eds., Meiner, Hamburg 1996, at 33 et seq.
31. Hegel, *Enzyklopädie*, in: *Werke in zwanzig Bänden*, supra note 21, § 382, at 25.
32. Hegel, *Vorlesungen über die Philosophie der Weltgeschichte. Berlin 1822/23*, supra note 30, at 72 et seq.; Georg Wilhelm Friedrich Hegel, *Vorlesungen über die Philosophie der Weltgeschichte* (1822–1831), Georg Lasson ed., Meiner, Leipziz 1917/1920, Volume 1, at 110 et seq.

(English translation by H. B. Nisbet: *Lectures on the Philosophy of World History*, Cambridge University Press, Cambridge/New York 1975, at 93 et seq.).
33. Hegel, *Phänomenologie des Geistes*, supra note 15, at 583 (English: at 460).
34. Ibid., at 431 et seq. (English: at 339).
35. Georg Wilhelm Friedrich Hegel, *Ästhetik* (1842), F. Bassenge ed., on the basis of H. G. Hotho's second edition, Aufbau-Verlag, Berlin/Weimar 1984, Volume 1, at 106 et seq (English translation by T. M. Knox: *Aesthetics*, Clarendon Press, Oxford 1975, Volume I, at 99).
36. Hegel, *Enzyklopädie*, in: *Werke in zwanzig Bänden*, supra note 21, § 385, at 32 et seq.
37. Karl Marx, Friedrich Engels, *Die deutsche Ideologie* (1845–1846), in: Karl Marx, Friedrich Engels, *Werke*, Volume 3, Dietz, Berlin/DDR 1969, 5–530, at 33 (English translation: *The German Ideology*, Prometheus Books, New York 1998, at 53).
38. Ibid.
39. Ibid., at 29 et seq. (English: at 48 et seq.).
40. Karl Marx, *Ökonomisch-philosophische Manuskripte* (1844), in: Marx/Engels, *Werke*, supra n. 37, Ergänzungsband (additional volume), Part 1, Dietz, Berlin/DDR 1968, 465–588, at 511 et seq. (English translation by Martin Milligan: Karl Marx, *Economic and Philosophic Manuscripts and the Communist Manifesto*, Prometheus Books, New York 1988, 13–168, at 71).
41. Ibid., at 512 (English: at 71 et seq.).
42. Ibid., at 514 (English: at 74).
43. Ibid., at 515 et seq. (English: at 75 et seq.).
44. Ibid., at 517 et seq. (English: at 78).
45. Ibid., at 484 et seq. (English: at 36 et seq.).
46. Karl Marx, *Das Kapital. Band I* (1867), in: Marx/Engels, *Werke*, supra note 37, Volume 23, 11–802, Dietz, Berlin /DDR 1962, at 226 (English translation by Ben Fowkes: *Capital. Volume I*, Penguin Books, London 1990 (1st ed. 1976), at 320).
47. Ibid.
48. Ibid., at 214 et seq. (English: at 307 et seq.).
49. Ibid., at 221 (English: at 315).
50. Marx, *Ökonomisch-philosophische Manuskripte*, supra note 40, at 502 (English: at 59).
51. Ibid., at 537 (English: at 103).
52. Ibid., at 536 (English: at 102).
53. Karl Marx, Friedrich Engels, *Manifest der Kommunistischen Partei* (1848), in: Marx/Engels, *Werke*, supra note 37, Volume 4, Dietz, Berlin/DDR 1959, 459–493, at 462 (English translation in: Marx,

*Economic and Philosophic Manuscripts and the Communist Manifesto*, supra n. 40, 203–243, at 209).
54. Ibid., at 493 (English: at 243).
55. Ibid., at 474 (English: at 222).
56. Karl Marx, *Das Kapital. Band III* (1894), in: Marx/Engels, *Werke*, supra note 37, Volume 25, Dietz, Berlin/DDR 1983, at 221 et seq. (English translation by David Fernbach: *Capital. Volume III*, Penguin Books, London 1981, at 317 et seq.).
57. Ibid., at 242 et seq. (English: at 339 et seq.).
58. Ibid., at 251 et seq. (English: at 349 et seq.).
59. John Dewey, *How We Think*, Heath and Company, Lexington (MA), 1933, at 4.
60. Ibid., at 5.
61. Ibid., at 4.
62. John Dewey, *Democracy and Education* (1915), Aakar Books, Dehly 2004, at 163.
63. Dewey, *How We Think*, supra note 59, at 9.
64. Ibid., at 5 et seq.
65. Dewey, *Democracy and Education*, supra note 62, at 163.
66. Dewey, *How We Think*, supra note 59, at 14.
67. John Dewey, *Reconstruction in Philosophy*, Henry Holt and Company, New York 1920, at 50.
68. Ibid., at 192.
69. Ibid., at 193.
70. Ibid., at 194.
71. Dewey, *Democracy and Education*, supra note 62.
72. Ibid., at 106.
73. John Dewey, *The Public and its Problems*, Alan Swallow, Denver 1927, at 158.
74. John Dewey, *Liberalism and Social Action* (1935), Capricorn Books, New York 1963, at 56 et seq.
75. Dewey, *The Public and Its Problems*, supra note 73, at 150.
76. Ibid., at 148.
77. Dewey, *Democracy and Education*, supra note 62, at 93 et seq.
78. Dewey, *Liberalism and Social Action*, supra note 74, at 71.
79. Ibid., at 79.
80. Hannah Arendt, *The Human Condition* (1958), University of Chicago Press, Chicago 1998, at 7.
81. Ibid.
82. Ibid., at 136.
83. Ibid., at 22.
84. Ibid., at 7.
85. Ibid., at 22 et seq.

86. Ibid., at 28 et seq.
87. Ibid., at 25 et seq.; 175 et seq.
88. Ibid., at 26 et seq.
89. Ibid., at 33 et seq.
90. Ibid., at 68.
91. Ibid.
92. Plato, *The Republic*, English translation by Tom Griffith, Cambridge University Press, Cambridge/New York 2003, 1st ed. 2000, Book VII, 514a et seq., at 220 et seq.
93. Ibid., Book VI, 484 a et seq., at 186 et seq.
94. Arendt, *The Human Condition*, supra note 80, at 222. For a different interpretation of Plato's political philosophy, see Sect. 2.1.2.1. Putting together the two approaches to Plato's position, it could be said that he was, to some extent, the last defender of the spirit of the *polis* as a community characterized by the citizens' full commitment of its wellbeing, as well as the first advocate of a more hierarchical and power-oriented understanding of the political life.
95. Arendt, *The Human Condition*, supra note 80, at 222.
96. Hannah Arendt, *The Origins of Totalitarianism* (1951), Harcourt Brace and Company, San Diego/New York/London 1973, at 305 et seq.
97. See Sect. 7.1.1.
98. Donald Davidson, *Problems of Rationality*, Clarendon, Oxford 2004, at 3 et seq., 15 et seq.
99. Donald Davidson, *Subjective, Intersubjective, Objective*, Clarendon, Oxford 2001, at 39 et seq.
100. Davidson, *Problems of Rationality*, supra note 98, at 18.
101. Davidson, *Subjective, Intersubjective, Objective*, supra note 99, at 107 et seq.
102. Ibid., at 120 et seq.
103. Davidson, *Problems of Rationality*, supra note 98, at 39 et seq.
104. Robert Brandom, *Making It Explicit*, Harvard University Press, Cambridge (MA) 1998 (1st ed. 1994), at 132 et seq., 618 et seq.
105. Jürgen Habermas, *Wahrheit und Rechtfertigung*, Suhrkamp, Frankfurt a. M. 2004, at 153 (English translation by Barbara Fultner: *Truth and Justification*, MIT Press, Cambridge (MA) 2003, at 144).
106. Brandom, *Making It Explicit*, supra note 104, at 622.
107. Ibid.
108. Habermas, *Wahrheit und Rechtfertigung*, supra note 105, at 138 et seq. (English: at 131 et seq.).
109. See Brandom's Hegel interpretations, available at http://www.pitt.edu/~rbrandom, accessed 25 August 2000.
110. Brandom, *Making It Explicit*, supra note 104, at 624.

111. Jürgen Habermas, *Vorstudien und Ergänzungen zur Theorie des kommunikativen Handelns*, Suhrkamp, Frankfurt a. M. 1984, at 598 et seq.; Jürgen Habermas, *Nachmetaphysisches Denken*, Suhrkamp, Frankfurt a. M. 1988, at 105 et seq. (English translation by William Mark Hohengarten: *Postmetaphysical Thinking*, The MIT Press, Cambridge (MA) 1992, at 57 et seq.); Habermas, *Wahrheit und Rechtfertigung*, supra n. 105, at 110 et seq. (English translation by Maeve Cooke: *On the Pragmatics of Communication*, MIT Press, Cambridge (MA) 1998, at 315 et seq.).
112. Habermas, *Nachmetaphysisches Denken*, supra note 111, at 72 (English translation: *Actions, Speech Acts, Linguistically Mediated Interactions and the Lifeworld*, in: Guttorn Fløistad (ed.), *Philosophical Problems Today. Volume I*, Kluwer, Dordrecht 1994, 45–74, at 53).
113. Ibid. (English: at 53).
114. Habermas, *Vorstudien und Ergänzungen zur Theorie des kommunikativen Handelns*, supra note 111, at 135 et seq.
115. See Sect. 1.2.
116. Habermas, *Vorstudien und Ergänzungen zur Theorie des kommunikativen Handelns*, supra note 111, at 174 et seq.
117. Habermas, *Wahrheit und Rechtfertigung*, supra note 105, at 249 (English: at 359).
118. Karl-Otto Apel, *Selected Essays. Volume Two: Ethics and the Theory of Rationality*, Eduardo Mendieta ed., Humanities Press, Atlantic Highlands (NJ) 1996, at 137 et seq.
119. Karl-Otto Apel, *Transformation der Philosophie*, Suhrkamp, Frankfurt a. M. 1999 (1st ed. 1973), Volume 2, 358–435 (English translation by Glyn Adey and David Frisby, in: Apel, *Selected Essays. Volume Two*, supra note 118, 1–67).
120. Ibid., at 423 et seq. (English: at 43 et seq.); Karl-Otto Apel, *Diskurs und Verantwortung. Das Problem des Übergangs zur postkonventionellen Moral*, Suhrkamp, Frankfurt a. M. 1990, at 141 et seq., 198 et seq. (English translation by Glyn Adey and David Frisby, in: Apel, *Selected Essays. Volume Two*, supra n. 118, at 233 et seq.).
121. Apel, *Transformation der Philosophie*, supra note 119, at 429 (English: at 47).
122. Hans Jonas, *Das Prinzip Verantwortung. Versuch einer Ethik für die technologische Zivilisation*, Suhrkamp, Frankfurt a. M. 1984, 1st ed. 1979 (English translation: *The Imperative of Responsibility*, University of Chicago Press, Chicago 1984).
123. Jürgen Habermas, *Erläuterungen zur Diskursethik*, Suhrkamp, Frankfurt a. M. 1991, at 219 et seq. (English translation by Ciaran P. Cronin: *Justification and Application*, MIT Press, Cambridge (MA) 2001, 1st ed. 1994, at 105 et seq.).

124. See Section 6.1.
125. Jürgen Habermas, *Theorie des kommunikativen Handelns*, 2 Volumes, Suhrkamp, Frankfurt a. M. 1988, 1st ed. 1981 (English translation by Thomas McCarthy: *The Theory of Communicative Action*, 2 Volumes, Beacon Press, Boston 1984 and 1987); Apel, *Selected Essays. Volume Two*, supra note 118, at 316 et seq.
126. Axel Honneth, *Kampf um Anerkennung*, Suhrkamp, Frankfurt a. M. 1992 (English translation by Joel Anderson: *The Struggle for Recognition*, Polity Press, Cambridge 1996); Jürgen Habermas, *Die Einbeziehung des Anderen*, Suhrkamp, Frankfurt a. M. 1996, at 237 et seq. (English translation by Ciaran Cronin and Pablo de Greiff: *The Inclusion of the Other*, MIT Press, Cambridge (MA) 1998, at 203 et seq.).
127. See Sect. 7.1.
128. Habermas, *Der philosophische Diskurs der Moderne*, supra note 4.
129. Jan Klabbers, *Setting the Scene*, in: Jan Klabbers, Anne Peters, Geir Ulfstein (eds.), *The Constitutionalization of International Law*, Oxford University Press, Oxford/New York 2009, 1–44, at 18.
130. See Sects. 3.3.4, 4.5, and 4.6.
131. Klabbers, *Setting the Scene*, supra note 129, at 18.
132. See Sect. 8.4.
133. Vicki C. Jackson, *Constitutional Engagement in a Transnational Era*, Oxford University Press, Oxford/New York 2010.
134. Tania Groppi, Marie-Claire Ponthoreau, *The Use of Foreign Precedents by Constitutional Judges: A Limited Practice, An Uncertain Future*, in: Tania Groppi, Marie-Claire Ponthoreau (eds.), *The Use of Foreign Precedents by Constitutional Judges*, Hart, Oxford/Portland (OR) 2013, 411–431.
135. Clara Marsan-Raventós, *From Judicial Dialogue to Cosmopolitan Norms: Enhancing Democracy in Globalised States*, in: Amrei Müller (ed.), *Judicial Dialogue and Human Rights*, Cambridge University Press, Cambridge/New York 2017, 435–466.
136. Eyal Benvenisti, George W. Downs, *Between Fragmentation and Democracy: The Role of National and International Courts*, Cambridge University Press, Cambridge/New York 2017.
137. Andreas Fischer-Lescano, Gunther Teubner, *Regime-Collisions: The Vain Search for Legal Unity in the Fragmentation of Global Law*, in: "Michigan Journal of International Law", Vol. 25 (2004), 999–1046, at 1018.
138. Paul Schiff Berman, *Global Legal Pluralism*, Cambridge University Press, Cambridge/New York 2012, at 294 et seq.
139. Geir Ulfstein, *The International Judiciary*, in: Klabbers/Peters/Ulfstein, *The Constitutionalization of International Law*, supra note 129, 126–152.

140. Jürgen Habermas, *Faktizität und Geltung*, Suhrkamp, Frankfurt a. M. 1992, at 151 et seq. (English translation by William Rehg: *Between Facts and Norms*, MIT Press, Cambridge (MA) 1996, at 118 et seq.).
141. Ibid., at 349 et seq. (English: at 287 et seq.).
142. Ibid., at 358 et seq. (English: at 295 et seq.); Habermas, *Die Einbeziehung des Anderen*, supra note 126, at 154 et seq. (English: at 129 et seq.).
143. Habermas, *Die Einbeziehung des Anderen*, supra note 126, at 156 et seq. (English: at 123).
144. Ibid., at 239 et seq. (English: at 205 et seq.).
145. Charles Taylor et al., *Multiculturalism*, Princeton University Press, Princeton (NJ) 1994.
146. See, in particular, the Constitutions of Ecuador (2008) and of Bolivia (2009).
147. Habermas, *Faktizität und Geltung*, supra note 140, at 399 et seq. (English: at 329 et seq.).
148. Ibid., at 324 et seq. (English: at 267 et seq.).
149. Frank Michelman, *Law's Republic*, in: "Yale Law Journal", Vol. 97 (1988), 1493–1537; Ernst Wolfgang Böckenförde, *Recht, Freiheit, Staat*, Suhrkamp, Frankfurt a. M. 1991.
150. Habermas, *Erläuterungen zur Diskursethik*, supra note 123, at 100 et seq. (English: at 1 et seq.).
151. Habermas, *Die Einbeziehung des Anderen*, supra note 126, at 257 et seq. (English: at 220 et seq.).
152. Jürgen Habermas, *Die postnationale Konstellation*, Suhrkamp, Frankfurt a. M. 1998, at 96 et seq. (English translation by Max Pensky: *The Postnational Constellation*, MIT Press, Cambridge (MA) 2001, at 62 et seq.).
153. See Sect. 4.4.
154. Jürgen Habermas, *Der gespaltene Westen*, Suhrkamp, Frankfurt a. M. 2001 (English translation by Ciaran Cronin: *The Divided West*, Polity Press, Cambridge 2006); Jürgen Habermas, *Eine politische Verfassung für die pluralistische Weltgesellschaft?*, in: "Kritische Justiz", Vol. 38 (2005), 222–247; Jürgen Habermas, *Kommunikative Rationalität und grenzüberschreitende Politik: eine Replik*, in: Peter Niesen, Benjamin Herborth (eds.), *Anarchie der kommunikativen Freiheit*, Suhrkamp, Frankfurt a. M. 2007, 406–459; Jürgen Habermas, *Konstitutionalisierung des Völkerrechts und die Legitimationsprobleme einer verfassten Weltgemeinschaft*, in: Winfried Brugger, Ulfried Neumann, Stephan Kirste (eds.), *Rechtsphilosophie im 21. Jahrhundert*, Suhrkamp, Frankfurt a. M. 2008, 360–379.
155. Thomas Nagel, *The Problem of Global Justice*, in: "Philosophy and Public Affairs", vol. 33 (2005), 113–147, at 121.

8 THE POST-UNITARY PARADIGMS OF ORDER III ...   447

156. Robert C. Paehlke, *Hegemony and Global Citizenship*, Palgrave Macmillan, New York 2014.
157. Seyla Benhabib, *The Rights of Others*, Cambridge University Press, Cambridge/New York 2004, at 17 et seq., 219 et seq.
158. Habermas, *Der gespaltene Westen*, supra note 154, at 113 et seq. (English: at 115 et seq.); Stefan Kadelbach, Thomas Kleinlein, *Überstaatliches Verfassungsrecht*, in: "Archiv des Völkerrechts", Vol. 44 (2006), 235–266.
159. Daniele Archibugi, *The Global Commonwealth of Citizens: Toward Cosmopolitan Democracy*, Princeton University Press, Princeton 2008.
160. Anne Peters, *Dual Democracy*, in: Klabbers/Peters/Ulfstein, *The Constitutionalization of International Law*, supra note 129, 263–341.
161. Apel, *Diskurs und Verantwortung*, supra note 120, at 179 et seq. (English: at 219 et seq.)
162. Ibid., at 203 (English: at 236).
163. Herbert Marcuse, *Eros and Civilization*, The Beacon Press, Boston (MA) 1966, 1st ed. 1955, at 112.

# Index

**A**
Absolutism
　according to Bodin, 44–46
　according to Hobbes, 217, 218
Aeschylus, 199, 203
Albert, Mathias, 322n38
Alexander VI, Pope, 123
Alienation (*Entäußerung*), 390
　according to Marx, 390–392
Althusius, Johannes, 162–165, 167–169
American War of Independence, 50
Anghie, Antony, 187n108
Anthropological pessimism
　according to Hobbes, 214–216
　according to Kant, 228
　according to Thucydides, 35
Antiphon, 100
Apel, Karl-Otto, 26, 266n161, 405, 413–418, 436
Archibugi, Daniele, 447n159
Arendt, Hannah, 26, 86n1, 397, 401–405, 424

Aristotle, 18, 37, 39–42, 45, 46, 49, 54, 61, 100, 102, 113, 122, 173, 210, 246, 276, 383
Arnim, Johannes von, 184
Atomism, 8
Augustine (Aurelius Augustinus), 106–110, 121, 139
Autocracy, 247
Autonomy
　according to Kant, 230–232
　according to Rousseau, 230–231
　political, 231
Azo, 112

**B**
Bach, Johann Sebastian, 437
Baldus de Ubaldi, 112
Bartolus de Saxoferrato, 112
Basic goods
　in New Natural Law, 174–178
Benedict XV, Pope, 189n144
Benhabib, Seyla, 447n157

Bentham, Jeremy, 51
Benvenisti, Eyal, 375n133, 445n136
Berger, Klaus Peter, 319
Bergman, Ingmar, 377–381
Berman, Harold J., 279, 289n31
Berman, Paul Schiff, 354, 355, 445n138
Bernstorff, Jochen von, 267n174
Bèze, Théodore de, 129
Biggar, Nigel, 195n315
"Billiard ball" theory, 82, 356, 357
Biology
 as leading science, 53
Biopower, 344
Black, Rufus, 195n315
Bobbio, Norberto, 193n261, 193n270, 259n28, 260n34, 260n47, 261n61, 261n66
Böckenförde, Ernst-Wolfgang, 183n6, 183n13, 184n23, 188n127, 192n235, 446n149
Bodin, Jean, 19, 41, 44–47, 163, 164
Bogdandy, Armin von, 27n13, 375n129, 375n130
Booysen, Hercules, 322n49
Boyle, Joseph, 172, 174, 178
Brandom, Robert, 371n27, 405, 407–409
Braudel, Fernand, 74
Brieskorn, Norbert, 260n35, 262n85
Brown Scott, James, 193n252
Brugger, Winfried, 324n72
Brumlik, Micha, 266n161
Brunkhorst, Hauke, 266n161, 323n65
Buckel, Sonja, 321n9
Buddhism, 13, 99
Burchill, Scott, 90n106

C
Calliess, Gralf-Peter, 321n9, 321n10
Calvin, Jean, 155, 156

Calvinism
 political doctrine of, 129, 155, 156, 164, 165
Campbell, R.H., 290n54
Capital
 composition of capital according to Marx, 393
 profitability of capital according to Adam Smith, 282, 283
Carey, Henry, 290n61
Carr, Craig L., 194n290
Categorical imperative, 229, 230
Catholicism
 backward-oriented conception of political power, 128–130
 doctrine of Catholic exceptionalism, 137–141
 political and legal theory of, 89–92, 98–100, 116–120
Cathrein, Viktor, 196n328
Chappell, Timothy, 195n321, 196n335
Charles I, King of England, 47, 49
Charlesworth, Hilary, 351–353
Cheneval, Francis, 195n306, 261n81
Chimni, Bhupinder S., 347–349
Christensen, Ralph, 321n9
Christianity
 concept of order in, 104–149
 persecution of the "others" in, 121–128
Chrysippus, 102
Cicero, Marcus Tullius, 103, 104, 276
Civilization
 clash of, 20, 72–75
 definition of, 73–74
*Civitas maxima*, 103, 104, 162, 168–172, 207, 208, 232, 255, 256, 291, 296
Cohen, Hermann, 253
Cohen, Jean L., 92n147

Colonization of the Americas, 122–128
Communication community (real and ideal), 413–417, 435, 436
Communicative paradigm, 26, 177, 181, 248, 255, 293, 342, 369, 381, 387, 390, 394, 403, 405, 408, 410, 413, 417, 419–421, 423–427, 429, 430, 434, 436–438
 and civil society, 426
 and cosmopolitan law, 429, 430
 and knowledge, 410–412
 and language, 405–410
 and moral theory, 413–417
 and systems theory, 417–419
 and the cultural community, 428
 and the national community, 428, 429
Communism
 according to Marx, 389, 394
Communitarianism, 83–86
 ethnocentric, 85, 86
 republican, 85, 86
*Communitas christiana*, 5, 14, 15, 105, 115, 123, 129, 234
Condorcet, Nicolas de, 52
Confederation of states (*Völkerbund*) according to Kant, 235–241
Conflict of norms
 in postmodern thinking, 353–355
 in the communicative paradigm, 419–423
Conservation, 148
Constitution
 according to Teubner, 317–319
 and the state according to Kant, 237–238
Constitutional adjudication, 427
Contextuality
 in postmodern thinking, 334–338

Contractualism (contract theory of the state), 162–165, 221–223, 228
Control
 society of control in postmodern thinking, 344, 345
*Corpus*
 metaphor of the, 14, 15, 107, 137, 157, 158, 164, 165, 179, 245, 246
Cosmological-ontological evidence of God's existence, 176
Cosmopolitanism, 103, 104, 233, 234, 254–258, 429–434
Coulmas, Peter, 183n12
Council of Constance, 121, 122
Cournot, Antoine-Augustin, 290n59
Courts
 dialogue between, 422, 423

D
Daniels, Joseph P., 325n86
Dann, Philipp, 375n129
Dante Alighieri, 95–98, 110–116
Davidson, Donald, 371n27, 405–408
Deitelhoff, Nicole, 93n163
Deleuze, Gilles, 344, 345
Delgado, Mariano, 188n128
Democracy
 according to Arendt, 402–405
 according to Dewey, 400, 401
 according to Kelsen, 246–249
 according to Rousseau, 222, 223
 according to the communicative paradigm, 248, 249, 424–427
 and Catholic doctrine, 134, 135
 and cosmopolitan order, 433, 434
 dual, 434
Democritus, 8, 100
Descartes, René, 22, 50, 204, 207, 210–213, 239, 241, 398, 406
Dewey, John, 397–401, 424

*Dharma*, 99
D'Holbach, Paul-Henry Dietrich, 51
Diels, Hermann, 183n7, 183n11
Diogenes Laertius, 184n20
Diogenes of Sinope, 103
Diplomacy, 65
Division of labour
  according to Marx, 389, 390
  according to Plato, 38
Dogliani, Mario, 266n156
Donahue, Charles Jr., 289n33
Dualism, 249, 250
Dunlap, Thomas, 267n174
Dunoff, Jeffrey L., 197n349, 325n87

## E

Elazar, Daniel J., 193n262
Empire
  neo-conservative concept of, 76–78
  postmodern concept of, 343–347
*Encomiendas*, 132
Endy, Melvin B., 262n85
Engels, Friedrich, 389, 390, 394–396
English Civil War, 47, 49
Epstein, Richard A., 289n32
Estrangement (*Entfremdung*)
  according to Marx, 391–396
Ethics
  of conviction, 142
  of responsibility, 142
  *see* Global ethic
Ethnos, 68
Eucken, Walter, 323n58
Eugene IV, Pope, 122
Experimentalism
  according to Dewey, 397–400

## F

Falsification
  theory of, 10
Familistic theory
  of the political community, 41, 42, 45–49, 163, 164, 171
Fassbender, Bardo, 197n349
Federalism
  universal federalism according to Althusius, 163–165
  universal federalism according to Höffe, 254–258
Feminism
  feminist criticism of international law, 352, 353
  feminist criticism of public law, 350–352
Fieschi, Sinibaldo (Pope Innocent IV), 115
Filmer, Robert, 47–49
Finnis, John, 172, 174, 176, 178
Fischer-Lescano, Andreas, 303, 304, 314
Fisch, Jörg, 186n84, 186n87, 186n90, 188n126
Formalism
  legal, 363–367
Foucault, Michel, 339–342, 344, 363
Francis, Pope, 147, 148
Frank, Manfred, 372n39
Freedom
  absolute, 388
  in the universal monarchy, 113
  negative. *See* Rights, citizens' rights
  according to Hobbes
  objective, 388
  positive. *See* Autonomy
  subjective, 388
Freud, Sigmund, 339
Freytag, Andreas, 325n86
Friedman, Milton, 308
Friend/enemy contraposition, 58

## G

Galilei, Galileo, 210

Gender, 350, 351
Gentili, Alberico, 119, 156–159, 161
George, Robert P., 172, 195n314
Glenn, H. Patrick, 374n114
Global ethic, 141–146
Glorious Revolution, 49, 50
Goldman, Berthold, 324n84
Goldmann, Matthias, 375n129, 375n130
Governance
  global, 360–363
Grewe, Wilhelm, 184n43
Grisez, Germain, 172–178
Groppi, Tania, 445n134
Grotius, Hugo, 158–161, 289n29

# H

Habermas, Jürgen, 27n6, 264n136, 266n163, 267n189, 297, 318, 320n2, 323n66, 371n27, 405, 411, 414, 418, 424, 425, 429
Hall, Peter A., 323n57
Hammer, Stefan, 267n185
Han Fei, 13
Happiness
  according to Aristotle, 40
  according to Dante, 112, 113, 116
  according to Hobbes, 145
  according to Thomas Aquinas, 112, 113
Hardimon, Michael O., 439n9
Hardt, Michael, 343–347, 349
Hart, H.L.A., 244
Hayek, Friedrich, 308
Hegel, Georg Wilhelm Friedrich, 17, 26, 84, 173, 179, 332, 335, 381–389
Hegemonism, 19, 20, 58, 60–63, 72, 75, 78, 79
Heidegger, Martin, 334–336, 339
Henricus Hostiensis, 115

Heraclitus, 100, 101
Herder, Johann Gottfried, 54
Hesiod, 1
Hobbes, Thomas, 22, 50, 51, 156, 160, 166, 167, 204–206, 212–219, 223, 224, 228–230, 238, 239, 255, 270, 282, 332
Höffe, Otfried, 183n6, 255–258
Holism, 15, 16, 32, 36–41, 49, 53, 54, 61, 97, 217, 244, 302, 380, 384, 386, 387, 406
Holistic particularism, 15, 18–20, 32, 41, 48–53, 57, 60–62, 72, 77, 79, 81, 83, 86
Holistic universalism, 15, 20, 21, 98, 116, 157, 165, 171, 172, 177, 178, 182, 224, 255, 269, 276, 278
  Christian-Catholic variant of, 116–149
  rationalist variant of, 149, 150, 155–172
Homer, 29
Honneth, Axel, 445n126
Hueglin, Thomas O., 193n262
Huntington, Samuel P., 72–75, 79

# I

Ideal speech situation
  according to Habermas, 414
Individualism
  gnoseological turn to, 208–212
  methodological, 228–241
  solipsism of modern individualism, 238–241, 333, 334
  unitary character of modern individualism, 238–241
  *see* Universalistic individualism
Industrial revolution, 52
Innocent III, Pope, 111
Instrumentalism
  according to Dewey, 397–400

International law
 according to Hegel, 386
 according to Slaughter, 357–360
 according to the communicative
  paradigm, 429, 430
 and state law according to Kelsen,
  249–254
 constitutionalization of, 178–183
 hegemonic concept of, 76, 77
 imperial concept of, 78
 priority of, 250–252
International Public Authority (IPA),
 360, 361
International regimes
 theory of, 83
International relations
 theory of, 63–67
Intersubjectivity, 26, 208, 239, 298,
 314, 331, 336, 380–382, 384,
 387, 401
 according to Arendt, 401–405
 according to Dewey, 399–401
 according to Hegel, 383–389
 according to the communicative
  paradigm, 405–438
 in political life, 400–405
Invisible hand, 283, 311, 348
Irving, John, 330
Irwin, Douglas A., 288n16, 289n19,
 289n23, 289n26, 289n30,
 290n62

J
Jackson, Vicki C., 445n133
Jellinek, Georg, 259n17
Jenks, C. Wilfred, 196n345
John Paul II, Pope, 137, 138
Johnson, Pierre Marc, 325n86
John XXIII, Pope, 134
Jonas, Hans, 444n122
*Jus*
 as derived from *justum*, 153
 as opposed to *lex*, 215
 *gentium*, 99, 110, 117, 118, 120,
  125, 127, 151, 153, 156, 157,
  161, 164, 168–170, 224, 279
 *in bello*, 5, 56, 126, 171
*Jus Publicum Europaeum*, 59, 65
Justice
 according to Aristotle, 40
 according to Plato, 38
 according to Rawls, 84
 and systems theory, 315–317
 in the universal monarchy, 113

K
Kadelbach, Stefan, 192n249, 447n158
Kadens, Emily, 279
Kagan, Robert, 79
Kallinos, 30
Kant, Immanuel, 22, 26, 35, 84,
 113, 162, 176, 177, 185, 206,
 207, 223, 227–244, 251, 252,
 255–258, 262, 263, 270, 332,
 334, 366, 398, 420, 429, 434
Kautilya, 13
Kelsen, Hans, 23, 56, 176, 178, 207,
 241, 243–254
 basic norm (*Grundnorm*), 178,
  179, 243, 244
 pure theory of law, 243, 252–254
Keohane, Robert O., 93n165
Kettner, Matthias, 323n65
Kierkegaard, Søren, 335, 380, 381
Kingsbury, Benedict, 375n132
Kipp, Heinrich, 88n45, 193n274
Kirste, Stephan, 324n72
Kirton, John J., 325n86
Klabbers, Jan, 421
Kleinlein, Thomas, 27n13, 192n249,
 194n293, 194n304, 447n158
Kögler, Hans Herbert, 372n41

Kohn, Hans, 91n111
Koskenniemi, Martti, 89n75, 266n173, 363–367
Krisch, Nico, 92n148, 323n67, 354, 374n132, 375n134
Kuhn, Thomas, 7, 411
Kumm, Mattias, 325n87
Kundera, Milan, 329–332
Küng, Hans, 142, 144, 146
Kunz, Karl-Ludwig, 321n9

L
Labour-power
 according to Marx, 393
Lal, Deepak, 78
La Mettrie, Julien Offray de, 50
Lang, Anthony F. Jr., 325n87
Langer, Stefan, 322n49
Lang, Fritz, 293
Language
 according to Brandom, 407, 408
 according to Davidson, 406, 407
 according to the communicative paradigm, 408–410
 truth content of, 336–338
Large-scale-order (*Großraumordnung*), 60, 72
Las Casas, Bartolomé de, 21, 106, 122, 130–133, 137, 147, 153, 188
Law
 and morals according to Kant, 242, 244
 and morals according to Kelsen, 241–244
 civic (*lex civilis*), 117, 118, 120, 153
 cosmopolitan, 233, 234, 430–434
 divine (*lex divina*), 110, 117, 130, 133, 149, 153, 158
 eternal (*lex aeterna*), 98, 117, 120

 fragmentation of, 304–306
 globalization of, 293, 303, 304
 heterarchical, 305
 independence of the law from God's command, 150–161
 natural. *See* Natural law
 polyarchic, 305
 positive (*lex humana*), 150, 151
 private law regimes. *See* Lex mercatoria
 rational (*lex rationalis*). *See* Natural law
League of Nations, 76, 251
Legal system
 multilevel, 120
Legitimacy, 361, 367, 369, 419, 421, 426, 433, 434
 input-oriented, 361
 output-oriented, 361
Leibniz, Gottfried Wilhelm, 301
Lemberg, Eugen, 91n111
Leo XIII, Pope, 188n143
Lex mercatoria, 348, 358
 and public law, 320, 321
 codification of, 319
 contemporary, 306–311
 of the Middle Ages, 23, 278–281, 307
 self-validation of, 310, 319
Liberalism, 21, 23, 77, 84, 85, 205, 218–220, 308
Lifeworld
 in the communicative paradigm, 417–419
List, Friedrich, 290n60
Locke, John, 22, 47, 84, 133, 166, 205, 218–220, 225, 238, 271, 356
Logos
 as the rational rule of the whole world, 101, 102
Lohmann, Georg, 268n198

Love, 97, 106, 438
Luhmann, Niklas, 24, 293, 296–303, 311, 313–316
Luther, Martin, 154

## M
Macdonald, Ronald St.John, 196n344
Machiavelli, Niccolò, 41–44, 51, 61, 63, 66, 158
MacIntyre, Alasdair, 86, 93n170
MacKinnon, Catharine, 350–352
Major (Mair), John, 122
Malthus, Thomas, 286
Malynes, Gerald de, 280
Mandeville, Bernard de, 271–274
Marcuse, Herbert, 436
Maritain, Jacques, 154
Marsan-Raventós, Clara, 445n135
Martin V, Pope, 122
Marx, Karl, 381, 382, 389–396, 402, 403, 419
Mattei, Ugo, 92n147
Maturana, Humberto R., 299
McCormick, John P., 260n149
Melos
  siege of, 33, 34
Mentalism. *See* Individualism, solipsism of modern individualism
Merle, Jean-Christophe, 268n198
Michelman, Frank, 446n149
Mill, John Stuart, 286, 287, 356
Mona, Martino, 321n9
Monarchy
  absolute, 44–46
  as a command of divine law, 128, 129
  independence of the individual monarchies from the universal monarchy, 111, 112
  universal, 112–116, 119, 235
Monism, 249–253

Moravcsik, Andrew, 92n160, 356
Morgenthau, Hans, 63–67, 75
Mosler, Hermann, 196n344
Müller, Adam, 53–56, 67
Müller, Harald, 93n163
Multilevel constitutionalism, 421, 422
Mustill, Rt. Hon. Lord Justice, 319

## N
Nagel, Thomas, 446n155
Napoleonic wars, 52
Nation
  as a daily plebiscite, 67
  concept of, 54, 64
  ethnic origins of the, 68
  identity of the, 54, 67
  in the globalization era, 69–71
Nationalism, 19, 20, 22, 55, 56, 60–64, 68, 71, 172, 249
Naturalistic fallacy
  in natural law theory, 172, 173
Natural law (*lex naturalis*)
  and *jus gentium*, 156–161, 165–172
  concept of, 103, 150
  New Natural Law, 172–178
Negri, Antonio, 343–347, 349
Neo-colonialism, 348, 349
Neo-conservatives, 75–80
Neo-liberalism
  in the theory of international relations, 358
Neo-realism, 63, 66
  structural, 20, 66
Networks
  theory of global networks, 357
Nicholas V, Pope, 122
Nobles, Richard, 321n15
Nomos
  as the law of the cosmopolitan community, 102
  as the law of the individual political community, 104

Normativity, 364, 367, 369, 409, 419
Nussbaum, Martha C., 184n21
Nys, Ernest, 185n59

O
Objectification (*Vergegenständlichung*)
  according to Marx, 390
Ockham, William of, 313, 336
Onuf, Nicholas Greenwood, 90n109
Order
  as opposed to chaos, 1
  as oppression, 342
  concept of, 3–6
  extension of, 13–15
  fragmentation of, 353–355
  ontological foundation of, 13–16
  pluralist structure of, 17, 353
  post-unitary, 14, 17, 24, 26, 292, 293, 296, 302, 306, 419–423
  public character of, 269
  reflexive character of, 269
Ordoliberalism, 308
Ovid, 2

P
Paehlke, Robert C., 447n156
Palacios Rubios, Juan López de, 123
Paradigm
  concept of, 7–12
  in human and natural sciences, 8–10
Paradigmatic revolution, 13–17
  failed, 269–288
  first, 14, 98
  second, 15, 204
  third, 17, 291–293
Paradigms of order
  concept of, 13
  post-unitary, 17
Parsons, Talcott, 295–297
Particularism, 13, 14, 16, 33–36

Particularistic individualism, 16, 23, 274, 380
Paulson, Stanley L., 267n185
Paul the Apostle, 150
Paulus, Andreas L., 197n356
Paul VI, Pope, 137
Payandeh, Mehrdad, 197n355
Peace
  according to Kant, 234
  and the teleological conception of history according to Kant, 236, 237
  in the universal monarchy, 113
  through accommodation, 65
  through law, 120, 250, 251
Peloponnesian War, 33, 34, 39
Penn, William, 226
People
  the concept of people according to Kelsen, 245, 246
Peters, Anne, 445n129, 447n160
Philo Judaeus (Philo of Alexandria), 277
Physics
  as leading science, 51, 53, 214
Picander (Christian Friedrich Henrici), 437
Pink Floyd, 353
Plato, 18, 37–41, 54, 61, 84, 102, 103, 167, 179, 276, 383, 401, 404
Pluralism
  legal, 207, 253, 254, 293, 304, 353–355, 363, 420
Plutarch, 276, 277
Polis
  according to Arendt, 403, 404
  according to Plato, 38
  and trade, 276
Ponthoreau, Marie-Claire, 445n134
Popper, Karl, 27n7
Populism, 71

Positivism
  legal, 56, 170, 171, 179, 241, 243, 244
Postmodernism, 25, 332–342
Pragmatism
  according to Dewey, 399
Primer, Irwin, 288n11
Property
  Marx's criticism of private property, 391, 392
  Rousseau's criticism of private property, 221, 222
Public interest
  as result of the "invisible hand", 283, 311, 348
Pufendorf, Samuel, 162, 165–169

## Q
Quaritsch, Helmut, 90n91

## R
Rabkin, Jeremy A., 76–78
Radbruch, Gustav, 195n313
Rational choice
  applied to international law, 81–83
Rationality
  according to Hobbes, 213, 229
  according to Kant, 229
  according to the communicative paradigm, 405–423
  criticism of universal rationality, 298, 365–367
Ratzinger, Joseph (pope Benedict XVI), 138
Rawls, John, 84
Realism, 13, 19, 20, 42, 44, 60–64, 66
Recognition
  struggle for, 382, 384–387, 419
Reflective thinking
  according to Dewey, 398
Reformation
  and natural law, 154–156
  and the unity of the Church, 208, 209
Renan, Ernest, 90n110
Republicanism
  according to Arendt, 404
  *see* Communitarianism, republican
*Requerimiento*, 123
Responsibility, 416, 417, 435, 436
*Rex regum* (papal bull), 122
Ricardo, David, 286
Rigaux, François, 267n184
Rights
  according to the communicative paradigm, 415–417, 424–427
  and duties, 143, 144
  and values, 144–146
  citizens' rights according to Hobbes, 216–218
  citizens' rights according to Locke, 220
  citizens' rights according to Rousseau, 223
  collective, 425, 426
  human rights according to Höffe, 255, 256
  human rights and Catholic doctrine, 134
  of non-citizens, 431–433
  women's rights, 352
Risse, Thomas, 93n163
Rivière, Jean, 185n46
Rodriguez-Pereyra, Gonzalo, 370n22
*Romanus pontifex* (papal bull of 1436), 122
*Romanus pontifex* (papal bull of 1455), 122
Roth, Joseph, 327–329, 331
Rousseau, Jean-Jacques, 22, 84, 133, 206, 218, 220–223, 227, 228, 230, 231, 238, 240

Russell, Bertrand, 27n5

**S**
Saint-Pierre, Charles-Irénée Castel Abbé de, 227
Sandel, Michael, 93n171
Savigny, Friedrich Carl von, 309
Scharpf, Fritz Wilhelm, 362
Schelkshorn, Hans, 260n35
Schieder, Siegfried, 90n106
Schiff, David, 321n15
Schmitt, Carl, 4, 19, 56–60, 65, 72, 75, 79, 217, 343
Schneider, Ulrich, 27n12
Scholasticism
  Spanish, 116–120, 123–133
Schopenhauer, Arthur, 335
Second Vatican Council, 21, 106, 133, 134, 138, 147, 154
Sellers, Mortimer N.S., 27n13, 94n180
Sen, Amartya, 290n51
Seneca, Lucius Annaeus, 104, 277
Sepúlveda, Juan Ginés de, 123, 125
Shakespeare, William, 199, 201–204
Simma, Bruno, 196n344
Simon, Dieter, 322n45
Skinner, A.S., 290n54
Slaughter, Anne-Marie, 92n160, 356–360
Smith, Adam, 281–285, 309, 392
Smith, Anthony D., 68–71
Smith, Steven B., 439n9
Snyder, Louis L., 91n111
Sociability
  criticism of the theory of universal human sociability, 181–183
  theory of the general human sociability, 159, 160, 165, 166
Social contract
  according to Rousseau, 206, 222, 223

Social systems, 295–302
  and environment, 299
  as communication operationalizing systems, 297
  autopoiesis of, 299, 300, 312–314
  binary code of, 299, 301
  globalization of, 301, 302
  interaction between, 300, 301
  in the communicative paradigm, 417–419
  operational closure of, 300, 312, 313
  plurality of, 297, 304, 305
  *see* Systems theory
Solidarity, 49, 52, 57, 67–69, 83, 86, 109, 140, 143, 147, 157, 162, 166, 171, 179, 242, 270, 332, 380, 395, 432, 437
Sophocles, 200, 201
Soskice, David, 323n57
Sovereignty
  according to Bodin, 44–46
  according to Kant, 238
  popular, 129, 130
Spengler, Oswald, 74
Spindler, Manuela, 90n106
Spinoza, Benedictus de (Baruch), 224, 225, 338
State
  according to Hegel, 386
  and the constitution according to Kant, 237, 238
  as a legal entity according to Kelsen, 244, 245
  disaggregated, 357
  individual states and international law, 179, 180
  role of the state in the economy, 285
  the rise of territorial states, 209

State of nature, 165–167, 170, 214–216, 219–222, 225, 227, 228, 230, 234, 238, 255, 256
Steiger, Heinhard, 268n198
Stewart, Richard B., 375n132
Stichweh, Rudolf, 322n38
Stoicism, 14, 100–104, 159
Suárez, Francisco, 105, 116, 117, 119, 120, 127–130, 138, 153, 154, 187
Subjectivity
  according to Hegel, 383, 384
  cognitive solipsism of, 333, 334
  criticism of modern subjectivity according to postmodern thinking, 340–342
  Dewey's criticism of modern subjectivity, 399
  internal unity of, 333
  self-referential hierarchy of, 333, 334
Surplus value
  according to Marx, 393
Systems theory, 24, 293–302
  and economic theory, 306–311
  and postmodernism, 311–312
  and supra-systemic rationality, 314, 315
  and the concept of constitution, 317–319
  individuals in systems theory, 297, 298
  rationality in systems theory, 298, 299
  *see* Social systems

**T**
Taylor, Charles, 86, 93n172, 93n174, 93n175, 93n176, 94n177, 94n178, 94n179
Technocracy
  critique of, 148

Tendential fall of the rate of profit
  according to Marx, 395, 396
Teson, Fernando, 351
Teubner, Gunther, 303, 304, 310, 311, 315, 317
Theory
  concept of, 7
Third World Approach to International Law (TWAIL), 347–349
Thomas Aquinas, 115, 129, 150, 155, 278
Thucydides, 18, 33–37, 42–44, 51, 61, 63, 66, 67, 81
Tietje, Christian, 324n85
Tirtaeus, 30, 31
Tomuschat, Christian, 179, 180
Totalitarianism
  according to Arendt, 404
Toynbee, Arnold, 74
Trade
  doctrine of free trade, 281–288
  international, 286, 308
  in the ancient world, 276–278
  in the Christian doctrine, 278, 279
*Translatio imperii*
  doctrine of the, 123, 131
Truth
  and knowledge, 410–412
  truth content of language, 336–368, 405–410
  truth content of the law, 363–367
Truyol y Serra, Antonio, 27n9
Tully, James, 325n87

**U**
Ulfstein, Geir, 445n129, 445n139
United Nations, 433
Universal economy
  Hellenistic doctrine of, 274, 276–278
Universalism
  and religion, 108

theory of the natural society and communication, 125, 126
Universalistic individualism, 22, 207, 208, 252, 254, 255, 258
criticism, 238–240
Utilitarianism, 51, 273

**V**
Varela, Francisco J., 299
Vasquez, John A., 27n8
Venzke, Ingo, 375n130
Verdross, Alfred, 178–180
Vitoria, Francisco de, 124–129, 131, 152, 153, 192n231, 234

**W**
Walzer, Michael, 192n244
War
theory of the just, 109, 127
Wasserstein Fassberg, Celia, 324n84

Weber, Max, 142, 294, 295, 362
Weckmann, Luis, 259n18
Weiler, Joseph H.H., 190n188
Weiss, Manfred, 322n45
Well-ordered society, 3–5, 13, 14, 16, 17, 20, 25, 37, 39, 80, 98, 292, 297, 367, 390, 394, 437
Westerman, Pauline C., 195n317, 195n322, 196n330
Wiener, Antje, 325n87
Wittgenstein, Ludwig, 336–339, 363, 405, 407
Wolff, Christian, 162, 168–171, 232
Wood, Allen W., 439n9
World republic (*Weltrepublik*)
according to Höffe, 254–258
according to Kant, 235–238

**Z**
Zeno of Citium, 101–103

Printed in the United States
by Baker & Taylor Publisher Services